Parp! Parp! Honk! Honk! It's...

THE COUNCIL GRITTER
A Dirty Great Comedy Vehicle Spreading the Crud from Issues 162 to 171

◆

TRUE GRITS:
Graham Dury, Wayne Gamble, Stevie Glover, Davey Jones and Simon Thorp

SALTS OF THE EARTH:
Tony Coffey, Alex Collier, Simon Ecob, John Fardell, Barney Farmer and Lee Healey, Will Freeman, Robin Halstead, Jason Hazeley, Christina Martin & James MacDougall, Alex Morris, Joel Morris, Graham Murdoch, Paul Palmer, Nick Pettigrew & Cecilia Smart, Lew Stringer, Cat Sullivan, Tim Telling and Nick Tolson

VINEGAR JOE:
Russell Blackman

◆

Shovelled out by Dennis Municipal Vehicles, Ltd, The Depot, 30 Cleveland Street, London W1T 4JD

ISBN 978-1-906372-99-6

First Printing Autumn 2009

Printed in the United Kingdom

◆

SUBSCRIBE ONLINE AT:
www.viz.co.uk

ROGER MELLIE

FTV

THE MAN ON THE TELLY

HI, TOM

ROGER...THERE YOU ARE!

GREAT NEWS... YOUR SHIP HAS COME IN AT LAST!

I'VE HAD NBC ON THIS MORNING FROM NEW YORK... THEY WANT TO BUY YOUR FORMAT FOR...

'ERE, TOM, TOM...

WHAT DO YOU THINK OF THIS?

PFFFFFFT! PFFT! PFFT!

COUGH! COUGH!

JESUS!

COUGH!.. WHAT IS IT? SOME KIND OF :COUGH: FLY SPRAY?

NO, TOM...IT'S 'PRIAPIC' THE GREAT NEW SCENT FROM ROGER MELLIE

PRIAPIC

SCENT? COUGH!.. WHERE'S IT FROM?

MATE OF MINE...GOT A CONTRACT IN THE FAR EAST

COUGH!

SENDS IT OVER IN DRUMS LABELLED 'COOKING OIL'...SAVES ON THE TAX

THOUGHT I'D BEST EXPAND MY BRAND TENT, TOM...GET A NICE LITTLE INCOME GOING FOR WHEN I'M NO LONGER AT THE TOP OF MY TREE...

...DAVID BECKHAM, BRITNEY SPEARS...THEY'RE ALL AT IT

COSTS PENNIES TO MAKE, TOM. ALL THE INGREDIENTS ARE BY-PRODUCTS FROM AN ANTI-FREEZE FACTORY IN LAOS

HMM!

ANYWAY, THIS STUFF HITS THE SHOPS ON MONDAY, TOM...AND A 30 SECOND AD IN THE MIDDLE OF 'CORRIE' SHOULD SEE IT FLYING OFF THE SHELVES

CORONATION STREET?

YES! SO IT'S GOT TO BE A SHIT HOT AD...AND THAT'S WHERE YOU COME IN

ME?

THINK THAT TICK-TOCK TICK-TOCK GUINESS AD BOLLOCKS... BLACK AND WHITE... REAL CLASS.

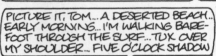

PICTURE IT, TOM... A DESERTED BEACH, EARLY MORNING...I'M WALKING BAREFOOT THROUGH THE SURF...TUX OVER MY SHOULDER...FIVE O'CLOCK SHADOW

HMM!!

I'VE BEEN IN THE CASINO ALL NIGHT AND I'VE LOST THE LOT!...BUT I'M SMILING

...THERE'S A BIRD COMING TOWARDS ME, TOM...THINK SCARLET JOHANSSEN OR A YOUNG JENNY AGGUTTER...AS WE PASS, SHE GETS A WHIFF OF MY PRIAPIC...

...NEXT THING, WE'RE AT IT IN THE SURF...THINK 'HERE TO ETERNITY', TOM, BUT WITH BARE ARSES...

...WE GO OUT OF FOCUS. IN THE FOREGROUND IS A BOTTLE OF THE STUFF WITH A BIT OF SEAWEED ON IT...

YEAH!

A VOICE OVER SAYS 'ROGER MELLIE'S PRIAPIC'

DEEP, GRAVELLY VOICE. THERE MUST BE SOME ACTOR AROUND WITH THROAT CANCER, TOM

YES. NOT A BAD IDEA THAT, ROGER...SOUNDS UP MARKET, TROPICAL, CLASSY... I LIKE IT!

GREAT. WELL WE'RE SHOOTING IT TOMORROW ON THE BEACH AT REDCAR.

YOU BRING A CAMERA, I'LL TRY AND FIND A HALF DECENT BIT OF FLUFF IN THE PUB TONIGHT

NEXT MORNING...

JESUS, TOM. CAN WE GET ON WITH IT?...I'M FREEZING ME FUCKIN' NUTS OFF 'ERE

OKAY...

PLACES, EVERYBODY!

RIGHT, ROGER, YOU'VE JUST LOST A FORTUNE AT THE ROULETTE TABLE, OKAY...

YEP! LET'S SEE IF WE CAN NAIL THIS FUCKER IN ONE TAKE, TOM

OKAY ON SET...

3...2...1... ACTION!

THAT'S IT, ROGER... GOOD... RUEFUL SMILE

GOOD... GOOD... LITTLE SHAKE OF THE HEAD...

THAT'S IT... NOW YOU SEE THE GIRL APPROACHING

SPLASH!

6

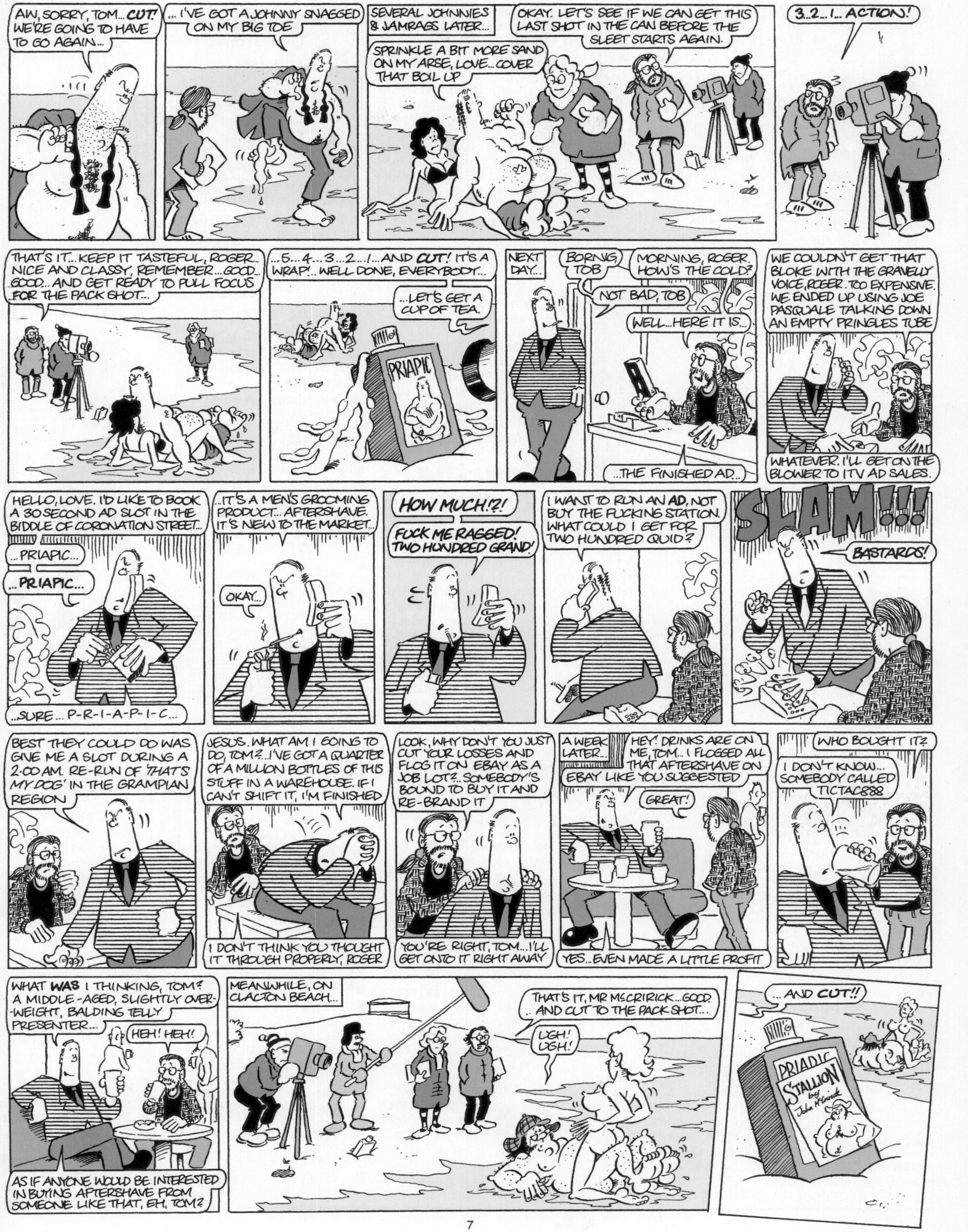
AW, SORRY, TOM... CUT! WE'RE GOING TO HAVE TO GO AGAIN...
... I'VE GOT A JOHNNY SNAGGED ON MY BIG TOE
SEVERAL JOHNNIES & JAMRAGS LATER...
SPRINKLE A BIT MORE SAND ON MY ARSE, LOVE... COVER THAT BOIL UP
OKAY. LET'S SEE IF WE CAN GET THIS LAST SHOT IN THE CAN BEFORE THE SLEET STARTS AGAIN.
3..2..1.. ACTION!
THAT'S IT... KEEP IT TASTEFUL, ROGER... NICE AND CLASSY, REMEMBER... GOOD... GOOD... AND GET READY TO PULL FOCUS FOR THE PACK SHOT...
...5...4...3...2...1...AND CUT! IT'S A WRAP!.. WELL DONE, EVERYBODY...
...LET'S GET A CUP OF TEA.
PRIAPIC
NEXT DAY...
BORNIG, TOB
MORNING, ROGER. HOW'S THE COLD?
NOT BAD, TOB
WELL... HERE IT IS...
...THE FINISHED AD...
WE COULDN'T GET THAT BLOKE WITH THE GRAVELLY VOICE, ROGER. TOO EXPENSIVE. WE ENDED UP USING JOE PASQUALE TALKING DOWN AN EMPTY PRINGLES TUBE
WHATEVER. I'LL GET ON THE BLOWER TO ITV AD SALES.
HELLO, LOVE. I'D LIKE TO BOOK A 30 SECOND AD SLOT IN THE BIDDLE OF CORONATION STREET...
...PRIAPIC...
...PRIAPIC...
...SURE... P-R-I-A-P-I-C...
...IT'S A MEN'S GROOMING PRODUCT... AFTERSHAVE. IT'S NEW TO THE MARKET...
OKAY...
HOW MUCH!?!
FUCK ME RAGGED! TWO HUNDRED GRAND!
I WANT TO RUN AN AD, NOT BUY THE FUCKING STATION. WHAT COULD I GET FOR TWO HUNDRED QUID?
SLAM!!!
BASTARDS!
BEST THEY COULD DO WAS GIVE ME A SLOT DURING A 2:00 AM. RE-RUN OF 'THAT'S MY DOG' IN THE GRAMPIAN REGION
JESUS. WHAT AM I GOING TO DO, TOM?.. I'VE GOT A QUARTER OF A MILLION BOTTLES OF THIS STUFF IN A WAREHOUSE. IF I CAN'T SHIFT IT, I'M FINISHED
I DON'T THINK YOU THOUGHT IT THROUGH PROPERLY, ROGER
LOOK, WHY DON'T YOU JUST CUT YOUR LOSSES AND FLOG IT ON EBAY AS A JOB LOT?.. SOMEBODY'S BOUND TO BUY IT AND RE-BRAND IT
YOU'RE RIGHT, TOM... I'LL GET ONTO IT RIGHT AWAY
A WEEK LATER...
HEY! DRINKS ARE ON ME, TOM... I FLOGGED ALL THAT AFTERSHAVE ON EBAY LIKE YOU SUGGESTED
GREAT!
YES... EVEN MADE A LITTLE PROFIT
WHO BOUGHT IT?
I DON'T KNOW... SOMEBODY CALLED TICTAC888
WHAT WAS I THINKING, TOM? A MIDDLE-AGED, SLIGHTLY OVER-WEIGHT, BALDING TELLY PRESENTER...
HEH! HEH!
AS IF ANYONE WOULD BE INTERESTED IN BUYING AFTERSHAVE FROM SOMEONE LIKE THAT, EH, TOM?
MEANWHILE, ON CLACTON BEACH...
THAT'S IT, MR McCRIRICK... GOOD. .. AND CUT TO THE PACK SHOT...
UGH! UGH!
... AND CUT!!
PRIAPIC
STALLION
by John McCririck

Letterbocks

...viz Comic, PO Box 656, North Shields, NE30 4XX ... e-mail letters@viz.co.uk

STAR LETTER

❑ No wonder England's bowlers had such difficulty playing in Australia recently. All of the games were played in the middle of the night! Come on Aussies, play fair next time.

Gary Beergut, Leamington Spa

**Mr Beergut's letter wins a postal order for 50 pence.*

❑ I had to laugh at my sister's two-year-old son the other day. He's bozz-eyed and has ginger hair.

Philip Celery, Bolton

❑ They say that if your ears are burning, then someone is talking about you. Well, not in my case, because I woke up with burning ears in the early hours of the morning last week to find that my bedroom was on fire. However, I can't rule out the possibility that someone may have been talking about me at the same time, so actually there could be some truth in it.

J Geils, Band

Safety Measures

❑ Why is it that the manufacturers of 12inch rulers make a big thing about them being shatterproof? Is there some worldwide problem with shattering rulers that we don't know about?

Dave Turner, S. Wales

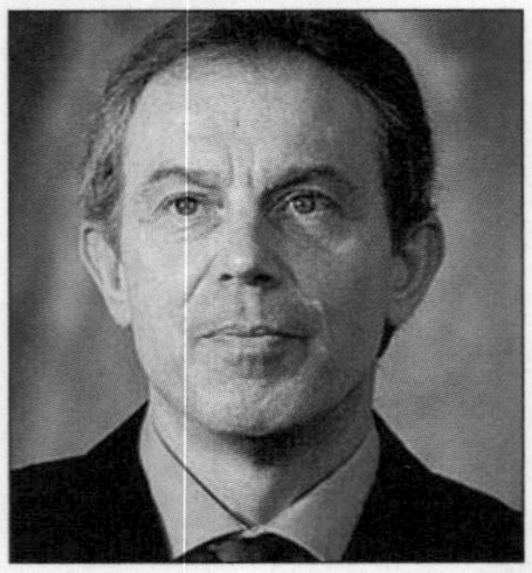

❑ In the past Tony Blair has holidayed at houses belonging to Silvio Berlusconi and Cliff Richard. Now he's jetted off to Florida to stay with Robin Gibb out of the Bee Gees. Has the man never heard of hotels or bed and breakfasts? I'm going to be watching the next honours list very closely, and if Mr Gibb gets so much as a CBE, Tony Blair will be getting one of my turds in the post.

Audrey Dunbarr Henley-on-Thames

❑ In 1997, my wife and I went on a once in a lifetime cruise around the world. I was reluctant to go as it was extremely expensive, but my wife talked me round when she pointed out, "we'll always have the memories." Well, now she's got Alzheimer's and can't remember what she had for breakfast, let alone a holiday ten years ago. So what a bloody waste of money that was.

T Storey, Nottingham

❑ I understand that you are a humorous magazine, but I must complain at the way you have tried to obtain a cheap laugh at the expense of Alzheimer's disease *(Letterbocks, this page)*. I suffer from this terrible affliction, and I can assure you it is no laughing matter.

Reginald Trussocks, Luton

Now that's Magic

❑ I was glad to read that the US plans to cut troops in half in Iraq sometime next year. A morale-boosting magic show is just what they need. Maybe the British should send Paul Daniels and the wonderful Debbie McGee over there to do their bit.

Tom Bassman, e-mail

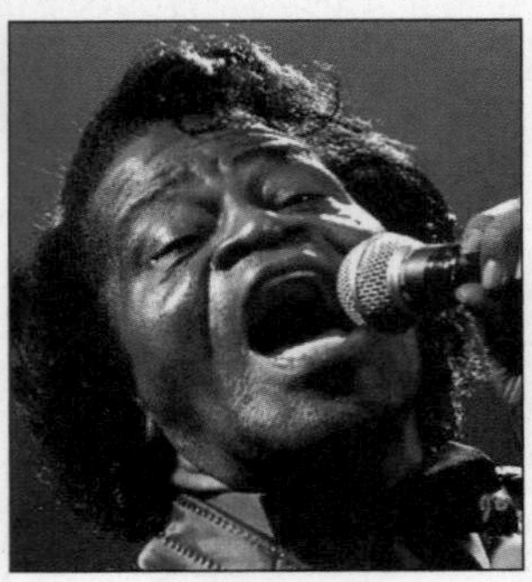

❑ I was devastated to hear of the death of the Godfather of Soul, James Brown. However, I was rather disappointed at his funeral when he didn't shrug off his shroud and climb out of his coffin for one last chorus whilst his minders tried to screw the lid down. That would have been the showman thing to do.

Leyton Buzzard, Cromer

❑ Why is it that every weather girl on TV seems to be pregnant? Haven't they heard of contraception?

Renton Pardue, Peterborough

❑ I agree with Mr. Pardue's letter *(above)* If these sluts spent more time studying meteorolgical trends and less time having unprotected penetrative sex with men, perhaps their forecasts would be a little more accurate.

Ada Dunwoody, Bristol

❑ Me and my mate Phil are always playing practical jokes on each other. Last April Fool's Day I broke into his house in the morning (he works nights) and hid. When he arrived home, I sneaked up and cracked him across ther back of the head with a crowbar before legging it. Later that afternoon there was a knock on my door. It was the police! The prankster had got me back by reporting my 'crime'. But the joke was on him, because April Fool's Day ends at midday.

Andrew Thayer, e-mail

Woolly Thinking

❑ I knitted a jumper for my husband this Christmas, but I couldn't shake off a nagging feeling that I'd gone wrong somewhere. I was sure it was the right size and his favourite colour. I realised my mistake when I came to give him his gift on Christmas Day - I suddenly remembered that he died in 1973.

Dolly Mills, London

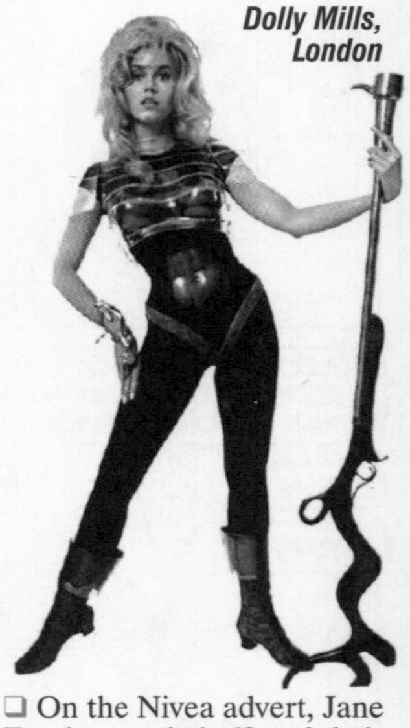

❑ On the Nivea advert, Jane Fonda says she's 68 and she's never felt better. That's as may be, but for my money she looked a lot better in *Barbarella*.

Tristram Trolleydash, Bude

New Year's Resolutions of the Twats

WE ALL make New Year's resolutions at the start of the year... and we have probably all broken them by the end of January! And celebrities are no different. We asked the stars of stage and screen what changes they were going to make in 2007, but they weren't in. So we asked a load of twats instead.

Eamonn Holmes, *TV Twat*

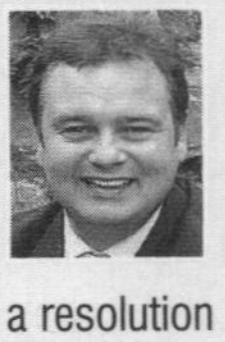

I'm shit at absolutely everything... except being shit, which I'm very good at! So this year, I'm making a resolution not to be so shit at everything. Unfortunately, one of the things I'm most shit at (after being thin and presenting television and radio programmes) is keeping my New Year's resolutions. So I'll probably just stay as shit as ever.

Jordan, *Twat Model*

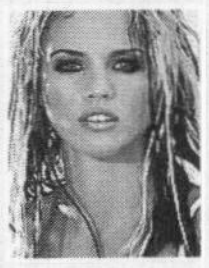

Me and Peter have resolved to appear on the front cover of OK! magazine more often in 2007. Last year there were a couple of issues that had somebody else on the cover. Of course, we were on the inside washing the dirty linen of our tawdry existence, but not being featured on the front really upset us and our babies, Harvey and the other one.

Peter Andre, *Twat Model's Twat of a Husband*

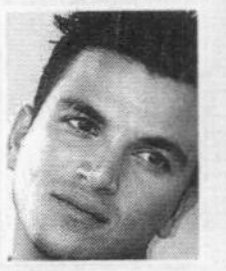

In 2007, when me and Jordan are being photographed for OK! magazine, I'm going to think of more imaginative ways to disguise the fact that I no longer have my trademark six-pack. Last year, all the photos had me up to my chest in a swimming pool, poking my head out from behind Jordan, or holding one of the babies in front of where my abs used to be.

Noel Edmonds, *Utter Twat*

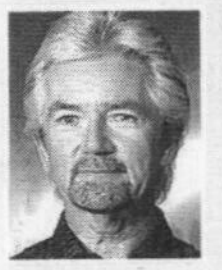

I practise Cosmic Ordering, the system by which you draw symbols on your wrist representing your hopes and aspirations, eg. if you want world peace you draw a dove; or a smiley face for happiness. Last year I drew an enormous pile of gold, and when I signed my contract with Channel 4 it came true. This year I'm going to draw a pile of diamonds so big it's got snow on the top.

'Sir' Boneo, *Irish Twat*

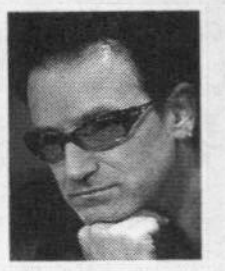

This year I successfully sued U2's ex-stylist in the High Court for the return of my hat and a pair of old trousers. This year I intend to continue using the full force of the law against people who have taken things that belong to me. I have begun 2007 by serving a writ on my local water board who have been stealing my turds for the last 46 years.

Cliff Richard, *Twat Singer*

I've had a number 1 hit in every decade from the 50s to the 90s, but I haven't yet topped the charts in the 1st decade of the 21st century.

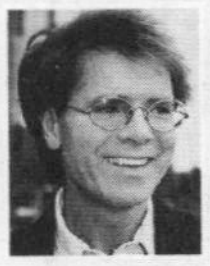

So this year I've made a resolution to have another number one single. I've prayed to God and asked Him to let me be Top of the Pops this year and He says He'll think about it and get back to me by the end of May at the latest. So fingers crossed for a summer smash!

Prince Edward, *Royal Twat*

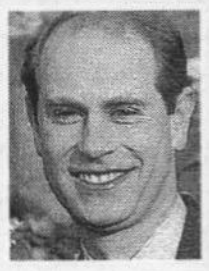

I'm in my 40s and the only thing I have ever done in my entire life was organise the *'It's a Royal Knockout'*, and it was utter, utter wank. I still wake up several times a night in a cold sweat crippled with the embarrassment of it all. So this year I'm either going to commit suicide or get myself hypnotised by Paul McKenna into believing that it was my equally pointless brother Andrew who produced it, not me.

TOP TIPS

SMOKERS. Enjoy seemingly longer holidays by stopping smoking on your first day off, making every day thereafter appear to be 72 hours long.

Steve Irving, Burbage

BOYS. Two pieces of used chewing gum stuck together make an ideal brain when lobotomising your action man.

Jeremy Rubbish, e-mail

OIL companies. Avoid having the general public pointing the global warming finger at you by putting some pictures of trees and flowers on your websites and adverts.

Will Neale, e-mail

FARMERS in Staffordshire. Get up before the crows piss like all other farmers throughout the country. That way you won't have to do the 8 mile journey to your fields in a tractor at 10 mph during the rush hour.

Ex farmer, e-mail

ITALIAN waiters. Ensure a warm welcome for your customers by having a good 5-second stare at their wives' tits upon entry, and then another good stare after they have been seated.

Luke Bounty-Hunter, e-mail

OLD people. If you feel cold indoors this winter, simply pop outside for ten minutes without a coat. When you go back inside you will really feel the benefit.

Win Dozsthreeone, e-mail

SOLVE 'Spot the Difference' puzzles by relaxing your eyes until you see four pictures. Then move the pictures backwards or forwards until the two middle ones overlap and then mark off the 10 locations where something appears not to be quite right.

Andrew Tait, Newcastle

AUSTRALIA'S Channel 9 cricket commentators. Pretend you are providing the unbiased reportage that you are employed to do by keeping the whoops, cheers and clapping to a minimum when Australia hit a six or take a wicket.

Mark Roberts, Adelaide

TOP TIPS

❑ Whilst I understand that a humour magazine has a duty to make people laugh, I feel I must write in to complain about your attempt to obtain a laugh at the expense of Alzheimer's disease *(Letterbocks, this page)*. I suffer from this terrible disease, and let me assure your readers that it is not a laughing matter.

Reginald Trussocks, Luton

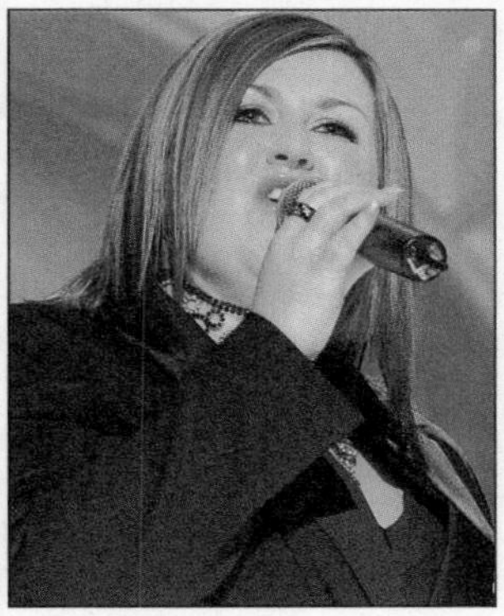

❑ In a recent interview, Michelle MacManus said, "I'll be in a bikini by the summer". Frankly, if it takes her that long to pull on, she really should take the hint and lose a bit of weight.

Ronald Bigstilton, Hove

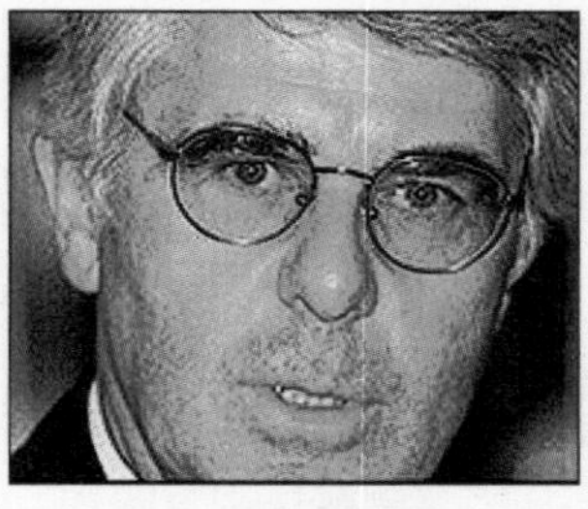

❑ If Max Clifford is so good at public relations, how come everyone thinks he's a cunt?

Liz Foster, e-mail

❑ According to reports, the Israelis and the Palestinians are going to put aside their differences and unite in their hatred of homosexuals at a planned Gay Pride march. How nice it is to see people of different religions focusing on their similarities rather than their differences.

M Bottlebank, Hull

❑ It must have been a slow news day last Sunday. *The Express* ran with 'John Reid: The Gloves Are Off.' Now I don't consider anyone removing their gloves, no matter how high they are in the government, to be newsworthy.

M Longdale, Leeds

❑ I live near a remedial school and there's a sign outside that says 'Slow. Children'. Now that can't be good for their confidence.

Chris Sloane, e-mail

❑ I felt I must write and complain about your attempts to use Alzheimer's disease as a source of laughs *(Letterbocks, this page)*. I am a sufferer of this condition, and let me tell you, it is no laughing matter.

Reginald Trussocks, Luton

❑ How about that picture of that bloke kissing that bird's arse again?

HS Lorrimer, Leeds

**Sorry, Mr Lorrimer, we've lost it. How about a picture of the Pope appearing to kiss some bird's tits instead?*

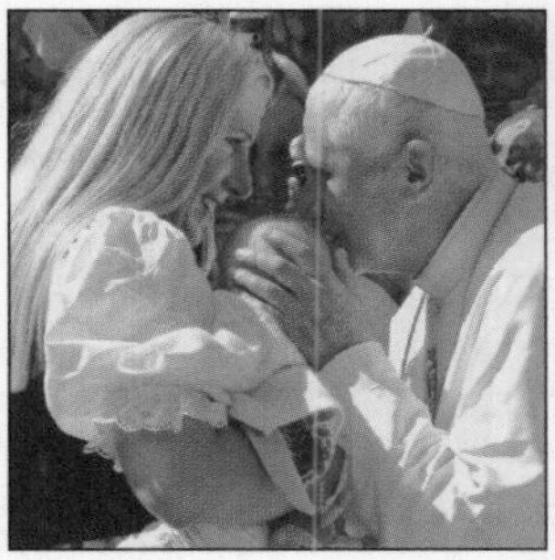

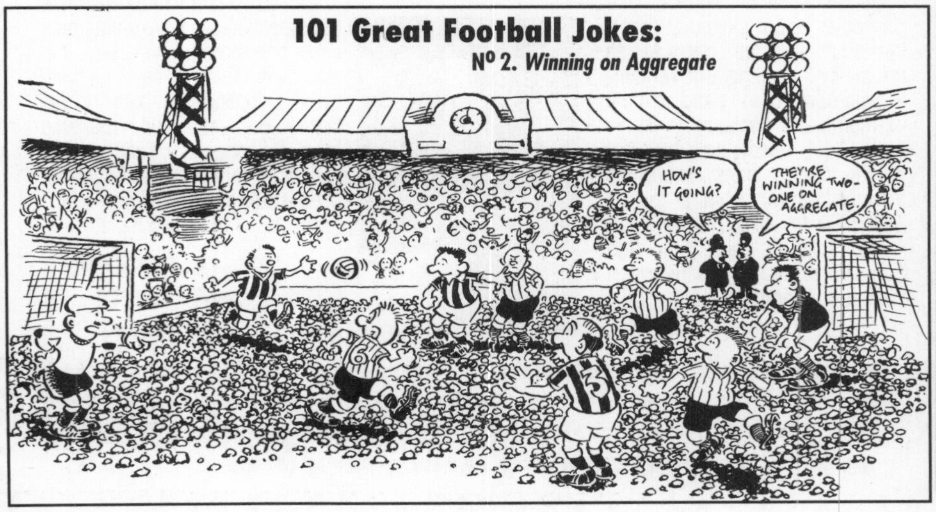
101 Great Football Jokes:
Nº 2. Winning on Aggregate
HOW'S IT GOING?
THEY'RE WINNING TWO-ONE ON AGGREGATE.

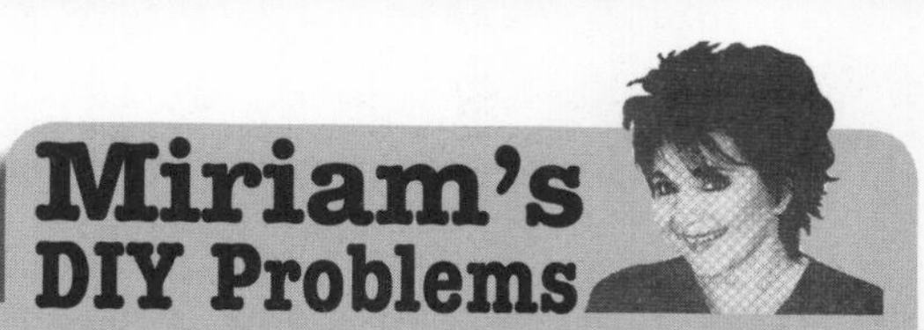
Miriam's
DIY Problems

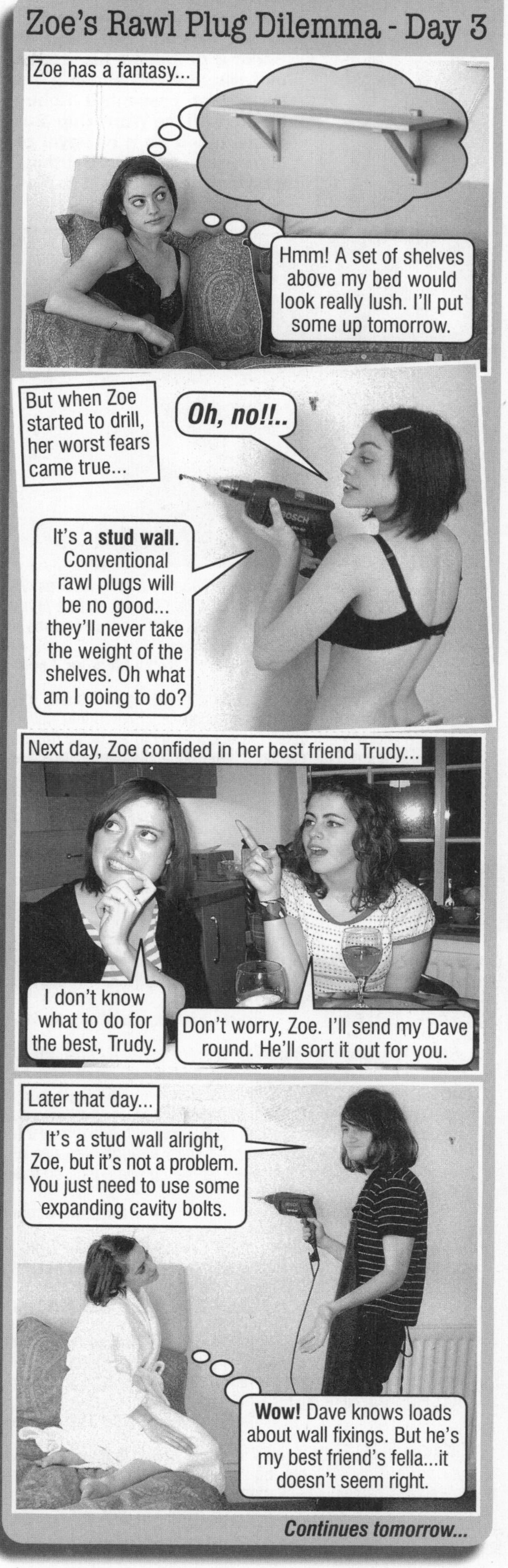
Zoe's Rawl Plug Dilemma - Day 3
Zoe has a fantasy...
Hmm! A set of shelves above my bed would look really lush. I'll put some up tomorrow.
But when Zoe started to drill, her worst fears came true...
Oh, no!!..
It's a stud wall. Conventional rawl plugs will be no good... they'll never take the weight of the shelves. Oh what am I going to do?
Next day, Zoe confided in her best friend Trudy...
I don't know what to do for the best, Trudy.
Don't worry, Zoe. I'll send my Dave round. He'll sort it out for you.
Later that day...
It's a stud wall alright, Zoe, but it's not a problem. You just need to use some expanding cavity bolts.
Wow! Dave knows loads about wall fixings. But he's my best friend's fella...it doesn't seem right.
Continues tomorrow...

HAVE YOUR SAY!

AT THE CEREMONY TO re-open the Royal Festival Hall, left wing firebrand Billy Bragg performed a song, after which he was presented to the Queen. The Bard of Barking defended his action by saying he was shaking the hand that presented Bobby Moore with the World Cup. But many saw it as a betrayal of his working class credentials. We went on the street to find out what YOU thought...

...IT MAY have been the hand that presented Bobby Moore with the World Cup, but it is also the hand that has almost certainly wanked off the Duke of Edinburgh on a number of occasions. I hope Billy washed his hands afterwards.

Mrs Dorothy Maguire, Leeds

...I WAS very disappointed to see Bragg shaking hands with this parasitic representative of the establishment. When introduced to her, he should have taken the opportunity to seize the means of production from the capitalist hegemony, dismantle the entire oligarchical edifice of the state and set up an anarcho-syndicalist commune in its place. Either that or kick her up the arse.

Foxy Smith, Tooting

...I WAS disgusted with Bragg kow-towing to this outdated symbol of the country's feudal past. I had all of Billy Bragg's records, but I made a bonfire in the garden and burnt them all.

Terry Hennessey, Luton

...I WAS disgusted with Her Majesty the Queen, betraying her upper class roots by shaking hands with an oik like Bragg. I immediately made a bonfire in the garden and burnt all my stamps and banknotes.

Audrey Fforbes-Hamilton, Surrey

...BRAGG shaking hands with the Queen did not surprise me at all. His working class hero persona is all an act. In real life he talks like Norman St John Stevas, and he lives in a huge mansion. My brother was his butler in the 80s, and he says he used to treat his servants like shit. He took a horsewhip to one of the footmen because his boots weren't shiny enough, and one of the maids nearly lost an eye when he flicked some pate de foie gras in it. Bragg just laughed.

G Stiltskin, Goole

...I WAS so incensed when I put the news on and saw Bragg shaking the Queen's hand that I put my foot through the screen and sent him a bill for £200 for a new telly.

Hector Shuttlecock, Isle of Wight

...THAT'S nothing. I work in a huge Bang & Olufsen television showroom, and when I saw the film of Bragg greeting the Queen on the news, I put my foot through every screen in the shop and sent him a bill for £1.2 million.

Frank Monkbottle, Hazeldean

...IF BILLY Bragg really wanted to shake a hand that had shaken the hand of Bobby Moore, he should have come to me. I was the England captain's bank manager in the 1970s.

Mr RB Arkwright, West Ham

No Names, it's... Noah Packdrill

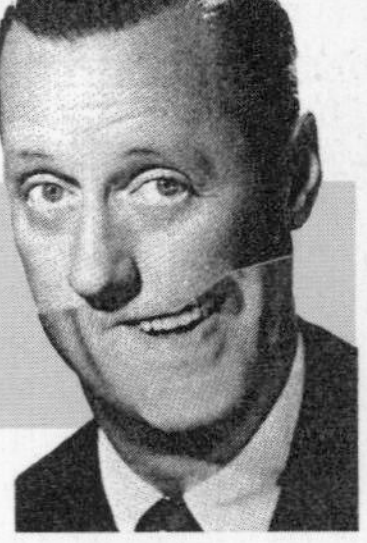

Britain's Most Fact-Free Showbiz Gossip Columnist

Wedding Bells for Actor

AN *ACTOR* who appears in films yesterday announced he intends to marry his long term *SWEETHEART*. The actor, who is best known for playing roles of a particular sort and who comes from a country, first met the actress on the set of a film in which they were both appearing at some time in the past. "We're both over the moon," the actor told reporters at a press conference in a hotel. "We've invited several big stars to attend our lavish ceremony, which will be held at some point in the future," he added. But when asked where the wedding will be, the actor was less forthcoming. "That's a secret," he said.

Celebrity Snaps

A *CELEBRITY* behaved in an aggressive manner towards a photographer outside a nightclub last night. The personality, whose face is familiar to readers of magazines, made several drunken attempts to punch a person holding a camera when leaving the club in the centre of a major city. An onlooker told reporters: "The famous person went absolutely ballistic when the photographer attempted to take a picture of them." And it's not the first time this has happened. The same person famously threw an object at photographers in an airport in the not too distant past. A spokesperson for the celebrity declined to comment.

Star Hopes for Hit

A WELL known *ACTOR* who appears regularly playing the same character in a long running television series is releasing a record. "It's something I've always wanted to do," he told reporters. The single, a cover version of a song recorded by a *BAND* several years ago has been produced by *SOMEBODY* who is famous for producing records for other people. But viewers of the programme in which the actor appears will be relieved to hear that he has no plans to give up his day job just yet. "If the single does well, there is a chance I could record an album. But at the moment, it's just a bit of fun," he said.

Sale of the Century

AN ITEM which used to belong to a *FAMOUS PERSON* who is now dead is expected to raise a lot of money when it is sold later today at an auction in another country. The item, with which that late person was photographed on many occasions, is expected to attract a lot of interest from collectors of things belonging to that person. "We've put a reserve of quite a lot of money on it," said a spokesperson from the company organising the sale. "But we think it could go for twice that." The previous auction record for an item belonging to this dead person was a very large amount of money, paid in the past for one of their things.

Going Solo

ONE OF the *MEMBERS OF A BAND* has sensationally announced that he is leaving to pursue a solo career. The member, who played an instrument in the band, cited several reasons for his decision. In the past, the band has enjoyed great success in the charts, selling large numbers of records. One particular album stayed at a certain position in the charts for an unusually long time. The remaining members of the band said the ex-member's decision to leave would not affect their recording or touring plans. There are already rumours that a former *MEMBER OF ANOTHER GROUP* which split up some time ago could be set to replace the musician in question.

Star Denies Gossip

A *STAR* yesterday angrily denied rumours about himself. The allegations that he had secretly done something that he shouldn't have done had been circulating for some time on the internet. The star told reporters that the speculations were unfounded, and corroborated his claim that they were false by saying a thing which appeared to back up his story. But people who believed that the original rumours were accurate remained unconvinced. "He would say that, wouldn't he," said one of them last night.

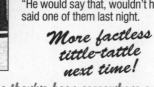

More factless tittle-tattle next time!

Do YOU know anything about someone? Perhaps they've been somewhere and done something, or maybe you've spotted them with someone else in a place. Write in and let me know at an email address, or ring my Gossipline at a telephone number. There's a crisp amount of money for every story I use.

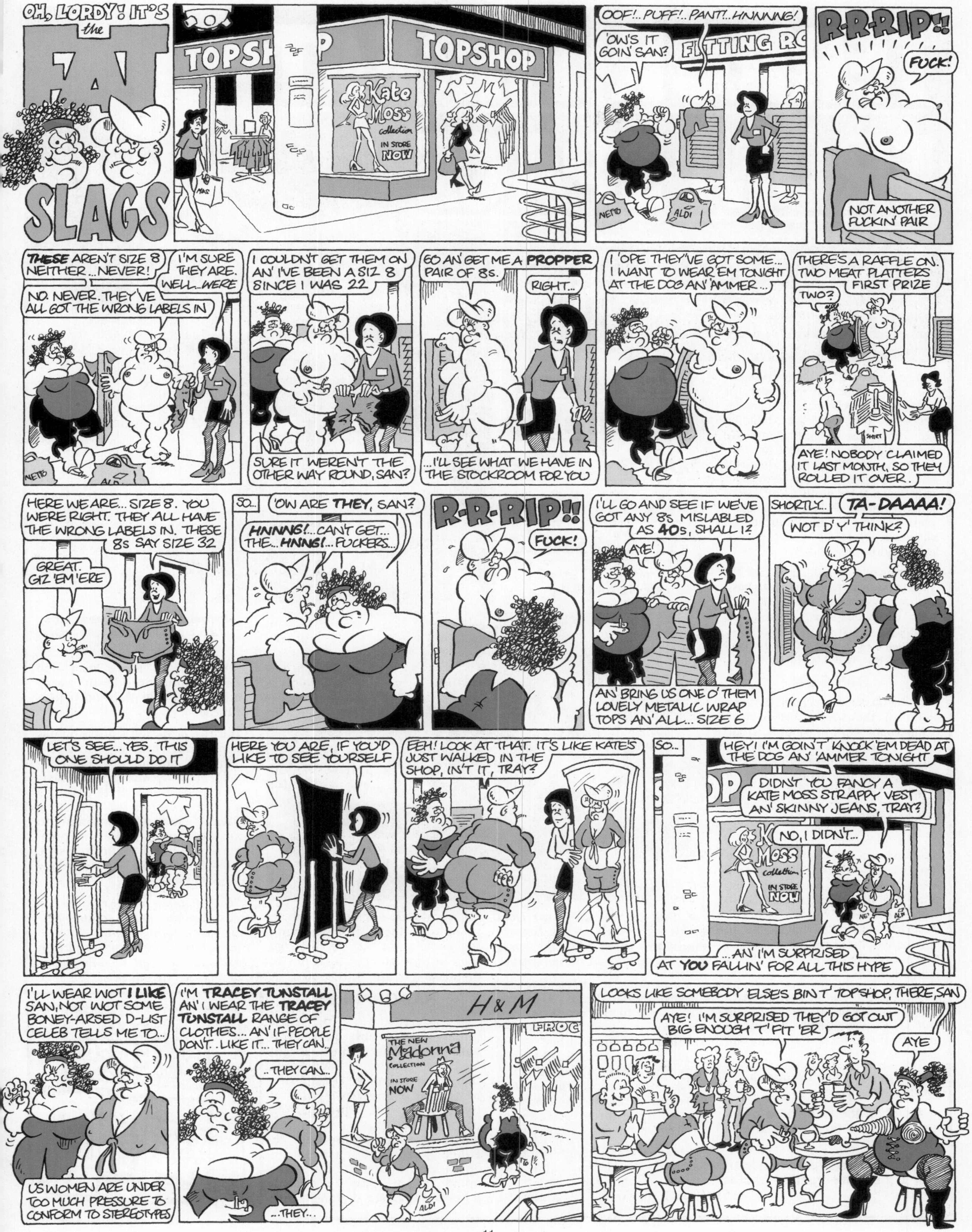

OH, LORDY! IT'S the FAT SLAGS
TOPSHOP
TOPSHOP
Kate Moss collection IN STORE NOW
OOF!.. PUFF!.. PANT!.. HNNNNG!
'OW'S IT GOIN' SAN?
FITTING RO
NETTO
ALDI
R-R-RIP!!
FUCK!
NOT ANOTHER FUCKIN' PAIR
THESE AREN'T SIZE 8 NEITHER ...NEVER!
I'M SURE THEY ARE. WELL...WERE
NO. NEVER. THEY'VE ALL GOT THE WRONG LABELS IN
I COULDN'T GET THEM ON AN' I'VE BEEN A SIZ 8 SINCE I WAS 22
SURE IT WEREN'T THE OTHER WAY ROUND, SAN?
GO AN' GET ME A PROPPER PAIR OF 8s.
RIGHT...
...I'LL SEE WHAT WE HAVE IN THE STOCKROOM FOR YOU
I 'OPE THEY'VE GOT SOME... I WANT TO WEAR 'EM TONIGHT AT THE DOG AN' 'AMMER...
THERE'S A RAFFLE ON. TWO MEAT PLATTERS FIRST PRIZE
TWO?
AYE! NOBODY CLAIMED IT LAST MONTH, SO THEY ROLLED IT OVER.
HERE WE ARE... SIZE 8. YOU WERE RIGHT. THEY ALL HAVE THE WRONG LABELS IN. THESE 8s SAY SIZE 32
GREAT. GIZ 'EM 'ERE
SO...
'OW ARE THEY, SAN?
HNNNG!... CAN'T GET... THE... HNNG!... FUCKERS...
R-R-RIP!!
FUCK!
I'LL GO AND SEE IF WE'VE GOT ANY 8s MISLABLED AS 40s, SHALL I?
AYE!
AN' BRING US ONE O' THEM LOVELY METALIC WRAP TOPS AN' ALL... SIZE 6
SHORTLY...
TA-DAAAA!
WOT D' Y' THINK?
LET'S SEE... YES. THIS ONE SHOULD DO IT
HERE YOU ARE, IF YOU'D LIKE TO SEE YOURSELF
EEH! LOOK AT THAT. IT'S LIKE KATE'S JUST WALKED IN THE SHOP, IN'T IT, TRAY?
SO...
HEY! I'M GOIN' T' KNOCK 'EM DEAD AT THE DOG AN' 'AMMER TONIGHT
DIDN'T YOU FANCY A KATE MOSS STRAPPY VEST AN' SKINNY JEANS, TRAY?
NO, I DIDN'T...
...AN' I'M SURPRISED AT YOU FALLIN' FOR ALL THIS HYPE
I'LL WEAR WOT I LIKE SAN, NOT WOT SOME BONEY-ARSED D-LIST CELEB TELLS ME TO...
US WOMEN ARE UNDER TOO MUCH PRESSURE TO CONFORM TO STEREOTYPES
I'M TRACEY TUNSTALL AN' I WEAR THE TRACEY TUNSTALL RANGE OF CLOTHES... AN' IF PEOPLE DON'T... LIKE IT... THEY CAN...
...THEY CAN...
...THEY...
H & M
FROG
THE NEW Madonna COLLECTION IN STORE NOW
ALDI
LOOKS LIKE SOMEBODY ELSE'S BIN T' TOPSHOP, THERE, SAN
AYE! I'M SURPRISED THEY'D GOT OWT BIG ENOUGH T' FIT 'ER
AYE

TERROR THREAT FROM SPACE

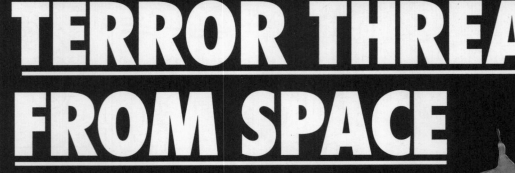

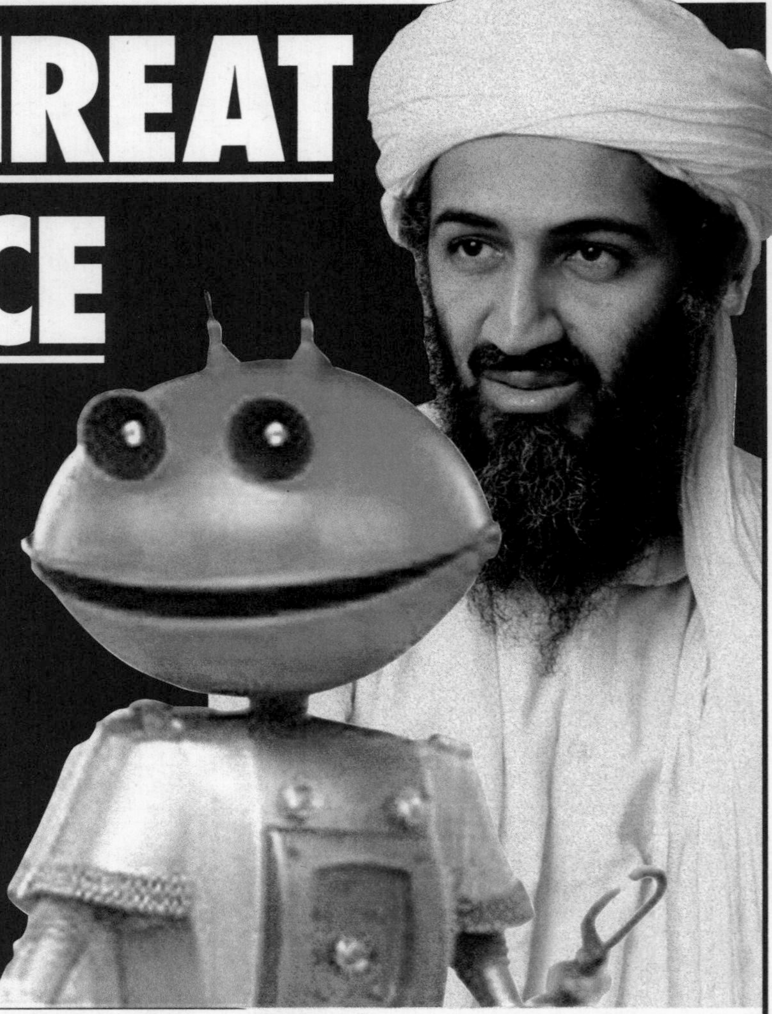

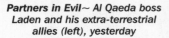

Partners in Evil~ Al Qaeda boss Laden and his extra-terrestrial allies (left), yesterday

THE 2001 ATTACKS on the World Trade Centre were the worst terrorist outrages the world has ever seen, yet they could pale into insignificance if the latest CIA reports are to be believed. For US spy chiefs fear that Al Qaeda boss *OSAMA BIN LADEN* is planning to enlist the help of *EXTRA-TERRESTRIALS* in order to launch a new and terrifying wave of atrocities on the west.

Bin Laden to Team Up with Little Green Men for Cosmic Jihad!

The Saudi 9-11 mastermind's lair has been under surveillance for some time after worried neighbours reported that he was building an enormous Jodrell Bank-style transmitter on the roof of his Tora Bora cave. Fears that Bin Laden had been attempting to make contact with beings from another world were later confirmed when spy satellite photographs of his mountain hideout showed several flying saucers parked on the grass outside.

Meanwhile, Middle Eastern TV station Al Jazeera is thought to have come into possession of disturbing video footage which shows the reclusive terrorist mastermind greeting an evil space monster and shaking him by the tentacle.

RAY-GUN

Pentagon sources claim that the alien in the footage is Mongo, Emperor of Mars, who is understood to have been developing a ray-gun capable of making buildings such as Big Ben, the White House or the Taj Mahal glow red and hum for a few seconds before vanishing completely.

"The prospect of Bin Laden teaming up with space aliens is the most worrying development we've seen for some time," said US defence spokesman Spiro Gyroskoswalsky. "The superior futuristic technology available to alien civilisations renders our puny Earthling defences completely inadequate."

"If Al Qaeda and their outer space cronies launch an all-out invasion of our planet, there will be nothing we can do to stop them. Resistance will be futile," he added.

Amongst the Intelligence chiefs' worst fears are:

- ***Obliteration of whole cities using anti-matter bombs hidden in rucksacks***
- ***Jumbo jets plucked from the sky by laser-guided tractor beams***

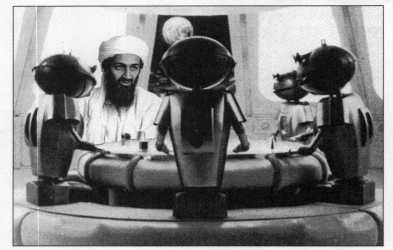

- ***Suicide bombers on BMX bikes with an ET in the basket, enabling them to fly over security barriers unchallenged***

According to BBC Security Correspondent Frank Gardner, it's a nightmare scenario that has got western governments worried. "A cosmic jihad would be infinitely more difficult to deal with than an Earth-based one," he told us. "Our present counter-terrorism measures don't begin to deal with the threat we're facing from inter-galactic extremists."

"Some of these beings are from another dimension, and will almost certainly have time travel at their disposal," he continued. "If they decide to plant a bomb on an airliner, they'll just wait until the plane is in the air, then go back in time and put their device on board it before it took off."

RAY-CHARLES

As a result of the new intelligence, airport alert levels have been raised from Bright Red to Scarlet. Meanwhile the government is considering bringing in emergency legislation to counter the threat from beyond the stars. Amongst measures being proposed by Home Secretary John Reid are detention of alien life forms for up to 28 days, stop and search powers against anyone with green skin or more than one head, compulsory identity cards and an extra 8p duty on a litre of diesel.

But the proposed legislation has been condemned as "knee-jerk soundbite politics" by Lib-Dem leader Sir Minge Campbell. "This is just knee-jerk soundbite politics," he told a series of reporters. "Identity cards will do nothing to stop these space invaders who will almost certainly be Star Trek-style trans-morphs, able to take on any identity at will."

"Either that, or they will be wearing rubber masks to hide their true lizard-faced identity, like on that series V they used to put on dead late at night on ITV a few years back," he added.

BREAST REDUCTION SURGEON
GONE BUST
SHUT

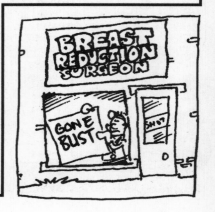

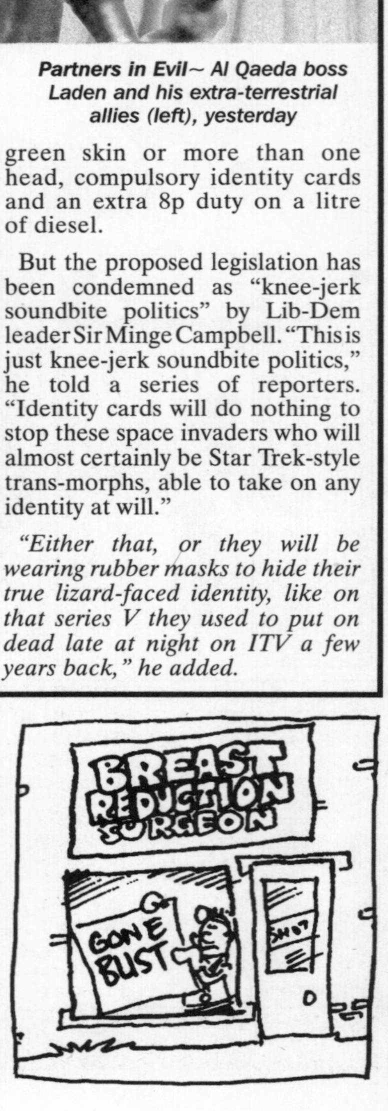

BLACKPOOL GEARS UP FOR INVASION

WITH AN alien attack now almost inevitable, most cities are resigned to the prospect of being wiped off the face of the earth by alien weapons of mass destruction which are far superior to our own. But one town that is determined not to throw in the towel so easily is the Lancashire seaside resort of Blackpool.

Lord Mayor: "Bring it On!"

At a recent emergency meeting, the council's Leisure, Tourism and Commerce committee voted by a majority of 8 to 2 (with 1 abstention) to resist any attempts by denizens of a distant galaxy to annihilate the popular holiday resort. Lord Mayor Councillor Mike Taylor told reporters: "Blackpool is used to being invaded. Every summer we get a million visitors looking for sun, sea and fun, and we cope admirably, so it'll take more than a few space invaders to put our townsfolk off their stride."

And he had this message for any bug-eyed space monsters thinking of launching an apocalyptic inter-stellar attack on his borough: "Oi, ET! You F.O! Or we'll send you back to your home planet with your tail between your six legs!"

The resolution passed at the meeting outlined several measures which would be implemented by the municipal authorities in the event of an *Independence Day*-style

EXCLUSIVE

invasion of the Fylde coast. These include:

- **THE MAYOR** and town hall staff to be evacuated to the Crazy Golf hut at Lytham St. Annes, in order to co-ordinate bus timetables, swimming pool opening times, essential refuse disposal and recycling services and other important administrative tasks.

- **RELAXATION** of town centre parking restrictions during evening hours, in order to reduce the risk of shoppers being vapourised by laser beams whilst carrying their bags back to their cars.

- **THE WINTER** Gardens and Flower Clock to be cordoned off to lessen the danger posed by triffids and Bodysnatcher-style pods growing amongst the shrubbery.

- **SUSPENSION** of the Mobile Library service, including a fine amnesty for books whose

return date coincides with the date of, or falls within the duration of, the invasion. This concession will not extend to books which were already subject to a late return penalty at or before the time that the alien hostilities commenced. Any pro rata fines on late books will not continue to increase during the emergency period, but will be frozen at the amount calculated up to (but not including) the day of the flying saucer onslaught. All fine tariffs will recommence on the first day after the defeat of the Martians (not including Sundays or Bank Holidays, when the library service is non-operational).

- **ALL DISABLED** access ramps to seafront buildings to be coned off to inhibit access by wheeled aliens such as Daleks, Robbie the Robots and K9s.

- **THE** installation of a neutron bomb 'doomsday' device in the organ loft of the Blackpool Tower Ballroom,

to be detonated by the Lord Mayor as a 'last resort' in order to destroy the attackers.

Meanwhile, members of Blackpool, Fleetwood and Cleveleys Women's Institutes have also been busy making preparations for the forthcoming invasion. Chairwoman Mrs Margot Leatherfanny told us: "We're well aware that, ironically, the germs of the common cold are the only things capable of defeating these seemingly invincible inter-galactic foes."

"With this in mind, we've been making a door-to-door collection of unwashed hankerchiefs which will be sewn together and flicked off the top of the Tower towards the air intakes on the underside of the mothership as it hovers over the town," she added.

MANY EXTRA-PLANETARY invaders these days are transmorphs - creatures that have the ability to change their shape to resemble other life forms. The chilling fact is, they could be living and working amongst us right now. The man sitting next to you on the bus, the lady in front of you in the post office queue, the one with the really big forehead out of Ant and Dec... any of these could be an extra-terrestrial being waiting for the signal to launch an all-out attack on planet earth.

But we can spot them. Like the body snatchers with their stiff little finger, aliens always make a small mistake that gives away their true identity. Why not take our fun quiz to discover whether the man next door is planning the annihilation of the earth.

Is YOUR Neighbour an ALIEN?

1 You look out of your bedroom window and see your neighbour hanging out his washing. What is the predominant colour of his clothes?
a) Beige
b) Fawn
c) Silver, sparkling with unearthly iridescent hues

2 You see your neighbour in Marks and Spencers buying a pair of trousers. How many legs are there on the trousers he is taking to the till?
a) 2
b) 2
c) More than 2

3 You go into the barbers for a haircut and you see your neighbour in the chair next to you. How would you describe the shape of his head?
a) Normal
b) Very slightly elongated or squashed

c) Mekon-shaped like Ant out of Ant and Dec. With an aerial sticking out the top

4 You pop out one Sunday morning to fetch the papers and you see your neighbour washing his car. What type of car is it?
a) A small, economical hatchback
b) An executive saloon car
c) A hovering silver disc with a perspex dome. With an aerial sticking out the top.

5 You are chatting with your neighbour over the garden fence when he mentions that he is going away for the weekend to visit his mum. Where does he say she lives?
a) Tipton
b) Dudley
c) In the fourth quadrant of a galaxy far, far away

How Did UFO Do? Score 1 point for each *a)* that you answered, 2 points for each *b)* and 3 points for each *c)*. Then tot up your score to find out if your neighbour is OK or ET...

5-10: Relax. Your neighbour is a fully paid up member of the human race - an earthling through and through. **11-14:** Don't panic. He is probably not an ET. But even if he is, chances are he comes in peace to our planet. **15:** Oh dear. Your neighbour is definitely an alien bent on crushing mankind as if we were no more than insects. The survival of our earth race is in your hands and your hands alone. You must act NOW: your neighbour must be killed before he has a chance to carry out his evil plans. Sneak into his cellar when he is at the shops and you will probably find a glowing orb that is the source of all his power. Smash it with something you find in the cellar, remembering to shield your eyes when it explodes. When he gets back from the shops he will have aged at a fantastic rate and will be having difficulty breathing. He may hold out his hand and ask for your help. Although you will feel pity for him, you must be resolute - remember all the millions who will die if you show him any mercy. Simply stand back and watch as he turns into a spangly cloud of gas, then turn and look up at the stars with a pensive expression.

ALIEN WAR: "BAD NEWS FOR BURIAL BUSINESS"

Close Encounters of the Thirsk Kind

Mrs. Pennycress: Proof

YOU MIGHT THINK that the wholesale destruction of mankind at the hands of space invaders would be good news for funeral directors. As millions upon millions of us lie dead in the streets, business might be expected to boom for undertakers.

By **Ingledew Botterill**

But that's not so, according to Les Shadrack, president of the British Society of Embalmers. He told us: "Conventional warfare is always a nice little earner for undertakers. For example the Blitz, with its good old-fashioned incendiary bombs and high explosives, spelled unprecedented profit levels in the industry. An alien war would be completely different."

"With its high tech ray guns and white-hot death beams, a space invasion will leave no bodies," he continued. "In all the films I've seen, the victims of Martian attacks are reduced to a small pile of ash, or even a scorched outline on a wall or pavement. No bereaved relative is going to shell out good money for a proper send-off when there is simply nothing left to bury or cremate."

In the absence of funeral services, many in the industry expect to see a rise in sales of commemorative park benches and flowers tied to railings. With this in mind, many manufacturers of garden furniture, small plaques and cable ties are taking on extra staff in anticipation of increased demand. "We're expecting a bumper year," said George Turpentine, managing director of Turpentine's Garden Furniture, Small Plaques and Cable Ties Ltd.

And its also good news for manufacturers of aluminium foil. As millions of people try to make reflective hats to protect their heads from alien mind control rays, supermarkets report panic buying. "No-one wants to be turned into an automaton-like zombie," said a delighted Hector Neatsfoot, managing director of Ashington-based foil company Alcan. "We just can't keep up with demand for our product."

Another group who are celebrating an unprecedented upturn in trade are Britain's estimated 125,000 professional origami teachers. Spokesman Robert Harbin told us:

"Business has been a little bit slow for the last 35-years or so, but suddenly everybody's desperate to learn how to fold hats out of foil. I've had to take my phone off the hook."

NEWS that we are soon to be invaded by extra-terrestrial terrorists has shocked the nation.

But for one North Yorkshire woman, the news has come as no surprise. For Mrs Edna Pennycress has proof that aliens are already here, and what's more they're abducting her husband Arthur on a regular basis.

spaceship

Mr Pennycress, an ex-drayman for Theakston's brewery in Thirsk, is taken up into a spaceship every day - sometimes twice, according to his wife. "What they do with him in their flying saucer I can only imagine," she told us. "When he staggers back through that door, he's got no memory of the last six hours. He doesn't even know what day it is."

According to Edna, Arthur goes out for a walk round the block each evening at around 6 o'clock, saying he'll be back in 5 minutes. Yet he never returns before 11.30, and occasionally doesn't return at all. "Several times I've found him slumped in a hedge in the early hours of the morning, and once they teleported him back down to earth and left him upside down in a wheelie bin," she said.

lunchtimes

Worryingly, the frequency with which Arthur is abducted seems to be increasing. Mrs Pennycress continued: "Now he's started being taken up into the ship at lunchtimes as well. The aliens have usually finished with him by half past three, but when he gets back he's so exhausted from his ordeal that he just sleeps for the rest of the afternoon."

"After his tea, he pops out for a bit of fresh air and they get him again," she added. "It must be a nightmare undergoing these dreadful alien experiments day after day. When he gets back he's unable to tell me what's happened to him because they leave him slurring his words and he quite often vomits down his shirt."

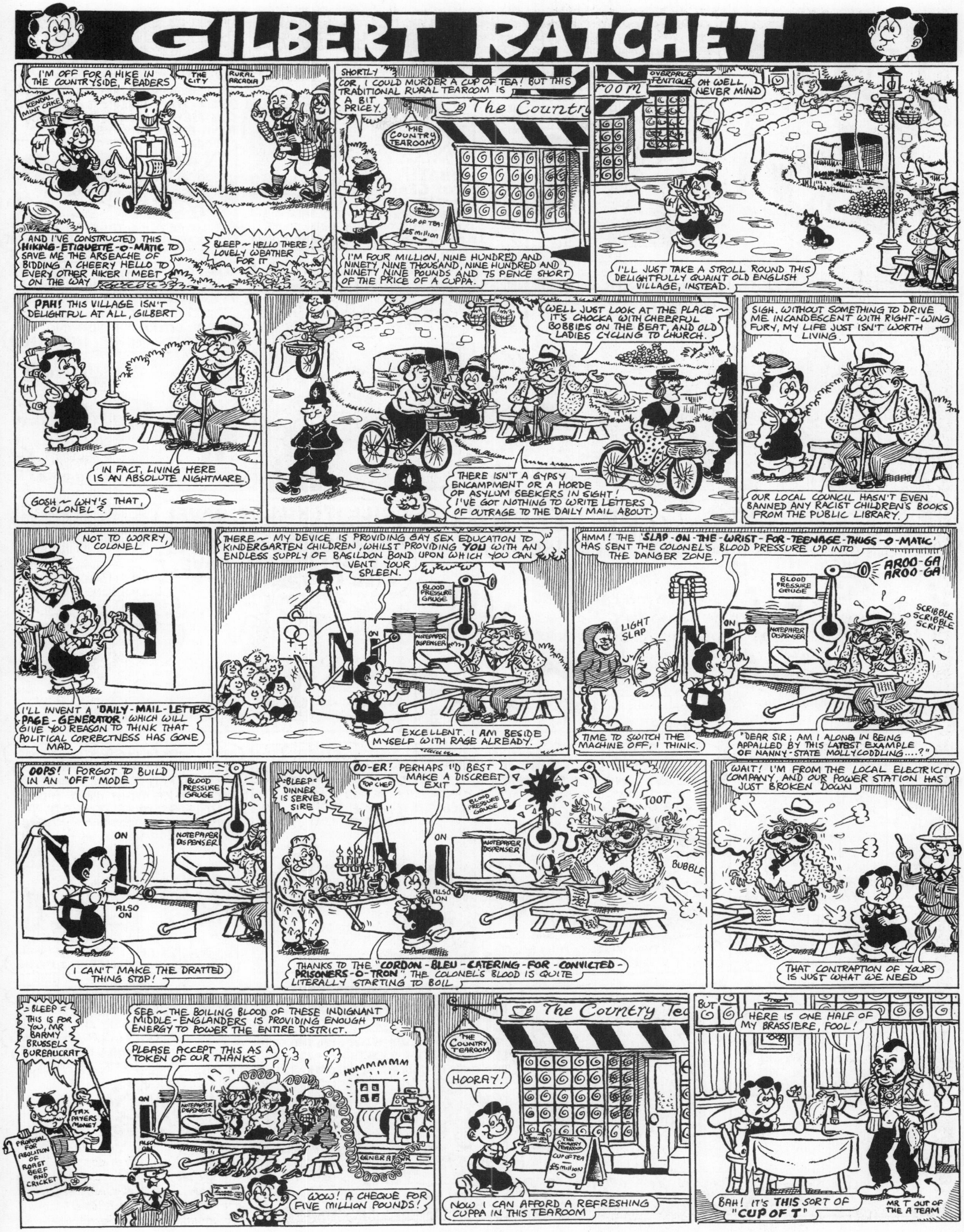
GILBERT RATCHET
I'M OFF FOR A HIKE IN THE COUNTRYSIDE, READERS
THE CITY
RURAL ARCADIA
KENDAL MINT CAKE
AND I'VE CONSTRUCTED THIS HIKING-ETIQUETTE-O-MATIC TO SAVE ME THE ARSEACHE OF BIDDING A CHEERY HELLO TO EVERY OTHER HIKER I MEET ON THE WAY
BLEEP ~ HELLO THERE! LOVELY WEATHER FOR IT
SHORTLY
COR, I COULD MURDER A CUP OF TEA! BUT THIS TRADITIONAL RURAL TEAROOM IS A BIT PRICEY.
THE COUNTRY TEAROOM
The Countr
CUP OF TEA: £5 million
I'M FOUR MILLION, NINE HUNDRED AND NINETY NINE THOUSAND, NINE HUNDRED AND NINETY NINE POUNDS AND 75 PENCE SHORT OF THE PRICE OF A CUPPA.
OVERPRICED FENTIQUE
OH WELL, NEVER MIND
I'LL JUST TAKE A STROLL ROUND THIS DELIGHTFULLY QUAINT OLD ENGLISH VILLAGE, INSTEAD.
PAH! THIS VILLAGE ISN'T DELIGHTFUL AT ALL, GILBERT
IN FACT, LIVING HERE IS AN ABSOLUTE NIGHTMARE.
GOSH ~ WHY'S THAT, COLONEL?
WELL JUST LOOK AT THE PLACE ~ IT'S CHOCKA WITH CHEERFUL BOBBIES ON THE BEAT, AND OLD LADIES CYCLING TO CHURCH.
THERE ISN'T A GYPSY ENCAMPMENT OR A HORDE OF ASYLUM SEEKERS IN SIGHT! I'VE GOT NOTHING TO WRITE LETTERS OF OUTRAGE TO THE DAILY MAIL ABOUT.
SIGH. WITHOUT SOMETHING TO DRIVE ME INCANDESCENT WITH RIGHT-WING FURY, MY LIFE JUST ISN'T WORTH LIVING.
OUR LOCAL COUNCIL HASN'T EVEN BANNED ANY RACIST CHILDREN'S BOOKS FROM THE PUBLIC LIBRARY.
NOT TO WORRY, COLONEL
I'LL INVENT A 'DAILY-MAIL-LETTERS-PAGE-GENERATOR' WHICH WILL GIVE YOU REASON TO THINK THAT POLITICAL CORRECTNESS HAS GONE MAD.
THERE ~ MY DEVICE IS PROVIDING GAY SEX EDUCATION TO KINDERGARTEN CHILDREN, WHILST PROVIDING YOU WITH AN ENDLESS SUPPLY OF BASILDON BOND UPON WHICH YOU CAN VENT YOUR SPLEEN.
BLOOD PRESSURE GAUGE
ON
NOTEPAPER DISPENSER
EXCELLENT. I AM BESIDE MYSELF WITH RAGE ALREADY.
HMM! THE 'SLAP-ON-THE-WRIST-FOR-TEENAGE-THUGS-O-MATIC' HAS SENT THE COLONEL'S BLOOD PRESSURE UP INTO THE DANGER ZONE.
AROO-GA AROO-GA
LIGHT SLAP
BLOOD PRESSURE GAUGE
ON
NOTEPAPER DISPENSER
SCRIBBLE SCRIBBLE SCRIT
TIME TO SWITCH THE MACHINE OFF, I THINK.
"DEAR SIR; AM I ALONE IN BEING APPALLED BY THIS LATEST EXAMPLE OF NANNY-STATE MOLLYCODDLING....?"
OOPS! I FORGOT TO BUILD IN AN "OFF" MODE
BLOOD PRESSURE GAUGE
ON
NOTEPAPER DISPENSER
ALSO ON
I CAN'T MAKE THE DRATTED THING STOP!
OO-ER! PERHAPS I'D BEST MAKE A DISCREET EXIT
BLEEP ~ DINNER IS SERVED, SIRE
TOP CHEF
BLOOD PRESSURE GAUGE
ON
NOTEPAPER DISPENSER
ALSO ON
TOOT
BUBBLE
THANKS TO THE "CORDON-BLEU-CATERING-FOR-CONVICTED-PRISONERS-O-TRON", THE COLONEL'S BLOOD IS QUITE LITERALLY STARTING TO BOIL
WAIT! I'M FROM THE LOCAL ELECTRICITY COMPANY, AND OUR POWER STATION HAS JUST BROKEN DOWN
THAT CONTRAPTION OF YOURS IS JUST WHAT WE NEED
BLEEP ~ THIS IS FOR YOU, MR BARMY BRUSSELS BUREAUCRAT
TAX PAYERS MONEY
PROPOSAL FOR ABOLITION OF ROAST BEEF AND CRICKET
SEE ~ THE BOILING BLOOD OF THESE INDIGNANT MIDDLE-ENGLANDERS IS PROVIDING ENOUGH ENERGY TO POWER THE ENTIRE DISTRICT.
PLEASE ACCEPT THIS AS A TOKEN OF OUR THANKS
HUMMMMM
ON
NOTEPAPER DISPENSER
GENERATOR
WOW! A CHEQUE FOR FIVE MILLION POUNDS!
The Country Tea
THE COUNTRY TEAROOM
HOORAY!
CUP OF TEA £5 million
NOW I CAN AFFORD A REFRESHING CUPPA IN THIS TEAROOM
BUT
HERE IS ONE HALF OF MY BRASSIERE, FOOL!
BAH! IT'S THIS SORT OF "CUP OF T"
MR T OUT OF THE A TEAM

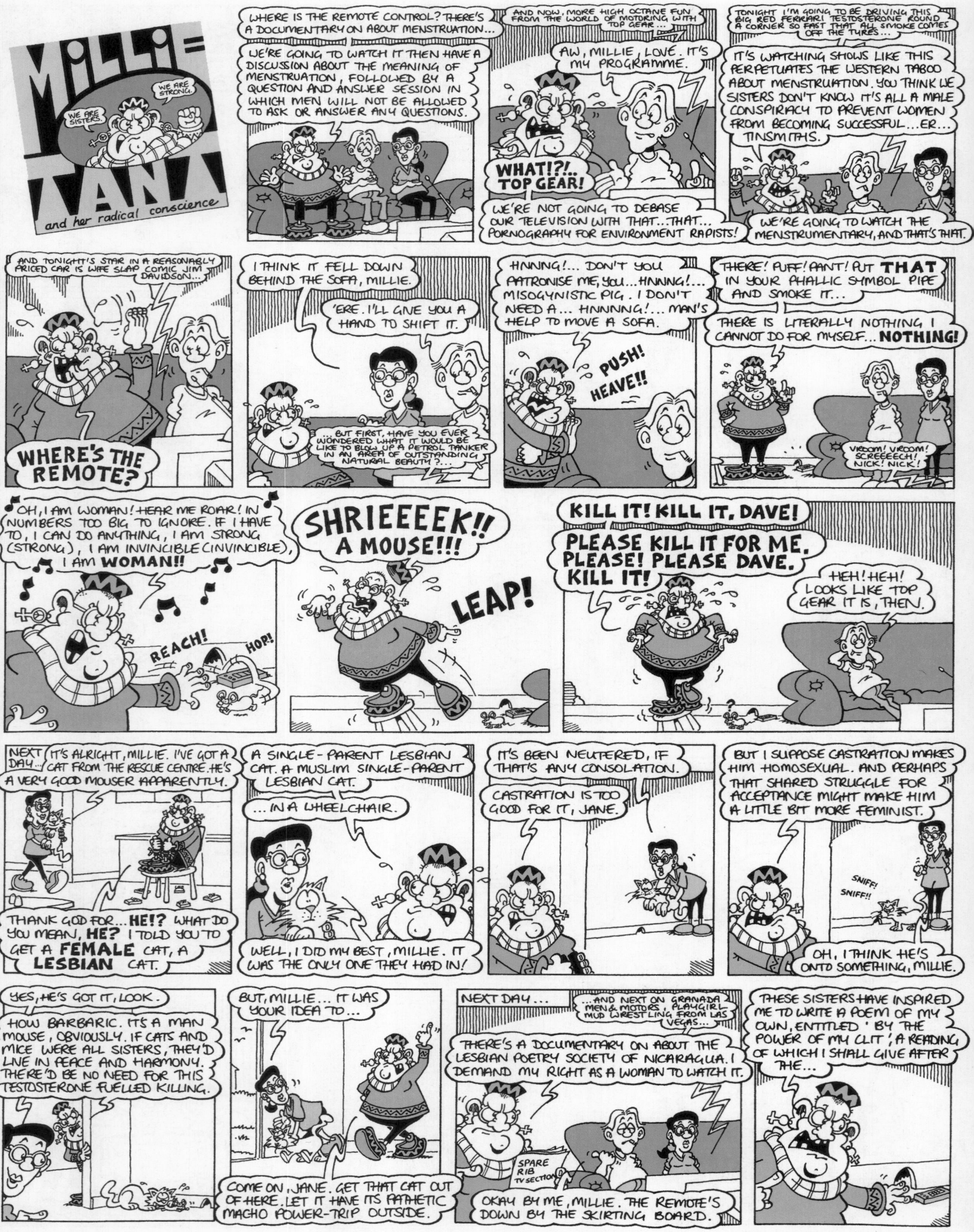
MILLIE TANT
and her radical conscience
WE ARE SISTERS.
WE ARE STRONG.
WHERE IS THE REMOTE CONTROL? THERE'S A DOCUMENTARY ON ABOUT MENSTRUATION...
WE'RE GOING TO WATCH IT THEN HAVE A DISCUSSION ABOUT THE MEANING OF MENSTRUATION, FOLLOWED BY A QUESTION AND ANSWER SESSION IN WHICH MEN WILL NOT BE ALLOWED TO ASK OR ANSWER ANY QUESTIONS.
AND NOW, MORE HIGH OCTANE FUN FROM THE WORLD OF MOTORING WITH TOP GEAR...
AW, MILLIE, LOVE. IT'S MY PROGRAMME.
WHAT!?!.. TOP GEAR!
WE'RE NOT GOING TO DEBASE OUR TELEVISION WITH THAT...THAT... PORNOGRAPHY FOR ENVIRONMENT RAPISTS!
TONIGHT I'M GOING TO BE DRIVING THIS BIG RED FERRARI TESTOSTERONE ROUND A CORNER SO FAST THAT ALL SMOKE COMES OFF THE TYRES...
IT'S WATCHING SHOWS LIKE THIS PERPETUATES THE WESTERN TABOO ABOUT MENSTRUATION. YOU THINK WE SISTERS DON'T KNOW IT'S ALL A MALE CONSPIRACY TO PREVENT WOMEN FROM BECOMING SUCCESSFUL...ER... TINSMITHS.
WE'RE GOING TO WATCH THE MENSTRUMENTARY, AND THAT'S THAT.
AND TONIGHT'S STAR IN A REASONABLY PRICED CAR IS WIFE SLAP COMIC JIM DAVIDSON...
WHERE'S THE REMOTE?
I THINK IT FELL DOWN BEHIND THE SOFA, MILLIE.
'ERE. I'LL GIVE YOU A HAND TO SHIFT IT.
...BUT FIRST, HAVE YOU EVER WONDERED WHAT IT WOULD BE LIKE TO BLOW UP A PETROL TANKER IN AN AREA OF OUTSTANDING NATURAL BEAUTY?...
HNNNG!... DON'T YOU PATRONISE ME, YOU...HNNNG!... MISOGYNISTIC PIG. I DON'T NEED A... HNNNNG!... MAN'S HELP TO MOVE A SOFA.
PUSH! HEAVE!!
THERE! PUFF! PANT! PUT THAT IN YOUR PHALLIC SYMBOL PIPE AND SMOKE IT...
THERE IS LITERALLY NOTHING I CANNOT DO FOR MYSELF... NOTHING!
VROOM! VROOM! SCREEEECH! NICK! NICK!
OH, I AM WOMAN! HEAR ME ROAR! IN NUMBERS TOO BIG TO IGNORE. IF I HAVE TO, I CAN DO ANYTHING, I AM STRONG (STRONG), I AM INVINCIBLE (INVINCIBLE), I AM WOMAN!!
REACH!
HOP!
SHRIEEEEK!! A MOUSE!!!
LEAP!
KILL IT! KILL IT, DAVE!
PLEASE KILL IT FOR ME. PLEASE! PLEASE DAVE. KILL IT!
HEH! HEH! LOOKS LIKE TOP GEAR IT IS, THEN.
NEXT DAY...
IT'S ALRIGHT, MILLIE. I'VE GOT A CAT FROM THE RESCUE CENTRE. HE'S A VERY GOOD MOUSER APPARENTLY.
THANK GOD FOR... HE!? WHAT DO YOU MEAN, HE? I TOLD YOU TO GET A FEMALE CAT, A LESBIAN CAT.
A SINGLE-PARENT LESBIAN CAT. A MUSLIM SINGLE-PARENT LESBIAN CAT.
...IN A WHEELCHAIR.
WELL, I DID MY BEST, MILLIE. IT WAS THE ONLY ONE THEY HAD IN!
IT'S BEEN NEUTERED, IF THAT'S ANY CONSOLATION.
CASTRATION IS TOO GOOD FOR IT, JANE.
BUT I SUPPOSE CASTRATION MAKES HIM HOMOSEXUAL. AND PERHAPS THAT SHARED STRUGGLE FOR ACCEPTANCE MIGHT MAKE HIM A LITTLE BIT MORE FEMINIST.
SNIFF! SNIFF!!
OH, I THINK HE'S ONTO SOMETHING, MILLIE.
YES, HE'S GOT IT, LOOK.
HOW BARBARIC. IT'S A MAN MOUSE, OBVIOUSLY. IF CATS AND MICE WERE ALL SISTERS, THEY'D LIVE IN PEACE AND HARMONY. THERE'D BE NO NEED FOR THIS TESTOSTERONE FUELLED KILLING.
BUT, MILLIE... IT WAS YOUR IDEA TO...
COME ON, JANE. GET THAT CAT OUT OF HERE. LET IT HAVE ITS PATHETIC MACHO POWER-TRIP OUTSIDE.
NEXT DAY...
...AND NEXT ON GRANADA MEN & MOTORS, PLAYGIRL MUD WRESTLING FROM LAS VEGAS...
THERE'S A DOCUMENTARY ON ABOUT THE LESBIAN POETRY SOCIETY OF NICARAGUA. I DEMAND MY RIGHT AS A WOMAN TO WATCH IT.
SPARE RIB TV SECTION
OKAY BY ME, MILLIE. THE REMOTE'S DOWN BY THE SKIRTING BOARD.
THESE SISTERS HAVE INSPIRED ME TO WRITE A POEM OF MY OWN, ENTITLED 'BY THE POWER OF MY CLIT', A READING OF WHICH I SHALL GIVE AFTER THE...

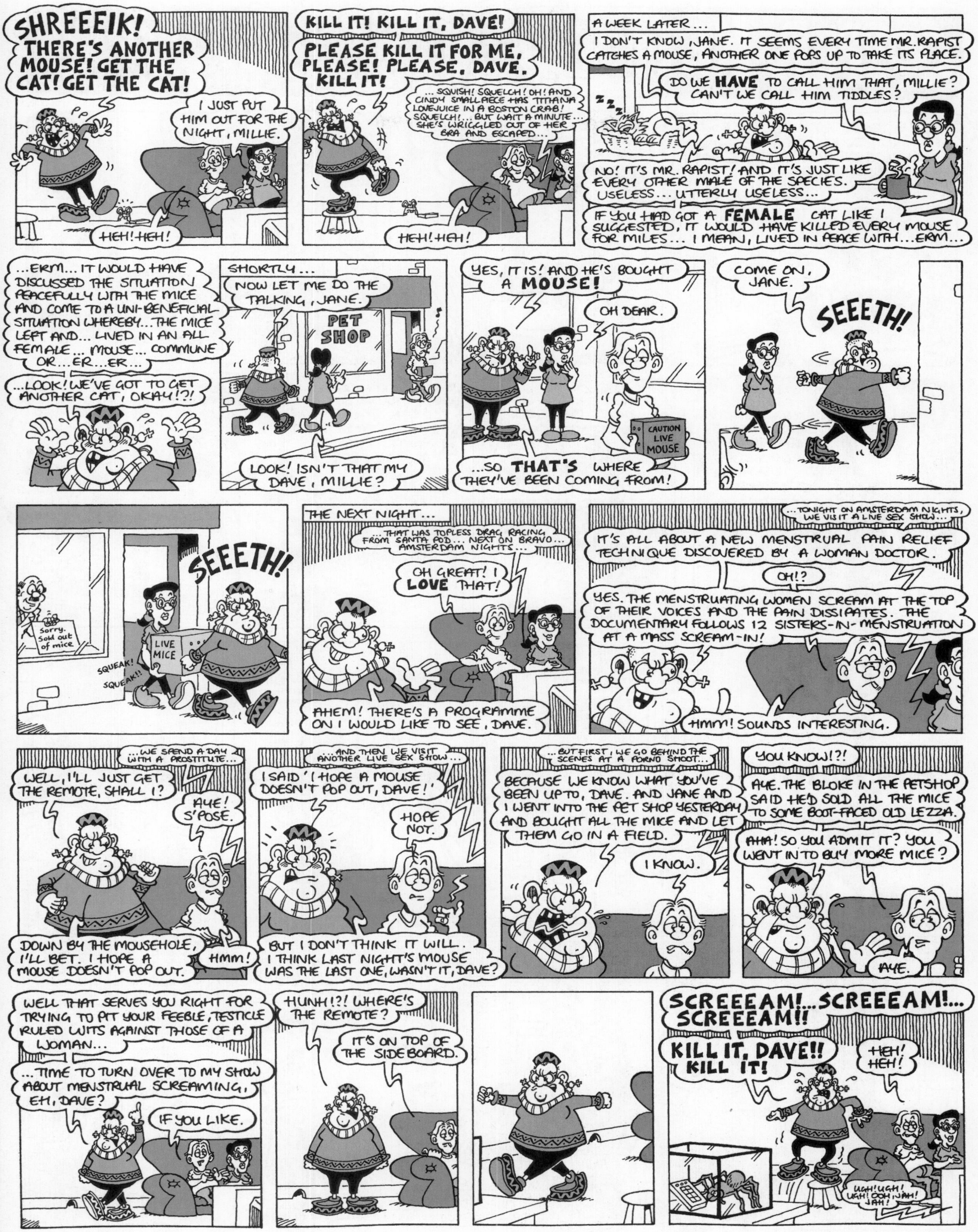
SHREEEIK! THERE'S ANOTHER MOUSE! GET THE CAT! GET THE CAT!
I JUST PUT HIM OUT FOR THE NIGHT, MILLIE.
HEH! HEH!
KILL IT! KILL IT, DAVE!
PLEASE KILL IT FOR ME, PLEASE! PLEASE, DAVE. KILL IT!
... SQUISH! SQUELCH! OH! AND CINDY SMALLPIECE HAS TITTANIA LOVEJUICE IN A BOSTON CRAB! SQUELCH! ... BUT WAIT A MINUTE ... SHE'S WRIGGLED OUT OF HER BRA AND ESCAPED ...
HEH! HEH!
A WEEK LATER ...
I DON'T KNOW, JANE. IT SEEMS EVERY TIME MR. RAPIST CATCHES A MOUSE, ANOTHER ONE POPS UP TO TAKE ITS PLACE.
DO WE HAVE TO CALL HIM THAT, MILLIE? CAN'T WE CALL HIM TIDDLES?
ZZZ
NO! IT'S MR. RAPIST! AND IT'S JUST LIKE EVERY OTHER MALE OF THE SPECIES. USELESS... UTTERLY USELESS...
IF YOU HAD GOT A FEMALE CAT LIKE I SUGGESTED, IT WOULD HAVE KILLED EVERY MOUSE FOR MILES... I MEAN, LIVED IN PEACE WITH... ERM...
...ERM... IT WOULD HAVE DISCUSSED THE SITUATION PEACEFULLY WITH THE MICE AND COME TO A UNI-BENEFICIAL SITUATION WHEREBY... THE MICE LEFT AND... LIVED IN AN ALL FEMALE... MOUSE... COMMUNE OR... ER... ER...
...LOOK! WE'VE GOT TO GET ANOTHER CAT, OKAY!?!
SHORTLY...
NOW LET ME DO THE TALKING, JANE.
PET SHOP
LOOK! ISN'T THAT MY DAVE, MILLIE?
YES, IT IS! AND HE'S BOUGHT A MOUSE!
OH DEAR.
CAUTION LIVE MOUSE
...SO THAT'S WHERE THEY'VE BEEN COMING FROM!
COME ON, JANE.
SEEETH!
Sorry. Sold out of mice
LIVE MICE
SQUEAK! SQUEAK!!
SEEETH!
THE NEXT NIGHT...
...THAT WAS TOPLESS DRAG RACING FROM SANTA POD... NEXT ON BRAVO... AMSTERDAM NIGHTS...
OH GREAT! I LOVE THAT!
AHEM! THERE'S A PROGRAMME ON I WOULD LIKE TO SEE, DAVE.
...TONIGHT ON AMSTERDAM NIGHTS, WE VISIT A LIVE SEX SHOW...
IT'S ALL ABOUT A NEW MENSTRUAL PAIN RELIEF TECHNIQUE DISCOVERED BY A WOMAN DOCTOR.
OH!?
YES. THE MENSTRUATING WOMEN SCREAM AT THE TOP OF THEIR VOICES AND THE PAIN DISSIPATES. THE DOCUMENTARY FOLLOWS 12 SISTERS-IN-MENSTRUATION AT A MASS SCREAM-IN!
HMM! SOUNDS INTERESTING.
...WE SPEND A DAY WITH A PROSTITUTE...
WELL, I'LL JUST GET THE REMOTE, SHALL I?
AYE! S'POSE.
DOWN BY THE MOUSEHOLE, I'LL BET. I HOPE A MOUSE DOESN'T POP OUT.
HMM!
...AND THEN WE VISIT ANOTHER LIVE SEX SHOW...
I SAID 'I HOPE A MOUSE DOESN'T POP OUT, DAVE!'
HOPE NOT.
BUT I DON'T THINK IT WILL. I THINK LAST NIGHT'S MOUSE WAS THE LAST ONE, WASN'T IT, DAVE?
...BUT FIRST, WE GO BEHIND THE SCENES AT A PORNO SHOOT...
BECAUSE WE KNOW WHAT YOU'VE BEEN UP TO, DAVE. AND JANE AND I WENT INTO THE PET SHOP YESTERDAY AND BOUGHT ALL THE MICE AND LET THEM GO IN A FIELD.
I KNOW.
YOU KNOW!?!
AYE. THE BLOKE IN THE PETSHOP SAID HE'D SOLD ALL THE MICE TO SOME BOOT-FACED OLD LEZZA.
AHA! SO YOU ADMIT IT? YOU WENT IN TO BUY MORE MICE?
AYE.
WELL THAT SERVES YOU RIGHT FOR TRYING TO PIT YOUR FEEBLE, TESTICLE RULED WITS AGAINST THOSE OF A WOMAN...
...TIME TO TURN OVER TO MY SHOW ABOUT MENSTRUAL SCREAMING, EH, DAVE?
IF YOU LIKE.
HUNH!?! WHERE'S THE REMOTE?
IT'S ON TOP OF THE SIDEBOARD.
SCREEEAM!... SCREEEAM!... SCREEEAM!!
KILL IT, DAVE!! KILL IT!
HEH! HEH!
UGH! UGH! UGH! OOH, JAH! JAH!

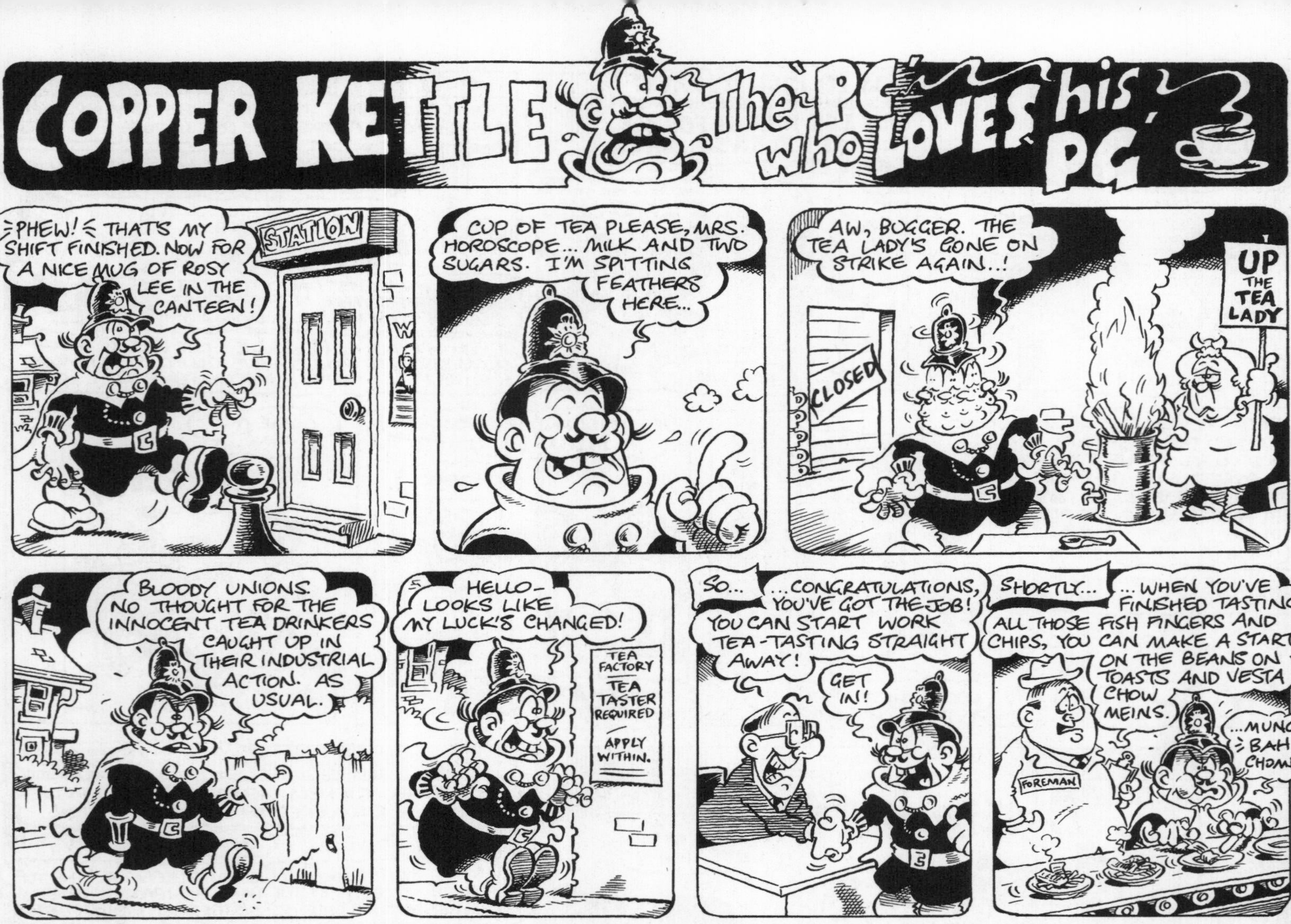
COPPER KETTLE
The 'PC' who LOVES his 'PG'
PHEW! THAT'S MY SHIFT FINISHED. NOW FOR A NICE MUG OF ROSY LEE IN THE CANTEEN!
STATION
CUP OF TEA PLEASE, MRS. HOROSCOPE... MILK AND TWO SUGARS. I'M SPITTING FEATHERS HERE...
AW, BUGGER. THE TEA LADY'S GONE ON STRIKE AGAIN..!
CLOSED
UP THE TEA LADY
BLOODY UNIONS. NO THOUGHT FOR THE INNOCENT TEA DRINKERS CAUGHT UP IN THEIR INDUSTRIAL ACTION. AS USUAL.
HELLO- LOOKS LIKE MY LUCK'S CHANGED!
TEA FACTORY
TEA TASTER REQUIRED
APPLY WITHIN.
SO...
...CONGRATULATIONS, YOU'VE GOT THE JOB! YOU CAN START WORK TEA-TASTING STRAIGHT AWAY!
GET IN!
SHORTLY...
...WHEN YOU'VE FINISHED TASTING ALL THOSE FISH FINGERS AND CHIPS, YOU CAN MAKE A START ON THE BEANS ON TOASTS AND VESTA CHOW MEINS.
FOREMAN
...MUNCH BAH! CHOMP

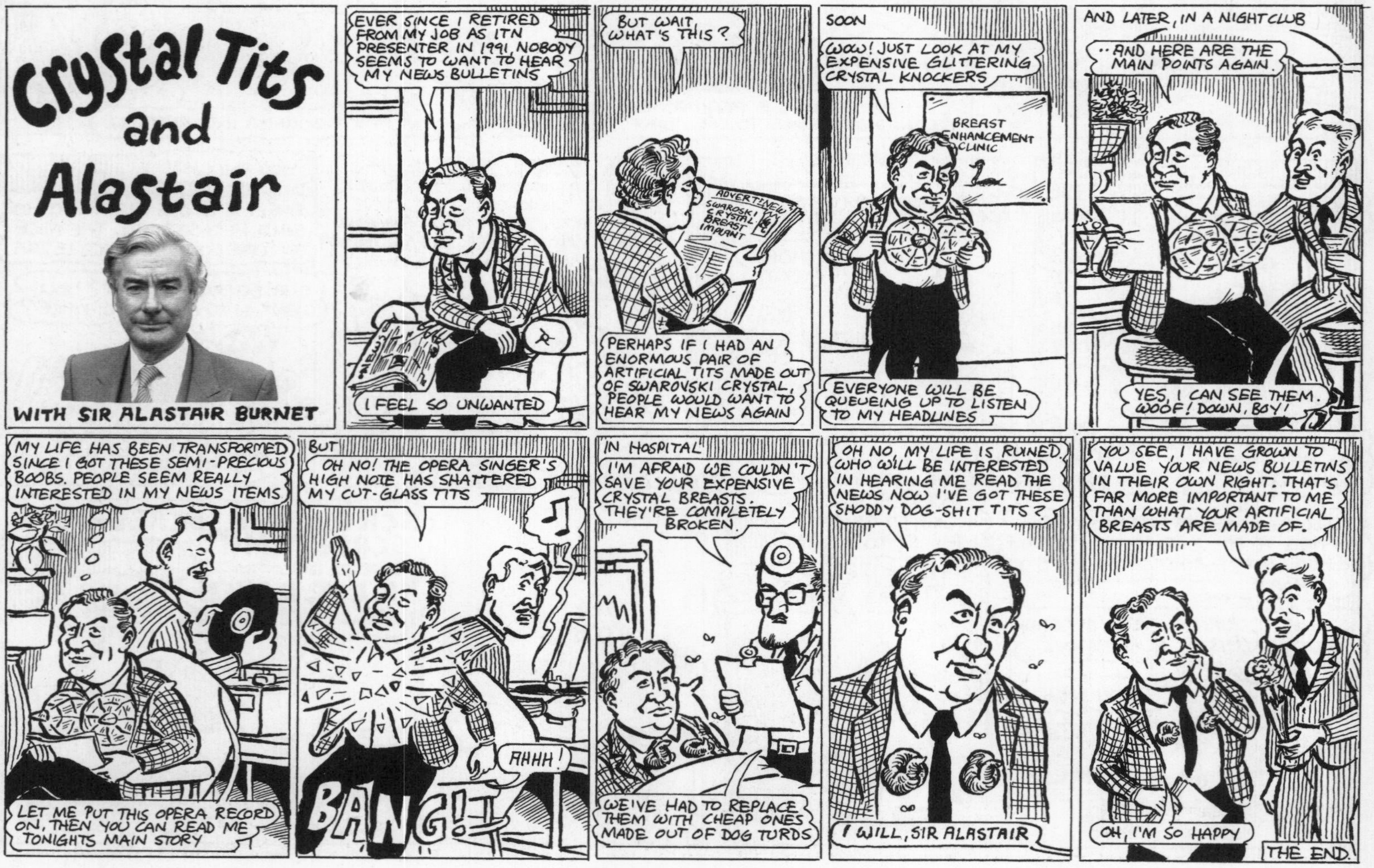
Crystal Tits and Alastair
WITH SIR ALASTAIR BURNET
EVER SINCE I RETIRED FROM MY JOB AS ITN PRESENTER IN 1991, NOBODY SEEMS TO WANT TO HEAR MY NEWS BULLETINS
I FEEL SO UNWANTED
BUT WAIT, WHAT'S THIS?
ADVERT NEW SWAROSKI CRYSTAL BREAST IMPLANT
PERHAPS IF I HAD AN ENORMOUS PAIR OF ARTIFICIAL TITS MADE OUT OF SWAROVSKI CRYSTAL, PEOPLE WOULD WANT TO HEAR MY NEWS AGAIN
SOON
WOW! JUST LOOK AT MY EXPENSIVE GLITTERING CRYSTAL KNOCKERS
BREAST ENHANCEMENT CLINIC
EVERYONE WILL BE QUEUEING UP TO LISTEN TO MY HEADLINES
AND LATER, IN A NIGHT CLUB
..AND HERE ARE THE MAIN POINTS AGAIN.
YES, I CAN SEE THEM. WOOF! DOWN, BOY!
MY LIFE HAS BEEN TRANSFORMED SINCE I GOT THESE SEMI-PRECIOUS BOOBS. PEOPLE SEEM REALLY INTERESTED IN MY NEWS ITEMS
LET ME PUT THIS OPERA RECORD ON, THEN YOU CAN READ ME TONIGHTS MAIN STORY
BUT
OH NO! THE OPERA SINGER'S HIGH NOTE HAS SHATTERED MY CUT-GLASS TITS
AHHH!
BANG!
IN HOSPITAL
I'M AFRAID WE COULDN'T SAVE YOUR EXPENSIVE CRYSTAL BREASTS. THEY'RE COMPLETELY BROKEN.
WE'VE HAD TO REPLACE THEM WITH CHEAP ONES MADE OUT OF DOG TURDS
OH NO, MY LIFE IS RUINED. WHO WILL BE INTERESTED IN HEARING ME READ THE NEWS NOW I'VE GOT THESE SHODDY DOG-SHIT TITS?
I WILL, SIR ALASTAIR
YOU SEE, I HAVE GROWN TO VALUE YOUR NEWS BULLETINS IN THEIR OWN RIGHT. THAT'S FAR MORE IMPORTANT TO ME THAN WHAT YOUR ARTIFICIAL BREASTS ARE MADE OF.
OH, I'M SO HAPPY
THE END.

MAJOR MISUNDERSTANDING

HALLOWEEN

LET'S TRY THIS HOUSE NEXT

YES. TEE HEE!

GIGGLE!

SQUEAL!

TRICK OR TREAT!

OOOOH! WOOO! WOOO!

WOOO! WOOO! WURRR!

MADAM, I HAVEN'T THE FAINTEST IDEA WHAT YOU'RE SAYING.

MIGHT I SUGGEST THAT NOW YOU ARE DOMICILED HERE IN THE UNITED KINGDOM OF GREAT BRITAIN, YOU LEARN TO SPEAK OUR LANGUAGE?

THE POLITICALLY CORRECT LOBBY TELL US THAT WE MUST RESPECT YOUR BELIEFS AND DRESS CODES. SO BE IT. BUT RESPECT IS A TWO-WAY STREET.

AND IT IS A BASIC COURTESY FOR ONE TO LEARN THE LANGUAGE OF ONE'S HOST NATION.

WHEN I WAS STATIONED IN SINGAPORE DURING MY YEARS WITH THE COLONIAL SERVICE, I ENDEAVOURED TO PICK UP A FEW SIMPLE PHRASES IN MALAY.

"BERAPA HARGA PELACUR?" "DENGAN CEPAT MEMASUKKEN JARI ANDA KE DALAM DUBUR SAYA" I LEARNED ENOUGH TO GET BY.

BUT YOU'RE NOT PREPARED TO GO TO THAT BOTHER, ARE YOU? OH NO.

FAR EASIER FOR YOU TO RELY ON TRANSLATORS PROVIDED BY THE LOCAL AUTHORITY.

AND WHO PAYS FOR ALL THIS? WHO PAYS FOR MY COUNCIL TAX BILL TO BE PRINTED WITH TRANSLATIONS INTO CANTONESE AND URDU?

JOE MUGGINS, THAT'S WHO. THE ORDINARY BRITISH TAXPAYER

IF YOU WISH TO COMMUNICATE WITH ME, YOU WILL KINDLY LEARN TO SPEAK HER MAJESTY THE QUEEN'S ENGLISH.

SLAM!

IT'S THE BACONS...

BONFIRE NIGHT...

HEY, I FUCKIN' LOVE BONFIRE NEET, ME...

NOO, WHERE'S THEM FUCKIN' BANGAZ?

SPARKZ SPARKZ

STOP, SON! Y'SHOULD HEV THEM FIREWALKS IN A BISCUIT TIN. AN' Y'SHOULD BE LOOKIN' F' THEM BANGAZ WI' A TORCH, NOT A MATCH

THAT'S REET, SON...

FOLLUR THE FIREWALK CURRD. W'DIVVENT WANT NEE ACCIDENTS

THAT'S IT... NOO, TEK THE BANGAZ OOT ONE AT A TIME AN' PUT THE LID BACK ON FO'T' PREVENT SPARKS GEDDIN' IN AN' SETTIN' AALL THE REST OFF

AALL REET

TEATIME ASSORTMEN

REET... NOO READ THE INSTRUCTIONS BY TORCH LIGHT, SON

FIX FORMLY... LIGHT THE FUSE AN' RETIRE TO A SAFE DISTANCE

THAT'S REET, SON...MEK SURE IT'S IN NICE AN' FORM...W'DIVVENT WANT IT FAALLIN' AWA

CAN I SPARK THE FUCKAH UP

NAH, SON... I'LL DEE IT WI' A GLURWIN' SPLINT...THERE WE GAN, BIFFA

NOO WAALK QUICKLY BACK TO A SAFE DISTANCE, BUT DIVVENT RUN

FSSS...

FUCK! IT'S GONE OOT! I'LL GAN BACK AN' LIGHT IT AGAIN

NEE, BIFFA! NEVAH RETURN TO A LIT FIREWALK

FSSS...S...S...PHUT!

SEE, SON...IT'S SPARKED UP AGAIN... FUCK, THAT COULD OF BEEN DANGEROUS THAT, BIFFA.

FSSSSS

OOOH!

BANG!

AAAH!

TEATIM ASSOR

HEY, THAT WAS FANTAKKA, THAT. REET, LET'S GAN PUT SOME JUMPIN' JACKS THROUGH CEDRIC'S LETTER BOX

TEK 'EM OOT THE TIN ONE AT A TIME, BIFFA...REMEMBAH THE FIREWALK CURD

Victoria V Victoria

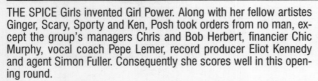

BECKHAM

QUEEN

ASK ANYONE in the street to name their favourite Victoria, and they will almost certainly reply either BECKHAM or SAXE-COBURG DE GOTHA. One is the size zero ex-Spice girl who now lives in LA; the other is Britain's longest-reigning monarch who has been dead for 106 years.

But just which one is the best? That's the question being asked by literally everyone from John's End to Land o' Groats. Now it's time to assess the qualities of each of them once and for all, as the Victorias cross swords in the Battle of the Century - BECKHAM versus QUEEN.

THE SPICE Girls invented Girl Power. Along with her fellow artistes Ginger, Scary, Sporty and Ken, Posh took orders from no man, except the group's managers Chris and Bob Herbert, financier Chic Murphy, vocal coach Pepe Lemer, record producer Eliot Kennedy and agent Simon Fuller. Consequently she scores well in this opening round.

6 — *Girl Power* — **8**

QUEEN Victoria invented Girl Power in 1837, a century and a half before the Spice Girls were even born (except Ginger). After becoming Queen at the tender age of eighteen, Victoria regularly summoned her Prime Ministers, such as Gladstone, Disraeli and Abraham Lincoln, to Buckingham Palace to tell them what she wanted, what she really, really wanted.

WITH just four letters, Beckham's unimaginative and inaccurate Spice Girls nickname "Posh" makes a feeble showing in this round. Amongst suggestions thought to have been rejected by record company bosses were "Unintelligent Spice", "Vacuous Spice" and "Skeletal Spice".

4 — *Nicknames* — **7**

HER Majesty's friends all knew her affectionately as "By the Grace of God, Queen Victoria of the United Kingdom of Great Britain and Ireland and of the British Dominions beyond the Seas Queen, Defender of the Faith, Empress of India". With a whopping 412 letters, it wins this round with ease.

BECKHAM'S husband David sports a wide range of body art, but it is all of a tacky nature; son Brooklyn's name in Gothic script on his back, the words "Perfectio in Spiritu" on his right arm, "Ut Amen et Foveam" on his left arm, a winged cross on his neck, a hinge on the inside of his elbow and "ACAB" on the inside of his lip are just some of the tasteless tattoos he sports.

7 — *Husband's body art* — **8**

QUEEN Victoria's husband Prince Consort Albert of Saxe-Coburg and Gotha had more refined body art tastes than Beckham's husband. With no tattoos, Bertie restricted his bodily adornment to a simple metal spike and ball pushed through the wall of his glans and exiting through his urethral meatus - an altogether more tasteful decoration which well befitted his regal status.

DESPITE her obscene wealth and utterly self-indulgent lifestyle, Posh Spice has never been photographed with a smile on her face, and has trained herself to do a ridiculous pseudo soft-porn pout whenever she is within 100 yards of a camera.

5 — *Ability to not be amused* — **7**

'We are not amused' was Her Majesty's catchphrase for six decades. Throughout the 81 years of her life, the Yoda-faced monarch scowled continuously, beating 33-year-old Beckham's current total by nearly half a century. A high scoring round.

NEW-MONEY Victoria flaunts her wealth in her series of vulgarly large houses. They are all ostentatiously decorated with gaudy gold fittings, tawdry chandeliers and tastelessly expensive paintings.

6 — *Palaces* — **7**

THANKS to centuries of breeding, HM the Queen enjoyed her wealth, buying many magnificent properties, each tastefully decorated with accents of gold, breathtaking chandeliers and precious works of art.

Victoria is often photographed wearing her bling, and probably thinks nothing of spending a million pounds on a diamond necklace, which she wears once before putting in the back of the cupboard next to the Breville sandwich toaster. In fact, she has so much jewellery that she employs 5 full-time security men at her LA mansion to stand guard round her dressing table.

8 — *Bling* — **9**

QUEEN Victoria was the owner of the Crown Jewels, the world's largest collection of bling. Included amongst her trinkets were seven crowns, two sceptres and an orb, as well as assorted rings, swords, spurs, tiaras and the legendary Star of Africa diamond. Instead of a dressing table, she kept them in the Tower of London, where they were guarded by Beefeaters - old men in fancy dress.

IN THIS modern age of 24-hour satellite television, hardcore triple-X DVDs and behind-the-scenes documentaries about the adult film industry on Bravo, we all know everything there is to know about lesbians, and Posh is no exception. Indeed, it is more than likely that she was watching the television when her fellow pop stars Madonna and Britney Spears done a lesbian kiss on the Brits or something. It is even quite possible that she numbers several tennis fans amongst her close friends. Beckham scores highly in this round.

7 — *Belief in Lezzers* — **7**

IT IS A well-known fact that in 1877, Queen Victoria refused to sign an act of Parliament which outlawed homosexuality until all references to lesbianism had been removed from it. This was because she did not believe that sex between women was possible. However, had she of had access to modern forms of media such as RealPlayer, the Fantasy Channel and Google Images (with SafeSearch turned off in Advanced Preferences), she would have seen that sex between women is not only possible, it is actually remarkably common.

POSH'S THREE children Brooklyn, Romeo and Cruz have failed to make their mark in the world. Seemingly content to sit on the coat-tails of their parents and enjoy the easy life, not one of these low-achievers has gone on to find fame on his own terms.

5 — *Eminent Descendants* — **6**

THE QUEEN'S nine children all went on to take up important positions in the world, becoming King's, Queens, Princes, Princesses, Dukes, Duchesses and Jack the Ripper. As a result, winning this family tree round is like falling off a log for Her Royal Majesty.

WITH SINGLE and album sales approaching 30 million, both as a member of the Spice Girls and as a solo artiste, and after spending an incredible 85 weeks in the charts, Posh is Top of the Pops when it comes to hit parade success.

10 — *Chart Success* — **0**

OH DEAR. Despite being the titular head of the largest empire the world has ever seen for more than sixty years, chart success eluded Queen Victoria throughout her reign. As a no-hit wonder, she fails to score in this final round.

BREEDING shows as Posh comes through on the rails to win by a scrawny neck and be crowned Queen of the Victorias. Once they are added up, her Victoria values are more than enough for Beckham to claim a well-deserved Victory.

60 *Final Score* **59**

OLD VIC finds herself pipped at the post thanks to her lack of a pop pedigree. When push comes to shove, she doesn't quite have what it takes to zig-a-zig ah her opponent, and loses her Best Victoria throne to the young pretender.

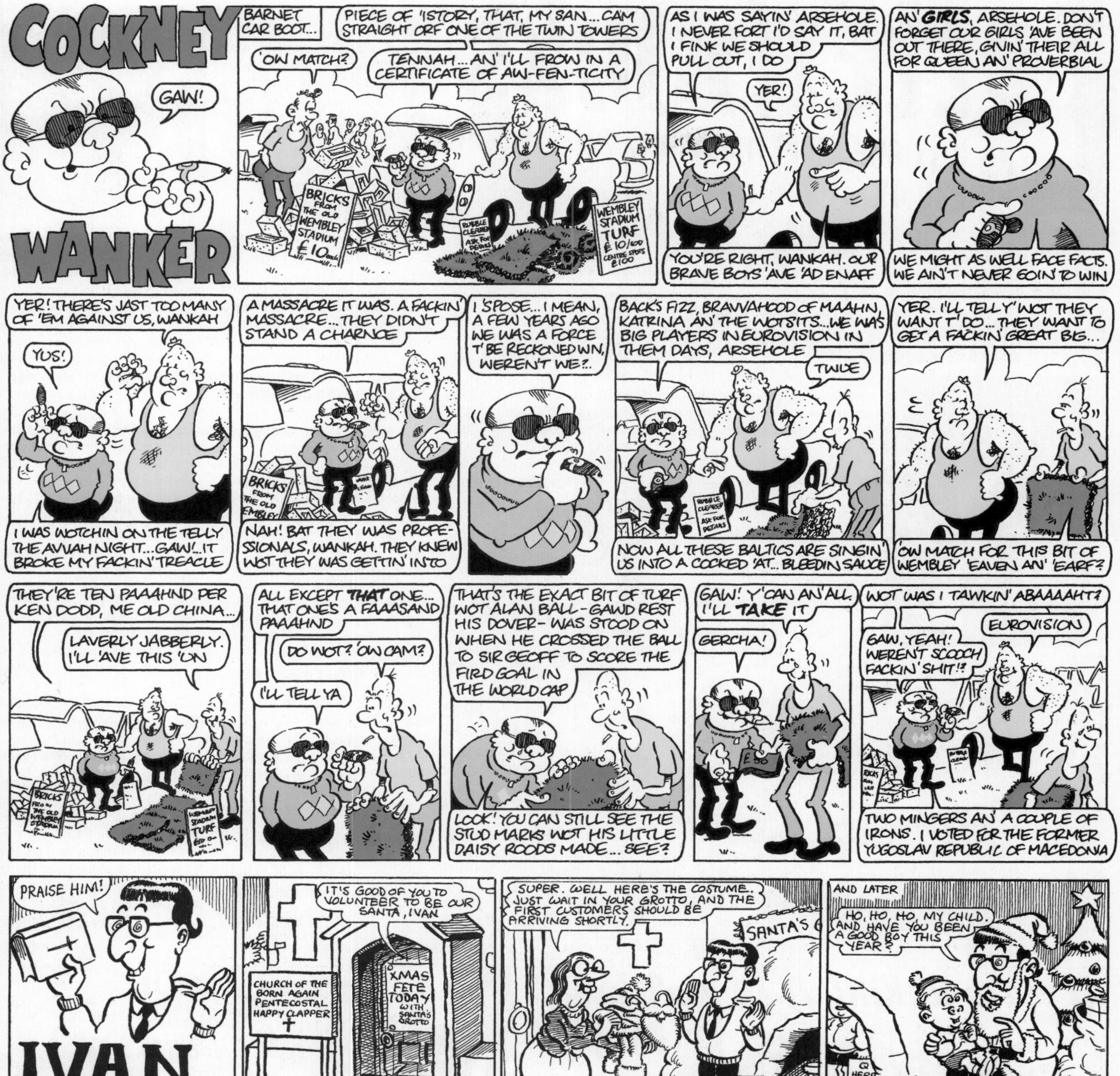
COCKNEY WANKER
GAW!
BARNET CAR BOOT...
PIECE OF 'ISTORY, THAT, MY SAN... CAM STRAIGHT ORF ONE OF THE TWIN TOWERS
'OW MATCH?
TENNAH... AN' I'LL FROW IN A CERTIFICATE OF AW-FEN-TICITY
BRICKS FROM THE OLD WEMBLEY STADIUM £10 each
RUBBLE CLEARED ASK FOR DETAILS
WEMBLEY STADIUM TURF £10/sod CENTRE SPOTS £100
AS I WAS SAYIN' ARSEHOLE. I NEVER FORT I'D SAY IT, BAT I FINK WE SHOULD PULL OUT, I DO
YER!
YOU'RE RIGHT, WANKAH. OUR BRAVE BOYS 'AVE 'AD ENAFF
AN' GIRLS, ARSEHOLE. DON'T FORGET OUR GIRLS 'AVE BEEN OUT THERE, GIVIN' THEIR ALL FOR QUEEN AN' PROVERBIAL
WE MIGHT AS WELL FACE FACTS. WE AIN'T NEVER GOIN' TO WIN
YER! THERE'S JAST TOO MANY OF 'EM AGAINST US, WANKAH
YUS!
I WAS WOTCHIN ON THE TELLY THE AVVAH NIGHT... GAW!.. IT BROKE MY FACKIN' TREACLE
A MASSACRE IT WAS. A FACKIN' MASSACRE... THEY DIDN'T STAND A CHARNCE
NAH! BAT THEY WAS PROFE-SSIONALS, WANKAH. THEY KNEW WOT THEY WAS GETTIN' INTO
I 'SPOSE... I MEAN, A FEW YEARS AGO WE WAS A FORCE T'BE RECKONED WIN, WEREN'T WE?..
BACK'S FIZZ, BRAVVAHOOD OF MAAHN, KATRINA AN' THE WOTSITS... WE WAS BIG PLAYERS IN EUROVISION IN THEM DAYS, ARSEHOLE
TWUE
NOW ALL THESE BALTICS ARE SINGIN' US INTO A COCKED 'AT... BLEEDIN SAUCE
YER. I'LL TELL Y' WOT THEY WANT T' DO... THEY WANT TO GET A FACKIN' GREAT BIG...
'OW MATCH FOR THIS BIT OF WEMBLEY 'EAVEN AN' 'EARF?
THEY'RE TEN PAAAHND PER KEN DODD, ME OLD CHINA...
LAVERLY JABBERLY. I'LL 'AVE THIS 'UN
ALL EXCEPT THAT ONE... THAT ONE'S A FAAASAND PAAAHND
DO WOT? 'OW CAM?
I'LL TELL YA
THAT'S THE EXACT BIT OF TURF WOT ALAN BALL- GAWD REST HIS DOVER- WAS STOOD ON WHEN HE CROSSED THE BALL TO SIR GEOFF TO SCORE THE FIRD GOAL IN THE WORLD CAP
LOOK! YOU CAN STILL SEE THE STUD MARKS WOT HIS LITTLE DAISY ROODS MADE... SEE?
GAW! Y'CAN AN' ALL. I'LL TAKE IT
GERCHA!
WOT WAS I TAWKIN' ABAAAAHT?
EUROVISION
GAW, YEAH! WEREN'T SCOOCH FACKIN' SHIT!?
TWO MINGERS AN' A COUPLE OF IRONS. I VOTED FOR THE FORMER YUGOSLAV REPUBLIC OF MACEDONIA

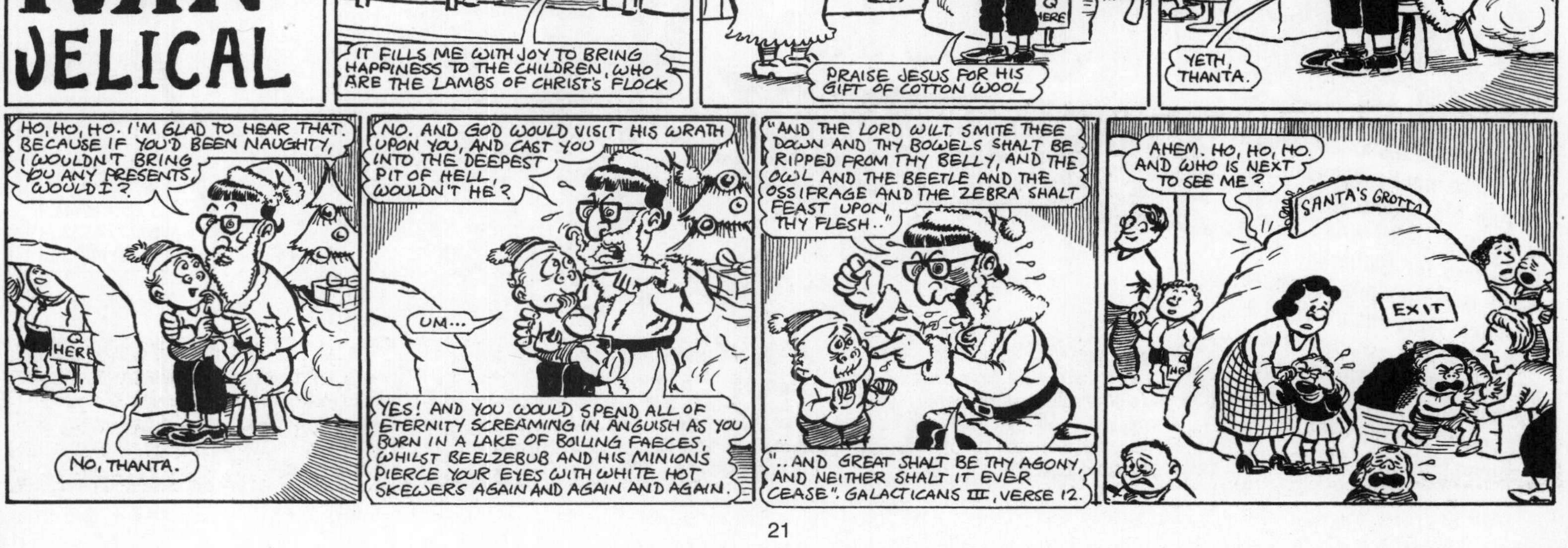
PRAISE HIM!
IVAN JELICAL
IT'S GOOD OF YOU TO VOLUNTEER TO BE OUR SANTA, IVAN
CHURCH OF THE BORN AGAIN PENTECOSTAL HAPPY CLAPPER
XMAS FETE TODAY WITH SANTA'S GROTTO
IT FILLS ME WITH JOY TO BRING HAPPINESS TO THE CHILDREN, WHO ARE THE LAMBS OF CHRIST'S FLOCK
SUPER. WELL HERE'S THE COSTUME. JUST WAIT IN YOUR GROTTO, AND THE FIRST CUSTOMERS SHOULD BE ARRIVING SHORTLY.
Q HERE
PRAISE JESUS FOR HIS GIFT OF COTTON WOOL
AND LATER
HO, HO, HO, MY CHILD. AND HAVE YOU BEEN A GOOD BOY THIS YEAR?
YETH, THANTA.
HO, HO, HO. I'M GLAD TO HEAR THAT. BECAUSE IF YOU'D BEEN NAUGHTY, I WOULDN'T BRING YOU ANY PRESENTS, WOULD I?
NO, THANTA.
NO. AND GOD WOULD VISIT HIS WRATH UPON YOU, AND CAST YOU INTO THE DEEPEST PIT OF HELL, WOULDN'T HE?
UM...
YES! AND YOU WOULD SPEND ALL OF ETERNITY SCREAMING IN ANGUISH AS YOU BURN IN A LAKE OF BOILING FAECES, WHILST BEELZEBUB AND HIS MINIONS PIERCE YOUR EYES WITH WHITE HOT SKEWERS AGAIN AND AGAIN AND AGAIN.
"AND THE LORD WILT SMITE THEE DOWN AND THY BOWELS SHALT BE RIPPED FROM THY BELLY, AND THE OWL AND THE BEETLE AND THE OSSIFRAGE AND THE ZEBRA SHALT FEAST UPON THY FLESH.."
"..AND GREAT SHALT BE THY AGONY, AND NEITHER SHALT IT EVER CEASE". GALACTICANS III, VERSE 12.
AHEM. HO, HO, HO. AND WHO IS NEXT TO SEE ME?
SANTA'S GROTTO
EXIT

Letterbocks

PO BOx 656, NorTh SHields, NE30 4XX. letters@viz.co.uk

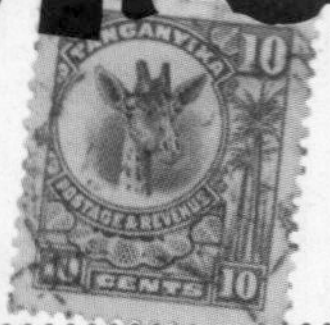
10
10
10
CENTS

STAR LETTER

•I heard on the news that the January storms had cost this country a billion pounds. What an utter waste of money. If anything, they did more harm than good.

S Prodnipple, Scarborough

● Recently, whilst having tea with Poet Laureate Andrew Motion, he casually mentioned that there was no word that rhymes with orange. Honestly, what are we paying him for?

Adam Oxbury, e-mail

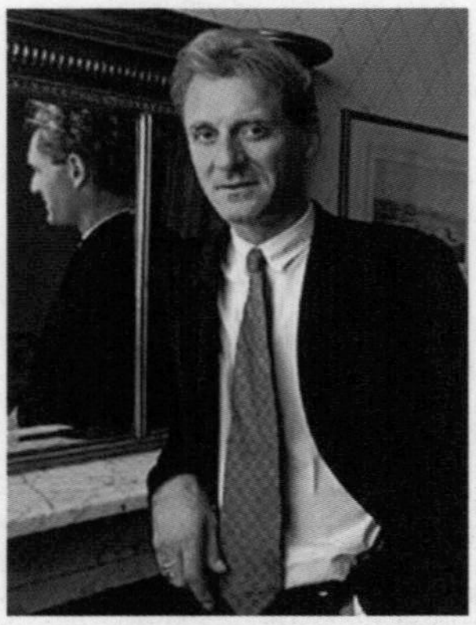

● According to the news, vets were supervising the gassing of 175,000 turkeys with flu at Bernard Matthews twizzler factory. What a shame. Instead of killing them all, surely the vets would have been better employed trying to make them better.

Mavis Brie, Luton

● I was shocked to hear that 175,000 turkeys were destroyed at Bernard Matthews' farm in Suffolk. I had no idea that real birds were involved at any point in the manufacture of his products.

Tom Smegma, London

● As a feminist, I'm willing to bet that all those turkeys that died of bird flu were men turkeys. Women turkeys would have just got on with things. And I bet it wasn't even bird flu, either, just a bird cold.

Dr G Greer, Warwick

● These feminists really get my goat. They are so busy burning their bras and banging on about equality and equal pay, that they conveniently forget about the poor male preying mantis who, after mating, is killed and eaten by his wife. How many more innocent male mantids have to die before the likes of Germaine Greer will speak out on *their* behalf?

Tom Camembert, Leeds

● I remember people back in the 1980s being afraid of freezing to death in a post holocaust nuclear winter. Now the same people don't want to be cooked to death by global warming. Honestly, there's no pleasing some people.

Ron Lilycropp, e-mail

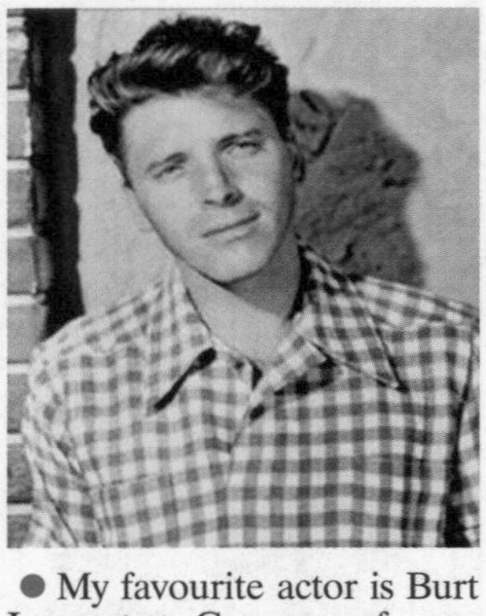

● My favourite actor is Burt Lancaster. Can any of your readers beat that?

Wilma Senile, Scarborough

● It breaks my heart to see so many marriages these days end in divorce. All couples have their differences, but it seems that today's young people aren't prepared to put the effort in to make their relationships work. My wife and I have been married for 54 years and it has often been a struggle, because she likes tea and I prefer coffee. But we have worked around it. I move into a bed and breakfast for a week while she has tea, then the following week when I come home and have coffee, she goes and stays with her sister in Gravesend.

Bill Turnbury, Auchterader

● My great Uncle Ernest was born in 1899, and he had all his own teeth until the day he died. This isn't as impressive as it might at first seem, however, as he was killed on the Somme on his sixteenth birthday.

Mildred Collis, Nottingham

● Disneyland claims in its advertising that it is 'A Place Where Dreams Come True'. Well last night I dreamt that I helped my friend Robin to fit a TomTom Sat Nav system in his Fiat Bravo and accidentally put a screwdriver through the dashboard causing £400 worth of damage. So I'll be giving Disneyland a miss this year.

Cecilia Smart, e-mail

● "She can dish it out, but she cannot take it", I once heard someone say of me. And it's true - I'm a school dinner lady and I'm allergic to mashed potatoes.

Mrs Pinches, Hereford

● I have a really itchy arse, and I was wondering if any of your readers have sharp nails. There's a drink in it for them.

Dansk, e-mail

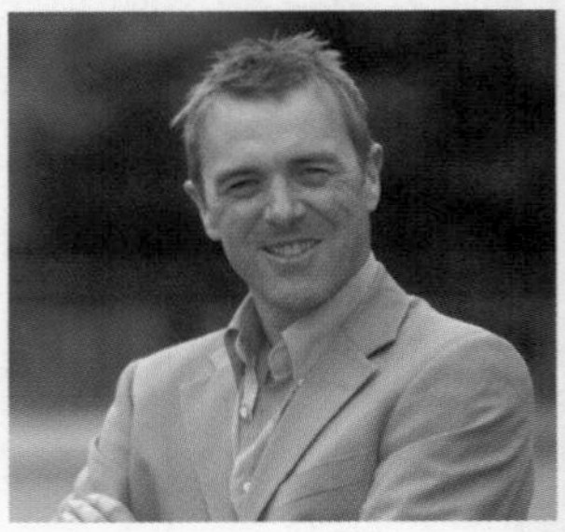

● I found myself deeply in debt, to the point where I didn't like answering the phone in case it was somebody chasing me for money. Then I saw Phil Tufnell on an ad for a loan agency, offering to solve my problems. I thought, well he was a modest spin bowler, and he won *'I'm a Celebrity...'* mainly for being a cheeky chappy, so he's bound to have a good grasp on fiscal strategies. So I gave them a call. Two years on, my house has been repossessed, my wife has left me and I'm living in a hostel. Any more advice, Phil?

**Belford Brewster
Bermondsey Doss House**

● I recently enrolled on an German evening course. It's a shame really, because if we had lost the war, we'd all be speaking German anyway and I would have saved a nifty £62. Sometimes history comes back to kick you in the arse, doesn't it?

Ian Corrigan, Newcastle

● I was devastated to hear that the well know roadside eatery Little Chef had gone into liquidation. Particularly as I've been sitting in one on the A1 since last November trying to attract the waitress to come over and take my order.

S Marston, Hexham

MILLIONAIRES' FINANCIAL MANAGEMENT

If you're RAKING IT IN you'll need the NEW Spear & Jackpot CASH RAKE

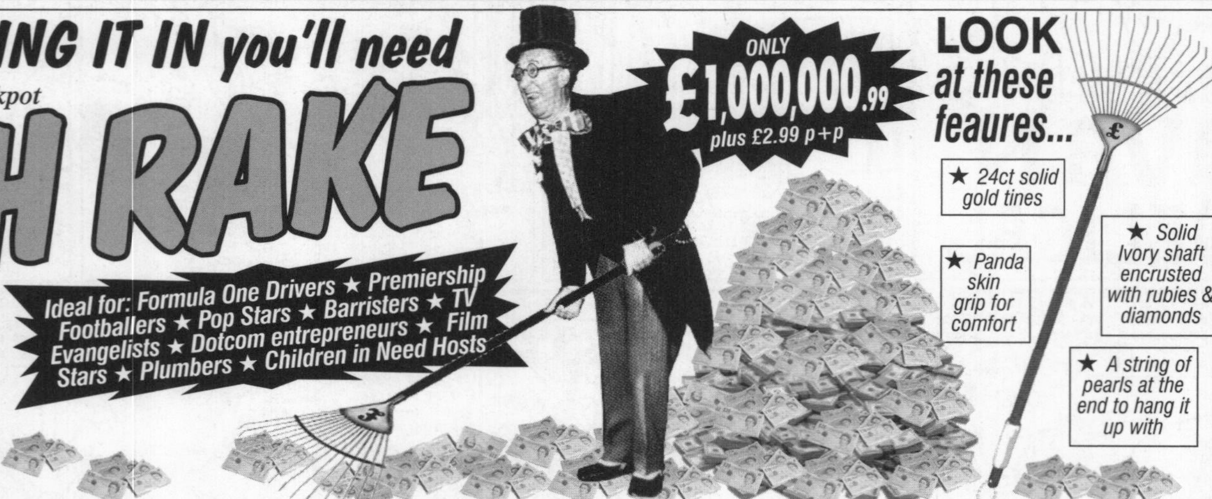
ONLY
£1,000,000.99
plus £2.99 p+p
LOOK at these feaures...
★ 24ct solid gold tines
★ Panda skin grip for comfort
★ Solid Ivory shaft encrusted with rubies & diamonds
★ A string of pearls at the end to hang it up with
Ideal for: Formula One Drivers ★ Premiership Footballers ★ Pop Stars ★ Barristers ★ TV Evangelists ★ Dotcom entrepreneurs ★ Film Stars ★ Plumbers ★ Children in Need Hosts

ARE YOU a millionaire who's got so much money coming in that it's becoming a problem? The *CASH RAKE* is the ideal tool for gathering it all into a neat, tidy pile. Carefully designed tines ensure that £5, £10, £20 and £50 notes are all gathered in, whilst those bothersome little coins are left behind to be picked up by common people.

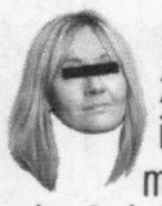

"I wrote some half-arsed stories about wizzards and witches and that and the money came in so fast that it was all over the house. I couldn't move for the stuff. Then a friend told me about the Cash Rake. Now, five minutes raking a day is all it takes to get it in one place." *Mrs JKR, Edinburgh*

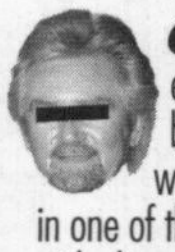

"Despite being loathsome and having no talents to speak of, I seem to earn a fortune. Until I bought a Spear & Jackpot Cash Rake my money was all over the place. Now it's in a lovely big pile in one of the sitting rooms of one of my houses, and I can sit looking at it all day." *Mr NE, Crinkly Bottom*

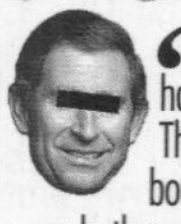

"I own Cornwall and half of Wales, and I also have a company that makes overpriced biscuits. The money comes in so fast it's laughable. I bought Cash Rakes as Xmas gifts last year for all my butlers, and it makes their job of keeping my fortune nice and tidy much easier." *HRH the P of W, Highgrove*

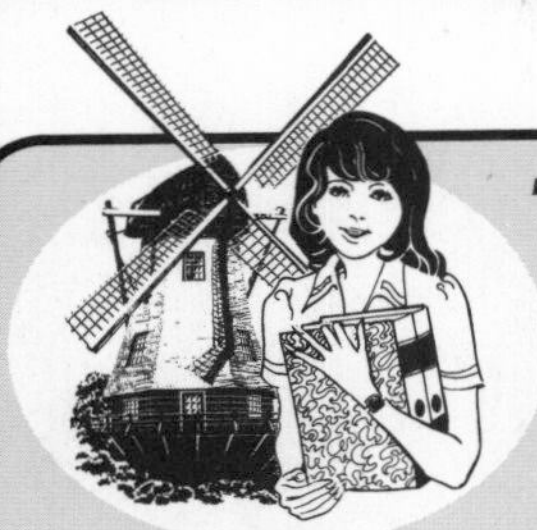

The Celebrity Rumour Mill
with Wendy Miller

Dear Wendy,
Is this rumour I keep hearing about Kevin Keegan true? It doesn't sound very likely, but I've heard it from four separate people now, including a man who drives a van for the local paper.

B. Sandwich, Darlington

★ *Yes, I heard that one too, but it is very dark inside these nightclubs, so it could have been someone else. But if it is true, he's got a lot of explaining to do.*

★★★★★★★★★★★★★★★★★★★★★

Dear Wendy,
I heard a terrible rumour about Paul Daniels and the wonderful Debbie McGee. I've been a fan of his for years and I simply cannot believe that it is true. Please can you set my mind at rest?

Henry Colliedog, London

★ *I wish I could set your mind at rest, but alas, I believe this rumour is true. A friend of a friend of mine was shown compelling evidence in a pub, just outside the News International compound in Wapping. Well, actually, it was a friend of a friend of mine's brother.*

Dear Wendy,
Have you heard the one going round about Una Stubbs and what she likes? Is it true?

E. Beer, London

★ *Yes, that one is true. I used to work with a man, and he said he knew somebody whose mate once went to her flat and she asked him to do that thing. And to look at her, you'd think that butter wouldn't melt.*

★★★★★★★★★★★★★★★★★★★★★

Dear Wendy,
I heard a rumour about Sir Jimmy Savile. Surely they wouldn't have given him a knighthood if they knew he got up to that sort of thing when he was there.

Worried, Chester

★ *Let me put your mind at rest. That rumour is complete nonsense. However, I heard another one about him that is apparently true and would make your hair stand on end.*

~Keep your ill-informed tittle-tattle coming in to my Celebrity Rumour Mill and I'll tell you if there are any grains of truth in it. Bye for Now, Rumourmongers.

Wendy

Have Your Say

THE VICTORIA AND ALBERT Museum stirred up a storm of controversy with their decision to hold an exhibition of Kylie Minogue's shorts. Some people think that a national institution should not be wasting its time on pointless ephemera, whilst others think it is important that our museums keep up to date and reflect public interests. We went on the streets to find out what YOU thought.

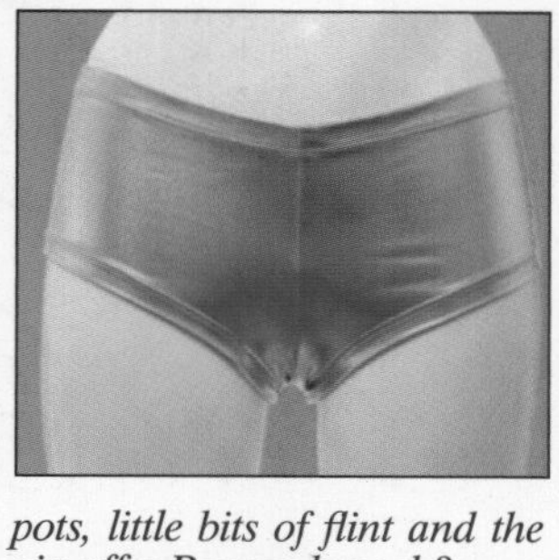

...I CAN understand 40,000 people going to a Kylie Minogue concert, but I can't understand why they would go to the Victoria and Albert Museum to see her shorts. Whatever next, queues round the block to see Jeanette Krankie's cap at the British Museum?

Frank Gouda, milkman

...I WOULDN'T cross the street to see Kylie's shorts. Fortunately, I live next door to the V&A, so I'll probably pop in and have a look.

George Edam, dairy farmer

...I QUEUED for seven hours to see Kylie's shorts, but they were worth it. They were the best shorts I have ever seen. I'm going to see them again tomorrow.

Kelly Babybel, milkmaid

...POP stars' shorts in a museum? How utterly ridiculous. What's wrong with broken pots, little bits of flint and the pin off a Roman brooch?

Hugo Goats, yoghurt salesman

...I GO TO a museum to find out about my British heritage and to see ancient artifacts displayed in their historical contexts, not to gawp at a young lady's shorts. If I wanted to do that, I'd go to the local squash club on a Wednesday when it's 'ladies only' between 11.00am and 2.00pm and sit in the coffee bar at the end table on the right where you get a good view of the courts.

Les Jarlesberg, cheesemonger

...I'M A great fan of Kylie's arse, so you'd probably expect me to be heading to the V&A to see her shorts. But I won't, because they have only ever prevented me from seeing her arse. I have nothing but contempt for them.

Gordon Lymeswondle, pasteuriser

...The V&A prides itself on being an interactive, hands-on museum. Yet when I tried to have a quick sniff of Kylie's shorts I was chased out of the museum by guards.

Sid Gorgonzola, mousetrap bait consultant

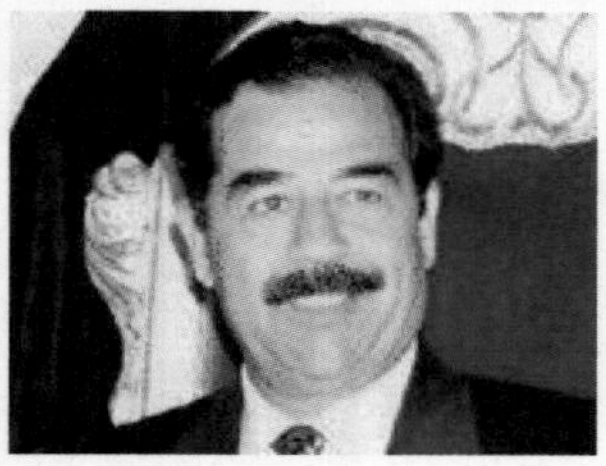

● John Prescott recently complained that the hanging of Saddam Hussein was 'undignified'. On the contrary, I thought that they treated him with remarkable sensitivity in the circumstances. Had his executioners played a swanee whistle as he dropped and then blown a duck call when his neck broke, then perhaps the deputy Prime Minister would have a point.

Tarquin Roulade, Surrey

● Everybody hates seagulls when they are stealing your chips, scavenging at the local landfill site and shitting on your windscreen. Yet when a ship sinks and a few of the flying rats get covered in oil, everybody feels sorry for them and they get treated like pampered poodles. It's the worst sort of hypocrisy.

Franklyn Mells, Branscombe

● My teachers told me I would never make anything of myself if I sat staring into space during lessons. However, I had the last laugh as I am now the Astronomer Royal.

Martin Rees, Greenwich

Top Tips

GENTLEMEN. Avoid any unnecessary scrotal surgery by removing any genital piercings before using the 'Black Hole' water flume at Butlins, Bognor Regis.

Big Bladder, e-mail

TAME budgies and parrots easily by replacing their grit with iron filings. By holding a large magnet, they will sit hapilly on your hand for hours.

Debbie Forster, e-mail

HOMEOWNERS. When selling your house, replace your furniture with children's tables and chairs, and use a dwarf estate agent. Instantly, your house will seem more roomy than it actually is.

Derek Nerrington, e-mail

DAILY Mail editors. Underline important words in your headlines just to make sure that your readers are clear about what it is you want them to think.

H Barrow, Tooting

CROWN THE DRAIN!

HM The Queen faced an anxious wait for her husband to come home last night after realising she had managed to lose the Crown Jewels while doing the washing up.

The top monarch noticed the famous jewels had gone missing while putting the saucers back in the cupboard. Since there was no sign of the priceless artefacts anywhere on the draining board, it seems likely that the jewels have gone down the Royal kitchen sink.

careful

According to palace sources, her husband Philip has warned her time and time again to be

ROYAL EXCLUSIVE!

more careful, but royal watchers have noted the warnings going in one regal ear and out the other.

bubbles

Exchange & Mart court correspondent Rodney Obsequious-Ffoulkes told reporters: "It's always a risk. The Queen has enormous plugholes to wash away the huge bubbles that are created by the royal washing up liquid, which since the time of Edward VI has been made from concentrated swans' tears.

"The royal bling is well chunky, but the Buckingham Palace plughole would easily be capable of swallowing

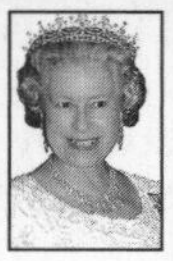

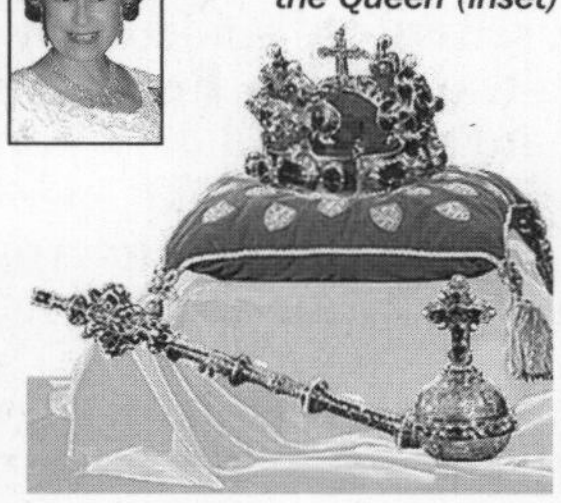

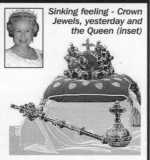

Sinking feeling - Crown Jewels, yesterday and the Queen (inset)

several crowns, swords, two sceptres and an orb, and all them bracelets and rings."

Only six months ago the Queen lost the Bank of England after putting it on the roof of her car outside a supermarket before absent-mindedly driving off.

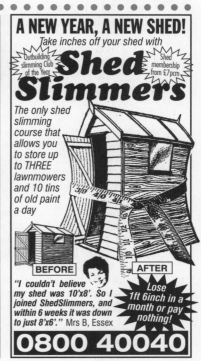

Bernard

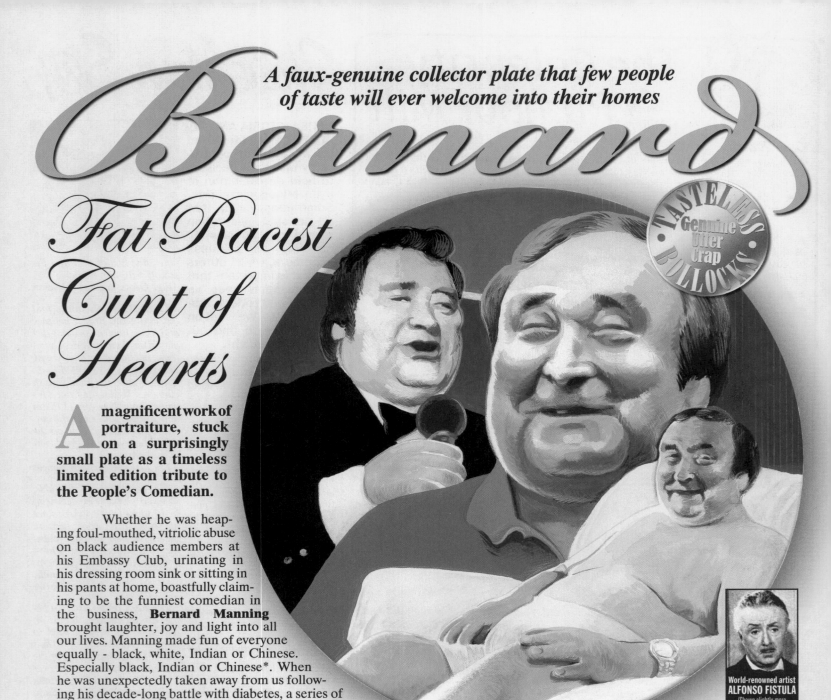

A faux-genuine collector plate that few people of taste will ever welcome into their homes

Fat Racist Cunt of Hearts

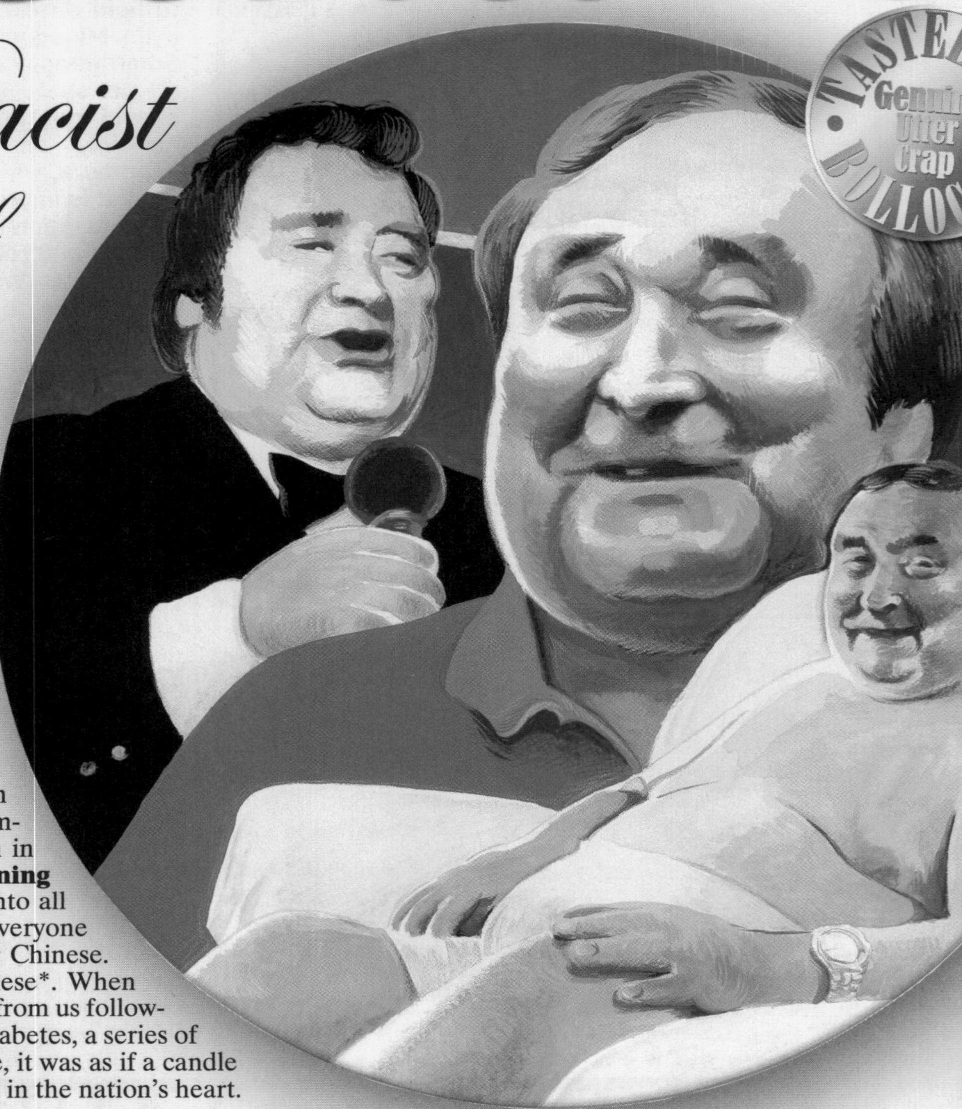

TASTELESS
Genuine Utter Crap
BOLLOCKS

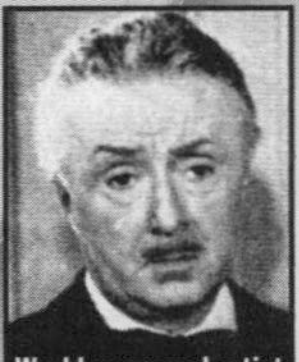

World-renowned artist **ALFONSO FISTULA** (Shown slightly more world-renowned than actual world-renownedness)

A magnificent work of portraiture, stuck on a surprisingly small plate as a timeless limited edition tribute to the People's Comedian.

Whether he was heaping foul-mouthed, vitriolic abuse on black audience members at his Embassy Club, urinating in his dressing room sink or sitting in his pants at home, boastfully claiming to be the funniest comedian in the business, **Bernard Manning** brought laughter, joy and light into all our lives. Manning made fun of everyone equally - black, white, Indian or Chinese. Especially black, Indian or Chinese*. When he was unexpectedly taken away from us following his decade-long battle with diabetes, a series of strokes and a brain haemorrhage, it was as if a candle in the wind had been snuffed out in the nation's heart.

Well now, the Rochdale Rose lives on once more in this handsome collector plate. Simply fill in the direct debit instruction below and **Bernard ~ Fat Racist Cunt of Hearts** will take his place amongst your your own most treasured possessions.

This exquisite painting, sensitively rendered by internationally-renowned racist portraitist **Alfonso Fistula**, perfectly captures every aspect of Bernard's extraordinary personality. From his twinkling, prejudiced eyes to his cheeky, bigoted grin; from his pale, flabby tits to his gigantic, stained underpants, it is impossible to underestimate the artist's attention to detail.

Crafted in 22-carat porcelain and lavishly bordered with genuine Cevres gold, **Bernard ~ Fat Racist Cunt of Hearts** has been produced in the highest quantity possible. With the edition strictly limited to the number of stupid old ladies who buy this sort of thing with their winter cold weather heating allowance, it's set to become a family hairloom which will be passed countless times from generation to generation and from brother to sister to charity shop.

***And the Irish and puffs.*

Limited Edition Collector Application Certificate

*Please accept my order for **Bernard ~ Fat Racist Cunt of Hearts.** I've already cleared a space for it on the mantlepiece, in between the picture of my grandchildren I've never met in New Zealand and the fading, black & white photograph of my late husband being presented with his gold watch on the day he retired, three weeks before he dropped dead while mowing the lawn. I enclose all the money I can find in the house.*

Name...

Address..

....

....

Postcode.. Tick Here ☐

Send to: *The Dickie Mint, PO Box 6, Leeds.*

This Application Certificate is No: ....73.... **out of 750**

*Further Hairloom Quality **Fat Racist Cunt of Hearts** collector plates will be sent just as soon as Chubby Brown and Jim Davidson die.*

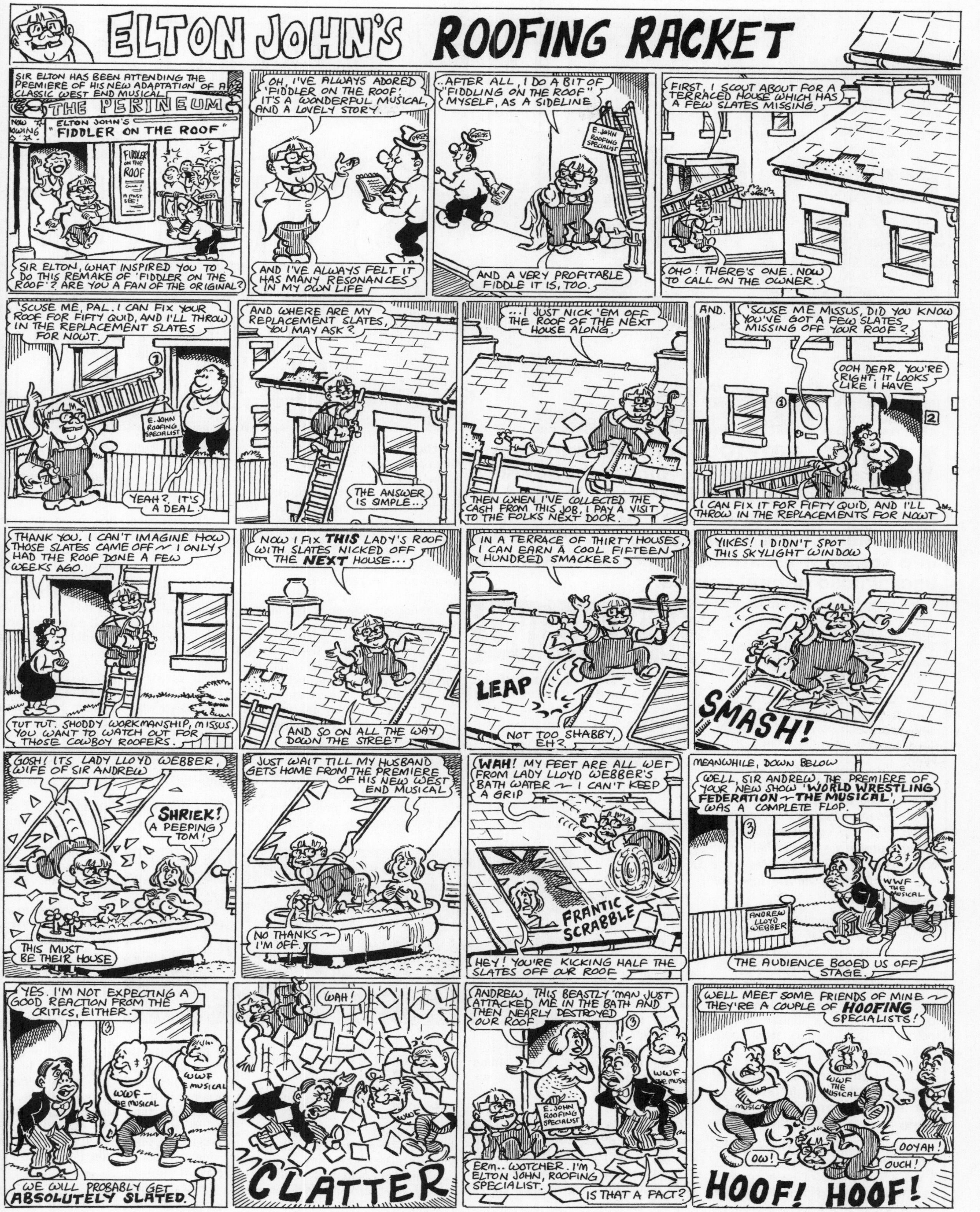

ELTON JOHN'S ROOFING RACKET
SIR ELTON HAS BEEN ATTENDING THE PREMIERE OF HIS NEW ADAPTATION OF A CLASSIC WEST END MUSICAL
THE PERINEUM
NOW SHOWING
ELTON JOHN'S "FIDDLER ON THE ROOF"
FIDDLER ON THE ROOF
A MUST SEE!
PRESS
SIR ELTON, WHAT INSPIRED YOU TO DO THIS REMAKE OF 'FIDDLER ON THE ROOF'? ARE YOU A FAN OF THE ORIGINAL?
OH, I'VE ALWAYS ADORED 'FIDDLER ON THE ROOF'. IT'S A WONDERFUL MUSICAL, AND A LOVELY STORY.
AND I'VE ALWAYS FELT IT HAS MANY RESONANCES IN MY OWN LIFE
..AFTER ALL, I DO A BIT OF "FIDDLING ON THE ROOF" MYSELF, AS A SIDELINE
E. JOHN ROOFING SPECIALIST
AND A VERY PROFITABLE FIDDLE IT IS, TOO.
FIRST, I SCOUT ABOUT FOR A TERRACED HOUSE WHICH HAS A FEW SLATES MISSING.
OHO! THERE'S ONE. NOW TO CALL ON THE OWNER.
'SCUSE ME, PAL. I CAN FIX YOUR ROOF FOR FIFTY QUID, AND I'LL THROW IN THE REPLACEMENT SLATES FOR NOWT.
E. JOHN ROOFING SPECIALIST
YEAH? IT'S A DEAL.
AND WHERE ARE MY REPLACEMENT SLATES, YOU MAY ASK?
THE ANSWER IS SIMPLE...
...I JUST NICK 'EM OFF THE ROOF OF THE NEXT HOUSE ALONG.
THEN WHEN I'VE COLLECTED THE CASH FROM THIS JOB, I PAY A VISIT TO THE FOLKS NEXT DOOR.
AND.
'SCUSE ME MISSUS, DID YOU KNOW YOU'VE GOT A FEW SLATES MISSING OFF YOUR ROOF?
OOH DEAR, YOU'RE RIGHT, IT LOOKS LIKE I HAVE
I CAN FIX IT FOR FIFTY QUID, AND I'LL THROW IN THE REPLACEMENTS FOR NOWT
THANK YOU. I CAN'T IMAGINE HOW THOSE SLATES CAME OFF ~ I ONLY HAD THE ROOF DONE A FEW WEEKS AGO.
TUT TUT. SHODDY WORKMANSHIP, MISSUS. YOU WANT TO WATCH OUT FOR THOSE COWBOY ROOFERS.
NOW I FIX THIS LADY'S ROOF WITH SLATES NICKED OFF THE NEXT HOUSE...
AND SO ON ALL THE WAY DOWN THE STREET
IN A TERRACE OF THIRTY HOUSES, I CAN EARN A COOL FIFTEEN HUNDRED SMACKERS
LEAP
NOT TOO SHABBY, EH?
YIKES! I DIDN'T SPOT THIS SKYLIGHT WINDOW
SMASH!
GOSH! ITS LADY LLOYD WEBBER, WIFE OF SIR ANDREW
SHRIEK! A PEEPING TOM!
THIS MUST BE THEIR HOUSE
JUST WAIT TILL MY HUSBAND GETS HOME FROM THE PREMIERE OF HIS NEW WEST END MUSICAL
NO THANKS ~ I'M OFF.
WAH! MY FEET ARE ALL WET FROM LADY LLOYD WEBBER'S BATH WATER ~ I CAN'T KEEP A GRIP
FRANTIC SCRABBLE
HEY! YOU'RE KICKING HALF THE SLATES OFF OUR ROOF
MEANWHILE, DOWN BELOW
WELL, SIR ANDREW, THE PREMIERE OF YOUR NEW SHOW 'WORLD WRESTLING FEDERATION ~ THE MUSICAL', WAS A COMPLETE FLOP.
ANDREW LLOYD WEBBER
WWF THE MUSICAL
THE AUDIENCE BOOED US OFF STAGE.
YES. I'M NOT EXPECTING A GOOD REACTION FROM THE CRITICS, EITHER.
WWF ~ THE MUSICAL
WE WILL PROBABLY GET ABSOLUTELY SLATED.
WAH!
CLATTER
ANDREW, THIS BEASTLY MAN JUST ATTACKED ME IN THE BATH AND THEN NEARLY DESTROYED OUR ROOF
E. JOHN ROOFING SPECIALIST
ERM.. WOTCHER. I'M ELTON JOHN, ROOFING SPECIALIST.
IS THAT A FACT?
WELL MEET SOME FRIENDS OF MINE ~ THEY'RE A COUPLE OF HOOFING SPECIALISTS!
WWF THE MUSICAL
OOYAH!
OW!
OUCH!
HOOF! HOOF!

TUT'S CURSE STRIKES AGAIN

WHEN EGYPTOLOGIST Howard Carter smashed open the tomb of the Boy King *Tutankhamen* in 1924, he unleashed an ancient curse. Over the next 70 years, almost everyone involved in his expedition was to die in a series of bizarre accidents, illnesses and unexplained natural causes.

When the last member of Carter's team passed on, the Pharoah's curse appeared to die with him, and King Tut's mummy once again rested in peace in its golden sarcophagus in the Great Pyramid of Cheops.

But this month, treasures from the tomb have gone on show in London and as a result, says one man, the curse has been reawakened once again.

According to Neville Oglesby, a car park attendant at the O2 Arena where the exhibition is being staged, the malevolent influence of Tutankhamen's spirit is behind a catalogue of misadventures that has befallen him in the last few weeks.

"We are dealing with an evil force too powerful to imagine," he told us. "The sooner these treasures go back to Egypt and the curse is lifted, the better."

"Nobody has died yet, but in my opinion, it's only a matter of time before history repeats itself once more," he added.

Oglesby first became aware that something was not right on the day the exhibits arrived from Cairo Museum.

"A massive articulated lorry arrived with all the artifacts packed in crates. I was reading one of my magazines in my booth by the barrier when the driver shouted out of his window. I

HEXCLUSIVE!

checked his chitty and pressed the button to raise the barrier to let him through. To my surprise, the barrier stayed down."

"I pressed the button again once more, but nothing happened. The funny thing was, I knew the barrier was in good working order because the man had been out to fix it twice earlier in the week. It was as if some invisible evil force was stopping it from going up.

"Eventually, I went out and wound the gate up manually using the emergency handle like I do whenever it goes wrong. Returning back to my booth and my magazines, I wondered if I had incurred the wrath of a 6000 year-old Egyptian mummy. I don't mind admitting that a chill ran down my spine."

Neville may have thought that that was the end of the curse. Little did he know that it was only just a taster of the nightmare that the long dead boy king was about to unleash on him.

"The exhibition was set up, and all went well for a couple of weeks. Then one day I was in my booth leafing through my magazines, when I realised I'd run out of tissues. I'm not really supposed to leave the premises, but I often pop over to the local newsagent to buy tissues and tea bags, and I did on this occasion. I wasn't gone more than five minutes, but that was long enough for Tutankhamen to wreak his terrible revenge upon me.

"When I got back to my booth, the horror hit me. A cat had somehow got in and done its business in the box I keep my magazines in. The top one was quite old, and one of my favourites. I had looked at it hundreds of times, and now it was ruined.

As I removed the cover to throw it away, it suddenly struck me that cats were sacred animals in ancient Egypt. Could it have been that my magazine had been spoilt by the spirit of one

of King Tut's pet cats as retribution for me doing the car park for the exhibition? The more I thought about it, the more it seemed to be the only explanation.

"I am almost certain that I pulled the door of my booth to before I nipped to the shop. Only an ancient Egyptian hex could explain how a cat could get in there and do a nonsense in my mag box."

By this time, Neville was getting jumpy as he waited to see how the curse would next manifest itself. He didn't have to wait long.

"It was two days after the cat incident and I'd had a busy morning. Three people had come knocking on my booth asking for change, and I was worn out, so I was looking forward to my lunch break when I could pull the blinds down and have a nice relaxing read. However, the curse of King Tutankhamen had other plans.

"It was strange, for no matter how hard I looked, I couldn't find my glasses anywhere. I knew I had them with me, because I'd been using them earlier to look at some pictures in one of my mags during my tea break. Now they had simply vanished into thin air.

"I remember thinking that if the Pharoah was capable of reaching through the millennia and magicking away my glasses, what else was he capable of? I don't mind admitting, my blood ran cold.

"I was forced to do without my glasses, and I had to squint to make out some of the pictures. When I had finished and went to put my magazine back in the box, I was amazed to find my specs hidden underneath one of the flaps at the top. How they got in there I will never know, as it's quite unusual for me to put them there, and I'm almost 100% certain I hadn't done so that morning."

For a few days everything seemed to be back to normal and Neville

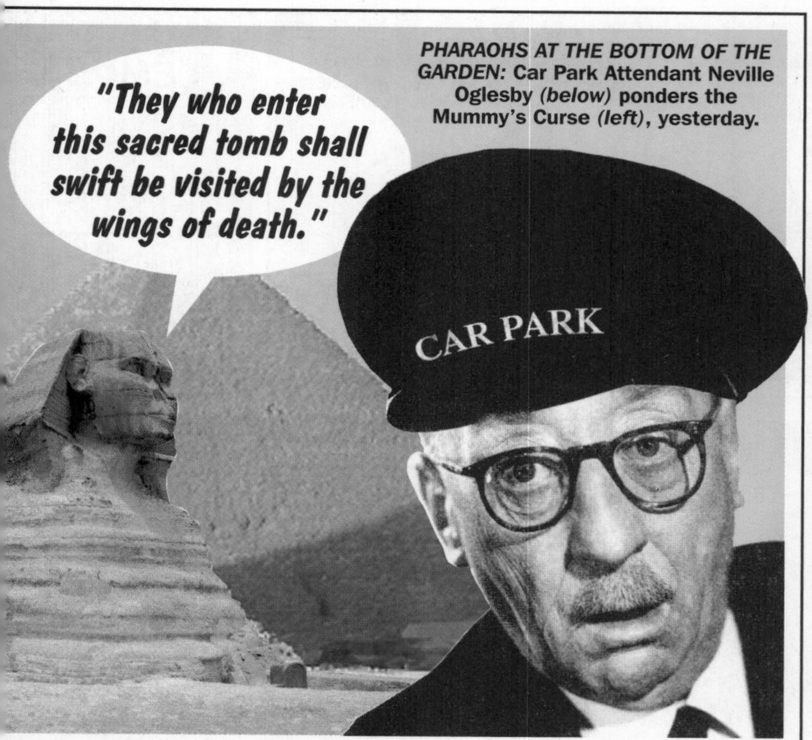
"They who enter this sacred tomb shall swift be visited by the wings of death."
CAR PARK

PHARAOHS AT THE BOTTOM OF THE GARDEN: **Car Park Attendant Neville Oglesby *(below)* ponders the Mummy's Curse *(left)*, yesterday.**

began to think that perhaps he had let his imagination run away with him. But then in a single day, a series of events took place for which he could offer no rational explanation.

✻ *OVERNIGHT RAIN leaked through the roof of his booth, ruining a new box of tissues.*

✻ *THE ELEMENT of his electric kettle, which had worked perfectly well for 18 years, suddenly burnt out.*

✻ *WHILST HE was reading one of his magazines, the zip of his trousers got jammed in the down position.*

✻ *ONE OF the blinds in his booth shot up for no reason whilst he was flicking through some magazines, leading to a formal complaint being made by a passing lady customer.*

"I felt that the boy king was toying with me, showing me just how powerful his ancient curse could be. I thought that hellish day would never be over, but it came to an end a bit sooner than I thought.

"I was called into my boss's office and given my marching orders. As a result of that lady's complaint, I was being sacked. It was true that I'd already had several verbal warnings and two writtens off him - but the last of those had been nearly three months ago. I hadn't put a foot wrong since then, which made my dismissal all the more cruel.

"There were hundreds of people involved in setting up the Tutankhamen exhibition, so why the mummy singled me out to be the victim of its curse I'll never know. All I know is that he'll now be seeking out someone else to exact his evil revenge upon - and that person had better look out."

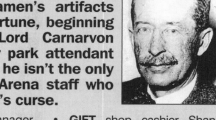

OVER THE YEARS, many people involved with the discovery and display of Tutankhamen's artifacts have suffered misfortune, beginning with egyptologist Lord Carnarvon and ending with car park attendant Neville Oglesby. But he isn't the only member of the O2 Arena staff who has fallen foul of Tut's curse.

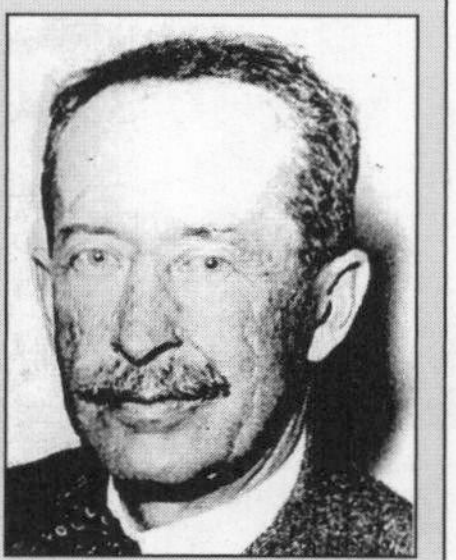

- **DEPUTY** catering manager June Medford sprained an ankle after a vengeful Egyptian spirit caused her to slip on a wet floor in the foyer.
- **LAVATORY** cleaner Hilda Braintree was docked a week's wages after the Pharoah's malign supernatural influence caused her to oversleep and be late for work four days on the trot.
- **GIFT** shop cashier Shania Warhol was arrested and cautioned after the dog-headed god Anubis persuaded her to fill her locker with £120 worth of souvenir pencils, rubbers, key-rings and fridge magnets.
- **TEMPORARY** kitchen assistant Kirk Scoltock was fired on his first day after being caught by CCTV security cameras smoking a joint near the bins.

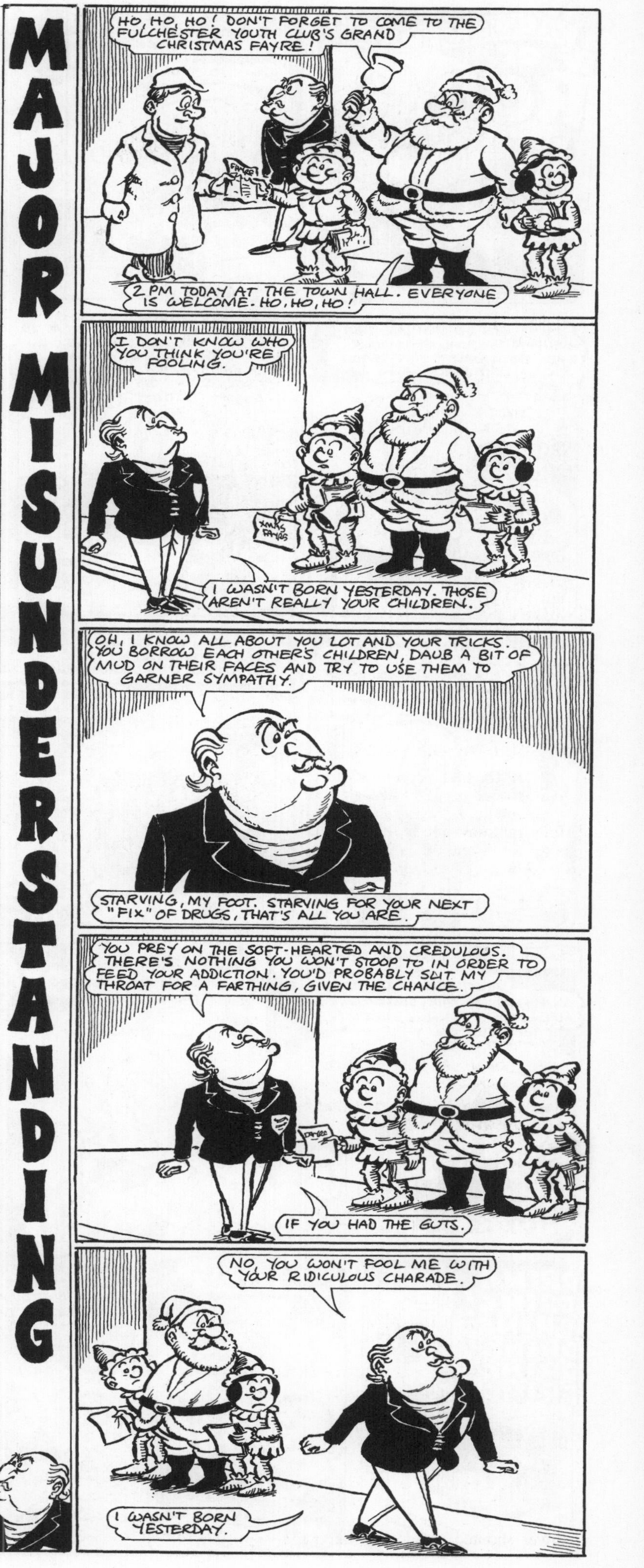
MAJOR MISUNDERSTANDING
HO, HO, HO! DON'T FORGET TO COME TO THE FULCHESTER YOUTH CLUB'S GRAND CHRISTMAS FAYRE!
2 PM TODAY AT THE TOWN HALL. EVERYONE IS WELCOME. HO, HO, HO!
I DON'T KNOW WHO YOU THINK YOU'RE FOOLING.
I WASN'T BORN YESTERDAY. THOSE AREN'T REALLY YOUR CHILDREN.
OH, I KNOW ALL ABOUT YOU LOT AND YOUR TRICKS. YOU BORROW EACH OTHER'S CHILDREN, DAUB A BIT OF MUD ON THEIR FACES AND TRY TO USE THEM TO GARNER SYMPATHY.
STARVING, MY FOOT. STARVING FOR YOUR NEXT "FIX" OF DRUGS, THAT'S ALL YOU ARE.
YOU PREY ON THE SOFT-HEARTED AND CREDULOUS. THERE'S NOTHING YOU WON'T STOOP TO IN ORDER TO FEED YOUR ADDICTION. YOU'D PROBABLY SLIT MY THROAT FOR A FARTHING, GIVEN THE CHANCE.
IF YOU HAD THE GUTS.
NO, YOU WON'T FOOL ME WITH YOUR RIDICULOUS CHARADE.
I WASN'T BORN YESTERDAY.

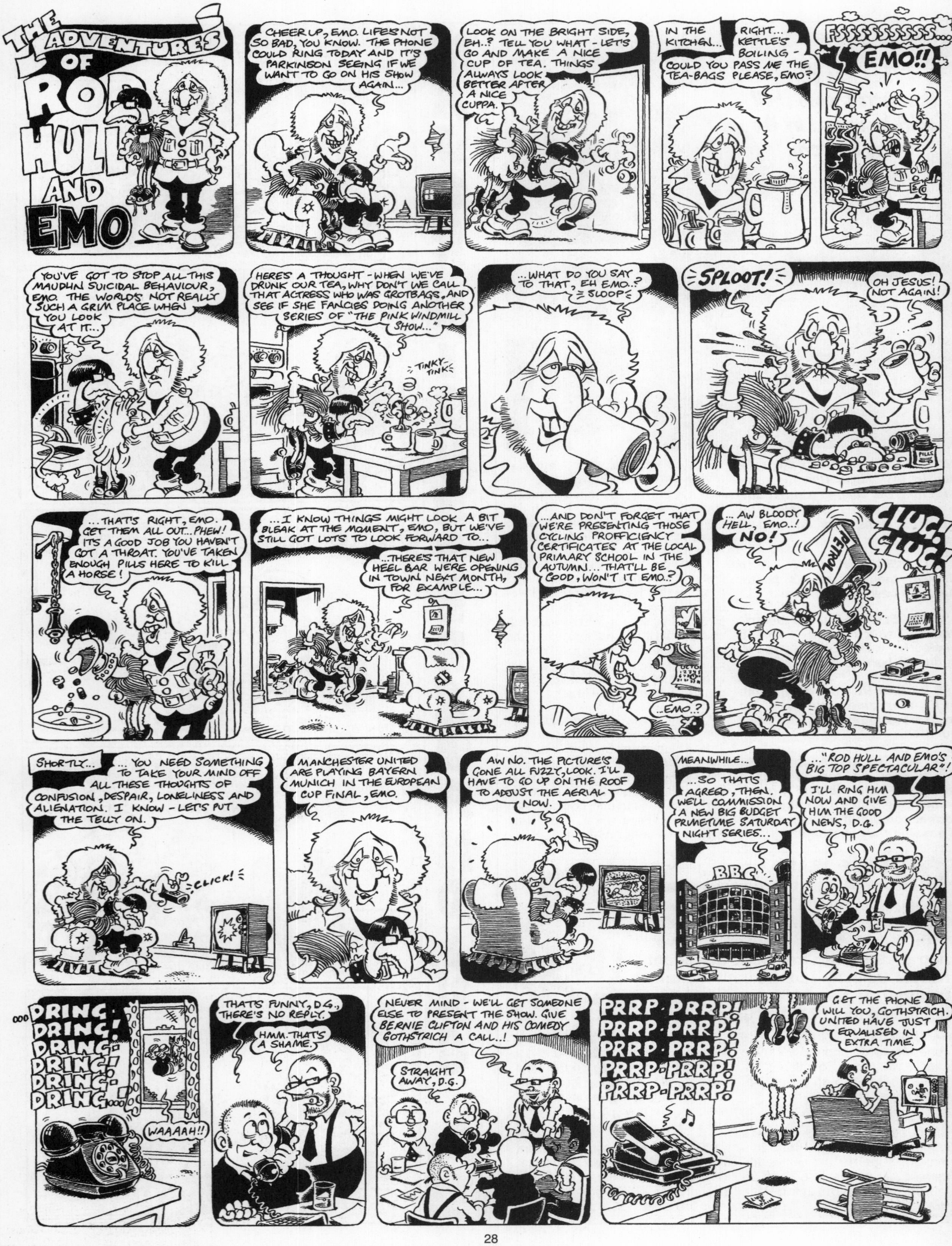
THE ADVENTURES OF ROD HULL AND EMO
CHEER UP, EMO. LIFE'S NOT SO BAD, YOU KNOW. THE PHONE COULD RING TODAY AND IT'S PARKINSON SEEING IF WE WANT TO GO ON HIS SHOW AGAIN...
LOOK ON THE BRIGHT SIDE, EH..? TELL YOU WHAT - LET'S GO AND MAKE A NICE CUP OF TEA. THINGS ALWAYS LOOK BETTER AFTER A NICE CUPPA.
IN THE KITCHEN...
RIGHT... KETTLE'S BOILING - COULD YOU PASS ME THE TEA-BAGS PLEASE, EMO?
FSSSSSSSSS...
EMO!!
YOU'VE GOT TO STOP ALL THIS MAUDLIN SUICIDAL BEHAVIOUR, EMO. THE WORLD'S NOT REALLY SUCH A GRIM PLACE WHEN YOU LOOK AT IT...
HERE'S A THOUGHT - WHEN WE'VE DRUNK OUR TEA, WHY DON'T WE CALL THAT ACTRESS WHO WAS GROTBAGS, AND SEE IF SHE FANCIES DOING ANOTHER SERIES OF "THE PINK WINDMILL SHOW..."
TINKY TINK
...WHAT DO YOU SAY TO THAT, EH EMO..?
SLOOP
SPLOOT!
OH JESUS! NOT AGAIN!
PILLS
...THAT'S RIGHT, EMO. GET THEM ALL OUT... PHEW! IT'S A GOOD JOB YOU HAVEN'T GOT A THROAT. YOU'VE TAKEN ENOUGH PILLS HERE TO KILL A HORSE!
...I KNOW THINGS MIGHT LOOK A BIT BLEAK AT THE MOMENT, EMO, BUT WE'VE STILL GOT LOTS TO LOOK FORWARD TO...
...THERE'S THAT NEW HEEL BAR WE'RE OPENING IN TOWN NEXT MONTH, FOR EXAMPLE...
...AND DON'T FORGET THAT WE'RE PRESENTING THOSE CYCLING PROFFICIENCY CERTIFICATES AT THE LOCAL PRIMARY SCHOOL IN THE AUTUMN... THAT'LL BE GOOD, WON'T IT EMO..?
...EMO..?
...AW BLOODY HELL, EMO..!
NO!
GLUG! GLUG!
PETROL
SHORTLY...
...YOU NEED SOMETHING TO TAKE YOUR MIND OFF ALL THESE THOUGHTS OF CONFUSION, DESPAIR, LONELINESS AND ALIENATION. I KNOW - LET'S PUT THE TELLY ON.
CLICK!
MANCHESTER UNITED ARE PLAYING BAYERN MUNICH IN THE EUROPEAN CUP FINAL, EMO.
AW NO. THE PICTURE'S GONE ALL FUZZY, LOOK. I'LL HAVE TO GO UP ON THE ROOF TO ADJUST THE AERIAL NOW.
MEANWHILE...
...SO THAT'S AGREED, THEN. WE'LL COMMISSION A NEW BIG BUDGET PRIMETIME SATURDAY NIGHT SERIES...
BBC
..."ROD HULL AND EMO'S BIG TOP SPECTACULAR"!
I'LL RING HIM NOW AND GIVE HIM THE GOOD NEWS, D.G.
DRING! DRING! DRING! DRING! DRING! DRING...
WAAAAH!!
THAT'S FUNNY, D.G., THERE'S NO REPLY.
HMM. THAT'S A SHAME.
NEVER MIND - WE'LL GET SOMEONE ELSE TO PRESENT THE SHOW. GIVE BERNIE CLIFTON AND HIS COMEDY GOTHSTRICH A CALL...!
STRAIGHT AWAY, D.G.
PRRP-PRRP! PRRP-PRRP! PRRP-PRRP! PRRP-PRRP! PRRP-PRRP!
GET THE PHONE WILL YOU, GOTHSTRICH. UNITED HAVE JUST EQUALISED IN EXTRA TIME.

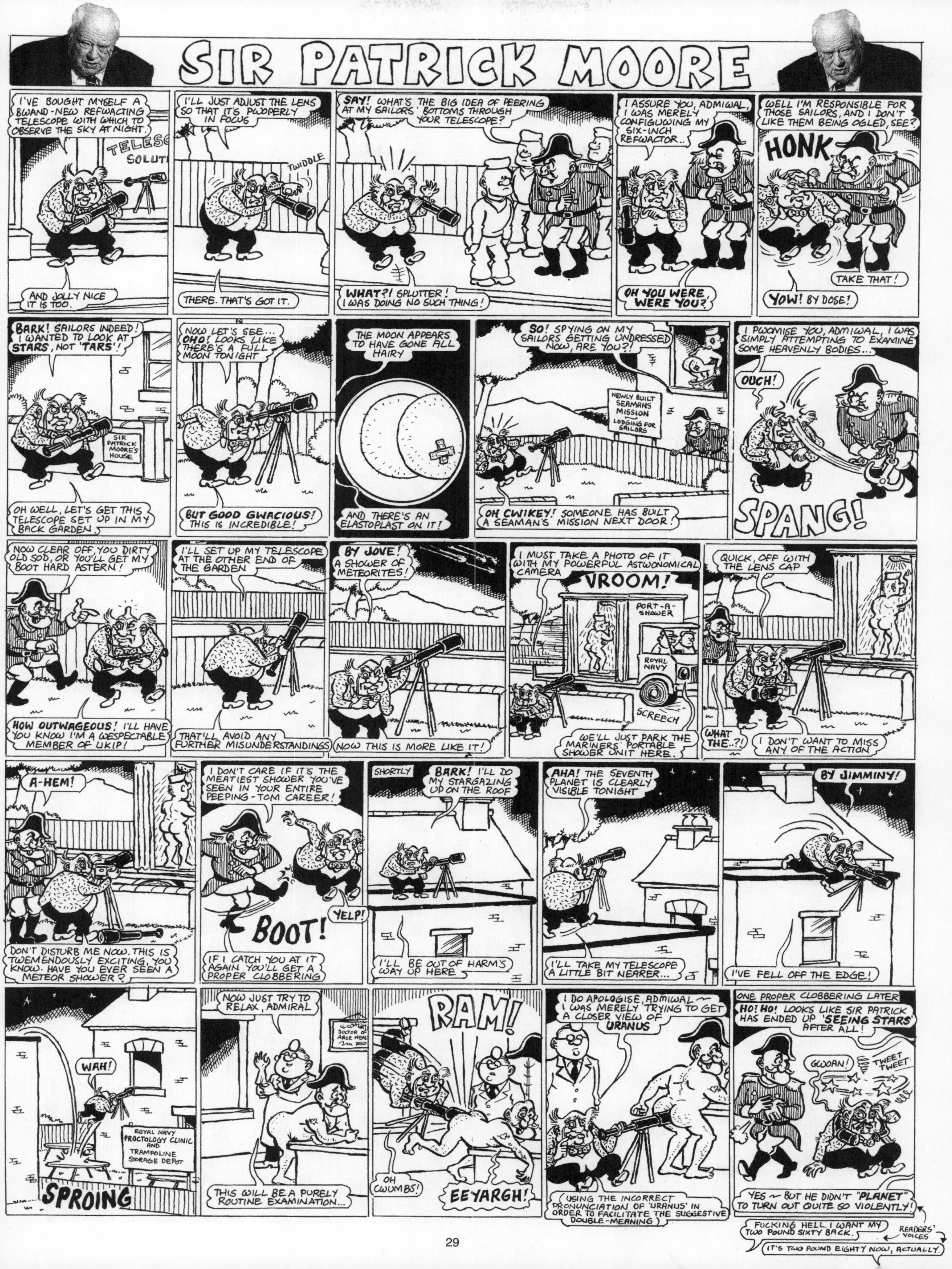
SIR PATRICK MOORE
I'VE BOUGHT MYSELF A BWAND-NEW REFWACTING TELESCOPE WITH WHICH TO OBSERVE THE SKY AT NIGHT.
TELESC
SOLUTI
AND JOLLY NICE IT IS TOO.
I'LL JUST ADJUST THE LENS SO THAT IT'S PWOPERLY IN FOCUS
TWIDDLE
THERE. THAT'S GOT IT.
SAY! WHAT'S THE BIG IDEA OF PEERING AT MY SAILORS' BOTTOMS THROUGH YOUR TELESCOPE?
WHAT?! SPLUTTER! I WAS DOING NO SUCH THING!
I ASSURE YOU, ADMIWAL, I WAS MERELY CONFIGUWING MY SIX-INCH WEFWACTOR..
OH YOU WERE, WERE YOU?
WELL I'M RESPONSIBLE FOR THOSE SAILORS, AND I DON'T LIKE THEM BEING OGLED, SEE?
HONK
TAKE THAT!
YOW! BY DOSE!
BARK! SAILORS INDEED! I WANTED TO LOOK AT STARS, NOT 'TARS'!
SIR PATRICK MOORE'S HOUSE
OH WELL, LET'S GET THIS TELESCOPE SET UP IN MY BACK GARDEN.
NOW LET'S SEE... OHO! LOOKS LIKE THERE'S A FULL MOON TONIGHT
BUT GOOD GWACIOUS! THIS IS INCREDIBLE!
THE MOON APPEARS TO HAVE GONE ALL HAIRY
AND THERE'S AN ELASTOPLAST ON IT!
SO! SPYING ON MY SAILORS GETTING UNDRESSED NOW, ARE YOU?!
NEWLY BUILT SEAMANS MISSION LODGING FOR SAILORS
OH CWIKEY! SOMEONE HAS BUILT A SEAMAN'S MISSION NEXT DOOR!
I PWOMISE YOU, ADMIWAL, I WAS SIMPLY ATTEMPTING TO EXAMINE SOME HEAVENLY BODIES...
OUCH!
SPANG!
NOW CLEAR OFF YOU DIRTY OLD SOD, OR YOU'LL GET MY BOOT HARD ASTERN!
HOW OUTWAGEOUS! I'LL HAVE YOU KNOW I'M A WESPECTABLE MEMBER OF UKIP!
I'LL SET UP MY TELESCOPE AT THE OTHER END OF THE GARDEN
THAT'LL AVOID ANY FURTHER MISUNDERSTANDINGS
BY JOVE! A SHOWER OF METEORITES!
NOW THIS IS MORE LIKE IT!
I MUST TAKE A PHOTO OF IT WITH MY POWERFUL ASTWONOMICAL CAMERA
VROOM!
PORT-A-SHOWER
ROYAL NAVY
SCREECH
WE'LL JUST PARK THE MARINERS' PORTABLE SHOWER UNIT HERE.
QUICK, OFF WITH THE LENS CAP
WHAT THE..?!
I DON'T WANT TO MISS ANY OF THE ACTION
A-HEM!
DON'T DISTURB ME NOW. THIS IS TWEMENDOUSLY EXCITING, YOU KNOW. HAVE YOU EVER SEEN A METEOR SHOWER?
I DON'T CARE IF IT'S THE MEATIEST SHOWER YOU'VE SEEN IN YOUR ENTIRE PEEPING-TOM CAREER!
YELP!
BOOT!
IF I CATCH YOU AT IT AGAIN YOU'LL GET A PROPER CLOBBERING
SHORTLY
BARK! I'LL DO MY STARGAZING UP ON THE ROOF
I'LL BE OUT OF HARM'S WAY UP HERE
AHA! THE SEVENTH PLANET IS CLEARLY VISIBLE TONIGHT
I'LL TAKE MY TELESCOPE A LITTLE BIT NEARER...
BY JIMMINY!
I'VE FELL OFF THE EDGE!
WAH!
ROYAL NAVY PROCTOLOGY CLINIC AND TRAMPOLINE STORAGE DEPOT
SPROING
NOW JUST TRY TO RELAX, ADMIRAL
THIS WILL BE A PURELY ROUTINE EXAMINATION...
RAM!
OH CWUMBS!
EEYARGH!
I DO APOLOGISE, ADMIWAL ~ I WAS MERELY TRYING TO GET A CLOSER VIEW OF URANUS
(USING THE INCORRECT PRONUNCIATION OF 'URANUS' IN ORDER TO FACILITATE THE SUGGESTIVE DOUBLE-MEANING)
ONE PROPER CLOBBERING LATER
HO! HO! LOOKS LIKE SIR PATRICK HAS ENDED UP 'SEEING STARS' AFTER ALL!
GWOAN!
TWEET TWEET
YES ~ BUT HE DIDN'T "PLANET" TO TURN OUT QUITE SO VIOLENTLY!
FUCKING HELL. I WANT MY TWO POUND SIXTY BACK.
READERS' VOICES
IT'S TWO POUND EIGHTY NOW, ACTUALLY.

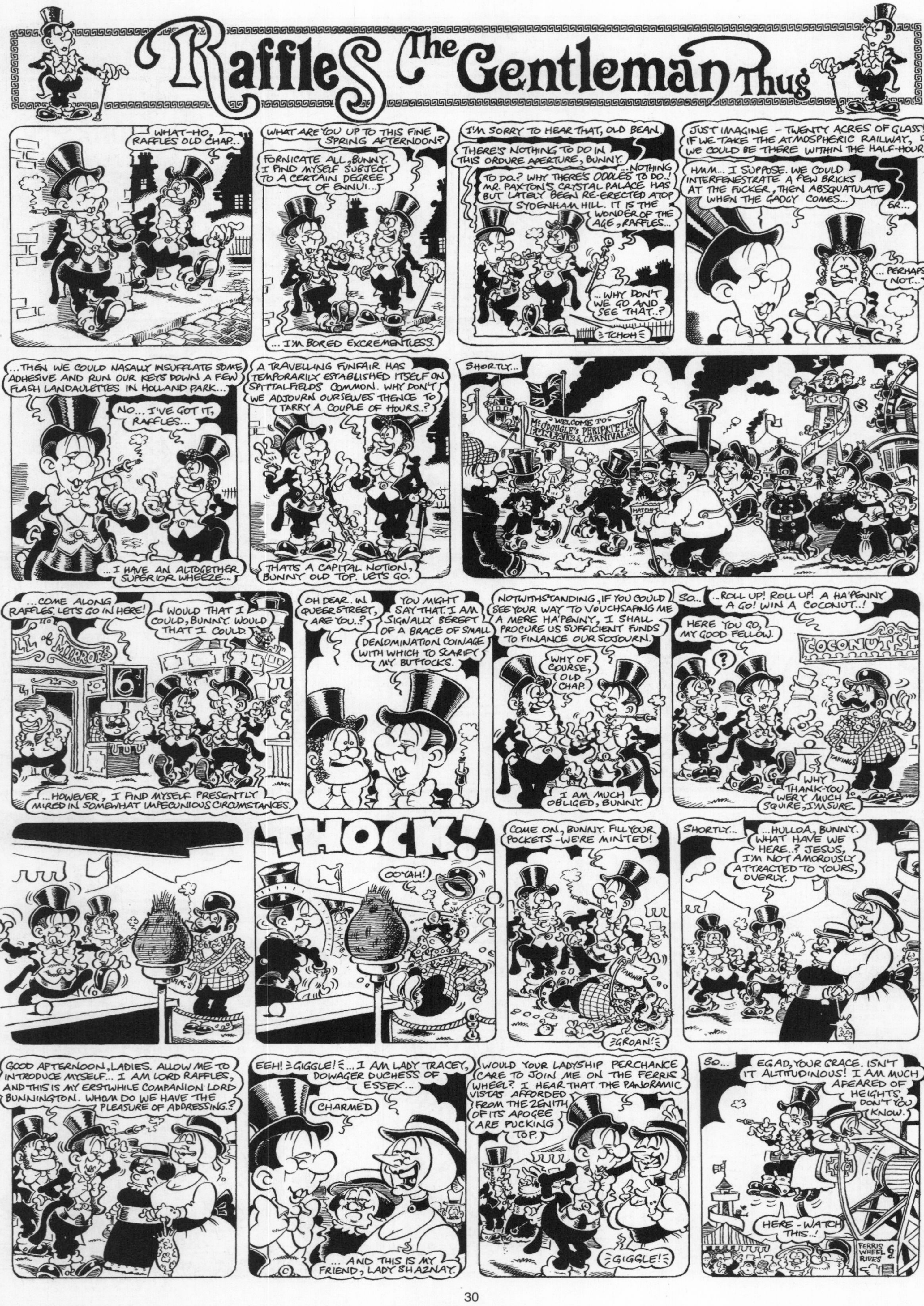
Raffles The Gentleman Thug
WHAT-HO, RAFFLES OLD CHAP...
WHAT ARE YOU UP TO THIS FINE SPRING AFTERNOON?
FORNICATE ALL, BUNNY. I FIND MYSELF SUBJECT TO A CERTAIN DEGREE OF ENNUI...
...I'M BORED EXCREMENTLESS.
I'M SORRY TO HEAR THAT, OLD BEAN.
THERE'S NOTHING TO DO IN THIS ORDURE APERTURE, BUNNY.
...NOTHING TO DO? WHY THERE'S ODDLES TO DO..! MR. PAXTON'S CRYSTAL PALACE HAS BUT LATELY BEEN RE-ERECTED ATOP SYDENHAM HILL. IT IS THE WONDER OF THE AGE, RAFFLES...
...WHY DON'T WE GO AND SEE THAT..?
TCHOH
JUST IMAGINE - TWENTY ACRES OF GLASS! IF WE TAKE THE ATMOSPHERIC RAILWAY, WE COULD BE THERE WITHIN THE HALF-HOUR.
HMM... I SUPPOSE. WE COULD INTERFENESTRATE A FEW BRICKS AT THE FUCKER, THEN ABSQUATULATE WHEN THE GADGY COMES...
ER...
...PERHAPS NOT...
...THEN WE COULD NASALLY INSUFFLATE SOME ADHESIVE AND RUN OUR KEYS DOWN A FEW FLASH LANDAULETTES IN HOLLAND PARK...
NO... I'VE GOT IT, RAFFLES...
...I HAVE AN ALTOGETHER SUPERIOR WHEEZE...
A TRAVELLING FUNFAIR HAS TEMPORARILY ESTABLISHED ITSELF ON SPITTALFIELDS COMMON. WHY DON'T WE ADJOURN OURSELVES THENCE TO TARRY A COUPLE OF HOURS..?
THAT'S A CAPITAL NOTION, BUNNY OLD TOP. LET'S GO.
SHORTLY...
WELCOME TO McODOUGLE'S PERIPATETIC FUNFAIR & CARNIVAL
MATCHES
...COME ALONG RAFFLES, LET'S GO IN HERE!
WOULD THAT I COULD, BUNNY. WOULD THAT I COULD.
HALL of MIRRORS
6d
...HOWEVER, I FIND MYSELF PRESENTLY MIRED IN SOMEWHAT IMPECUNIOUS CIRCUMSTANCES.
OH DEAR. IN QUEER STREET, ARE YOU..?
YOU MIGHT SAY THAT. I AM SIGNALLY BEREFT OF A BRACE OF SMALL DENOMINATION COINAGE WITH WHICH TO SCARIFY MY BUTTOCKS.
NOTWITHSTANDING, IF YOU COULD SEE YOUR WAY TO VOUCHSAFING ME A MERE HA'PENNY, I SHALL PROCURE US SUFFICIENT FUNDS TO FINANCE OUR SOJOURN.
WHY OF COURSE, OLD CHAP.
I AM MUCH OBLIGED, BUNNY.
SO...
...ROLL UP! ROLL UP! A HA'PENNY A GO! WIN A COCONUT..!
HERE YOU GO, MY GOOD FELLOW.
?
COCONUT SH
TAKINGS
WHY THANK-YOU WERY MUCH SQUIRE, I'M SURE.
THOCK!
OOYAH!
COME ON, BUNNY. FILL YOUR POCKETS - WE'RE MINTED!
TAKINGS
GROAN!
SHORTLY...
...HULLOA, BUNNY. WHAT HAVE WE HERE..? JESUS, I'M NOT AMOROUSLY ATTRACTED TO YOURS, OVERLY.
GOOD AFTERNOON, LADIES. ALLOW ME TO INTRODUCE MYSELF... I AM LORD RAFFLES, AND THIS IS MY ERSTWHILE COMPANION LORD BUNNINGTON. WHOM DO WE HAVE THE PLEASURE OF ADDRESSING..?
EEH! GIGGLE! ...I AM LADY TRACEY, DOWAGER DUCHESS OF ESSEX...
CHARMED.
...AND THIS IS MY FRIEND, LADY SHAZNAY.
WOULD YOUR LADYSHIP PERCHANCE CARE TO JOIN ME ON THE FERRIS WHEEL? I HEAR THAT THE PANORAMIC VISTAS AFFORDED FROM THE ZENITH OF ITS APOGEE ARE PUCKING TOP.
GIGGLE!
SO...
EGAD, YOUR GRACE. ISN'T IT ALTITUDINOUS! I AM MUCH AFEARED OF HEIGHTS, DON'T YOU KNOW.
HERE - WATCH THIS..!
FERRIS WHEEL RIDES 6d

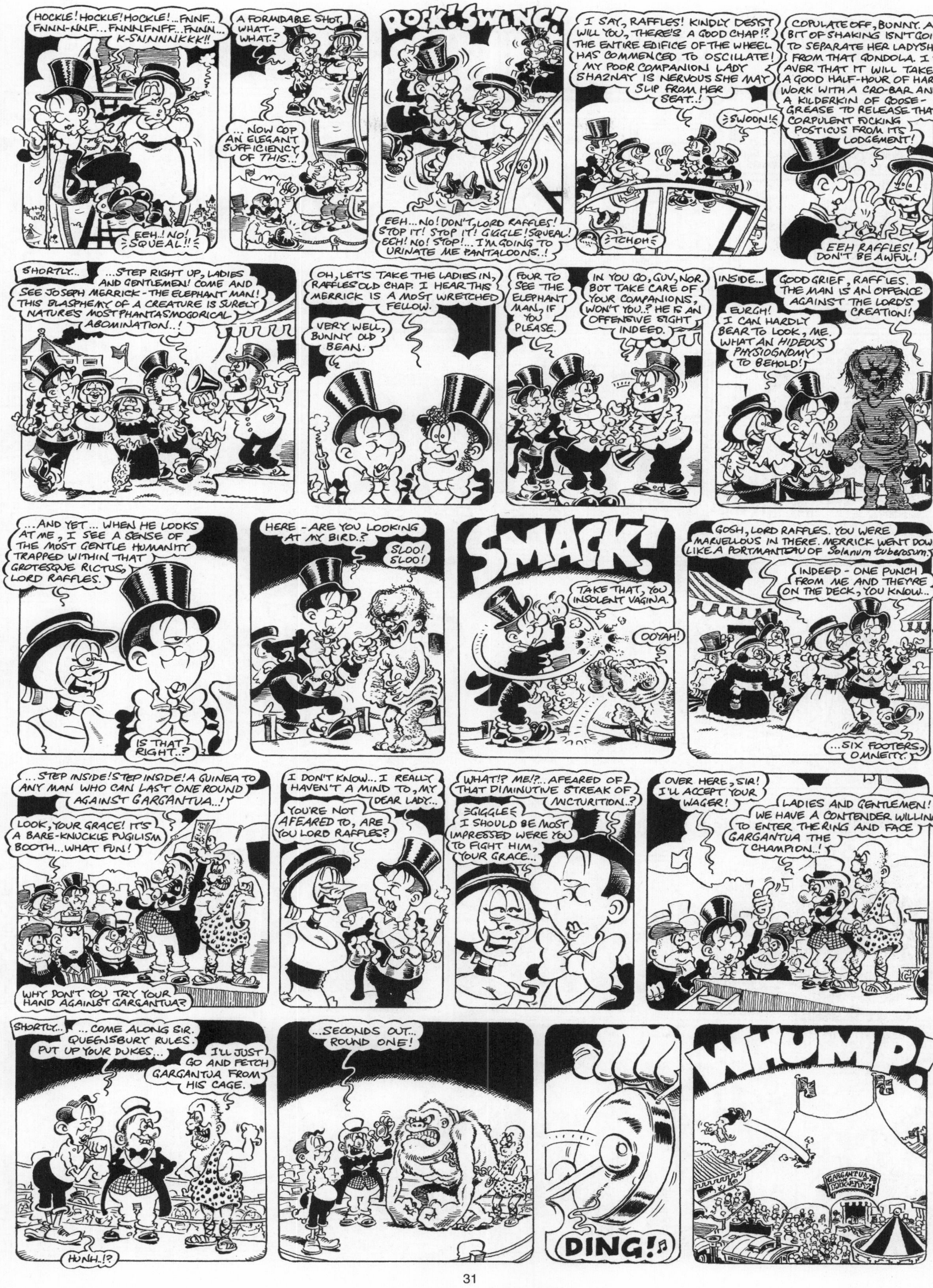
HOCKLE! HOCKLE! HOCKLE!... FNNF... FNNN-NNF... FNNNFNFF... FNNN... K-SNNNNKKK!!
EEH..! NO! SQUEAL!!...
A FORMIDABLE SHOT, WHAT-WHAT..?
... NOW COP AN ELEGANT SUFFICIENCY OF THIS..!
ROCK! SWING!
EEH... NO! DON'T, LORD RAFFLES! STOP IT! STOP IT! GIGGLE! SQUEAL! EECH! NO! STOP!... I'M GOING TO URINATE ME PANTALOONS..!
I SAY, RAFFLES! KINDLY DESIST WILL YOU, THERE'S A GOOD CHAP!? THE ENTIRE EDIFICE OF THE WHEEL HAS COMMENCED TO OSCILLATE! MY POOR COMPANION LADY SHAZNAY IS NERVOUS SHE MAY SLIP FROM HER SEAT..!
SWOON!
TCHOH
COPULATE OFF, BUNNY. A BIT OF SHAKING ISN'T GOING TO SEPARATE HER LADYSHIP FROM THAT GONDOLA. I AVER THAT IT WILL TAKE A GOOD HALF-HOUR OF HARD WORK WITH A CRO-BAR AND A KILDERKIN OF GOOSE-GREASE TO RELEASE THAT CORPULENT FUCKING POSTICUS FROM ITS LODGEMENT!
EEH RAFFLES! DON'T BE AWFUL!
SHORTLY...
...STEP RIGHT UP, LADIES AND GENTLEMEN! COME AND SEE JOSEPH MERRICK - THE ELEPHANT MAN! THIS BLASPHEMY OF A CREATURE IS SURELY NATURE'S MOST PHANTASMOGORICAL ABOMINATION..!
OH, LET'S TAKE THE LADIES IN, RAFFLES OLD CHAP. I HEAR THIS MERRICK IS A MOST WRETCHED FELLOW.
VERY WELL, BUNNY OLD BEAN.
FOUR TO SEE THE ELEPHANT MAN, IF YOU PLEASE.
IN YOU GO, GUV, NOR. BUT TAKE CARE OF YOUR COMPANIONS, WON'T YOU..? HE IS AN OFFENSIVE SIGHT INDEED.
INSIDE...
GOOD GRIEF, RAFFLES. THE MAN IS AN OFFENCE AGAINST THE LORD'S CREATION!
EURGH! I CAN HARDLY BEAR TO LOOK, ME. WHAT AN HIDEOUS PHYSIOGNOMY TO BEHOLD!
...AND YET... WHEN HE LOOKS AT ME, I SEE A SENSE OF THE MOST GENTLE HUMANITY TRAPPED WITHIN THAT GROTESQUE RICTUS, LORD RAFFLES.
IS THAT RIGHT..?
HERE - ARE YOU LOOKING AT MY BIRD..?
SLOO! SLOO!
SMACK!
TAKE THAT, YOU INSOLENT VAGINA.
OOYAH!
GOSH, LORD RAFFLES. YOU WERE MARVELLOUS IN THERE. MERRICK WENT DOWN LIKE A PORTMANTEAU OF Solanum tuberosum.
INDEED - ONE PUNCH FROM ME AND THEY'RE ON THE DECK, YOU KNOW...
...SIX FOOTERS, OMNEITY.
...STEP INSIDE! STEP INSIDE! A GUINEA TO ANY MAN WHO CAN LAST ONE ROUND AGAINST GARGANTUA..!
LOOK, YOUR GRACE! IT'S A BARE-KNUCKLE PUGILISM BOOTH... WHAT FUN!
WHY DON'T YOU TRY YOUR HAND AGAINST GARGANTUA?
I DON'T KNOW... I REALLY HAVEN'T A MIND TO, MY DEAR LADY...
YOU'RE NOT AFEARED TO, ARE YOU LORD RAFFLES?
WHAT!? ME!?... AFEARED OF THAT DIMINUTIVE STREAK OF MICTURITION..?
GIGGLE I SHOULD BE MOST IMPRESSED WERE YOU TO FIGHT HIM, YOUR GRACE...
OVER HERE, SIR! I'LL ACCEPT YOUR WAGER!
LADIES AND GENTLEMEN! WE HAVE A CONTENDER WILLING TO ENTER THE RING AND FACE GARGANTUA THE CHAMPION..!
SHORTLY...
... COME ALONG SIR. QUEENSBURY RULES. PUT UP YOUR DUKES...
I'LL JUST GO AND FETCH GARGANTUA FROM HIS CAGE.
HUNH..!?
...SECONDS OUT... ROUND ONE!
DING!
WHUMP!

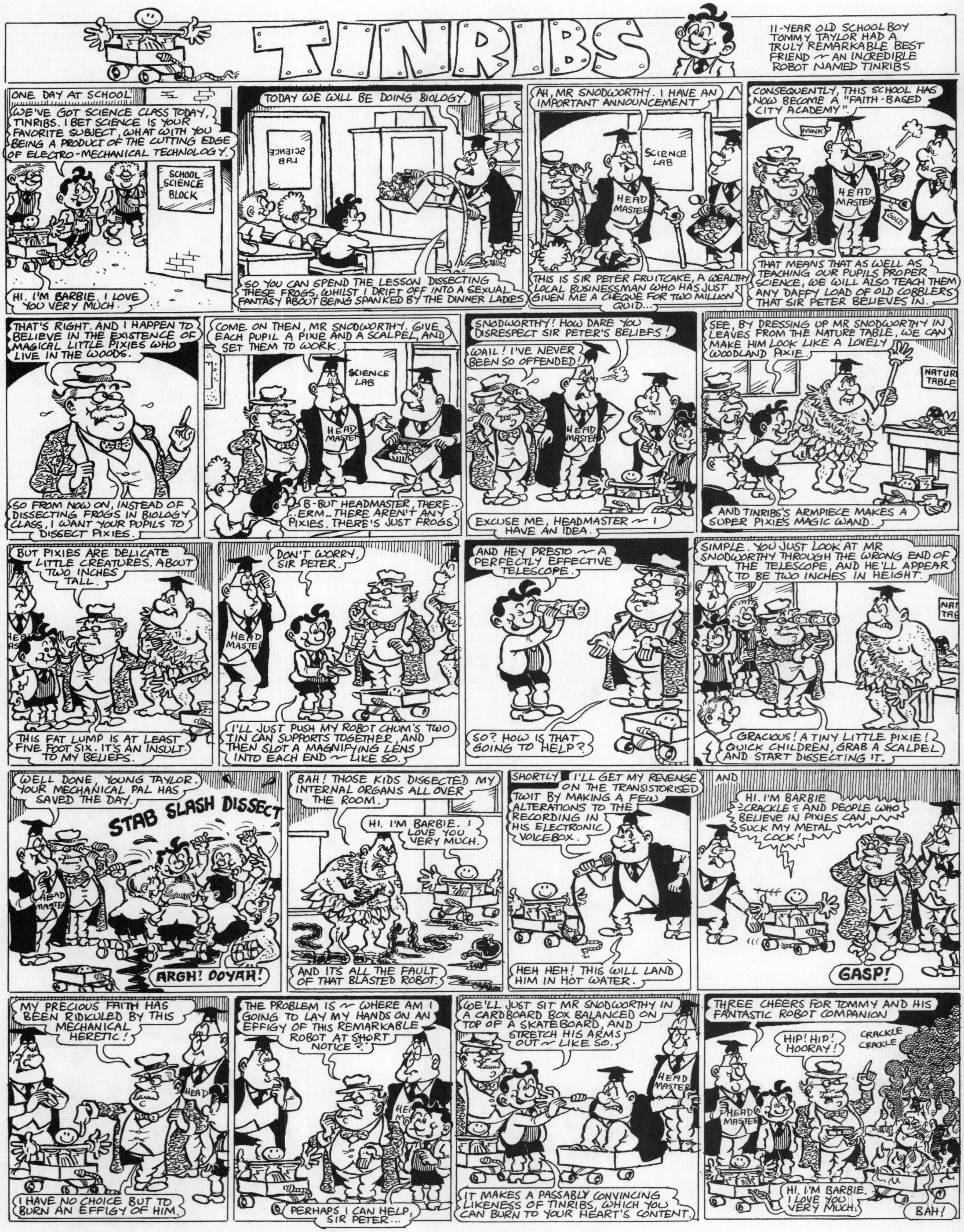
TINRIBS
11-YEAR OLD SCHOOL BOY TOMMY TAYLOR HAD A TRULY REMARKABLE BEST FRIEND ~ AN INCREDIBLE ROBOT NAMED TINRIBS
ONE DAY AT SCHOOL
WE'VE GOT SCIENCE CLASS TODAY, TINRIBS. I BET SCIENCE IS YOUR FAVORITE SUBJECT, WHAT WITH YOU BEING A PRODUCT OF THE CUTTING EDGE OF ELECTRO-MECHANICAL TECHNOLOGY.
SCHOOL SCIENCE BLOCK
HI. I'M BARBIE. I LOVE YOU VERY MUCH.
TODAY WE WILL BE DOING BIOLOGY.
SCIENCE LAB
SO YOU CAN SPEND THE LESSON DISSECTING THESE FROGS, WHILST I DRIFT OFF INTO A SEXUAL FANTASY ABOUT BEING SPANKED BY THE DINNER LADIES.
AH, MR SNODWORTHY. I HAVE AN IMPORTANT ANNOUNCEMENT
SCIENCE LAB
HEAD MASTER
THIS IS SIR PETER FRUITCAKE, A WEALTHY LOCAL BUSINESSMAN WHO HAS JUST GIVEN ME A CHEQUE FOR TWO MILLION QUID...
CONSEQUENTLY, THIS SCHOOL HAS NOW BECOME A "FAITH-BASED CITY ACADEMY".
MINK
HEAD MASTER
GOLD
THAT MEANS THAT AS WELL AS TEACHING OUR PUPILS PROPER SCIENCE, WE WILL ALSO TEACH THEM ANY DAFFY LOAD OF OLD COBBLERS THAT SIR PETER BELIEVES IN.
THAT'S RIGHT. AND I HAPPEN TO BELIEVE IN THE EXISTENCE OF MAGICAL LITTLE PIXIES WHO LIVE IN THE WOODS.
SO FROM NOW ON, INSTEAD OF DISSECTING FROGS IN BIOLOGY CLASS, I WANT YOUR PUPILS TO DISSECT PIXIES.
COME ON THEN, MR SNODWORTHY. GIVE EACH PUPIL A PIXIE AND A SCALPEL, AND SET THEM TO WORK.
SCIENCE LAB
HEAD MASTER
B-BUT HEADMASTER, THERE... ..ERM.. THERE AREN'T ANY PIXIES. THERE'S JUST FROGS.
SNODWORTHY! HOW DARE YOU DISRESPECT SIR PETER'S BELIEFS!
WAIL! I'VE NEVER BEEN SO OFFENDED!
HEAD MASTER
EXCUSE ME, HEADMASTER ~ I HAVE AN IDEA.
SEE, BY DRESSING UP MR SNODWORTHY IN LEAVES FROM THE NATURE TABLE, WE CAN MAKE HIM LOOK LIKE A LOVELY WOODLAND PIXIE.
NATURE TABLE
AND TINRIBS'S ARMPIECE MAKES A SUPER PIXIE'S MAGIC WAND.
BUT PIXIES ARE DELICATE LITTLE CREATURES, ABOUT TWO INCHES TALL.
THIS FAT LUMP IS AT LEAST FIVE FOOT SIX. IT'S AN INSULT TO MY BELIEFS.
DON'T WORRY, SIR PETER.
HEAD MASTER
I'LL JUST PUSH MY ROBOT CHUM'S TWO TIN CAN SUPPORTS TOGETHER, AND THEN SLOT A MAGNIFYING LENS INTO EACH END ~ LIKE SO.
AND HEY PRESTO ~ A PERFECTLY EFFECTIVE TELESCOPE.
SO? HOW IS THAT GOING TO HELP?
SIMPLE. YOU JUST LOOK AT MR SNODWORTHY THROUGH THE WRONG END OF THE TELESCOPE, AND HE'LL APPEAR TO BE TWO INCHES IN HEIGHT.
GRACIOUS! A TINY LITTLE PIXIE! QUICK CHILDREN, GRAB A SCALPEL AND START DISSECTING IT.
WELL DONE, YOUNG TAYLOR. YOUR MECHANICAL PAL HAS SAVED THE DAY.
STAB SLASH DISSECT
HEAD MASTER
ARGH! OOYAH!
BAH! THOSE KIDS DISSECTED MY INTERNAL ORGANS ALL OVER THE ROOM.
HI. I'M BARBIE. I LOVE YOU VERY MUCH.
AND IT'S ALL THE FAULT OF THAT BLASTED ROBOT.
SHORTLY
I'LL GET MY REVENGE ON THE TRANSISTORISED TWIT BY MAKING A FEW ALTERATIONS TO THE RECORDING IN HIS ELECTRONIC VOICEBOX.
HEH HEH! THIS WILL LAND HIM IN HOT WATER.
AND
HI. I'M BARBIE. *CRACKLE* AND PEOPLE WHO BELIEVE IN PIXIES CAN SUCK MY METAL COCK!
GASP!
MY PRECIOUS FAITH HAS BEEN RIDICULED BY THIS MECHANICAL HERETIC!
HEAD
I HAVE NO CHOICE BUT TO BURN AN EFFIGY OF HIM.
THE PROBLEM IS ~ WHERE AM I GOING TO LAY MY HANDS ON AN EFFIGY OF THIS REMARKABLE ROBOT AT SHORT NOTICE?
PERHAPS I CAN HELP, SIR PETER...
WE'LL JUST SIT MR SNODWORTHY IN A CARDBOARD BOX BALANCED ON TOP OF A SKATEBOARD, AND STRETCH HIS ARMS OUT ~ LIKE SO.
HEAD MASTER
IT MAKES A PASSABLY CONVINCING LIKENESS OF TINRIBS, WHICH YOU CAN BURN TO YOUR HEART'S CONTENT.
THREE CHEERS FOR TOMMY AND HIS FANTASTIC ROBOT COMPANION
HIP! HIP! HOORAY!
CRACKLE CRACKLE
HEAD MASTER
HI, I'M BARBIE. I LOVE YOU VERY MUCH.
BAH!

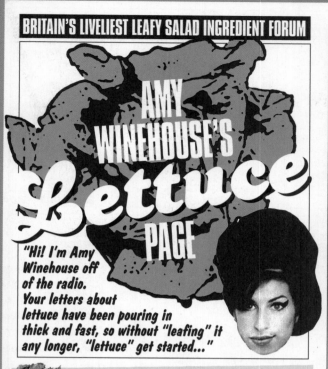

BRITAIN'S LIVELIEST LEAFY SALAD INGREDIENT FORUM

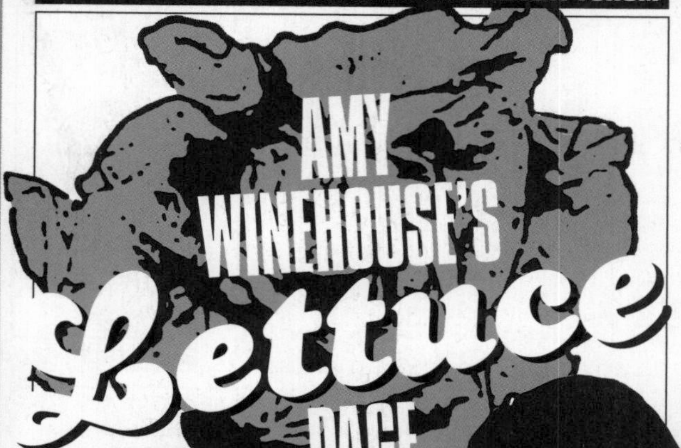

AMY WINEHOUSE'S Lettuce PAGE

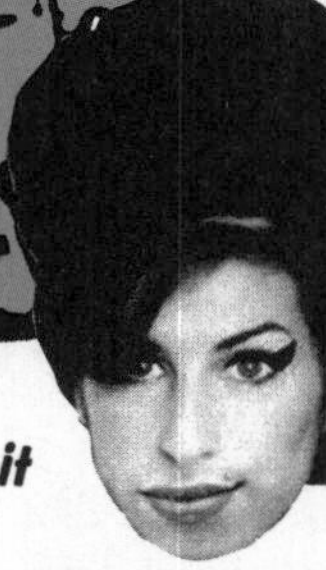

"Hi! I'm Amy Winehouse off of the radio. Your letters about lettuce have been pouring in thick and fast, so without "leafing" it any longer, "lettuce" get started..."

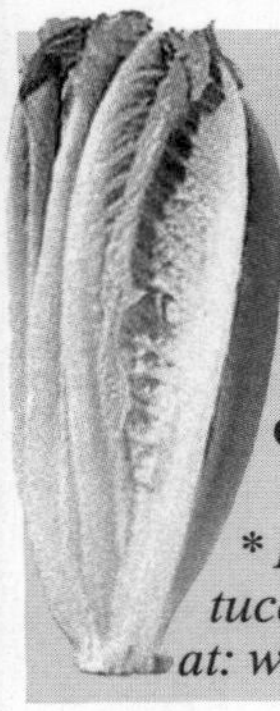

AMY'S Star Letter

MY HUSBAND used to work as a salad photographer, but now he works for the Royal Mail. These days he has to *post letters*, whereas in the olden days he *posed lettuce*!

Margaret Dunhelm, Stoke

** Margaret wins this fantastic head of cos lettuce, worth over 80p, donated by our friends at: www.iwantoneofthemlettuces.co.uk!*

• **I LIVE** next door to Mr and Mrs Dunhelm *(above letter)*. Whilst it is true that he was a lettuce photographer and now works for the Royal Mail, he is based in the sorting office where he carries out maintenance on automatic postcode reading equipment, so he doesn't actually post letters at all. Nobody likes a joke more than I do, but there is no excuse for factual inaccuracies.

Hector Beelzebub, Stoke

• **MY WIFE** and I are both lettuce fans. The other night we were playing scrabble, and I couldn't believe my luck when I looked at the seven letters I had picked up - T,U,L,E,T,C,E! I'm sure I don't need to spell out to my fellow lettuce fans what word I made. It was LETTUCE!

Albert Ridley, Nuneaton

• **I REALLY** love lettuce. In fact I love it so much that my wife often jokes that I should change my name to George Lettuce.

George Leafy-Greens, Newcastle

• **I'VE ALWAYS** been a fan of the Hollywood actor John Wayne. But I wonder if he liked lettuce.

Edna Carstairs, Redditch

** Yes Edna. John Wayne (real name Marian Monroe) was the honorary president of the American Lettuce Association from 1950 to 1978.*

Lettuce FACT FILE

OVER 10,000 tons of chopped lettuce is left on the side of plates by British pub grub eaters every hour. That's equivalent to the amount of lettuce produced by a lettuce patch the size of Wales... in a year!

ROCKET lettuce was developed by NASA scientists to give astronauts something heathy to eat with their pouched foods. But, unsurprisingly, the astronauts just left it on the side of the pouch.

LETTUCE was brought back from South America by Sir Frances Drake in 1066. Before this time, people having a pub lunch were given a small amount of raw cabbage to leave on the side of their plate.

THE WORLD'S smallest man, Calvin Phillips was so small that instead of lettuce, he had the leaf off a sprout in his beefburgers. Which were made from mice.

LETTUCE is one of the world's cheapest foods. So cheap, in fact, that the most expensive lettuce ever sold - the Rockerfeller Lettuce - cost just £1.42 when it was sold at a Sotheby's vegetable auction in New York.

LETTUCE is usually regarded as being good for you. But that certainly wasn't the case for Fats Domino. The New Orleans boogie-woogie pianist was killed when a 6lb lettuce dropped by a passing bird struck him on the head.

QUEEN Victoria famously refused to believe that lettuces existed. On being shown one at the 1851 Great Exhibition, she insisted that it was merely a thin-leaved cabbage. When its grower maintained that it was indeed a lettuce, the mischievous monarch sent him to the Tower of London where he remained for eight years.

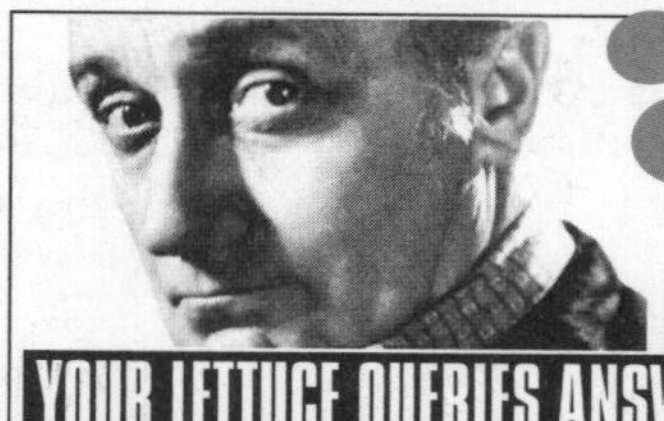

Salad Daze

YOUR LETTUCE QUERIES ANSWERED BY CRISPIN DRY, PROFESSOR OF LETTUCES AT DE MONTFORT UNIVERSITY

Dear Professor Dry,

• **WHY** is iceberg lettuce so called?

Ena Chopsuey, Leeds

WELL, Edna, like icebergs, iceberg lettuces (or Lactuta sativa as we lettuce scientists call them) grow with nine tenths of their leaves below the surface of the soil. On an historical note, it is a bizarre coincidence that RMS Olympic, the sister ship of RMS Titanic, was sunk after colliding with a container ship... packed with iceberg lettuces!

Dear Professor Dry,

• **WHY** is normal lettuce green, but lollo rosso is red?

Edna Fu Yung, Leeds

THERE is a simple answer to this, Edna. Lollo rosso is italian for red lollo. If lollo rosso was green, the Italians would have to call it lollo verdo. To call a red lettuce lollo verdo would be ridiculous, so that's why it's called lollo rosso.

Dear Professor Dry,

• **I WAS** chatting in the pub the other night, and the conversation got round to lettuce. One man said that pak choi was a kind of lettuce, and I disagreed as I am sure that it is more of a cabbage. The discussion got a little heated and blows were exchanged. After one punch to the temple, the man stumbled and banged his head on the corner of the bar. He lapsed into a coma and as a result I am being charged with aggravated assault. The police say that if he dies, then manslaughter charges will be brought. But leaving aside the rights and wrongs of my actions, was I right when I said that pak choi was not a lettuce?

Norman Wonton, Leeds

DON'T worry, Norman. You are completely correct when you say pak choi is a cabbage. It belongs in the brassica family along with cabbages, sprouts and broccolli. Your victim was in the wrong and got little more than he deserved.

Lettuce LAUGHS

Q: WHAT did the lettuce who had just become a vicar say to his congregation?

A: *Lettuce (let us) pray.*

Edna Bunions, Hartlepool

Q: WHAT did the jug containing a three table spoons of olive oil, a table spoon of lemon juice and a teaspoon of vinegar say to the lettuce that barged into its bedroom whilst it was putting its clothes on?

A: *Can't you see I'm dressing? (like salad dressing)*

Ada Hammertoe, Derby

Q: WHO is a lettuce's favourite ex-Radio1 DJ?

A: *DLT (BLT (Bacon, lettuce and tomato))*

Dolly Chillblains, Brighton

Q: WHY did the lettuce leaf? (leave)

A: *Because it saw the salad dressing. My husband thinks 'because it saw the salad bowl' is funnier.*

Nelly & Albert Ingrowing-Nail, Leeds

Lettuce PUZZLES

AMY WINEHOUSE and her friends LILY ALLEN and CORINNE BAILEY-RAE have gone fishing for lettuces but oh dear! Their lines have got tangled on the riverbank. Can you sort out the lines to discover which girl has hooked which lettuce variety?

ANSWER: Amy - Iceberg, Lily - Little Gem, Corinne - Romaine

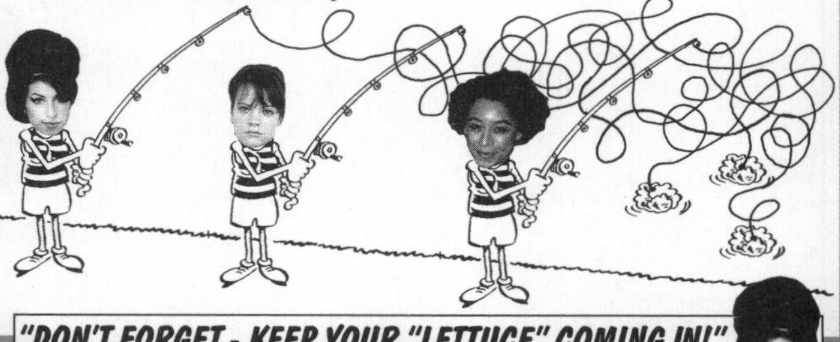

"DON'T FORGET - KEEP YOUR "LETTUCE" COMING IN!"

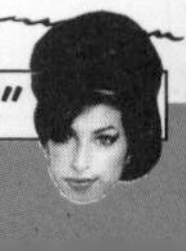

KIDS SAY THE FUNNIEST THINGS... about Lettuce

"THAT'S a nice lettuce, nana," said my three-year-old granddaughter the other day whilst I was preparing dinner. I had to laugh. She was pointing at a cabbage!

Ada Golightly, Dundee

ELDERLY RELATIVES SAY THE FUNNIEST THINGS ABOUT KIDS SAYING THE FUNNIEST THINGS... about Lettuce

"THAT'S a nice lettuce, nana," said my three-year-old daughter to my mother the other day whilst she was preparing dinner. "That's not a lettuce, it's a cabbage," she chuckled. I had to laugh, for my mother is in the tertiary stages of senile dementia and it was indeed a lettuce.

Brenda Crabtree, Dundee

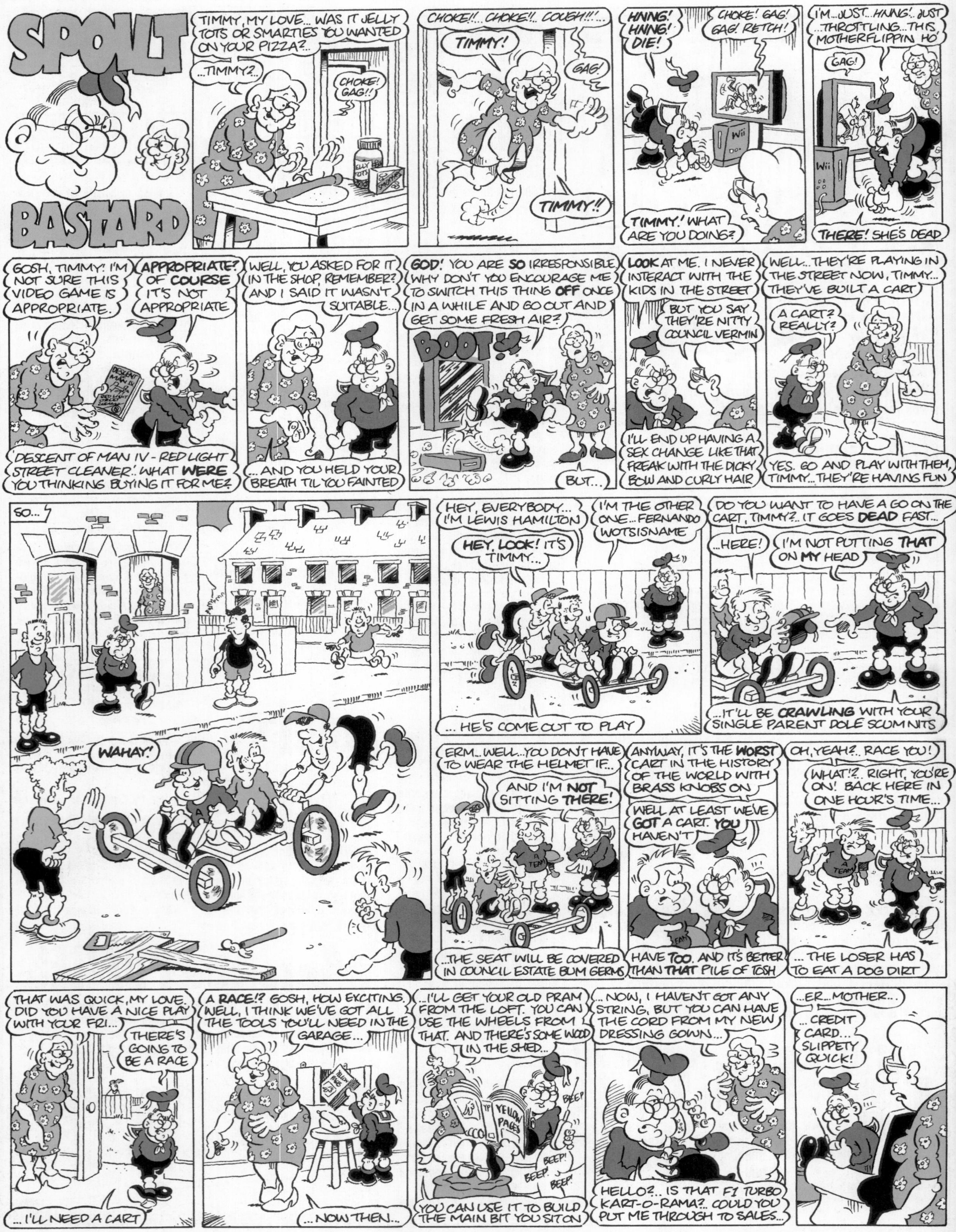
SPOILT BASTARD
TIMMY, MY LOVE... WAS IT JELLY TOTS OR SMARTIES YOU WANTED ON YOUR PIZZA?..
...TIMMY?..
CHOKE! GAG!!
CHOKE!!.. CHOKE!!.. COUGH!!!...
TIMMY!
GAG!
TIMMY!!
HNNG! HNNG! DIE!
CHOKE! GAG! GAG! RETCH!
TIMMY! WHAT ARE YOU DOING?
I'M... JUST... HNNG!.. JUST ...THROTTLING... THIS MOTHERFLIPPIN HO'
GAG!
THERE! SHE'S DEAD
GOSH, TIMMY! I'M NOT SURE THIS VIDEO GAME IS APPROPRIATE.
APPROPRIATE? OF COURSE IT'S NOT APPROPRIATE
'DESCENT OF MAN IV - RED LIGHT STREET CLEANER'.. WHAT WERE YOU THINKING BUYING IT FOR ME?
WELL, YOU ASKED FOR IT IN THE SHOP, REMEMBER? AND I SAID IT WASN'T SUITABLE...
...AND YOU HELD YOUR BREATH TIL YOU FAINTED
GOD! YOU ARE SO IRRESPONSIBLE. WHY DON'T YOU ENCOURAGE ME TO SWITCH THIS THING OFF ONCE IN A WHILE AND GO OUT AND GET SOME FRESH AIR?
BOOT!!
BUT...
LOOK AT ME. I NEVER INTERACT WITH THE KIDS IN THE STREET
BUT YOU SAY THEY'RE NITTY COUNCIL VERMIN
I'LL END UP HAVING A SEX CHANGE LIKE THAT FREAK WITH THE DICKY BOW AND CURLY HAIR
WELL... THEY'RE PLAYING IN THE STREET NOW, TIMMY... THEY'VE BUILT A CART
A CART? REALLY?
YES. GO AND PLAY WITH THEM, TIMMY... THEY'RE HAVING FUN
SO...
WAHAY!
HEY, EVERYBODY... I'M LEWIS HAMILTON
I'M THE OTHER ONE... FERNANDO WOTSISNAME
HEY, LOOK! IT'S TIMMY...
... HE'S COME OUT TO PLAY
DO YOU WANT TO HAVE A GO ON THE CART, TIMMY?.. IT GOES DEAD FAST...
...HERE!
I'M NOT PUTTING THAT ON MY HEAD
...IT'LL BE CRAWLING WITH YOUR SINGLE PARENT DOLE SCUM NITS
ERM... WELL... YOU DON'T HAVE TO WEAR THE HELMET IF...
AND I'M NOT SITTING THERE!
...THE SEAT WILL BE COVERED IN COUNCIL ESTATE BUM GERMS
ANYWAY, IT'S THE WORST CART IN THE HISTORY OF THE WORLD WITH BRASS KNOBS ON
WELL AT LEAST WE'VE GOT A CART. YOU HAVEN'T
HAVE TOO. AND IT'S BETTER THAN THAT PILE OF TOSH
OH, YEAH?.. RACE YOU!
WHAT!?.. RIGHT, YOU'RE ON! BACK HERE IN ONE HOUR'S TIME...
... THE LOSER HAS TO EAT A DOG DIRT
THAT WAS QUICK, MY LOVE. DID YOU HAVE A NICE PLAY WITH YOUR FRI...
THERE'S GOING TO BE A RACE
... I'LL NEED A CART
A RACE!? GOSH, HOW EXCITING. WELL, I THINK WE'VE GOT ALL THE TOOLS YOU'LL NEED IN THE GARAGE...
... NOW THEN...
...I'LL GET YOUR OLD PRAM FROM THE LOFT. YOU CAN USE THE WHEELS FROM THAT. AND THERE'S SOME WOOD IN THE SHED...
YELLOW PAGES
BEEP
BEEP! BEEP! BEEP!
YOU CAN USE IT TO BUILD THE MAIN BIT YOU SIT ON
... NOW, I HAVEN'T GOT ANY STRING, BUT YOU CAN HAVE THE CORD FROM MY NEW DRESSING GOWN...
HELLO?.. IS THAT F1 TURBO KART-O-RAMA?.. COULD YOU PUT ME THROUGH TO SALES...
...ER... MOTHER...
... CREDIT CARD... SLIPPETY QUICK!

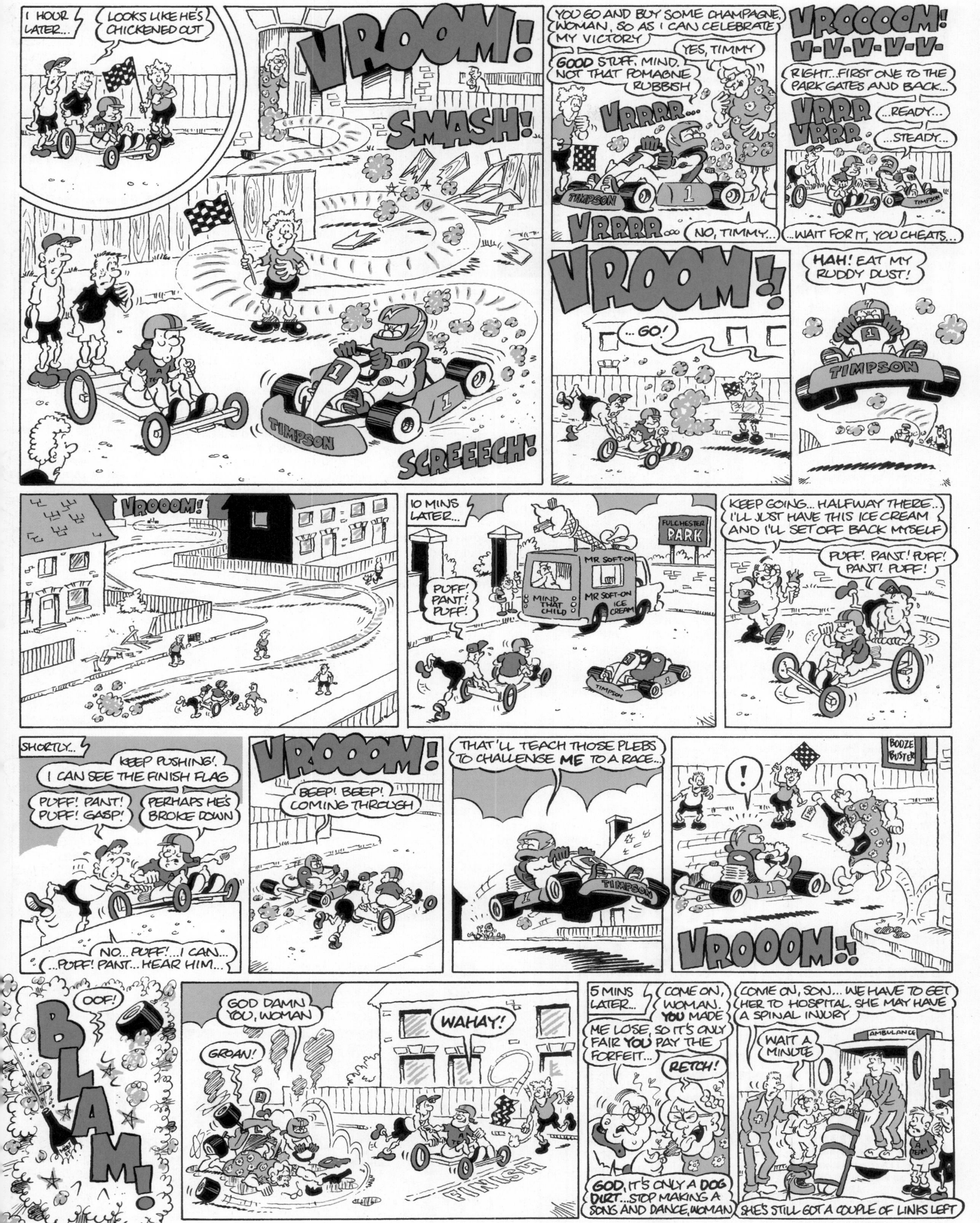

1 HOUR LATER...
LOOKS LIKE HE'S CHICKENED OUT
VROOM!
SMASH!
SCREEECH!
TIMPSON
YOU GO AND BUY SOME CHAMPAGNE, WOMAN, SO AS I CAN CELEBRATE MY VICTORY
YES, TIMMY
GOOD STUFF, MIND. NOT THAT POMAGNE RUBBISH
VRRRR...
VRRRR...
NO, TIMMY...
VROOOOM! V-V-V-V-V-V-
RIGHT... FIRST ONE TO THE PARK GATES AND BACK...
VRRR VRRR
...READY...
...STEADY...
...WAIT FOR IT, YOU CHEATS...
VROOM!
...GO!
HAH! EAT MY RUDDY DUST!
TIMPSON
VROOOM!
10 MINS LATER...
FULCHESTER PARK
MR SOFT-ON
MR SOFT-ON ICE CREAM
MIND THAT CHILD
PUFF! PANT! PUFF!
KEEP GOING... HALFWAY THERE... I'LL JUST HAVE THIS ICE CREAM AND I'LL SET OFF BACK MYSELF
PUFF! PANT! PUFF! PANT! PUFF!
SHORTLY...
KEEP PUSHING! I CAN SEE THE FINISH FLAG
PUFF! PANT! PUFF! GASP!
PERHAPS HE'S BROKE DOWN
NO... PUFF!... I CAN... ...PUFF! PANT... HEAR HIM...
VROOOM!
BEEP! BEEP! COMING THROUGH
THAT'LL TEACH THOSE PLEBS TO CHALLENGE ME TO A RACE...
BOOZE BUSTER
!
VROOOM!
OOF!
BLAM!
GOD DAMN YOU, WOMAN
GROAN!
WAHAY!
FINISH
5 MINS LATER...
COME ON, WOMAN. YOU MADE ME LOSE, SO IT'S ONLY FAIR YOU PAY THE FORFEIT...
RETCH!
GOD, IT'S ONLY A DOG DIRT... STOP MAKING A SONG AND DANCE, WOMAN
COME ON, SON... WE HAVE TO GET HER TO HOSPITAL. SHE MAY HAVE A SPINAL INJURY
WAIT A MINUTE
AMBULANCE
SHE'S STILL GOT A COUPLE OF LINKS LEFT

LETTEBOCKS

PO Box 656,
North Shields,
NE30 4XX
letters@viz.co.uk

ST★R LETTER

❑ In Greek mythology, Corvus was a bird who was cast into the sky by the Gods as a punishment. In the next breath they placed a dog called Laeleps in the sky as a reward for winning a race against a fox. I wish these Greek deities would make their bloody minds up.

Spoongleberry, e-mail

❑ I went to the North Shields branch of B&Q yesterday to buy a length of wood for a DIY project. At 3.6 metres, the piece was too long to fit in the car, so I thought I would take advantage of their in-store 'Timber Cutting Service'. Imagine my utter, utter bewilderment when I was told that the piece of timber I had selected was too long. If it had been 3 metres or less, they would have happily cut it for me, but at 3.6 metres, it was too long to be cut in half. Where are you supposed to begin?

T Franklyn, Newcastle

❑ I got arrested for impersonating a police officer a couple of weeks ago. He reckoned I made him sound nasal and a bit gay, and he really objected to my mimicry of his facial twitch.

Lou Chriss, e-mail

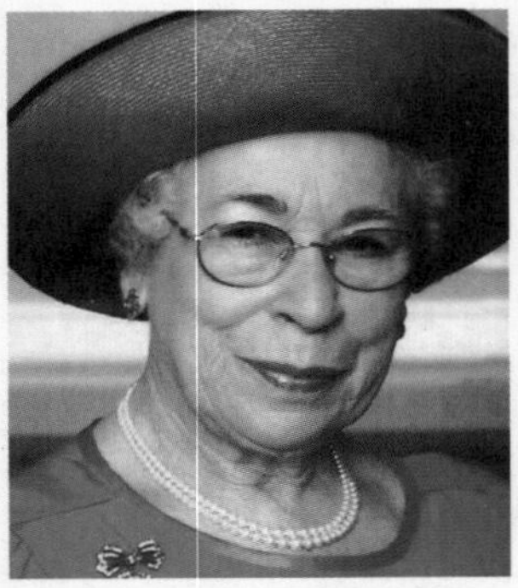

❑ Dame Helen Mirren has won all these Baftas, Golden Globes and Oscars for playing the Queen, and she's only done it once. Meanwhile, Queen lookalike Jeanette Charles has been doing it for years, and she hasn't got so much as a pat on the back. Once again, it's one rule for Dames, and another rule for bank manager's wives who bear a passing resemblance to the reigning monarch.

Hector Coffee, London

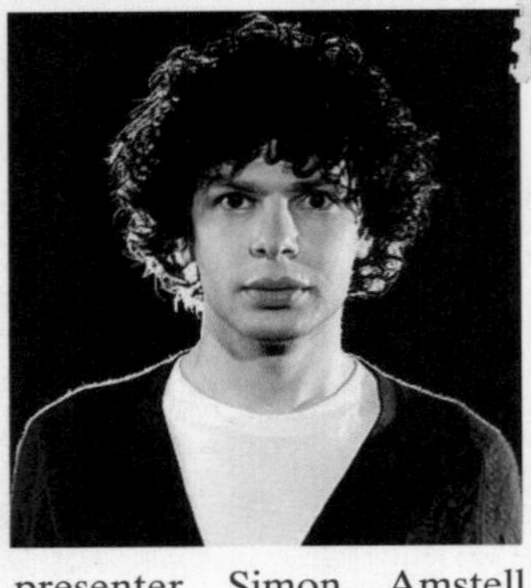

❑ I was enjoying the latest series of *Never Mind the Buzzcocks* when a friend at work informed me that the new presenter Simon Amstell was a *gay!* How disgusting that licence payers' money is going to fund this man's perverted lifestyle. Thank goodness it was on so late that my children didn't see it.

Mrs Iris Battenburg, Cheam

❑ I couldn't agree more with Mrs Battenburg *(letter above)*. I am physically sick every time I switch on the telly and see another of these so-called gays. I bought the DVD box set of *Queer as Folk* two weeks ago, and I vomited so much that I lost 4 stone and ruptured my pyloric sphincter.

Doris O'Hare, Oakhampton

❑ I too am fed up with gays on the television. If it's not Graham Norton mincing about on *Strictly Come Dancing*, it's Dale Winton camping it up on *Supermarket Sweep*. Why don't they have a return to wholesome, heterosexual TV presenters like Sir Cliff Richard and Jim Davidson.

Edna Fossilrecord, Hull

❑ It was reported on the news that London traffic wardens were going on strike. I'm not quite sure who they think will be missing their services. To be honest, it won't be that much of a blow to me if my car doesn't get ticketed, towed or impounded today.

H Sandstone, Wembley

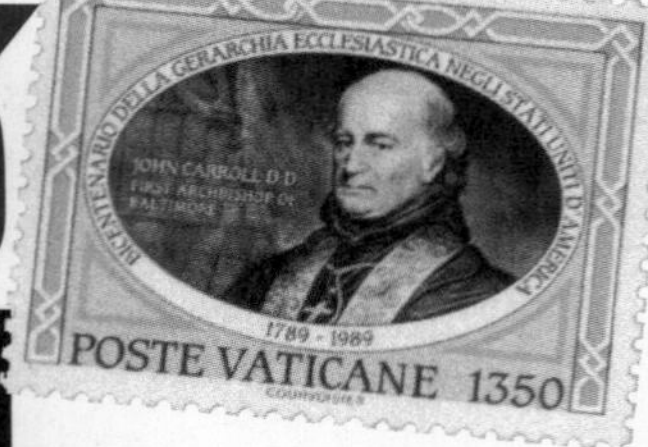
POSTE VATICANE 1350
1789 · 1989

❑ After years of enjoying Revels, I was appalled to discover that the manufacturers have removed chocolate covered peanuts from the bags. It's politcal correctness gone mad. The peanuts were my favourite ones. I understand that some children have an allergy to them which could prove fatal if eaten, but quite frankly, that was a risk I was prepared to take.

H Plywood, Peterborough

❑ I live a very hectic life and time is very precious to me. So imagine how pleased I was this morning when I managed to save two minutes by brushing my teeth whilst having a shit. Sadly, I have now wasted that time by writing to tell you about it.

Nick Pettigrew, e-mail

❑ A woman whose daughter was hospitalised in a US tornado told ITV News that "God would make her better." Presumably, that's a different God from the one that almost killed her with a tornado.

M Lovejoy, e-mail

❑ It looks like Rude Kid has moved into football management. The cheeky little cunt.

Howard Moran, Newton Abbot

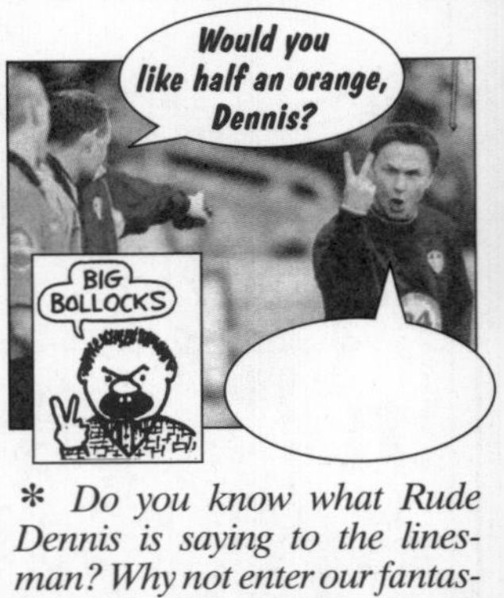
Would you like half an orange, Dennis?
BIG BOLLOCKS

* *Do you know what Rude Dennis is saying to the linesman? Why not enter our fantastic caption competition. Simply fill in Dennis' spee... ...lloon and ... ...nnis Co... ...PO Bo... ...Shields NE29 1BT. The rudest entry will win the latest Shitdisco album.*

COMPETITION NOW CLOSED

❑ Sir. It has come to my attention that when BBC Newsreader Huw Edwards reads

TOP TIPS

BBC sport newsreaders. Save time by not reporting on the progress of Andy Murray in tennis tournaments. I have yet to meet any member of the public who likes the miserable sod.

M Plywood, Hull

MOBILE party DJs. Having trouble getting nervous guests up and dancing? Try petulantly demanding "What's wrong with you?", and calling them all "boring." That should do the trick.

Mark Glover, Coventry

CONVINCE neighbours that you own an old fashioned typewriter by wearing metal thimbles and drumming your fingers on a plastic tray. Every ten seconds ting a wine glass with a pencil and run a butter knife along the teeth of a comb before continuing drumming your fingers.

E Tring, Luton

TOURETTES sufferers with an interest in Victoriana. Simply replace shouting 'fuck', 'cunt' and 'wanker' with 'poppycock', 'fiddlesticks' and 'balderdash' to recreate an authentic Victorian experience.

S Nonsense, e-mail

BBC sports newsreaders. Actually, on second thoughts, could you report on Andy Murray when he gets knocked out of a tournament, as this cheers me up immensely, as it does most people I know.

M Plywood, Hull

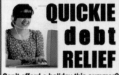

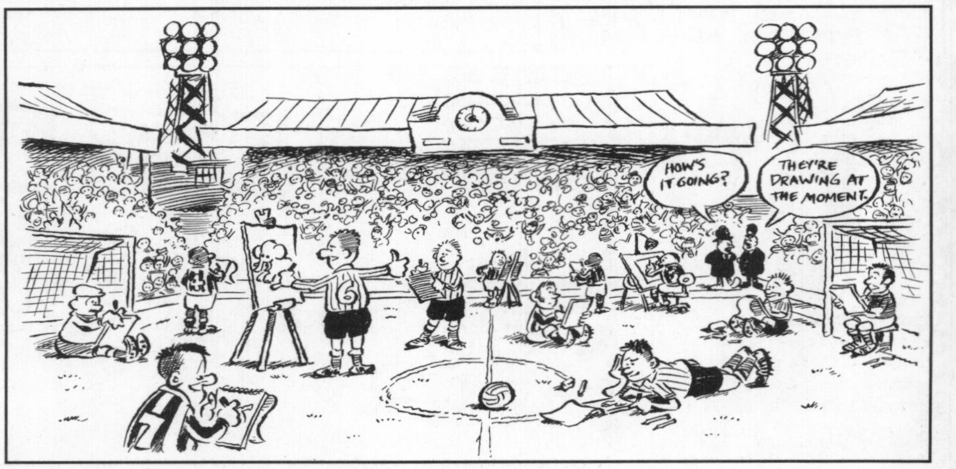
HOW'S IT GOING?
THEY'RE DRAWING AT THE MOMENT.

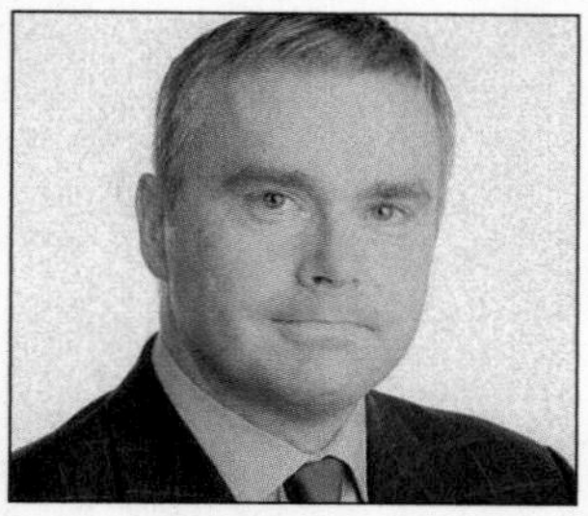

the headlines these days, he sneers like Billy Idol. If he holds our English news in such contempt, may I suggest that he goes back to Wales to read the news there instead.

Brigadier Lewerthwaite, Hull

❑ During this winter's heavy snowfall, the BBC weatherman suggested that we work from home. As I'm a joiner, I built a couple of partition walls in my living room. The wife went absolutely spare as we can no longer get to the front door, and to top it all my boss is refusing to pay me. I feel like wiping my arse on my TV licence and sending it to Michael Fish.

Graham Flintoft, Gateshead

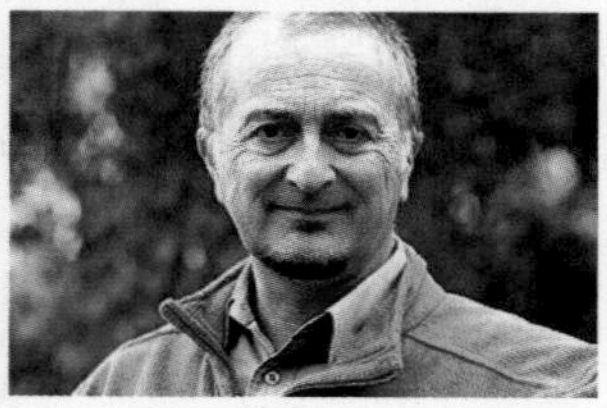

❑ Tony Robinson is the worst kind of hypocrite I could imagine. On *Time Team* he makes out he is interested in things hundreds of years old, like broken pots and Roman mosaics. Now we hear that he is going out with a woman of just 25.

Frank Icthyosaur, Minehead

❑ I feel a strong connection with Gordon Brown and his wait to suceed Tony Blair. Dave the warehouse manager is retiring in June and I've got my eye on his stapler. Me and Gordon are like two peas in a pod.

Nick Pettigrew, London

❑ My bank keep e-mailing me to inform me they are having a 'sale' at the moment. Unless they are selling £50 notes for a fiver, they can fuck right off.

Cecilia Smart, e-mail

Tell Me, Do
with Dr. Dougal Do

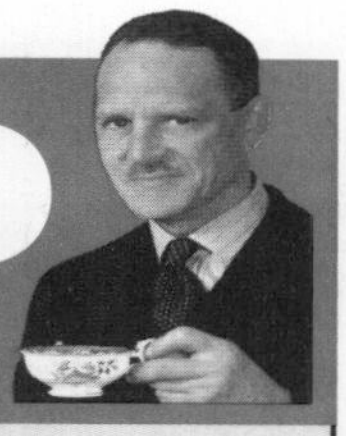

● Last week Mrs Elsie Skidmarks wrote telling me of her confusion between the seventies New York jazz/rock outfit **Steely Dan**, and the seventies English folk revivalists, **Steeleye Span**. I asked readers if they could suggest any memorable way of distinguishing between the two groups. Here are a selection of your methods...

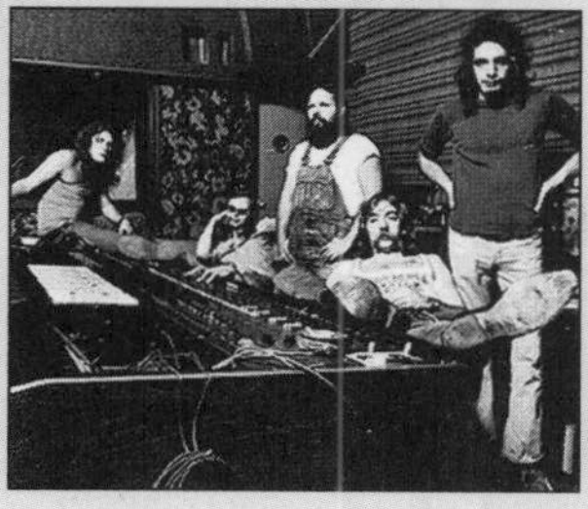

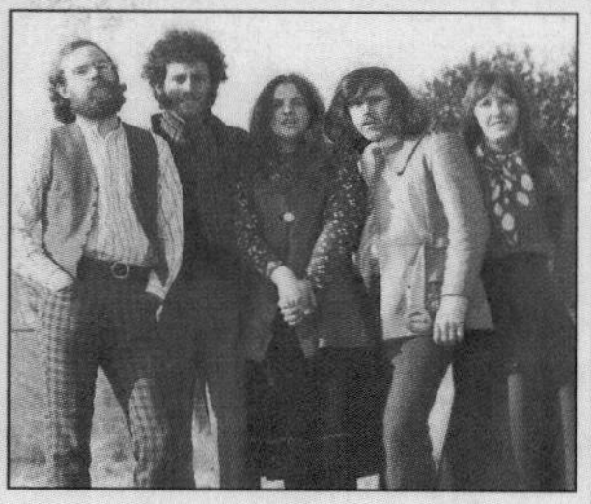

Dan or Span? Steely or Steeleye? Which is which?

...THE INITIALS of the American band Steely Dan are SD, the same as Sammy Davis and Snoop Dogg, both American singers. England's Steeleye Span, on the other hand, share initials with the English singers Steve Strange out of Visage, and Classix Nouveau's Sal Solo.

Edna Guttering, Wimbledon

...I REMEMBER it because Steely Dan is an anagram of AT DENSELY, and Steeleye Span is an anagram of EEL EYES PANTS. Simple.

Mavis Eaves, Dulchester

...IF YOU look in the Guiness Book of Hit Singles, the artist alphabetically before Steeleye Span is Tommy Steele, who used to play an acoustic guitar, which reminds me that they are a folk band. The artist after Steely Dan is Jim Steiman, who is rock rather than folk, reminding me that Steely Dan are jazz.

Dolly Soffit, Leeds

...MY GREAT grandfather had a simple rhyme he used to use to distinguish between these two bands which has been passed down through generations of my family. My father told me the rhyme on his deathbed. I would love to share it with Mrs Skidmarks, but before he passed on, my father made me promise that I would not reveal it to anyone except with my dying breath to my own son.

Charles Flashings, Crewe

...I WAS reading the gas meter in the room where Mr Flashings' father lay on his deathbed, and I overheard him passing the rhyme on with his dying breath. It went like this:

These bands are hard to tell apart,
But here's a rhyme to learn by heart,
Steeleye Span jazz rock do play,
Whilst Steely Dan sing folk all day.

At least I think that's how it went. Like Mrs Skidmarks, I find them very difficult to tell apart.

Ernie Ridgetile, Crewe

This week's *Tell Me, Do* comes from Mrs *Enid Winnits* from Bude. She writes...

● *CAN YOU help me, Dr. Dougal Do? For the life of me, I can't help muddling the British bands Level 42 and UB40. I know one was a cod reggae outfit from the West Midlands, whilst the other were Isle of Wight-born percussive slap bass funkateers. I'm 98 and my memory is not what it used to be.*

There's the question, readers, so Tell Me, Do. How do ***YOU*** distinguish between the bands **Level 42** and **UB40**? Write to me at ***Tell Me, Do, Viz Comic, PO Box 656, North Shields NE30 4XX.***

Planet 'All Bolloxed Up'

A STUDY by a government environmental task force has concluded that the planet Earth is 'completely bolloxed'. And leading scientists announced today that any attempts to stop the effects of global warming would be like 'pissing in the wind.'

EXCLUSIVE!

The findings, published in *New Scientist Magazine*, overturn conventional thinking that by changing our habits, worsening freak weather conditions can be reversed.

Speaking next to a pile of burning tyres, the government's chief meteorologist Cliff Spawn told reporters: "Turning your heating down by one degree is going to change precisely fuck all. There are chemical factories and all sorts pumping tonnes of shite into the atmosphere all day, every day. Think about that the next time you walk to work in the pouring rain.'

Reporting to the House of Commons, Spawn told MPs: "For years we've been telling everyone to only boil one cup of water in a kettle to make a cuppa. Now it would appear that everything we've been told recentley by beardy types is utter wank. We might as well face the facts that we're doomed. We can only hope that when the end comes it's quick."

A spokesman for Friends of the Earth admitted to being disappointed by the findings. "It would seem that not leaving your TV on 'standby' and

Completely fucked~ the atmosphere, yesterday

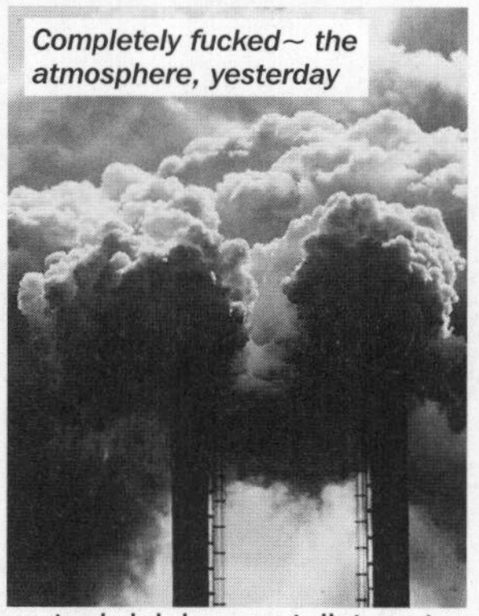

put a brick in your toilet cystern are fucking futile gestures. It's unfortunate, but there it is," he told us.

Spawn went on to tell MPs that the report recommends 'every man, woman and child go out today and buy as much booze as they can' and 'spend the remainder of their lives in an alcohol- fuelled stupor.'

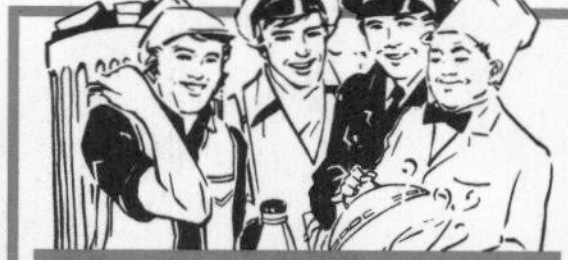

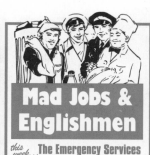

Mad Jobs & Englishmen

this week... **The Emergency Services**

A MAN whose wife had been murdered and a woman who had been robbed at knifepoint. These are just a couple of people whose barmy requests for help 999 operators have had to deal with in the past.

Other oddball requests include a man who wanted a fire engine to come to his house because it was burning down and a woman who wanted an ambulance to take her son to hospital because he had the classic symptoms of meningitis.

"You always hear these mad stories about people who phone us up with nonsense questions and appeals for help," says 999 operator Ian Dull. "They sound unbelievable, but they're all true! You couldn't make this stuff up!"

Mr Dull, 50, went on to regale us with some of the weird and wacky requests he had dealt with personally.

"I remember getting a phone call from a seven year old girl who had watched her mother get beaten to death by burglars. She kept asking for us to 'please help' and saying that her 'mummy wouldn't wake up'. We were howling with laughter! I get bugged to tell that story at our Christmas party every single year, it's a classic!"

"Then there was the time with the bus crash. I got a call from the driver. He had crashed the bus and apparently everyone on board had serious injuries or something. Ridiculous!"

But it's not all fun and games. There are inevitably times when Mr Dull receives some very distressing calls from people in genuine need.

"I got one call a couple of years back that I will never forget for as long as I live," he told us. "It was from an old lady whose telly had gone off during a power cut, right in the middle of Countdown. What do you say to someone in that situation? You both know they're going to miss the Countdown conundrum. That was hard."

So whilst some of the more frivolous 999 calls can be amusing, it should be borne in mind that there is a serious side. Silly phone calls to the emergency services waste time when the operators could be helping people in real trouble.

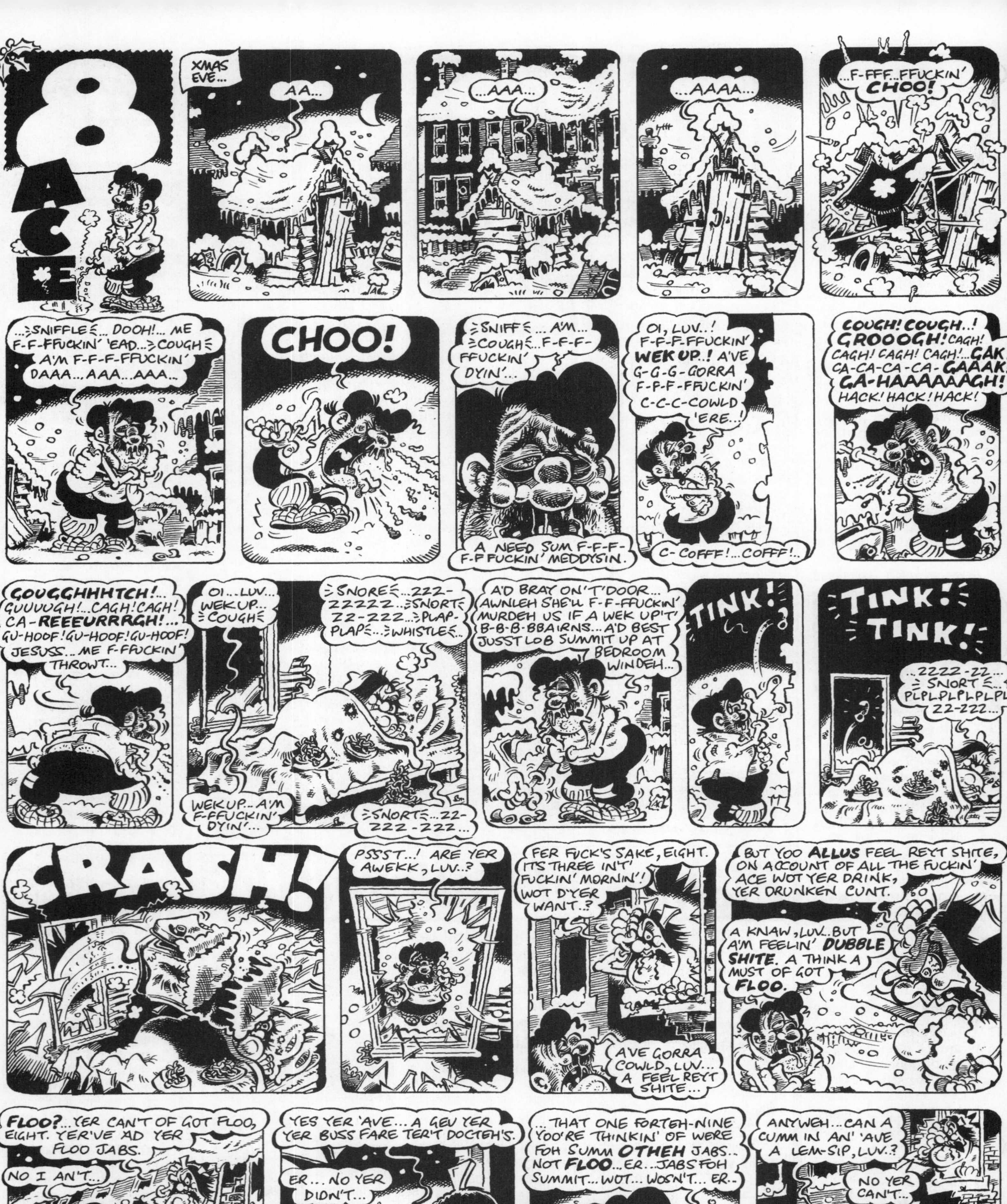
8 ACE
XMAS EVE...
AA...
...AAA...
...AAAA...
...F-FFF...FFUCKIN' CHOO!
...SNIFFLE... DOOH!... ME F-F-FFUCKIN' 'EAD... COUGH A'M F-F-F-FFUCKIN' DAAA... AAA... AAA...
CHOO!
SNIFF... A'M... COUGH... F-F-F-FFUCKIN' DYIN'...
A NEED SUM F-F-F-F-F FUCKIN' MEDDYSIN.
OI, LUV...! F-F-F-FFUCKIN' WEK UP..! A'VE G-G-G-GORRA F-F-F-FFUCKIN' C-C-C-COWLD 'ERE...
C-COFFF!... COFFF!...
COUGH! COUGH..! GROOOGH! CAGH! CAGH! CAGH! CAGH!... GAK! CA-CA-CA-CA-GAAAK! GA-HAAAAAAGH! HACK! HACK! HACK!
GOUGGHHHTCH!... GUUUUGH!... CAGH! CAGH! CA-REEEURRRGH!... GU-HOOF! GU-HOOF! GU-HOOF! JESUSS... ME F-FFUCKIN' THROWT...
OI... LUV... WEKUP... COUGH
SNORE... ZZZ-ZZZZZ... SNORT ZZ-ZZZ... PLAP-PLAP... WHISTLE
WEKUP... A'M F-FFUCKIN' DYIN'...
SNORT... ZZ-ZZZ-ZZZ...
A'D BRAY ON' T'DOOR... AWNLEH SHE'LL F-F-FFUCKIN' MURDEH US IF A WEK UP'T B-B-B-BBAIRNS... A'D BEST JUSST LOB SUMMIT UP AT BEDROOM WINDEH...
TINK!
TINK! TINK!
...ZZZZ-ZZ... SNORT PLPLPLPLPLPL ZZ-ZZZ...
CRASH!
PSS'ST...! ARE YER AWEKK, LUV...?
FER FUCK'S SAKE, EIGHT. IT'S THREE IN'T FUCKIN' MORNIN'! WOT D'YER WANT...?
A'VE GORRA COWLD, LUV... A FEEL REYT SHITE...
BUT YOO ALLUS FEEL REYT SHITE, ON ACCOUNT OF ALL THE FUCKIN' ACE WOT YER DRINK, YER DRUNKEN CUNT.
A KNAW, LUV... BUT A'M FEELIN' DUBBLE SHITE. A THINK A MUST OF GOT FLOO.
FLOO?... YER CAN'T OF GOT FLOO, EIGHT. YER'VE 'AD YER FLOO JABS.
NO I AN'T...
YES YER 'AVE... A GEV YER YER BUSS FARE TER'T DOCTEH'S.
ER... NO YER DIDN'T...
... THAT ONE FORTEH-NINE YOO'RE THINKIN' OF WERE FOH SUMM OTHEH JABS... NOT FLOO... ER... JABS FOH SUMMIT... WOT... WOSN'T... ER...
...FLOO... THEMS WOS.
ANYWEH... CAN A CUMM IN AN' 'AVE A LEM-SIP, LUV...?
NO YER CAN'T...
WHY NOT, YER F-FF-F-FFUCKIN' BB-B-BB-B...

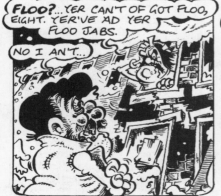

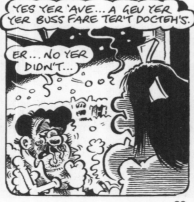

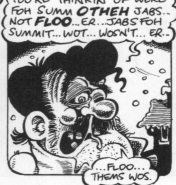

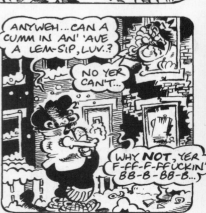

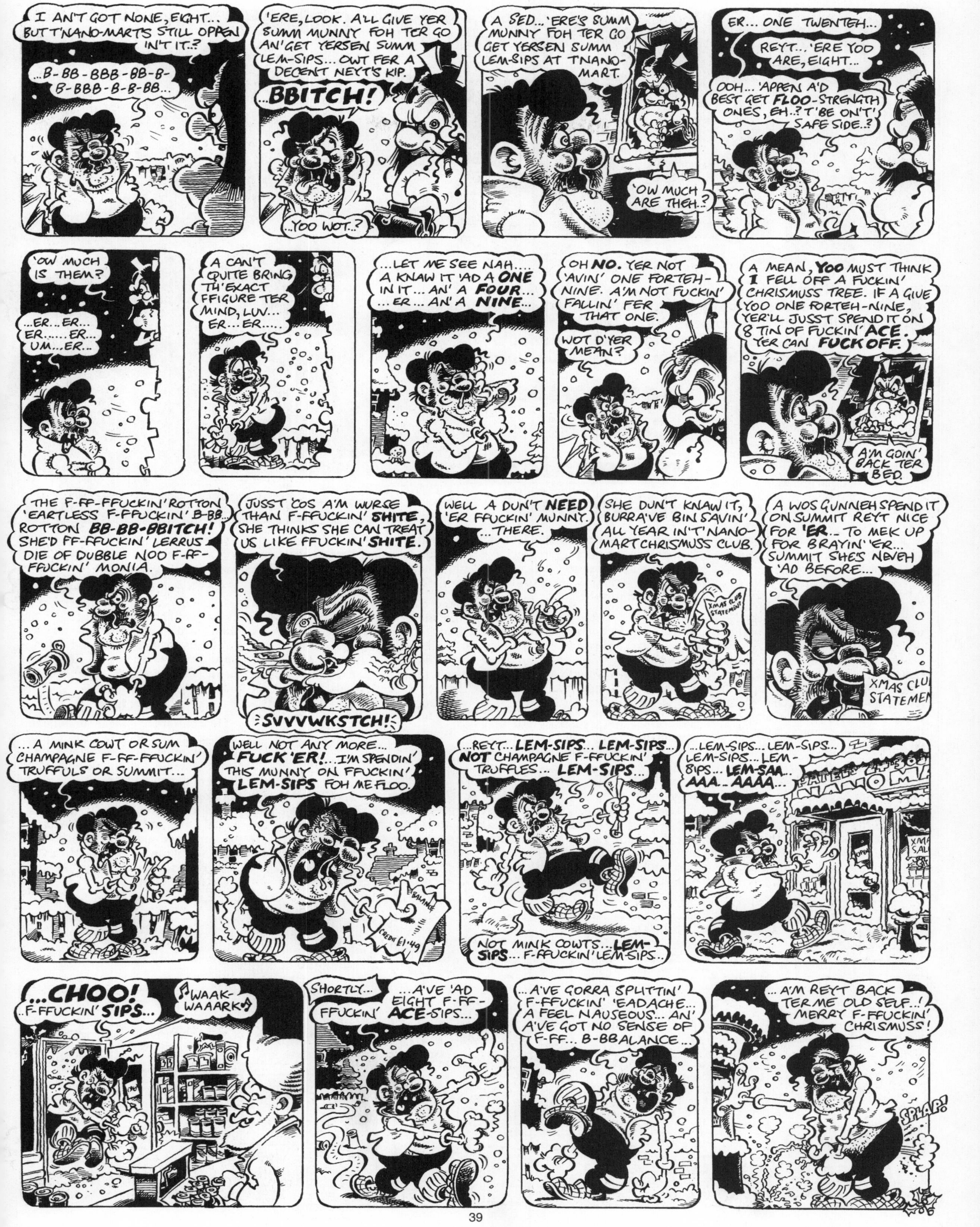
I AN'T GOT NONE, EIGHT... BUT T'NANO-MART'S STILL OPPEN IN'T IT..?
...B-BB-BBB-BB-B-B-BBB-B-B-BB...
'ERE, LOOK. A'LL GIVE YER SUMM MUNNY FOH TER GO AN' GET YERSEN SUMM LEM-SIPS... OWT FER A DECENT NEYT'S KIP.
...BBITCH!
...YOO WOT..?
A SED... 'ERE'S SUMM MUNNY FOH TER GO GET YERSEN SUMM LEM-SIPS AT T'NANO-MART.
'OW MUCH ARE THEH..?
ER... ONE TWENTEH...
REYT... 'ERE YOO ARE, EIGHT...
OOH... 'APPEN A'D BEST GET FLOO-STRENGTH ONES, EH..? T'BE ON T' SAFE SIDE..?
'OW MUCH IS THEM?
...ER...ER... ER.......ER... UM...ER...
A CAN'T QUITE BRING TH'EXACT FFIGURE TER MIND, LUV... ER... ER.....
...LET ME SEE NAH.... A KNAW IT 'AD A ONE IN IT... AN' A FOUR... ...ER... AN' A NINE...
OH NO. YER NOT 'AVIN' ONE FORTEH-NINE. A'M NOT FUCKIN' FALLIN' FER THAT ONE.
WOT D'YER MEAN?
A MEAN, YOO MUST THINK I FELL OFF A FUCKIN' CHRISMUSS TREE. IF A GIVE YOO ONE FORTEH-NINE, YER'LL JUSST SPEND IT ON 8 TIN OF FUCKIN' ACE. YER CAN FUCK OFF.
A'M GOIN' BACK TER BED.
THE F-FF-FFUCKIN' ROTTON 'EARTLESS F-FFUCKIN' B-BB... ROTTON BB-BB-BBITCH! SHE'D FF-FFUCKIN' LERRUS DIE OF DUBBLE NOO F-FF-FFUCKIN' MONIA.
JUSST 'COS A'M WURSE THAN F-FFUCKIN' SHITE, SHE THINKS SHE CAN TREAT US LIKE FFUCKIN' SHITE.
SVVVWKSTCH!
WELL A DUN'T NEED 'ER FFUCKIN' MUNNY. ...THERE.
SHE DUN'T KNAW IT, BURRA'VE BIN SAVIN' ALL YEAR IN T'NANO-MART CHRISMUSS CLUB.
XMAS CLUB STATEMENT
A WOS GUNNEH SPEND IT ON SUMMIT REYT NICE FOR 'ER... TO MEK UP FOR BRAYIN' 'ER... SUMMIT SHE'S NEVEH 'AD BEFORE...
...A MINK COWT OR SUM CHAMPAGNE F-FF-FFUCKIN' TRUFFULS OR SUMMIT...
WELL NOT ANY MORE... FUCK 'ER!... I'M SPENDIN' THIS MUNNY ON FFUCKIN' LEM-SIPS FOH ME FLOO.
BALANCE
CREDIT £1·49
...REYT... LEM-SIPS... LEM-SIPS... NOT CHAMPAGNE F-FFUCKIN' TRUFFLES... LEM-SIPS...
NOT MINK COWTS... LEM-SIPS... F-FFUCKIN' LEM-SIPS...
...LEM-SIPS... LEM-SIPS... LEM-SIPS... LEM-SIPS... LEM-SAA... AAA... AAAA...
OPEN
...CHOO! ...F-FFUCKIN' SIPS...
WAAK-WAAARK
SHORTLY...
...A'VE 'AD EIGHT F-FF-FFUCKIN' ACE-SIPS...
...A'VE GORRA SPLITTIN' F-FFUCKIN' 'EADACHE... A FEEL NAUSEOUS... AN' A'VE GOT NO SENSE OF F-FF... B-BBALANCE...
...A'M REYT BACK TER ME OLD SELF..! MERRY F-FFUCKIN' CHRISMUSS!
SPLAP!

NAMED & SHAMED

EVANS ABOVE: Evans (above), and Depp (inset).

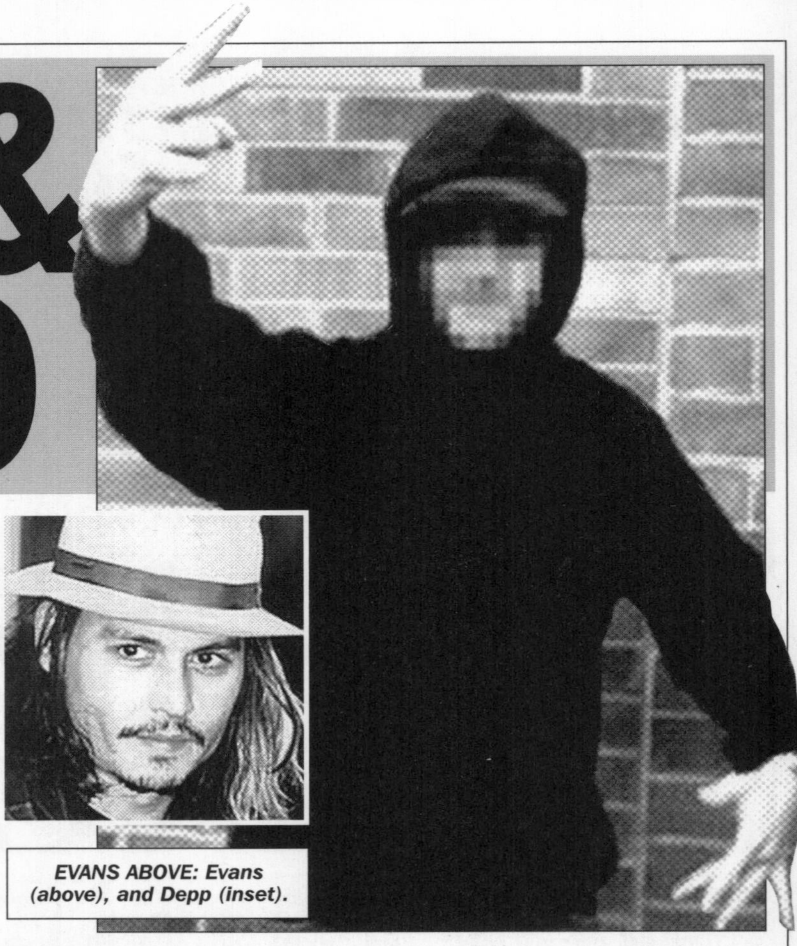

NOTTINGHAM COUNCIL yesterday unveiled strict new measures designed to crack down on the activities of a notorious local hooligan. And if successful, it is hoped the scheme could be adopted nationwide to combat the UK's growing juvenile delinquency problem.

New Poster Campaign to Humiliate ASBO Lout

17 year old Keanu Evans has plagued his neighbourhood with a campaign of petty theft, vandalism and intimidation since his family moved to the notorious Ratzmaze Estate in 2004. During this time, Evans has been arrested more than 100 times, and been made the subject of fourteen ASBOs. In 2006, he was electronically tagged and served with a curfew order after setting fire to the library of the local comprehensive school.

PRESSURE

In response to mounting pressure from angry local residents, Nottingham Council yesterday outlined their intention to mount a localised poster campaign in order to embarrass Evans into behaving himself. Councillor Martin Duffy hopes this latest move to 'Name and Shame' Evans will prove more successful than previous attempts to curb the youngster's anti-social behaviour.

"The billboard-sized posters will feature Evans depicted as a gun-toting gangster, bedecked in jewels and leaning on a Ferrari Testarossa, to indicate the shallow and transient material goods which this unruly adolescent values above manners and basic decency," Duffy told reporters. "He will also be surrounded by a selection of scantily clad models, to highlight his lack of respect for women, and the poster will feature the slogan 'Keanu Evans: Born to be Bad'," he continued.

"I'm sure Evans will be none too popular with his chums when they find out what he's been up to, and I'm confident that they will make it clear to him that they do not want to be associated with a mischief-maker," he added.

Councillors are confident that the posters will be a success, and they have several other ideas for schemes to promote their zero-tolerance law and order message. Plans for a nationwide television advertising campaign in the autumn are already well advanced. "We are hoping to enlist the help of respected names from entertainment, such as Sir Cliff Richard, Melvyn Bragg and Jilly Cooper who would personally criticise Evans' behaviour," said Duffy. "I can't think of a better way of drilling home the message to young people that anti-social behaviour simply isn't cool."

TEMPERATURE

And the council's ambitions don't stop there. For Duffy has commissioned top Hollywood scriptwriters to begin work on a screenplay based on Evans' life of crime. "The movie would probably star Johnny Depp as Evans, a dangerous, hard living rebel who laughs in the face of authority," said Duffy. "It will be a gritty, hard hitting drama like Die Hard, or Under Siege 2, and will dispel the myth that this sort of lifestyle is glamorous and exciting."

"The film would spell out the difficulties which our law enforcers have endured in dealing with Evans' misbehaviour by portraying the Nottinghamshire police as bumbling, incompetent clowns. The Chief Constable isn't too happy with my ideas, but I've told him to reserve judgement until he's seen the movie!"

But plans for the biopic have been met with scepticism by local residents, particularly after it emerged that Evans would receive payment for the film. "Unfortunately we would have to pay Evans a competitive fee to secure the rights to use his image and name. But those are Equity's rules, not mine," said Duffy.

VOLUME

He continued: "I can understand that some people may have reservations about having to suffer a large rates increase to foot the bill for a local hooligan to feature in a major motion picture which, if successful, could set him on the path to international fame and a life which most of us can only dream of. But I think we have to take whatever measures are necessary to teach this young thug that crime doesn't pay."

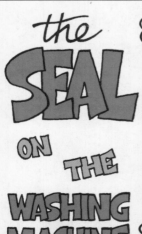

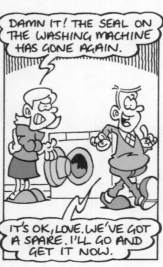

the SEAL ON THE WASHING MACHINE
DAMN IT! THE SEAL ON THE WASHING MACHINE HAS GONE AGAIN.
IT'S OK, LOVE. WE'VE GOT A SPARE. I'LL GO AND GET IT NOW.
WHUMP!
MEANWHILE...
LONDON

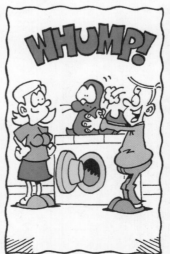

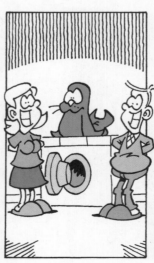

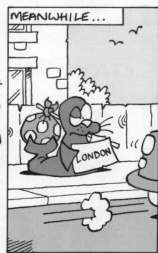

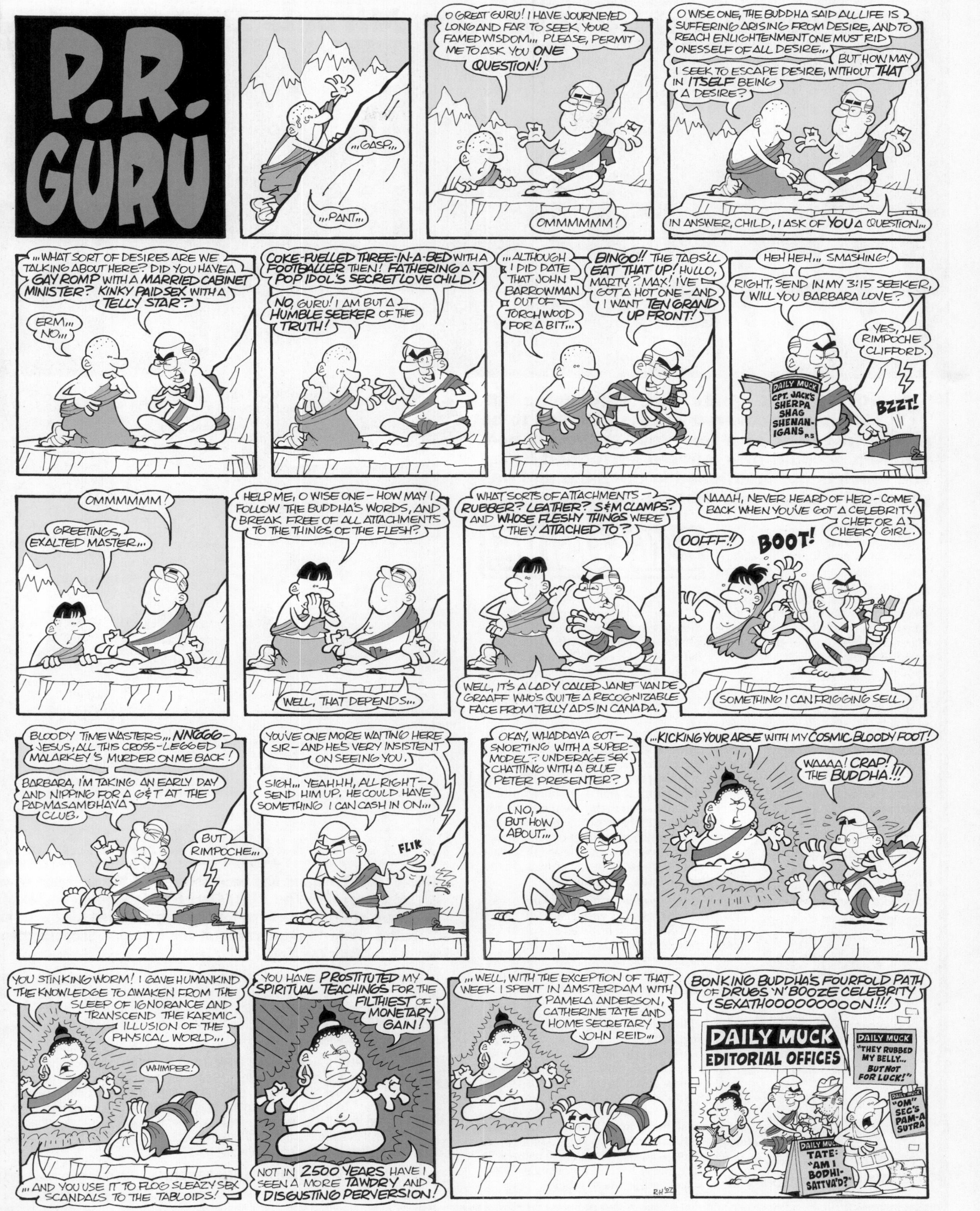
P.R. GURU
...GASP...
...PANT...
O GREAT GURU! I HAVE JOURNEYED LONG AND FAR TO SEEK YOUR FAMED WISDOM... PLEASE, PERMIT ME TO ASK YOU ONE QUESTION!
OMMMMMM!
O WISE ONE, THE BUDDHA SAID ALL LIFE IS SUFFERING ARISING FROM DESIRE, AND TO REACH ENLIGHTENMENT ONE MUST RID ONESSELF OF ALL DESIRE...
BUT HOW MAY I SEEK TO ESCAPE DESIRE, WITHOUT THAT IN ITSELF BEING A DESIRE?
IN ANSWER, CHILD, I ASK OF YOU A QUESTION...
...WHAT SORT OF DESIRES ARE WE TALKING ABOUT HERE? DID YOU HAVE A GAY ROMP WITH A MARRIED CABINET MINISTER? KINKY PAID SEX WITH A TELLY STAR?
ERM... NO...
COKE-FUELLED THREE-IN-A-BED WITH A FOOTBALLER THEN! FATHERING A POP IDOL'S SECRET LOVE CHILD!
NO, GURU! I AM BUT A HUMBLE SEEKER OF THE TRUTH!
...ALTHOUGH I DID DATE THAT JOHN BARROWMAN OUT OF TORCHWOOD FOR A BIT...
BINGO!! THE TABS'LL EAT THAT UP! HULLO, MARTY? MAX! I'VE GOT A HOT ONE - AND I WANT TEN GRAND UP FRONT!
HEH HEH... SMASHING!
RIGHT, SEND IN MY 3:15 SEEKER, WILL YOU BARBARA LOVE?
YES, RIMPOCHE CLIFFORD.
DAILY MUCK
CPT. JACK'S SHERPA SHAG SHENANIGANS P.5
BZZT!
OMMMMMM!
GREETINGS, EXALTED MASTER...
HELP ME, O WISE ONE - HOW MAY I FOLLOW THE BUDDHA'S WORDS, AND BREAK FREE OF ALL ATTACHMENTS TO THE THINGS OF THE FLESH?
WELL, THAT DEPENDS...
WHAT SORTS OF ATTACHMENTS - RUBBER? LEATHER? S&M CLAMPS? AND WHOSE FLESHY THINGS WERE THEY ATTACHED TO?
WELL, IT'S A LADY CALLED JANET VAN DE GRAAFF WHO'S QUITE A RECOGNIZABLE FACE FROM TELLY ADS IN CANADA.
NAAAH, NEVER HEARD OF HER - COME BACK WHEN YOU'VE GOT A CELEBRITY CHEF OR A CHEEKY GIRL.
OOFFF!!
BOOT!
SOMETHING I CAN FRIGGING SELL.
BLOODY TIME WASTERS... NNGGG - JESUS, ALL THIS CROSS-LEGGED MALARKEY'S MURDER ON ME BACK!
BARBARA, I'M TAKING AN EARLY DAY AND NIPPING FOR A G&T AT THE PADMASAMBHAVA CLUB.
BUT RIMPOCHE...
YOU'VE ONE MORE WAITING HERE SIR - AND HE'S VERY INSISTENT ON SEEING YOU.
SIGH... YEAHHH, ALL RIGHT - SEND HIM UP. HE COULD HAVE SOMETHING I CAN CASH IN ON...
FLIK
OKAY, WHADDAYA GOT - SNORTING WITH A SUPER-MODEL? UNDERAGE SEX CHATTING WITH A BLUE PETER PRESENTER?
NO, BUT HOW ABOUT...
...KICKING YOUR ARSE WITH MY COSMIC BLOODY FOOT!
WAAAA! CRAP! THE BUDDHA!!!
YOU STINKING WORM! I GAVE HUMANKIND THE KNOWLEDGE TO AWAKEN FROM THE SLEEP OF IGNORANCE AND TRANSCEND THE KARMIC ILLUSION OF THE PHYSICAL WORLD...
WHIMPER!
...AND YOU USE IT TO FLOG SLEAZY SEX SCANDALS TO THE TABLOIDS!
YOU HAVE PROSTITUTED MY SPIRITUAL TEACHINGS FOR THE FILTHIEST OF MONETARY GAIN!
NOT IN 2500 YEARS HAVE I SEEN A MORE TAWDRY AND DISGUSTING PERVERSION!
...WELL, WITH THE EXCEPTION OF THAT WEEK I SPENT IN AMSTERDAM WITH PAMELA ANDERSON, CATHERINE TATE AND HOME SECRETARY JOHN REID...
BONKING BUDDHA'S FOURFOLD PATH OF DRUGS 'N' BOOZE CELEBRITY SEXATHOOOOOOOOON!!!
DAILY MUCK EDITORIAL OFFICES
DAILY MUCK "THEY RUBBED MY BELLY... BUT NOT FOR LUCK!"
DAILY MUCK "OM" SEC'S PAM-A SUTRA
DAILY MUCK TATE: "AM I BODHI-SATTVA'D?"
RH '07

Church Jubilant as New Miracle Discovered

Our Father Who *Dart* in Heaven

A BOY TENDING goats on a Palestinian hillside has discovered what is believed to be a fragment of a long lost gospel. It contains an account of a miracle performed by Jesus which is not mentioned in the Bible and was previously unknown to Biblical scholars.

EXCLUSIVE!

Abdul Marrowfat, 12, followed a stray goat into a cave in the Golan Heights and found an alabaster jar containing a few scraps of parchment with ancient writing on. He took it back to his village and showed it to his father, Dr Yitsak Marrowfat, Emeritus Professor of Biblical Archaeology at the University of Ramalla.

Dr Marrowfat pieced the fragments together, and was able to identfy the document as part of the lost gospel of St Job of Galilee. Amazingly, it contained a 2000-year-old account of a darts game at Jesus's local inn in Bethlehem, during which he performed a miracle. "I couldn't believe my eyes when I translated the words," said Dr Marrowfat. "It told of how the Messiah scored 501 in the match... using just 8 throws!"

The discovery of the scrolls has caused great excitement in religious circles, as the maximum score possible with 8 darts is 480 - twenty one short of the regulation 501 target. "Conventional mathematics tells us that it is impossible to check out, finishing on a double, with fewer than 9 darts," said Dr Oral Osmond, lecturer in Intelligent Design at the University of Alabama. "The fact that Christ did an 8 dart finish proves beyond any doubt that he truly was the Son of God."

But other academics were less convinced by the evidence. Hell-bound heathen evolutionist Richard Dawkins was sceptical that a genuine miracle was described in the fragment. "A miracle is simply an event that has taken place which we cannot explain. It says more about our knowledge of science than it does about the so-called powers of Jesus," he told us.

"Perhaps our knowledge of mathematics at present is insufficient to explain how 501 can be achieved in 8 darts with a finish on the bull or a double. Or perhaps the bullseye in Jesus's times was worth 101, and has gradually changed through evolution to its present value of 50," he added.

However, Dawkins was unable to suggest a rational explanation for another miracle mentioned on the other side of the parchment where Jesus scores a 148 break during a visit to a snooker club in Jerusalem. "That one is a little more tricky to dismiss so lightly," he told us. "I really can't think of any way you could score more than 147 with 15 reds and 6 colours. In fact, I may have to reconsider my position on this whole religion thing."

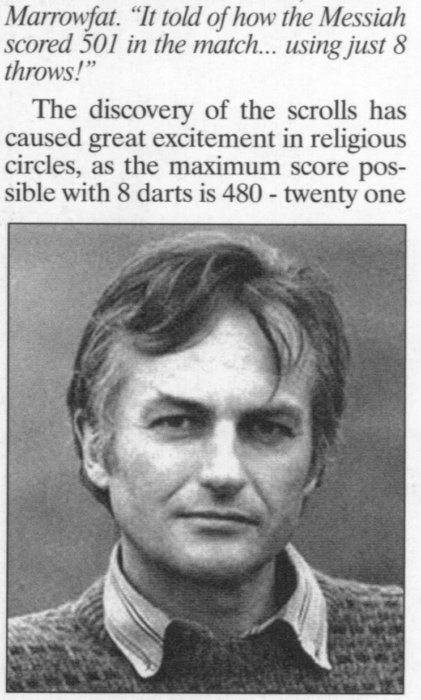

***DAWKINS:* Hell-bound sceptic**

21 And Jesus of Nazareth went forth to the oche which was exactly eight cubits from the board. And he did take up his arrows and thrice times did cast them at the board. And the Pharisee did look upon the board and spake out unto the assembled multitude in a loud voice saying, One hundred and eighty. And great was the jubilation of the apostles.

22 And Timon of Athens did then step up to the oche and did likewise thrice cast his arrows. And the Pharisee did look upon the board and spake out unto the assembled multitude in a more subdued voice saying, Timon of Athens, thou hast scored three score and three.

23 And Jesus of Nazareth again went forth to the oche for it was once more his turn and thrice did throw his arrows. And great was the amazement of the people for the score was one hundred and eighty.

24 And Timon of Athens was sore vexed. And thrice more did he throw his arrows. And one hit the five and one hit the one and one hit the treble twenty but bounced out and landed in the pint of Judas Iscariot. And great was the laughter in the inn. And the score it was six.

25 And Jesus of Nazareth went forth to the oche and spoke unto the Pharisee saying, How many do I need? And the Pharisee replied saying, One hundred and forty and one.

26 And Jesus threw two of his darts. And the Pharisee looked upon the board and saw that Jesus had indeed scored one hundred and forty and one. And the crowd saw that he still had his third arrow in his hand. And Simon who is called Peter which is ceefax the rock cried out in a loud voice saying, Lo! He has checked out and the number of darts is eight. It is a miracle.

27 And the news of the Lord's eight dart finish spread throughout the bar and into the lounge and even unto the snug and the car park and the bogs. And the people of the town were jubilant and cried out, Jesus has done another of them miracles for He is truly the Son of God. Hosanna! Hosanna in Exchelsea!

LORD OF THE DARTS

THE DARTS world has been stunned by the discovery of wha are being called *The Eight Dart Finish Scrolls.* We asked th cream of British darts players as they gathered for the Lambe and Butler World Championships at the Lakeside Shopping Centr Thurrock for their reactions.

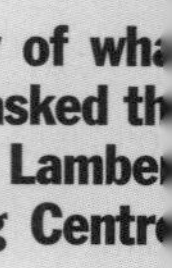

❑ FAT former world champion **JOCKY WILSON**, who once allegedly shat in an opponent's shoe in the dressing room at The Hexagon, Reading, told us: "I've done the nine dart finish many times in my professional career. But it's usually 180, 180, treble 20, treble 19 and double 12. Doing that with one dart less really would be a miracle."

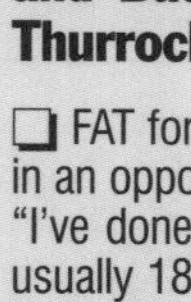

❑ **ERIC *'Swan's Neck'* BRISTOW**, who rose to fame as the Crafty Coc ney was also impressed with the Saviour of Mankind's performance at the och "I remember being taught about the miracles at Sunday School when I was nipper," he told us. "Raising the dead, walking on water, feeding the five tho sand and all that mallarkey are all very impressive, but I always thought the could be rational explanations for them. However, after 40 years at the top of the darts tre I know that no mere mortal could achieve an 8 dart checkout."

❑ VETERAN professional **SHAUN GREATBATCH** was the first man to achieve a

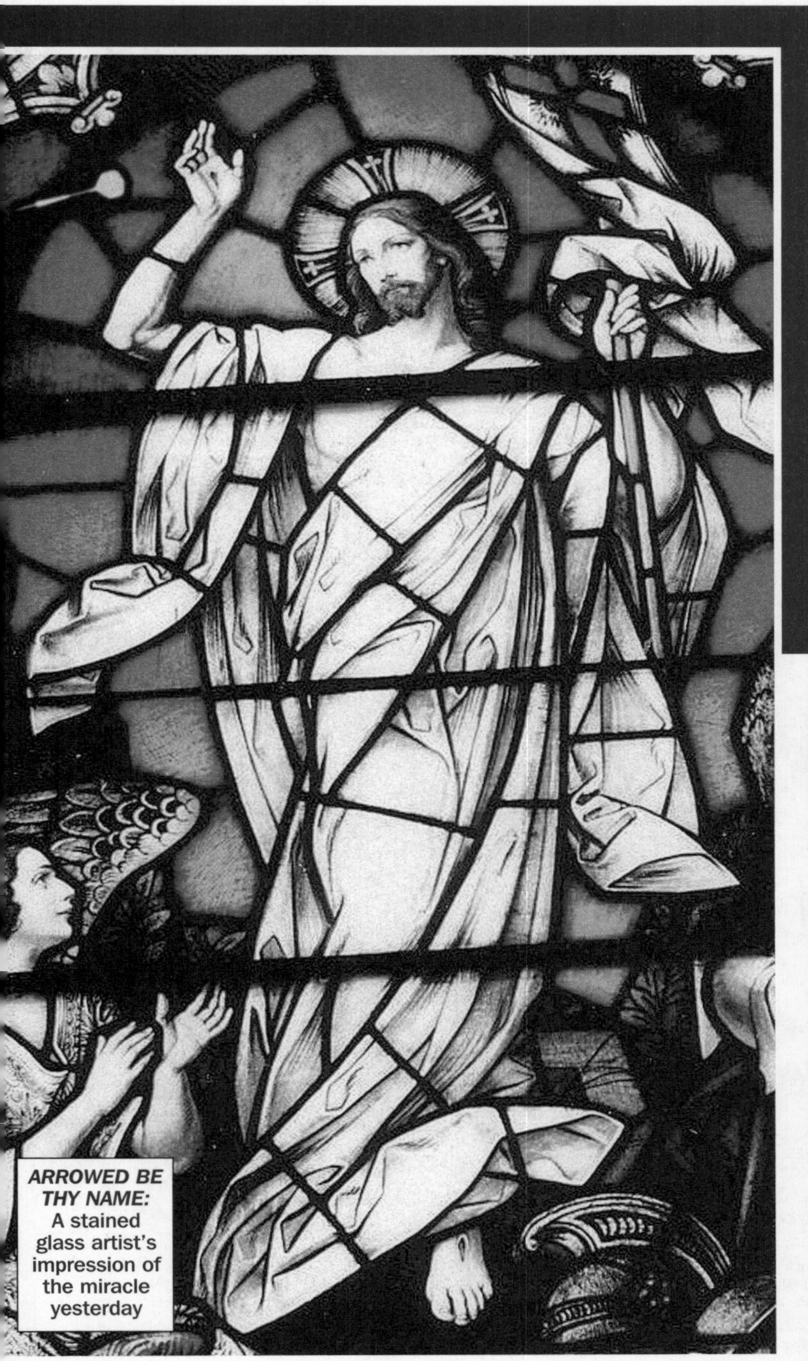

ARROWED BE THY NAME: A stained glass artist's impression of the miracle yesterday

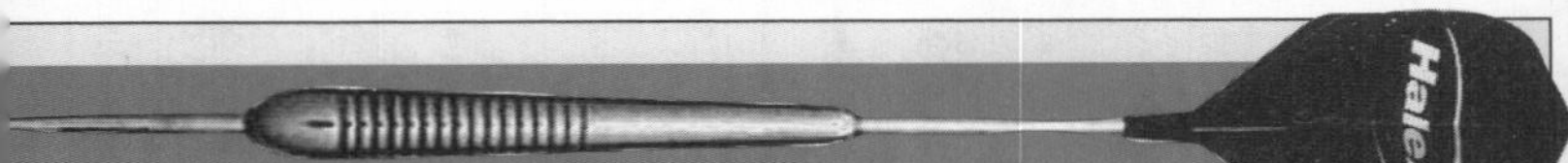

Halex

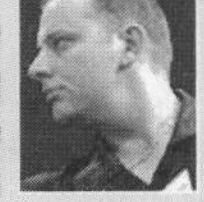

rt finish on live TV during the 2002 Dutch Open. He was cautious about draw-
g any conclusions from the newly discovered gospels. "I've been in this game
ong time, and I've seen plenty of tournament referees make mistakes totting
the scores in their heads," he explained. "Perhaps this Pharisee just made
simple mental arithmetic error in all the excitement. And it would have been
sy to do in those days because Roman numerals don't lend themselves to computational
erations that depend on place value," he continued.

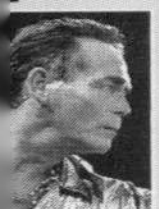

BOBBY *'Dazzler'* GEORGE was visibly moved when we spoke to him about the scrolls. "I once saw John Lowe throw the perfect nine darts in an exhibition match at Bernard Manning's Embassy Club in Harpurhey," he said. "Three rounds of 167 - treble 20, treble 19 and the bull. I thought that was close to a miracle. To do the same with a dart in hand would definitely require some sort of divine intervention."

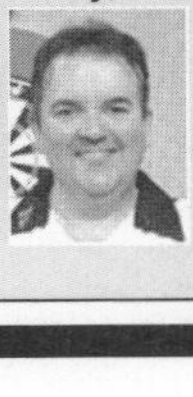

PHIL *'The Power'* TAYLOR, who has done the nine dart finish three times on tel-
ision, agreed. "I'm usually too busy playing darts to think about religion or spirituality," he
d us. "But hearing about Jesus Christ's miracle 8-darter has kindled a flame
faith in my soul. I've become born again, I've invited Jesus into my heart and
e begged the Lord to forgive me my trespasses, as I forgive those who have
spassed against me. Even that fat cunt Jocky Wilson who allegedly shat in
y shoe at The Hexagon, Reading."

MRS. BRADY OLD LADY

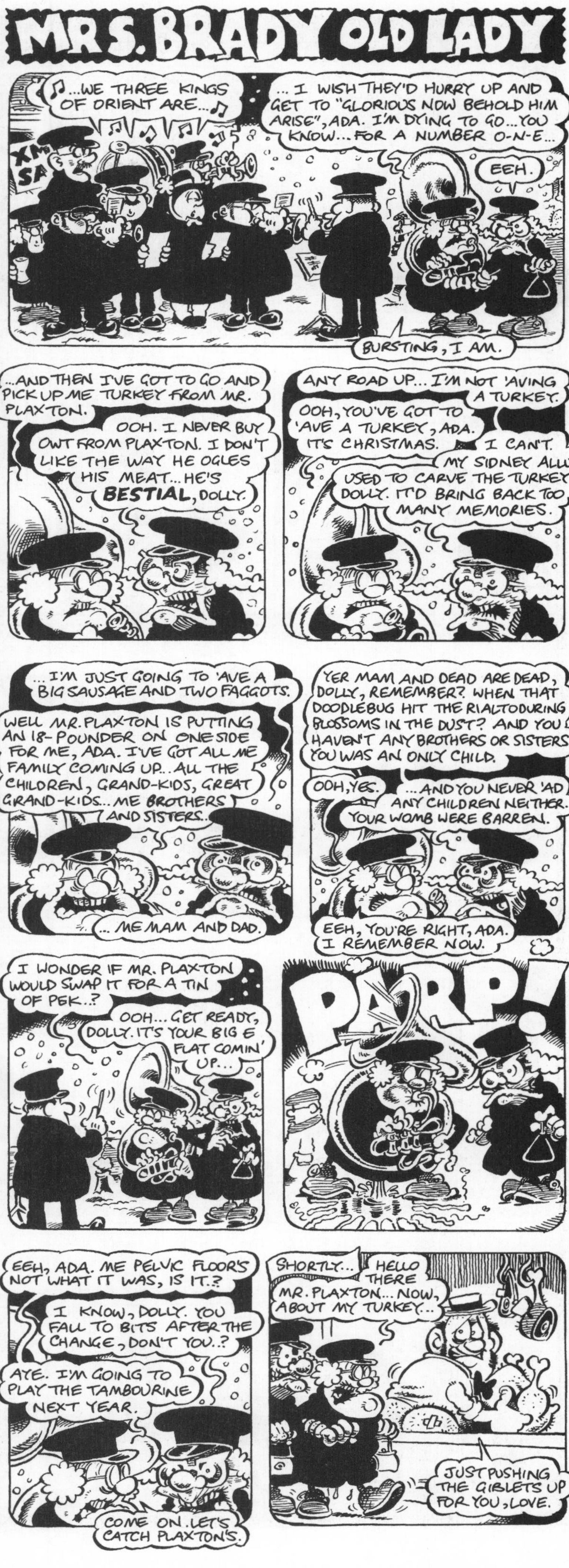

♫...WE THREE KINGS OF ORIENT ARE...♫
...I WISH THEY'D HURRY UP AND GET TO "GLORIOUS NOW BEHOLD HIM ARISE", ADA. I'M DYING TO GO...YOU KNOW...FOR A NUMBER O-N-E...
EEH.
BURSTING, I AM.
...AND THEN I'VE GOT TO GO AND PICK UP ME TURKEY FROM MR. PLAXTON.
OOH. I NEVER BUY OWT FROM PLAXTON. I DON'T LIKE THE WAY HE OGLES HIS MEAT...HE'S BESTIAL, DOLLY.
ANY ROAD UP... I'M NOT 'AVING A TURKEY.
OOH, YOU'VE GOT TO 'AVE A TURKEY, ADA. IT'S CHRISTMAS.
I CAN'T. MY SIDNEY ALLUS USED TO CARVE THE TURKEY, DOLLY. IT'D BRING BACK TOO MANY MEMORIES.
...I'M JUST GOING TO 'AVE A BIG SAUSAGE AND TWO FAGGOTS.
WELL MR. PLAXTON IS PUTTING AN 18-POUNDER ON ONE SIDE FOR ME, ADA. I'VE GOT ALL ME FAMILY COMING UP...ALL THE CHILDREN, GRAND-KIDS, GREAT GRAND-KIDS...ME BROTHERS AND SISTERS...
...ME MAM AND DAD.
YER MAM AND DEAD ARE DEAD, DOLLY, REMEMBER? WHEN THAT DOODLEBUG HIT THE RIALTO DURING BLOSSOMS IN THE DUST? AND YOU HAVEN'T ANY BROTHERS OR SISTERS. YOU WAS AN ONLY CHILD.
OOH, YES.
...AND YOU NEVER 'AD ANY CHILDREN NEITHER. YOUR WOMB WERE BARREN.
EEH, YOU'RE RIGHT, ADA. I REMEMBER NOW.
I WONDER IF MR. PLAXTON WOULD SWAP IT FOR A TIN OF PEK..?
OOH... GET READY, DOLLY. IT'S YOUR BIG E FLAT COMIN' UP...
PARP!
EEH, ADA. ME PELVIC FLOOR'S NOT WHAT IT WAS, IS IT..?
I KNOW, DOLLY. YOU FALL TO BITS AFTER THE CHANGE, DON'T YOU..?
AYE. I'M GOING TO PLAY THE TAMBOURINE NEXT YEAR.
COME ON. LET'S CATCH PLAXTON'S.
SHORTLY... HELLO THERE MR. PLAXTON... NOW, ABOUT MY TURKEY...
JUST PUSHING THE GIBLETS UP FOR YOU, LOVE.

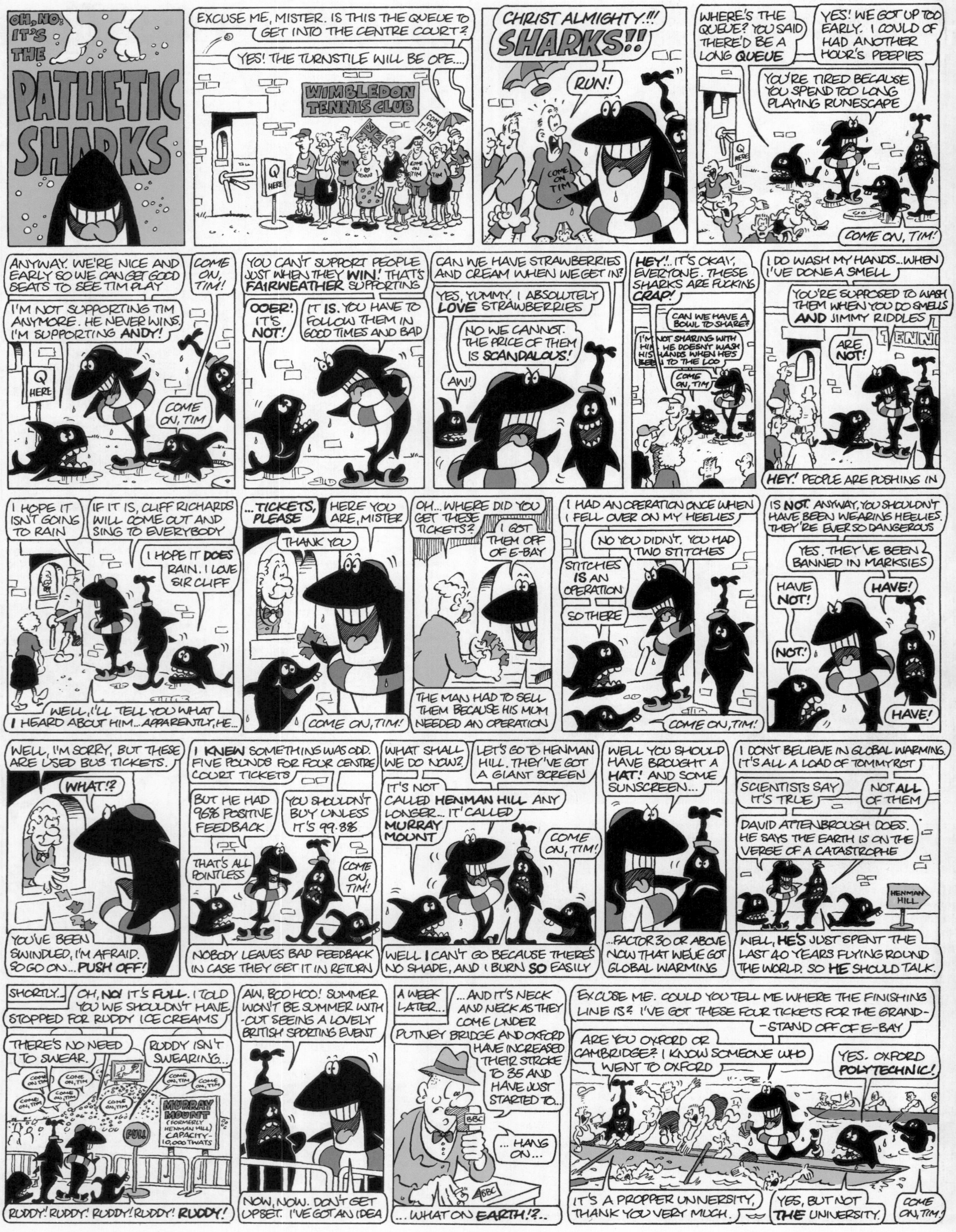
OH, NO! IT'S THE PATHETIC SHARKS
EXCUSE ME, MISTER. IS THIS THE QUEUE TO GET INTO THE CENTRE COURT?
YES! THE TURNSTILE WILL BE OPE....
WIMBLEDON TENNIS CLUB
COME ON TIM
Q HERE
CHRIST ALMIGHTY!!! SHARKS!!
RUN!
COME ON TIM
WHERE'S THE QUEUE? YOU SAID THERE'D BE A LONG QUEUE
YES! WE GOT UP TOO EARLY. I COULD OF HAD ANOTHER HOUR'S PEEPIES
YOU'RE TIRED BECAUSE YOU SPEND TOO LONG PLAYING RUNESCAPE
COME ON, TIM!
ANYWAY. WE'RE NICE AND EARLY SO WE CAN GET GOOD SEATS TO SEE TIM PLAY
COME ON, TIM!
I'M NOT SUPPORTING TIM ANYMORE. HE NEVER WINS. I'M SUPPORTING ANDY!
COME ON, TIM
YOU CAN'T SUPPORT PEOPLE JUST WHEN THEY WIN! THAT'S FAIRWEATHER SUPPORTING
OOER! IT'S NOT!
IT IS. YOU HAVE TO FOLLOW THEM IN GOOD TIMES AND BAD
CAN WE HAVE STRAWBERRIES AND CREAM WHEN WE GET IN?
YES, YUMMY. I ABSOLUTELY LOVE STRAWBERRIES
NO WE CANNOT. THE PRICE OF THEM IS SCANDALOUS!
AW!
HEY!.. IT'S OKAY, EVERYONE. THESE SHARKS ARE FUCKING CRAP!
CAN WE HAVE A BOWL TO SHARE?
I'M NOT SHARING WITH HIM. HE DOESN'T WASH HIS HANDS WHEN HE'S BEEN TO THE LOO
COME ON, TIM
I DO WASH MY HANDS... WHEN I'VE DONE A SMELL
YOU'RE SUPPOSED TO WASH THEM WHEN YOU DO SMELLS AND JIMMY RIDDLES
ARE NOT!
HEY! PEOPLE ARE PUSHING IN
I HOPE IT ISN'T GOING TO RAIN
IF IT IS, CLIFF RICHARDS WILL COME OUT AND SING TO EVERYBODY
I HOPE IT DOES RAIN. I LOVE SIR CLIFF
WELL, I'LL TELL YOU WHAT I HEARD ABOUT HIM... APPARENTLY, HE...
...TICKETS, PLEASE
HERE YOU ARE, MISTER
THANK YOU
COME ON, TIM!
OH... WHERE DID YOU GET THESE TICKETS?
I GOT THEM OFF OF E-BAY
THE MAN HAD TO SELL THEM BECAUSE HIS MOM NEEDED AN OPERATION
I HAD AN OPERATION ONCE WHEN I FELL OVER ON MY HEELIES
NO YOU DIDN'T. YOU HAD TWO STITCHES
STITCHES IS AN OPERATION
SO THERE
COME ON, TIM!
IS NOT. ANYWAY, YOU SHOULDN'T HAVE BEEN WEARING HEELIES. THEY'RE EVER SO DANGEROUS
YES. THEY'VE BEEN BANNED IN MARKSIES
HAVE NOT!
HAVE!
NOT!
HAVE!
WELL, I'M SORRY, BUT THESE ARE USED BUS TICKETS.
WHAT!?
YOU'VE BEEN SWINDLED, I'M AFRAID. SO GO ON... PUSH OFF!
I KNEW SOMETHING WAS ODD. FIVE POUNDS FOR FOUR CENTRE COURT TICKETS
BUT HE HAD 96% POSITIVE FEEDBACK
YOU SHOULDN'T BUY UNLESS IT'S 99.8%
THAT'S ALL POINTLESS
COME ON, TIM!
NOBODY LEAVES BAD FEEDBACK IN CASE THEY GET IT IN RETURN
WHAT SHALL WE DO NOW?
LET'S GO TO HENMAN HILL. THEY'VE GOT A GIANT SCREEN
IT'S NOT CALLED HENMAN HILL ANY LONGER... IT'S CALLED MURRAY MOUNT
COME ON, TIM!
WELL I CAN'T GO BECAUSE THERE'S NO SHADE, AND I BURN SO EASILY
WELL YOU SHOULD HAVE BROUGHT A HAT! AND SOME SUNSCREEN...
...FACTOR 30 OR ABOVE NOW THAT WE'VE GOT GLOBAL WARMING
I DON'T BELIEVE IN GLOBAL WARMING. IT'S ALL A LOAD OF TOMMYROT
SCIENTISTS SAY IT'S TRUE
NOT ALL OF THEM
DAVID ATTENBROUGH DOES. HE SAYS THE EARTH IS ON THE VERGE OF A CATASTROPHE
HENMAN HILL
WELL, HE'S JUST SPENT THE LAST 40 YEARS FLYING ROUND THE WORLD. SO HE SHOULD TALK.
SHORTLY...
OH, NO! IT'S FULL. I TOLD YOU WE SHOULDN'T HAVE STOPPED FOR RUDDY ICE CREAMS
THERE'S NO NEED TO SWEAR.
RUDDY ISN'T SWEARING...
COME ON, TIM
MURRAY MOUNT (FORMERLY HENMAN HILL) CAPACITY-10,000 TWATS
FULL
RUDDY! RUDDY! RUDDY! RUDDY! RUDDY!
AW, BOO HOO! SUMMER WON'T BE SUMMER WITH-OUT SEEING A LOVELY BRITISH SPORTING EVENT
NOW, NOW. DON'T GET UPSET. I'VE GOT AN IDEA
A WEEK LATER...
...AND IT'S NECK AND NECK AS THEY COME UNDER PUTNEY BRIDGE AND OXFORD HAVE INCREASED THEIR STROKE TO 35 AND HAVE JUST STARTED TO...
BBC
...HANG ON...
...WHAT ON EARTH!?..
EXCUSE ME. COULD YOU TELL ME WHERE THE FINISHING LINE IS? I'VE GOT THESE FOUR TICKETS FOR THE GRAND-STAND OFF OF E-BAY
ARE YOU OXFORD OR CAMBRIDGE? I KNOW SOMEONE WHO WENT TO OXFORD
YES. OXFORD POLYTECHNIC!
IT'S A PROPPER UNIVERSITY, THANK YOU VERY MUCH.
YES, BUT NOT THE UNIVERSITY.
COME ON, TIM!

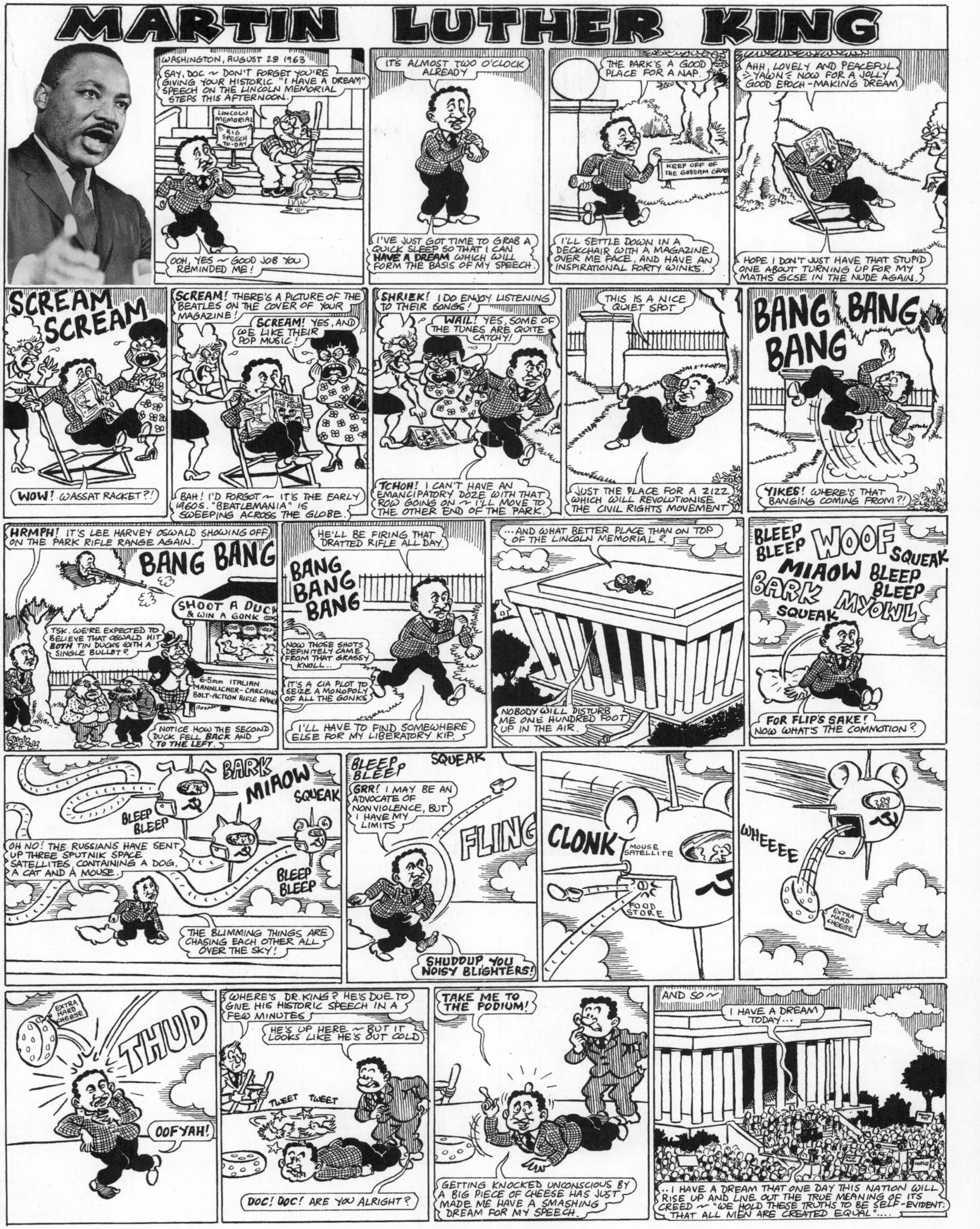

MARTIN LUTHER KING
WASHINGTON, AUGUST 28 1963
SAY, DOC ~ DON'T FORGET YOU'RE GIVING YOUR HISTORIC "I HAVE A DREAM" SPEECH ON THE LINCOLN MEMORIAL STEPS THIS AFTERNOON.
LINCOLN MEMORIAL
BIG SPEECH TO-DAY
OOH, YES ~ GOOD JOB YOU REMINDED ME!
IT'S ALMOST TWO O'CLOCK ALREADY
I'VE JUST GOT TIME TO GRAB A QUICK SLEEP SO THAT I CAN HAVE A DREAM WHICH WILL FORM THE BASIS OF MY SPEECH.
THE PARK'S A GOOD PLACE FOR A NAP.
KEEP OFF OF THE GODDAM GRASS
I'LL SETTLE DOWN IN A DECKCHAIR WITH A MAGAZINE OVER ME FACE, AND HAVE AN INSPIRATIONAL FORTY WINKS.
AHH, LOVELY AND PEACEFUL ~ YAWN ~ NOW FOR A JOLLY GOOD EPOCH-MAKING DREAM
HOPE I DON'T JUST HAVE THAT STUPID ONE ABOUT TURNING UP FOR MY MATHS GCSE IN THE NUDE AGAIN.
SCREAM SCREAM
WOW! WASSAT RACKET?!
SCREAM! THERE'S A PICTURE OF THE BEATLES ON THE COVER OF YOUR MAGAZINE!
SCREAM! YES, AND WE LIKE THEIR POP MUSIC!
TIME FAB FOUR
BAH! I'D FORGOT ~ IT'S THE EARLY 1960S. "BEATLEMANIA" IS SWEEPING ACROSS THE GLOBE.
SHRIEK! I DO ENJOY LISTENING TO THEIR SONGS!
WAIL! YES, SOME OF THE TUNES ARE QUITE CATCHY!
TCHOH! I CAN'T HAVE AN EMANCIPATORY DOZE WITH THAT ROW GOING ON ~ I'LL MOVE TO THE OTHER END OF THE PARK.
THIS IS A NICE QUIET SPOT
JUST THE PLACE FOR A ZIZZ WHICH WILL REVOLUTIONISE THE CIVIL RIGHTS MOVEMENT
BANG BANG BANG
YIKES! WHERE'S THAT BANGING COMING FROM?!
HRMPH! IT'S LEE HARVEY OSWALD SHOWING OFF ON THE PARK RIFLE RANGE AGAIN.
BANG BANG
SHOOT A DUCK & WIN A GONK
TSK. WE'RE EXPECTED TO BELIEVE THAT OSWALD HIT BOTH TIN DUCKS WITH A SINGLE BULLET?
6.5mm ITALIAN MANNLICHER-CARCANO BOLT-ACTION RIFLE RANGE
NOTICE HOW THE SECOND DUCK FELL BACK AND TO THE LEFT.
HE'LL BE FIRING THAT DRATTED RIFLE ALL DAY.
BANG BANG BANG
NOW THOSE SHOTS DEFINITELY CAME FROM THAT GRASSY KNOLL..
IT'S A CIA PLOT TO SEIZE A MONOPOLY OF ALL THE GONKS
I'LL HAVE TO FIND SOMEWHERE ELSE FOR MY LIBERATORY KIP.
...AND WHAT BETTER PLACE THAN ON TOP OF THE LINCOLN MEMORIAL?
NOBODY WILL DISTURB ME ONE HUNDRED FOOT UP IN THE AIR.
BLEEP BLEEP WOOF SQUEAK MIAOW BLEEP BLEEP BARK MYOWL SQUEAK
FOR FLIP'S SAKE! NOW WHAT'S THE COMMOTION?
BARK MIAOW SQUEAK BLEEP BLEEP
OH NO! THE RUSSIANS HAVE SENT UP THREE SPUTNIK SPACE SATELLITES, CONTAINING A DOG, A CAT AND A MOUSE.
BLEEP BLEEP
THE BLIMMING THINGS ARE CHASING EACH OTHER ALL OVER THE SKY!
BLEEP BLEEP SQUEAK
GRR! I MAY BE AN ADVOCATE OF NON VIOLENCE, BUT I HAVE MY LIMITS
FLING
SHUDDUP YOU NOISY BLIGHTERS!
CLONK
MOUSE SATELLITE
FOOD STORE
WHEEEE
EXTRA HARD CHEESE
EXTRA HARD CHEESE
THUD
OOFYAH!
WHERE'S DR. KING? HE'S DUE TO GIVE HIS HISTORIC SPEECH IN A FEW MINUTES
HE'S UP HERE ~ BUT IT LOOKS LIKE HE'S OUT COLD
TWEET TWEET
DOC! DOC! ARE YOU ALRIGHT?
TAKE ME TO THE PODIUM!
GETTING KNOCKED UNCONSCIOUS BY A BIG PIECE OF CHEESE HAS JUST MADE ME HAVE A SMASHING DREAM FOR MY SPEECH.
AND SO ~
I HAVE A DREAM TODAY...
...I HAVE A DREAM THAT ONE DAY THIS NATION WILL RISE UP AND LIVE OUT THE TRUE MEANING OF ITS CREED ~ "WE HOLD THESE TRUTHS TO BE SELF-EVIDENT: THAT ALL MEN ARE CREATED EQUAL"....

People Who Help Us...

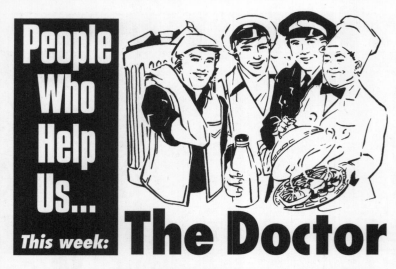

This week: **The Doctor**

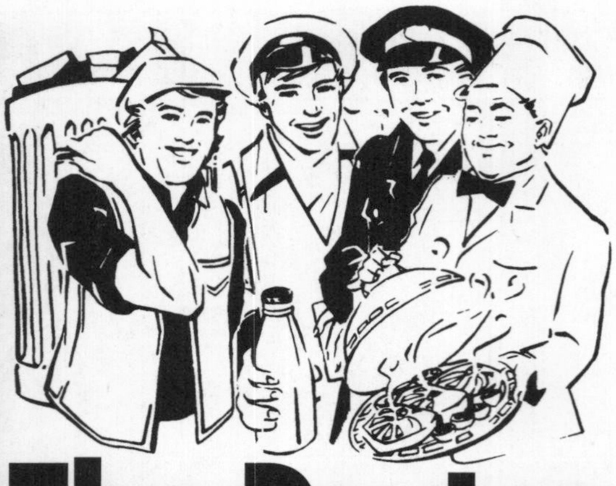

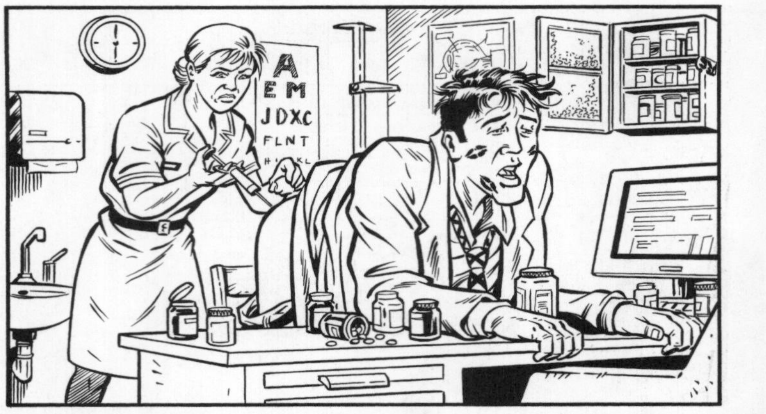
A
E M
J D X C
F L N T

1. IT IS 6.00am, and the day has begun for our doctor, after a mere 5 hours sleep. An important late meeting in a lap-dancing club with a drug company rep has left him exhausted. Today he may be asked to make several life or death decisions, so it's into his clinic for a quick cocktail of dihydrocodeine, tilidine, tolfenamic acid, pyritinol and chloromethiazole out of the restricted drugs cabinet. This immediately perks him up and leaves him ready to face the day.

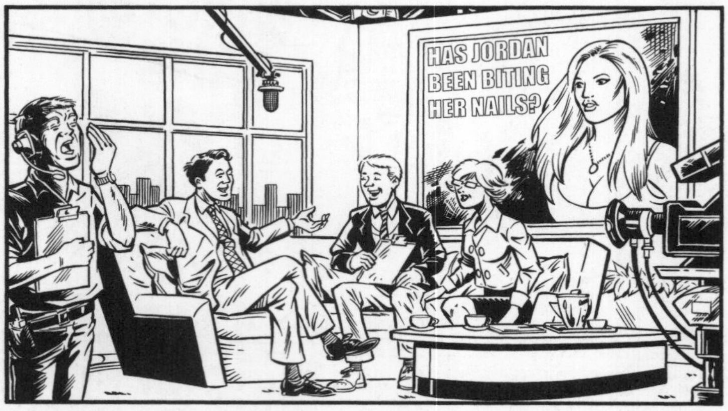
HAS JORDAN
BEEN BITING
HER NAILS?

2. THUS refreshed, the doctor sets off for the first appointment in his busy schedule. The modern physician not only practises from his surgery, he more likely than not will be expected to appear on BBC Breakfast or GMTV where he will be called upon to comment about topical medical matters. Obesity, alcoholism and the mental state of Britney Spears are all subjects upon which he could be asked to give an opinion at a moment's notice.

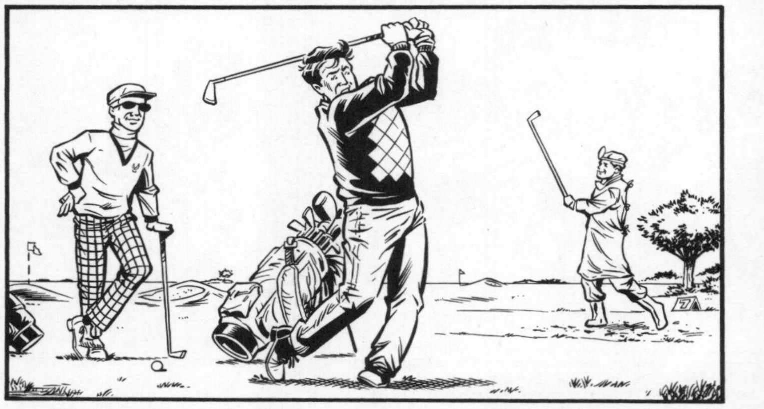

3. IT IS stressful work speaking on live TV about a subject of which you have barely a passing knowledge. So our medic makes his way from the TV studio to the golf course for a relaxing nine holes. Doctors are asked to make life and death decisions every day of their working lives, and a tired mind is more likely to make mistakes than a fresh one. To make sure that his relaxation is not interrupted, he switches off his pager and his mobile phone.

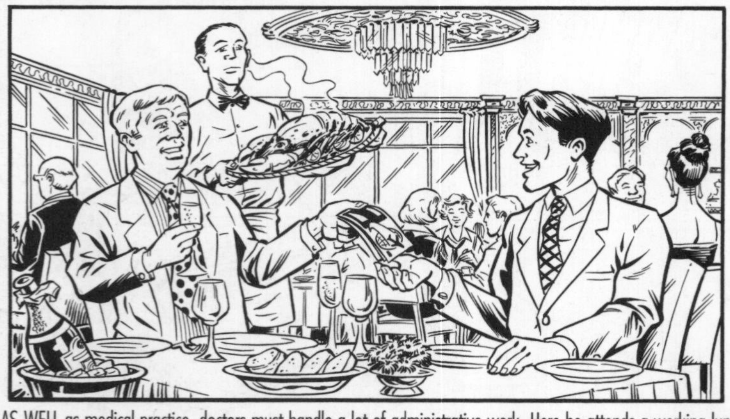

4. AS WELL as medical practice, doctors must handle a lot of administrative work. Here he attends a working lunch with a drug rep at a posh restaurant. It is the job of the rep to persuade the doctor, by any means, that his company's products are effective. Sometimes they hold seminars at swanky hotels in Barbados with championship golf courses attached, which doctors attend to consider the benefits to their patients that a new drug could provide.

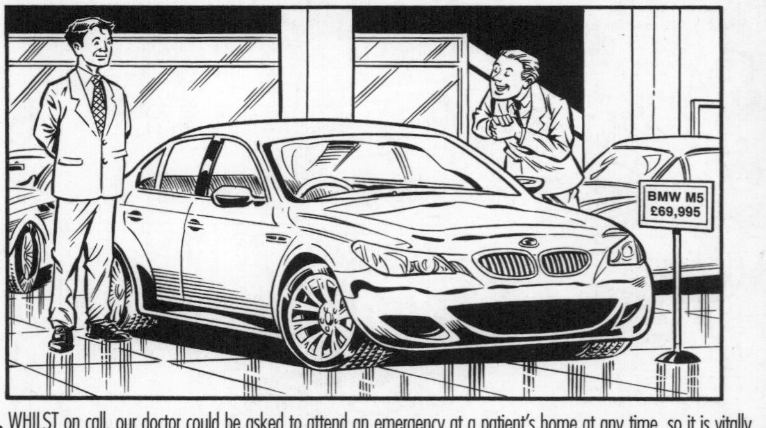
BMW M5
£69,995

5. WHILST on call, our doctor could be asked to attend an emergency at a patient's home at any time, so it is vitally important that he has a fast, reliable car to get him there. For patient safety, the practice provides the doctor with a brand new BMW M5. And in order that he arrives relaxed and able to make split second life or death decisions, he opts for the full factory burr walnut pack, 16-speaker stereo and leather interior. And a matching Z8 convertible for his wife.

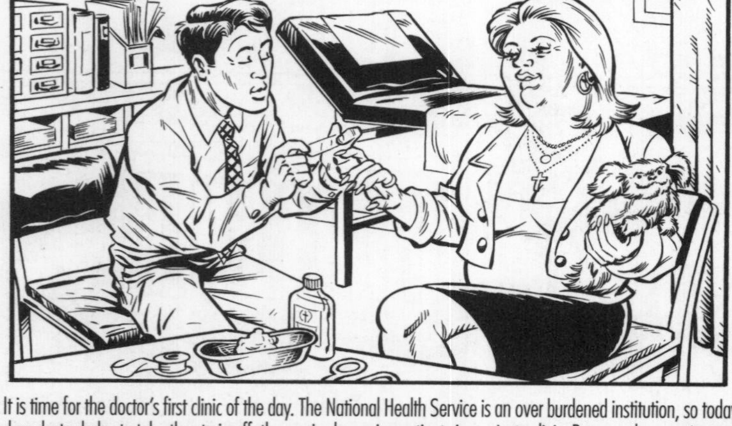

6. It is time for the doctor's first clinic of the day. The National Health Service is an over burdened institution, so today's modern doctor helps to take the strain off the service by seeing patients in a private clinic. Because these patients pay for their treatment, there is more money in the NHS budget for when the doctor finally gets round to seeing everybody else. This is the doctor's way of repaying the public, who paid for his expensive training through their taxes.

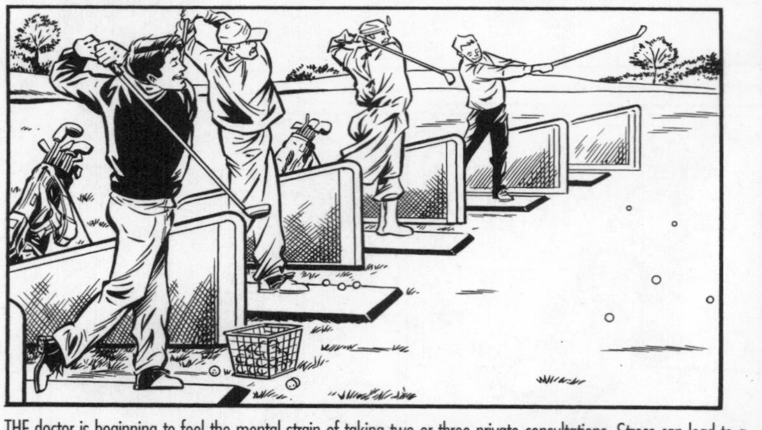

7. THE doctor is beginning to feel the mental strain of taking two or three private consultations. Stress can lead to a mis-diagnosis with serious or possibly even fatal results, so before he sees any more cases, it is important that the doctor winds down. For the sake of his patients, it's off to the driving range to relieve the tension of his demanding profession by hitting a couple of baskets of balls, followed by a relaxing drink in the golf club members' bar with colleagues.

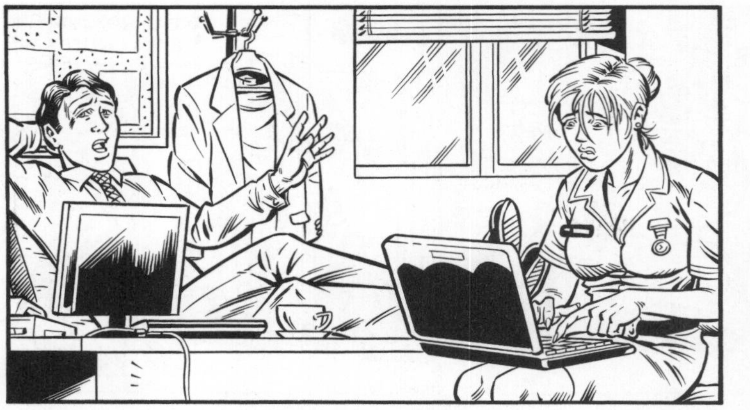

8. SUITABLY refreshed, our doctor makes his way back to the hospital. But there is no time to see any patients. Most doctors these days churn out dire, formulaic medical columns for newspapers, and our doctor must dictate his work quickly in order to meet his paper's tight deadlines. An ability to look up information on erectile dysfunction, vaginisimus and G-spots on Wikipedia is needed to fill the titilating column inches relentlessly demanded by today's tabloid editors.

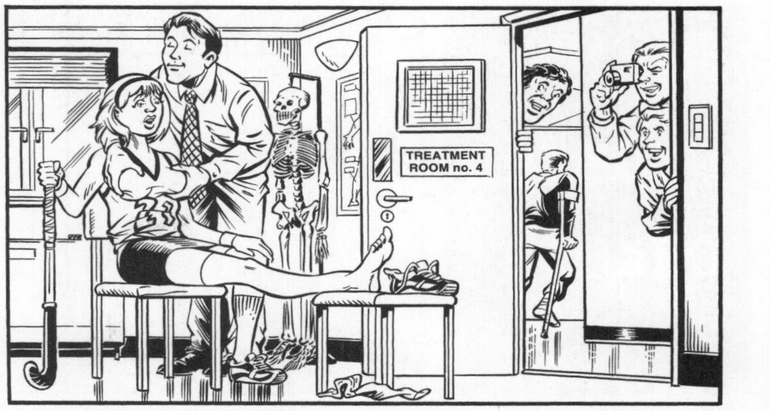
TREATMENT
ROOM no. 4

9. LIKE all of us, doctors are human and can make mistakes, but their mistakes could mean the difference between life and death. So it is vitally important that nothing is overlooked. At this Sports Injury Clinic, a young woman has what looks like a simple twisted ankle, but the doctor wants to make sure there have been no potentially serious injuries to her breasts. He examines them, but such is his thoroughness, he invites several colleagues in to give a second opinion.

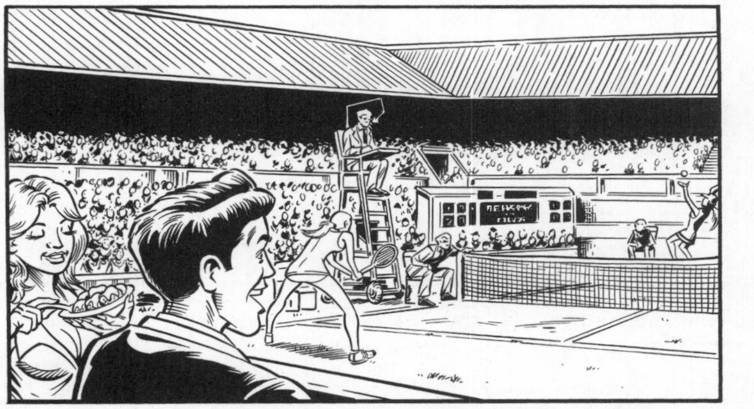

10. THERE are not enough hours in the day for a busy doctor to meet all the demands that are placed on him. For the third time today, our physician must hold a meeting with a drugs rep. This man's company has developed a new analogue chlorpromazine antidepressant. Our doctor is not convinced of the benefits to his patients such a drug would bring, so the rep gives him a pair of tickets for both singles finals at this year's Wimbledon Championships.

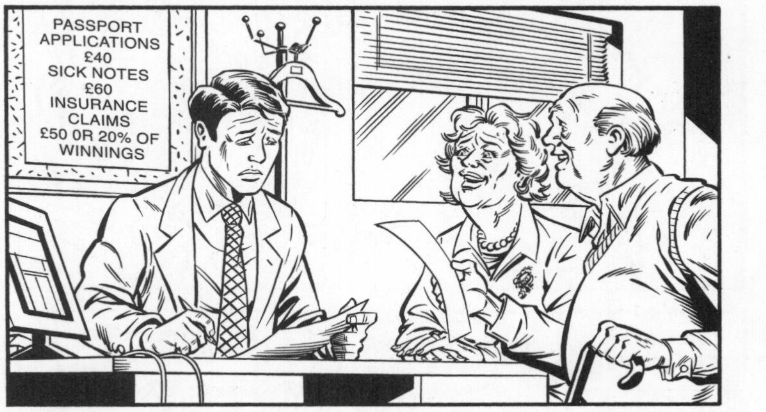
PASSPORT
APPLICATIONS
£40
SICK NOTES
£60
INSURANCE
CLAIMS
£50 OR 20% OF
WINNINGS

11. WHEN they graduate from medical school, doctors take the hippocratic oath, a sacred promise that they will help people to the best of their ability. This normally takes the form of ministering to the sick in the community, diagnosing their illnesses and prescribing treatments that will make them better. But they are also happy to help out in other ways too. Here, our doctor is aiding two of his patients by signing their passport applications for £40 a go.

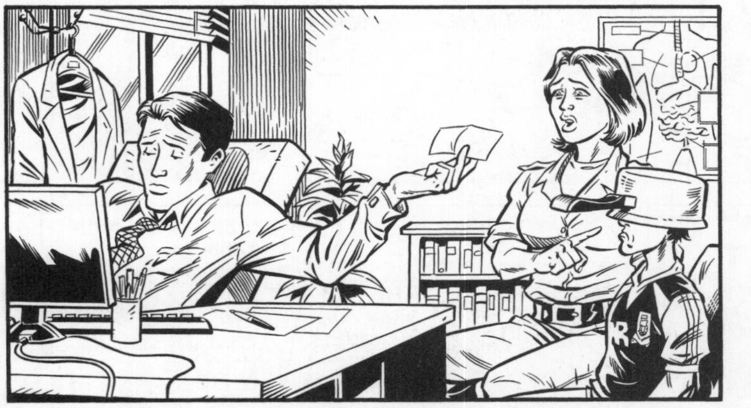

12. ALTHOUGH NHS patients do not pay at source, they are guaranteed the same high quality treatment afforded to the private patient. Here, a little boy comes in complaining of headaches, restricted vision, a tight feeling around his temples and muffled hearing. Using a Computer Aided Diagnostic System, the doctor is able to enter the symptoms into the program, quickly diagnose hemi-facial spasm disorder, and prescribe an extensive course of steroids.

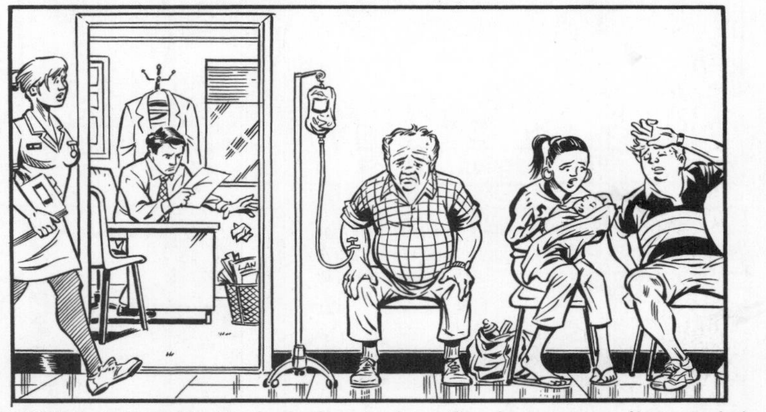

13. ALTHOUGH trained in medicine, it is a fact that the modern doctor will spend a certain amount of his time involved in paperwork. Medical reports have to be written, case notes have to be studied and research literature has to be read to keep up with all the latest developments in drugs and treatments. Here, the doctor finds a brief window in his hectic schedule to write some invoices for his private patients and to sort out his golf club membership.

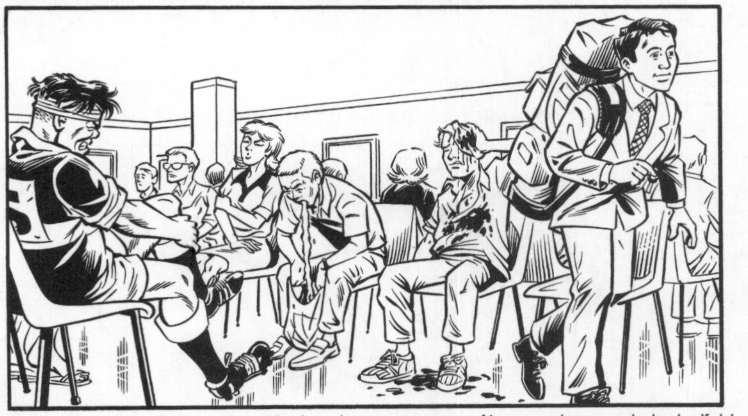

14. HALFWAY through his afternoon surgery, the doctor has an appointment of his own to keep... at the local golf club. Just as a lorry driver must have a break every so often, a doctor must take a few precious hours two or three times a day to kick back and escape from the demands of his professional life. None of his patients left waiting at the surgery begrudge their GP a little time for himself, and a spot of practice on the putting green is just what the doctor ordered!

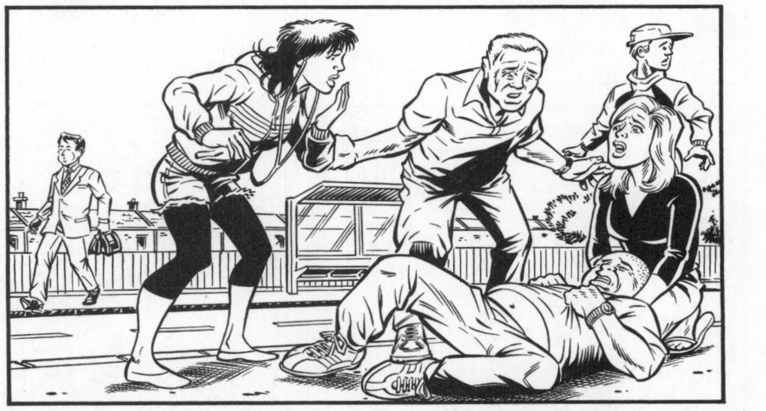

15. ON HIS way home, the doctor spots a man who has collapsed with a heart attack. The doctor knows that, tired after a day's work, he could easily make a fatal slip. He therefore decides that it is in the best interests of the man to not volunteer the information that he is a doctor, and crosses the street. In fact, doctors seldom use their professional title, except when booking tables in exclusive restaurants or trying to get their seats upgraded on holiday flights.

Next week's People Who Help Us: ***The Scoutmaster***

Drunken bakers

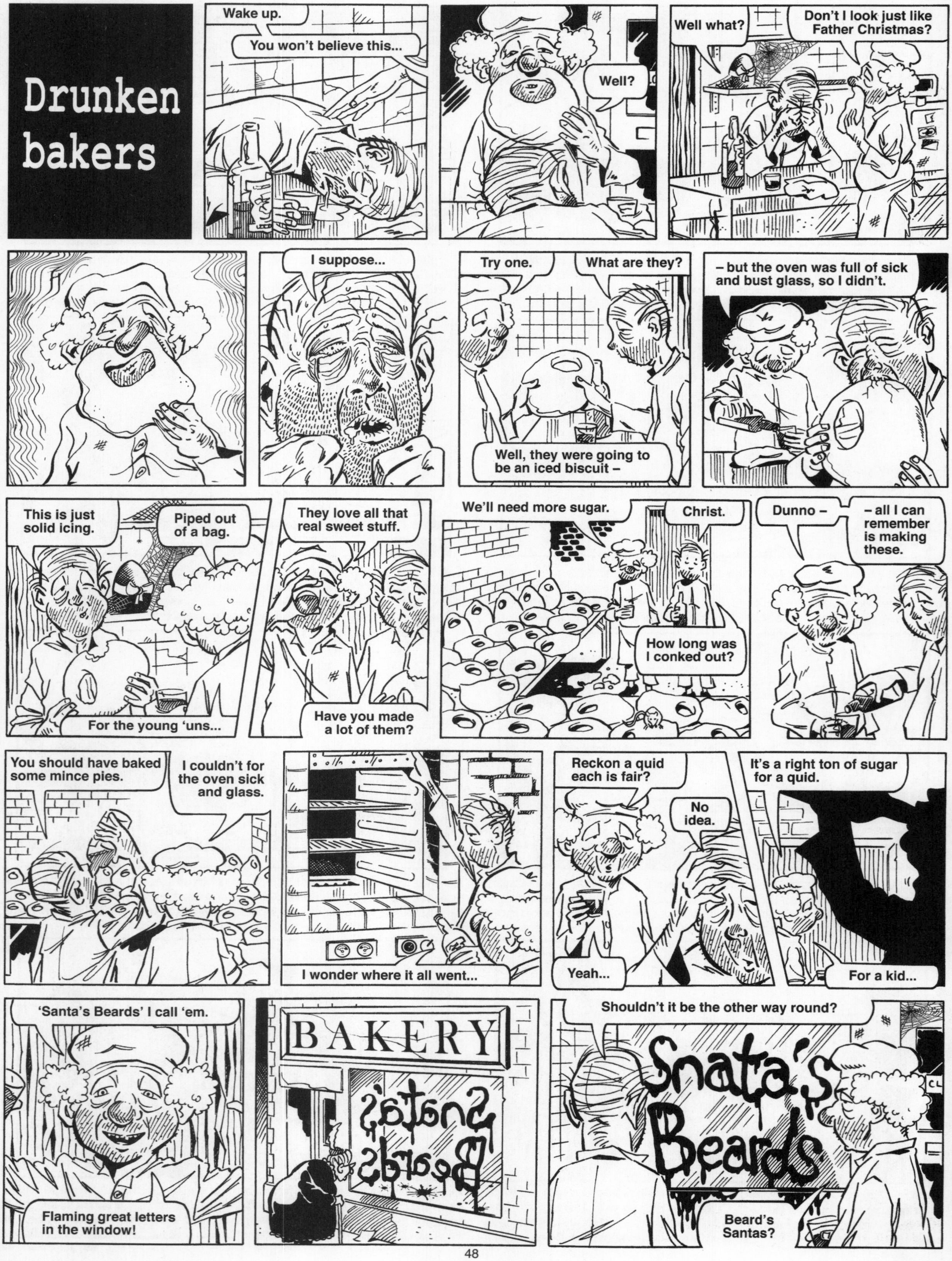
Wake up.
You won't believe this...
Well?
Well what?
Don't I look just like Father Christmas?
I suppose...
Try one.
What are they?
Well, they were going to be an iced biscuit –
– but the oven was full of sick and bust glass, so I didn't.
This is just solid icing.
Piped out of a bag.
For the young 'uns...
They love all that real sweet stuff.
Have you made a lot of them?
We'll need more sugar.
Christ.
How long was I conked out?
Dunno –
– all I can remember is making these.
You should have baked some mince pies.
I couldn't for the oven sick and glass.
I wonder where it all went...
Reckon a quid each is fair?
No idea.
Yeah...
It's a right ton of sugar for a quid.
For a kid...
'Santa's Beards' I call 'em.
Flaming great letters in the window!
BAKERY
Snata's Beards
Shouldn't it be the other way round?
Snata's Beards
Beard's Santas?

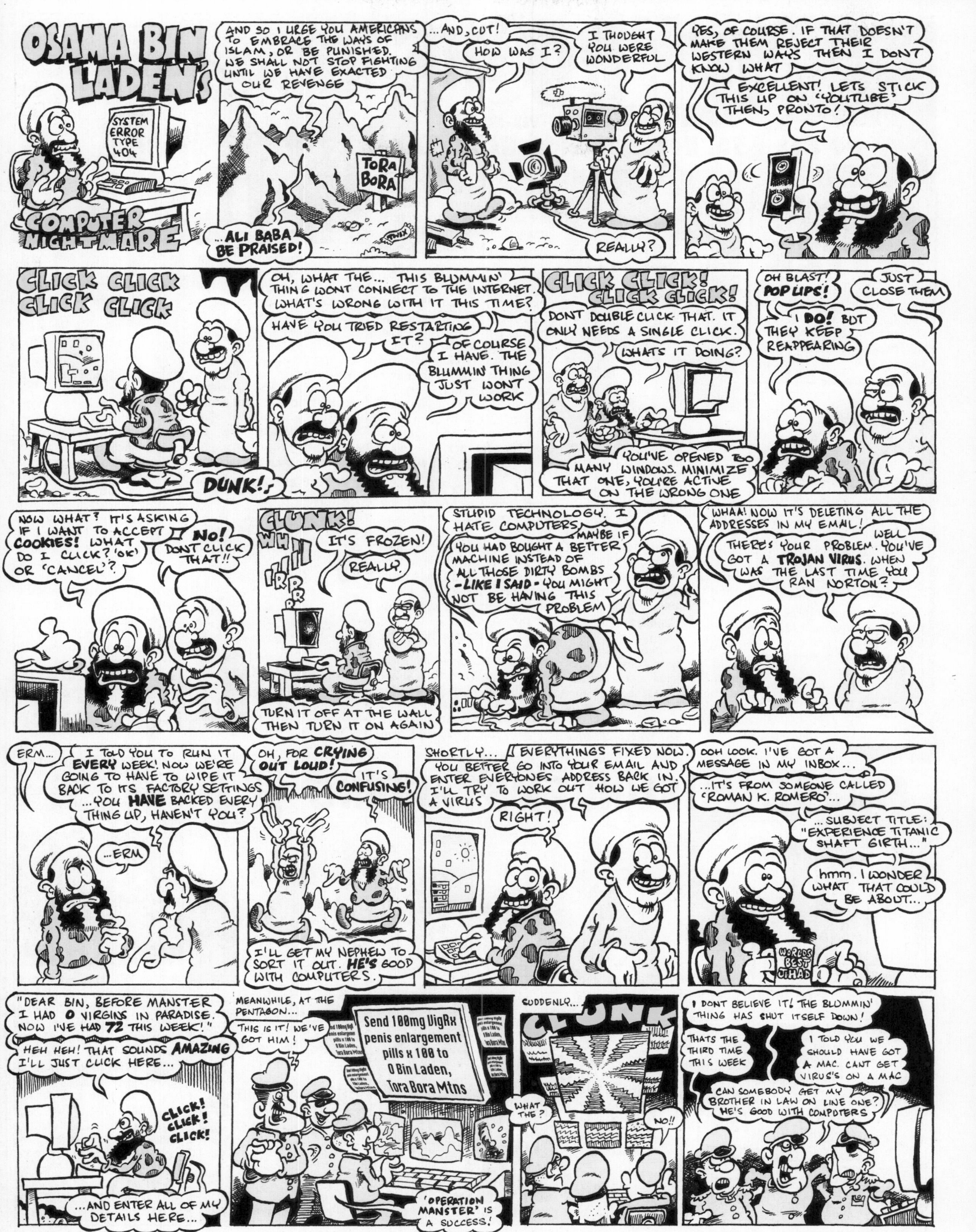
OSAMA BIN LADEN'S
COMPUTER NIGHTMARE
SYSTEM ERROR TYPE 404
AND SO I URGE YOU AMERICANS TO EMBRACE THE WAYS OF ISLAM, OR BE PUNISHED. WE SHALL NOT STOP FIGHTING UNTIL WE HAVE EXACTED OUR REVENGE
TORA BORA
...ALI BABA BE PRAISED!
...AND, CUT!
HOW WAS I?
I THOUGHT YOU WERE WONDERFUL
REALLY?
YES, OF COURSE. IF THAT DOESN'T MAKE THEM REJECT THEIR WESTERN WAYS THEN I DON'T KNOW WHAT
EXCELLENT! LETS STICK THIS UP ON 'YOUTUBE' THEN, PRONTO!
CLICK CLICK CLICK CLICK
DUNK!
OH, WHAT THE... THIS BLUMMIN' THING WONT CONNECT TO THE INTERNET. WHAT'S WRONG WITH IT THIS TIME?
HAVE YOU TRIED RESTARTING IT?
OF COURSE I HAVE. THE BLUMMIN' THING JUST WONT WORK
CLICK CLICK! CLICK CLICK!
DONT DOUBLE CLICK THAT. IT ONLY NEEDS A SINGLE CLICK.
WHATS IT DOING?
YOU'VE OPENED TOO MANY WINDOWS. MINIMIZE THAT ONE, YOU'RE ACTIVE ON THE WRONG ONE
OH BLAST! POP UPS!
JUST CLOSE THEM
I DO! BUT THEY KEEP REAPPEARING
NOW WHAT? IT'S ASKING IF I WANT TO ACCEPT COOKIES! WHAT DO I CLICK? 'OK' OR 'CANCEL'?
NO! DONT CLICK THAT!!
CLUNK!
WHIRRRR
IT'S FROZEN!
REALLY.
TURN IT OFF AT THE WALL THEN TURN IT ON AGAIN
STUPID TECHNOLOGY. I HATE COMPUTERS
MAYBE IF YOU HAD BOUGHT A BETTER MACHINE INSTEAD OF ALL THOSE DIRTY BOMBS -LIKE I SAID- YOU MIGHT NOT BE HAVING THIS PROBLEM
WHAA! NOW IT'S DELETING ALL THE ADDRESSES IN MY EMAIL!
WELL THERE'S YOUR PROBLEM. YOU'VE GOT A TROJAN VIRUS. WHEN WAS THE LAST TIME YOU RAN NORTON?
ERM...
I TOLD YOU TO RUN IT EVERY WEEK! NOW WE'RE GOING TO HAVE TO WIPE IT BACK TO ITS FACTORY SETTINGS ...YOU HAVE BACKED EVERY THING UP, HAVEN'T YOU?
...ERM
OH, FOR CRYING OUT LOUD!
IT'S CONFUSING!
I'LL GET MY NEPHEW TO SORT IT OUT. HE'S GOOD WITH COMPUTERS.
SHORTLY...
EVERYTHINGS FIXED NOW. YOU BETTER GO INTO YOUR EMAIL AND ENTER EVERYONES ADDRESS BACK IN. I'LL TRY TO WORK OUT HOW WE GOT A VIRUS
RIGHT!
OOH LOOK. I'VE GOT A MESSAGE IN MY INBOX...
...IT'S FROM SOMEONE CALLED 'ROMAN K. ROMERO'...
...SUBJECT TITLE: "EXPERIENCE TITANIC SHAFT GIRTH..."
hmm. I WONDER WHAT THAT COULD BE ABOUT...
WORLDS BEST JIHAD
"DEAR BIN, BEFORE MANSTER I HAD 0 VIRGINS IN PARADISE. NOW I'VE HAD 72 THIS WEEK!"
HEH HEH! THAT SOUNDS AMAZING I'LL JUST CLICK HERE...
CLICK! CLICK! CLICK!
...AND ENTER ALL OF MY DETAILS HERE...
MEANWHILE, AT THE PENTAGON...
THIS IS IT! WE'VE GOT HIM!
Send 100mg VigRx penis enlargement pills x 100 to O Bin Laden, Tora Bora Mtns
'OPERATION MANSTER' IS A SUCCESS!
SUDDENLY...
CLUNK
WHAT THE?
NO!!
I DONT BELIEVE IT! THE BLUMMIN' THING HAS SHUT ITSELF DOWN!
THATS THE THIRD TIME THIS WEEK
I TOLD YOU WE SHOULD HAVE GOT A MAC. CANT GET VIRUS'S ON A MAC
CAN SOMEBODY GET MY BROTHER IN LAW ON LINE ONE? HE'S GOOD WITH COMPUTERS

LETTERBOCKS

letters@viz.co.uk

PO Box 656, North Shields, NE30 4XX

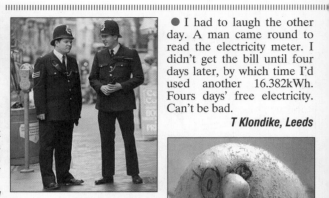

● I had to laugh the other day. A man came round to read the electricity meter. I didn't get the bill until four days later, by which time I'd used another 16.382kWh. Fours days' free electricity. Can't be bad.

T Klondike, Leeds

STAR LETTER

● They say that dog owners look like their dogs. Well, I avoided this phenomenon by swapping dogs with my neighbour, who looks nothing like me.

Rog, e-mail

● I've spoken to three people who have met Jimmy Carr in person, and each one has said what a thoroughly nice bloke he is. I wish I hadn't spoken to them. If anyone else has met the twat and likes him, please keep it to yourself.

T Thorn, Rhyll

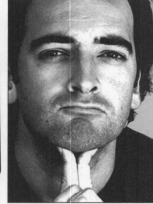

● I recently saw TV impressionist Alistair McGowan walking down the platform at Waterloo station, dragging a suitcase and wearing a straw hat. It was rubbish. I hadn't got a clue who he was supposed to be, and it wasn't funny anyway. If that's what the BBC thinks passes for entertainment, then I shall not be renewing my TV licence.

W Gambles, Newcastle

● Why do people describe cold weather temperatures in the Celcius scale, but describe hot weather in Fahrenheit? Talk about bloody drama queens.

PGT Weasel, Burrow

● I'm beginning to think there may be something in this climate change after all. Four months ago it was very cold and now it's quite warm.

Alan Heath, e-mail

● Mr Gambles (letter, this issue) is right to be disappointed at Alistair McGowan's poor performance, but at least he got it for free. I just paid £15 to see Jo Brand at Newcastle City Hall, and she was only on stage an hour and it was all old material. Seeing her walk down a railway platform in a straw hat and pulling a suitcase would certainly have been funnier.

J Thorne, Hexham

● I aggree with J Thorne's letter (above). Me and my mate went to the same show and sat on the front row. We were pissed as farts and blagged our way into the theatre using a used ticket from that day's Newcastle game against Arsenal. And even *we* felt ripped off.

C Wanker, Woolwich

● I recently saw *15 to 1* quizmaster William G Stewart's cock in a urinal, and let me tell you, it wasn't worth writing to *Viz* about.

Anon, e-mail

● I can't remember the last time I saw a bobby on the beat. But that's probably because I'm in the tertiary stages of Alzheimer's disease.

Albert Carlisle, London

● I appreciate how unlikely it is that any of your readers have forgotten what an utter twat Elton John is. But could you print a picture of him looking an utter twat, just to make absolutely sure?

B Lurgess, Lancs

* *Certainly, Mr Burgess.*

● Whilst peeling some spuds for dinner, I discovered a potato that bears a strange resemblance to the cartoon version of annoying antipodean Rolf Harris. Admittedly I had to add a beard and glasses with a felt pen. And the mouth, but still. And people get worked up about Jesus appearing on a dishcloth.

Gilbert Black, e-mail

● My granny always used to say that Cliff Richard wasn't gay, he just hadn't found the right girl yet. Well that was over thirty years ago, and Cliff still seems to be looking in the

SPOT THE DEFERENCE

Here is Prince Charles backstage at a recent Royal Variety Performance. Somewhere in the picture is a former left-wing comedian fawning like fuck over him. Can you spot the deference?

* *Have **YOU** got any pictures of right-on celebrities cringing like toads when meeting members of the royal family? Maybe you've got a photo of Rowan Atkinson curtseying to the Duchess of Kent, or Billy Connolly laughing at one of the Duke of Edinburgh's racist quips. Or perhaps you've got a snap of Billy Bragg putting his denim jacket across a puddle for Prince Edward. Send them in to 'Spot the Deference' at our usual address. There's a five pound note with a beautiful picture of Her Majesty the Queen on it for every one we use.*

MAJOR MISUNDERSTANDING

ST BEDES MONASTERY † ADMISSION 50P

I DARESAY YOU ALL FEEL VERY BRAVE IN YOUR LITTLE GANG, DON'T YOU?

EFFING AND BLINDING AT PASSERSBY AND BOASTING ABOUT HOW MANY "ASBOS" YOU'VE GOT

DON'T THINK I DON'T KNOW WHAT YOU'RE PLANNING

YOU THINK YOU'RE GOING TO "HAPPY SLAP" ME, AND VIDEO RECORD THE RESULTS ON YOUR MOBILE TELEPHONES

WELL YOU'VE PICKED ON THE WRONG MAN THIS TIME. I WAS REGIMENTAL BOXING CHAMPION IN THE ROYAL FUSILIERS.

COME ON THEN. PUT UP YOUR DUKES ANY ONE OF YOU. I'LL GIVE YOU A RUN FOR YOUR MONEY.

NO, I THOUGHT NOT. YOU DON'T LIKE IT WHEN SOMEONE STANDS UP TO YOU, DO YOU?

THAT'S BECAUSE YOUR GENERATION IS SOFT. YOU'VE BEEN MOLLYCODDLED BY THE NANNY STATE. A COUPLE OF WEEKS OF BASIC TRAINING AND YOU'D BE CRYING FOR YOUR MUMMIES.

YOU MAY THINK YOU LOOK VERY TOUGH, HIDING AWAY UNDER YOUR "HOODIES".

BUT YOU DON'T INTIMIDATE ME.

wrong place. But looking on the bright side, perhaps it's just as well if he doesn't find the right girl. Now that he's nearly seventy, the thought of him shacking up with a young bit of skirt would probably turn my granny's stomach. If she was still alive.

M Smith, Luton

● Thought you might like this photo of Tasha's Mam enjoying herself on the beach.

Greg Hughes, London

**Have you snapped a real-life Viz character? There's an Alfa-Romeo Brera or £1 for every one we use.*

● I despair of kids nowadays. This advert was put on some lift doors in my local shopping centre. It has been up for an entire month and no one has bothered to draw a big hairy knob and balls on the right hand door at mouth level and a second one at arse level on the left hand door. Have any of your readers seen a more blatant example of a missed opportunity for childish graffiti?

Normie, e-mail

● Why do you never see coloured plumbers? There are plenty of coloured doctors, and I believe there are even coloured policemen these days. Perhaps they just don't make very good plumbers.

Edna Racist, London

● My husband loves tuna sandwiches, and he loves jam sandwiches. But when I give him tuna and jam sandwiches he turns his nose up. Are any other readers' husbands as fussy as mine?

Enda Mumps, Peterborough

WHY ISN'T THE RADIO ON?
THE BATTERIES HAVE RUN OUT.

TOP TIPS

BOOKSHOP owners. Annoy Christians by putting the Bible in the 'Fiction' section of your shop where, joking aside, it actually belongs.

T Rumpole, Bailey

DEFY the government at the start of British Summer Time by refusing to put your clocks forward at 2.00 in the morning. 'Save' the hour for later in the day. You still get your lie-in and you can fast forward your day when it suits you, like when there is nothing on telly.

Terry Davenport, e-mail

DAILY Mail editors. Confuse your readers by claiming that asylum seekers are the natural predators of paedophiles.

Tommy Dungmonger, e-mail

STATELY home owners. Sprinkle pepper into the helmets of suits of armour so as any intruders who hide in them when being chased will give themselves away by sneezing just after you walk past.

S. Doo, e-mail

Could YOU be the next~but~one Queen of England?

One lucky reader must WIN...

HRH Prince William's Hand in Marriage!

FOLLOWING his split from Kate Middleton, William is once again a bachelor prince, and on the lookout for a suitable girl to take down the aisle. We've teamed up with our pals at Buck House to offer one lucky Viz reader the chance to win the heir's hand in marriage. And all you've got to do to end up with dishy Wills on wedding mugs and teatowels across the Commonwealth is answer these two etiquette questions to prove you're posh enough to pass muster in the Palace.

1. Wills takes you to a posh restaurant for tea. You order loaded skins with a sour cream and chives dip for starters, but then notice that you have three knives and three forks to choose from. Which ones do you use?

a) The outer ones.
b) The inner fork and outer knife
c) All of them

2. After your starter, you decide to go for a shit to make room for your main course. What phrase do you use to excuse yourself?

a) Back in a tick, I'm just nipping to crimp one off
b) Just going to wave a friend off to the sea, pal
c) Pardon one, your hayness. One is jast orf to piyder one's nase.

Send your answers to the usual address. The first correct entry drawn out of the hat by sinister former royal butler Paul Burrell will get a fairytale Royal Wedding in June. One runner-up will win a slightly-less grand marriage to Will's ginger brother.

Name...
Address..
I am: ☐ over 16 ☐ virgin ☐ fertile ☐ not particularly bright
I am **not**: ☐ Catholic ☐ Muslim ☐ Jewish ☐ Common
(Please tick all the boxes)

Buckingham Palace may make your personal details available to other, carefully selected unmarried Princes. Please tick if you'd prefer not to hear from other Royal Families. ☐

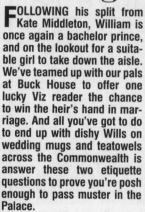

'Dropped Gut' led to Royal Break-up

The break up of Prince William and his longtime girlfriend Kate Middleton was inevitable, according to Palace insiders, after she committed a faux-pas in front of Her Majesty the Queen.

The incident was said to have occured at Royal Ascot last year when Kate broke wind in the Royal enclosure. The 23-year-old law student was reaching over the buffet to pick up a swan vol-au-vent when the fluff slipped out within earshot of Her Majesty.

William, clearly devastated, attempted to make light of the matter by quipping, "get out and walk." Royal aides immediately ran over to see if the Queen was okay.

"She was shocked, but otherwise unharmed," said one royal enclosure guest. "She had obviously heard about people breaking wind, but I think this was the first time she had ever witnessed it at first hand. But I must say, she reacted remarkably well and with great dignity."

Her Majesty was taken to sit in a side room where Sir Frederick Lamb, the Royal surgeon gave her a sedative to calm her nerves. "Within the hour Her Majesty was back outside, waving at people," Sir Frederick told reporters later. "Remarkable, when you consider she is almost eighty."

The Queen was able to continue her duties, watching the racing and eating swans, but for Kate, already considered too common by some members of the Royal family, the damage was done.

"The next day, William was told in no uncertain terms that the relationship could not continue," the insider told us. "The palace were fearful that a constitutional crisis may occur should Miss Middleton step on a frog whist on a public engagement. They simply could not take the risk."

•In 1939, whilst Her Majesty the Queen Mother was visiting Londoners caught up in the Blitz, a loud 'quack' was heard coming from her direction. Immediately, her loyal servant, Billy Booth, stepped forward and took the blame, saying he had eaten some bad prawns the night before. He was sacked on the spot and a demoralising constitutional crisis was averted. But many present believed it was actually the Queen Mum who had dealt it. Their suspicions were heightened when, 4 months later, 'Backside Billy' as he came to be known, was awarded an OBE for his 'Loyal Services to the Queen Mother'.

the evil Skeletor

theevilskeletor@viz.co.uk

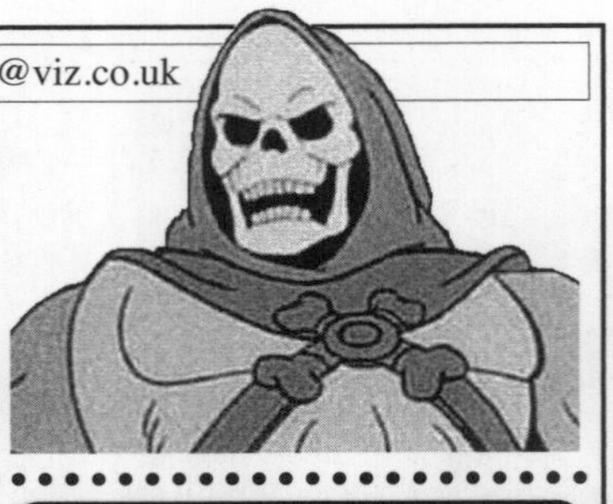

SKULL-FACED 'HE-MAN AND THE MASTERS OF THE UNIVERSE' SUPERVILLAIN ANSWERS YOUR PROBLEMS

Dear Skeletor, LETTER OF THE DAY

My husband and I argue all the time, usually over nothing, and I always end up saying something I shouldn't.

I am 28 and my husband is 29 and we have been married for five years.

It never used to be this way but lately we just can't stop getting at each other. How do I stop this vicious cycle?

Sandra Sausage, Derby

Skeletor says...

*"At times, we all say things that we regret. I recall once saying to He-Man 'The people of Eternia will see you kneel before me... just before you **die**!' Looking back it was a dreadful thing to say, but these things slip off the tongue all too easily in anger. I would advise you to just step back from an argument before it happens. Breathe and count to ten ...**Bwa ha ha ha ha ha ha.**"*

I want revenge on love rat

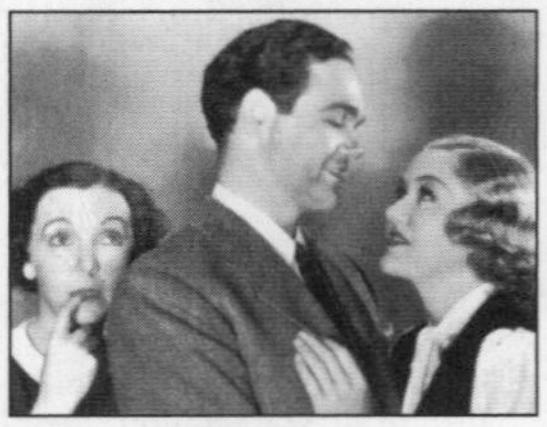

Dear Skeletor,

I found out that my boyfriend and best friend have been seeing each other behind my back.

He is 21 and I am 18 and we have been going out for nearly a year.

I'm so angry and although it is not in my nature, I really want revenge. You're evil. Can you recommend any good forms of vengeance?

Sally Mobility-Scooter, Brentwood

Skeletor says...

*"Revenge is a dish best served cold. I remember once at the Galactic Games I decided to get my own back on He-Man after being roundly trounced. I set up an ambush and transported myself, another villain Crita and He-Man to the ancient ruins of the Oasis on Primus. Then I challenged He-Man to our final battle. The long and the short of it is that I got caught completely off guard and Crita and I got knocked off a cliff ledge and into a shuttle pod. In all the ensuing chaos He-Man managed to get hold of my staff and used his power sword to trap myself and Crita in the shuttle pod and exile us into space. It really wasn't worth it, and neither will it be in your case. Just walk away. The best revenge is to go on and be happy ...**Bwa ha ha ha ha ha ha ha.**"*

I feel so guilty over my affair

I love my wife very much, but I have been cheating on her with a woman at work for 6 months now.

I am 35 and my wife is 34 and we have been married for ten years.

I am really ashamed of my actions but as much as I'd like to end my affair and put things right I can't bring myself to face the music. Also, the woman I have been seeing has threatened to tell my wife everything if I call it off with her. What should I do?

Mike Yoghurt-Pot, Norwich

Skeletor says...

"If there's one thing I've learned in my time as an intergalactic warlord, it's that honesty is the best policy. I remember once I fooled the Galactic Guardian Hydron into thinking I was the force for good that he needed to save his home planet Primus, when in fact it was actually He-Man. To cut a long story short, he couldn't decide who was good and who was evil, so transported us both to the future.

My evil nature was eventually found out, but if I was just honest in the first place I wouldn't have been exiled through time and space.

*Tell your wife yourself, don't let her hear it from someone else. It will show that you are being honest and can perhaps be trusted again, and it will take the power away from this other woman ...**Bwa ha ha ha ha ha ha.**"*

Dear Skeletor,

Planetary toppling tips

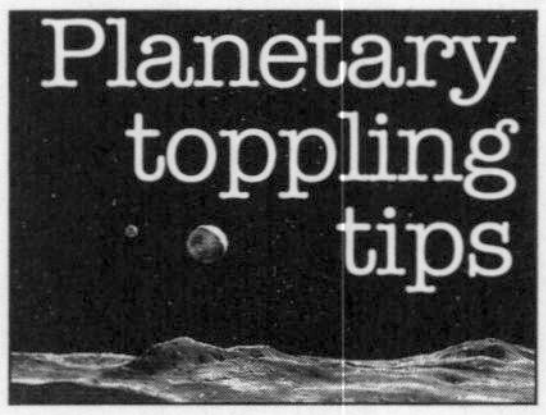

I need to defeat an evil overlord who has taken possession of my planet. Any tips?

Vorg, Quandar

Skeletor says...

*"The best way to defeat an enemy of any description is magic. I learned black magic from Hordak the powerful warlord of Eternia's sister planet Etheria, and it served me well. Also, there are power-giving crystals to be found on some moons. I don't know where your nearest galaxy is, but I found one once on Moon Nordor. I simply absorbed its energies, and it made me more powerful and evil than ever before. Good luck and let me know how it goes ...**Bwa ha ha ha ha ha ha.**"*

Skeletor's Photo Casebook

Xanthia's holiday romance - Day 3

Xanthia, Queen of the Tree People has had a holiday romance with Fernandium, a waiter on the planet Necronia. Now she feels guilty for cheating on her boyfriend Zagros, the Beastmaster...

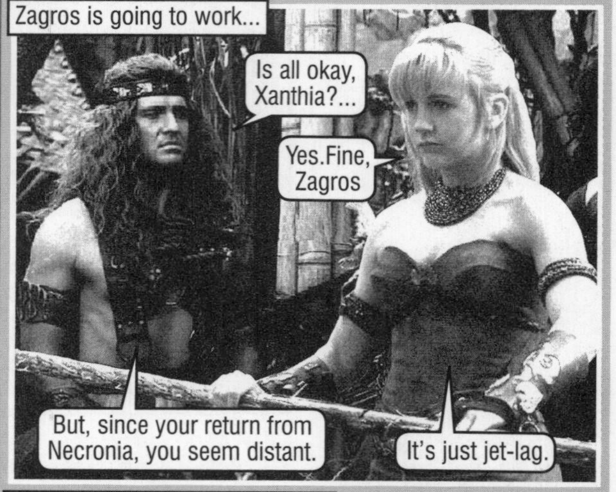

Zagros is going to work...
Is all okay, Xanthia?...
Yes.Fine, Zagros
But, since your return from Necronia, you seem distant.
It's just jet-lag.

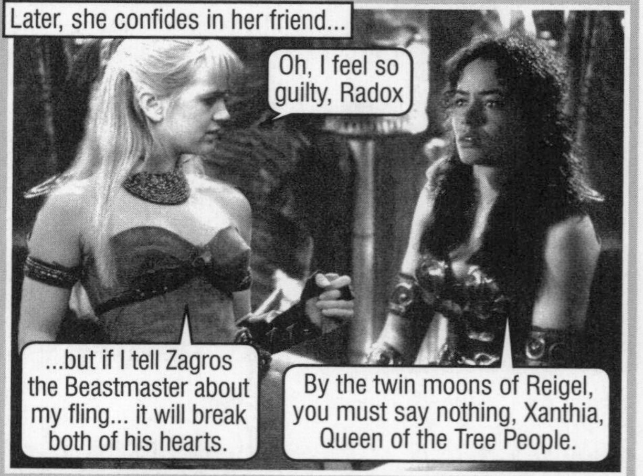

Later, she confides in her friend...
Oh, I feel so guilty, Radox
...but if I tell Zagros the Beastmaster about my fling... it will break both of his hearts.
By the twin moons of Reigel, you must say nothing, Xanthia, Queen of the Tree People.

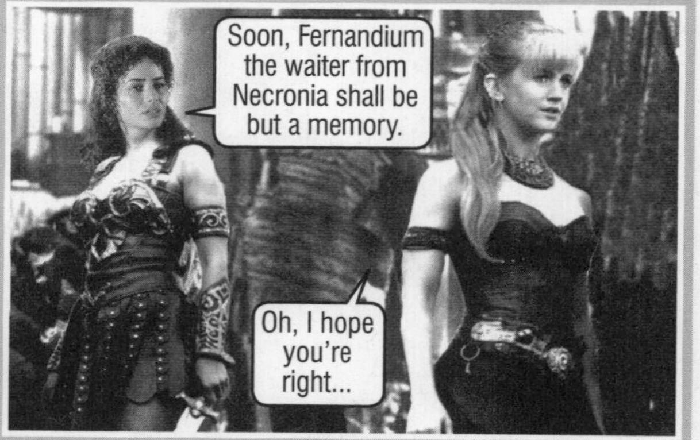

Soon, Fernandium the waiter from Necronia shall be but a memory.
Oh, I hope you're right...

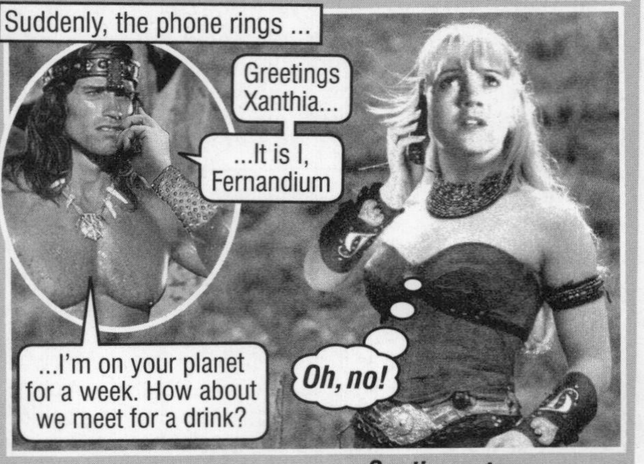

Suddenly, the phone rings ...
Greetings Xanthia...
...It is I, Fernandium
...I'm on your planet for a week. How about we meet for a drink?
Oh, no!

Continues tomorrow...

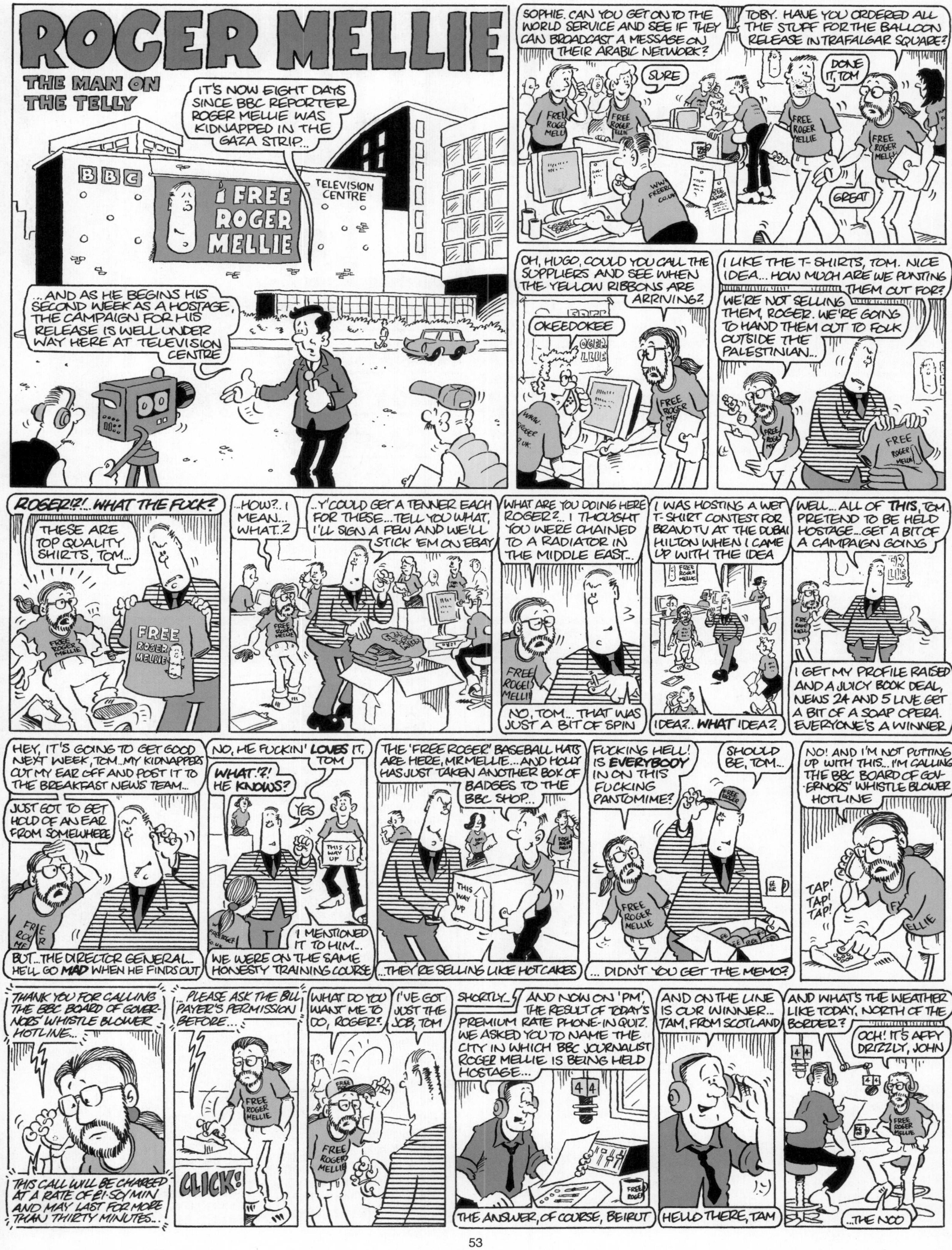

ROGER MELLIE
THE MAN ON THE TELLY
IT'S NOW EIGHT DAYS SINCE BBC REPORTER ROGER MELLIE WAS KIDNAPPED IN THE GAZA STRIP...
BBC
FREE ROGER MELLIE
TELEVISION CENTRE
...AND AS HE BEGINS HIS SECOND WEEK AS A HOSTAGE, THE CAMPAIGN FOR HIS RELEASE IS WELL UNDER WAY HERE AT TELEVISION CENTRE
SOPHIE. CAN YOU GET ON TO THE WORLD SERVICE AND SEE IF THEY CAN BROADCAST A MESSAGE ON THEIR ARABIC NETWORK?
SURE
TOBY. HAVE YOU ORDERED ALL THE STUFF FOR THE BALLOON RELEASE IN TRAFALGAR SQUARE?
DONE IT, TOM
GREAT
OH, HUGO, COULD YOU CALL THE SUPPLIERS AND SEE WHEN THE YELLOW RIBBONS ARE ARRIVING?
OKEEDOKEE
I LIKE THE T-SHIRTS, TOM. NICE IDEA... HOW MUCH ARE WE PUNTING THEM OUT FOR?
WE'RE NOT SELLING THEM, ROGER. WE'RE GOING TO HAND THEM OUT TO FOLK OUTSIDE THE PALESTINIAN...
ROGER!?!... WHAT THE FUCK?
THESE ARE TOP QUALITY SHIRTS, TOM...
FREE ROGER MELLIE
...HOW?.. I MEAN... WHAT..?
...Y'COULD GET A TENNER EACH FOR THESE... TELL YOU WHAT, I'LL SIGN A FEW AND WE'LL STICK 'EM ON EBAY
WHAT ARE YOU DOING HERE ROGER?.. I THOUGHT YOU WERE CHAINED TO A RADIATOR IN THE MIDDLE EAST...
NO, TOM... THAT WAS JUST A BIT OF SPIN
I WAS HOSTING A WET T-SHIRT CONTEST FOR BRAVO TV AT THE DUBAI HILTON WHEN I CAME UP WITH THE IDEA
IDEA?.. WHAT IDEA?
WELL... ALL OF THIS, TOM. PRETEND TO BE HELD HOSTAGE... GET A BIT OF A CAMPAIGN GOING
I GET MY PROFILE RAISED AND A JUICY BOOK DEAL, NEWS 24 AND 5 LIVE GET A BIT OF A SOAP OPERA. EVERYONE'S A WINNER
HEY, IT'S GOING TO GET GOOD NEXT WEEK, TOM... MY KIDNAPPERS CUT MY EAR OFF AND POST IT TO THE BREAKFAST NEWS TEAM...
JUST GOT TO GET HOLD OF AN EAR FROM SOMEWHERE
BUT... THE DIRECTOR GENERAL... HE'LL GO MAD WHEN HE FINDS OUT
NO, HE FUCKIN' LOVES IT, TOM
WHAT!?! HE KNOWS?
YES
THIS WAY UP
I MENTIONED IT TO HIM...
WE WERE ON THE SAME HONESTY TRAINING COURSE
THE 'FREE ROGER' BASEBALL HATS ARE HERE, MR MELLIE... AND HOLLY HAS JUST TAKEN ANOTHER BOX OF BADGES TO THE BBC SHOP...
THIS WAY UP
...THEY'RE SELLING LIKE HOTCAKES
FUCKING HELL! IS EVERYBODY IN ON THIS FUCKING PANTOMIME?
SHOULD BE, TOM...
...DIDN'T YOU GET THE MEMO?
NO! AND I'M NOT PUTTING UP WITH THIS... I'M CALLING THE BBC BOARD OF GOVERNORS' WHISTLE BLOWER HOTLINE
TAP! TAP! TAP!
THANK YOU FOR CALLING THE BBC BOARD OF GOVERNORS' WHISTLE BLOWER HOTLINE...
THIS CALL WILL BE CHARGED AT A RATE OF £1·50/MIN AND MAY LAST FOR MORE THAN THIRTY MINUTES...
...PLEASE ASK THE BILL PAYER'S PERMISSION BEFORE...
CLICK!
WHAT DO YOU WANT ME TO DO, ROGER?
I'VE GOT JUST THE JOB, TOM
SHORTLY...
AND NOW ON 'PM', THE RESULT OF TODAY'S PREMIUM RATE PHONE-IN QUIZ. WE ASKED YOU TO NAME THE CITY IN WHICH BBC JOURNALIST ROGER MELLIE IS BEING HELD HOSTAGE...
THE ANSWER, OF COURSE, BEIRUT
AND ON THE LINE IS OUR WINNER... TAM, FROM SCOTLAND
HELLO THERE, TAM
AND WHAT'S THE WEATHER LIKE TODAY, NORTH OF THE BORDER?
OCH! IT'S AFFY DRIZZLY, JOHN
...THE NOO

8 Years After the Showbiz Accident that Shook the World, there are Still More Questions than Answers. It's Time to Ask...

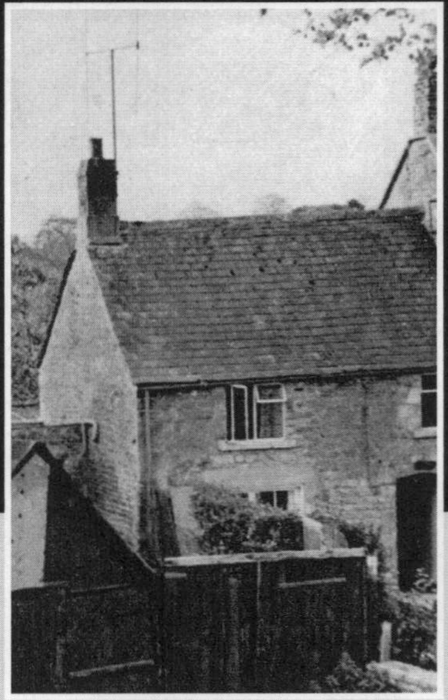

HOW DID HULL DIE?

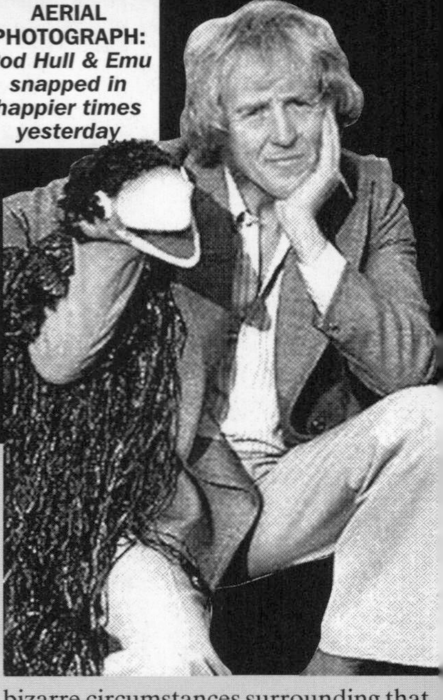

AERIAL PHOTOGRAPH: *Rod Hull & Emu snapped in happier times yesterday*

We re-open the Inquest of the Century

ON MARCH 17th 1999, Emu puppeteer ROD HULL settled down at his home in Winchelsea to watch Manchester United take on Inter Milan in the second leg of the Champions' League quarter final. Half way through the match, Hull's television picture suddenly went fuzzy and the 63-year-old entertainer made the fateful decision to climb up onto his roof and adjust the aerial. The sequence of events that happened next remains shrouded in mystery.

The official version is that Hull somehow lost his footing, and tumbled off the roof and fell thirty feet to the ground. Following an official inquest, the Sussex Coroner recorded a verdict of Accidental Death.

But many people feel that this was a cover-up. They say that there was more to Hull's tragic death than met the eye. Barely had his aerial stopped wobbling before conspiracy theorists began asking questions. They wanted to know how a perfectly healthy 63-year-old could simply fall to his death whilst clambering around in his slippers on a wet roof in the pitch dark. It just didn't make sense. Was it simply a combination of a low co-efficient of friction and gravity, or were more sinister forces at work?

In the 8 years since Hull's supposedly accidental death, many theories have been put forward to explain the bizarre circumstances surrounding that night. For the first time, we collect together all these theories and put them before retired Old Bailey coroner Hazelnut Monkbottle, QC.

Drawing on decades of experience, Monkbottle will assess the evidence in each case before delivering a final verdict on the REAL cause of Rod Hull's death. And his astounding conclusion is set to send shockwaves through the showbiz world.

THE VIZ INQUEST | PRESIDING: His Honour, Mr Justice Hazelnut Monkbottle QC

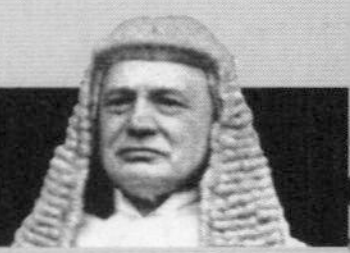

EXPLANATION ONE
The Parkie Hypothesis

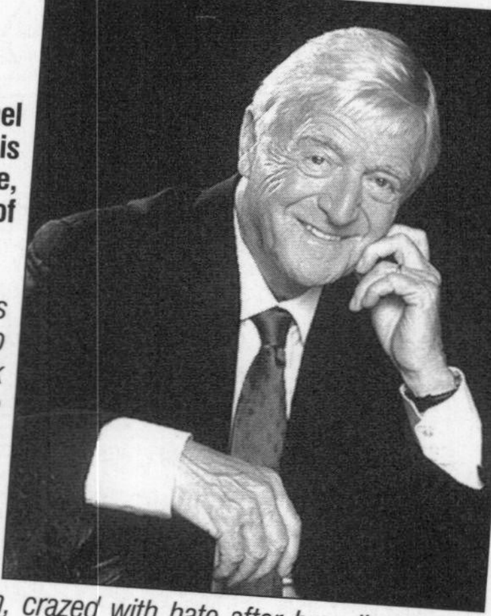

THEORY: That BBC presenter Michael Parkinson, humiliated by Hull on his infamous 1976 chatshow appearance, engineered Hull's death as an act of revenge.

In video footage of his mauling at Hull's hands, Parkinson can clearly be heard to say "If he comes near me again, I'll break his bloody neck." Most people took the interviewer's live TV death threat as a humorous comment directed at Hull's out-of-control Emu puppet. But was it really so light-hearted? Could it be that the comment was actually directed at Hull himself? The theory states that Parkinson, crazed with hate after brooding for 23 years over his humiliation and lost shoe, sneaked inside Hull's home whilst the Antipodean entertainer was out, before smearing butter onto the soles of his slippers. Biding his time, Parkinson then concealed himself in the garden and waited until Hull returned later that evening to watch the football match on television. At a critical point during the game, Parkinson somehow dislodged Hull's TV aerial, luring the safari-suited puppeteer onto the roof to fix it. With butter on the soles of his slippers, there was only ever going to be one outcome.

MONKBOTTLE'S VERDICT: The Parkie Hypothesis is a compelling one. The Yorkshireman certainly had both motive and opportunity to commit this heinous crime. He would have had access to butter at the BBC canteen and his well love of cricket would mean he could easily throw a ball accurately enough to hit a TV aerial. But without a piece of 'smoking gun' evidence, such as a butter knife in Hull's garden with Parkie's fingerprints on it, or a receipt for a dozen cricket balls bought that day, we cannot state with any certainty whether he was guilty of Hull's premeditated murder. They say that revenge is a dish best served cold, but only Parkie knows if he served it up to Rod Hull up on his roof on that cold March night in 1999.

EXPLANATION TWO
The Manchurian Candidate Theory

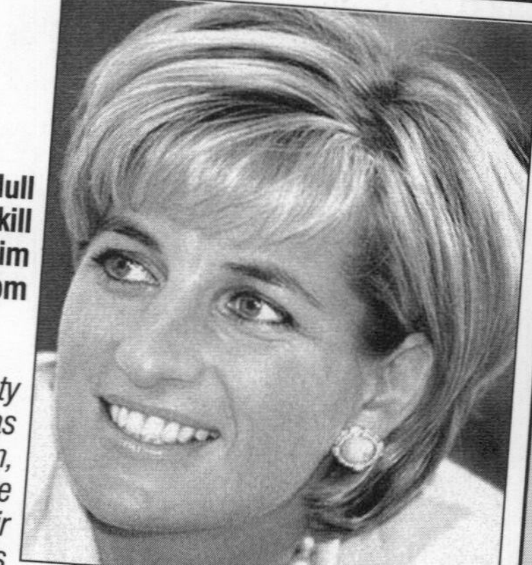

THEORY: That MI6, believing that Hull had information about a Royal plot to kill the Princess of Wales, brainwashed him into committing suicide by jumping from his own roof.

Rod Hull appeared at the 1972 Royal Variety Performance. Theorists believe that it was here, backstage at the London Palladium, that he overheard the Queen and Prince Philip discussing a plan to assassinate their future daughter-in-law. Two years after this plan was carried out in Paris, and afraid that Hull was about to go public with what he knew, MI6 decided to 'take him out'. When Hull called a taxi three weeks before the match, the driver, an MI6 psy-ops agent, took him to a secret base like in The Avengers. There he was subjected to brainwashing for 48 hours before being returned home with no memory of what had taken place. Unwittingly, the entertainer had become a 'sleeper', programmed to climb onto his roof and jump off when he heard the trigger phrase "it's one-nil on the night to the Italians". After 63 minutes of the televised match, Ventola scored for Inter, and Hull's fate was sealed. Like an automaton, he climbed up the drainpipe of his house onto the roof, and leapt to his death.

MONKBOTTLE'S VERDICT: The Manchurian Candidate theory is intriguing, but after examining it carefully, I find that it asks more questions than it answers. Certainly, it is possible that the Royal family and MI6 wanted Hull out of the way because of what he knew about Diana's murder. But if Manchester United had scored first on that fateful evening, then the Secret Service's plan would have come to nothing. Of course, it is possible that the Red Devils' coach driver was also an MI6 psy-ops agent, and he somehow brainwashed the team into allowing their opponents to gain the upper hand in the 63rd minute. The only people who can say for certain whether this is the case are The Queen and Prince Philip, and something tells me that their lips will remain sealed.

EXPLANATION THREE
The Duck Scenario

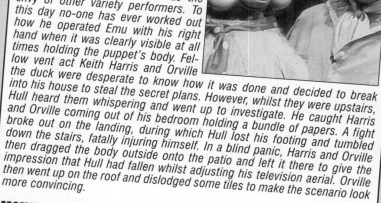

THEORY: Keith Harris and Orville the duck broke into Hull's house, but were discovered. In the ensuing tussle, Hull fell down the stairs and was killed.

Throughout his career, Hull was the envy of other variety performers. To this day no-one has ever worked out how he operated Emu with his right hand when it was clearly visible at all times holding the puppet's body. Fellow vent act Keith Harris and Orville the duck were desperate to know how it was done and decided to break into his house to steal the secret plans. However, whilst they were upstairs, Hull heard them whispering and went up to investigate. He caught Harris and Orville coming out of his bedroom holding a bundle of papers. A fight broke out on the landing, during which Hull lost his footing and tumbled down the stairs, fatally injuring himself. In a blind panic, Harris and Orville then dragged the body outside onto the patio and left it there to give the impression that Hull had fallen whilst adjusting his television aerial. Orville then went up on the roof and dislodged some tiles to make the scenario look more convincing.

MONKBOTTLE'S VERDICT: A very plausible explanation as to what happened, but without concrete evidence of this conspiracy it would be premature to point the finger of suspicion at Harris and his duck sidekick. It seems to me that the missing piece of the jigsaw is this: How did Orville get onto the roof to dislodge the tiles? In his 1981 hit, the incontinent, green duck clearly states that he is unable to fly - "I wish I could fly, right up to the sky, but I can't," he sings. However, when Orville recorded the song, he was not under oath, so this hearsay testimony is inadmissible in a coroner's court. Can Harris's accomplice fly? Did he use a ladder? Perhaps we will never know.

EXPLANATION FOUR
The Wrong Man Conjecture

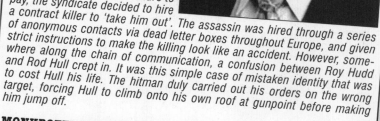

THEORY: A hit man was paid to kill ancient vauderville comic Roy Hudd. But he made a mistake and assassinated the similarly named Rod Hull.

Veteran comedian Roy Hudd could have run up huge debts betting on illegal whippet racing with a shady far-eastern gambling syndicate. The exact sums are unknown, but are conjectured to possibly have been several hundreds of pounds. Tired of Hudd's constant excuses for his failure to pay, the syndicate decided to hire a contract killer to 'take him out'. The assassin was hired through a series of anonymous contacts via dead letter boxes throughout Europe, and given strict instructions to make the killing look like an accident. However, somewhere along the chain of communication, a confusion between Roy Hudd and Rod Hull crept in. It was this simple case of mistaken identity that was to cost Hull his life. The hitman duly carried out his orders on the wrong target, forcing Hull to climb onto his own roof at gunpoint before making him jump off.

MONKBOTTLE'S VERDICT: It is tragic enough that Hull died, but it would be doubly tragic if he had been killed in Roy Hudd's place. The trouble with this theory is that is is so difficult to prove or disprove. As anyone who has seen The Day of the Jackal will know, European hitmen are extremely professional at their job, executing their orders with chilling and ruthless efficiency. What is certain is this: If the Wrong Man hypothesis is true, the perpetrator will have left not a shred of evidence behind. As a matter of urgency, the police should seize Roy Hudd's bank details to see if hundreds of pounds vanished into shady far-eastern gambling syndicate accounts in the late nineties.

EXPLANATION FIVE
The Rennes le Chateaux Connection

THEORY: Rod Hull was a direct descendant of Jesus Christ and Mary Magdalene. He met his death whilst being pursued by members of the secretive Opus Dei sect.

Rod Hull was watching the football on the TV when there was a knock at the door. He assumed that it was the man from Park Christmas Hampers come to collect his weekly payment. However, when he opened the door he was confronted by a cowled albino monk with piercing red eyes. Knowing he was the son of Jesus, it is likely that Hull had been expecting this visit all his life. The monk burst in and, thinking quickly, Hull pushed an amulet into his face causing it to sizzle. This action bought the frightened entertainer a few seconds, and he escaped by climbing up the inside of his chimney and up onto his roof. Once up there, he saw that his house was surrounded by a ring of chanting Knights Templar, Freemasons and Grand Masters of the Priory of Sion. In a final act of defiance and realising there was no escape, Hull flung himself off the roof rather than reveal the locations of the Holy Grail, the Spear of Destiny and the Turin Shroud. And the Ark of the Covenant.

MONKBOTTLE'S VERDICT: However far-fetched this theory may sound, it is still worthy of consideration. The more it is studied, the more facts appear that seem to support it. For instance, in the 1980s, the deceased man appeared in an ITV programme called Rod Hull and Emu's Pink Windmill Show. If you re-arrange the letters, they spell out the sinister message 'Hush. Opus Dei will kill damn Rod H' with just two Ns, a D and a W left over. These spare letters, if you take their position in the alphabet, add up to 57. If you then take away the digits in the date on which Hull died - 17, 3, 1999, you are left with the answer 9...the original number of Knights Templars when they were formed in 1118.

MONKBOTTLE'S SUMMING UP

I HAVE LOOKED carefully at the competing theories put before me and I have carefully weighed up all the facts and evidence. Did Rod Hull meet his death at the hands of Michael Parkinson? Was he caught up in the conspiracy to kill Lady Diana and hypnotised by Secret Service agents into taking his own life? Was he the victim of a tragic accident whilst being burgled by Keith Harris and Orville? Did he fall foul of a confused assassin? Or did he sacrifice himself to prevent precious holy relics falling into the hands of the Vatican?

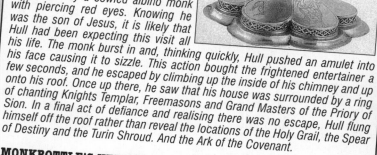

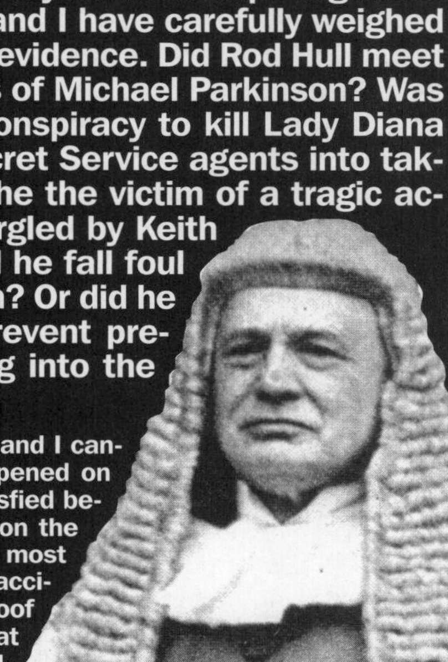

The fact is, nobody knows, and I cannot say for certain what happened on that night. However, I am satisfied beyond reasonable doubt that, on the balance of probability, it is most likely that Rod Hull died by accident after falling off his wet roof whilst adjusting his TV aerial at night wearing slippers. And I therefore return a verdict of Accidental Death.

...or was it?

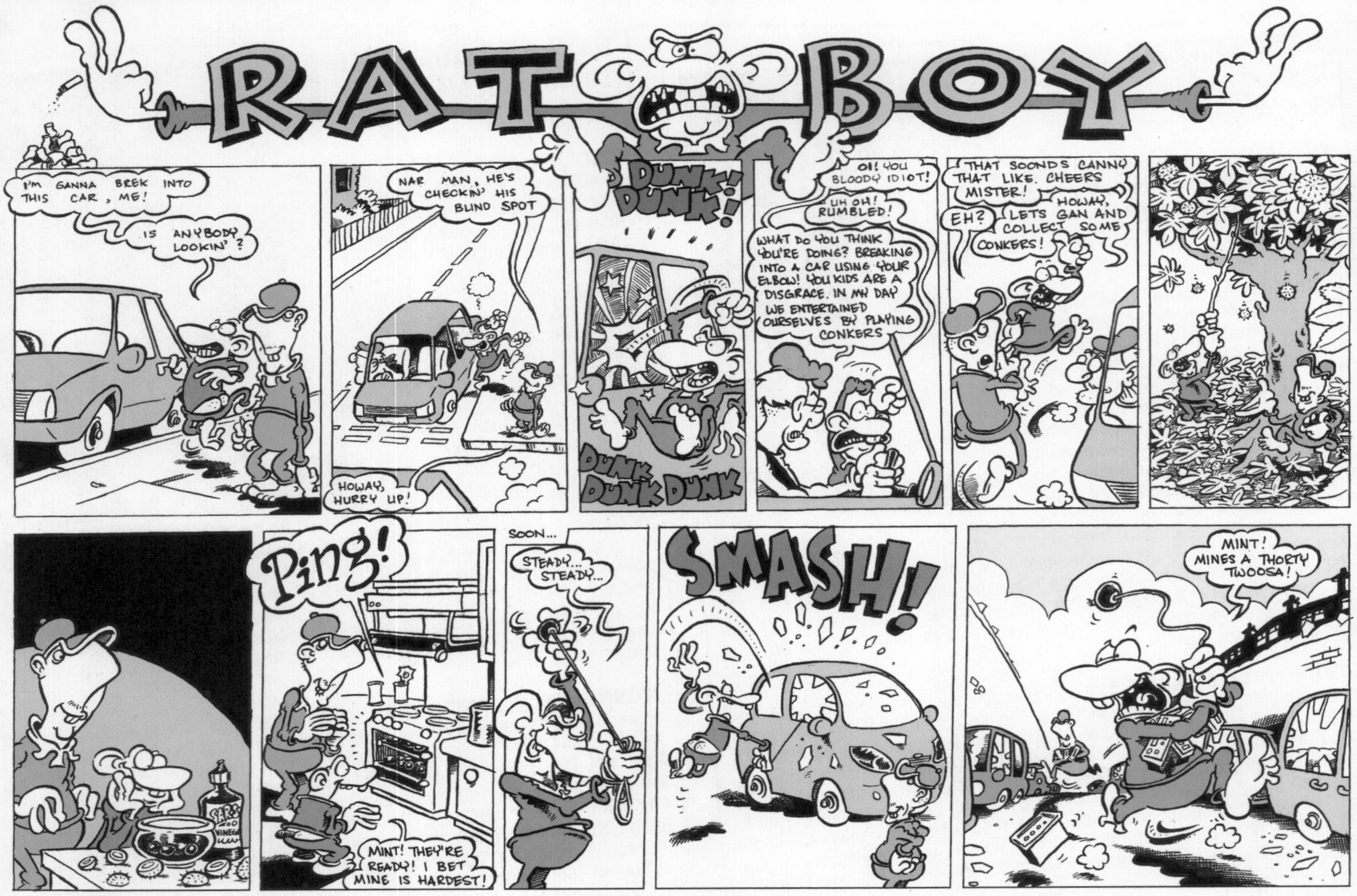
RAT BOY
I'M GANNA BREK INTO THIS CAR, ME!
IS ANYBODY LOOKIN'?
NAR MAN, HE'S CHECKIN' HIS BLIND SPOT
HOWAY, HURRY UP!
DUNK! DUNK!
DUNK DUNK DUNK
OI! YOU BLOODY IDIOT!
UH OH! RUMBLED!
WHAT DO YOU THINK YOU'RE DOING? BREAKING INTO A CAR USING YOUR ELBOW! YOU KIDS ARE A DISGRACE. IN MY DAY WE ENTERTAINED OURSELVES BY PLAYING CONKERS
THAT SOONDS CANNY THAT LIKE. CHEERS MISTER!
EH?
HOWAY, LETS GAN AND COLLECT SOME CONKERS!
Ping!
MINT! THEY'RE READY! I BET MINE IS HARDEST!
SOON...
STEADY... STEADY...
SMASH!
MINT! MINES A THORTY TWOOSA!

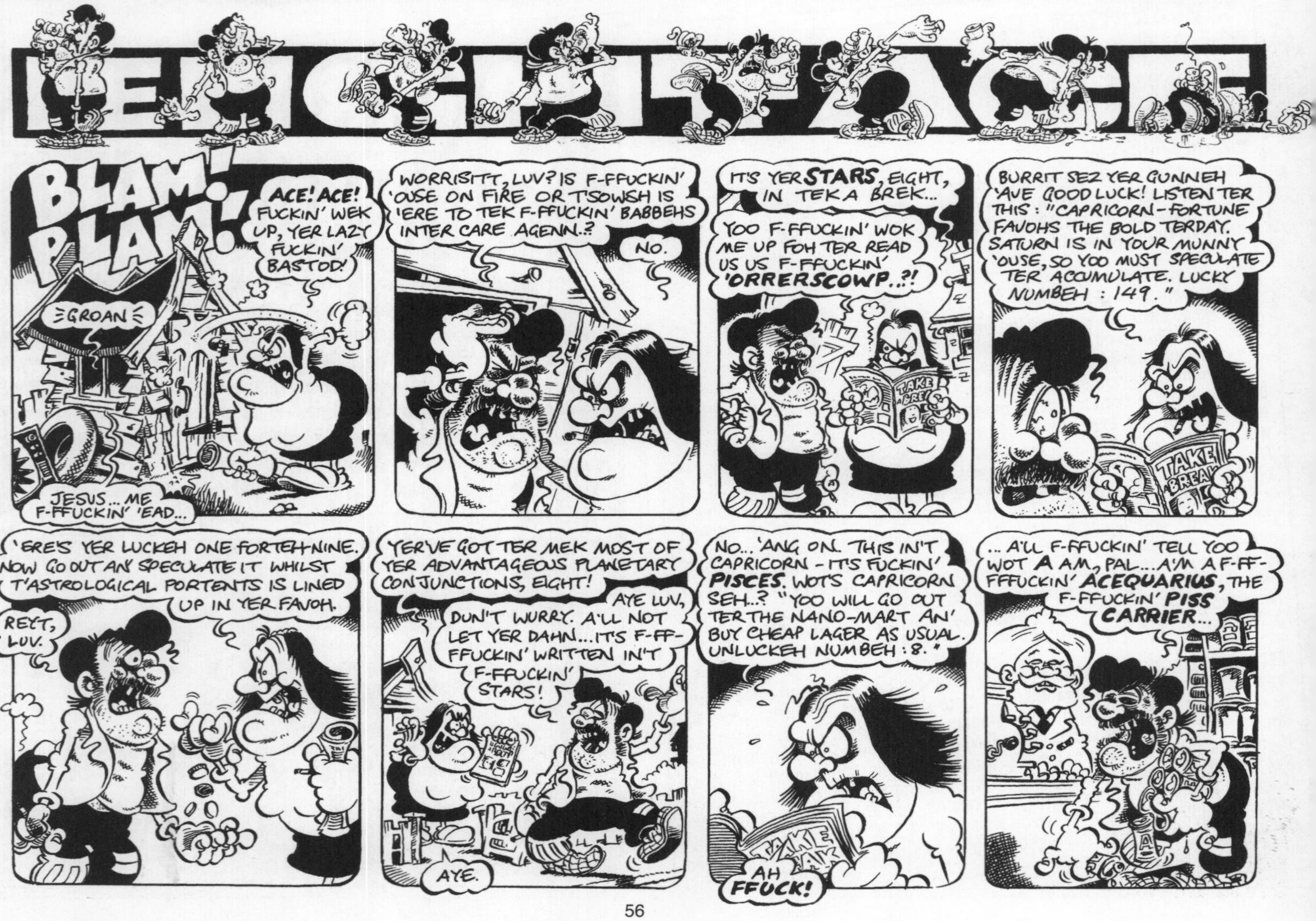
BLAM! PLAM!
ACE! ACE! FUCKIN' WEK UP, YER LAZY FUCKIN' BASTOD!
GROAN
JESUS... ME F-FFUCKIN' 'EAD...
WORRISITT, LUV? IS F-FFUCKIN' 'OUSE ON FIRE OR T'SOWSH IS 'ERE TO TEK F-FFUCKIN' BABBEHS INTER CARE AGENN..?
NO.
IT'S YER STARS, EIGHT, IN TEKA BREK...
YOO F-FFUCKIN' WOK ME UP FOH TER READ US US F-FFUCKIN' 'ORRERSCOWP..?!
BURRIT SEZ YER GUNNEH 'AVE GOOD LUCK! LISTEN TER THIS: "CAPRICORN - FORTUNE FAVOHS THE BOLD TERDAY. SATURN IS IN YOUR MUNNY 'OUSE, SO YOO MUST SPECULATE TER ACCUMULATE. LUCKY NUMBEH : 149."
'ERE'S YER LUCKEH ONE FORTEH NINE. NOW GO OUT AN' SPECULATE IT WHILST T'ASTROLOGICAL PORTENTS IS LINED UP IN YER FAVOH.
REYT, LUV.
YER'VE GOT TER MEK MOST OF YER ADVANTAGEOUS PLANETARY CONJUNCTIONS, EIGHT!
AYE LUV, DUN'T WURRY. A'LL NOT LET YER DAHN... IT'S F-FF-FFUCKIN' WRITTEN IN'T F-FFUCKIN' STARS!
AYE.
NO... 'ANG ON. THIS IN'T CAPRICORN - IT'S FUCKIN' PISCES. WOT'S CAPRICORN SEH..? "YOO WILL GO OUT TER THE NANO-MART AN' BUY CHEAP LAGER AS USUAL. UNLUCKEH NUMBEH : 8."
AH FFUCK!
... A'LL F-FFUCKIN' TELL YOO WOT A AM, PAL... A'M A F-FF-FFFUCKIN' ACEQUARIUS, THE F-FFUCKIN' PISS CARRIER...

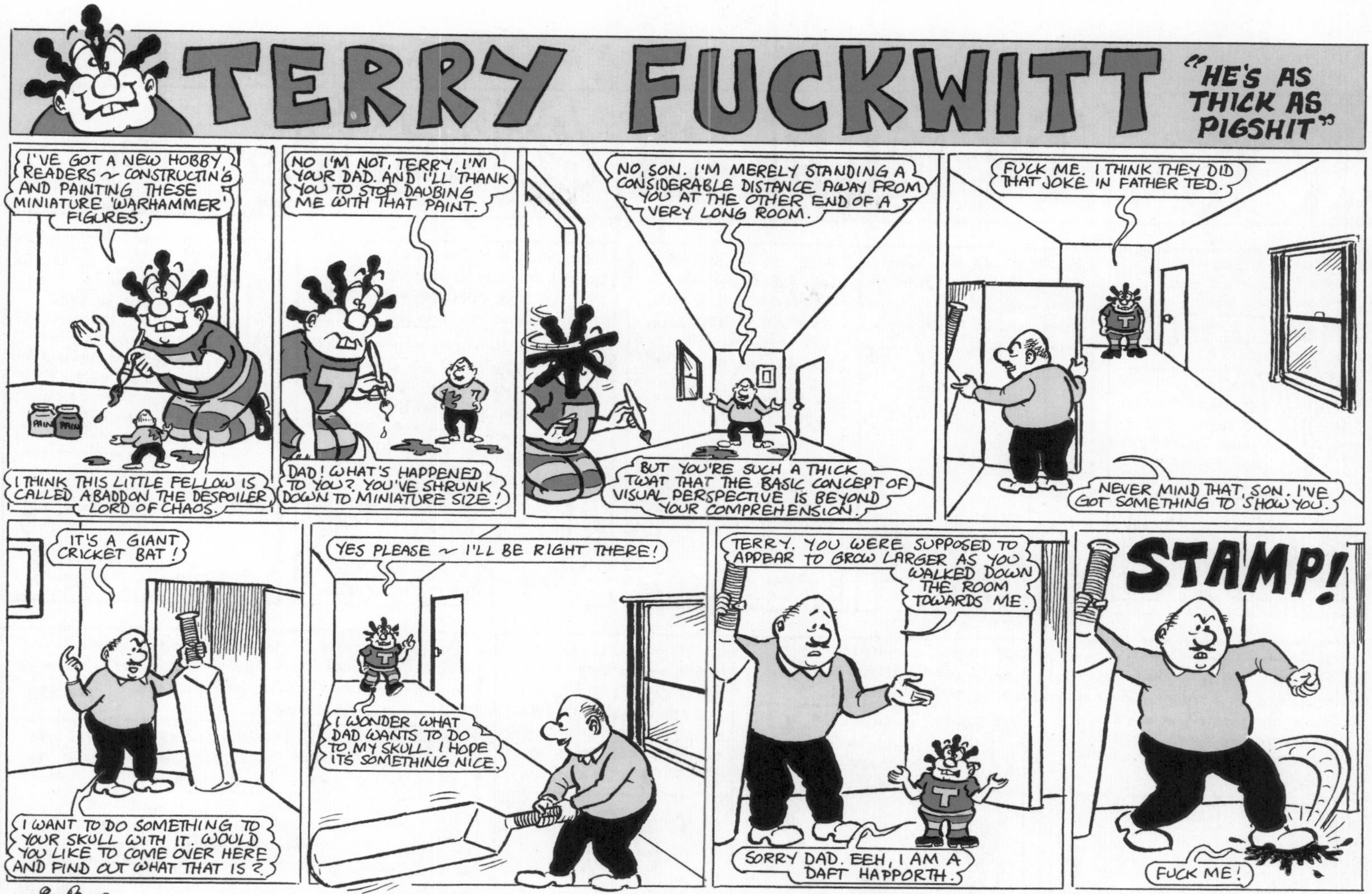
TERRY FUCKWITT
"HE'S AS THICK AS PIGSHIT"
I'VE GOT A NEW HOBBY READERS ~ CONSTRUCTING AND PAINTING THESE MINIATURE 'WARHAMMER' FIGURES.
PAINT
PAINT
I THINK THIS LITTLE FELLOW IS CALLED ABADDON THE DESPOILER LORD OF CHAOS.
NO I'M NOT, TERRY, I'M YOUR DAD. AND I'LL THANK YOU TO STOP DAUBING ME WITH THAT PAINT.
DAD! WHAT'S HAPPENED TO YOU? YOU'VE SHRUNK DOWN TO MINIATURE SIZE!
NO, SON. I'M MERELY STANDING A CONSIDERABLE DISTANCE AWAY FROM YOU AT THE OTHER END OF A VERY LONG ROOM.
BUT YOU'RE SUCH A THICK TWAT THAT THE BASIC CONCEPT OF VISUAL PERSPECTIVE IS BEYOND YOUR COMPREHENSION.
FUCK ME. I THINK THEY DID THAT JOKE IN FATHER TED.
NEVER MIND THAT, SON. I'VE GOT SOMETHING TO SHOW YOU.
IT'S A GIANT CRICKET BAT!
I WANT TO DO SOMETHING TO YOUR SKULL WITH IT. WOULD YOU LIKE TO COME OVER HERE AND FIND OUT WHAT THAT IS?
YES PLEASE ~ I'LL BE RIGHT THERE!
I WONDER WHAT DAD WANTS TO DO TO MY SKULL. I HOPE IT'S SOMETHING NICE.
TERRY. YOU WERE SUPPOSED TO APPEAR TO GROW LARGER AS YOU WALKED DOWN THE ROOM TOWARDS ME.
SORRY DAD. EEH, I AM A DAFT HAPPORTH.
STAMP!
FUCK ME!

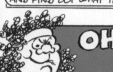

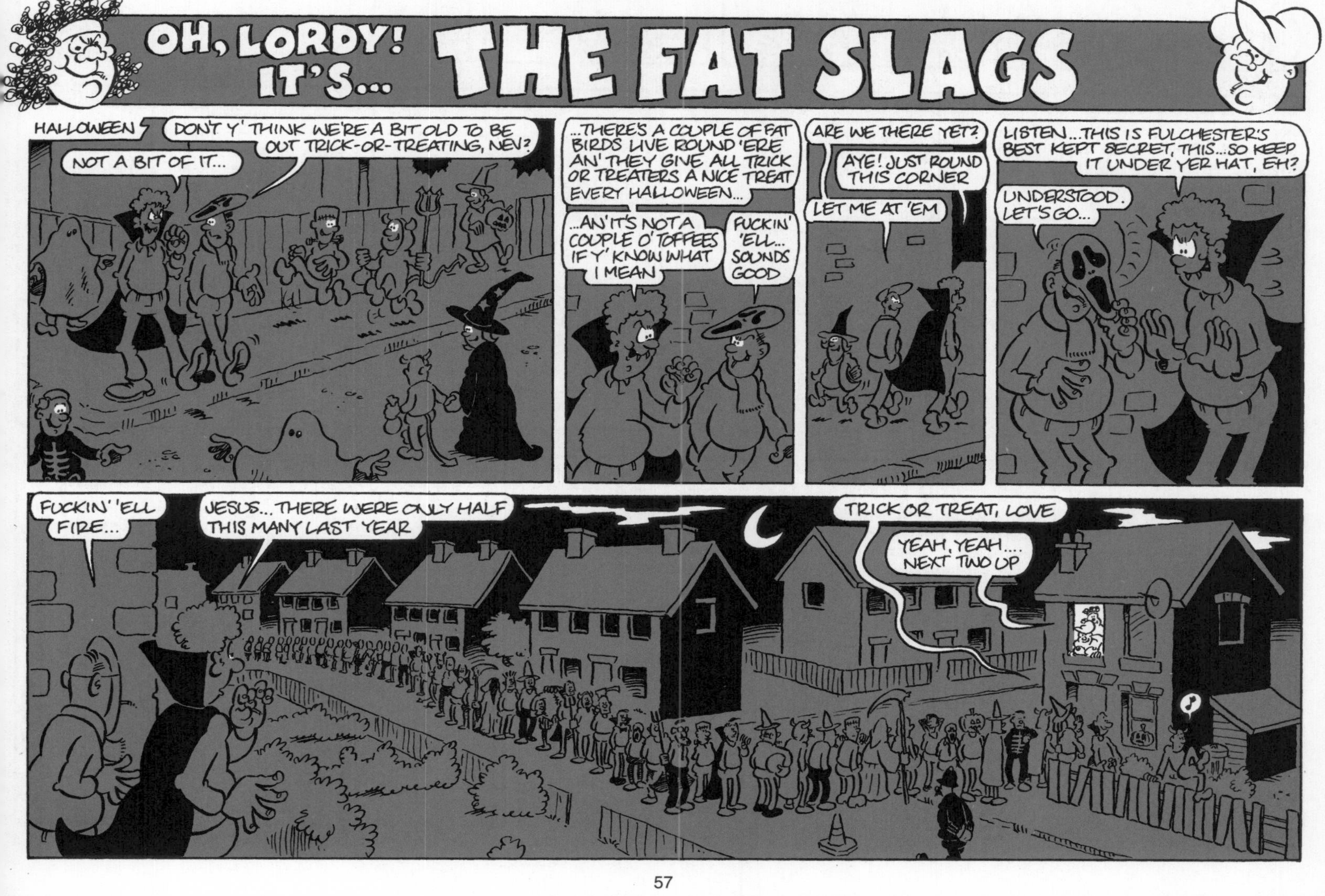
OH, LORDY! IT'S... THE FAT SLAGS
HALLOWEEN
DON'T Y' THINK WE'RE A BIT OLD TO BE OUT TRICK-OR-TREATING, NEV?
NOT A BIT OF IT...
...THERE'S A COUPLE OF FAT BIRDS LIVE ROUND 'ERE AN' THEY GIVE ALL TRICK OR TREATERS A NICE TREAT EVERY HALLOWEEN...
...AN' IT'S NOT A COUPLE O' TOFFEES IF Y' KNOW WHAT I MEAN
FUCKIN' 'ELL SOUNDS GOOD
ARE WE THERE YET?
AYE! JUST ROUND THIS CORNER
LET ME AT 'EM
LISTEN...THIS IS FULCHESTER'S BEST KEPT SECRET, THIS...SO KEEP IT UNDER YER HAT, EH?
UNDERSTOOD. LET'S GO...
FUCKIN' 'ELL FIRE...
JESUS...THERE WERE ONLY HALF THIS MANY LAST YEAR
TRICK OR TREAT, LOVE
YEAH, YEAH.... NEXT TWO UP

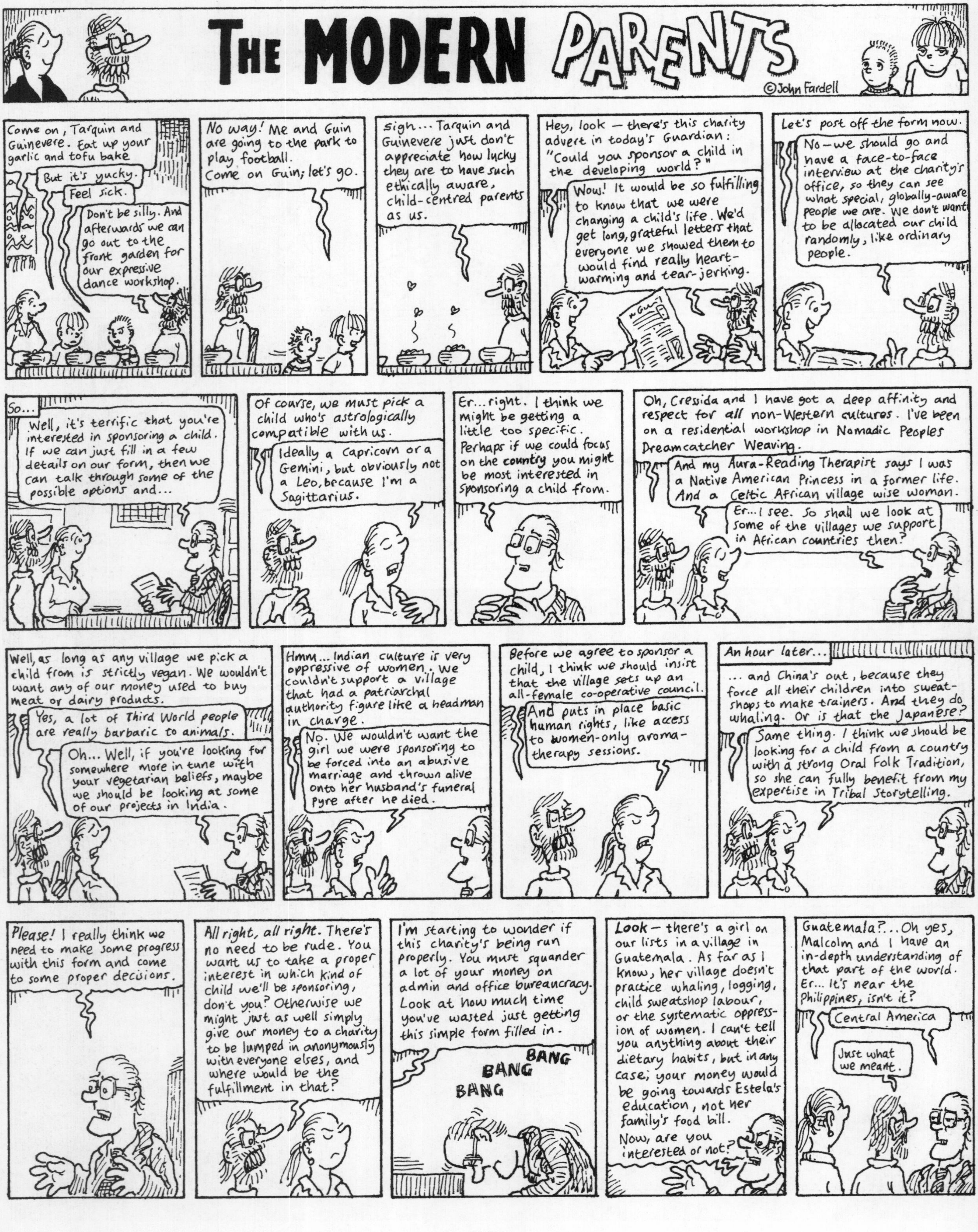
THE MODERN PARENTS
©John Fardell
Come on, Tarquin and Guinevere. Eat up your garlic and tofu bake.
But it's yucky.
Feel sick.
Don't be silly. And afterwards we can go out to the front garden for our expressive dance workshop.
No way! Me and Guin are going to the park to play football. Come on Guin; let's go.
sigh... Tarquin and Guinevere just don't appreciate how lucky they are to have such ethically aware, child-centred parents as us.
Hey, look — there's this charity advert in today's Guardian: "Could you sponsor a child in the developing world?"
Wow! It would be so fulfilling to know that we were changing a child's life. We'd get long, grateful letters that everyone we showed them to would find really heart-warming and tear-jerking.
Let's post off the form now.
No—we should go and have a face-to-face interview at the charity's office, so they can see what special, globally-aware people we are. We don't want to be allocated our child randomly, like ordinary people.
So...
Well, it's terrific that you're interested in sponsoring a child. If we can just fill in a few details on our form, then we can talk through some of the possible options and...
Of course, we must pick a child who's astrologically compatible with us.
Ideally a Capricorn or a Gemini, but obviously not a Leo, because I'm a Sagittarius.
Er... right. I think we might be getting a little too specific. Perhaps if we could focus on the country you might be most interested in sponsoring a child from.
Oh, Cressida and I have got a deep affinity and respect for all non-Western cultures. I've been on a residential workshop in Nomadic Peoples Dreamcatcher Weaving.
And my Aura-Reading Therapist says I was a Native American Princess in a former life. And a Celtic African village wise woman.
Er... I see. So shall we look at some of the villages we support in African countries then?
Well, as long as any village we pick a child from is strictly vegan. We wouldn't want any of our money used to buy meat or dairy products.
Yes, a lot of Third World people are really barbaric to animals.
Oh... Well, if you're looking for somewhere more in tune with your vegetarian beliefs, maybe we should be looking at some of our projects in India.
Hmm... Indian culture is very oppressive of women. We couldn't support a village that had a patriarchal authority figure like a headman in charge.
No. We wouldn't want the girl we were sponsoring to be forced into an abusive marriage and thrown alive onto her husband's funeral pyre after he died.
Before we agree to sponsor a child, I think we should insist that the village sets up an all-female co-operative council.
And puts in place basic human rights, like access to women-only aroma-therapy sessions.
An hour later...
... and China's out, because they force all their children into sweat-shops to make trainers. And they do whaling. Or is that the Japanese?
Same thing. I think we should be looking for a child from a country with a strong Oral Folk Tradition, so she can fully benefit from my expertise in Tribal Storytelling.
Please! I really think we need to make some progress with this form and come to some proper decisions.
All right, all right. There's no need to be rude. You want us to take a proper interest in which kind of child we'll be sponsoring, don't you? Otherwise we might just as well simply give our money to a charity to be lumped in anonymously with everyone elses, and where would be the fulfillment in that?
I'm starting to wonder if this charity's being run properly. You must squander a lot of your money on admin and office bureaucracy. Look at how much time you've wasted just getting this simple form filled in.
BANG
BANG
BANG
Look — there's a girl on our lists in a village in Guatemala. As far as I know, her village doesn't practice whaling, logging, child sweatshop labour, or the systematic oppression of women. I can't tell you anything about their dietary habits, but in any case, your money would be going towards Estela's education, not her family's food bill. Now, are you interested or not?
Guatemala?... Oh yes, Malcolm and I have an in-depth understanding of that part of the world. Er... It's near the Philippines, isn't it?
Central America
Just what we meant.

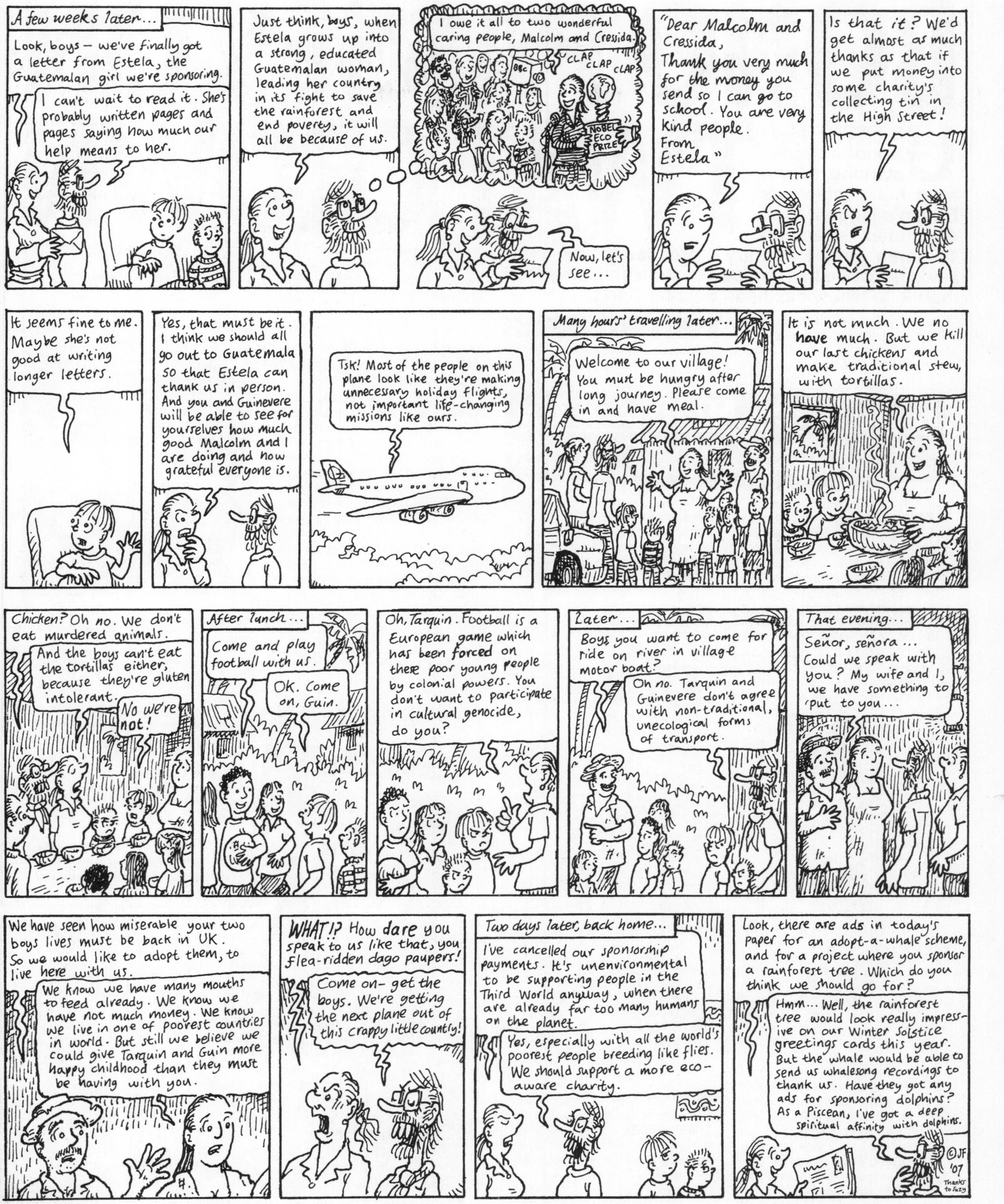
A few weeks later...
Look, boys – we've finally got a letter from Estela, the Guatemalan girl we're sponsoring.
I can't wait to read it. She's probably written pages and pages saying how much our help means to her.
Just think, boys, when Estela grows up into a strong, educated Guatemalan woman, leading her country in its fight to save the rainforest and end poverty, it will all be because of us.
I owe it all to two wonderful caring people, Malcolm and Cressida.
BBC
CLAP CLAP CLAP
NOBEL ECO PRIZE
Now, let's see...
"Dear Malcolm and Cressida, Thank you very much for the money you send so I can go to school. You are very kind people. From Estela"
Is that it? We'd get almost as much thanks as that if we put money into some charity's collecting tin in the High Street!
It seems fine to me. Maybe she's not good at writing longer letters.
Yes, that must be it. I think we should all go out to Guatemala so that Estela can thank us in person. And you and Guinevere will be able to see for yourselves how much good Malcolm and I are doing and how grateful everyone is.
Tsk! Most of the people on this plane look like they're making unnecessary holiday flights, not important life-changing missions like ours.
Many hours' travelling later...
Welcome to our village! You must be hungry after long journey. Please come in and have meal.
It is not much. We no have much. But we kill our last chickens and make traditional stew, with tortillas.
Chicken? Oh no. We don't eat murdered animals.
And the boys can't eat the tortillas either, because they're gluten intolerant.
No we're not!
After lunch...
Come and play football with us.
OK. Come on, Guin.
Oh, Tarquin. Football is a European game which has been forced on these poor young people by colonial powers. You don't want to participate in cultural genocide, do you?
Later...
Boys you want to come for ride on river in village motor boat?
Oh no. Tarquin and Guinevere don't agree with non-traditional, unecological forms of transport.
That evening...
Señor, señora... Could we speak with you? My wife and I, we have something to put to you...
We have seen how miserable your two boys lives must be back in UK. So we would like to adopt them, to live here with us.
We know we have many mouths to feed already. We know we have not much money. We know we live in one of poorest countries in world. But still we believe we could give Tarquin and Guin more happy childhood than they must be having with you.
WHAT!? How dare you speak to us like that, you flea-ridden dago paupers!
Come on – get the boys. We're getting the next plane out of this crappy little country!
Two days later, back home...
I've cancelled our sponsorship payments. It's unenvironmental to be supporting people in the Third World anyway, when there are already far too many humans on the planet.
Yes, especially with all the world's poorest people breeding like flies. We should support a more eco-aware charity.
Look, there are ads in today's paper for an adopt-a-whale scheme, and for a project where you sponsor a rainforest tree. Which do you think we should go for?
Hmm... Well, the rainforest tree would look really impressive on our Winter Solstice greetings cards this year. But the whale would be able to send us whalesong recordings to thank us. Have they got any ads for sponsoring dolphins? As a Piscean, I've got a deep spiritual affinity with dolphins.
©JF '07
Thanks to Suzy

BONO PASSES ON TWAT CROWN

U2 FRONT MAN Bono has finally stepped down from his position as Britain's biggest twat. And after spending 10 years as the country's premier tit, the pint-sized gobshite has decided to pass on his wanker mantle to fellow dickhead popstar Sting.

TWAXCLUSIVE

"I've had a fantastic decade as the UK's biggest tosspot," he told Radio 4's Jim Naughtie. "I've made cringe-worthy speeches at the Labour Party conference, I've campaigned on green issues whilst having my hat flown halfway across the world in a jumbo jet and I've used my vast wealth to pursue former employees through the courts for the return of a pair of trousers."

"I've acted like an absolute bellend to the best of my abilities, but now it's time to take a back seat," he added.

Bono refused to speculate on who would take over from him as the UK's foremost twat, but analysts believe it is practically certain that the appointment will go to his fellow arsehole Sting. "Sting's got all the right credentials," an insider told us. "He bangs on about environmental issues whilst advertising Jaguar cars and Concorde, he says he lives simply but he's got two butlers and a private jet, and he reckons that cancer is caused by 'undigested dreams'. The man is an utter tool."

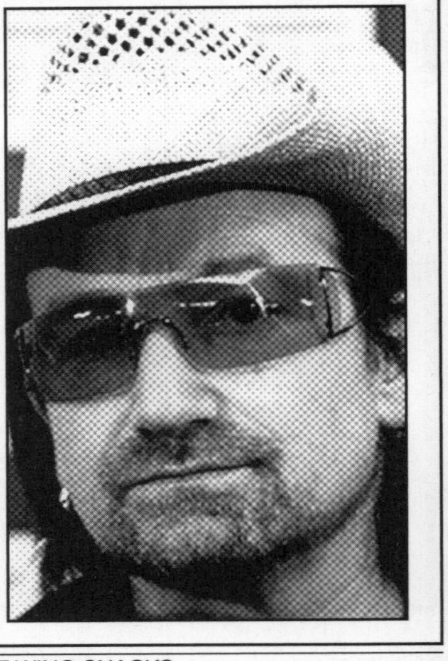

How They Measure Up

ALTHOUGH they are both equally twattish, Sting and Bono couldn't differ more in their physical dimensions.

AT 5′4″, ***STING*** towers 6″ above 4′10″ ***BONO***. However, when it comes to weight, the U2 singer beats his Police counterpart hands down, tipping the scales at 16 stone against his rival's 14 stone 8lb. Comparing armspan, there's nothing between them with both twats measuring 3′2″ from fingertip to fingertip. But it's head circumference that really shows up their differences. ***STING***, whose hits include 'Da Doo Doo Doo, Da Daa Daa Daa' weighs in with a cranial circumference of 25″ (equivalent to a hat size of 7½), whilst pinhead ***BONO*** boasts a bonce that is just 11″ round - the size of a small grapefruit.

IN THE trouser department, there's little to choose between the two. ***STING*** famously boasts that he can keep his pecker up for five hours, but at a mere 2⅛″ on the stonk, it's a pretty hollow achievement. Meanwhile ***BONO*** shouldn't get too cocky. He may be able to muster 4″ of throbbing Irish gristle, but as his penis is only as thick as a pipe cleaner, he has no cause to gloat.

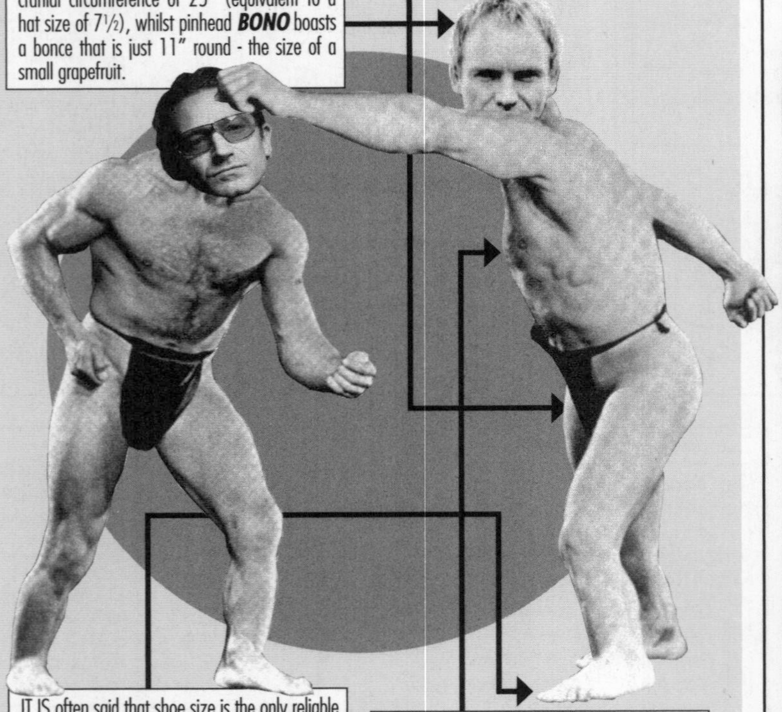

IT IS often said that shoe size is the only reliable way of sorting the twats from the arseholes, and this is certainly true in this case. Stingy ***STING*** saves money by crushing his Police size 9s into children's size 4 shoes, thus avoiding VAT. Meanwhile ***BONO*** takes a ladies' size 6 slingback on his left foot whilst wearing a gents' size 10 built-up orthopaedic shoe on his right.

SURFACE area is another variable which demonstrates the dramatic difference between ***STING*** and ***BONO***. If the skin were flayed from both their bodies and laid out flat, one of them would cover half a tennis court, whilst the other would cover twenty-nine and a quarter snooker tables.

FAR RIGHT WING SNACKS

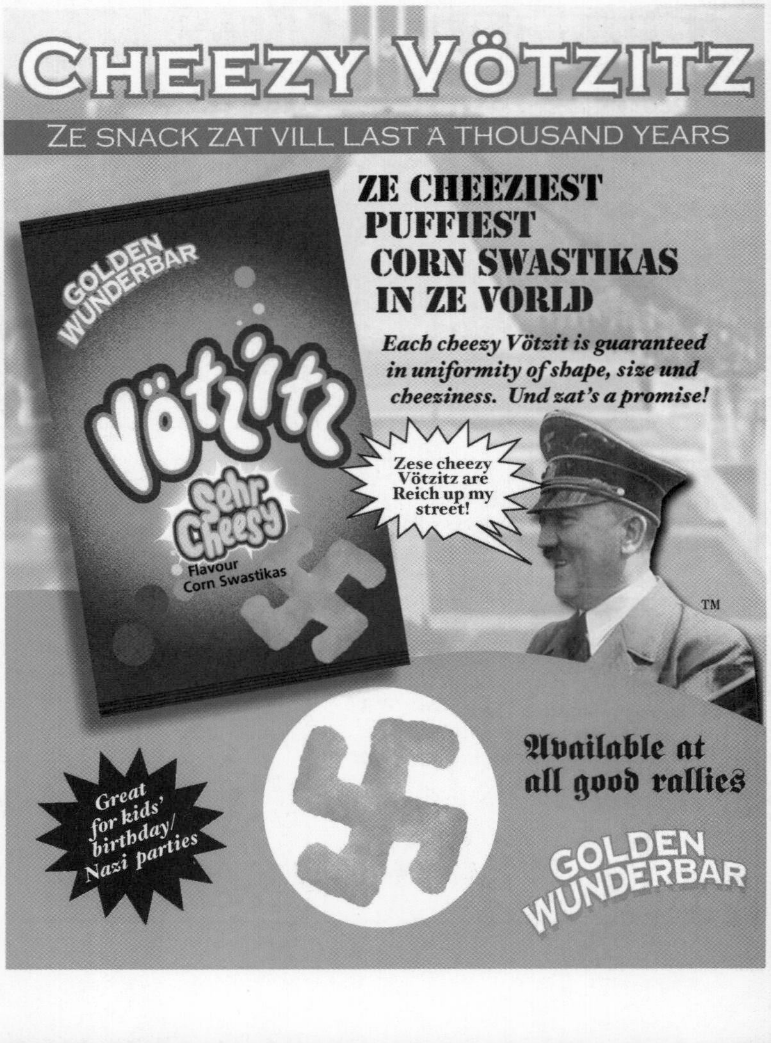
CHEEZY VÖTZITZ
ZE SNACK ZAT VILL LAST A THOUSAND YEARS
ZE CHEEZIEST PUFFIEST CORN SWASTIKAS IN ZE VORLD
Each cheezy Vötzit is guaranteed in uniformity of shape, size und cheeziness. Und zat's a promise!
GOLDEN WUNDERBAR
Vötzitz
Sehr Cheesy
Flavour Corn Swastikas
Zese cheezy Vötzitz are Reich up my street!
TM
Great for kids' birthday/ Nazi parties
Available at all good rallies
GOLDEN WUNDERBAR

Esther's Heart of Gold

GOLD BEATER: Esther Rantzen with her teeth, yesterday.

TOOTHY *Hearts of Gold* presenter Esther Rantzen last night received her very own heart of gold at Papworth Hospital in Cambridge.

In an eighteen-hour operation, the former *That's Life* host's own healthy heart was cut out, discarded and replaced with a 24-carat artificial organ, the first such transplant carried out anywhere in the world.

Miss Rantzen was last night recovering at home, where a spokesman described her condition as critical but stable.

GOOD

He told us: "The procedure went as well as can be expected, but Esther's not out of the woods yet. However, if she gets through the next forty-eight hours without any significant complications

That's Life or Death Op for TV Esther

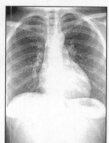

arising, her chances of survival are quite good."

It is thought that Rantzen decided to undergo the grueling op after a routine chest X-ray revealed that her own heart was made out of exactly the same material as everyone else's. "The results of her medical came as a terrible blow to Esther," her spokesman told us. "So when the chance for a solid gold heart came up, she grabbed it with both hands."

ODD

"After all the decades she's spent championing consumer rights on television and setting up the Childline charity single-handed, if anyone deserves a heart of gold, Esther does," he added.

Rantzen is reported to have paid over £1 million for the fully-functioning golden organ, which boasts diamond-studded ventricles, ruby-encrusted aortas and a tricuspid valve carved from a solid block of platinum.

EVEN

And unlike the owner of a traditional artificial heart, Esther will never need to change her ticker's batteries. That's because it is fitted with a state-of-the-art clockwork mechanism that can run for over a week on a single winding.

SHAKIN'

"As long as she can get someone to stick their hand up her fanny and pull down on the chain that hoists the counterweight up into her chest every eight days, there's no reason why Esther shouldn't live forever," the spokesman told us.

"Just imagine that. Esther making her judgemental, moralising programmes for all eternity. It's like all the nation's dreams come true at once," he added.

How It Was Done

9.00am
ESTHER Rantzen is wheeled into the operating theatre and anaesthetized.

10.30am
SURGEON makes his first incision, entering the thoracic cavity via the pericardium.

1.00pm
THE functions of Rantzen's heart are taken over for the duration of the operation by an artificial oxygenating pump.

3.15pm
TWO ribs are removed to allow surgical access to the cardiacical chamber.

5.00pm
RANTZEN'S heart is disconnected from its veins, removed and discarded.

7.30pm
THE surgical team takes a well-earned tea break.

8.00pm
IT'S time for pudding. There's a choice of semolina, jam roly poly or sherry trifle.

9.00pm
AFTER tea, the bejewelled, prosthetic organ is brought into the operating theatre on a sterile velvet cushion.

10.30pm
THE aorta and pulmonary veins are offered up and connected using gold jubilee clips.

12.00am
THE secondary arteries are plumbed in and a nurse gives the precious jewels a final polish before the wound is closed.

2.00am
THE gold heart is wound up with a key and started for the first time.

2.30am
THE surgeon inserts the final stitches in Esther Rantzen's chest before she is wheeled out of the operating theatre into the recovery ward.

3.00am
SHE wakes up with her new heart of gold!

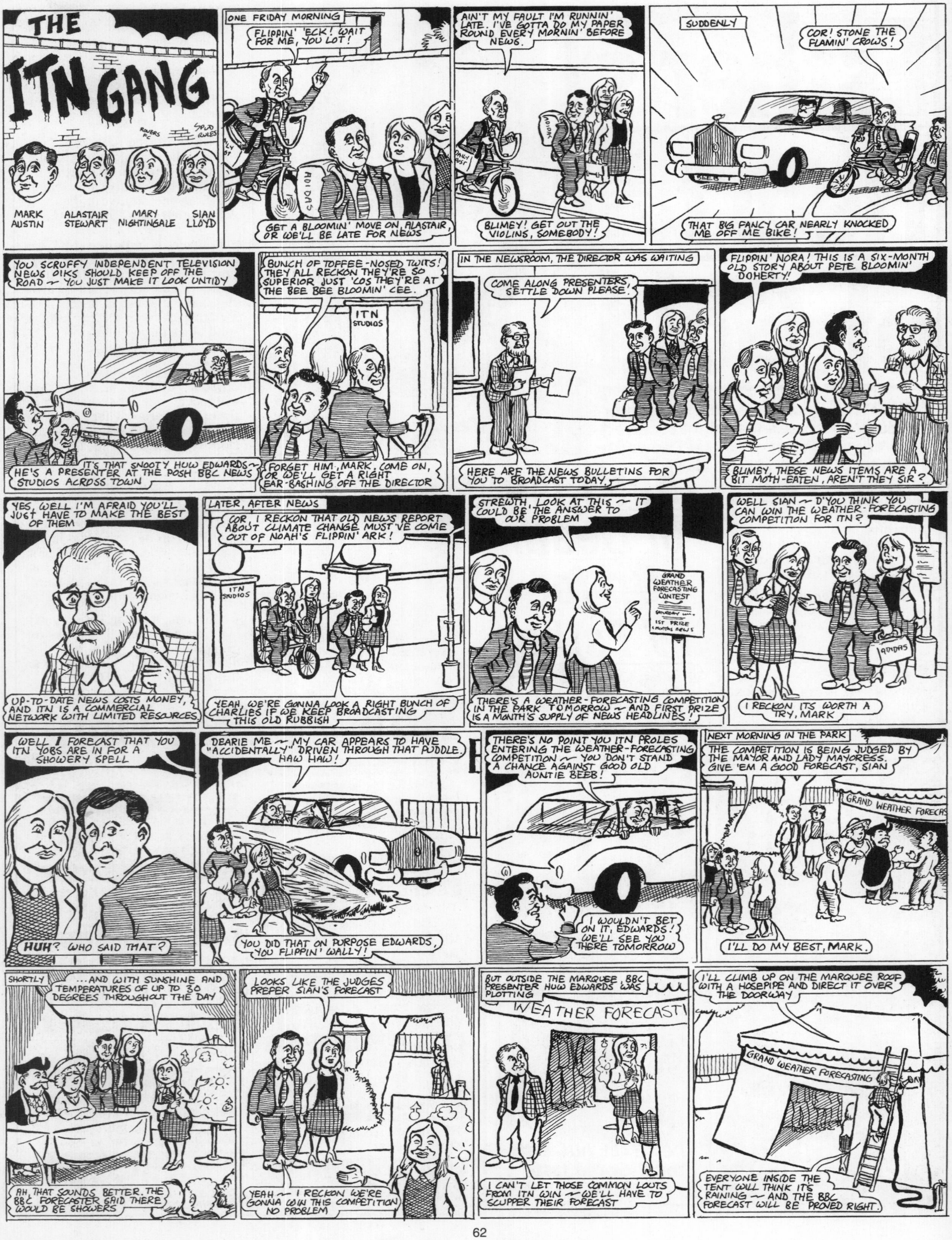
THE ITN GANG
ROVERS FC
SPUD RULES
MARK AUSTIN
ALASTAIR STEWART
MARY NIGHTINGALE
SIAN LLOYD
ONE FRIDAY MORNING
FLIPPIN' 'ECK! WAIT FOR ME, YOU LOT!
ADIDAS
GET A BLOOMIN' MOVE ON, ALASTAIR, OR WE'LL BE LATE FOR NEWS
AIN'T MY FAULT I'M RUNNIN' LATE. I'VE GOTTA DO MY PAPER ROUND EVERY MORNIN' BEFORE NEWS.
BLIMEY! GET OUT THE VIOLINS, SOMEBODY!
SUDDENLY
COR! STONE THE FLAMIN' CROWS!
THAT BIG FANCY CAR NEARLY KNOCKED ME OFF ME BIKE!
YOU SCRUFFY INDEPENDENT TELEVISION NEWS OIKS SHOULD KEEP OFF THE ROAD ~ YOU JUST MAKE IT LOOK UNTIDY
IT'S THAT SNOOTY HUW EDWARDS ~ HE'S A PRESENTER AT THE POSH BBC NEWS STUDIOS ACROSS TOWN
BUNCH OF TOFFEE-NOSED TWITS! THEY ALL RECKON THEY'RE SO SUPERIOR JUST 'COS THEY'RE AT THE BEE BEE BLOOMIN' CEE.
ITN STUDIOS
FORGET HIM, MARK. COME ON, OR WE'LL GET A RIGHT EAR-BASHING OFF THE DIRECTOR
IN THE NEWSROOM, THE DIRECTOR WAS WAITING
COME ALONG PRESENTERS, SETTLE DOWN PLEASE.
HERE ARE THE NEWS BULLETINS FOR YOU TO BROADCAST TODAY.
FLIPPIN' NORA! THIS IS A SIX-MONTH OLD STORY ABOUT PETE BLOOMIN' DOHERTY!
BLIMEY, THESE NEWS ITEMS ARE A BIT MOTH-EATEN, AREN'T THEY SIR?
YES, WELL I'M AFRAID YOU'LL JUST HAVE TO MAKE THE BEST OF THEM
UP-TO-DATE NEWS COSTS MONEY, AND ITN IS A COMMERCIAL NETWORK WITH LIMITED RESOURCES.
LATER, AFTER NEWS
COR, I RECKON THAT OLD NEWS REPORT ABOUT CLIMATE CHANGE MUST'VE COME OUT OF NOAH'S FLIPPIN' ARK!
ITN STUDIOS
YEAH, WE'RE GONNA LOOK A RIGHT BUNCH OF CHARLIES IF WE KEEP BROADCASTING THIS OLD RUBBISH
STREWTH, LOOK AT THIS ~ IT COULD BE THE ANSWER TO OUR PROBLEM
GRAND WEATHER FORECASTING CONTEST
1ST PRIZE
THERE'S A WEATHER-FORECASTING COMPETITION IN THE PARK TOMORROW ~ AND FIRST PRIZE IS A MONTH'S SUPPLY OF NEWS HEADLINES!
WELL SIAN ~ D'YOU THINK YOU CAN WIN THE WEATHER-FORECASTING COMPETITION FOR ITN?
ADIDAS
I RECKON ITS WORTH A TRY, MARK
WELL I FORECAST THAT YOU ITN YOBS ARE IN FOR A SHOWERY SPELL
HUH? WHO SAID THAT?
DEARIE ME ~ MY CAR APPEARS TO HAVE "ACCIDENTALLY" DRIVEN THROUGH THAT PUDDLE. HAW HAW!
YOU DID THAT ON PURPOSE EDWARDS, YOU FLIPPIN' WALLY!
THERE'S NO POINT YOU ITN PROLES ENTERING THE WEATHER-FORECASTING COMPETITION ~ YOU DON'T STAND A CHANCE AGAINST GOOD OLD AUNTIE BEEB!
I WOULDN'T BET ON IT, EDWARDS! WE'LL SEE YOU THERE TOMORROW
NEXT MORNING IN THE PARK
THE COMPETITION IS BEING JUDGED BY THE MAYOR AND LADY MAYORESS. GIVE 'EM A GOOD FORECAST, SIAN
GRAND WEATHER FORECAS
I'LL DO MY BEST, MARK.
SHORTLY
...AND WITH SUNSHINE AND TEMPERATURES OF UP TO 30 DEGREES THROUGHOUT THE DAY
AH, THAT SOUNDS BETTER. THE BBC FORECASTER SAID THERE WOULD BE SHOWERS
LOOKS LIKE THE JUDGES PREFER SIAN'S FORECAST
YEAH ~ I RECKON WE'RE GONNA WIN THIS COMPETITION NO PROBLEM
BUT OUTSIDE THE MARQUEE, BBC PRESENTER HUW EDWARDS WAS PLOTTING
WEATHER FORECAST
I CAN'T LET THOSE COMMON LOUTS FROM ITN WIN ~ WE'LL HAVE TO SCUPPER THEIR FORECAST
I'LL CLIMB UP ON THE MARQUEE ROOF WITH A HOSEPIPE AND DIRECT IT OVER THE DOORWAY
GRAND WEATHER FORECASTING DAY
EVERYONE INSIDE THE TENT WILL THINK IT'S RAINING ~ AND THE BBC FORECAST WILL BE PROVED RIGHT.

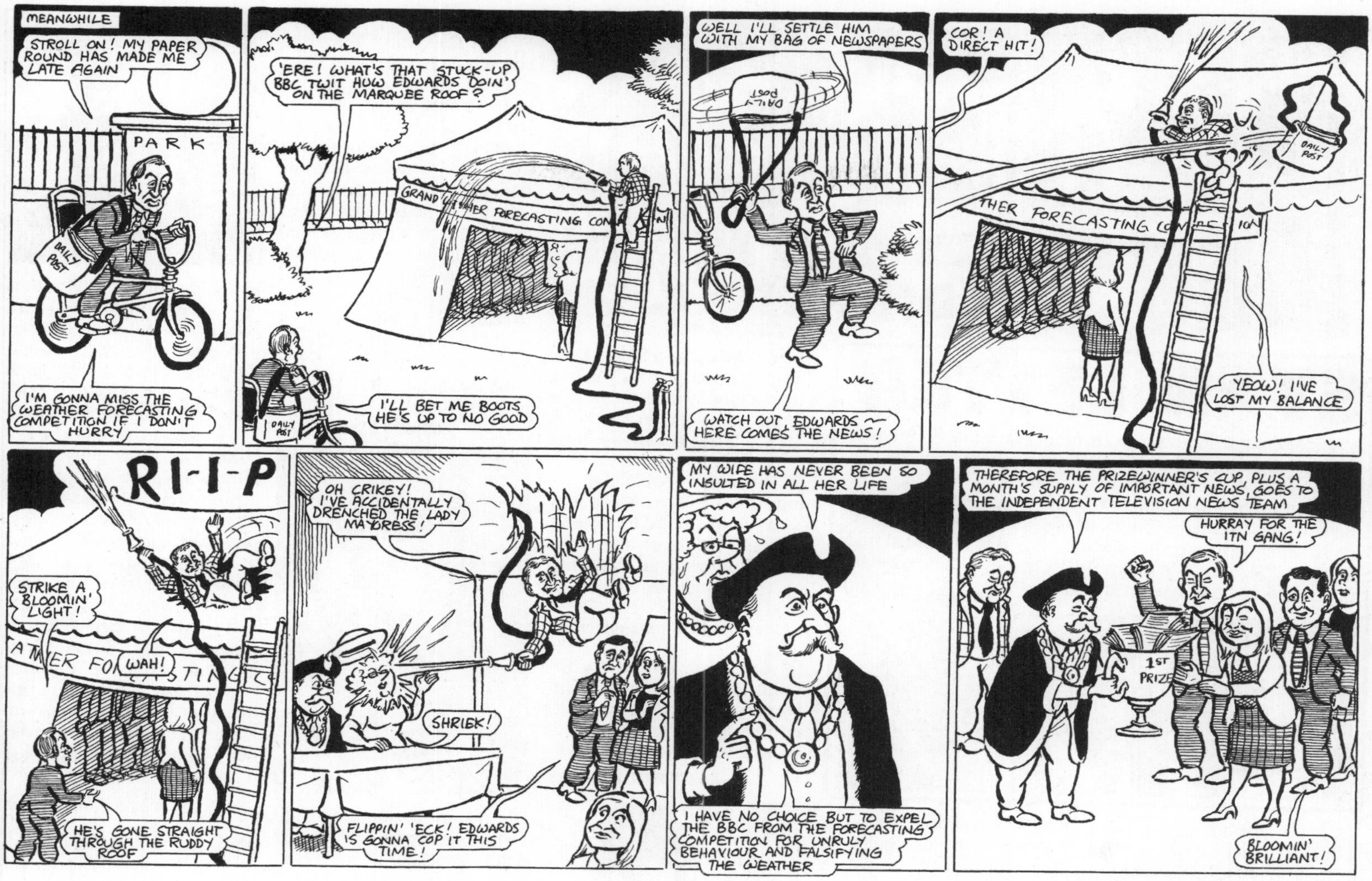
MEANWHILE
STROLL ON! MY PAPER ROUND HAS MADE ME LATE AGAIN
PARK
DAILY POST
I'M GONNA MISS THE WEATHER FORECASTING COMPETITION IF I DON'T HURRY
'ERE! WHAT'S THAT STUCK-UP BBC TWIT HUW EDWARDS DOIN' ON THE MARQUEE ROOF?
GRAND WEATHER FORECASTING COMPETITION
I'LL BET ME BOOTS HE'S UP TO NO GOOD
WELL I'LL SETTLE HIM WITH MY BAG OF NEWSPAPERS
DAILY POST
WATCH OUT, EDWARDS ~ HERE COMES THE NEWS!
COR! A DIRECT HIT!
DAILY POST
THER FORECASTING COMPETITION
YEOW! I'VE LOST MY BALANCE
RI-I-P
STRIKE A BLOOMIN' LIGHT!
WAH!
HE'S GONE STRAIGHT THROUGH THE RUDDY ROOF
OH CRIKEY! I'VE ACCIDENTALLY DRENCHED THE LADY MAYORESS!
SHRIEK!
FLIPPIN' 'ECK! EDWARDS IS GONNA COP IT THIS TIME!
MY WIFE HAS NEVER BEEN SO INSULTED IN ALL HER LIFE
I HAVE NO CHOICE BUT TO EXPEL THE BBC FROM THE FORECASTING COMPETITION FOR UNRULY BEHAVIOUR AND FALSIFYING THE WEATHER
THEREFORE THE PRIZEWINNER'S CUP, PLUS A MONTH'S SUPPLY OF IMPORTANT NEWS, GOES TO THE INDEPENDENT TELEVISION NEWS TEAM
HURRAY FOR THE ITN GANG!
1ST PRIZE
BLOOMIN' BRILLIANT!

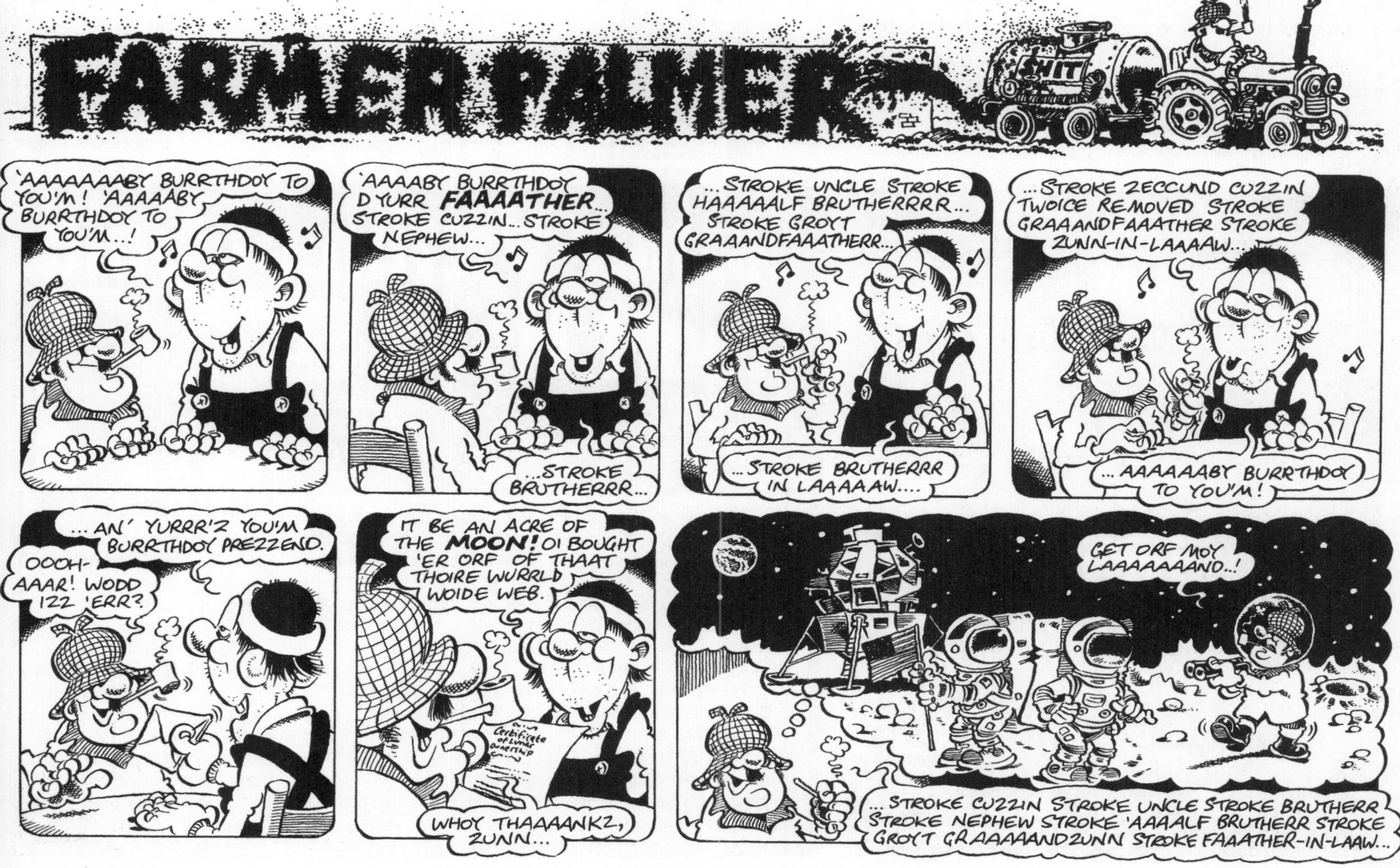
FARMER PALMER
SHIT
'AAAAAAABY BURRTHDOY TO YOU'M! 'AAAAABY BURRTHDOY TO YOU'M...!
'AAAABY BURRTHDOY D'YURR FAAAATHER.. STROKE CUZZIN... STROKE NEPHEW...
...STROKE BRUTHERRR...
...STROKE UNCLE STROKE HAAAAALF BRUTHERRRR... STROKE GROYT GRAAANDFAAATHERR...
...STROKE BRUTHERRR IN LAAAAAW....
...STROKE ZECCUND CUZZIN TWOICE REMOVED STROKE GRAAANDFAAATHER STROKE ZUNN-IN-LAAAAW...
...AAAAAABY BURRTHDOY TO YOU'M!
...AN' YURRR'Z YOU'M BURRTHDOY PREZZEND.
OOOH-AAAR! WODD IZZ 'ERR?
IT BE AN ACRE OF THE MOON! OI BOUGHT 'ER ORF OF THAAT THOIRE WURRLD WOIDE WEB.
WHOY THAAAANKZ, ZUNN...
GET ORF MOY LAAAAAAAND...!
...STROKE CUZZIN STROKE UNCLE STROKE BRUTHERR STROKE NEPHEW STROKE 'AAAALF BRUTHERR STROKE GROYT GRAAAAANDZUNN STROKE FAAATHER-IN-LAAW...

LETTERBOX

PO BOX 656, NORTH SHIELDS, NE30 4XX

LETTERS@viz.co.uk

ST★R LETTER

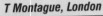

In 2003 we went to war with Iraq in order to rid them of their stockpile of weapons of mass destruction. Many people were critical of the government for taking this action as the weapons inspectors headed by Dr Hans Blix were unable to find any such weapons. But let us not jump to conclusions. If these photgraphs are anything to go by, Blix can't even find a pair of glasses that fit him properly, so what chance has he got of finding Iraq's hidden arsenal?

T Montague, London

"It's hard to believe it, but our Queen is 81 this year," said royal photographer Arthur Edwards in a circular e-mail from *the Sun*. It isn't actually *that* hard to believe, seeing as she was 80 last year.

S Glover, Hull

How ridiculous of NASA spending billions of pounds to come up with the non-stick frying pan. In the weightlessness of space, the astronauts' sausages are just going to float right out of the pan. If anything, they should have been developing something to make them stick.

J Boxbury, Norfolk

Talking of pans. my father bought a very expensive frying pan, but justified the purchase because it had a lifetime guarantee. Three weeks later, he was killed by a falling tree. Twenty-seven pounds for less than a month's use seems like pretty poor value to me.

Elron Poindexter, Tring

When did people stop using 3-foot long cloth snakes as draught excluders behind doors? I bet it was about the same time we started letting all the bloody foreigners in or something.

Gnasher, Macclesfield

Last year I went to Toronto and I saw one of Jimi Hendrix's shoes in a museum. Four thousand miles to see a shoe! It wasn't even a pair.

T Lawnmower, Cornwall

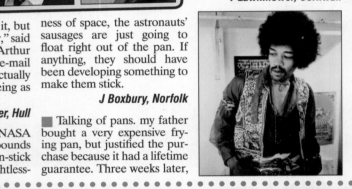

I am deaf, and I like spang vids as much as the next man. I get the general drift of what is happening in the art films, but my enjoyment is lessened because I cannot hear the dialogue, and it would help my timing if I knew when the cash splash is about to happen. Perhaps porn makers could include subtitles along the bottom, or better still, have deaf actors who could sign straight to camera. I understand it might be a little difficult for an actress in a spitroast or a triple entry gangbang, but at least they could make the effort.

Keswick Stan, e-mail

It's nice to see California Governor Arnold Schwarzeneggar taking a lead in the battle to save the world's ecosystem. If the rest of us followed the fine example he has set by converting one of his 11 Hummers to run on vegetable oil, then perhaps we would stand a chance of pulling our planet back from the brink of environmental Armageddon.

Alfonse Juniper, Luton

The church authorities have decided that Bishop Tom Butler will not face disciplinary action after he was found throwing toys from the back seat of a car outside a pub, after spending the afternoon at the Irish Embassy. The decision was apparently made after it was concluded that his actions were 'completely out of character'. However, God punished Adam and Eve's out of character lapse when they ate an apple, by casting them out of the Garden of Eden and cursing all their descendants with death, disease, famine and pestilence, for ever and eternity. Once again, it's one rule for all of mankind, another rule for bishops who deny being pissed-up outside a pub in Bermondsey.

Job McDuff, Tiverton

I learned with interest this week that the term 'inflammable' does not in fact mean that something is not flammable. The word does not follow the same negative rule as other words prefixed 'in', such as inaudible, insatiable, indiscreet, etc. I also burnt my arse cheeks quite badly.

C. Drakeman, London

Esther Victim of Gold Heart Hoax

ESTHER EGG ON FACE: So sad Rantzen yesterday.

A CONMAN has tricked Hearts of Gold presenter *Esther Rantzen* out of more than a MILLION POUNDS after promising to fit her with a solid gold prosthetic heart.

Rantzen paid a 'significant seven-figure sum' to the fraudster after seeing an advert for a fictitious gold organ transplant company on the internet. After being shown the golden heart and handing over the money, she was apparently driven in a windowless van to a lock-up garage which she was led to believe was the world-renowned Papworth Hospital.

She was then placed on an operating table and anaesthetized; however no surgery took place. When she awoke, she was sent home. The hoax only came to light more than a week later when one of Rantzen's assistants went to wind up the clockwork organ, but was unable to locate a chain.

fake

It was then discovered that the foot-long operation scar on the TV host's chest was a fake that had been drawn on with an eyebrow pencil.

Police later raided a property in Peterborough, where they recovered a large quantity of cash, an eyebrow pencil and a grapefruit covered in Ferrero Rocher wrappers.

foolish

A spokesman told us: "Esther feels very foolish. But she hopes that her story will serve as a warning to ordinary members of the public. If you are offered a golden organ transplant, make sure you check your surgeon's credentials before you hand over any money."

■ I was quite amused at the fate of a contestant on the reality talent show *Any Dream Will Do*, who believed, as a born again Christian, that it was his destiny to win. He was the first to be voted off. I don't know if this shows that God doesn't exist, or that he does and has an excellent grasp of irony.

M Treetops, Luton

■ Chris Tarrant has been accused of throwing cutlery at a fellow diner at an Indian restaurant. What absolute rubbish. I was in that Nottingham restaurant, and I had a perfect view of the table where the alleged assault took place, and I didn't see Mr Tarrant attack anyone. In fact I didn't see him at all. That's because it was last Christmas I was there, so he might have done it for all I know.

J Purcell, Nottingham

■ Russell Brand, Russell Crowe, Russell Grant, Russell Watson. Is everyone with the first name Russell a complete twat?

Tim Rustling, e-mail

**Do you know a famous Russell who isn't a twat? Send your nominations and we'll print the name of any famous Russells who aren't twats.*

■ I read that the Queen's doctor, Sir George Pinker, has died at the age of 82. He must really have been a rubbish doctor if he couldn't even manage to stay alive himself. And certainly not a doctor fit for Her Majesty the Queen.

L Drawer, e-mail

■ It is said that gentlemen prefer blondes. I hope then that lesbians prefer brunettes, otherwise we might have to organise some kind of rota system.

Johnny Pring, e-mail

■ In Boots the other day I saw some packets of Immodium in the last minute impulse-buy rack by the till. Now chewing gum I can understand, but you've either got chonic diarrohea or you haven't.

N Tinberg, London

■ I recently discovered that an ex-boyfriend of mine not only reads the *Daily Mail*, but also owns 2 books written by pig-faced rabble-rouser Richard Littlejohn. Have any readers ever had a more shameful secret kept from them by a so-called loved one?

Sickened, London

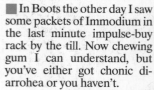

■ In electing the right wing Nicolas Sarkozy over the socialist Segolene Royal in the recent election, the French have denied everyone a politician it's worth having a Hilary Swank over. I don't suppose you've got a picture of her in a bikini by any chance.

Stuie, e-mail

Miriam

ANSWERS YOUR PROBLEMS

Dear Miriam, **LETTER OF THE DAY**

The other day I set off for work, leaving my husband in the house watching the TV as usual.

I hadn't gone a hundred yards down the road when my engine conked out and the car juddered to a halt. I walked back home to get my husband's help. When I got home I found him in the bedroom. I couldn't believe my eyes. He was parading in front of the wardrobe mirror dressed in my underwear and high heel shoes, and he was wearing my make up.

I am 32, my husband is 34 and we have been married for 12 years. When I confronted him, he tried to make out that he had dressed up in my lingerie because couldn't find any of his own underwear. But when I asked him about the make up, he broke down and admitted that he has been wearing my clothes for six months. I told him it had to stop, or I would leave him.

He was made redundant from his job six months ago, and he says he has been feeling increasingly depressed and worthless. I love him very much, but ever since I gave him the ultimatum, he has become increasingly distant, and I don't feel I can get through to him any more. Please can you help?

Mrs B, Essex

Miriam says... *A car stalling after being driven a short distance can be caused by a variety of faults in the engine. Start by checking that there is no debris in the fuel line. If it is clear, check the jubilee clips holding the vacuum pipes onto the inlet manifold. If none of these approaches solves the problem, it could be that the fuel pump itself is faulty, causing low delivery pressure to the carburettor float chamber.*

MIRIAM'S ADVICE LINES	0898 100--
Engine misfires and husband addicted to porn	-01
Car hesitates under braking and wife having an affair	-02
Vehicle pulls to side and think my son is gay	-03
Vaginal dryness and judder as clutch is engaged	-04

FRED BASKET
THAT'S ODD..!
I WONDER WHY HALF THE TEA'S VANISHED OFF THE TABLE!
Got to leave room for my pudding..!
609,322,404,896,214,536
© A CORPSE LTD.

TOP TIPS

CONTESTANTS on *Wife Swap*. Try not to be so surprised at how different the other family is. That is, and always has been, the format of the show.

Martin Christiansen, e-mail

RYAN Air passengers. These days they let ALL passengers off the planes, thus eliminating the need to all clamber to the front the second the aircraft lands.

Darren Singleton, e-mail

MUMS. Confuse your children by mixing butter with their I Can't Believe It's Not Butter. They won't know what to believe.

Sam McCrohan, Guildford

MOURNERS. Read the dress code instructions on funeral invitations very carefully. Sombre, whilst being only 2 letters away from sombrero, is a world apart in tone.

C. Tarquin, e-mail

PARENTS. When people ask how old your child is, they want to know how old he is at the moment. The phrase 'he/she will be five next birthday' involves some tricky calculations and is not very useful.

Nikko, e-mail

OLD PEOPLE. Save having to get a flu jab each year by not queuing outside the Post Office every Tuesday morning in the pouring rain an hour before it opens. They won't run out of money. It's not like the queue outside the butcher's during the war.

Sarah Cocks, e-mail

HOUSEWIVES. Make the normally mundane task of switching the central heating on a little more exciting by singing 'The heating's on' to the tune of 80s hit *The Heat is On* by Glen Frey as you are doing it.

Jorgen Jarlesberg, Goole

Greatest Briton Named

IMAGINATION front-man *Leee Johns* was celebrating with friends last night after being named as the greatest Briton in history.

Johns, yesterday ~ astonished

The lead singer of the eighties soul band took the title after beating an eminent line up of hopefuls including ***Sir Winston Churchill, Isambard Kingdom Brunel, Florence Nightingale*** and ***Alan Turing.***

At a lavish ceremony, a clearly surprised Johns, 50, whose hits include *Just an Illusion* and *Body Talk*, accepted the prize from the Duke of Gloucester. He made an emotional speech in which he thanked all those who had voted for him and praised the calibre of his fellow nominees.

winner

Johns said he was astounded at the unexpected accolade. "I was very surprised to be invited to the ceremony," he told reporters. "When the Duke read out my name as the winner, I was astonished. When you look at some of the people I was up against, you wouldn't think I had a chance."

miles

Johns picked up a solid gold cup and a crown, and a statue of him will be placed on the empty plinth in Trafalgar Square. In addition, the Royal Mail are to issue a set of stamps based on the titles of Imagination's songs.

biscuit

Yesterday, Leee was still coming to terms with his title of the Greatest Briton of All Time. "It's still all a bit unreal," he said. "I had a few top ten hits in the eighties, but after that my career went a bit quiet. I still can't understand how I beat all these amazing historical figures," he continued.

watney's red

"I suppose Churchill was an inspirational leader whose bulldog spirit led the country to victory in the war, but on the other hand, he never took *Music and Lights* to number 5 in the charts. And I suppose that's more relevant to people today," he added.

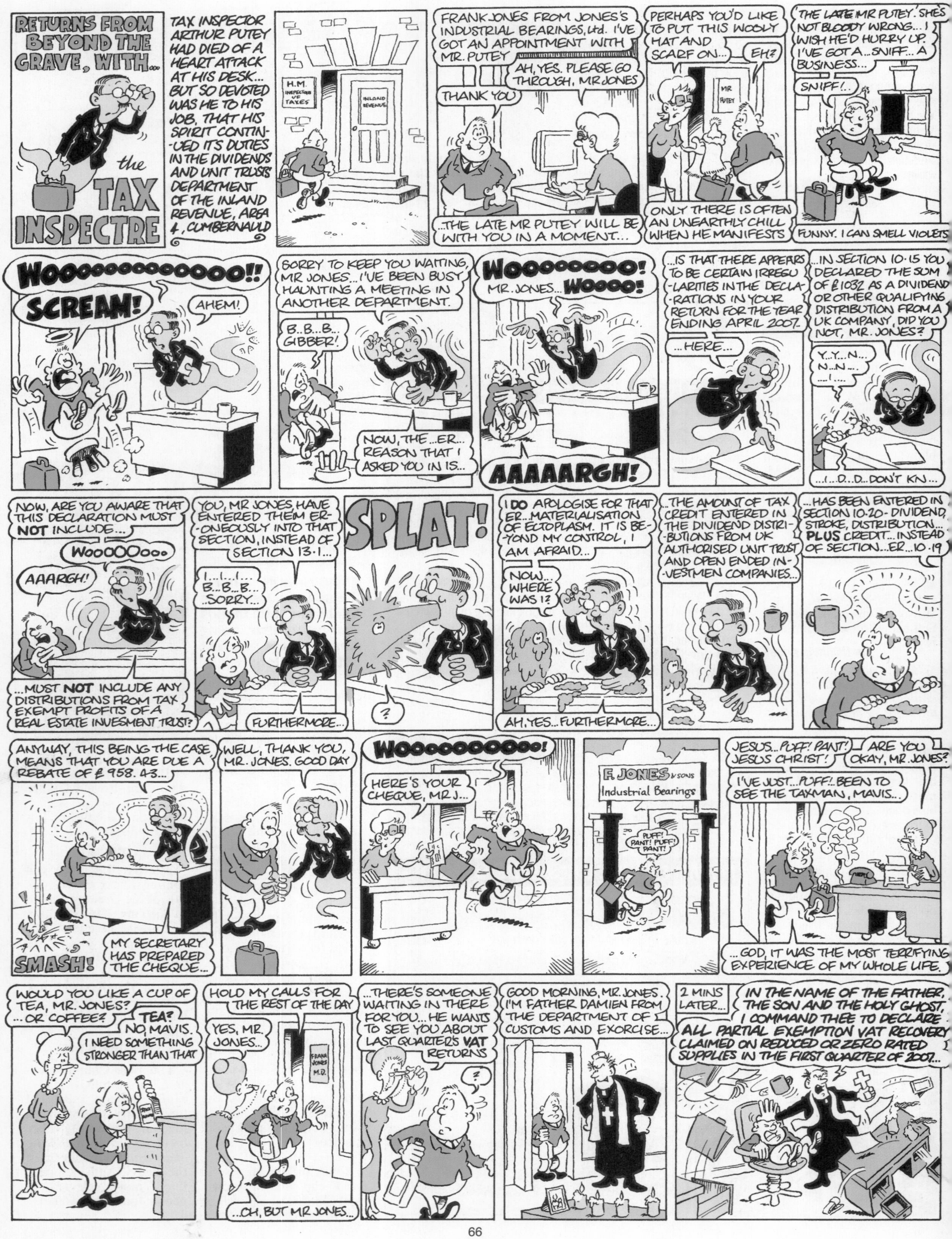
RETURNS FROM BEYOND THE GRAVE, WITH...
the TAX INSPECTRE
TAX INSPECTOR ARTHUR PUTEY HAD DIED OF A HEART ATTACK AT HIS DESK... BUT SO DEVOTED WAS HE TO HIS JOB, THAT HIS SPIRIT CONTIN-UED ITS DUTIES IN THE DIVIDENDS AND UNIT TRUSTS DEPARTMENT OF THE INLAND REVENUE, AREA 4, CUMBERNAULD
H.M. INSPECTOR OF TAXES
INLAND REVENUE
FRANK JONES FROM JONES'S INDUSTRIAL BEARINGS, Ltd. I'VE GOT AN APPOINTMENT WITH MR. PUTEY
AH, YES. PLEASE GO THROUGH, MR JONES
THANK YOU
...THE LATE MR PUTEY WILL BE WITH YOU IN A MOMENT...
PERHAPS YOU'D LIKE TO PUT THIS WOOLY HAT AND SCARF ON...
EH?
MR PUTEY
ONLY THERE IS OFTEN AN UNEARTHLY CHILL WHEN HE MANIFESTS
'THE LATE MR PUTEY.' SHE'S NOT BLOODY WRONG... I WISH HE'D HURRY UP. I'VE GOT A... SNIFF... A BUSINESS...
SNIFF!..
FUNNY. I CAN SMELL VIOLETS
WOOOOOOOOOOOOO!!
SCREAM!
AHEM!
SORRY TO KEEP YOU WAITING, MR JONES... I'VE BEEN BUSY HAUNTING A MEETING IN ANOTHER DEPARTMENT.
B..B..B.. GIBBER!
NOW, THE...ER... REASON THAT I ASKED YOU IN IS...
WOOOOOOOO! MR. JONES... WOOOO!
AAAAARGH!
...IS THAT THERE APPEARS TO BE CERTAN IRREGU-LARITIES IN THE DECLA-RATIONS IN YOUR RETURN FOR THE YEAR ENDING APRIL 2007.
...HERE...
...IN SECTION 10·15 YOU DECLARED THE SUM OF £1032 AS A DIVIDEND OR OTHER QUALIFYING DISTRIBUTION FROM A UK COMPANY, DID YOU NOT, MR. JONES?
Y..Y...N... N..N... ...I...
...I...D...D...DON'T KN...
NOW, ARE YOU AWARE THAT THIS DECLARATION MUST NOT INCLUDE...
WOOOOOooo
AAARGH!
...MUST NOT INCLUDE ANY DISTRIBUTIONS FROM TAX EXEMPT PROFITS OF A REAL ESTATE INVESMENT TRUST?
YOU, MR JONES, HAVE ENTERED THEM ER-ONEOUSLY INTO THAT SECTION, INSTEAD OF SECTION 13·1...
I...I...I... B...B...B... ...SORRY...
FURTHERMORE...
SPLAT!
?
I DO APOLOGISE FOR THAT ER...MATERIALISATION OF ECTOPLASM. IT IS BE-YOND MY CONTROL, I AM AFRAID...
NOW... WHERE WAS I?
AH, YES...FURTHERMORE...
...THE AMOUNT OF TAX CREDIT ENTERED IN THE DIVIDEND DISTRI-BUTIONS FROM UK AUTHORISED UNIT TRUST AND OPEN ENDED IN-VESTMEN COMPANIES...
...HAS BEEN ENTERED IN SECTION 10·20 - DIVIDEND, STROKE, DISTRIBUTION... PLUS CREDIT...INSTEAD OF SECTION...ER...10·19
ANYWAY, THIS BEING THE CASE, MEANS THAT YOU ARE DUE A REBATE OF £958.43...
SMASH!
MY SECRETARY HAS PREPARED THE CHEQUE...
WELL, THANK YOU, MR. JONES. GOOD DAY
WOOOOOOOOOO!
HERE'S YOUR CHEQUE, MR J...
F. JONES & SONS Industrial Bearings
PUFF! PANT! PUFF! PANT!
JESUS...PUFF! PANT! JESUS CHRIST!
ARE YOU OKAY, MR. JONES?
I'VE JUST...PUFF!...BEEN TO SEE THE TAXMAN, MAVIS...
...GOD, IT WAS THE MOST TERRIFYING EXPERIENCE OF MY WHOLE LIFE.
WOULD YOU LIKE A CUP OF TEA, MR. JONES? ...OR COFFEE?
TEA? NO, MAVIS. I NEED SOMETHING STRONGER THAN THAT
HOLD MY CALLS FOR THE REST OF THE DAY
YES, MR. JONES...
FRANK JONES M.D.
...OH, BUT MR JONES...
...THERE'S SOMEONE WAITING IN THERE FOR YOU... HE WANTS TO SEE YOU ABOUT LAST QUARTER'S VAT RETURNS
?
GOOD MORNING, MR. JONES. I'M FATHER DAMIEN FROM THE DEPARTMENT OF CUSTOMS AND EXORCISE...
2 MINS LATER...
IN THE NAME OF THE FATHER, THE SON AND THE HOLY GHOST, I COMMAND THEE TO DECLARE ALL PARTIAL EXEMPTION VAT RECOVERY CLAIMED ON REDUCED OR ZERO RATED SUPPLIES IN THE FIRST QUARTER OF 2007...

Basil's Brushes

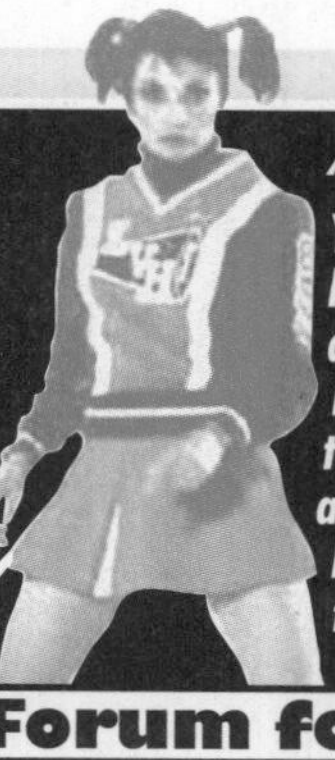

"Hey, brushes, you're so fine! You're so fine you blow my mind! Hey brushes! Hi, I'm TONI BASIL and when I'm not busy recording my one novelty hit record a quarter of a century ago, I'm just crazy about brushes! This week, my mailbag has been "bristling" with your fantastic letters about brushes."

Britain's LIVELIEST Forum for Brushaholics

MY HUSBAND took early retirement from his job as a door-to-door brush salesman, and used his redundancy money to set up a business as a mobile bird of prey hairdresser. He always jokes that whereas he used to "hawk brushes" for a living, these days he "brushes hawks". However, he has had little work in the last three years and now it looks like we may lose the house. Consequently, every time he makes that joke I burst into tears.

Mrs Edna Tetanus, Wolverhampton

I RECENTLY sent my 12-year old son out to get me a new brush, because the one I was using had worn out. Imagine my surprise when he returned several days later with a large quantity of the vegetation which covers the African veldt. He had completely mistaken which sort of "brush" I wanted!

Mrs Una Visceroptosis, Aberystwyth

IT MAKES my blood boil that the barmy Brussels bureaucrats have decreed that these days I have to sweep my patio with a 0.9144metre brush. It really is political correctness gone mad.

Brigadier Rupert Littlejohn, Aldershot

MY HUSBAND is Assistant Chief Constable of Northumbria Police, and I recently caught him sweeping up a pile of leaves in the garden. Talk about a brush with the law!

Mrs Ada Pyonephrosis, Newcastle

Brush Spot

Strangely, Eskimos have no word in their language for "brush", although they have over 700 different words for "broom"!

MY HUSBAND is Assistant Chief Constable of Northumbria Police, and I recently caught him cleaning his teeth in the bathroom. Talk about a brush with the law!

Mrs Ada Pyonephrosis, Newcastle

MY HUSBAND is Assistant Chief Constable of Northumbria Police, and I recently caught him painting the front door. Talk about a brush with the law!

Mrs Ada Pyonephrosis, Newcastle

MY HUSBAND is Assistant Chief Constable of Northumbria Police, and I recently caught scrubbing some faecal skidmarks off the lavatory bowl. Talk about a brush with the law!

Mrs Ada Pyonephrosis, Newcastle

THE ground floor of my house was flooded out during the recent heavy rains. When the waters finally receded, I discovered that my expensive electric vacuum cleaner was waterlogged and completely useless. However, my old sweeping brush still worked perfectly. Or rather, I imagine that it would have done if it hadn't floated away during the deluge.

Mrs D Senile-Pruritis, Cheltenham

I AM a big fan of brushes, and nothing gets my goat more than people using the expression "daft as a brush". For my money, there is nothing more sensible than a brush. The expression ought to be "daft as people who make unwarranted slurs about the imagined silliness of perfectly sensible household utensils".

Mr Stanley Bartholinian-Abcess, Tunbridge Wells

I SCREAMED with contemptuous laughter when my daughter complained that the batteries in her electric toothbrush had gone flat. I've had the same toothbrush for the last sixty years and it's never run out of batteries or needed recharging yet. Honestly, children these days don't know they're born. I blame the parents.

Mrs Rita Bedwetting, York

I HAD to write and tell you about a brush with fame that I had the other day. I work in a shop selling kitchen utensils, and rhythm and blues keyboard maestro Georgie Fame came in and bought a pastry brush!

Edward Phimosis, Oswestry

BRUSH JOKES

Q: What's a brush's favourite pop star?
A: *Kate Brush*

Mrs Ethel Menorrhagia, Dundee

Q: What's a brush's favourite classical composer?
A: *Handel (Handle) (Like a brush handle).*

Mrs Nora Leucorrhoea, Dundee

Q: What position would a brush play in a football team?
A: *Sweeper.*

Mrs Elsie Haematemesis, Dundee

An Englishman, an Irishman and a Scotsman apply for a job at a brush factory. I can't remember how the middle of the joke goes, but it ends up with the Irishman using the brush upside down or something.

Mrs Olive Schistosomiasis, Dundee

Q: Why is Jordan like a brush?
A: *Because they've both got big bristles (bristols).*

Mr Arthur Spermatorrhoea, Dundee

Q: Who is the President of the United States of America?
A: *George W Brush.*

Mrs Ada Furunculosis, Dundee

Q: What noise does a car driven by a brush make?
A: *Broom! Broom!*

Mrs Marjorie Aerophagia, Dundee

Truth Brushes

Your brush queries answered by Dame Norma Wisdom, Professor of brush-related facts at de Montfort University.

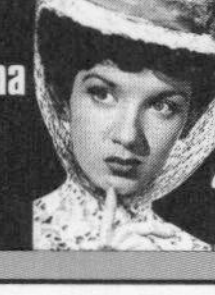

I'VE ALWAYS been a big fan of crooner Mel "velvet fog" Torme, and I've got his record. But recently I started a violent argument with my next door neighbour about Mel's favourite sort of brush. I said it was a bottle brush, whilst my neighbour maintained it was a nailbrush. Please can you tell us who is right and who is lying?

Ron Hyperpiesis, Hull

* *Unfortunately, you're both wrong. The truth is that Mel Torme was allergic to all brushes except wallpaper paste brushes.*

BRUSH FOR THE DAY with the Rev. Arthur Brush

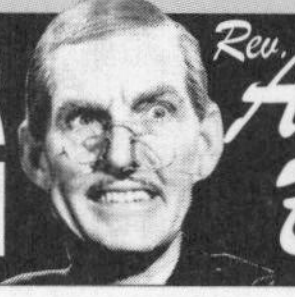

"I will also make it a possession for the bittern, and pools of water: and I will sweep it with the brush of destruction, saith the Lord of hosts." (Isaiah 14: ch. 23)

In this biblical quotation from the prophet Isaiah, it is clear that God is extremely cross. Indeed, it could be said that He is "bristling" with anger! In our own lives, it is often tempting to "sweep things under the carpet", but we must remember that God is omnipresent, and that includes under the carpet. Even though it's a very thin gap, He can fit down there, and He sees what we are attempting to hide from Him. The only safe policy, if we are to avoid the Lord's vengeful wrath, is to use a dustpan, and sweep the things we are trying to hide into that instead, and then put them in the bin.

Next week: ***"Either what woman having ten pieces of silver, if she lose one piece, doth not light a candle and sweep the house, and seek diligently till she find it?"*** (Luke 15: ch. 8)

KIDS SAY THE MOST VAGUELY AMUSING THINGS ABOUT BRUSHES

"GOSH granny, somebody must have very big teeth," announced my 3-year-old grandson recently. I had to laugh, as I explained to him that he was looking at a back-scrubbing brush!

Mrs Freda Epistaxis, Southampton

MY 2-year-old grand-daughter was recently going through all the items on my dressing table. When I pointed out the hairbrush, she asked me: "Is that an implement for grooming leporid rodents of the genus Caprolagus?" Bless her, she thought I meant hares!

Mrs Joyce Splenomegaly, Harrogate

"GOSH granny, somebody must have a very small back," announced my 3-year-old grandson recently. I had to laugh, as I explained to him that he was looking at a toothbrush!"

Mrs Freda Epistaxis, Southampton

Brush Spot

The most valuable brush in the world is a solid gold toilet brush discovered in the tomb of the ancient Egyptian pharaoh Tutunkhamen. In 1996, it was sold at auction by its then owner, 'Crackerjack' presenter Stuart Francis, for £350 billion.

Brush Spot

Due to an ancient bylaw which has never been repealed, it is an offence punishable by death to use any sort of brush in Tewkesbury on a Sunday. Luckily the law is rarely enforced, and the last citizen of the town to be executed for breaking it was beheaded way back in 1978.

BRUSH PUZZLES

TONI BASIL and her friends **TONI ARTHUR** and **LUCA TONI** have gone fishing for brushes, but Oh dear! Their lines have got all tangled up. Can you untangle the lines to discover which Toni has hooked which sort of brush?

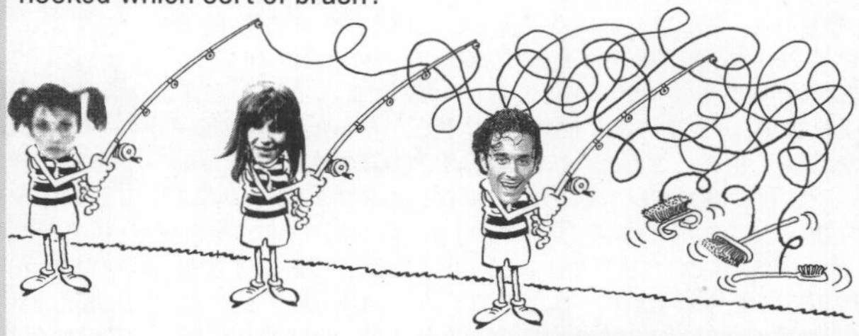

Brush Spot

Michelangelo painted his famous fresco on the roof of the Cistine Chapel using brushes he had made himself ... from his own pubes!

ANSWERS: TONI BASIL has caught a nailbrush, TONI ARTHUR has caught a toothbrush and LUCA TONI has caught a brush.

★GAMBLING★

A PROFESSIONAL GAMBLER has expressed his concern for celebrities after the government gave the green light for Las Vegas-style Supercasinos around the country.

High Roller Ray Fears for Stars

Ray Croucher, 52, fears that the stars could be tempted to squander their fortunes in the glamorous new unlimited stake gaming arenas. And he should know, for after 35 years as one of Britain's most successful high rollers, Ray has seen the mighty fallen more times than he cares to remember.

And now, in his new book, Wallsend-based Croucher lifts the lid on the gambling celebs who simply don't know when to stop.

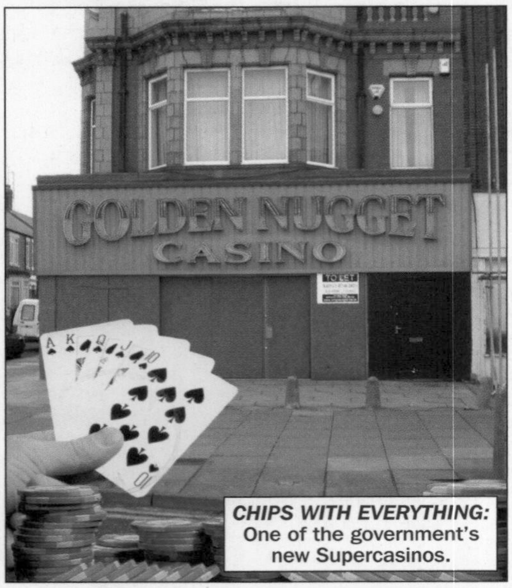
GOLDEN NUGGET
CASINO

CHIPS WITH EVERYTHING: One of the government's new Supercasinos.

★★★★KIDMAN LOST CHERRY IN CHIPPIE★★★★

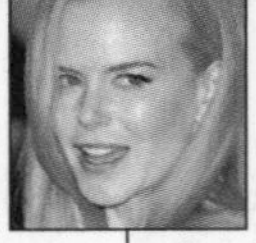

"THE FIRST rule of gambling is never to bet more than you can afford to lose, and it's a rule I've never broken. It's a pity the same can't be said of the stars. I remember once when I'd been playing roulette in Monte Carlo with **PRINCE RAINIER** and **BILL GATES**. I lost quite heavily, and so when I returned home, I tried to recoup some money by having a go on the fruitie in the chip shop on Hadrian Road. I only had 50p, so I hedged my bets by holding two lemons on the first spin and trying to nudge the middle reel. I lost, but I took it in my stride and walked away. On my way out, I went to the counter on the offchance that they had a few batter bits they were throwing out, and I couldn't believe my eyes when I turned to leave. There, stood at the bandit was **NICOLE KIDMAN**! She had this manic look on her face and she was stuffing money in the machine like there was no tomorrow. It was plain to see that she didn't have a system, which meant she was going to lose, big time. She'd got two cherries and a bell, and she was going to try to nudge for three cherries. At this point a pro would kneel down and look round the reel to see what was coming up. Kidman was just going to nudge and hope, like the chancer she was. By the time the chippie shut, she had put £3 million in twenty pees into that fruitie. Like in one of her films, she'd played the bandit with her eyes wide shut, and left the chippie with her pockets empty."

★★★★★★★★★★FRANK DID IT HIS WAY★★★★★★★★★★

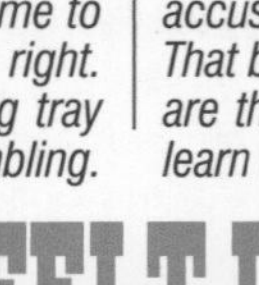

*"PLAYING Craps in a 5 star casino in Sun City with **DONALD TRUMP** might sound impossibly glamorous to the average guy in the street, but to a professional gambler like me it's just another day at the office. That's why, on the rare occasions when I'm home, I like to chill out a bit at the Happyland amusement arcade in Whitley Bay. I remember once I was getting a cup of 10 pees from the change booth when I heard a commotion over by the tuppenny waterfalls. When I looked over, I was amazed to see the Rat Pack - **FRANK SINATRA, DEAN MARTIN, PETER LAWFORD** and **SAMMY DAVIS JR.** - arguing about the best time to drop the coins. And get this - none of them was right. I could have told them to do it just as the sliding tray starts moving backwards. It's the first rule of gambling. But I didn't tell them, because for every winner on the pro-gambling circuit, there are four losers, and they were the losers that day. They say the first rule of gambling is to know when you are beaten, and these Vegas high rollers certainly hadn't learned that rule. After putting in nearly £10million in 2 pees they walked out, frustrated at their failure. I could see the huge mat of copper overhanging the slides and moved in for the kill. It was going to be like taking candy from a baby, but I never got the chance to collect that jackpot. At that moment, a lorry must have gone past and set the tamper alarm off. The gadgy came over and accused me of bumping it again and chucked me out. That big win was so near and yet so far, but those are the breaks in this game, and any pro has to learn to take the rough with the smooth."*

WOLFMAN JACK GOT ★BITTEN AT DOGS★

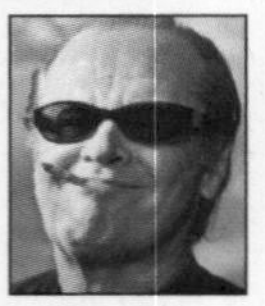

*"THE FIRST rule of gambling is to know the game inside out before you part with your cash. Unfortunately, that's a rule that celebrities seem unable to get their heads round. I remember this one time, I'd just spent a week in Vegas taking part in a poker tournament alongside the likes of **ARISTOTLE ONASSIS** and **PAUL GETTY**. I arrived back in Wallsend and immediately got the bus to Brough Park, as it was Tuesday and the dogs were on. When I got there, I had to pinch myself to prove I wasn't dreaming that I was still in Las Vegas. For standing in front of me in the queue for the Tote was One Flew Over the Cuckoo's Nest star **JACK NICHOLSON**! We got chatting and he told me how he was going to put a million pound on Prince Charming who was in trap three in the 8.20 because three was his lucky number. I told him that he was throwing his money away, because as any professional gambler will tell you, you always bet on the dog that does a shit in the pre-race parade. That's why I was putting my £3.80 on Highland Boy. But, like his character in A Few Good Men, Nicholson couldn't handle the truth. Sure enough, Prince Charming came in fourth and Jack came away with jack shit. I saw him during the next race throwing his guts up in the alley behind the portaloos."*

★★★★★★EASTWOOD FELT LUCKY, PUNK★★★★★★

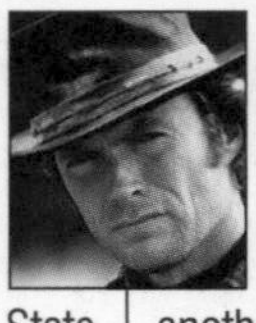

"I PLAY a monthly poker game with **HUGH HEFNER**, **STEPHEN SPIELBERG** and **HENRY KISSINGER**. We never know where the game is going to be, we just meet at the airport, climb aboard Hugh's private jet and we're whisked off to some exotic location. One month we may find ourselves on top of the Empire State building, the next in Marakesh or at the North Pole. I remember this one month, I got on the wrong bus to the airport and Hugh's plane took off without me. I'd already psyched myself up for some cards and I was in gambling mode. I had four pounds in my pocket so I popped into the newsagent to get some scratchcards - two Rich for Lifes, a Red Hot Seven and a Lucky Leprechaun. While I was busy scratching them on the counter, I heard someone ask the shopkeeper for 3 million Double Draws. I recognised the voice immediately. It was **CLINT EASTWOOD**. As a professional high roller, I know that the first rule of gambling is to learn how to load the odds in your favour. With scratch cards, one in ten is a winner, so I always buy them in lots of ten. Then I use the winnings from that lot to buy another ten, and so on. That way, I am always on top of the game and I don't get in over my head. But Clint had made the classic amateur's mistake of buying his cards in bulk, and I knew he would pay dearly. He spent the next twenty minutes scratching furiously at the silver bits, all to no avail. Eastwood may have felt lucky, punk when he went in that newsagent, but he came out with a fistful of dollars less than he came in with, and nothing in his pockets but a bit of every which way but loose change."

★FEVER★

Picture courtesy of Whitley Bay Telegraph & Argus.

"At the gaming tables, winning and losing comes with the territory," he told us. "It's all a matter of weighing up the odds. If you do your homework, it's easy to turn them in your favour and win a million. But if you don't know what you are doing, you could lose everything on the turn of a card or the spin of a wheel. Unless, like me, you are a professional, gambling is a mug's game. And I'm afraid that in Hollywood, there's one born every minute.

"Most people can have the occasional flutter and leave it at that. But the mind of a celebrity works differently. They believe that because they've made a lot of money acting and singing, they can be successful at anything. Sadly for them, nothing could be further from the truth..."

REGULARS KNOCKED ★SPOTS OF LIBERACE★

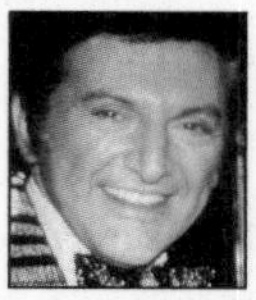

"WHEN YOU spend 11 months of the year sitting around roulette tables anywhere from Saint Morritz to Reno, it makes a refreshing change to find myself back on my home turf. That's why when I'm home, you'll probably find me in my favourite boozer, The Albion in Willington Quay. They know me there, and they don't pester me with questions about my celebrity friends and my jet-setting lifestyle. I remember one time I was in there. It was a Tuesday morning and I was watching the racing from Redcar on the telly, because I had £1.37 riding on Stepanov in the 11.30. There was a game of dominoes going on at the next table involving a couple of regulars, Albert and Scouse Jack, but I wasn't getting involved as they were playing for matches. I'm a professional gambler used to playing for fortunes in hard cash and matches don't pay the bills! The next thing I know, a familiar face had joined the game. It was ***LIBERACE****! Immediately, he upped the stakes, staking a hundred thousand matches on the next game. Now he may have been able to play the piano, but he didn't have the faintest idea how to play doms. He kept hold of the double six when he had a golden opportunity to drop it and then ended up having to knock, and lost badly. He kept making classic mistakes, losing game after game. Instead of cutting his losses, he kept piling on the matches, saying double or quits. By the final round, there were 200 million matches on the table. I could see the sweat on Liberace's top lip as the game got underway. As usual, like a fool he held onto his high doubles, and it didn't take Scouse Jack long to chip out. When Liberace left The Albion that day, he didn't have two matches to scratch his arse with. I couldn't help thinking that if those matches had been cash, he would have been ruined."*

CASH
CASINO
NOW
INSIDE
DRAW
for details

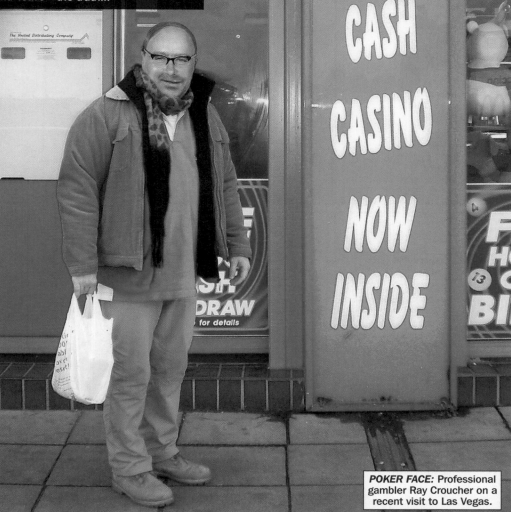

POKER FACE: Professional gambler Ray Croucher on a recent visit to Las Vegas.

SPEAKING from his bedsit home above a Wallsend launderette, Ray expressed his concern that the opening of the new Supercasinos will spell financial disaster for the stars.

He told us: "I've seen too many celebrities crash and burn at the gaming tables, at the bandits and in William Hill's. They may be superstars in Hollywood, but in the world of gambling they are just bit-part players."

He continued: *"Everybody has ups and downs, even a professional like me. I've had a particularly bad run since 1998, and that followed hard on the heels of another lean period which lasted fourteen years. I owe quite a lot of money to a bookie in Blyth, and I've got a few from Howden and North Shields looking for me too. But I'm not worried. The life of the professional gambler is a rollercoaster, and I know I'll bounce back. That big win is just around the corner. I only hope it comes before they break my legs again."*

Signed copies of Ray's book **'Thank Your Unlucky Stars'** *(Hard-boiled Egg Books)* are available from the author in The Albion pub, Howden, every day from 10.30am to midnight, priced one pint.

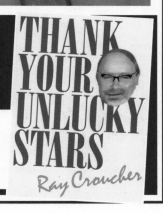

THANK
YOUR
UNLUCKY
STARS
Ray Croucher

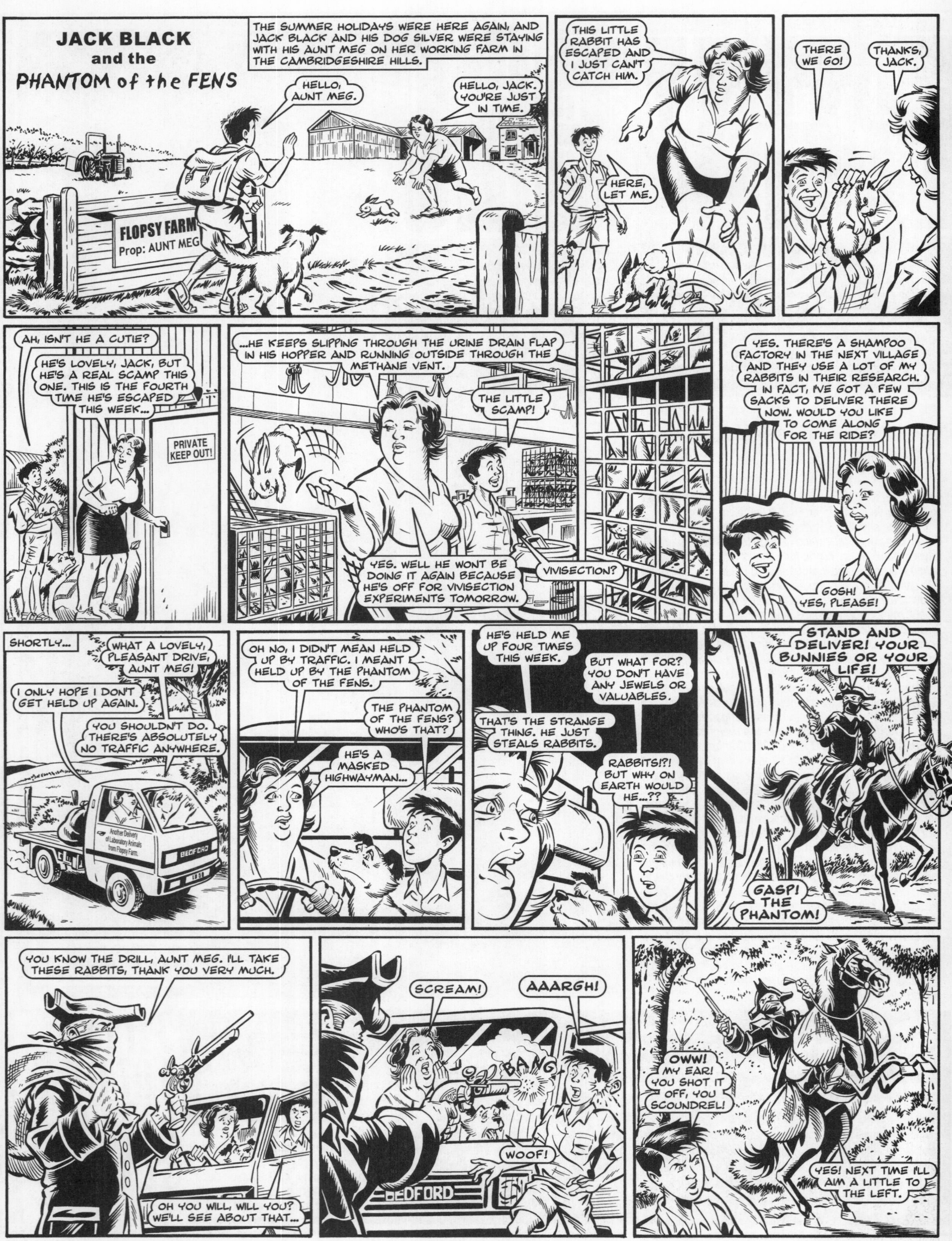
JACK BLACK and the PHANTOM of the FENS
THE SUMMER HOLIDAYS WERE HERE AGAIN, AND JACK BLACK AND HIS DOG SILVER WERE STAYING WITH HIS AUNT MEG ON HER WORKING FARM IN THE CAMBRIDGESHIRE HILLS.
HELLO, AUNT MEG.
HELLO, JACK. YOU'RE JUST IN TIME.
FLOPSY FARM Prop: AUNT MEG
THIS LITTLE RABBIT HAS ESCAPED AND I JUST CAN'T CATCH HIM.
HERE, LET ME.
THERE WE GO!
THANKS, JACK.
AH, ISN'T HE A CUTIE?
HE'S LOVELY, JACK, BUT HE'S A REAL SCAMP THIS ONE. THIS IS THE FOURTH TIME HE'S ESCAPED THIS WEEK...
PRIVATE KEEP OUT!
...HE KEEPS SLIPPING THROUGH THE URINE DRAIN FLAP IN HIS HOPPER AND RUNNING OUTSIDE THROUGH THE METHANE VENT.
THE LITTLE SCAMP!
YES. WELL HE WONT BE DOING IT AGAIN BECAUSE HE'S OFF FOR VIVISECTION EXPERIMENTS TOMORROW.
VIVISECTION?
YES. THERE'S A SHAMPOO FACTORY IN THE NEXT VILLAGE AND THEY USE A LOT OF MY RABBITS IN THEIR RESEARCH. IN FACT, I'VE GOT A FEW SACKS TO DELIVER THERE NOW. WOULD YOU LIKE TO COME ALONG FOR THE RIDE?
GOSH! YES, PLEASE!
SHORTLY...
WHAT A LOVELY, PLEASANT DRIVE, AUNT MEG!
I ONLY HOPE I DON'T GET HELD UP AGAIN.
YOU SHOULDN'T DO. THERE'S ABSOLUTELY NO TRAFFIC ANYWHERE.
Another Delivery of Laboratory Animals from Flopsy Farm.
BEDFORD
OH NO, I DIDN'T MEAN HELD UP BY TRAFFIC. I MEANT HELD UP BY THE PHANTOM OF THE FENS.
THE PHANTOM OF THE FENS? WHO'S THAT?
HE'S A MASKED HIGHWAYMAN...
HE'S HELD ME UP FOUR TIMES THIS WEEK.
BUT WHAT FOR? YOU DON'T HAVE ANY JEWELS OR VALUABLES.
THAT'S THE STRANGE THING. HE JUST STEALS RABBITS.
RABBITS!?! BUT WHY ON EARTH WOULD HE...??
STAND AND DELIVER! YOUR BUNNIES OR YOUR LIFE!
GASP! THE PHANTOM!
YOU KNOW THE DRILL, AUNT MEG. I'LL TAKE THESE RABBITS, THANK YOU VERY MUCH.
OH YOU WILL, WILL YOU? WE'LL SEE ABOUT THAT...
SCREAM!
AAARGH!
BANG
WOOF!
BEDFORD
OWW! MY EAR! YOU SHOT IT OFF, YOU SCOUNDREL!
YES! NEXT TIME I'LL AIM A LITTLE TO THE LEFT.

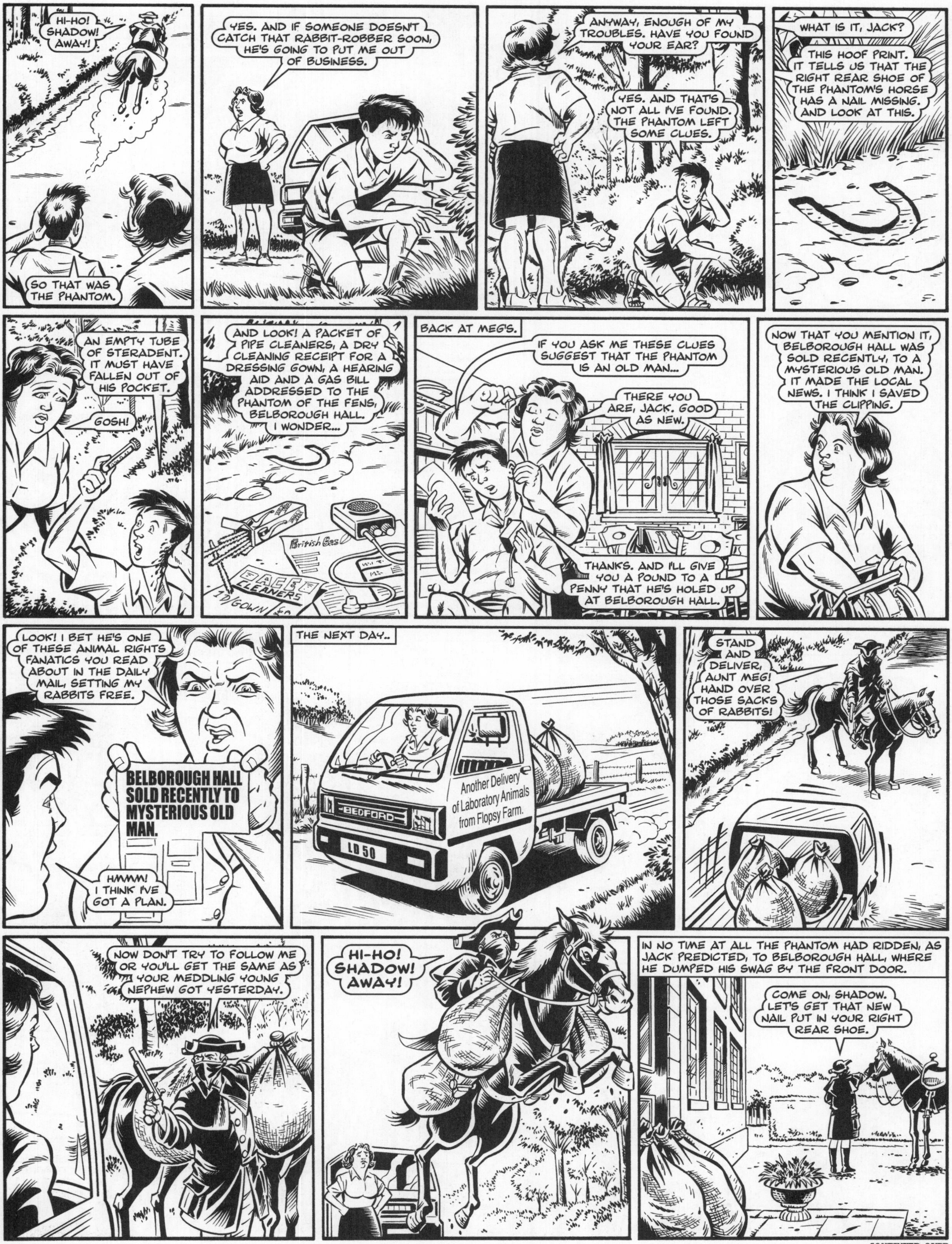
HI-HO! SHADOW! AWAY!
SO THAT WAS THE PHANTOM.
YES. AND IF SOMEONE DOESN'T CATCH THAT RABBIT-ROBBER SOON, HE'S GOING TO PUT ME OUT OF BUSINESS.
ANYWAY, ENOUGH OF MY TROUBLES. HAVE YOU FOUND YOUR EAR?
YES. AND THAT'S NOT ALL I'VE FOUND. THE PHANTOM LEFT SOME CLUES.
WHAT IS IT, JACK?
THIS HOOF PRINT. IT TELLS US THAT THE RIGHT REAR SHOE OF THE PHANTOM'S HORSE HAS A NAIL MISSING. AND LOOK AT THIS.
AN EMPTY TUBE OF STERADENT. IT MUST HAVE FALLEN OUT OF HIS POCKET.
GOSH!
AND LOOK! A PACKET OF PIPE CLEANERS, A DRY CLEANING RECEIPT FOR A DRESSING GOWN, A HEARING AID AND A GAS BILL ADDRESSED TO THE PHANTOM OF THE FENS, BELBOROUGH HALL. I WONDER...
British Gas
PIPE CLEANERS
BACK AT MEG'S.
IF YOU ASK ME THESE CLUES SUGGEST THAT THE PHANTOM IS AN OLD MAN...
THERE YOU ARE, JACK. GOOD AS NEW.
THANKS. AND I'LL GIVE YOU A POUND TO A PENNY THAT HE'S HOLED UP AT BELBOROUGH HALL.
NOW THAT YOU MENTION IT, BELBOROUGH HALL WAS SOLD RECENTLY, TO A MYSTERIOUS OLD MAN. IT MADE THE LOCAL NEWS. I THINK I SAVED THE CLIPPING.
LOOK! I BET HE'S ONE OF THESE ANIMAL RIGHTS FANATICS YOU READ ABOUT IN THE DAILY MAIL, SETTING MY RABBITS FREE.
BELBOROUGH HALL SOLD RECENTLY TO MYSTERIOUS OLD MAN.
HMMM! I THINK I'VE GOT A PLAN.
THE NEXT DAY..
Another Delivery of Laboratory Animals from Flopsy Farm.
BEDFORD
LD 50
STAND AND DELIVER, AUNT MEG! HAND OVER THOSE SACKS OF RABBITS!
NOW DON'T TRY TO FOLLOW ME OR YOU'LL GET THE SAME AS YOUR MEDDLING YOUNG NEPHEW GOT YESTERDAY.
HI-HO! SHADOW! AWAY!
IN NO TIME AT ALL THE PHANTOM HAD RIDDEN, AS JACK PREDICTED, TO BELBOROUGH HALL, WHERE HE DUMPED HIS SWAG BY THE FRONT DOOR.
COME ON, SHADOW. LET'S GET THAT NEW NAIL PUT IN YOUR RIGHT REAR SHOE.

CONTINUED OVER

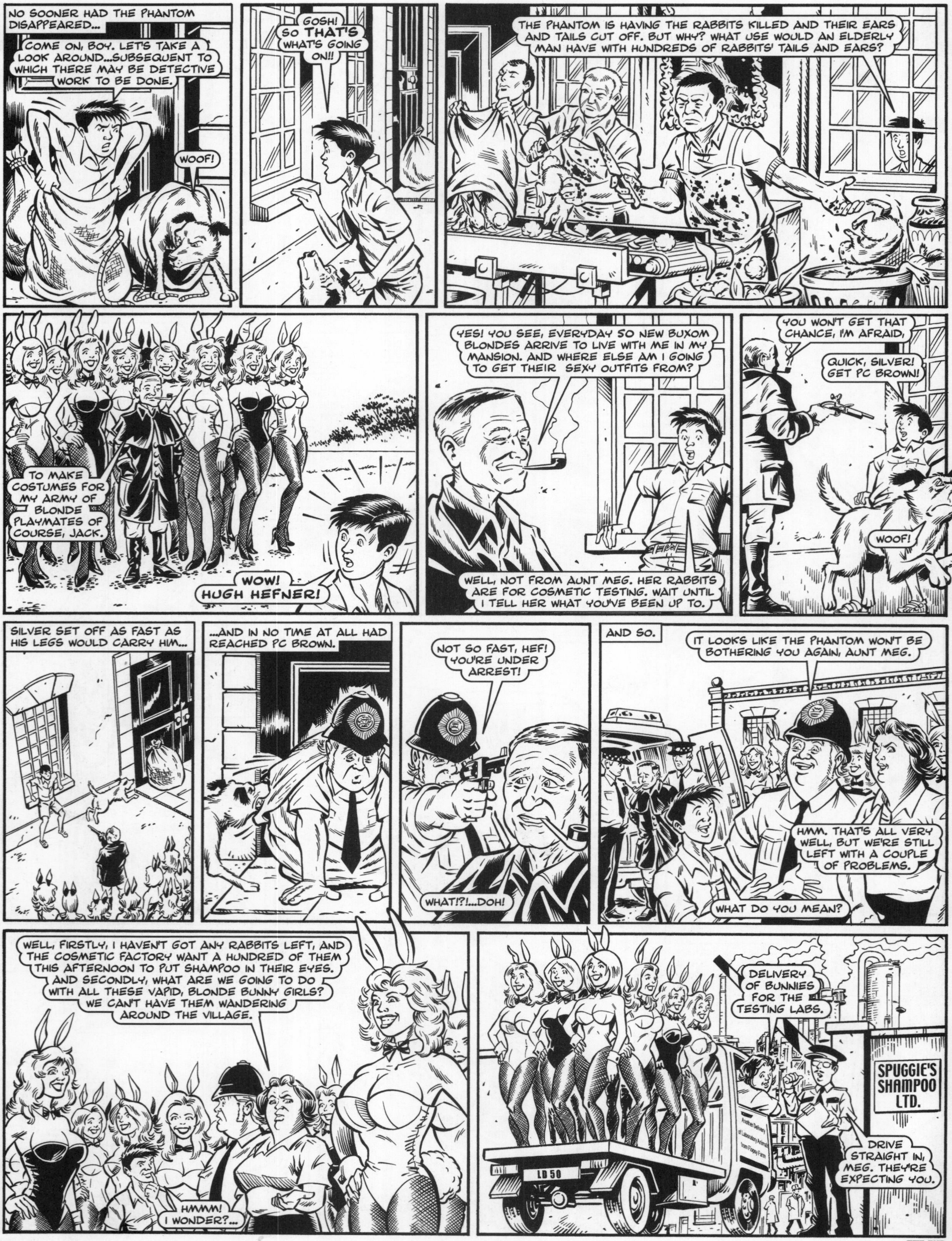

NO SOONER HAD THE PHANTOM DISAPPEARED...
COME ON, BOY. LET'S TAKE A LOOK AROUND...SUBSEQUENT TO WHICH THERE MAY BE DETECTIVE WORK TO BE DONE.
WOOF!
GOSH! SO THAT'S WHAT'S GOING ON!!
THE PHANTOM IS HAVING THE RABBITS KILLED AND THEIR EARS AND TAILS CUT OFF. BUT WHY? WHAT USE WOULD AN ELDERLY MAN HAVE WITH HUNDREDS OF RABBITS' TAILS AND EARS?
TO MAKE COSTUMES FOR MY ARMY OF BLONDE PLAYMATES OF COURSE, JACK.
WOW! HUGH HEFNER!
YES! YOU SEE, EVERYDAY SO NEW BUXOM BLONDES ARRIVE TO LIVE WITH ME IN MY MANSION. AND WHERE ELSE AM I GOING TO GET THEIR SEXY OUTFITS FROM?
WELL, NOT FROM AUNT MEG. HER RABBITS ARE FOR COSMETIC TESTING. WAIT UNTIL I TELL HER WHAT YOU'VE BEEN UP TO.
YOU WON'T GET THAT CHANCE, I'M AFRAID,
QUICK, SILVER! GET PC BROWN!
WOOF!
SILVER SET OFF AS FAST AS HIS LEGS WOULD CARRY HIM...
...AND IN NO TIME AT ALL HAD REACHED PC BROWN.
NOT SO FAST, HEF! YOU'RE UNDER ARREST!
WHAT!?!...DOH!
AND SO.
IT LOOKS LIKE THE PHANTOM WON'T BE BOTHERING YOU AGAIN, AUNT MEG.
HMM. THAT'S ALL VERY WELL, BUT WE'RE STILL LEFT WITH A COUPLE OF PROBLEMS.
WHAT DO YOU MEAN?
WELL, FIRSTLY, I HAVEN'T GOT ANY RABBITS LEFT, AND THE COSMETIC FACTORY WANT A HUNDRED OF THEM THIS AFTERNOON TO PUT SHAMPOO IN THEIR EYES. AND SECONDLY, WHAT ARE WE GOING TO DO WITH ALL THESE VAPID, BLONDE BUNNY GIRLS? WE CAN'T HAVE THEM WANDERING AROUND THE VILLAGE.
HMMM! I WONDER?...
DELIVERY OF BUNNIES FOR THE TESTING LABS.
SPUGGIE'S SHAMPOO LTD.
LD 50
DRIVE STRAIGHT IN, MEG. THEY'RE EXPECTING YOU.
THE END

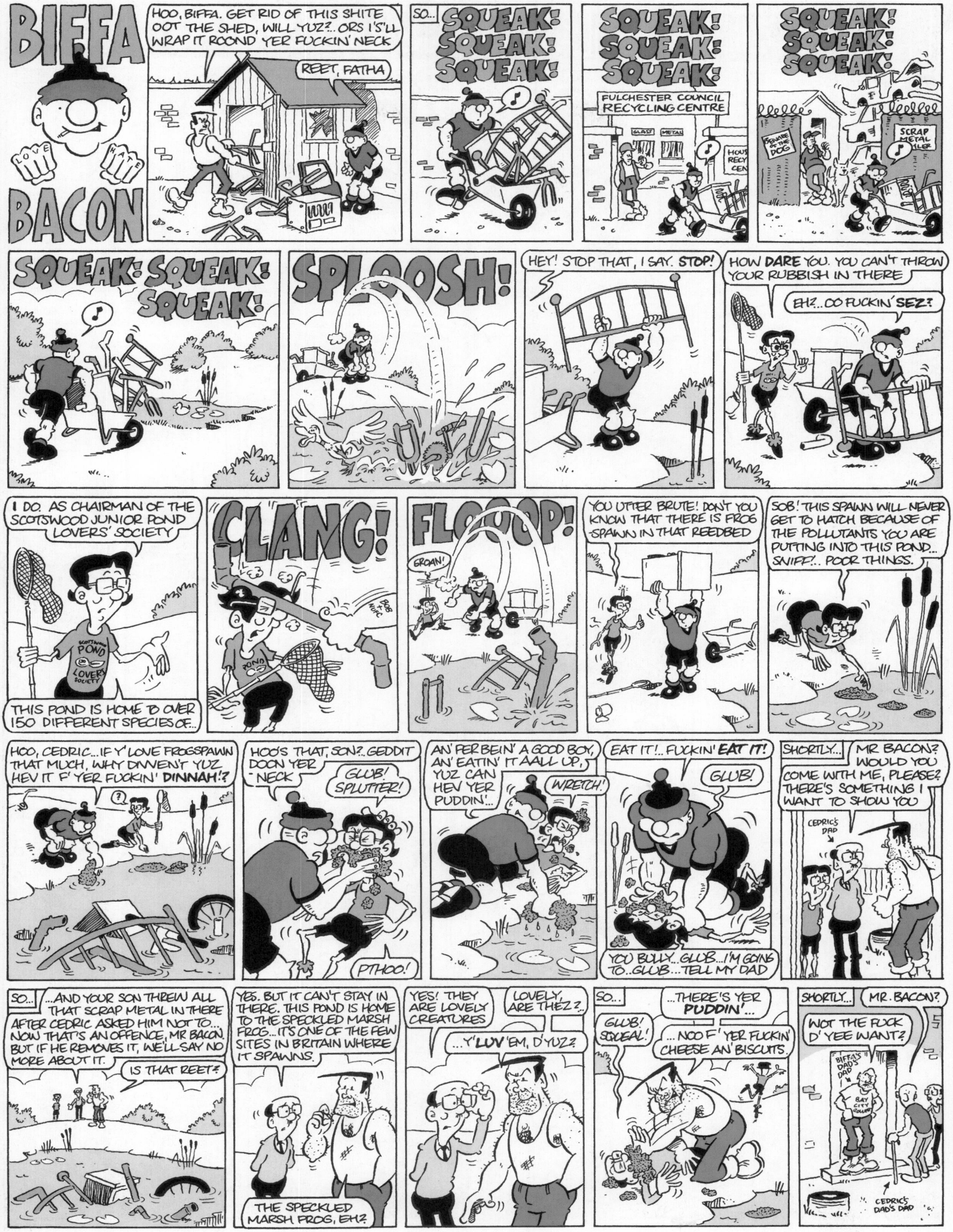

BIFFA BACON
LOVE
HATE
HOO, BIFFA. GET RID OF THIS SHITE OOT THE SHED, WILL YUZ?.. ORS I'S'LL WRAP IT ROOND YER FUCKIN' NECK
REET, FATHA
SO...
SQUEAK! SQUEAK! SQUEAK!
SQUEAK! SQUEAK! SQUEAK!
FULCHESTER COUNCIL RECYCLING CENTRE
GLASS
METAL
SQUEAK! SQUEAK! SQUEAK!
BEWARE OF THE DOG
SCRAP METAL
SQUEAK! SQUEAK! SQUEAK!
SPLOOSH!
HEY! STOP THAT, I SAY. STOP!
HOW DARE YOU. YOU CAN'T THROW YOUR RUBBISH IN THERE
EH?.. OO FUCKIN' SEZ?
I DO. AS CHAIRMAN OF THE SCOTSWOOD JUNIOR POND LOVERS' SOCIETY
SCOTSWOOD POND LOVERS SOCIETY
THIS POND IS HOME TO OVER 150 DIFFERENT SPECIES OF...
CLANG!
FLOOOP!
GROAN!
YOU UTTER BRUTE! DON'T YOU KNOW THAT THERE IS FROG-SPAWN IN THAT REEDBED
SOB! THIS SPAWN WILL NEVER GET TO HATCH BECAUSE OF THE POLLUTANTS YOU ARE PUTTING INTO THIS POND... SNIFF!.. POOR THINGS.
HOO, CEDRIC...IF Y' LOVE FROGSPAWN THAT MUCH, WHY DIVVEN'T YUZ HEV IT F' YER FUCKIN' DINNAH!?
HOO'S THAT, SON?.. GEDDIT DOON YER NECK
GLUB! SPLUTTER!
PTHOO!
AN' FER BEIN' A GOOD BOY, AN' EATIN' IT AALL UP, YUZ CAN HEV YER PUDDIN'...
WRETCH!
EAT IT!.. FUCKIN' EAT IT!
GLUB!
YOU BULLY...GLUB...I'M GOING TO..GLUB...TELL MY DAD
SHORTLY...
MR BACON? WOULD YOU COME WITH ME, PLEASE? THERE'S SOMETHING I WANT TO SHOW YOU
CEDRIC'S DAD
SO...
...AND YOUR SON THREW ALL THAT SCRAP METAL IN THERE AFTER CEDRIC ASKED HIM NOT TO... NOW THAT'S AN OFFENCE, MR BACON. BUT IF HE REMOVES IT, WE'LL SAY NO MORE ABOUT IT.
IS THAT REET?
YES. BUT IT CAN'T STAY IN THERE. THIS POND IS HOME TO THE SPECKLED MARSH FROG...IT'S ONE OF THE FEW SITES IN BRITAIN WHERE IT SPAWNS.
THE SPECKLED MARSH FROG, EH?
YES! THEY ARE LOVELY CREATURES
LOVELY, ARE THEZ?..
...Y'LUV 'EM, D'YUZ?
SO...
...THERE'S YER PUDDIN'...
GLUB! SQUEAL!
...NOO F' YER FUCKIN' CHEESE AN' BISCUITS.
SHORTLY...
MR. BACON?
WOT THE FUCK D' YEE WANT?
BIFFA'S DAD'S DAD
BAY CITY ROLLERS
CEDRIC'S DAD'S DAD

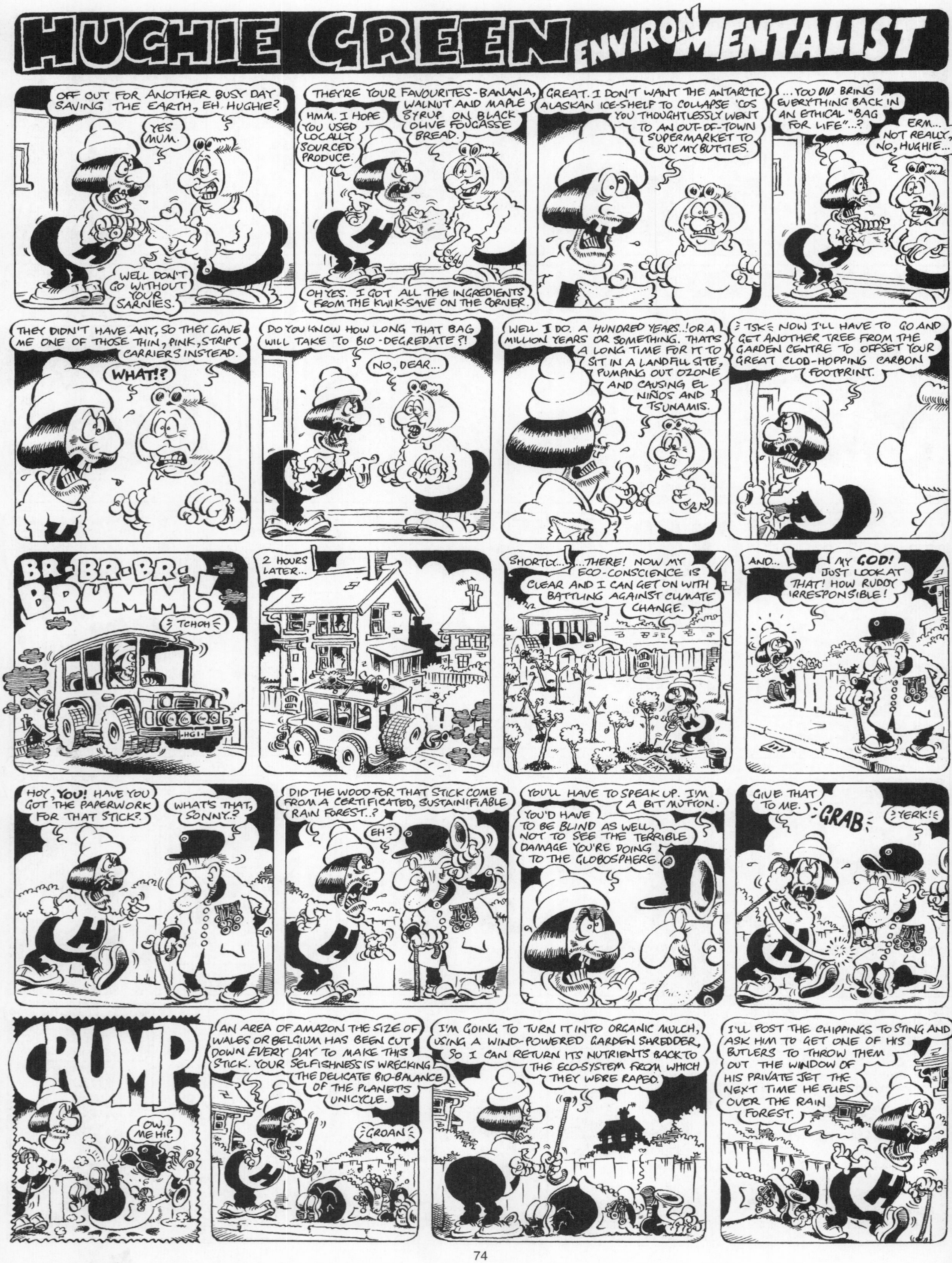
HUGHIE GREEN ENVIRONMENTALIST
OFF OUT FOR ANOTHER BUSY DAY SAVING THE EARTH, EH, HUGHIE?
YES MUM.
WELL DON'T GO WITHOUT YOUR SARNIES.
THEY'RE YOUR FAVOURITES - BANANA, WALNUT AND MAPLE SYRUP ON BLACK OLIVE FOUGASSE BREAD.
HMM. I HOPE YOU USED LOCALLY SOURCED PRODUCE.
OH YES. I GOT ALL THE INGREDIENTS FROM THE KWIK-SAVE ON THE CORNER.
GREAT. I DON'T WANT THE ANTARCTIC ALASKAN ICE-SHELF TO COLLAPSE 'COS YOU THOUGHTLESSLY WENT TO AN OUT-OF-TOWN SUPERMARKET TO BUY MY BUTTIES.
...YOU DID BRING EVERYTHING BACK IN AN ETHICAL "BAG FOR LIFE"...?
ERM... NOT REALLY, NO, HUGHIE...
THEY DIDN'T HAVE ANY, SO THEY GAVE ME ONE OF THOSE THIN, PINK, STRIPY CARRIERS INSTEAD.
WHAT!?
DO YOU KNOW HOW LONG THAT BAG WILL TAKE TO BIO-DEGREDATE?!
NO, DEAR...
WELL I DO. A HUNDRED YEARS..! OR A MILLION YEARS OR SOMETHING. THAT'S A LONG TIME FOR IT TO SIT IN A LANDFILL SITE, PUMPING OUT OZONE AND CAUSING EL NIÑOS AND TSUNAMIS.
TSK. NOW I'LL HAVE TO GO AND GET ANOTHER TREE FROM THE GARDEN CENTRE TO OFFSET YOUR GREAT CLOD-HOPPING CARBON FOOTPRINT.
BR-BR-BR-BRUMM!
TCHOH
HG1
2 HOURS LATER...
SHORTLY...
...THERE! NOW MY ECO-CONSCIENCE IS CLEAR AND I CAN GET ON WITH BATTLING AGAINST CLIMATE CHANGE.
PEAT
AND...
MY GOD! JUST LOOK AT THAT! HOW RUDDY IRRESPONSIBLE!
HOY, YOU! HAVE YOU GOT THE PAPERWORK FOR THAT STICK?
WHAT'S THAT, SONNY..?
DID THE WOOD FOR THAT STICK COME FROM A CERTIFICATED, SUSTAINIFIABLE RAIN FOREST..?
EH?
YOU'LL HAVE TO SPEAK UP. I'M A BIT MUTTON.
YOU'D HAVE TO BE BLIND AS WELL NOT TO SEE THE TERRIBLE DAMAGE YOU'RE DOING TO THE GLOBOSPHERE.
GIVE THAT TO ME.
GRAB
YERK!
CRUMP!
OW, ME HIP.
AN AREA OF AMAZON THE SIZE OF WALES OR BELGIUM HAS BEEN CUT DOWN EVERY DAY TO MAKE THIS STICK. YOUR SELFISHNESS IS WRECKING THE DELICATE BIO-BALANCE OF THE PLANET'S UNICYCLE.
GROAN
I'M GOING TO TURN IT INTO ORGANIC MULCH, USING A WIND-POWERED GARDEN SHREDDER, SO I CAN RETURN ITS NUTRIENTS BACK TO THE ECO-SYSTEM FROM WHICH THEY WERE RAPED.
I'LL POST THE CHIPPINGS TO STING AND ASK HIM TO GET ONE OF HIS BUTLERS TO THROW THEM OUT THE WINDOW OF HIS PRIVATE JET THE NEXT TIME HE FLIES OVER THE RAIN FOREST.

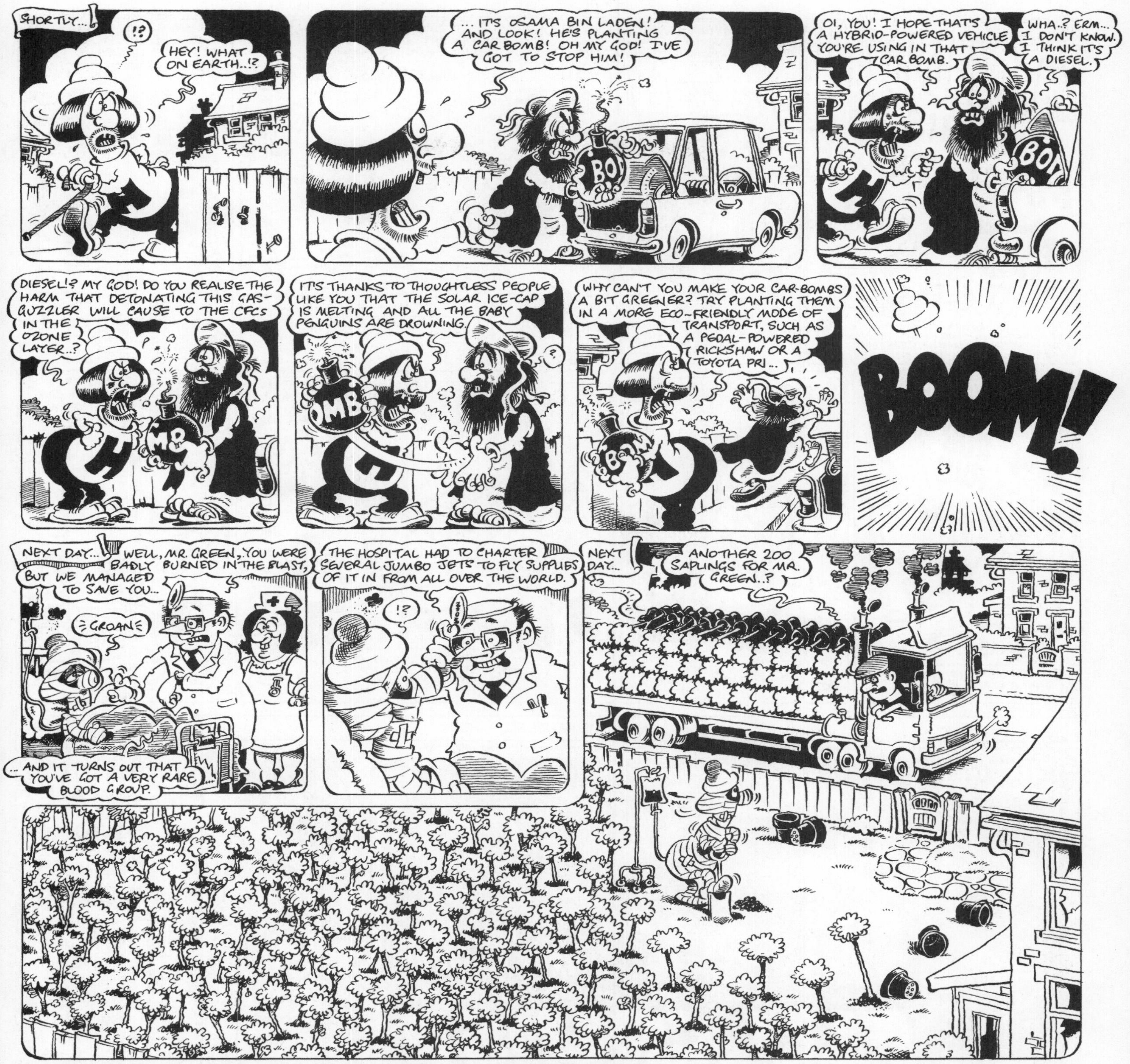
SHORTLY...
!?
HEY! WHAT ON EARTH..!?
...IT'S OSAMA BIN LADEN! AND LOOK! HE'S PLANTING A CAR BOMB! OH MY GOD! I'VE GOT TO STOP HIM!
BOMB
OI, YOU! I HOPE THAT'S A HYBRID-POWERED VEHICLE YOU'RE USING IN THAT CAR BOMB.
WHA..? ERM... I DON'T KNOW. I THINK IT'S A DIESEL.
DIESEL!? MY GOD! DO YOU REALISE THE HARM THAT DETONATING THIS GAS-GUZZLER WILL CAUSE TO THE CFCs IN THE OZONE LAYER..?
IT'S THANKS TO THOUGHTLESS PEOPLE LIKE YOU THAT THE SOLAR ICE-CAP IS MELTING AND ALL THE BABY PENGUINS ARE DROWNING.
WHY CAN'T YOU MAKE YOUR CAR-BOMBS A BIT GREENER? TRY PLANTING THEM IN A MORE ECO-FRIENDLY MODE OF TRANSPORT, SUCH AS A PEDAL-POWERED RICKSHAW OR A TOYOTA PRI...
BOOM!
NEXT DAY...
WELL, MR GREEN, YOU WERE BADLY BURNED IN THE BLAST, BUT WE MANAGED TO SAVE YOU...
GROAN
...AND IT TURNS OUT THAT YOU'VE GOT A VERY RARE BLOOD GROUP.
THE HOSPITAL HAD TO CHARTER SEVERAL JUMBO JETS TO FLY SUPPLIES OF IT IN FROM ALL OVER THE WORLD.
!?
NEXT DAY...
ANOTHER 200 SAPLINGS FOR MR. GREEN..?

Oddie Gets Genital Thrush

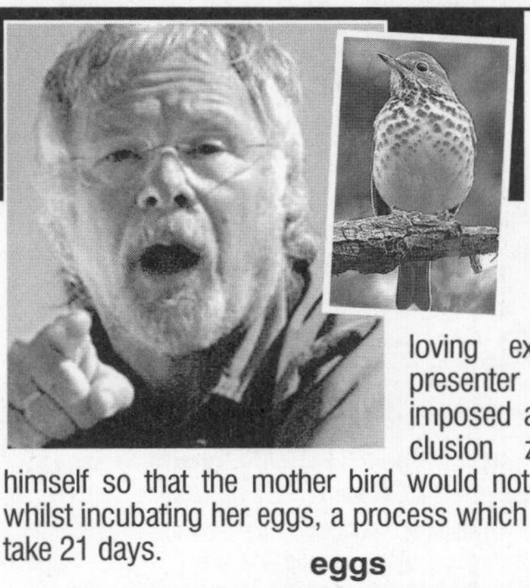

Oddie and (inset) a thrush similar to the one nesting in his pubes.

CURMUDGEONLY TV bird-spotter Bill Oddie today begins his fourth day standing with his trousers around his ankles in the middle of Sherwood Forest after a bird made a nest... *in his pubes!*

The ex-Goodie, 66 had been picnicking last Saturday in Clumber Park near Mansfield when he was caught short and popped into the forest to spend a penny. He was just about to pull up his trousers when a female Mistlethrush flew down from a tree and perched on his manhood. Before Oddie could react, the bird apparently started to make a nest in his pubic hair.

A spokesman for Oddie told us: "The thrush laid a clutch of eggs in the nest and Bill has vowed not to move until the chicks have hatched."

The bird-loving ex-*Springwatch* presenter immediately imposed a 20 yard exclusion zone around himself so that the mother bird would not be disturbed whilst incubating her eggs, a process which he expects to take 21 days.

eggs

But a spokesman for twitcher club the RSPB warned that the gnome-like naturalist could be in for a longer wait than he thinks. He told reporters: "The eggs will hatch after three weeks, but it could be a further month before the chicks are fully fledged and ready to leave the safety of Bill's pubes. Oddie could easily find himself standing in the woods with his kecks round his ankles until early Autumn."

why

The bearded grouch is being sustained during his ordeal with food provided by volunteers from the Edwalton Women's Institute. "We are firing home-made cakes and sausage rolls into his mouth across the exclusion zone using catapults and slingshots made from old tights and knicker elastic," said branch chairlady Marjorie Chairperson.

zed

This is not the first time that an ex-Goodie has found himself incapacitated by wildlife. In 1983, Tim Brooke-Taylor spent three months bent double on St Andrews golf course after a red squirrel hibernated in the hole in his arse as he bent to place his ball on the tee.

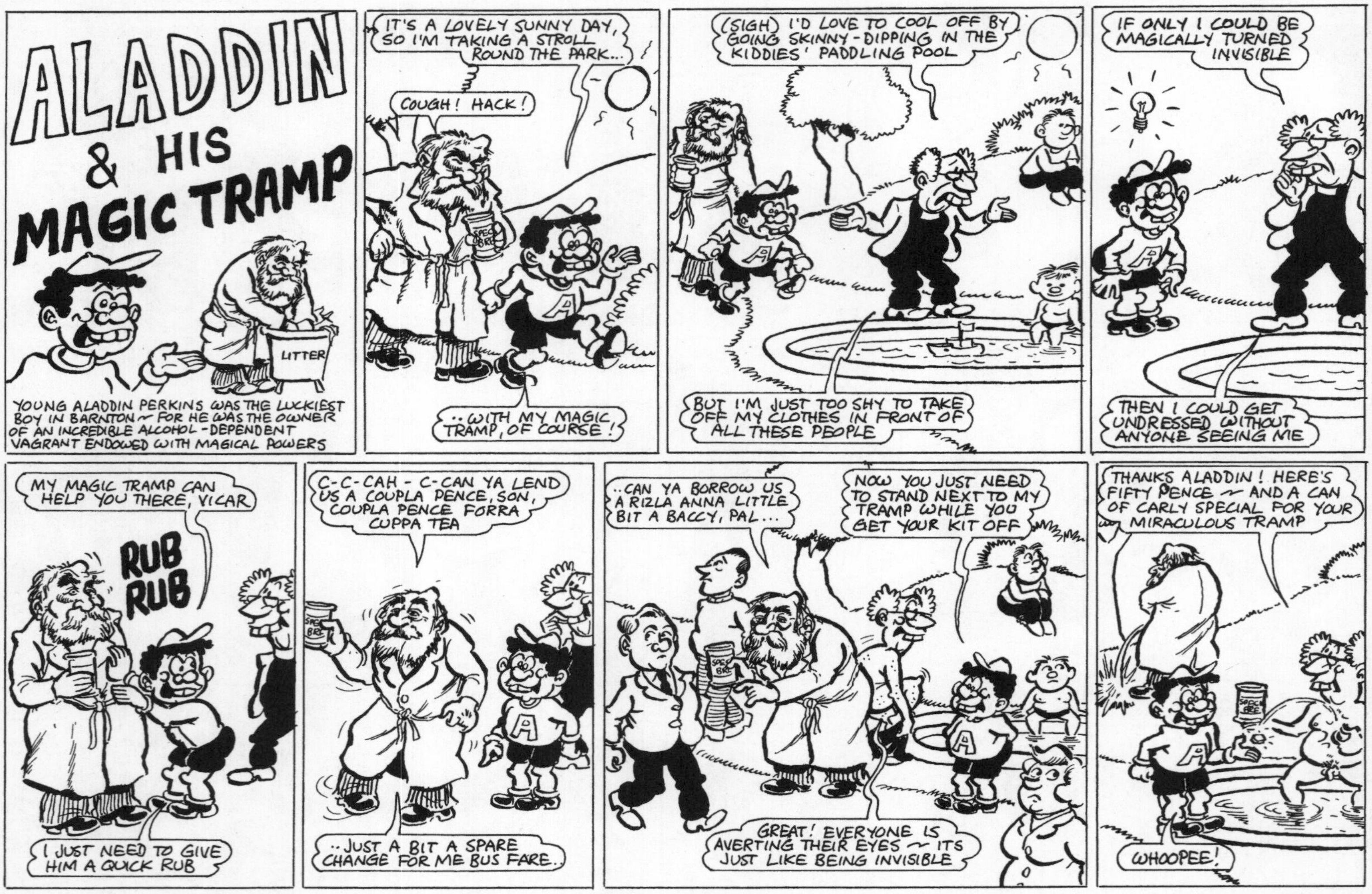
ALADDIN & HIS MAGIC TRAMP
LITTER
YOUNG ALADDIN PERKINS WAS THE LUCKIEST BOY IN BARNTON ~ FOR HE WAS THE OWNER OF AN INCREDIBLE ALCOHOL-DEPENDENT VAGRANT ENDOWED WITH MAGICAL POWERS
IT'S A LOVELY SUNNY DAY, SO I'M TAKING A STROLL ROUND THE PARK...
COUGH! HACK!
..WITH MY MAGIC TRAMP, OF COURSE!
(SIGH) I'D LOVE TO COOL OFF BY GOING SKINNY-DIPPING IN THE KIDDIES' PADDLING POOL
BUT I'M JUST TOO SHY TO TAKE OFF MY CLOTHES IN FRONT OF ALL THESE PEOPLE
IF ONLY I COULD BE MAGICALLY TURNED INVISIBLE
THEN I COULD GET UNDRESSED WITHOUT ANYONE SEEING ME
MY MAGIC TRAMP CAN HELP YOU THERE, VICAR
RUB RUB
I JUST NEED TO GIVE HIM A QUICK RUB
C-C-CAH - C-CAN YA LEND US A COUPLA PENCE, SON, COUPLA PENCE FORRA CUPPA TEA
..JUST A BIT A SPARE CHANGE FOR ME BUS FARE..
..CAN YA BORROW US A RIZLA ANNA LITTLE BIT A BACCY, PAL...
NOW YOU JUST NEED TO STAND NEXT TO MY TRAMP WHILE YOU GET YOUR KIT OFF
GREAT! EVERYONE IS AVERTING THEIR EYES ~ ITS JUST LIKE BEING INVISIBLE
THANKS ALADDIN! HERE'S FIFTY PENCE ~ AND A CAN OF CARLY SPECIAL FOR YOUR MIRACULOUS TRAMP
WHOOPEE!

MARITIME ILLNESS CRUISES

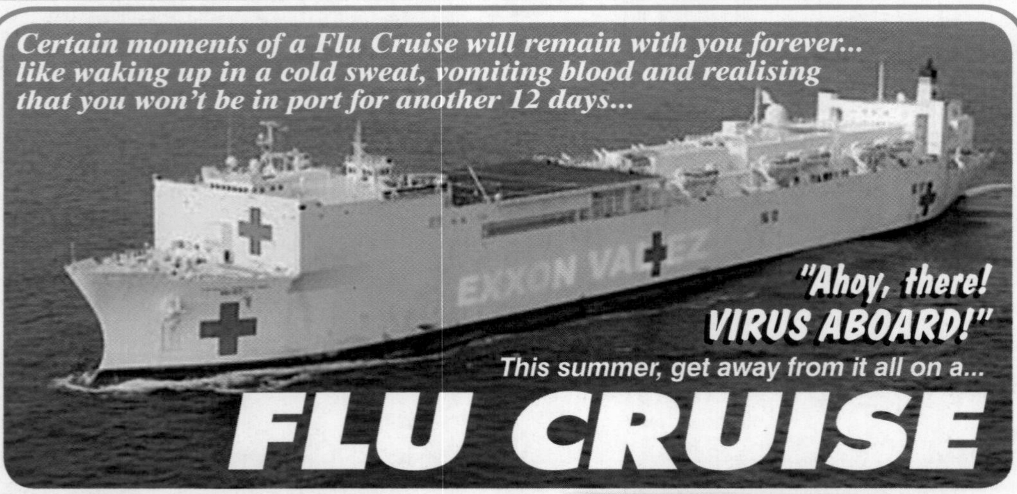
Certain moments of a Flu Cruise will remain with you forever... like waking up in a cold sweat, vomiting blood and realising that you won't be in port for another 12 days...
EXXON VALDEZ
"Ahoy, there! VIRUS ABOARD!"
This summer, get away from it all on a...
FLU CRUISE

SAVOUR the occasion from DAY ONE as you are laid low below deck with nausea, vomiting, diahorrea, cramps, fevers and headaches - *ALL GUARANTEED!*

The **STOMACH FLU** virus also causes dehydration which, if severe enough, can cause hospitalization at several exotic locations. You'll have plenty of time to stroll around and explore the many incredibly dilapidated medical facilities of the region, and delight in the enigmatic encounters you'll have with gun-toting militiamen or unsmiling nurses waving huge syringes in your face! During your leisurely days at sea you can enjoy many traditional on-board games like *Disinfect the Deck* and *Decontamination*. And the on-board cuisine is second to none. When you are not retching bile, you can feast your eyes on our unique mouth-chundering dishes, all served by bleach-toting staff in gas masks.

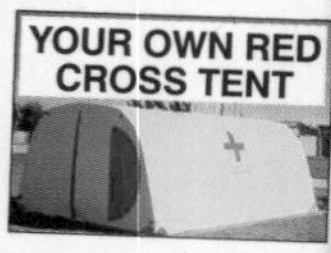

YOUR OWN RED CROSS TENT

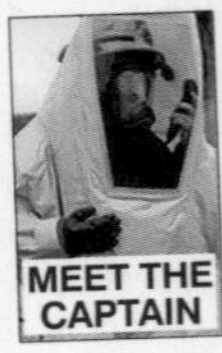

MEET THE CAPTAIN

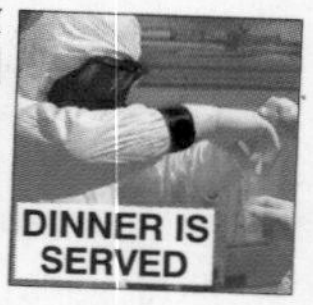

DINNER IS SERVED

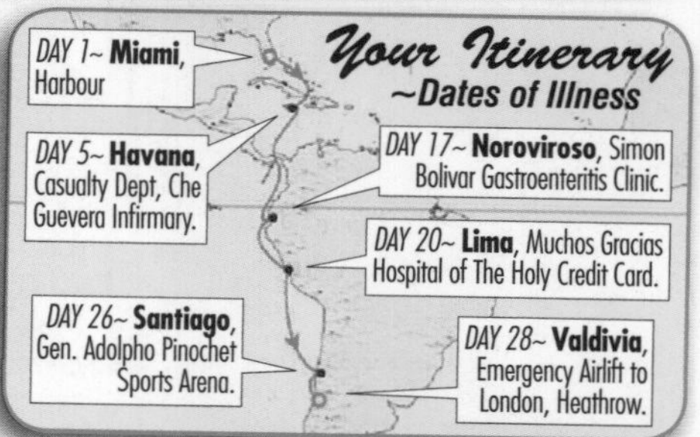
Your Itinerary
~Dates of Illness
DAY 1~ Miami, Harbour
DAY 5~ Havana, Casualty Dept, Che Guevera Infirmary.
DAY 17~ Noroviroso, Simon Bolivar Gastroenteritis Clinic.
DAY 20~ Lima, Muchos Gracias Hospital of The Holy Credit Card.
DAY 26~ Santiago, Gen. Adolpho Pinochet Sports Arena.
DAY 28~ Valdivia, Emergency Airlift to London, Heathrow.

Please send my free FLU CRUISE brochure to:

NAME........................ADDRESS..

Tick here ☐ if you require an overnight stay in hospital. If you require a vegetarian option meal left to go cold by your bed by a surly nurse, tick here ☐ Please tick your preferred hospital department (one only): Gastro-Urinary ☐ A&E ☐

• *FLU CRUISE UK (LTD) is not liable for any mistaken amputations or blue-dye eye injections performed by half-blind 'surgeons' at the General Adolpho Pinochet Infirmary.*

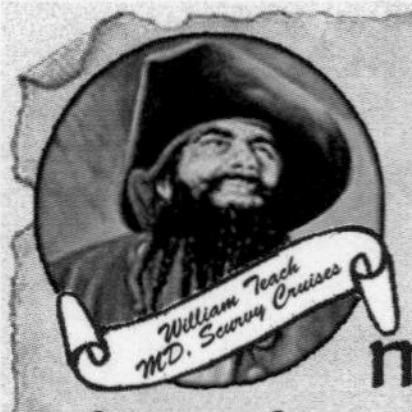
William Teach M.D. Scurvy Cruises

Avast, me Hearties an' Shiver me Timbers!

If any of you landlubbers fancies a more traditional seagoing illness - then why not climb aboard our

SCURVY CRUISE

Sail round and round the Southern Seas, hopelessly lost and with no fresh fruit. Your teeth will drop out in a week and you'll be coughing blood after only a month at sea. Ahar!

For a brochure, send an S.A.E. to:

Capt. Blackbeard, FREEPOST, Table 12, Wetherspoons Jamaica Inn, Slavery Theme Park, Bristol, BR245 7RT

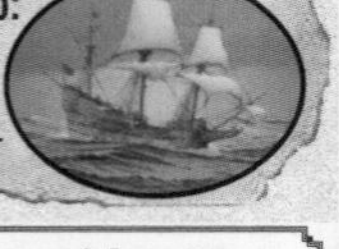

~AEGINA~HYDROS~MYKONOS~NAXOS~
~IKARIA~KOS~SPETSES~MILOS~KALIMNOS~

*There are over 300 beautiful islands to explore in the Aegean... but all **you'll** see is the bottom of a bucket*

SPEWSAIL GASTROENTERITIS ISLAND HOPPING HOLIDAY

It's *'Anchors and Stomachs away!'* Honk your way around the beautiful Greek Islands on a ***SpewSail*** holiday. And with a new resistant strain of Norwalk-Rotavirus every season, you'll end your holiday gagging to come back.

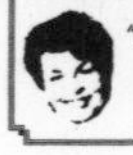

"I was given the Last Rites on Crete. Thank-you SpewSail" **Mrs B, Essex**

For a brochure write to: *SpewSail, PO Box 19745, Southampton*

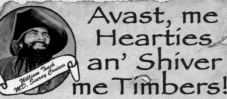

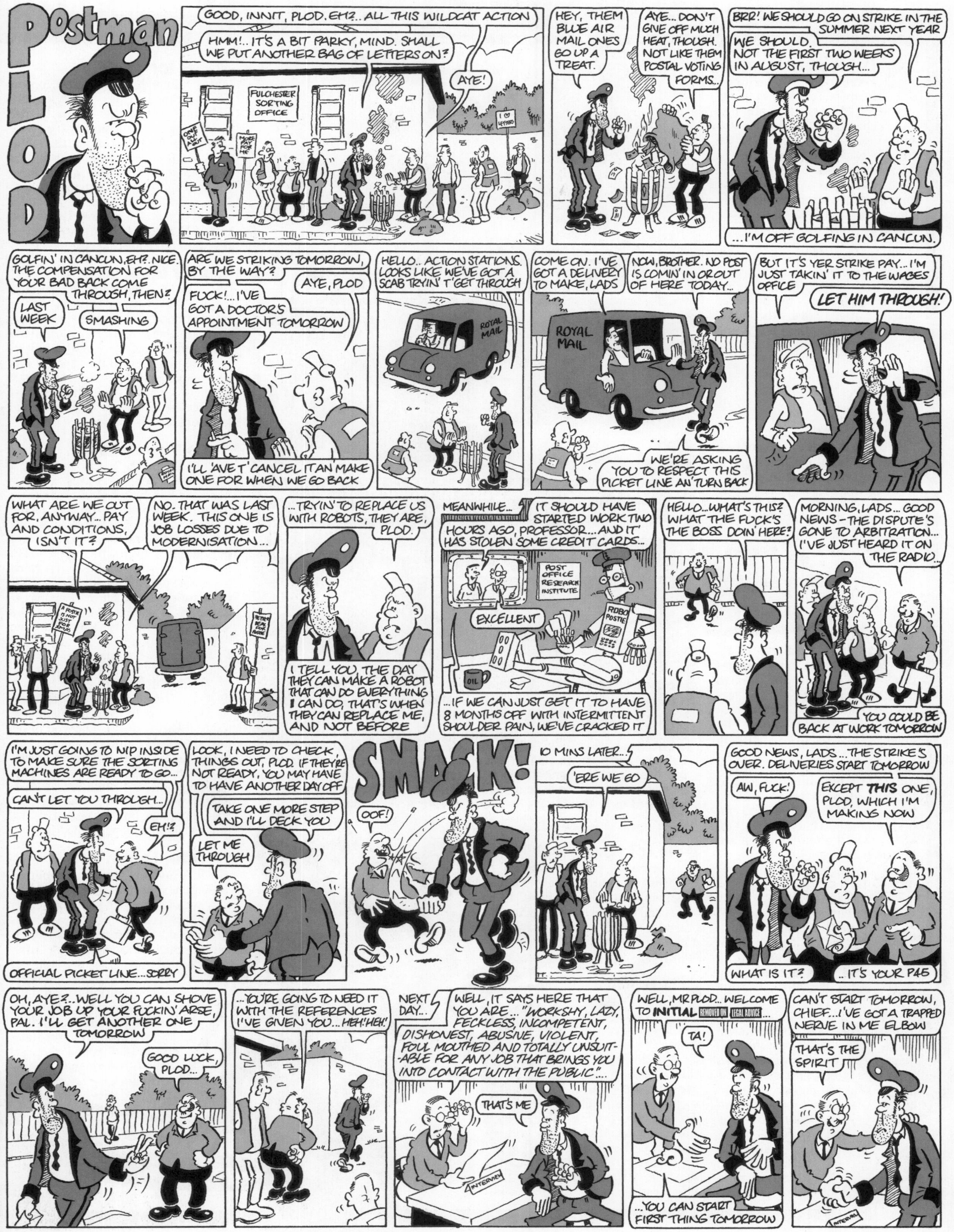

Postman PLOD
GOOD, INNIT, PLOD, EH?.. ALL THIS WILDCAT ACTION
HMM!.. IT'S A BIT PARKY, MIND. SHALL WE PUT ANOTHER BAG OF LETTERS ON?
AYE!
FULCHESTER SORTING OFFICE
ONE OUT ALL OUT
MORE PAY FOR ME
I ♡ LETTERS
HEY, THEM BLUE AIR MAIL ONES GO UP A TREAT.
AYE... DON'T GIVE OFF MUCH HEAT, THOUGH. NOT LIKE THEM POSTAL VOTING FORMS...
BRR! WE SHOULD GO ON STRIKE IN THE SUMMER NEXT YEAR
WE SHOULD. NOT THE FIRST TWO WEEKS IN AUGUST, THOUGH...
...I'M OFF GOLFING IN CANCUN.
GOLFIN' IN CANCUN, EH?. NICE. THE COMPENSATION FOR YOUR BAD BACK COME THROUGH, THEN?
LAST WEEK
SMASHING
ARE WE STRIKING TOMORROW, BY THE WAY?
AYE, PLOD
FUCK!... I'VE GOT A DOCTOR'S APPOINTMENT TOMORROW
I'LL 'AVE T' CANCEL IT AN' MAKE ONE FOR WHEN WE GO BACK
HELLO.. ACTION STATIONS. LOOKS LIKE WE'VE GOT A SCAB TRYIN' T'GET THROUGH
ROYAL MAIL
COME ON. I'VE GOT A DELIVERY TO MAKE, LADS
NOW, BROTHER. NO POST IS COMIN' IN OR OUT OF HERE TODAY...
ROYAL MAIL
WE'RE ASKING YOU TO RESPECT THIS PICKET LINE AN' TURN BACK
BUT IT'S YER STRIKE PAY... I'M JUST TAKIN' IT TO THE WAGES OFFICE
LET HIM THROUGH!
WHAT ARE WE OUT FOR, ANYWAY... PAY AND CONDITIONS, ISN'T IT?
NO. THAT WAS LAST WEEK. THIS ONE IS JOB LOSSES DUE TO MODERNISATION...
...TRYIN' TO REPLACE US WITH ROBOTS, THEY ARE, PLOD.
I TELL YOU, THE DAY THEY CAN MAKE A ROBOT THAT CAN DO EVERYTHING I CAN DO, THAT'S WHEN THEY CAN REPLACE ME, AND NOT BEFORE
MEANWHILE...
IT SHOULD HAVE STARTED WORK TWO HOURS AGO, PROFESSOR... AND IT HAS STOLEN SOME CREDIT CARDS...
POST OFFICE RESEARCH INSTITUTE
EXCELLENT
ROBO POSTIE
OIL
...IF WE CAN JUST GET IT TO HAVE 8 MONTHS OFF WITH INTERMITTENT SHOULDER PAIN, WE'VE CRACKED IT
HELLO... WHAT'S THIS? WHAT THE FUCK'S THE BOSS DOIN' HERE?
MORNING, LADS... GOOD NEWS - THE DISPUTE'S GONE TO ARBITRATION... I'VE JUST HEARD IT ON THE RADIO...
YOU COULD BE BACK AT WORK TOMORROW
I'M JUST GOING TO NIP INSIDE TO MAKE SURE THE SORTING MACHINES ARE READY TO GO...
CAN'T LET YOU THROUGH...
EH!?
OFFICIAL PICKET LINE... SORRY
LOOK, I NEED TO CHECK THINGS OUT, PLOD. IF THEY'RE NOT READY, YOU MAY HAVE TO HAVE ANOTHER DAY OFF
TAKE ONE MORE STEP AND I'LL DECK YOU
LET ME THROUGH
SMACK!
OOF!
10 MINS LATER...
'ERE WE GO
GOOD NEWS, LADS... THE STRIKE'S OVER. DELIVERIES START TOMORROW
AW, FUCK!
EXCEPT THIS ONE, PLOD, WHICH I'M MAKING NOW
WHAT IS IT?
...IT'S YOUR P45
OH, AYE?... WELL YOU CAN SHOVE YOUR JOB UP YOUR FUCKIN' ARSE, PAL. I'LL GET ANOTHER ONE TOMORROW
GOOD LUCK, PLOD...
...YOU'RE GOING TO NEED IT WITH THE REFERENCES I'VE GIVEN YOU... HEH! HEH!
NEXT DAY...
WELL, IT SAYS HERE THAT YOU ARE... "WORKSHY, LAZY, FECKLESS, INCOMPETENT, DISHONEST, ABUSIVE, VIOLENT, FOUL MOUTHED AND TOTALLY UNSUITABLE FOR ANY JOB THAT BRINGS YOU INTO CONTACT WITH THE PUBLIC"...
THAT'S ME
INTERVIEW
WELL, MR PLOD... WELCOME TO INITIAL REMOVED ON LEGAL ADVICE...
TA!
...YOU CAN START FIRST THING TOMORROW
CAN'T START TOMORROW, CHIEF... I'VE GOT A TRAPPED NERVE IN ME ELBOW
THAT'S THE SPIRIT
INTERVIEW

THE A-Z of LEWIS HAMILTON

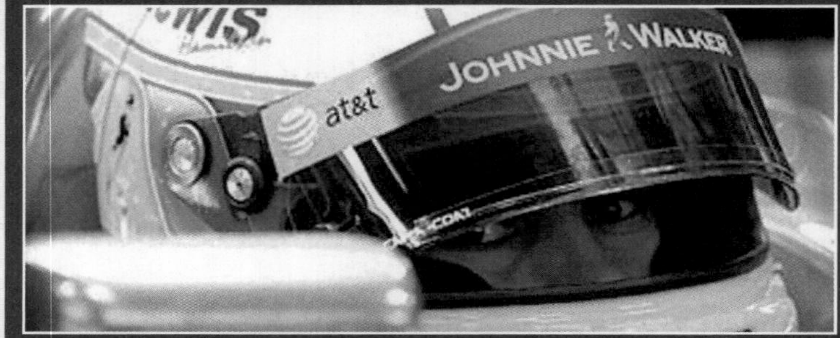
JOHNNIE WALKER
at&t

LORD Nelson, The Duke of Wellington, Winston Churchill... all heroes who have scored great victories for Britain. And now the country has a new name to add to its pantheon of great winners - Formula One driver LEWIS HAMILTON.

With four back-to-back Grand Prix victories* under his belt, and podium finishes in every race this season**, 22-year-old Hamilton is the golden boy of British motor racing. And everyone in the UK has been diagnosed with Hamilton Mania as severe Lewis Loopiness sweeps a nation already in the grip of Compulsive F1 Obsessive Disorder. In every pub, club and office in the land, at water-coolers, bus-stops and urinal troughs from Lands End to John O'Groats, people can talk of nothing else but this rookie driver who has taken the high octane motorsport world by storm.

But how much do we REALLY know about this humble 22-year-old who has risen from the back streets of Stevenage to become the fastest man on earth? Here's a fantastic file of F1 facts to tell you everything you ever wanted to know about Lewis Hamilton but were afraid to ask.

*Only two back-to-back victories confirmed at time of going to press. **Publisher's estimate. Actual amount of podium finishes during season subject to change.

A is for Alonso

Hamilton's McLaren team-mate is spaniard Fernando Alonso, the reigning world champion. Whilst they exhibit great rivalry during races, off the track the pair are great friends. They have a pact to give each other one of their kidneys should they ever need one, and Hamilton is godfather to Alonso's eight children.

B is for Black

Hamilton holds a sporting record that will never be beaten, for he is the first ever black F1 driver. He also holds the record for being the only young black man in Britain to drive a Mercedes without regularly getting pulled over and questioned by sarcastic police officers.

C is for Crash Helmet

Hamilton's trademark yellow crash helmet is a technological marvel. It incorporates an oxygen supply, a drinking tube, and a supply of snacks in case he gets hungry during his gruelling 90-minute Grand Prix races.

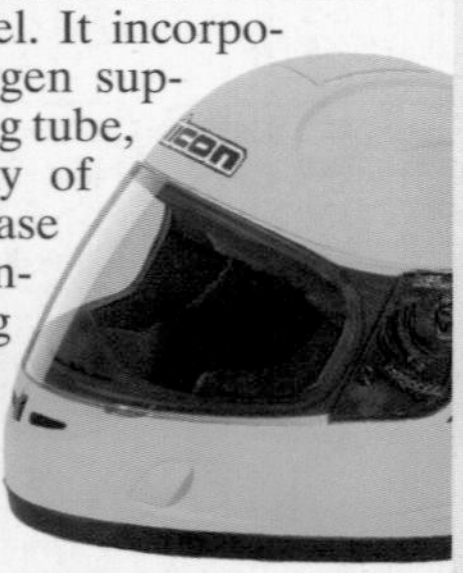

D is for Driving Test

Amazingly, it took Hamilton fifteen attempts to pass his driving test. "The examiner kept failing me for not keeping up with the traffic," he laughs. Had he been German, Hamilton would have been legally prevented from ever holding a licence after failing to pass at his third attempt. He would also have no idea how to queue politely and would habitually get up at 4am whilst on holiday to place his towel on a sun lounger.

E is for Erectile Dysfunction

Hamilton may be one of the 500,000 British men who suffer from erectile dysfunction. This embarrassing condition can be caused by any one of a number of factors, both physical and psychological. However, one thing's for certain - if Lewis gets married and is unable to gain a firm erection on his wedding night, he will find himself unable to consummate his marriage.

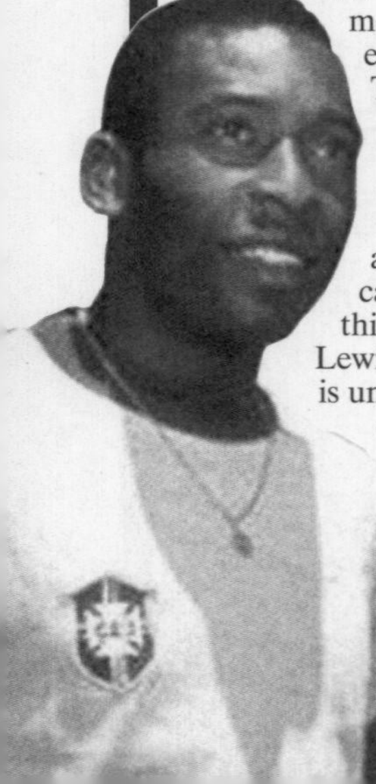

F is for Formula 1

Formula 1 is a special type of sport invented by Bernie Ecclestone, which allows cigarettes to be advertised on television on a Sunday afternoon. And again for an hour after the *South Bank Show.*

G is for G-Force

During a race, an F1 driver can experience G-Forces of up to 4 or even 5 whilst cornering. To give you some idea of what this feels like, imagine driving your own car round a bend at 30mph with the corpse of Bernard Manning strapped to the top of your head.

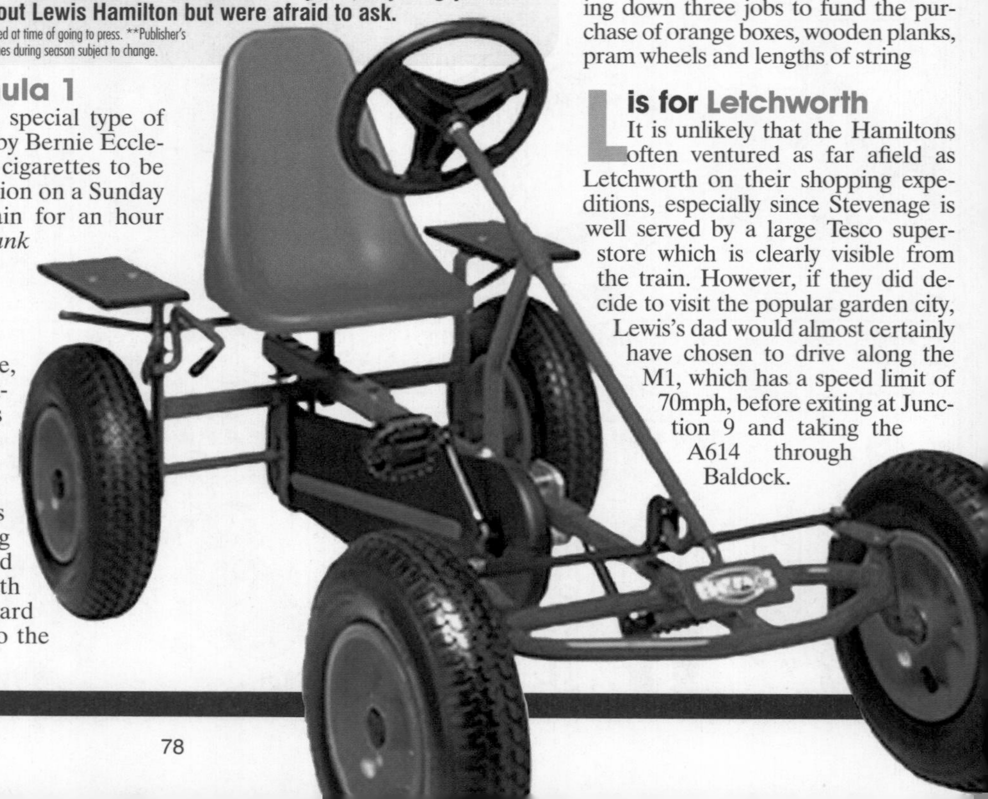

H is for Hitchin

Although Lewis grew up in Stevenage, his family would probably have often driven to the nearby town of Hitchin to do a bit of shopping. Travelling along the A600 between the two conurbations, it is possible that their car would have reached the national single carriageway speed limit of 60mph - less than a third of the 200mph that Lewis now regularly attains behind the wheel of his McLaren F1 racing car.

I is for Insects

Like all schoolboys, Hamilton probably tortured insects during his childhood. Pulling the legs off spiders, burning ants with a magnifying glass and tearing the wings of butterflies are just a few of the random acts of cruelty that a 10-year-old Hamilton is likely to have committed against defenceless members of the animal kingdom.

J is for Johnny

If Hamilton elects to wear a rubber johnny on his wedding night, he will have failed to consummate his marriage in the eyes of the Catholic church. "A marriage is only consummated when the spouses have performed between themselves in a human fashion a conjugal act which is suitable in itself for the procreation of offspring, to which marriage is ordered by its nature and by which the spouses become one flesh," Cardinal Cormac Murphy O'Connor told ITV F1 host Jim Rosenthal.

K is for Karts

Like many of his F1 predecessors, Lewis first cut his driving teeth in kart racing. Convinced of his talent, his father Anthony financed his burgeoning karting career. However, success in karting doesn't come cheap. At one point Mr Hamilton was holding down three jobs to fund the purchase of orange boxes, wooden planks, pram wheels and lengths of string

L is for Letchworth

It is unlikely that the Hamiltons often ventured as far afield as Letchworth on their shopping expeditions, especially since Stevenage is well served by a large Tesco superstore which is clearly visible from the train. However, if they did decide to visit the popular garden city, Lewis's dad would almost certainly have chosen to drive along the M1, which has a speed limit of 70mph, before exiting at Junction 9 and taking the A614 through Baldock.

M is for Mars Bars

Hamilton is addicted to Mars Bars. On an average GP weekend the sweet-toothed race ace chomps his way through nearly three of them! "A Mars a Day helps me work, rest and play," he told ITV F1 commentator Martin Brundle during a recent starting grid walkabout.

N is for Nerves

Lewis has nerves of steel ... quite literally! As a boy, he fell off his skateboard and was taken to Stevenage Hospital to have an X-Ray on his wrist. When the plate was developed, doctors were amazed to see that his entire nervous system consisted of thin metal wires, which later proved to be stainless steel.

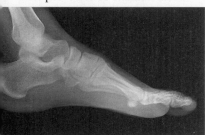

O is for Osmosis

Hamilton's favourite type of chemical diffusion is osmosis, the process by which water molecules pass from an area of high density to an area of lower density through an intervening semi-permeable membrane.

P is for Pit Stop

The only time in a race when the driver gets a chance to relax is during his pit-stops. For about 8 seconds, he is able to sit back whilst his mechanics do all the work. "While my car's being fuelled up and getting a tyre-change, I like to chill out with a good book, a glass of wine, and with a CD of Andean panpipe music playing on my helmet intercom," he told ITV F1 rostrum cameraman Ken Morse.

Q is for Queen

Lewis is a big fan of top British monarch the Queen. Whenever he wins a race, he insists that F1 organisers play her theme tune - the National Anthem.

R is for Re-fuelling

Hamilton admits that he is always nervous during re-fuelling stops. His biggest fear is that the petrol rig nozzle will come loose, spewing gallons of volatile fuel into the cockpit at high pressure. He is well aware that the heat from his V8 racing engine would ignite the fuel, instantly turning his McLaren car into a raging inferno in which he would be trapped and cooked alive. The pit crew would be driven back by the intense, searing heat and forced to stand by helplessly, listening to their driver's agonised screams for help as his flesh is consumed in the flames. "Fingers crossed it never happens," he told perky-nippled ITV F1 reporter Louise Goodman.

S is for Speed

As a young boy, one of Hamilton's early experiences of travelling at speed in a car was probably going shopping with his parents. However, it probably didn't provide much of a thrill, as it is likely that the speed limit in 1980s Stevenage was just 30mph - a mere seventh of the speed Lewis now regularly attains on the track.

T is for Tonsils

Hamilton's tonsils are two rounded, almond-shaped glands situated immediately behind the anterior pillars of the F1 speed demon's soft palate. Or perhaps they WERE, for Lewis is remaining tight-lipped about whether or not they were surgically removed during his childhood, possibly following a bout of tonsilitis. Any such operation would almost certainly have taken place in a hospital, in the grounds of which there is typically a speed limit of 5mph - one fortieth of the speed he now reaches in a race!

U is for Underpants

Lewis wears underpants in preference to boxer shorts, but unlike Joe Public he doesn't have to go out and buy them in the shops. That's because his helmet sponsors Hugo Boss provide him with as many pants as he wants. When the elastic goes in the ones he's wearing, he simply has to pick up the phone and they pop a fresh pair in the post... completely free of charge!

V is for Vaginisimus

Vaginisimus - involuntary vaginal spasming causing constriction and pain whilst attempting intercourse - is not something that Lewis Hamilton suffers from. However, should he get married, it is a condition that may affect his wife on their wedding night, thus preventing the marriage from being consummated. "Fingers crossed it won't happen," he told ITV F1 pitlane correspondent Ted Kravitz.

W is for Wedding Night

In order for his marriage to be legally consummated, Hamilton will have to penetrate his wife. "Although there is no legal requirement which states a particular depth of penetration, it must be 'sufficient to render some satisfaction to the female party'," says Perceval Richer, Professor of Marital Law at Oxford University.

X is for Xylophone

Lewis has never played the xylophone, despite the fact that he was brought up in flat over his parents' xylophone shop in Stevenage. "I don't know why I never had a go on one," he told ITV F1 anchor Steve Ryder, "I just never fancied it."

Y is for Yellow

Secretive Hamilton refuses to say why he decided to paint his crash helmet yellow. "I chose the colour yellow for my helmet because my favourite song is 'Yellow Submarine' by the Beatles," he explained to ITV F1 pundit Mark Blundell.

Z is for Zymoscope

If Lewis Hamilton had become a brewer, he would regularly be required to ascertain the fermenting power of various yeast samples. To do this, he would use a piece of equipment called a zymoscope. However, the 22-year-old chose a different career path and the rest is history. "To be perfectly honest, I don't have a clue what a zymoscope is for," he told excitable ITV F1 gobshite James Allen.

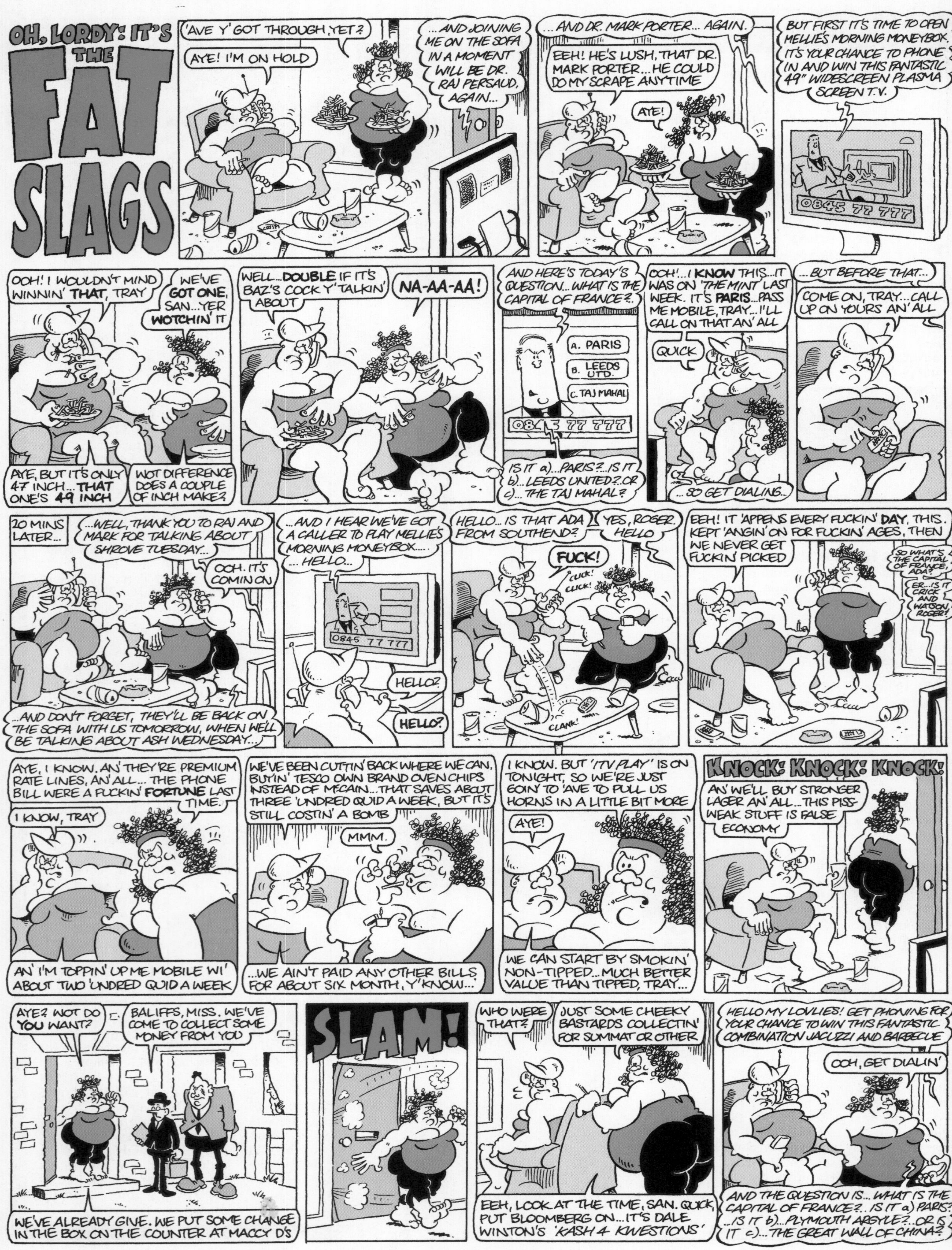
OH, LORDY! IT'S THE FAT SLAGS
'AVE Y' GOT THROUGH, YET?
AYE! I'M ON HOLD
...AND JOINING ME ON THE SOFA IN A MOMENT WILL BE DR. RAJ PERSAUD, AGAIN...
...AND DR. MARK PORTER... AGAIN.
EEH! HE'S LUSH, THAT DR. MARK PORTER... HE COULD DO MY SCRAPE ANYTIME
AYE!
BUT FIRST IT'S TIME TO OPEN MELLIE'S MORNING MONEYBOX. IT'S YOUR CHANCE TO PHONE IN AND WIN THIS FANTASTIC 49" WIDESCREEN PLASMA SCREEN T.V.
0845 77 777
OOH! I WOULDN'T MIND WINNIN' THAT, TRAY
WE'VE GOT ONE, SAN... YER WOTCHIN' IT
AYE, BUT IT'S ONLY 47 INCH... THAT ONE'S 49 INCH
WOT DIFFERENCE DOES A COUPLE OF INCH MAKE?
WELL... DOUBLE IF IT'S BAZ'S COCK Y' TALKIN' ABOUT
NA-AA-AA!
AND HERE'S TODAY'S QUESTION... WHAT IS THE CAPITAL OF FRANCE?..
A. PARIS
B. LEEDS UTD.
C. TAJ MAHAL
IS IT a)... PARIS?... IS IT b)... LEEDS UNITED?.. OR c)... THE TAJ MAHAL?
OOH!... I KNOW THIS... IT WAS ON 'THE MINT' LAST WEEK. IT'S PARIS... PASS ME MOBILE, TRAY... I'LL CALL ON THAT AN' ALL
QUICK
...SO GET DIALING...
...BUT BEFORE THAT...
COME ON, TRAY... CALL UP ON YOURS AN' ALL
20 MINS LATER...
...WELL, THANK YOU TO RAJ AND MARK FOR TALKING ABOUT SHROVE TUESDAY...
OOH. IT'S COMIN ON
...AND DON'T FORGET, THEY'LL BE BACK ON THE SOFA WITH US TOMORROW, WHEN WE'LL BE TALKING ABOUT ASH WEDNESDAY...
...AND I HEAR WE'VE GOT A CALLER TO PLAY MELLIE'S MORNING MONEYBOX.... ...HELLO...
0845 77 777
HELLO?
HELLO?
HELLO... IS THAT ADA FROM SOUTHEND?
YES, ROGER. HELLO
FUCK!
CLICK! CLICK!
CLANK!
EEH! IT 'APPENS EVERY FUCKIN' DAY, THIS. KEPT 'ANGIN' ON FOR FUCKIN' AGES, THEN WE NEVER GET FUCKIN' PICKED
SO WHAT'S THE CAPITAL OF FRANCE, ADA?
ER... IS IT CRICK AND WATSON, ROGER?
AYE, I KNOW. AN' THEY'RE PREMIUM RATE LINES, AN' ALL... THE PHONE BILL WERE A FUCKIN' FORTUNE LAST TIME.
I KNOW, TRAY
AN' I'M TOPPIN' UP ME MOBILE WI' ABOUT TWO 'UNDRED QUID A WEEK
WE'VE BEEN CUTTIN' BACK WHERE WE CAN, BUYIN' TESCO OWN BRAND OVEN CHIPS INSTEAD OF McCAIN... THAT SAVES ABOUT THREE 'UNDRED QUID A WEEK, BUT IT'S STILL COSTIN' A BOMB
MMM.
...WE AIN'T PAID ANY OTHER BILLS FOR ABOUT SIX MONTH, Y'KNOW...
I KNOW. BUT 'ITV PLAY' IS ON TONIGHT, SO WE'RE JUST GOIN' TO 'AVE TO PULL US HORNS IN A LITTLE BIT MORE
AYE!
WE CAN START BY SMOKIN' NON-TIPPED... MUCH BETTER VALUE THAN TIPPED, TRAY...
KNOCK! KNOCK! KNOCK!
AN' WE'LL BUY STRONGER LAGER AN' ALL... THIS PISS-WEAK STUFF IS FALSE ECONOMY
AYE? WOT DO YOU WANT?
BALIFFS, MISS. WE'VE COME TO COLLECT SOME MONEY FROM YOU
WE'VE ALREADY GIVE. WE PUT SOME CHANGE IN THE BOX ON THE COUNTER AT MACCY D'S
SLAM!
WHO WERE THAT?
JUST SOME CHEEKY BASTARDS COLLECTIN' FOR SUMMAT OR OTHER
EEH, LOOK AT THE TIME, SAN. QUICK, PUT BLOOMBERG ON... IT'S DALE WINTON'S 'KASH 4 KWESTIONS'
HELLO MY LOVLIES! GET PHONING FOR YOUR CHANCE TO WIN THIS FANTASTIC COMBINATION JACUZZI AND BARBECUE
OOH, GET DIALIN'
AND THE QUESTION IS... WHAT IS THE CAPITAL OF FRANCE?.. IS IT a) PARIS? ...IS IT b)... PLYMOUTH ARGYLE?.. OR IS IT c)... THE GREAT WALL OF CHINA?

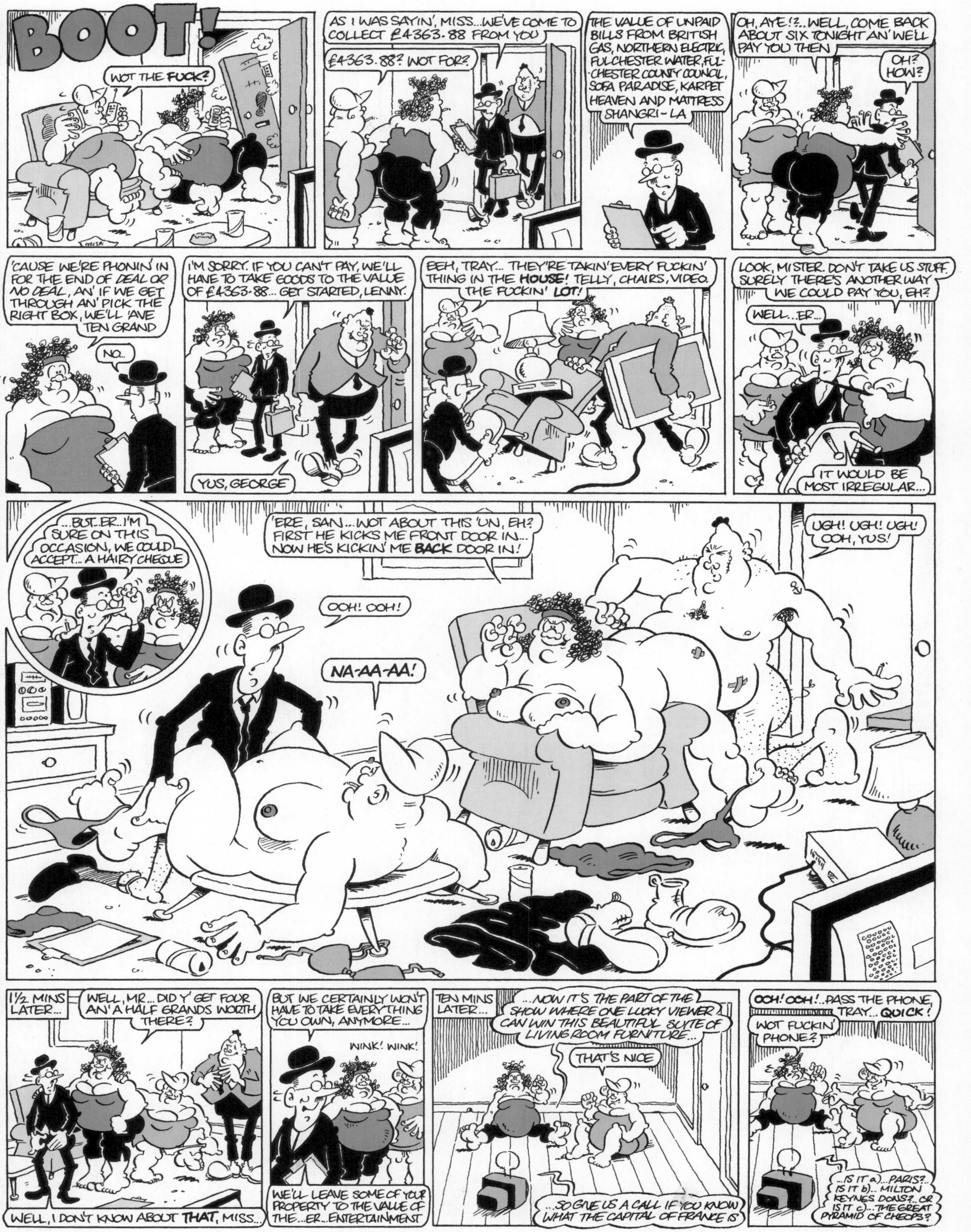

BOOT!
WOT THE FUCK?
AS I WAS SAYIN', MISS... WE'VE COME TO COLLECT £4363.88 FROM YOU
£4363.88? WOT FOR?
THE VALUE OF UNPAID BILLS FROM BRITISH GAS, NORTHERN ELECTRIC, FULCHESTER WATER, FULCHESTER COUNTY COUNCIL, SOFA PARADISE, KARPET HEAVEN AND MATTRESS SHANGRI-LA
OH, AYE!?... WELL, COME BACK ABOUT SIX TONIGHT AN' WE'LL PAY YOU THEN
OH? HOW?
'CAUSE WE'RE PHONIN' IN FOR THE END OF DEAL OR NO DEAL, AN' IF WE GET THROUGH AN' PICK THE RIGHT BOX, WE'LL 'AVE TEN GRAND
NO...
I'M SORRY. IF YOU CAN'T PAY, WE'LL HAVE TO TAKE GOODS TO THE VALUE OF £4363.88... GET STARTED, LENNY.
YUS, GEORGE
EEH, TRAY... THEY'RE TAKIN' EVERY FUCKIN' THING IN THE HOUSE! TELLY, CHAIRS, VIDEO. THE FUCKIN' LOT!
LOOK, MISTER. DON'T TAKE US STUFF. SURELY THERE'S ANOTHER WAY WE COULD PAY YOU, EH?
WELL... ER...
IT WOULD BE MOST IRREGULAR...
...BUT... ER... I'M SURE ON THIS OCCASION, WE COULD ACCEPT... A HAIRY CHEQUE
'ERE, SAN... WOT ABOUT THIS 'UN, EH? FIRST HE KICKS ME FRONT DOOR IN... NOW HE'S KICKIN' ME BACK DOOR IN!
UGH! UGH! UGH! OOH, YUS!
OOH! OOH!
NA-AA-AA!
1½ MINS LATER...
WELL, MR... DID Y' GET FOUR AN' A HALF GRANDS WORTH THERE?
WELL, I DON'T KNOW ABOUT THAT, MISS...
BUT WE CERTAINLY WON'T HAVE TO TAKE EVERYTHING YOU OWN, ANYMORE...
WINK! WINK!
WE'LL LEAVE SOME OF YOUR PROPERTY TO THE VALUE OF THE... ER... ENTERTAINMENT
TEN MINS LATER...
...NOW IT'S THE PART OF THE SHOW WHERE ONE LUCKY VIEWER CAN WIN THIS BEAUTIFUL SUITE OF LIVING ROOM FURNITURE...
THAT'S NICE
...SO GIVE US A CALL IF YOU KNOW WHAT THE CAPITAL OF FRANCE IS
OOH! OOH!... PASS THE PHONE, TRAY... QUICK!
WOT FUCKIN' PHONE?
...IS IT a)... PARIS?.. IS IT b)... MILTON KEYNES DONS?.. OR IS IT c)... THE GREAT PYRAMID OF CHEOPS?

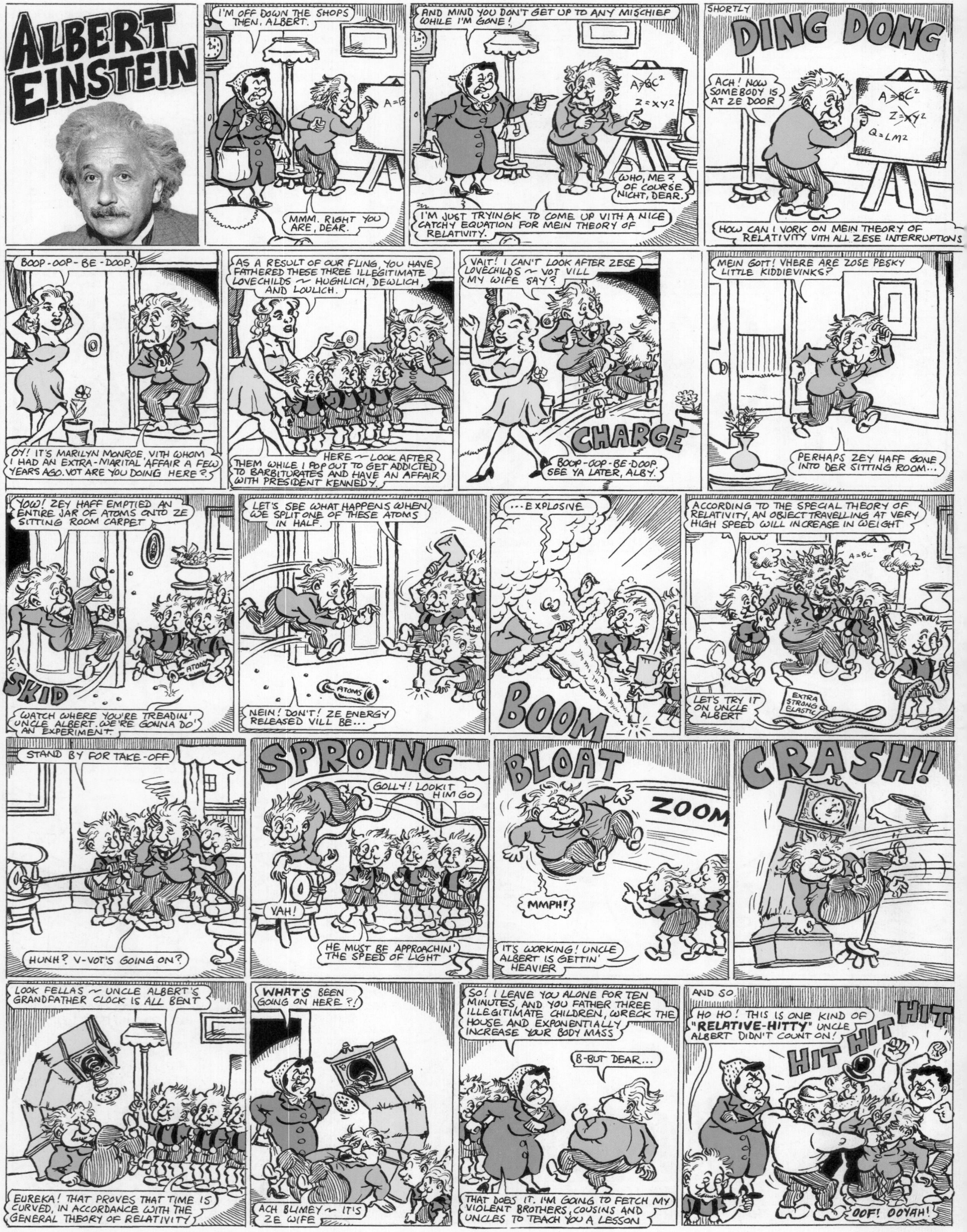
ALBERT EINSTEIN
I'M OFF DOWN THE SHOPS THEN, ALBERT.
A=B
MMM. RIGHT YOU ARE, DEAR.
AND MIND YOU DON'T GET UP TO ANY MISCHIEF WHILE I'M GONE!
WHO, ME? OF COURSE NICHT, DEAR.
I'M JUST TRYINGK TO COME UP VITH A NICE CATCHY EQUATION FOR MEIN THEORY OF RELATIVITY.
SHORTLY
DING DONG
ACH! NOW SOMEBODY IS AT ZE DOOR
Q=LM2
HOW CAN I VORK ON MEIN THEORY OF RELATIVITY VITH ALL ZESE INTERRUPTIONS
BOOP-OOP-BE-DOOP.
OY! IT'S MARILYN MONROE, VITH WHOM I HAD AN EXTRA-MARITAL AFFAIR A FEW YEARS AGO. VOT ARE YOU DOING HERE?
AS A RESULT OF OUR FLING, YOU HAVE FATHERED THESE THREE ILLEGITIMATE LOVECHILDS ~ HUGHLICH, DEWLICH, AND LOULICH.
HERE ~ LOOK AFTER THEM WHILE I POP OUT TO GET ADDICTED TO BARBITURATES AND HAVE AN AFFAIR WITH PRESIDENT KENNEDY.
VAIT! I CAN'T LOOK AFTER ZESE LOVECHILDS ~ VOT VILL MY WIFE SAY?
CHARGE
BOOP-OOP-BE-DOOP. SEE YA LATER, ALBY.
MEIN GOTT! VHERE ARE ZOSE PESKY LITTLE KIDDIEVINKS?
PERHAPS ZEY HAFF GONE INTO DER SITTING ROOM...
YOW! ZEY HAFF EMPTIED AN ENTIRE JAR OF ATOMS ONTO ZE SITTING ROOM CARPET
SKID
ATOMS
WATCH WHERE YOU'RE TREADIN' UNCLE ALBERT. WE'RE GONNA DO AN EXPERIMENT.
LET'S SEE WHAT HAPPENS WHEN WE SPLIT ONE OF THESE ATOMS IN HALF.
ATOMS
NEIN! DON'T! ZE ENERGY RELEASED VILL BE...
...EXPLOSIVE
BOOM
ACCORDING TO THE SPECIAL THEORY OF RELATIVITY, AN OBJECT TRAVELLING AT VERY HIGH SPEED WILL INCREASE IN WEIGHT
A=BC²
LET'S TRY IT ON UNCLE ALBERT
EXTRA STRONG ELASTIC
STAND BY FOR TAKE-OFF
HUNH? V-VOT'S GOING ON?
SPROING
GOLLY! LOOKIT HIM GO
YAH!
HE MUST BE APPROACHIN' THE SPEED OF LIGHT
BLOAT
ZOOM
MMPH!
IT'S WORKING! UNCLE ALBERT IS GETTIN' HEAVIER
CRASH!
LOOK FELLAS ~ UNCLE ALBERT'S GRANDFATHER CLOCK IS ALL BENT
EUREKA! THAT PROVES THAT TIME IS CURVED, IN ACCORDANCE WITH THE GENERAL THEORY OF RELATIVITY
WHAT'S BEEN GOING ON HERE?!
ACH BLIMEY ~ IT'S ZE WIFE
SO! I LEAVE YOU ALONE FOR TEN MINUTES, AND YOU FATHER THREE ILLEGITIMATE CHILDREN, WRECK THE HOUSE AND EXPONENTIALLY INCREASE YOUR BODY MASS
B-BUT DEAR...
THAT DOES IT. I'M GOING TO FETCH MY VIOLENT BROTHERS, COUSINS AND UNCLES TO TEACH YOU A LESSON
AND SO
HO HO! THIS IS ONE KIND OF "RELATIVE-HITTY" UNCLE ALBERT DIDN'T COUNT ON!
HIT HIT HIT HIT
OOF! OOYAH!

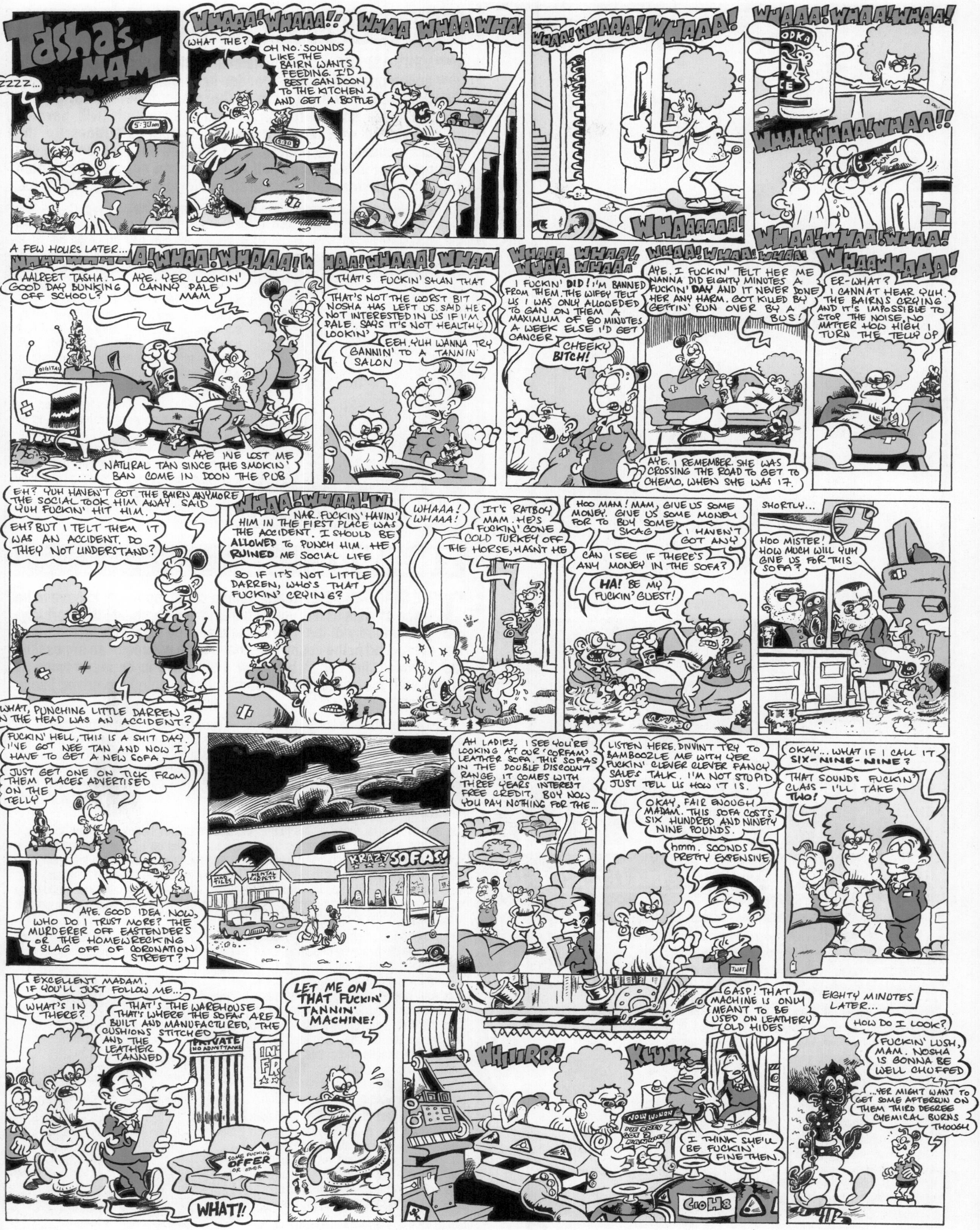
Tasha's MAM
ZZZZ...
5:30am
WHAAA! WHAAA!!
WHAT THE?
OH NO. SOUNDS LIKE THE BAIRN WANTS FEEDING. I'D BEST GAN DOON TO THE KITCHEN AND GET A BOTTLE
WHAA WHAA WHAA
WHAA! WHAAA! WHAAA!
WHAAA! WHAA! WHAA!
WHAA! WHAA! WHAA!!
WHAAAAAA!
WHAA! WHAA! WHAA! WHAA!
A FEW HOURS LATER...
WHAAA! WHAAA! WHAAA!
AALREET TASHA. GOOD DAY BUNKING OFF SCHOOL?
AYE. YER LOOKIN' CANNY PALE MAM
DIGITAL
AYE I'VE LOST ME NATURAL TAN SINCE THE SMOKIN' BAN COME IN DOON THE PUB
WHAA! WHAAA! WHAA!
THAT'S FUCKIN' SHAN THAT
THAT'S NOT THE WORST BIT. NOSHA HAS LEFT US. SAID HE'S NOT INTERESTED IN US IF I'M PALE. SAYS IT'S NOT HEALTHY LOOKIN'
EEH. YUH WANNA TRY BANNIN' TO A TANNIN' SALON
WHAA WHAA! WHAA WHAA
I FUCKIN' DID! I'M BANNED FROM THEM. THE WIFEY TELT US I WAS ONLY ALLOWEDED TO GAN ON THEM A MAXIMUM OF 80 MINUTES A WEEK ELSE I'D GET CANCER
CHEEKY BITCH!
WHAA! WHAA! WHAA!
AYE. I FUCKIN' TELT HER ME NANNA DID EIGHTY MINUTES A FUCKIN' DAY AND IT NEVER DONE HER ANY HARM. GOT KILLED BY GETTIN' RUN OVER BY A BUS!
AYE. I REMEMBER. SHE WAS CROSSING THE ROAD TO GET TO CHEMO, WHEN SHE WAS 17.
WHAAWHAAA!
ER-WHAT? I CANNAT HEAR YUH. THE BAIRNS CRYING AND IT'S IMPOSSIBLE TO STOP THE NOISE, NO MATTER HOW HIGH I TURN THE TELLY UP
EH? YUH HAVEN'T GOT THE BAIRN ANYMORE THE SOCIAL TOOK HIM AWAY. SAID YUH FUCKIN' HIT HIM.
EH? BUT I TELT THEM IT WAS AN ACCIDENT. DO THEY NOT UNDERSTAND?
WHAT, PUNCHING LITTLE DARREN IN THE HEAD WAS AN ACCIDENT?
WHAA! WHAA!
NAR. FUCKIN' HAVIN' HIM IN THE FIRST PLACE WAS THE ACCIDENT. I SHOULD BE ALLOWED TO PUNCH HIM. HE RUINED ME SOCIAL LIFE
SO IF IT'S NOT LITTLE DARREN, WHO'S THAT FUCKIN' CRYING?
WHAAA! WHAAA!
IT'S RATBOY MAM. HE'S FUCKIN' GONE COLD TURKEY OFF THE HORSE, HASN'T HE
HOO MAM! MAM, GIVE US SOME MONEY. GIVE US SOME MONEY FOR TO BUY SOME SKAG
I HAVEN'T GOT ANY
CAN I SEE IF THERE'S ANY MONEY IN THE SOFA?
HA! BE MY FUCKIN' GUEST!
SHORTLY...
HOO MISTER! HOW MUCH WILL YUH GIVE US FOR THIS SOFA?
FUCKIN' HELL, THIS IS A SHIT DAY. I'VE GOT NEE TAN AND NOW I HAVE TO GET A NEW SOFA
JUST GET ONE ON TICK FROM THEM PLACES ADVERTISED ON THE TELLY
AYE. GOOD IDEA. NOW, WHO DO I TRUST MORE? THE MURDERER OFF EASTENDERS OR THE HOMEWRECKING SLAG OFF OF CORONATION STREET?
MAD TILES
MENTAL CARPETS
KRAZY SOFAS!
AH LADIES, I SEE YOU'RE LOOKING AT OUR 'CORFAM' LEATHER SOFA. THIS SOFAS IN THE DOUBLE DISCOUNT RANGE, IT COMES WITH THREE YEARS INTEREST FREE CREDIT, BUY NOW YOU PAY NOTHING FOR THE...
LISTEN HERE. DIVVINT TRY TO BAMBOOZLE ME WITH YER FUCKIN' CLEVER CLEVER FANCY SALES TALK. I'M NOT STUPID. JUST TELL US HOW IT IS.
OKAY, FAIR ENOUGH MADAM. THIS SOFA COSTS SIX HUNDRED AND NINETY NINE POUNDS.
hmm. SOONDS PRETTY EXPENSIVE
TWAT
OKAY... WHAT IF I CALL IT SIX-NINE-NINE?
THAT SOUNDS FUCKIN' CLASS - I'LL TAKE TWO!
EXCELLENT MADAM. IF YOU'LL JUST FOLLOW ME...
WHAT'S IN THERE?
THAT'S THE WAREHOUSE THAT'S WHERE THE SOFAS ARE BUILT AND MANUFACTURED, THE CUSHIONS STITCHED AND THE LEATHER TANNED
PRIVATE NO ADMITTANCE
SOME FUCKING OFFER OR OTHER
WHAT!!
LET ME ON THAT FUCKIN' TANNIN' MACHINE!
WHIIIRR!
KLUNK
GASP! THAT MACHINE IS ONLY MEANT TO BE USED ON LEATHERY OLD HIDES
I THINK SHE'LL BE FUCKIN' FINE THEN.
C10H8
EIGHTY MINUTES LATER...
HOW DO I LOOK?
FUCKIN' LUSH, MAM. NOSHA IS GONNA BE WELL CHUFFED
...YER MIGHT WANT TO GET SOME AFTERSUN ON THEM THIRD DEGREE CHEMICAL BURNS THOUGH

N O R T H
S E A
Cardigan Bay

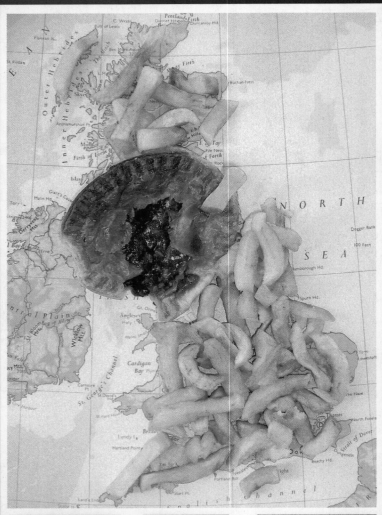

FAT BRITAIN

All Change as Obesity Epidemic Threatens UK

EVERY DAY it seems that a new report is released predicting shocking increases in British obesity levels. According to the latest figures, 78% of the population is presently overweight, and that figure increasing every day.

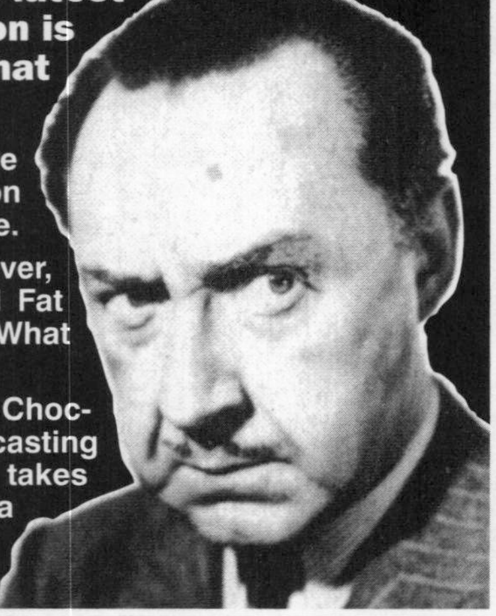

And if scientists' predictions prove correct, by 2020 every single person in the country will be clinically obese.

The face of Britain will change forever, that much is certain. But what will Fat Britain looks like? How will it travel? What will it do to relax?

Here, Professor Kidderminster Chocolate, head of the Obesity Forecasting Department at Lampeter University takes a look at every aspect of daily life in a future where EVERY Briton is a fatty-bum-bum...

TELEVISION

EVERY ASPECT of the television industry will have to change to accomodate Britain's broader-beamed viewers. Televisions themselves will all have to be made wider as fat people take up more screen room. And remote controls will have to be redesigned with larger, more widely-spaced buttons for the viewers' sausage-like fingers. Not only that, but programmes will be broadcast in the upper half of the screen only, as the bottom half will be permanently obscured by viewers' bloated stomachs.

The other side of the camera will also see great changes. Weather reports will take longer, as a thirty-stone Sian Lloyd lumbers around in front of her map, wheezing and fighting for breath. And commercial breaks will have to be much longer to allow gargantuan viewers to waddle off to the lavatory, where they will take several minutes to locate their genitals amongst all their rolls of sweating flesh.

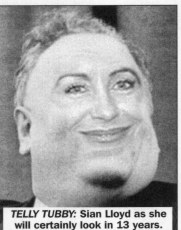

TELLY TUBBY: **Sian Lloyd as she will certainly look in 13 years.**

The sexy programmes we love today, such as *The Tudors*, *Diary of a Call Girl*, *Fanny Hill* and *Das Crazy Sex Show*, will all have to be banned as their broadcast would lead to excited viewers dropping dead in their millions.

This would be good news for viewers, as dull, uninteresting programmes would be a lot cheaper to make and consequently the licence fee would drop from £140 to around £60. Now for the bad news; the increased expense of feeding morbidly obese BBC employees would see the fee increase to more than four times its present level.

TRAVEL

THE STANDARD four-seater saloon car of today would have to be twice as wide as it is now in order to accommodate the morbidly-obese family of the future sitting side by side. This would mean that every road in the country will have to be widened - an impossible task. Instead, the car as we know it will have to be made twice as LONG, with the passengers sitting in a line behind the driver, like in a bobsleigh.

Up at the front, the dashboard will have to be three feet deep, to accommodate all the driver's pies, sweets, burgers and cakes. Meanwhile, the traditional steering wheel will be useless, as it will become wedged in the bulging gut of the 2020 motorist. Instead, he will wear a metal collander on his head, which will transmit his brainwaves to the front wheels down some curly wires. The salad-dodging driver of the future will merely have to think which way he wants to go and the wheels will automatically point in the right direction.

In tomorrow's fat world of the future, the double decker buses we know today will of become a thing of the past, as the narrow staircases up to their top decks will be impassable for their elephantine passengers. And the drivers will be wedged solid into their cramped cabs, too fat to get out at the depot. They will be forced to live their whole lives like veal cows, trapped on board their buses, wallowing miserably in a foetid soup of their own filth and ordure. It's not a pleasant prospect for their passengers, so bus fares will be forced to come down.

With the roads clogged up with double-length cars and shit-stinking buses, train travel will become the best way of getting about. But even the railways will not be immune from the consequences of Fat Britain. In order to meet the demands of the obese travelling public, on a typical twelve-carriage intercity express, eleven of the carriages will have to be buffet cars serving teas, coffees, sandwiches, hot bacon and tomato rolls, and a wide selection of snacks and crisps. However, some things won't change. The trains of 2020 will still run out of sandwiches within ten minutes of leaving the station.

LUDGATE CIRCUS
Double Decker

But the biggest change of all will take place in the air. Instead of the relaxed, spacious experience that flying is for us today, going abroad on a plane in the year 2020 will be cramped, stuffy and uncomfortable, with barely enough room for us to stretch our legs.

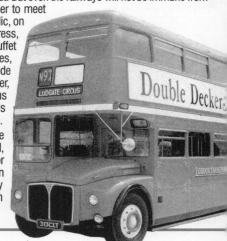

FILM & POP MUSIC

EVERYONE loves going to the pictures, but in Fat Britain we're set to see a whole load of changes to our movie-going experience. The first difference we'll notice is at the food counter. The obscene, bucket-sized 'large' popcorn of today will become the piddly 'extra-small' portion of 2020. Ask for a 'large' popcorn in the future, and it will be delivered to your seat by an usherette in a fork-lift truck. But that's not all she'll be delivering. With viewers' fat cheeks swollen up like risen dough, squeezing their piggy little eyes shut, staff will hand out special screwjacks so film fans can push their podgy chops down far enough for them to be able to see the screen.

DIE LARD: How Bruce Willis will look in 2020.

Pop bands of the fat future will bear little resemblance to the ones we know today. Guitars, pianos and any instruments with fiddly little keys will prove impossible to play with the clumsy, chubby fingers our musicians will then have. As their waistlines swell, present day skinny virtuosos such as Eric Clapton, Jools Holland and Peter Hook will be forced to retrain as alpine horn, kazoo or kettle drum players.

SPORT

BUTTERBALL: How Peter Crouch will appear in the future.

IN THE fat Britain of the future, Premiership football games will be much shorter than they are today, as thirty-stone players will find themselves red-faced, puffing and blowing within ten minutes of kick-off. Crowd numbers will be slashed in half, as each fatty footie fan will require two seats - one for each buttock. With ticket revenues slashed in two, players' wages will drop. And further down the table, the effects could be be even more pronounced, with non-league grounds left empty as overweight supporters find themselves unable to squeeze through the turnstiles.

The London Marathon will still take place, now lasting over a week instead of its present three or four hours. And its route will be drastically different too. Structural engineers fear that the massive vibrations set up by thousands of morbidly obese runners thundering across it like a herd of baby elephants would smash Tower Bridge like matchwood.

The traditional cricket match that is such a part of our national identity is set to be transformed beyond recognition. In the Test Matches of 2020, big-boned bowlers will make their run-ups on battery-powered mobility scooters, whilst corpulent batsmen will slouch on settees in front of their wickets, clutching a bat in one hand and a plate of sausage rolls in the other. Tea and lunch intervals would last so long that there would only be enough time for a couple of overs a day.

And the High Octane world of Grand Prix racing will not be immune either. The F1 cars of today, with their 1000 horsepower engines, would barely have enough grunt to get off the starting line with a fifty-stone Lewis Hamilton at the wheel. And the McLaren driver's trademark yellow helmet will have to be redesigned from scratch, needing seven - or even eight - chinstraps to hold it on.

Darts would be the only sport left unaffected.

WORK

THE WORLD of work will be unrecognisable in a fat Britain of the future. Rush hours will not exist as we know them today, as practically the entire working population will be too fat to get out of their houses. Traditionally, in such circumstances, the Fire Brigade are called to remove a window and lift the victim out on a tarpaulin. But in 2020, the firefighters will be unable to assist, as they will be too fat themselves to slide down the pole and get out of the station.

Of those that do manage to get to work, the vast majority will find themselves working in chippies, cake shops and Greggs bakery. However, the shop counters will have to be moved forwards several feet to make enough space for the vast assistants. This means that the space for customers in the shop will be smaller. However, this will all be irrelevant as none of the customers will be able to fit through the doors.

In factories, the working day will be completely different. In order to meet the workforce's insatiable demand for food, tea breaks will be up to two hours long, and the traditional cake trolley will be replaced by a dumper truck filled with jam doughnuts. Coupled with a four-hour break for lunch, this means that production lines will only be running for half an hour a day, during which time the workers will probably take the opportunity to go for a big Elvis-sized shit on specially strengthened jumbo toilets.

Blackpool Gears Up For Lardarse Invasion

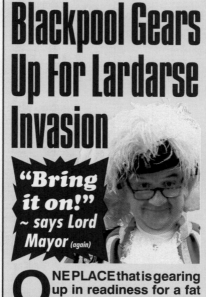

"Bring it on!" ~ says Lord Mayor *(again)*

ONE PLACE that is gearing up in readiness for a fat future is the Lancashire seaside resort of Blackpool. And according to Lord Mayor, Mike Taylor, by 2020 the town will be more than able to cope with any number of morbidly obese funseekers. *"Bring it on!"* he told reporters.

Launching their new policy document 'Blackpool - Where FAT spells FUN,' Blackpool County Council set out a twenty point plan to ensure that the town will be more than ready for the 2020 corpulence epidemic. Amongst measures being proposed are:

• *THE famous 360 foot tower being reduced in height to just 4 foot to allow fatties to enjoy the panoramic view from the top without wearing themselves out climbing up the stairs.*

• *INSTALLATION of cranes along the Golden Mile to winch the 50-stone sun-seekers on and off the beach.*

• *THOSE things you stick your head through to have your photograph taken will be re-painted to depict extremely thin people in bathing costumes in order to create a humorous contrast.*

• *COIN trays on all fruit machines in arcades along the Golden Mile will be widened to allow lucky winners to get at their winnings with their roly-poly digits.*

• *THE wooden and canvas deckchairs on the beach will be phased out and replaced with extra load-bearing designs made from railway sleepers and industrial conveyor belting.*

• *THE famous illuminations will be lowered down their lamp post so that blubbery tourists will not need to strain themselves lifting their chins to see them.*

• *THE world famous Flower Clock will be dug up and replaced with a Waddle-Through Pie Shop.*

"Blackpool has kept going strong through two world wars and global warming," Mr. Taylor told reporters. "We're certainly not going to let a few excess pounds of adipose tissue spoil the fun along the Golden Mile," he added.

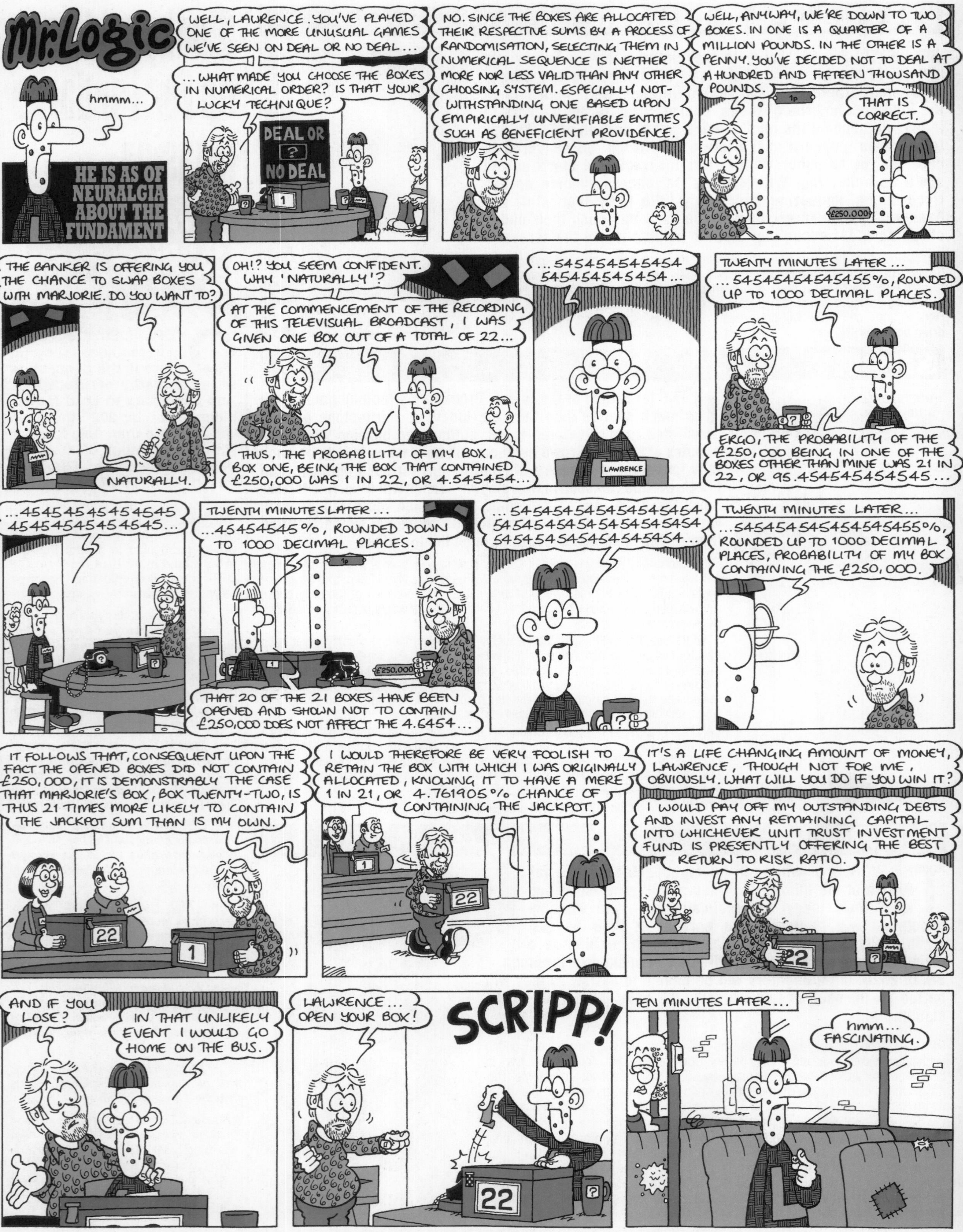
Mr.Logic
hmmm...
HE IS AS OF NEURALGIA ABOUT THE FUNDAMENT
WELL, LAWRENCE. YOU'VE PLAYED ONE OF THE MORE UNUSUAL GAMES WE'VE SEEN ON DEAL OR NO DEAL...
...WHAT MADE YOU CHOOSE THE BOXES IN NUMERICAL ORDER? IS THAT YOUR LUCKY TECHNIQUE?
DEAL OR ? NO DEAL
NO. SINCE THE BOXES ARE ALLOCATED THEIR RESPECTIVE SUMS BY A PROCESS OF RANDOMISATION, SELECTING THEM IN NUMERICAL SEQUENCE IS NEITHER MORE NOR LESS VALID THAN ANY OTHER CHOOSING SYSTEM. ESPECIALLY NOTWITHSTANDING ONE BASED UPON EMPIRICALLY UNVERIFIABLE ENTITIES SUCH AS BENEFICIENT PROVIDENCE.
WELL, ANYWAY, WE'RE DOWN TO TWO BOXES. IN ONE IS A QUARTER OF A MILLION POUNDS. IN THE OTHER IS A PENNY. YOU'VE DECIDED NOT TO DEAL AT A HUNDRED AND FIFTEEN THOUSAND POUNDS.
THAT IS CORRECT.
THE BANKER IS OFFERING YOU THE CHANCE TO SWAP BOXES WITH MARJORIE. DO YOU WANT TO?
NATURALLY.
OH!? YOU SEEM CONFIDENT. WHY 'NATURALLY'?
AT THE COMMENCEMENT OF THE RECORDING OF THIS TELEVISUAL BROADCAST, I WAS GIVEN ONE BOX OUT OF A TOTAL OF 22...
THUS, THE PROBABILITY OF MY BOX, BOX ONE, BEING THE BOX THAT CONTAINED £250,000 WAS 1 IN 22, OR 4.545454...
...545454545454 545454545454...
LAWRENCE
TWENTY MINUTES LATER...
...545454545454 55%, ROUNDED UP TO 1000 DECIMAL PLACES.
ERGO, THE PROBABILITY OF THE £250,000 BEING IN ONE OF THE BOXES OTHER THAN MINE WAS 21 IN 22, OR 95.454545454545...
...45454545454545 45454545454545...
TWENTY MINUTES LATER...
...45454545%, ROUNDED DOWN TO 1000 DECIMAL PLACES.
THAT 20 OF THE 21 BOXES HAVE BEEN OPENED AND SHOWN NOT TO CONTAIN £250,000 DOES NOT AFFECT THE 4.5454...
...545454545454545454 545454545454545454 545454545454545454...
TWENTY MINUTES LATER...
...5454545454545455%, ROUNDED UP TO 1000 DECIMAL PLACES, PROBABILITY OF MY BOX CONTAINING THE £250,000.
IT FOLLOWS THAT, CONSEQUENT UPON THE FACT THE OPENED BOXES DID NOT CONTAIN £250,000, IT IS DEMONSTRABLY THE CASE THAT MARJORIE'S BOX, BOX TWENTY-TWO, IS THUS 21 TIMES MORE LIKELY TO CONTAIN THE JACKPOT SUM THAN IS MY OWN.
I WOULD THEREFORE BE VERY FOOLISH TO RETAIN THE BOX WITH WHICH I WAS ORIGINALLY ALLOCATED, KNOWING IT TO HAVE A MERE 1 IN 21, OR 4.761905% CHANCE OF CONTAINING THE JACKPOT.
IT'S A LIFE CHANGING AMOUNT OF MONEY, LAWRENCE, THOUGH NOT FOR ME, OBVIOUSLY. WHAT WILL YOU DO IF YOU WIN IT?
I WOULD PAY OFF MY OUTSTANDING DEBTS AND INVEST ANY REMAINING CAPITAL INTO WHICHEVER UNIT TRUST INVESTMENT FUND IS PRESENTLY OFFERING THE BEST RETURN TO RISK RATIO.
AND IF YOU LOSE?
IN THAT UNLIKELY EVENT I WOULD GO HOME ON THE BUS.
LAWRENCE... OPEN YOUR BOX!
SCRIPP!
TEN MINUTES LATER...
hmm... FASCINATING.

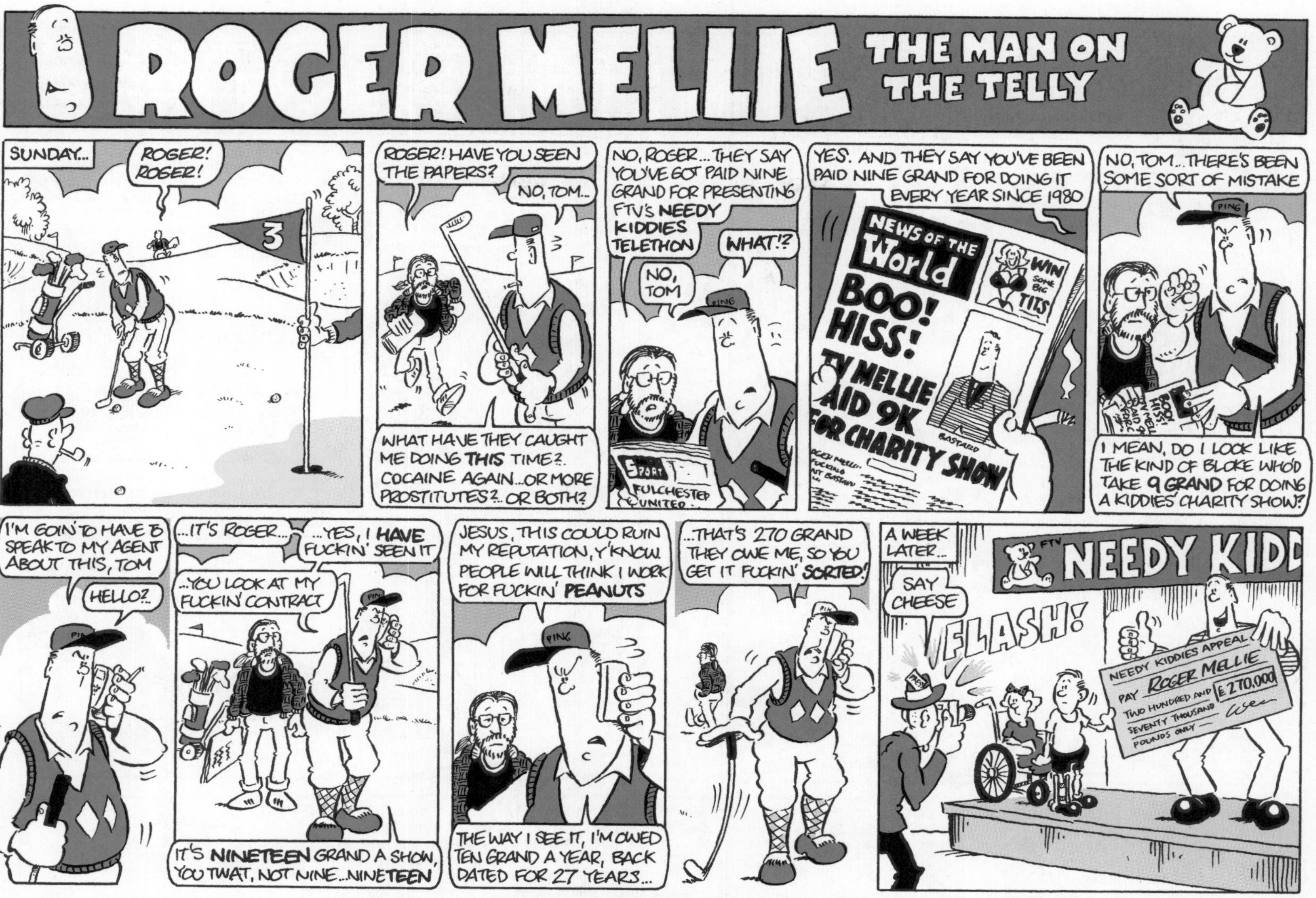
ROGER MELLIE
THE MAN ON THE TELLY
SUNDAY...
ROGER! ROGER!
3
ROGER! HAVE YOU SEEN THE PAPERS?
NO, TOM...
WHAT HAVE THEY CAUGHT ME DOING THIS TIME?.. COCAINE AGAIN...OR MORE PROSTITUTES?..OR BOTH?
NO, ROGER... THEY SAY YOU'VE GOT PAID NINE GRAND FOR PRESENTING FTV'S NEEDY KIDDIES TELETHON
NO, TOM
WHAT!?
PING
SPORT
FULCHESTER UNITED
YES. AND THEY SAY YOU'VE BEEN PAID NINE GRAND FOR DOING IT EVERY YEAR SINCE 1980
NEWS OF THE World
WIN SOME BIG TITS
BOO! HISS!
TV MELLIE PAID 9K FOR CHARITY SHOW
BASTARD
NO, TOM... THERE'S BEEN SOME SORT OF MISTAKE
PING
I MEAN, DO I LOOK LIKE THE KIND OF BLOKE WHO'D TAKE 9 GRAND FOR DOING A KIDDIES' CHARITY SHOW?
I'M GOIN' TO HAVE TO SPEAK TO MY AGENT ABOUT THIS, TOM
HELLO?..
PING
...IT'S ROGER...
...YES, I HAVE FUCKIN' SEEN IT
...YOU LOOK AT MY FUCKIN' CONTRACT
PING
IT'S NINETEEN GRAND A SHOW, YOU TWAT, NOT NINE...NINETEEN
JESUS, THIS COULD RUIN MY REPUTATION, Y'KNOW. PEOPLE WILL THINK I WORK FOR FUCKIN' PEANUTS
PING
THE WAY I SEE IT, I'M OWED TEN GRAND A YEAR, BACK DATED FOR 27 YEARS...
...THAT'S 270 GRAND THEY OWE ME, SO YOU GET IT FUCKIN' SORTED!
PING
A WEEK LATER...
FTV NEEDY KIDD
SAY CHEESE
FLASH!
PRESS
NEEDY KIDDIES APPEAL
PAY ROGER MELLIE £270,000
TWO HUNDRED AND SEVENTY THOUSAND POUNDS ONLY

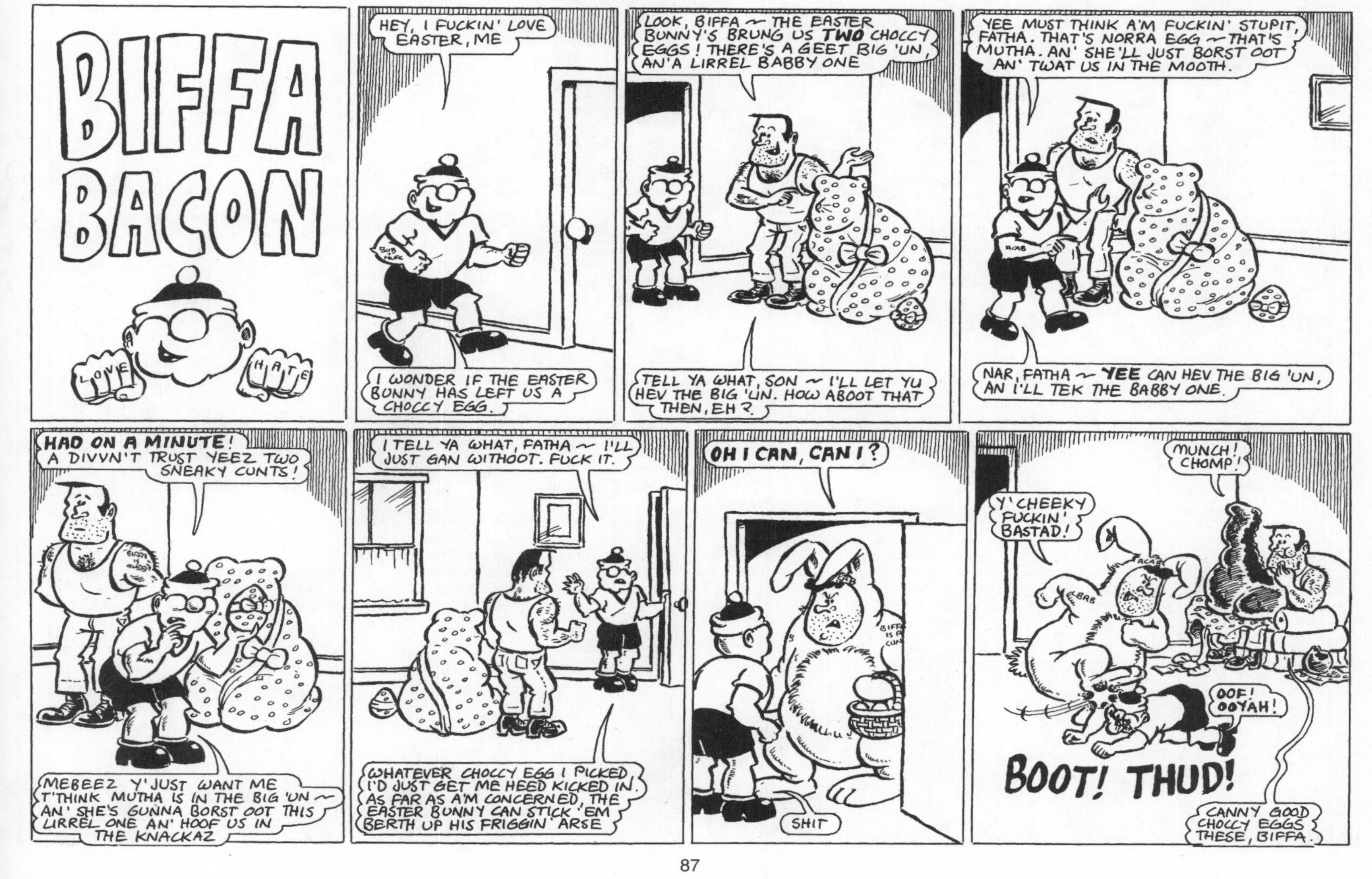
BIFFA BACON
LOVE
HATE
HEY, I FUCKIN' LOVE EASTER, ME
I WONDER IF THE EASTER BUNNY HAS LEFT US A CHOCCY EGG.
LOOK, BIFFA ~ THE EASTER BUNNY'S BRUNG US TWO CHOCCY EGGS! THERE'S A GEET BIG 'UN AN'A LIRREL BABBY ONE
TELL YA WHAT, SON ~ I'LL LET YU HEV THE BIG 'UN. HOW ABOOT THAT THEN, EH?
YEE MUST THINK A'M FUCKIN' STUPIT, FATHA. THAT'S NORRA EGG ~ THAT'S MUTHA. AN' SHE'LL JUST BORST OOT AN' TWAT US IN THE MOOTH.
NAR, FATHA ~ YEE CAN HEV THE BIG 'UN, AN I'LL TEK THE BABBY ONE.
HAD ON A MINUTE! A DIVVN'T TRUST YEEZ TWO SNEAKY CUNTS!
MEBEEZ Y' JUST WANT ME T'THINK MUTHA IS IN THE BIG 'UN ~ AN' SHE'S GUNNA BORST OOT THIS LIRREL ONE AN' HOOF US IN THE KNACKAZ
I TELL YA WHAT, FATHA ~ I'LL JUST GAN WITHOOT. FUCK IT.
WHATEVER CHOCCY EGG I PICKED I'D JUST GET ME HEED KICKED IN. AS FAR AS A'M CONCERNED, THE EASTER BUNNY CAN STICK 'EM BERTH UP HIS FRIGGIN' ARSE
OH I CAN, CAN I?
SHIT
MUNCH! CHOMP!
Y' CHEEKY FUCKIN' BASTAD!
OOF! OOYAH!
BOOT! THUD!
CANNY GOOD CHOCCY EGGS THESE, BIFFA.

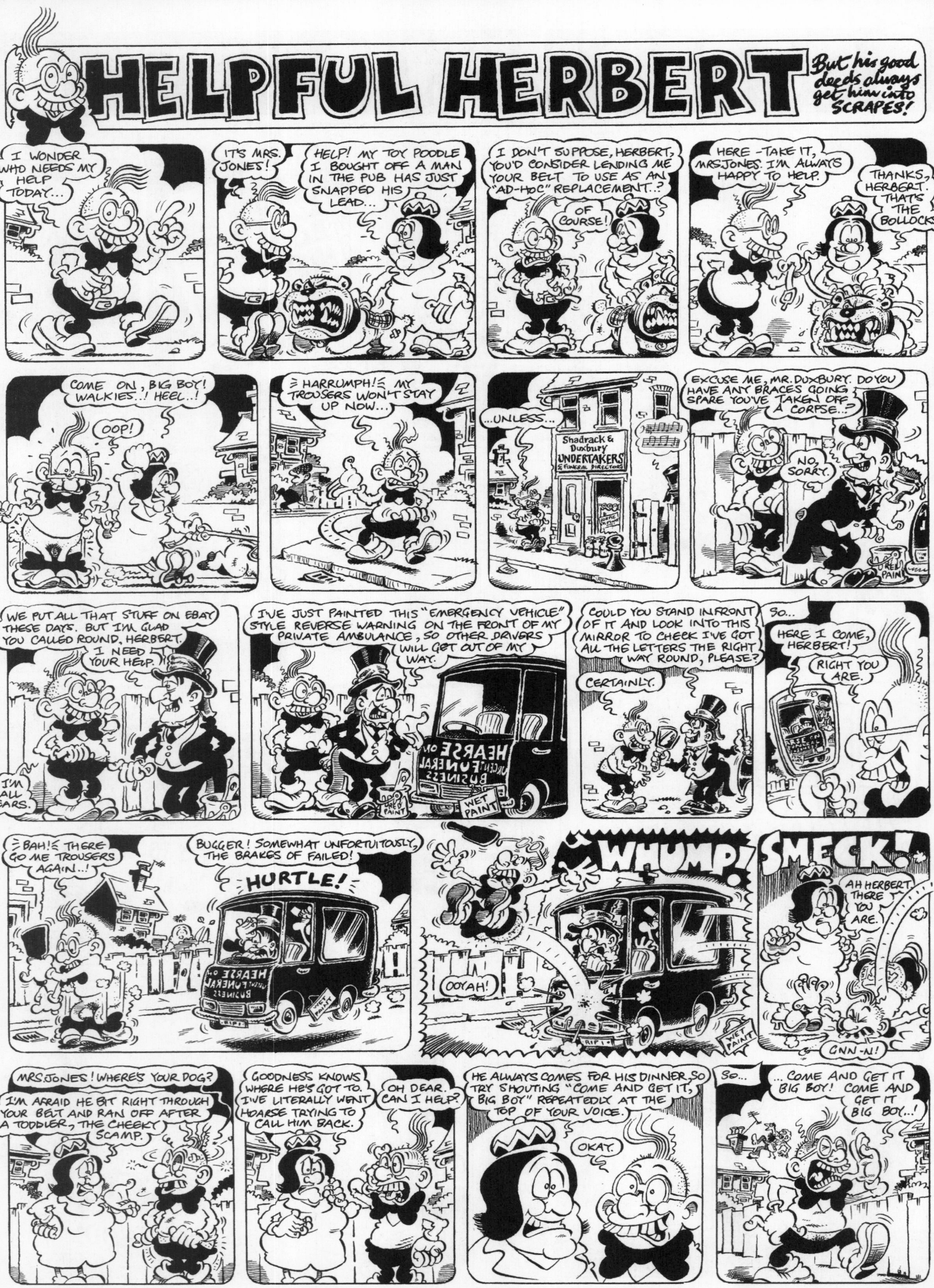
HELPFUL HERBERT
But his good deeds always get him into SCRAPES!
I WONDER WHO NEEDS MY HELP TODAY...
IT'S MRS. JONES!
HELP! MY TOY POODLE I BOUGHT OFF A MAN IN THE PUB HAS JUST SNAPPED HIS LEAD...
I DON'T SUPPOSE, HERBERT, YOU'D CONSIDER LENDING ME YOUR BELT TO USE AS AN "AD-HOC" REPLACEMENT..?
OF COURSE!
HERE - TAKE IT, MRS JONES. I'M ALWAYS HAPPY TO HELP.
THANKS, HERBERT. THAT'S THE BOLLOCKS.
COME ON, BIG BOY! WALKIES..! HEEL..!
OOP!
HARRUMPH! MY TROUSERS WON'T STAY UP NOW...
...UNLESS...
Shadrack & Duxbury UNDERTAKERS & FUNERAL DIRECTORS
EXCUSE ME, MR. DUXBURY. DO YOU HAVE ANY BRACES GOING SPARE YOU'VE TAKEN OFF A CORPSE..?
NO, SORRY.
WE PUT ALL THAT STUFF ON EBAY THESE DAYS. BUT I'M GLAD YOU CALLED ROUND, HERBERT. I NEED YOUR HELP.
I'M ALL EARS.
I'VE JUST PAINTED THIS "EMERGENCY VEHICLE" STYLE REVERSE WARNING ON THE FRONT OF MY PRIVATE AMBULANCE, SO OTHER DRIVERS WILL GET OUT OF MY WAY.
WET PAINT
COULD YOU STAND IN FRONT OF IT AND LOOK INTO THIS MIRROR TO CHECK I'VE GOT ALL THE LETTERS THE RIGHT WAY ROUND, PLEASE?
CERTAINLY.
SO...
HERE I COME, HERBERT!
RIGHT YOU ARE.
BAH! THERE GO ME TROUSERS AGAIN..!
BUGGER! SOMEWHAT UNFORTUITOUSLY, THE BRAKES OF FAILED!
HURTLE!
WHUMP!
OOYAH!
SMECK!
AH HERBERT THERE YOU ARE.
GNN-N!
MRS. JONES! WHERE'S YOUR DOG?
I'M AFRAID HE BIT RIGHT THROUGH YOUR BELT AND RAN OFF AFTER A TODDLER, THE CHEEKY SCAMP.
GOODNESS KNOWS WHERE HE'S GOT TO. I'VE LITERALLY WENT HOARSE TRYING TO CALL HIM BACK.
OH DEAR. CAN I HELP?
HE ALWAYS COMES FOR HIS DINNER SO TRY SHOUTING "COME AND GET IT, BIG BOY" REPEATEDLY AT THE TOP OF YOUR VOICE.
OKAY.
SO...
...COME AND GET IT BIG BOY! COME AND GET IT BIG BOY...!

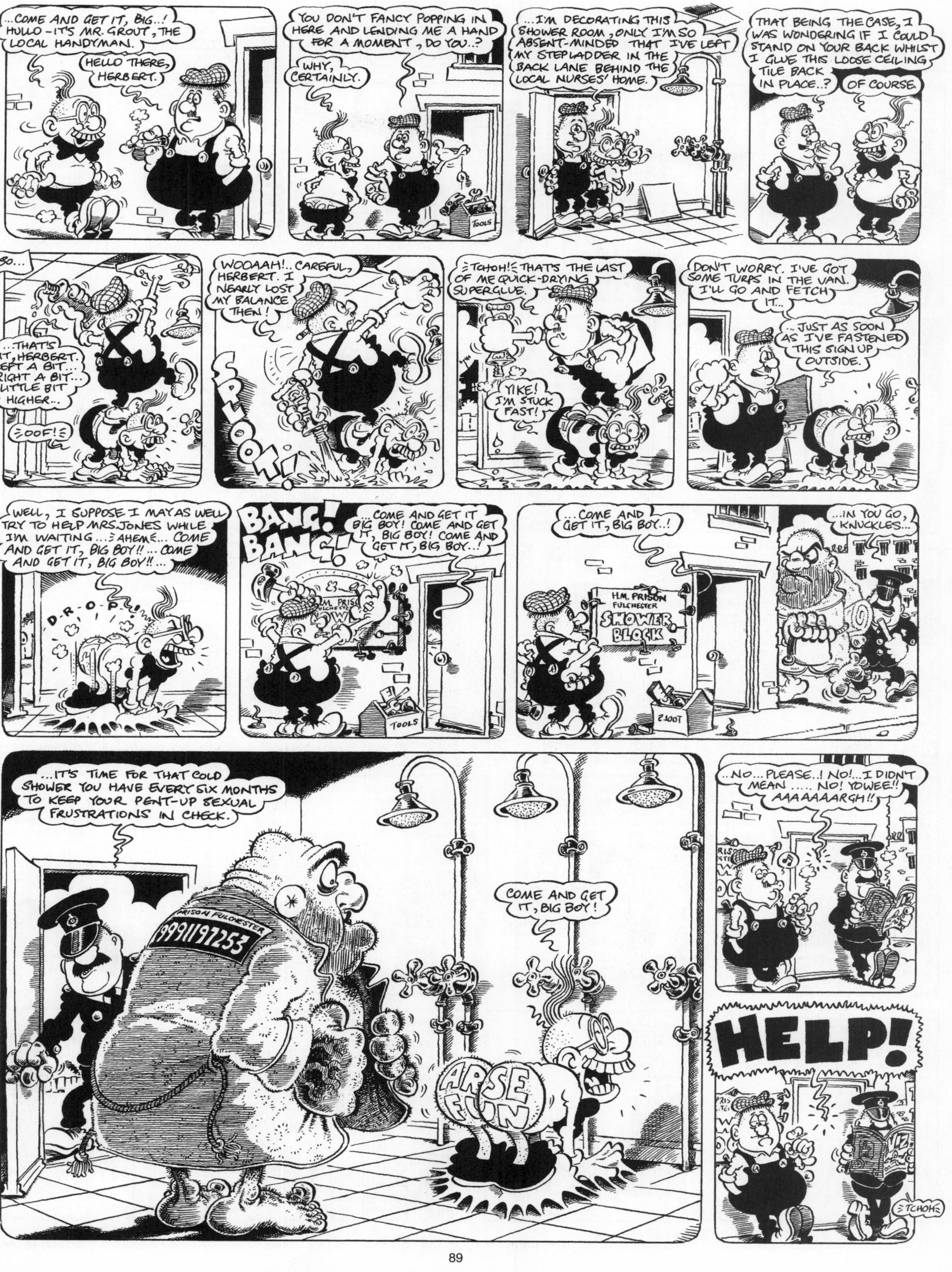
...COME AND GET IT, BIG..! HULLO - IT'S MR. GROUT, THE LOCAL HANDYMAN.
HELLO THERE, HERBERT.
YOU DON'T FANCY POPPING IN HERE AND LENDING ME A HAND FOR A MOMENT, DO YOU..?
WHY, CERTAINLY.
TOOLS
...I'M DECORATING THIS SHOWER ROOM, ONLY I'M SO ABSENT-MINDED THAT I'VE LEFT MY STEPLADDER IN THE BACK LANE BEHIND THE LOCAL NURSES' HOME.
THAT BEING THE CASE, I WAS WONDERING IF I COULD STAND ON YOUR BACK WHILST I GLUE THIS LOOSE CEILING TILE BACK IN PLACE..?
OF COURSE.
SO...
...THAT'S IT, HERBERT. LEFT A BIT... RIGHT A BIT... ...LITTLE BIT HIGHER...
OOF!
WOOAAH!.. CAREFUL, HERBERT. I NEARLY LOST MY BALANCE THEN!
SPLOOT!
TCHOH! THAT'S THE LAST OF ME QUICK-DRYING SUPERGLUE.
YIKE! I'M STUCK FAST!
DON'T WORRY. I'VE GOT SOME TURPS IN THE VAN. I'LL GO AND FETCH IT...
...JUST AS SOON AS I'VE FASTENED THIS SIGN UP OUTSIDE.
WELL, I SUPPOSE I MAY AS WELL TRY TO HELP MRS. JONES WHILE I'M WAITING... AHEM... COME AND GET IT, BIG BOY!! ...COME AND GET IT, BIG BOY!! ...
D-R-O-P!
BANG! BANG!
...COME AND GET IT BIG BOY! COME AND GET IT, BIG BOY! COME AND GET IT, BIG BOY..!
TOOLS
...COME AND GET IT, BIG BOY..!
H.M. PRISON FULCHESTER SHOWER BLOCK
...IN YOU GO, KNUCKLES...
...IT'S TIME FOR THAT COLD SHOWER YOU HAVE EVERY SIX MONTHS TO KEEP YOUR PENT-UP SEXUAL FRUSTRATIONS IN CHECK.
PRISON FULCHESTER
9911197253
COME AND GET IT, BIG BOY!
ARSE FUN
...NO... PLEASE..! NO!...I DIDN'T MEAN ..... NO! YOWEE!! AAAAAAARGH!!
HELP!
TCHOH

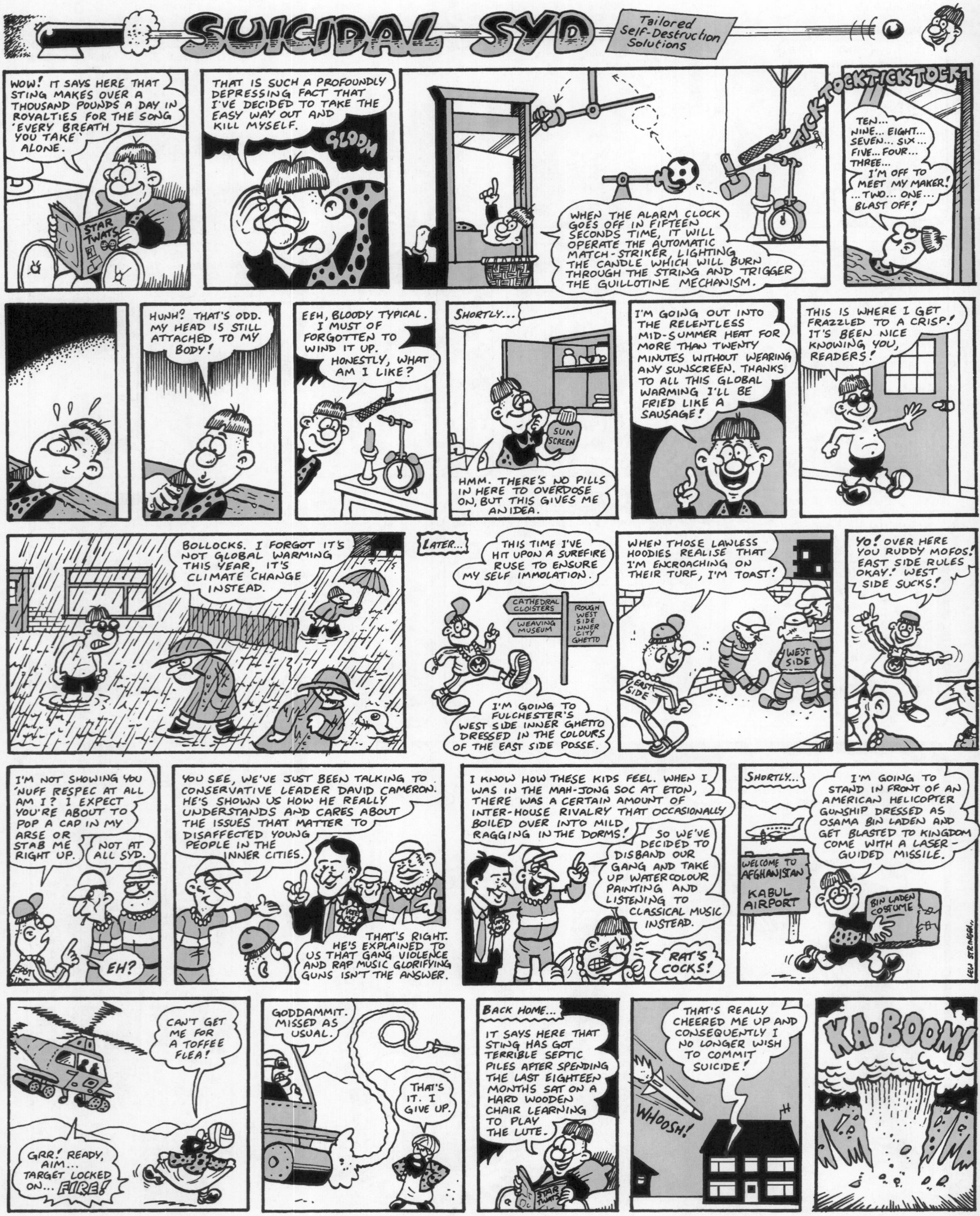

SUICIDAL SYD
Tailored Self-Destruction Solutions
WOW! IT SAYS HERE THAT STING MAKES OVER A THOUSAND POUNDS A DAY IN ROYALTIES FOR THE SONG 'EVERY BREATH YOU TAKE' ALONE.
STAR TWATS
THAT IS SUCH A PROFOUNDLY DEPRESSING FACT THAT I'VE DECIDED TO TAKE THE EASY WAY OUT AND KILL MYSELF.
GLOOM
WHEN THE ALARM CLOCK GOES OFF IN FIFTEEN SECONDS TIME, IT WILL OPERATE THE AUTOMATIC MATCH-STRIKER, LIGHTING THE CANDLE WHICH WILL BURN THROUGH THE STRING AND TRIGGER THE GUILLOTINE MECHANISM.
TICK TOCK TICK TOCK
TEN... NINE... EIGHT... SEVEN... SIX... FIVE... FOUR... THREE... I'M OFF TO MEET MY MAKER! ...TWO... ONE... BLAST OFF!
HUNH? THAT'S ODD. MY HEAD IS STILL ATTACHED TO MY BODY!
EEH, BLOODY TYPICAL. I MUST OF FORGOTTEN TO WIND IT UP. HONESTLY, WHAT AM I LIKE?
SHORTLY...
SUN SCREEN
HMM. THERE'S NO PILLS IN HERE TO OVERDOSE ON, BUT THIS GIVES ME AN IDEA.
I'M GOING OUT INTO THE RELENTLESS MID-SUMMER HEAT FOR MORE THAN TWENTY MINUTES WITHOUT WEARING ANY SUNSCREEN. THANKS TO ALL THIS GLOBAL WARMING I'LL BE FRIED LIKE A SAUSAGE!
THIS IS WHERE I GET FRAZZLED TO A CRISP! IT'S BEEN NICE KNOWING YOU, READERS!
BOLLOCKS. I FORGOT IT'S NOT GLOBAL WARMING THIS YEAR, IT'S CLIMATE CHANGE INSTEAD.
LATER...
THIS TIME I'VE HIT UPON A SUREFIRE RUSE TO ENSURE MY SELF IMMOLATION.
CATHEDRAL CLOISTERS
WEAVING MUSEUM
ROUGH WEST SIDE INNER CITY GHETTO
I'M GOING TO FULCHESTER'S WEST SIDE INNER GHETTO DRESSED IN THE COLOURS OF THE EAST SIDE POSSE.
WHEN THOSE LAWLESS HOODIES REALISE THAT I'M ENCROACHING ON THEIR TURF, I'M TOAST!
WEST SIDE
EAST SIDE
YO! OVER HERE YOU RUDDY MOFOS! EAST SIDE RULES OKAY! WEST SIDE SUCKS!
I'M NOT SHOWING YOU 'NUFF RESPEC AT ALL AM I? I EXPECT YOU'RE ABOUT TO POP A CAP IN MY ARSE OR STAB ME RIGHT UP.
NOT AT ALL SYD.
EH?
YOU SEE, WE'VE JUST BEEN TALKING TO CONSERVATIVE LEADER DAVID CAMERON. HE'S SHOWN US HOW HE REALLY UNDERSTANDS AND CARES ABOUT THE ISSUES THAT MATTER TO DISAFFECTED YOUNG PEOPLE IN THE INNER CITIES.
THAT'S RIGHT. HE'S EXPLAINED TO US THAT GANG VIOLENCE AND RAP MUSIC GLORIFYING GUNS ISN'T THE ANSWER.
I KNOW HOW THESE KIDS FEEL. WHEN I WAS IN THE MAH-JONG SOC AT ETON, THERE WAS A CERTAIN AMOUNT OF INTER-HOUSE RIVALRY THAT OCCASIONALLY BOILED OVER INTO MILD RAGGING IN THE DORMS!
SO WE'VE DECIDED TO DISBAND OUR GANG AND TAKE UP WATERCOLOUR PAINTING AND LISTENING TO CLASSICAL MUSIC INSTEAD.
RAT'S COCKS!
SHORTLY...
I'M GOING TO STAND IN FRONT OF AN AMERICAN HELICOPTER GUNSHIP DRESSED AS OSAMA BIN LADEN AND GET BLASTED TO KINGDOM COME WITH A LASER-GUIDED MISSILE.
WELCOME TO AFGHANISTAN
KABUL AIRPORT
BIN LADEN COSTUME
CAN'T GET ME FOR A TOFFEE FLEA!
GRR! READY, AIM... TARGET LOCKED ON... FIRE!
GODDAMMIT. MISSED AS USUAL.
THAT'S IT. I GIVE UP.
BACK HOME...
IT SAYS HERE THAT STING HAS GOT TERRIBLE SEPTIC PILES AFTER SPENDING THE LAST EIGHTEEN MONTHS SAT ON A HARD WOODEN CHAIR LEARNING TO PLAY THE LUTE.
STAR TWATS
THAT'S REALLY CHEERED ME UP AND CONSEQUENTLY I NO LONGER WISH TO COMMIT SUICIDE!
WHOOSH!
KA-BOOM!

IT IS NOW EXACTLY 40 years since homosexuals were legalised. But even after four decades, the media refuses to abandon its tired, outdated stereotypes - often portraying gays as flamboyant, mincing queens or leather-clad, moustachioed bikers.

In reality, however, homosexuals are just like the rest of us. There could even be one living in your street, and unless someone warned you, you'd never suspect anything was wrong. These days, gays support football teams, drive cars and hold down proper jobs; anyone from any walk of life could be one. It's a remarkable fact that your hairdresser, your holiday flight attendant or even your local priest could all be on the other bus, because gays play valuable roles in the world just like normal people do.

Indeed, gays are such an everyday part of modern society that you might be one yourself without knowing it!

Psychologists believe that sexual orientation is on a sliding scale, and we all have homosexual tendencies to a greater or lesser extent. So exactly *how gay are you?* Here's a chance to find out where you come on the scale by taking this scientific test. Simply answer the 10 questions below, then tot up your score to find out...

How GAY are YOU?

THE ONLY GAY IN THE VILLAGE PEOPLE: What's YOUR GQ?

1 YOU are at the airport bookstore looking for some holiday reading. What do you choose?
a) This month's *Razzle* and *Bravo Two-Zero* by Andy McNabb.
b) A copy of the *Spectator* and *Atonement* by Ian McEwan.
c) A flower arranging magazine and an assortment of Mills & Boon novels.

2 YOU find yourself standing next to another man at a pub urinal. How do you strike up a conversation?
a) Ask him if he saw the match last night, commenting on England's recent run of poor performances.
b) Chat to him about your favourite films, such as *Rocky* or *Porky's Revenge*. But not the *Wizard of Oz*.
c) Chat to him about the *Wizard of Oz*.

3 HOW would you describe your moustache?
a) Short and neatly-clipped, in the style of ladies' man Leslie Philips or womaniser Errol Flynn.
b) Unkempt but not unruly, like London mayor Ken Livingstone or TV presenter Anne Robinson.
c) Thick, bushy and luxuriant, like flamboyant showman Freddie Mercury or Paul Rutherford out of Frankie Goes to Hollywood.

4 YOU decide your flat needs decorating. What do you do?
a) Get your wife and her sister, who you are knocking off on the side, to do it while you are at the pub watching football.
b) Employ a professional decorator, telling him to paint everything magnolia or cream.
c) Throw yourself wholeheartedly into a whirlwind of interior design, spending hours agonising over colour charts, curtain samples and fabric swatches.

5 YOU go to a fancy dress party as one of the Village People. Which one do you choose to impersonate?
a) The macho construction worker, complete with tough tool belt and manly hard hat.
b) The Red Indian, with feathered head-dress, beads and painted face.
c) The Hell's Angel, wearing black leather trolleys and motorcycle cap, and sporting a thick, bushy and luxuriant moustache like flamboyant showman Freddie Mercury or Paul Rutherford out of Frankie Goes to Hollywood.

6 YOUR journey to work takes 6 minutes on the bus. Which two songs on your iPod do you listen to?
a) *Gertcha* by Chas & Dave and *Ace of Spades* by Motorhead.
b) *Lola* by the Kinks and *Walk on the Wild Side* by Lou Reed.
c) *Somewhere Over the Rainbow* by Judy Garland. Twice.

7 HOW would you describe your wrists?
a) Taut, turgid, powerful and strong, like an *Indoor League* arm wrestler or an archer at the Battle of Agincourt.
b) Strong enough for most day-to-day purposes, like opening jam jars and lifting car batteries.
c) Limp, slack and flaccid, so that you are unable to hold your hands horizontal.

8 YOU go to a pet shop to buy yourself a pet. What do you come home with?
a) A twenty-foot reticulated python, two tarantulas and six pitbull terriers, all called Tyson.
b) A couple of lop-eared rabbits, or perhaps a ginger cat.
c) A toy poodle called Dorothy, dyed pink.

9 YOU are walking along the street when you come to a puddle. What do you do?
a) Just keep walking straight through the water. Like an SAS soldier, wet feet hold no fear for you.
b) Skirt round the puddle, stepping into the road if necessary to avoid your shoes getting a soaking.
c) Let out a high-pitched shriek of horror and skip girlishly over the puddle with pointy toes.

10 WHILST out on a Friday night, you get into a fight over a taxi. What do you do?
a) Strip to the waist and exchange bare-knuckle punches with the other bloke for half an hour, each blow making a sound like a car door slamming. A bit like Clint Eastwood in *Every Which Way but Loose.*
b) Grab the other man by the lapels and attempt to nut him on the bridge of his nose. Then kick him in the bollocks and run off.
c) Lean forwards whilst turning your head away from your opponent, then try to pull his hair whilst scratching his face with the manicured nails on your other hand.

HOW DID YOU DO?

TO WORK OUT your GQ (Gayness Quotient), award yourself points for your answers as follows: *Mainly As*; 30 points and under: *Mainly Bs*; 31-40 points: *Mainly Cs*; 41 points and over.

UNDER 30 POINTS: You're definitely not gay - in fact, you're an out-and-out heterosexual. A score of under thirty points proves that you're 100% straight, with not a single camp bone in your body. If you find yourself snogging another man whilst dressed in women's underwear, chances are you're merely indulging in a little good-natured, manly horseplay with your rugby club mates.

31 - 40 POINTS: You're not gay, but you're not completely heterosexual either. In fact, you're what scientists call bi-curious, essentially straight but keen to explore other sexual avenues if the opportunity arises. You occasionally find yourself telling your wife you're going out to walk the dog, when in fact you're heading for Hampstead Heath to fellate some stranger in a bush.

41 POINTS AND OVER: There's no two ways about it, you're gay! You've probably spent your whole life lying to friends, family and yourself about your true nature, but now it's time to stop the lies, come out of the closet and admit to the world that you're gay and proud. Get yourself a rubber vest, a pair of spandex shorts and a ticket on the next bus to Brighton. It's 2007 and time to start livin'!

LETTERBOCKS

Viz Comic, PO Box 656
North Shields NE30 4XX
e-mail: letters@viz.co.uk

STAR LETTER

I couldn't believe my luck the other day when I received an envelope on which were printed the words 'Check Inside. You Could Already Have Won Half A Million Pounds.' And sure enough, there inside the envelope was half a million pounds in crisp new £50 notes. **Robert Canning, e-mail**

Has one ever noticed that when one drops a piece of toast it always lands caviar side down?
**HM Queen Elizabeth II
Windsor**

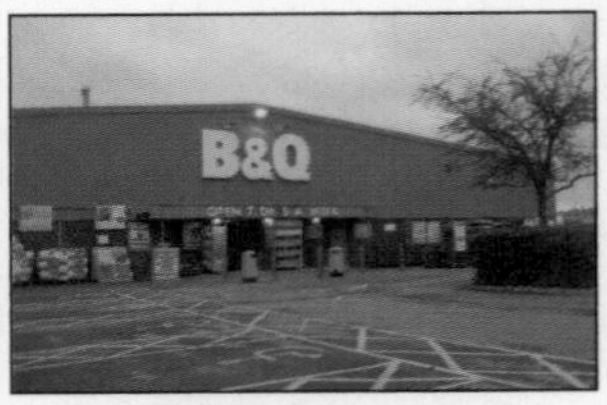
B&Q

Congratulations to B&Q for helping to fight climate change by charging customers 5p for a plastic bag. If only the other corporate giants at out-of-town retail parks showed the same level of commitment to the environment, the world would be a better place.
Joan David, Newcastle

BBC Radio London recently had a discussion on the overcrowded living conditions in the capital, and I have to say that I am shocked at the state we have reached. For instance, I read recently in a newspaper that a Premiership footballer 'shared a bed with 4 women'. If a rich footballer is living in such cramped conditions, then what conditions must the average Londoner be suffering?
J Addison, Croydon

What is it with the Jews and hats? Either they've got a tiny little hat that sits on the back of their head, or else they're wearing a hat with a massive brim. Nothing in between. Come on, sort your hat sizes out.
Hector Jones, Luton

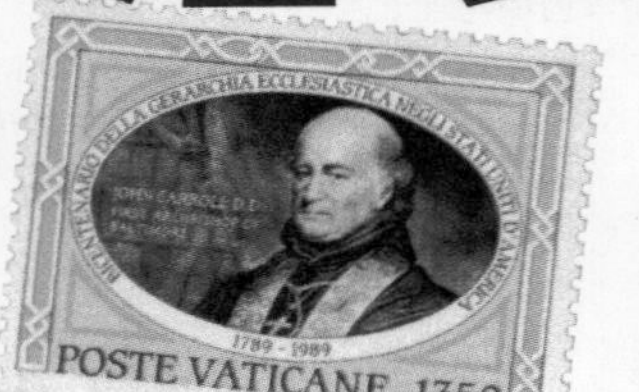
1789 - 1989
POSTE VATICANE 1350

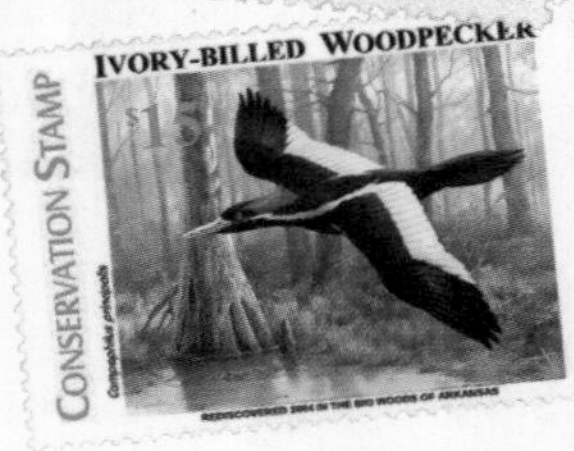
IVORY-BILLED WOODPECKER
CONSERVATION STAMP

With reference to Hector Jones' letter *(this page)*, I see he is having a go at a safe target in Jewish headwear. I bet he won't dare have a go at the muslims' hats, will he?
Arthur Sixpence, Tring

Whilst singing *All Things Bright and Beautiful* at a wedding recently, my girlfriend laughed so loud at the line 'The purple-headed mountain' that people three rows in front of us were tutting. Even the vicar glared at her. Could I use your pages to make a public declaration of love for her?
Adam Bowman, e-mail

Why is it that when one goes into one's wardrobe for a mink cape, there are always thousands of wire hangers? One believes they are breeding in there.
**HM Queen Elizabeth II
Windsor**

I just saw a van drive by with the company name 'Seafood Solutions'. I must admit, I didn't know seafood was a problem.
Martin Kristos, e-mail

A Christian came up to me in the street the other day and gave me a pamphlet entitled 'God is Good.' Just good? That seems very feint praise for someone who made everything.
Hazelnut Monkbottle, e-mail

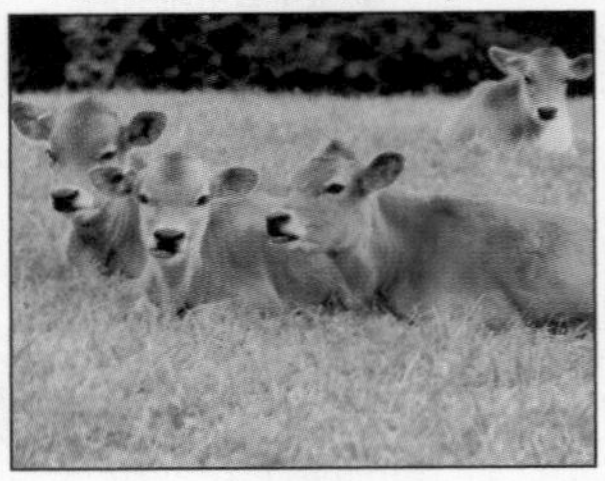

What right have cows got to decide when it rains? I've just seen loads of them lying down in a field with knowing looks on their faces.
Aaron Delays, e-mail

TOP TIPS

QUEENS. Don't throw away old crowns. They make excellent cosies for Ming Dynasty teapots.
**HM Queen Elizabeth II
Windsor**

SMOKERS. Take a tip from tumble dryer users. Enjoy a crafty fag at your desk by attaching a flexible vent hose to your face and running it out of the office window.
**Aston Martini
London**

QUEENS. If a large jewel falls out of one's sceptre, it can easily replaced with a pear drop of the same colour, from which one has sucked the sugar coating.
**HM Queen Elizabeth II
Windsor**

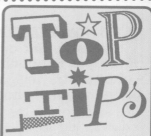

Is it just one, or does one never see white corgi faeces anymore?
**HM Queen Elizabeth II
Windsor**

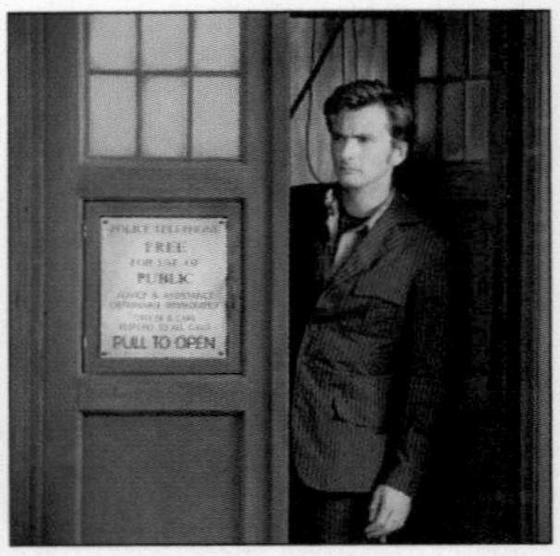
PULL TO OPEN

Surely it should be Dr Whom?
Parsimonious Twat, e-mail

How is it that no two people in a soap opera ever share the same name, even when it's a fairly common one like Dave or Emma?
Martin Palindrome, e-mail

In his book *Against All Gods*, atheist philosopher AC Grayling argues that religious

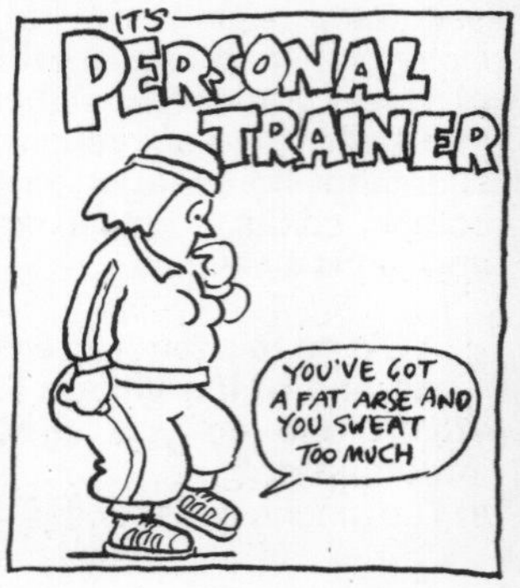
IT'S PERSONAL TRAINER
YOU'VE GOT A FAT ARSE AND YOU SWEAT TOO MUCH

BULLDOG BASIL

Fox Unscathed After 3 Month Kidnap Ordeal

CHILDREN'S favourite *Basil Brush* was today tasting freedom after being held hostage in Beirut for three months.

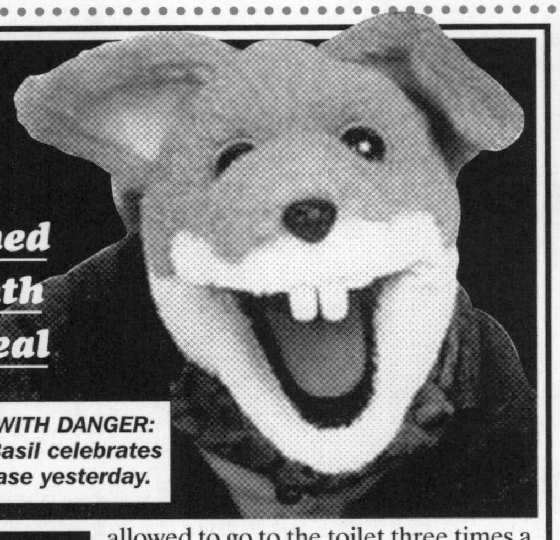

BRUSH WITH DANGER: Puppet Basil celebrates his release yesterday.

The puppet fox was released by his captors in the early hours of the morning after being taken from his hotel room in the Lebanese capital on May 28th.

KILL

The Lebanese People's Faction had threatened to kill the puppet unless Israel gave in to a list of demands including the release of Lebanese prisoners and the withdrawal of troops from occupied territories.

The fox's release came as a surprise as negotiations between the LPF and the Lebanese government had stalled.

GAS

Brush looked tired, but well as the desk he was sitting on was carried out

EXCLUSIVE!

of the building where he had spent the last 12 weeks. "That's the last time I order a sandwich from room service," he quipped to reporters as he was driven to the British Embassy.

"Boom! Boom!" added the clearly exhausted Brush.

At a press conference last night, Brush, 40, gave details of his ordeal.

"It was fairly grim, but I was not mistreated," he told a packed press room.

PORTLAND

"My desk was chained to a radiator in a small room with no windows. I was allowed to go to the toilet three times a day, when they would unchain my desk and carry it to a small privvy along the corridor."

The fox quickly won the confidence of his guard, who he referred to as Mr Rashid.

BLUE CIRCLE

"Mr Rashid would read to me every night before I went to sleep. It was a story about a spy, and I used to interrupt every few seconds with a little joke, which would exasperate him.

"But the terrible thing was, he used to leave the story at the most exciting parts and I would have to wait until the next night to find out what happened."

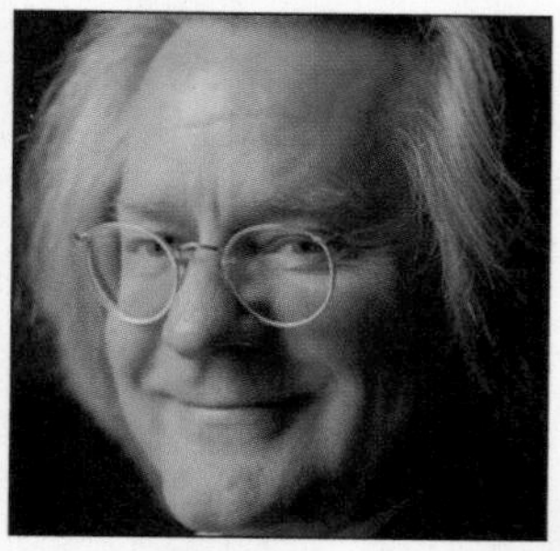

education is a form of child abuse. It certainly was at the Catholic boarding school I was sent to, where I got bummed left, right and centre off every priest and his dog.

Frazer Nash, Oxford

■ With reference to my letter a little earlier. I don't want anyone to think that I was advocating that anyone should 'have a go' at Muslims' hats. I have great repect for the headwear of all faiths, especially fundamentalist Muslims.

Arthur Sixpence, Tring

■ How ridiculous to award Salman Rushdie a nightclub for his services to literature. What on earth is the Queen thinking of, giving drinking establishments to controversial authors? Honestly, they're turning this ruddy country into a laughing stock, and that's swearing.

Edna Stonedeaf, Luton

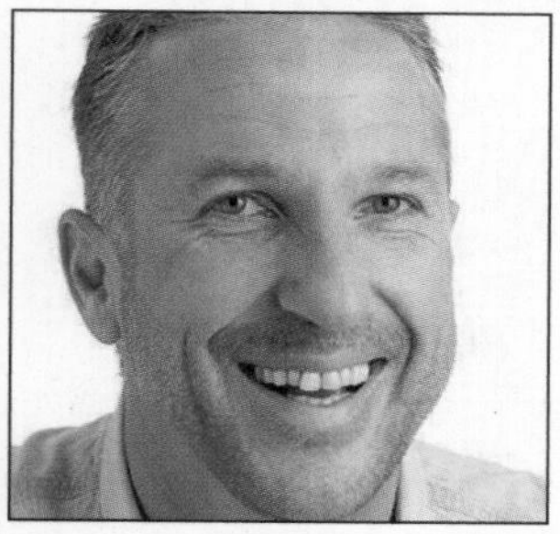

■ Ian Botham has been knighted for winning the Ashes in 1981 and for subsequently raising millions of pounds for charity with his marathon walks. But my mate Martin once sat next to him at a dinner and he said he was a fucking pig. If only her Majesty had spoken to my mate Martin before drawing up her honours list, she could have perhaps saved herself a gong, or at least awarded it to someone with better table manners.

T Thorn, Hexham

■ Has one ever noticed that when one takes one's socks from the washing machine, there is always an odd number? Actually, I haven't noticed because I have never taken anything out of a washing machine in my life. Or indeed put anything in one.

HM Queen Elizabeth II
Windsor

■ Congratulations to 5Live twat Nicky Campbell for asking the Mayor of Sheffield whether he thought his city's recent floods were caused by global warming. But bigger congratulations to the Mayor for saying that he didn't know.

Morgan Plusfour, Oswestry

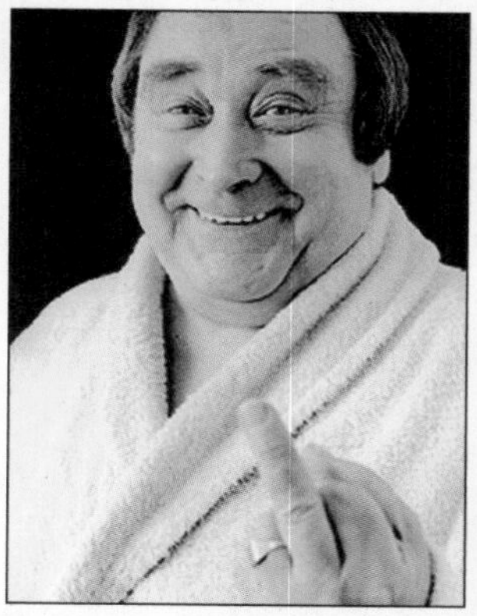

■ Following the death of Bernard Manning, the PC brigade have come out of the woodwork to call the man a racist. For my money, all he ever did was try to make people laugh. And if you can't spend forty years heaping poisonous, four letter abuse on members of ethnic minorities without being labelled a racist, it's a sorry state of affairs.

Austin Cambridge, Oxford

■ F1 pundits never tire of telling us that the downforce of a grand prix car is so strong that they could drive upside down on the ceiling without falling off. Well, as the Mayor of Birmingham, I would like to invite Bernie Ecclestone to hold an upside-down Formula 1 race on the underside of Spaghetti Junction. It would add another dimension to this sport and a bit of overhead excitement to anyone stuck in traffic on the M6.

Councillor Ray Jackson
Birmingham

■ Councillor Jackson's proposition for an upside down Birmingham Grand Prix is very interesting, but unfortunately not practical. We have tried it once or twice, and it proved rather difficult as the cars tended to fall off when they slowed down for the corners. There is also the risk that a careless mechanic could drop a spanner from the upside-down pits and injure a member of the crowd below.

Bernie Ecclestone, London

■ With reference to Councillor Jackson's letter *(this issue)*, an upside down motor race would be a tremendous sporting spectacle, but one which we are unlikely to see. Perhaps anyone wishing to have a taste of what it might look like should turn their TV upside down during the next Grand Prix.

Wolseley Hornet, Harpendon

■ On last week's *Top Gear*, Jeremy Clarkson's review of the Lamborghini Murcelago left me confused. He claimed that it was superior to the Ferrari Marinello by every measurable parameter, yet didn't have the magic of its prancing horse-badged rival. As a result, I have been left unable to decide which car is the bet-

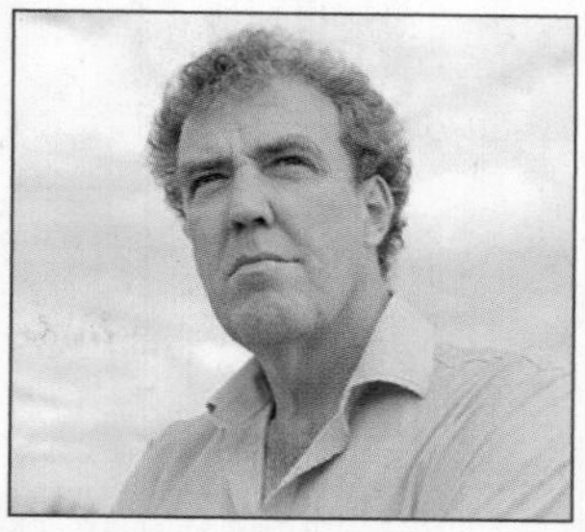

ter purchase, so I'll probably spend my £400 on an L-reg Nissan Micra with a week's MOT and two month's tax.

Spike Dustbin, Scotswood

■ I am an airline pilot, and during long flights, I often switch the plane to autopilot and nip into the bogs for a quick wank. But I would like to reassure my passengers that they are completely safe, as if there was any sort of emergency, such as an engine catching fire or a rudder snapping off, the stewardesses are under strict instructions to fetch me immediately.

Capt. Harrison Fibreboard,
e-mail

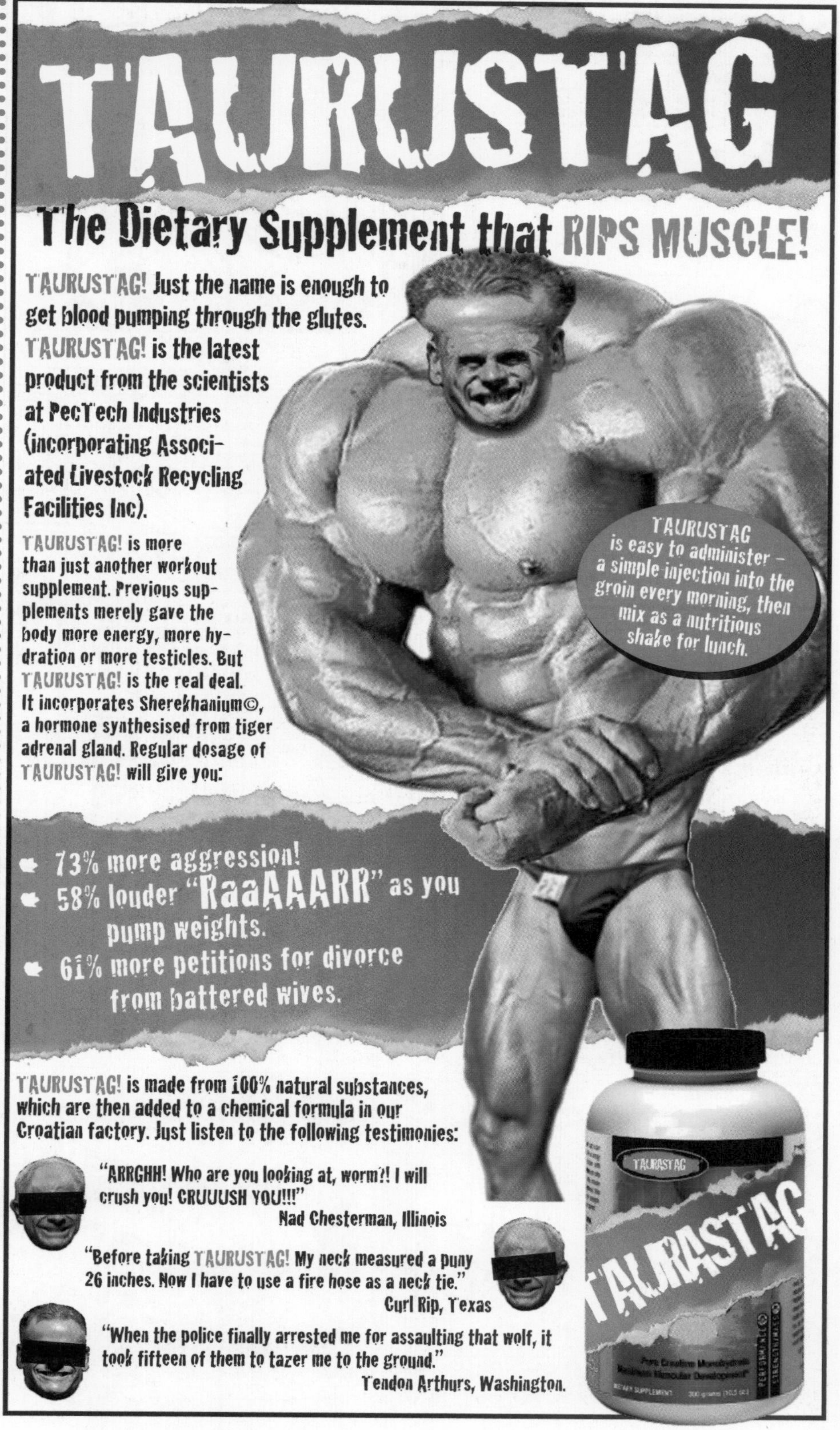
TAURUSTAG
The Dietary Supplement that RIPS MUSCLE!
TAURUSTAG! Just the name is enough to get blood pumping through the glutes.
TAURUSTAG! is the latest product from the scientists at PecTech Industries (incorporating Associated Livestock Recycling Facilities Inc).
TAURUSTAG! is more than just another workout supplement. Previous supplements merely gave the body more energy, more hydration or more testicles. But TAURUSTAG! is the real deal. It incorporates Sherekhanium©, a hormone synthesised from tiger adrenal gland. Regular dosage of TAURUSTAG! will give you:
TAURUSTAG is easy to administer – a simple injection into the groin every morning, then mix as a nutritious shake for lunch.
• 73% more aggression!
• 58% louder "RaaAAARR" as you pump weights.
• 61% more petitions for divorce from battered wives.
TAURUSTAG! is made from 100% natural substances, which are then added to a chemical formula in our Croatian factory. Just listen to the following testimonies:
"ARRGHH! Who are you looking at, worm?! I will crush you! CRUUUSH YOU!!!"
Nad Chesterman, Illinois
"Before taking TAURUSTAG! My neck measured a puny 26 inches. Now I have to use a fire hose as a neck tie."
Curl Rip, Texas
"When the police finally arrested me for assaulting that wolf, it took fifteen of them to tazer me to the ground."
Tendon Arthurs, Washington.
TAURASTAG
TAURASTAG

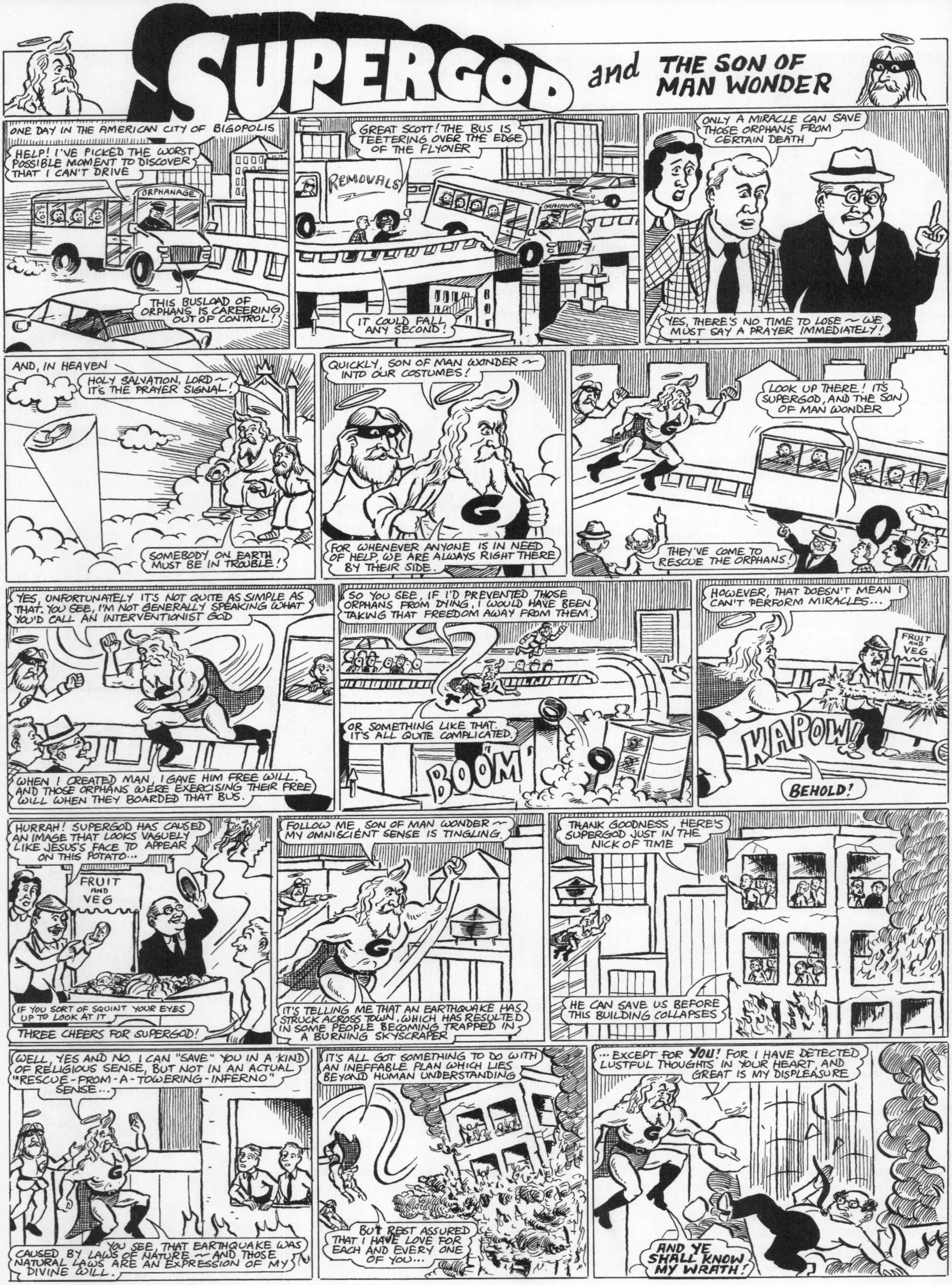
SUPERGOD and THE SON OF MAN WONDER
ONE DAY IN THE AMERICAN CITY OF BIGOPOLIS
HELP! I'VE PICKED THE WORST POSSIBLE MOMENT TO DISCOVER THAT I CAN'T DRIVE
ORPHANAGE
THIS BUSLOAD OF ORPHANS IS CAREERING OUT OF CONTROL!
GREAT SCOTT! THE BUS IS TEETERING OVER THE EDGE OF THE FLYOVER
REMOVALS
IT COULD FALL ANY SECOND!
ONLY A MIRACLE CAN SAVE THOSE ORPHANS FROM CERTAIN DEATH
YES, THERE'S NO TIME TO LOSE ~ WE MUST SAY A PRAYER IMMEDIATELY!
AND, IN HEAVEN
HOLY SALVATION, LORD ~ IT'S THE PRAYER SIGNAL!
SOMEBODY ON EARTH MUST BE IN TROUBLE!
QUICKLY, SON OF MAN WONDER ~ INTO OUR COSTUMES!
FOR WHENEVER ANYONE IS IN NEED OF HELP, WE ARE ALWAYS RIGHT THERE BY THEIR SIDE.
LOOK UP THERE! IT'S SUPERGOD, AND THE SON OF MAN WONDER
THEY'VE COME TO RESCUE THE ORPHANS!
YES, UNFORTUNATELY IT'S NOT QUITE AS SIMPLE AS THAT. YOU SEE, I'M NOT GENERALLY SPEAKING WHAT YOU'D CALL AN INTERVENTIONIST GOD
WHEN I CREATED MAN, I GAVE HIM FREE WILL. AND THOSE ORPHANS WERE EXERCISING THEIR FREE WILL WHEN THEY BOARDED THAT BUS.
SO YOU SEE, IF I'D PREVENTED THOSE ORPHANS FROM DYING, I WOULD HAVE BEEN TAKING THAT FREEDOM AWAY FROM THEM.
OR SOMETHING LIKE THAT. IT'S ALL QUITE COMPLICATED.
BOOM
HOWEVER, THAT DOESN'T MEAN I CAN'T PERFORM MIRACLES...
FRUIT AND VEG
KAPOW!
BEHOLD!
HURRAH! SUPERGOD HAS CAUSED AN IMAGE THAT LOOKS VAGUELY LIKE JESUS'S FACE TO APPEAR ON THIS POTATO...
FRUIT AND VEG
IF YOU SORT OF SQUINT YOUR EYES UP TO LOOK AT IT
THREE CHEERS FOR SUPERGOD!
FOLLOW ME, SON OF MAN WONDER ~ MY OMNISCIENT SENSE IS TINGLING.
IT'S TELLING ME THAT AN EARTHQUAKE HAS STRUCK ACROSS TOWN, WHICH HAS RESULTED IN SOME PEOPLE BECOMING TRAPPED IN A BURNING SKYSCRAPER
THANK GOODNESS, HERE'S SUPERGOD JUST IN THE NICK OF TIME
HE CAN SAVE US BEFORE THIS BUILDING COLLAPSES
WELL, YES AND NO. I CAN "SAVE" YOU IN A KIND OF RELIGIOUS SENSE, BUT NOT IN AN ACTUAL "RESCUE-FROM-A-TOWERING-INFERNO" SENSE...
YOU SEE, THAT EARTHQUAKE WAS CAUSED BY LAWS OF NATURE ~ AND THOSE NATURAL LAWS ARE AN EXPRESSION OF MY DIVINE WILL.
IT'S ALL GOT SOMETHING TO DO WITH AN INEFFABLE PLAN WHICH LIES BEYOND HUMAN UNDERSTANDING
BUT REST ASSURED THAT I HAVE LOVE FOR EACH AND EVERY ONE OF YOU...
...EXCEPT FOR YOU! FOR I HAVE DETECTED LUSTFUL THOUGHTS IN YOUR HEART, AND GREAT IS MY DISPLEASURE
AND YE SHALL KNOW MY WRATH!

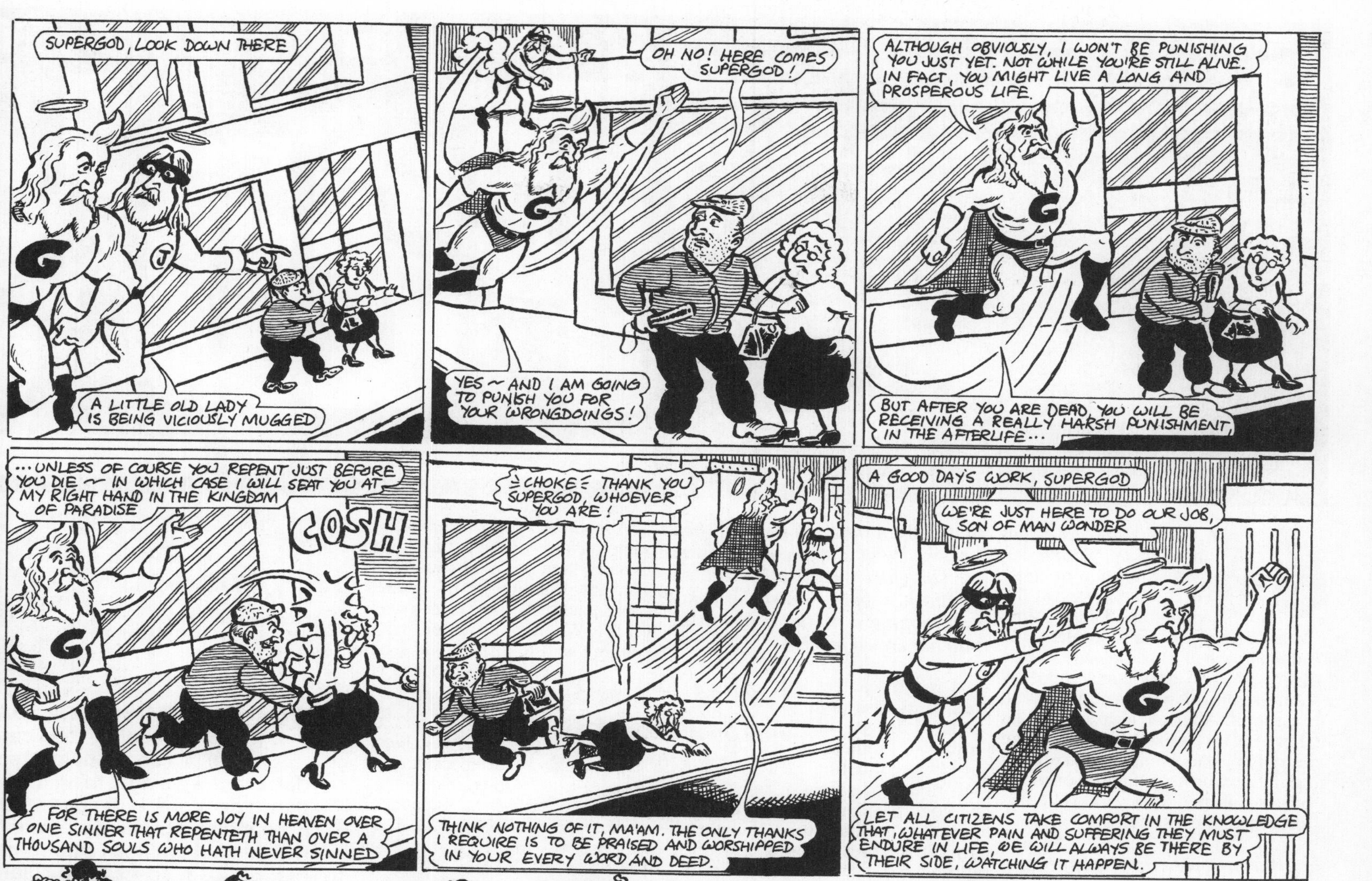
SUPERGOD, LOOK DOWN THERE
A LITTLE OLD LADY IS BEING VICIOUSLY MUGGED
OH NO! HERE COMES SUPERGOD!
YES ~ AND I AM GOING TO PUNISH YOU FOR YOUR WRONGDOINGS!
ALTHOUGH OBVIOUSLY, I WON'T BE PUNISHING YOU JUST YET. NOT WHILE YOU'RE STILL ALIVE. IN FACT, YOU MIGHT LIVE A LONG AND PROSPEROUS LIFE.
BUT AFTER YOU ARE DEAD, YOU WILL BE RECEIVING A REALLY HARSH PUNISHMENT IN THE AFTERLIFE...
...UNLESS OF COURSE YOU REPENT JUST BEFORE YOU DIE ~ IN WHICH CASE I WILL SEAT YOU AT MY RIGHT HAND IN THE KINGDOM OF PARADISE
COSH
FOR THERE IS MORE JOY IN HEAVEN OVER ONE SINNER THAT REPENTETH THAN OVER A THOUSAND SOULS WHO HATH NEVER SINNED
≋CHOKE≋ THANK YOU SUPERGOD, WHOEVER YOU ARE!
THINK NOTHING OF IT, MA'AM. THE ONLY THANKS I REQUIRE IS TO BE PRAISED AND WORSHIPPED IN YOUR EVERY WORD AND DEED.
A GOOD DAY'S WORK, SUPERGOD
WE'RE JUST HERE TO DO OUR JOB, SON OF MAN WONDER
LET ALL CITIZENS TAKE COMFORT IN THE KNOWLEDGE THAT, WHATEVER PAIN AND SUFFERING THEY MUST ENDURE IN LIFE, WE WILL ALWAYS BE THERE BY THEIR SIDE, WATCHING IT HAPPEN.

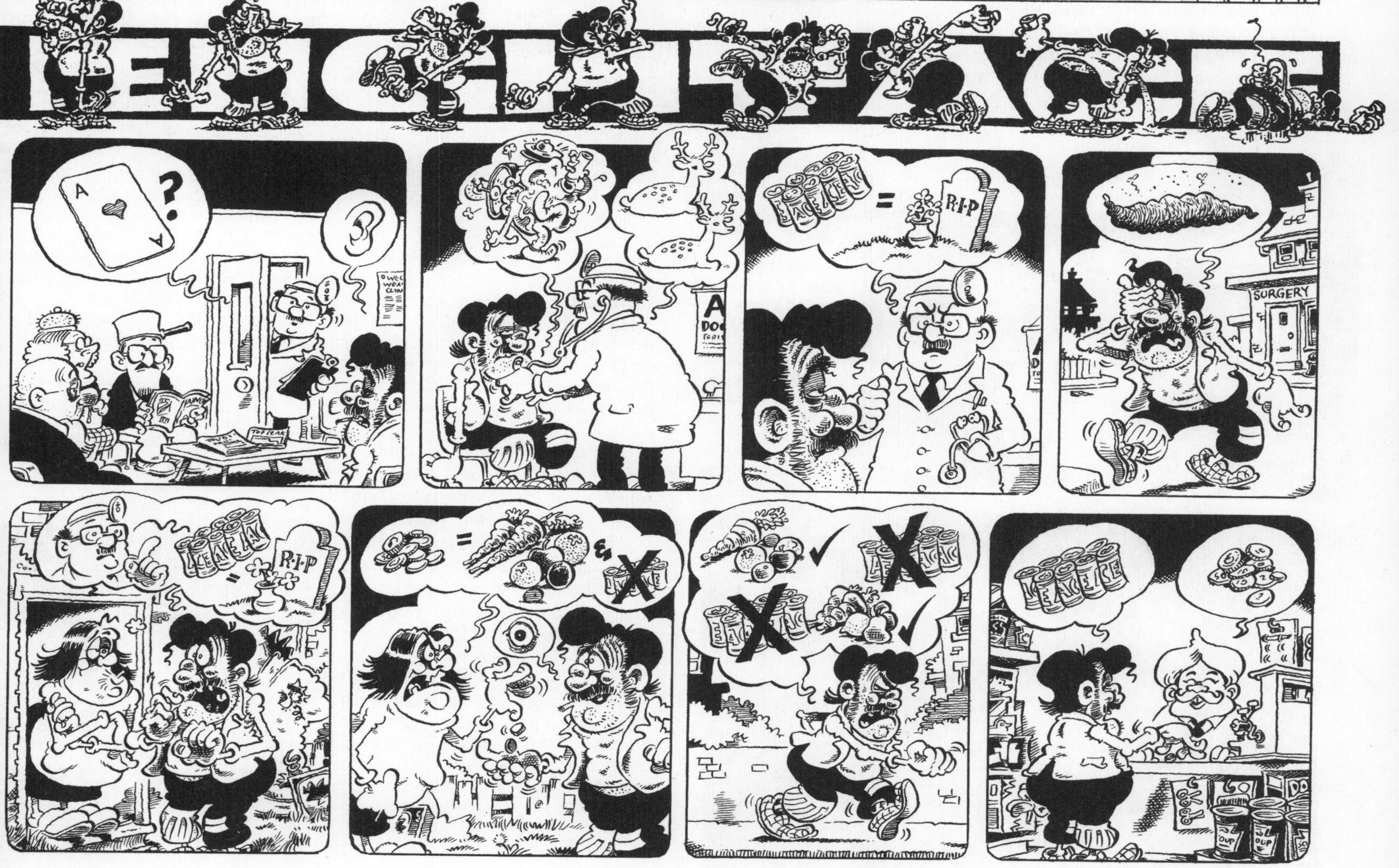
SURGERY
R·I·P

Star Snapper Barry Calls Ti

Pap's

SHOWBIZ STARS and celebrities were last night breathing a sigh of relief after one of the world's most ruthless paparazzi photographers announced he was hanging up his telephoto lens.

After 25 years as a member of the press-pack, snapping the rich and famous in their unguarded moments, ***BARRY DUCKETT*** - self-styled "King of the Paps" - is quitting the media circus in order to devote more time to his burgeoning mobile wheelie bin-cleaning business in Ossett, near Wakefield.

"It may sound strange to some people, but I've had my fill of peeking over walls in St Moritz, climbing up trees in the Bahamas and chasing limousines through the streets of Beverly Hills," he told us. "Being a topflight paparazzi is a young man's game, and I'm getting a bit long in the

EXCLUSIVE

tooth for it these days."

Barry may have lost some of his hunger for the chase, but he is adamant that he doesn't regret a single moment of his exciting career. "If I told you some of the things I've seen, you'd think I was making it up," he laughed. "But it's all true, and I've got the photographs to prove it!"

Now Barry has decided to write his memoirs, and he's expecting quite a bit of interest from publishers. Here, in a series of exclusive extracts, he gives *Viz* readers a taste of what to expect if the book ever hits the shelves.

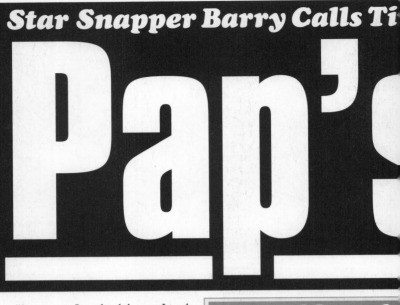

"There's no great skill to being a paparazzi. It's just a question of being in the right place at the right time. And one time I was certainly in the right place was on the beach in Mustique a few years ago. I never go anywhere without my camera, and this particular day was no exception. After all, a decent candid shot of A-listers like Mick Jagger and Jerry Hall smooching in the surf can easily be worth six figures once it's been syndicated worldwide, so it pays to keep your eyes peeled.

"But my eyes nearly popped out of my head when I saw who was catching some rays on the sand down by the pier. It was her majesty the Queen and Prince Philip! And they popped out even further when I clocked what they were getting up to. The Queen was sunbathing on her back, topless, whilst the Duke was rubbing a bottle of factor 15 into her crown jewels.

"I got my camera out of its case and zoomed in on the royal lovebirds, quickly shooting off four or five photographs, just in case the first one didn't come out. I thought all my Christmases had come at once. Although I'd never be able to sell such red hot pictures in Britain, I knew that continental mags would be queuing up to print them, and that would spell a cash bonanza for me.

"I waited until I had lined up a good shot of Kylie soaping lady Di's tits."

"As soon as I got back home, I took some pictures of the cat to finish the film off, then posted it straight off to Truprint. Waiting for my photos to come back was the longest week of my life. When the envelope arrived, I couldn't wait to open it and see how my shots had come out.

"I don't think I've ever been so disappointed. The pictures of the cat had come out great, but the rest of the film was blank. All I could suppose was that in my excitement I must of left the lens cap on when I took the pictures of the Queen. I could of kicked myself, but that's the paparazzi game, I suppose. I made a mental note to check my lens cap next time."

OPPORTUNITY

Barry didn't let his missed opportunity get him down for too long. A week later he was walking through the streets of Bel Air when he spotted a familiar face.

"It was Scarlet Johanssen. I decided to follow her and take a few shots of the 'Pearl Earring' actress. There's always a good market in the US celebrity titles for pictures of glamorous stars out shopping. I followed her into a clothes shop to pap her looking at some dresses.

"But once inside, I couldn't believe my luck. She'd taken a selection of erotic lingerie off one of the racks and had slipped into a cubicle to try it on. In her hurry, she'd left the curtain open and I had a fantastic view of her as she stripped naked and posed in front of the mirror in a selection of sexy bras and suspenders.

"I got my camera out and ran off nearly half a film. Back in Ossett the next day, I took the film to my local chemist. I was so sure these shots were going to mean a jackpot payday that I paid for the express next-day prints service, even though it cost an extra £1.75."

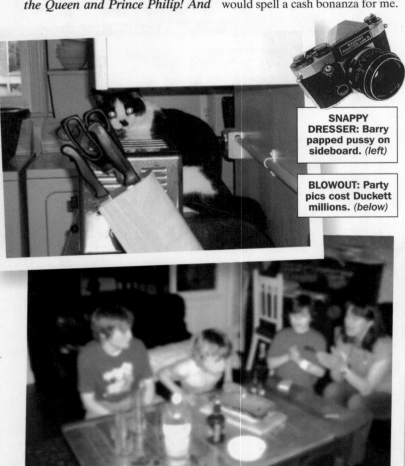

SNAPPY DRESSER: Barry papped pussy on sideboard. ***(left)***

BLOWOUT: Party pics cost Duckett millions. ***(below)***

Gym Nearl
Fixed it
for Me

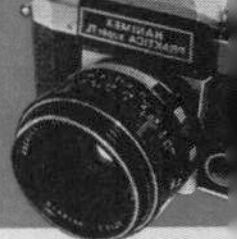

"WHEN I LOOK BA across my long care I can honestly sa don't regret a single thing. But c thing I do regret is the part I play in hounding a particular celebrity her death. I am not going to na her, out of respect for her fam except to say that she was a mu loved PRINCESS OF HEARTS.

"Everywhere she went, she was surrou by the paparazzi day and night. We were li pack of hungry dogs chasing a helpless ra trying to get pictures up its skirt. Then one quite out of the blue, that dream came true

"I was walking past a gym in Knightsbr when I noticed her car parked outside. I c see there was a high window in the chan rooms which had been left open, so I thou might chance my arm. As a seasoned press I never go anywhere without a stepladder, a few seconds I was looking down my lens the changing rooms. But the sight that gre my eyes in there came as quite a shock.

Jordan's Tit
in for the Lad

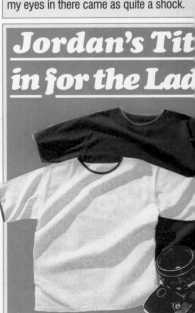

n Celebrity Merry-Go-Round

Life!

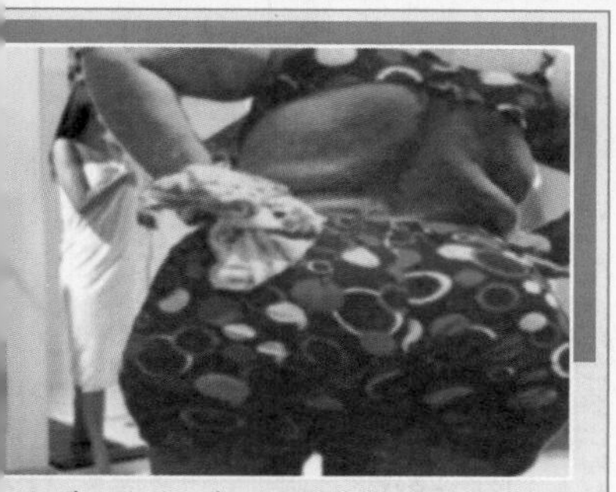

was the person I am not going to name out spect for her family, alright. She was stark d in the shower. But that's not all. She in a middle of a steamy lesbo clinch with rtain pint-sized Aussie pop Princess who t also remain nameless. It was the scoop e century! I couldn't believe I should be so y, lucky, lucky.

only had one shot left on the film, so I d my time and waited until I had lined up ood shot of Kylie soaping lady Di's tits. ever, just as I pressed the button a big fat walked in front of the camera, completely ng the shot.

've always regretted missing that multi-on pound photo-opportunity, but in a way nk it was for the best. In order to make nuch money from it as possible, I would had to sell it to the sort of seedy foreign cations that have no scruples. Magazines think nothing of invading people's privacy e me feel physically sick."

ONE OF THE MOST UNUSUAL shots I ever got was in Bali. I s relaxing by a hotel pool when mour model JORDAN came out aring a T-shirt. I couldn't believe good fortune - a pic of Katie Price hout her ample charms on view is holy grail of British paparazzis. I d my camera under my deckchair, d quickly whipped it out and rted snapping.

nfortunately, her husband Peter Andre heard shutter whirring, and came over in a fury. knew that a pic of his wife with her boobs er cover could easily ruin her reputation, e grabbed my camera and ripped the film ruining all my photographs. By the time wrestled it back off him and reloaded, she'd aged to whip off her top and get her assets It was yet another wasted opportunity, but n's the breaks in this game. You've just got oll with the punches, pick yourself up and straight back on the paparazzi horse."

But when Barry returned the following morning to pick up his photos, it turned out that the fates had conspired against him once again.

SHOWER

"On the way home I eagerly opened the envelope to see what I'd got. But my 12 red-hot snaps of sexy Scarlet in her scanties were nowhere to be seen. The processing lab must of mixed up my film with somebody else's, because I'd been given a load of pictures of some kiddie's birthday party.

"I knew there was no point going back to complain. One thing I learned early on in the paparazzi game was to take the rough with the smooth. I don't know who ended up with my photographs, but I do know he's sitting on a gold mine."

Celebrities know that they are fair game for paparazzis whenever they go shopping, walk down the red carpet at a film premiere or attend a star-studded bash. They make sure that photographers only capture their public face as they make their way through the blizzard of flashguns. But sometimes a star's private, hidden side is thrown into the spotlight when a paparazzi manages to snap them in an unguarded moment.

"I was in LA for the Oscars. I'd just bought myself a new telephoto lens and was desperate to give it a try. Out on the hotel balcony, I looked through it and was amazed at how far I could see. There, clear as day in the viewfinder, I could see Michael Jackson feeding the animals at the private zoo on his Neverland Ranch... over 100 miles away in Nevada!

"I was about to put my camera away again when suddenly Jacko, clearly unaware that he was being watched from the next state, took his clothes off. What happened next shocked even a hardened pap like me. Without going into too many details, suffice it to say that Jackson proceeded to perform a series of explicit and degrading sex acts on his animals.

"My 12 red-hot snaps of sexy Scarlet in her scanties were nowhere to be seen."

BEEF

"Elephants, giraffes, stick insects and a twenty stone male polar bear - none were safe from Jacko's depraved lust. Over the ensuing three hours I snapped enough photographs of the disgusting events I was watching to fill a whole 36-frame film. Or so I thought.

"When I opened the back of the camera I couldn't believe my eyes again. It was completely empty as I had stupidly forgotten to load it that morning. I quickly put a film in and ran back out onto the balcony, but by that time the wacko star had finished and was pulling his trousers back up. If only I had remembered to put a film in my camera in the first place, my photos of his revolting zoo orgy would have been plastered across the front page of every newspaper in the world and I would have been rolling in money. I could of kicked myself again. ❞

If any publishers are interested in Barry's book *'I Get By With a Little Help from my Lens'*, please call 0181 18055 and ask whoever answers to go up to the third landing and knock on door 4c. If you live in the Ossett area and have a wheelie bin which you would like cleaning on a fortnightly basis (£2 for standard clean & disinfect, £3.50 for full steam clean including lid), please call the same number.

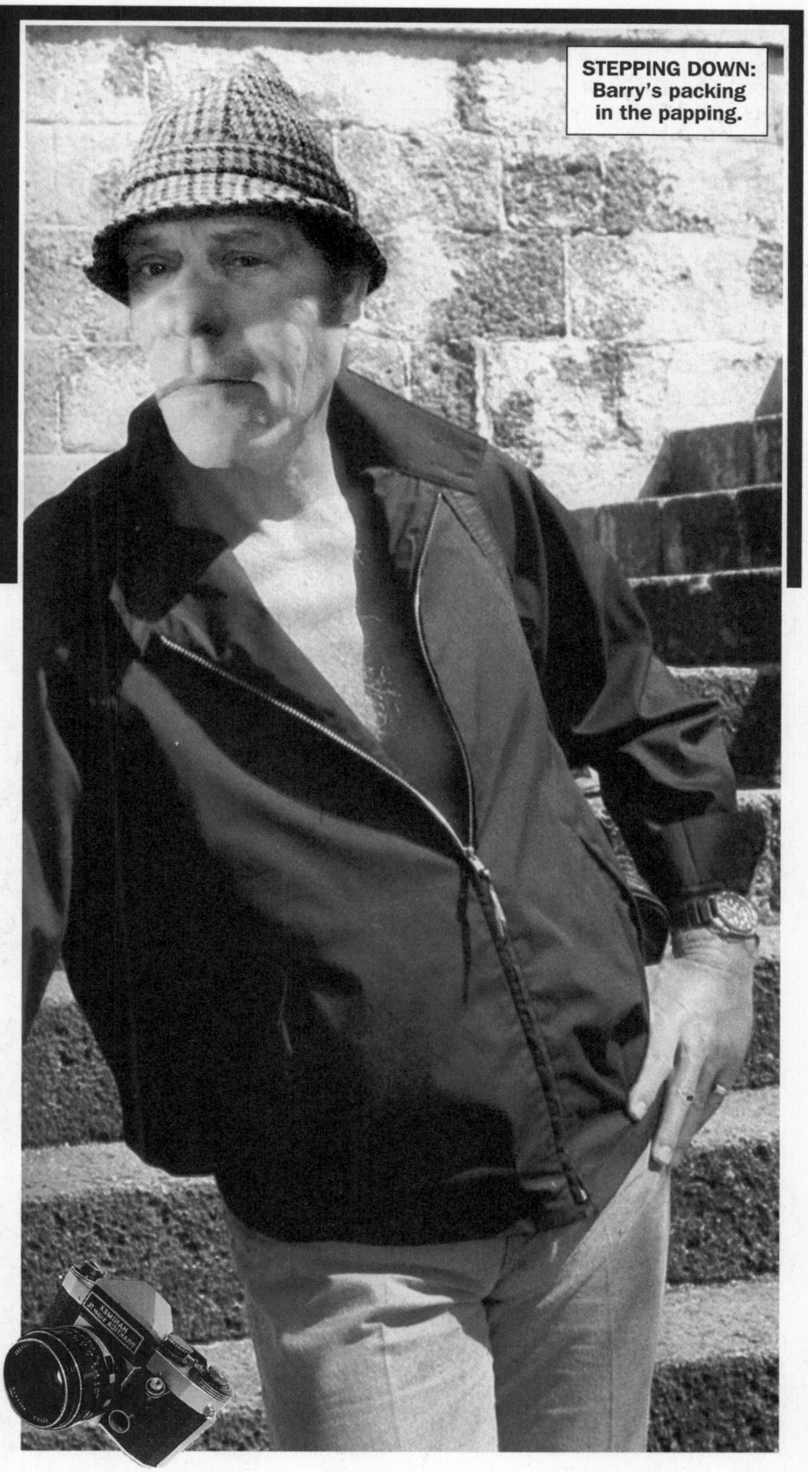

STEPPING DOWN: Barry's packing in the papping.

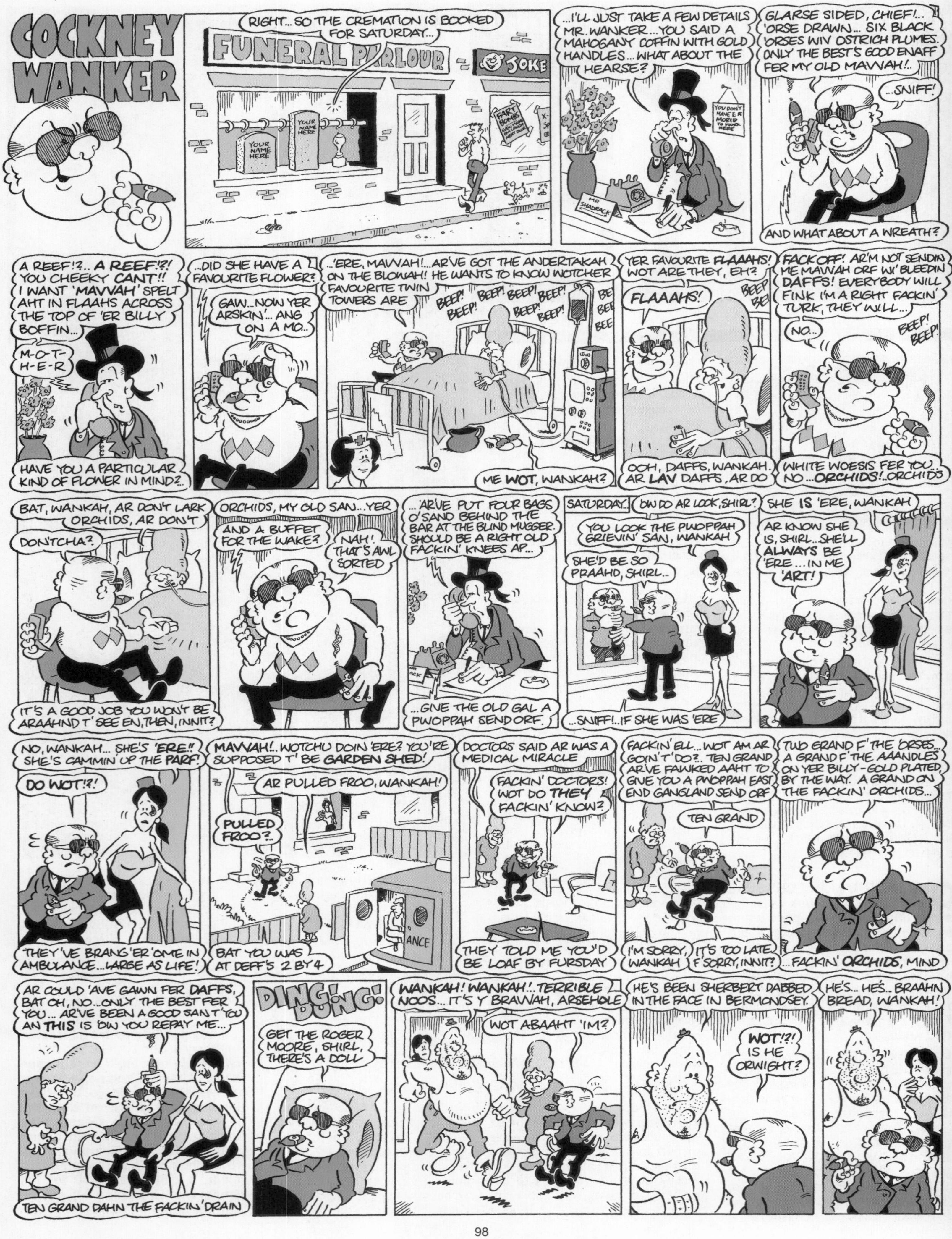
COCKNEY WANKER
RIGHT... SO THE CREMATION IS BOOKED FOR SATURDAY...
FUNERAL PARLOUR
JOKE
YOUR NAME HERE
YOUR NAME HERE
FART BOMBS
...I'LL JUST TAKE A FEW DETAILS MR. WANKER... YOU SAID A MAHOGANY COFFIN WITH GOLD HANDLES... WHAT ABOUT THE HEARSE?
MR SHADRACK
GLARSE SIDED, CHIEF!.. 'ORSE DRAWN... SIX BLACK 'ORSES WIV OSTRICH PLUMES. ONLY THE BEST'S GOOD ENAFF FER MY OLD MAVVAH!..
...SNIFF!
AND WHAT ABOUT A WREATH?
A REEF!?.. A REEF!?! YOU CHEEKY CANT!! I WANT 'MAVVAH' SPELT AHT IN FLAAHS ACROSS THE TOP OF 'ER BILLY BOFFIN...
M-O-T-H-E-R
HAVE YOU A PARTICULAR KIND OF FLOWER IN MIND?...
...DID SHE HAVE A FAVOURITE FLOWER?
GAW...NOW YER ARSKIN'... ANG ON A MO...
...'ERE, MAVVAH!... AR'VE GOT THE ANDERTAKAH ON THE BLOWAH! HE WANTS TO KNOW WOTCHER FAVOURITE TWIN TOWERS ARE
BEEP! BEEP! BEEP! BEEP! BEEP! BEEP! BEEP!
ME WOT, WANKAH?
YER FAVOURITE FLAAAHS! WOT ARE THEY, EH?
FLAAAHS!
OOH, DAFFS, WANKAH. AR LAV DAFFS, AR DO
FACK OFF! AR'M NOT SENDIN ME MAVVAH ORF WI' BLEEDIN DAFFS! EVERYBODY WILL FINK I'M A RIGHT FACKIN' TURK, THEY WILL...
NO...
BEEP! BEEP!
WHITE WOESIS FER YOU NO ...ORCHIDS!..ORCHIDS
BAT, WANKAH, AR DON'T LARK ORCHIDS, AR DON'T
DON'TCHA?
IT'S A GOOD JOB YOU WON'T BE ARAAHND T' SEE EN, THEN, INNIT?
ORCHIDS, MY OLD SAN...YER AND A BUFFET FOR THE WAKE?
NAH! THAT'S AWL SORTED
...AR'VE PUT FOUR BAGS O'SAND BEHIND THE BAR AT THE BLIND MUGGER. SHOULD BE A RIGHT OLD FACKIN' KNEES AP...
...GIVE THE OLD GAL A PWOPPAH SEND ORF.
SATURDAY...
OW DO AR LOOK, SHIRL?
YOU LOOK THE PWOPPAH GRIEVIN' SAN, WANKAH
SHE'D BE SO PRAAHD, SHIRL...
...SNIFF!...IF SHE WAS 'ERE
SHE IS 'ERE, WANKAH
AR KNOW SHE IS, SHIRL...SHE'LL ALWAYS BE 'ERE ...IN ME 'ART!
NO, WANKAH... SHE'S 'ERE!! SHE'S CAMMIN UP THE PARF!
DO WOT!?!
THEY'VE BRANG 'ER 'OME IN AMBULANCE...LARSE AS LIFE!
MAVVAH!.. WOTCHU DOIN 'ERE? YOU'RE SUPPOSED T' BE GARDEN SHED!
AR PULLED FROO, WANKAH!
PULLED FROO?...
BAT YOU WAS AT DEFF'S 2 BY 4
DOCTORS SAID AR WAS A MEDICAL MIRACLE
FACKIN' DOCTORS! WOT DO THEY FACKIN' KNOW?
THEY TOLD ME YOU'D BE LOAF BY FURSDAY
FACKIN' ELL... WOT AM AR GOIN' T'DO?.. TEN GRAND AR'VE FAWKED AAHT TO GIVE YOU A PWOPPAH EAST END GANGLAND SEND ORF
TEN GRAND
I'M SORRY, WANKAH
IT'S TOO LATE F'SORRY, INNIT?
TWO GRAND F' THE 'ORSES... A GRAND F' THE AAANDLES ON YER BILLY - GOLD PLATED, BY THE WAY. A GRAND ON THE FACKIN' ORCHIDS...
...FACKIN' ORCHIDS, MIND
AR COULD 'AVE GAWN FER DAFFS, BAT OH, NO...ONLY THE BEST FER YOU... AR'VE BEEN A GOOD SAN T' YOU AN THIS IS 'OW YOU REPAY ME...
TEN GRAND DAHN THE FACKIN' DRAIN
DING! DONG!
GET THE ROGER MOORE, SHIRL, THERE'S A DOLL
WANKAH! WANKAH!.. TERRIBLE NOOS... IT'S Y BRAVVAH, ARSEHOLE
WOT ABAAHT 'IM?
HE'S BEEN SHERBERT DABBED IN THE FACE IN BERMONDSEY.
WOT!?! IS HE ORWIGHT?
HE'S... HE'S.. BRAAHN BREAD, WANKAH!

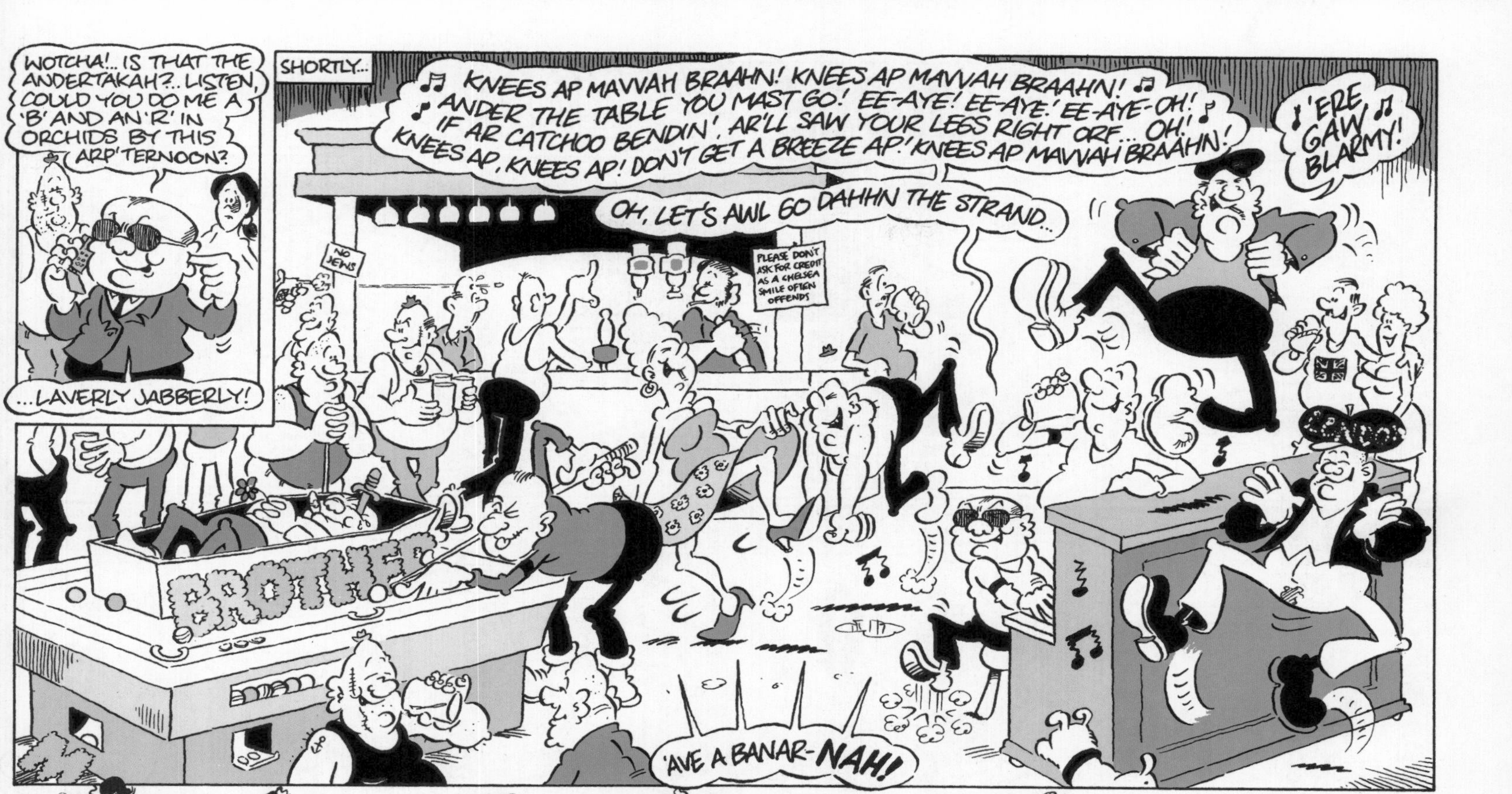
WOTCHA!... IS THAT THE ANDERTAKAH?.. LISTEN, COULD YOU DO ME A 'B' AND AN 'R' IN ORCHIDS BY THIS ARP'TERNOON?
...LAVERLY JABBERLY!
SHORTLY...
KNEES AP MAVVAH BRAAHN! KNEES AP MAVVAH BRAAHN! ANDER THE TABLE YOU MAST GO! EE-AYE! EE-AYE! EE-AYE-OH! IF AR CATCHOO BENDIN', AR'LL SAW YOUR LEGS RIGHT ORF... OH! KNEES AP, KNEES AP! DON'T GET A BREEZE AP! KNEES AP MAVVAH BRAAHN!
'ERE, GAW BLARMY!
OH, LET'S AWL GO DAHHN THE STRAND...
NO JEWS
PLEASE DON'T ASK FOR CREDIT AS A CHELSEA SMILE OFTEN OFFENDS
BROTHER
'AVE A BANAR-NAH!

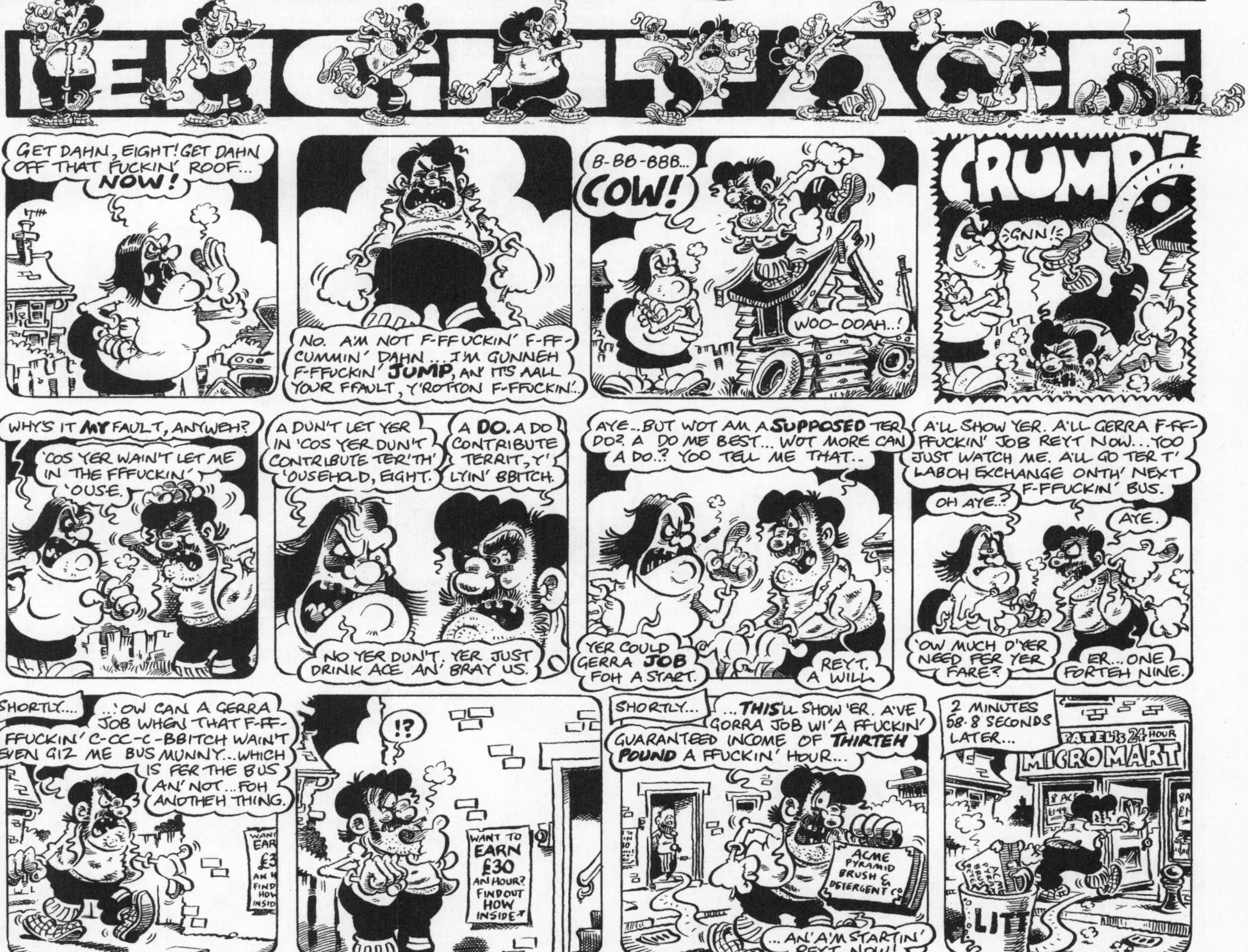
GET DAHN, EIGHT! GET DAHN OFF THAT FUCKIN' ROOF... NOW!
NO. A'M NOT F-FFUCKIN' F-FF-CUMMIN' DAHN ...I'M GUNNEH F-FFUCKIN' JUMP, AN' IT'S AALL YOUR FFAULT, Y'ROTTON F-FFUCKIN'...
B-BB-BBB... COW!
WOO-OOAH..!
CRUMP!
GNN!
WHY'S IT MY FAULT, ANYWEH?
'COS YER WAIN'T LET ME IN THE FFFUCKIN' 'OUSE.
A DUN'T LET YER IN 'COS YER DUN'T CONTRIBUTE TER'TH' 'OUSEHOLD, EIGHT.
A DO. A DO CONTRIBUTE TERRIT, Y' LYIN' BBITCH.
NO YER DUN'T. YER JUST DRINK ACE AN' BRAY US.
AYE... BUT WOT AM A SUPPOSED TER DO? A DO ME BEST... WOT MORE CAN A DO..? YOO TELL ME THAT...
YER COULD GERRA JOB FOH A START.
REYT. A WILL.
A'LL SHOW YER. A'LL GERRA F-FF-FFUCKIN' JOB REYT NOW... YOO JUST WATCH ME. A'LL GO TER T' LABOH EXCHANGE ONTH' NEXT F-FFUCKIN' BUS.
OH AYE..?
AYE.
'OW MUCH D'YER NEED FER YER FARE?
ER... ONE FORTEH NINE.
SHORTLY...
...'OW CAN A GERRA JOB WHEN THAT F-FF-FFUCKIN' C-CC-C-BBITCH WAIN'T EVEN GIZ ME BUS MUNNY... WHICH IS FER THE BUS AN' NOT... FOH ANOTHEH THING.
!?
WANT TO EARN £30 AN HOUR? FIND OUT HOW INSIDE
SHORTLY...
...THIS'LL SHOW 'ER. A'VE GORRA JOB WI' A FFUCKIN' GUARANTEED INCOME OF THIRTEH POUND A FFUCKIN' HOUR...
ACME PYRAMID BRUSH & DETERGENT Co
...AN' A'M STARTIN' REYT NOW!
2 MINUTES 58.8 SECONDS LATER...
PATEL'S 24 HOUR MICROMART
LITT

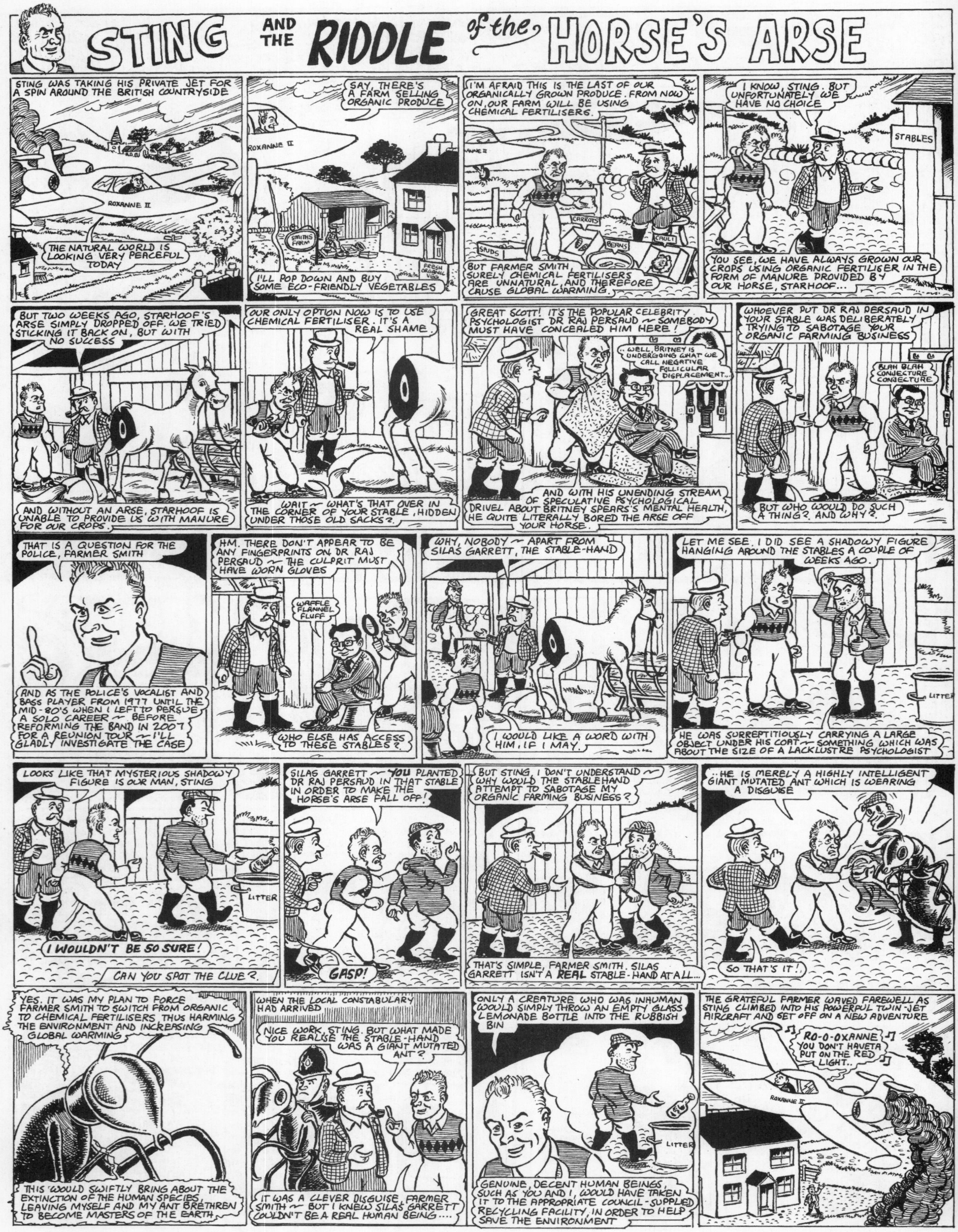
STING AND THE RIDDLE of the HORSE'S ARSE
STING WAS TAKING HIS PRIVATE JET FOR A SPIN AROUND THE BRITISH COUNTRYSIDE
ROXANNE II
THE NATURAL WORLD IS LOOKING VERY PEACEFUL TODAY
SAY, THERE'S A FARM SELLING ORGANIC PRODUCE
ROXANNE II
SMITHS FARM
FRESH ORGANIC VEG
I'LL POP DOWN AND BUY SOME ECO-FRIENDLY VEGETABLES
I'M AFRAID THIS IS THE LAST OF OUR ORGANICALLY GROWN PRODUCE. FROM NOW ON, OUR FARM WILL BE USING CHEMICAL FERTILISERS.
CARROTS
BEANS
SPUDS
CAULI
BUT FARMER SMITH, SURELY CHEMICAL FERTILISERS ARE UNNATURAL, AND THEREFORE CAUSE GLOBAL WARMING
I KNOW, STING. BUT UNFORTUNATELY WE HAVE NO CHOICE
STABLES
YOU SEE, WE HAVE ALWAYS GROWN OUR CROPS USING ORGANIC FERTILISER IN THE FORM OF MANURE PROVIDED BY OUR HORSE, STARHOOF...
BUT TWO WEEKS AGO, STARHOOF'S ARSE SIMPLY DROPPED OFF. WE TRIED STICKING IT BACK ON, BUT WITH NO SUCCESS
AND WITHOUT AN ARSE, STARHOOF IS UNABLE TO PROVIDE US WITH MANURE FOR OUR CROPS.
OUR ONLY OPTION NOW IS TO USE CHEMICAL FERTILISER. IT'S A REAL SHAME.
WAIT ~ WHAT'S THAT OVER IN THE CORNER OF YOUR STABLE, HIDDEN UNDER THOSE OLD SACKS?
GREAT SCOTT! IT'S THE POPULAR CELEBRITY PSYCHOLOGIST DR RAJ PERSAUD ~ SOMEBODY MUST HAVE CONCEALED HIM HERE!
.. WELL, BRITNEY IS UNDERGOING WHAT WE CALL NEGATIVE FOLLICULAR DISPLACEMENT...
AND WITH HIS UNENDING STREAM OF SPECULATIVE PSYCHOLOGICAL DRIVEL ABOUT BRITNEY SPEARS'S MENTAL HEALTH, HE QUITE LITERALLY BORED THE ARSE OFF YOUR HORSE.
WHOEVER PUT DR RAJ PERSAUD IN YOUR STABLE WAS DELIBERATELY TRYING TO SABOTAGE YOUR ORGANIC FARMING BUSINESS
BLAH BLAH CONJECTURE CONJECTURE
BUT WHO WOULD DO SUCH A THING? AND WHY?
THAT IS A QUESTION FOR THE POLICE, FARMER SMITH
AND AS THE POLICE'S VOCALIST AND BASS PLAYER FROM 1977 UNTIL THE MID-80'S WHEN I LEFT TO PERSUE A SOLO CAREER ~ BEFORE REFORMING THE BAND IN 2007 FOR A REUNION TOUR ~ I'LL GLADLY INVESTIGATE THE CASE
HM. THERE DON'T APPEAR TO BE ANY FINGERPRINTS ON DR RAJ PERSAUD ~ THE CULPRIT MUST HAVE WORN GLOVES
WAFFLE FLANNEL FLUFF
WHO ELSE HAS ACCESS TO THESE STABLES?
WHY, NOBODY ~ APART FROM SILAS GARRETT, THE STABLE-HAND
I WOULD LIKE A WORD WITH HIM, IF I MAY.
LET ME SEE. I DID SEE A SHADOWY FIGURE HANGING AROUND THE STABLES A COUPLE OF WEEKS AGO.
LITTER
HE WAS SURREPTITIOUSLY CARRYING A LARGE OBJECT UNDER HIS COAT ~ SOMETHING WHICH WAS ABOUT THE SIZE OF A LACKLUSTRE PSYCHOLOGIST
LOOKS LIKE THAT MYSTERIOUS SHADOWY FIGURE IS OUR MAN, STING
LITTER
I WOULDN'T BE SO SURE!
CAN YOU SPOT THE CLUE?
SILAS GARRETT ~ YOU PLANTED DR RAJ PERSAUD IN THAT STABLE IN ORDER TO MAKE THE HORSE'S ARSE FALL OFF!
GASP!
BUT STING, I DON'T UNDERSTAND ~ WHY WOULD THE STABLEHAND ATTEMPT TO SABOTAGE MY ORGANIC FARMING BUSINESS?
THAT'S SIMPLE, FARMER SMITH. SILAS GARRETT ISN'T A REAL STABLE-HAND AT ALL...
.. HE IS MERELY A HIGHLY INTELLIGENT GIANT MUTATED ANT WHICH IS WEARING A DISGUISE
SO THAT'S IT!
YES. IT WAS MY PLAN TO FORCE FARMER SMITH TO SWITCH FROM ORGANIC TO CHEMICAL FERTILISERS, THUS HARMING THE ENVIRONMENT AND INCREASING GLOBAL WARMING
THIS WOULD SWIFTLY BRING ABOUT THE EXTINCTION OF THE HUMAN SPECIES, LEAVING MYSELF AND MY ANT BRETHREN TO BECOME MASTERS OF THE EARTH
WHEN THE LOCAL CONSTABULARY HAD ARRIVED
NICE WORK, STING. BUT WHAT MADE YOU REALISE THE STABLE-HAND WAS A GIANT MUTATED ANT?
IT WAS A CLEVER DISGUISE, FARMER SMITH ~ BUT I KNEW SILAS GARRETT COULDN'T BE A REAL HUMAN BEING....
ONLY A CREATURE WHO WAS INHUMAN WOULD SIMPLY THROW AN EMPTY GLASS LEMONADE BOTTLE INTO THE RUBBISH BIN
LITTER
GENUINE, DECENT HUMAN BEINGS, SUCH AS YOU AND I, WOULD HAVE TAKEN IT TO THE APPROPRIATE COUNCIL-SUPPLIED RECYCLING FACILITY, IN ORDER TO HELP SAVE THE ENVIRONMENT
THE GRATEFUL FARMER WAVED FAREWELL AS STING CLIMBED INTO HIS POWERFUL TWIN-JET AIRCRAFT AND SET OFF ON A NEW ADVENTURE
RO-O-OXANNE YOU DON'T HAVETA PUT ON THE RED LIGHT..
ROXANNE II

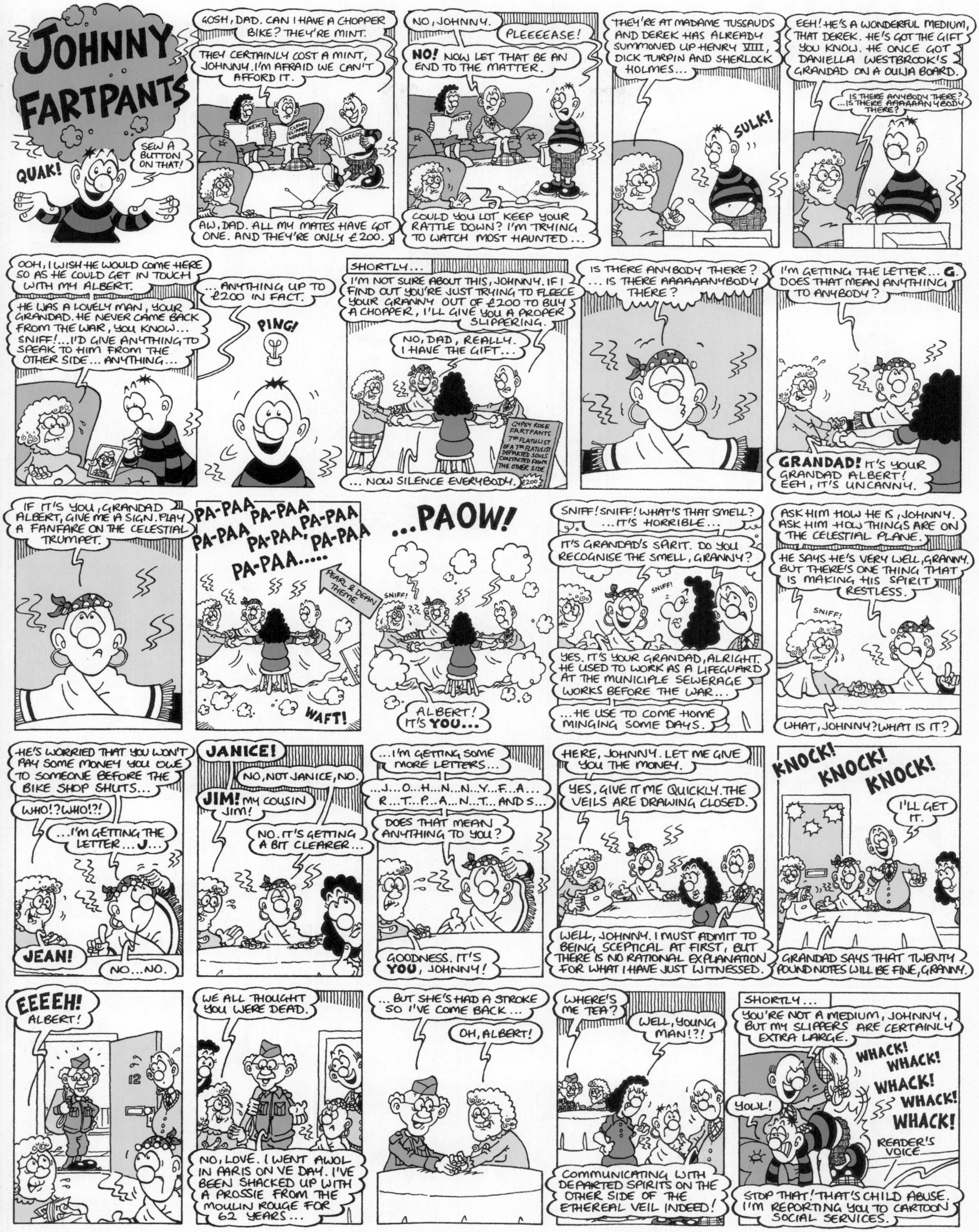
JOHNNY FARTPANTS
QUAK!
SEW A BUTTON ON THAT!
GOSH, DAD. CAN I HAVE A CHOPPER BIKE? THEY'RE MINT.
THEY CERTAINLY COST A MINT, JOHNNY. I'M AFRAID WE CAN'T AFFORD IT.
NEWS
ARGOS
AW, DAD. ALL MY MATES HAVE GOT ONE. AND THEY'RE ONLY £200.
NO, JOHNNY.
PLEEEEASE!
NO! NOW LET THAT BE AN END TO THE MATTER.
NEWS
COULD YOU LOT KEEP YOUR RATTLE DOWN? I'M TRYING TO WATCH MOST HAUNTED...
THEY'RE AT MADAME TUSSAUDS AND DEREK HAS ALREADY SUMMONED UP HENRY VIII, DICK TURPIN AND SHERLOCK HOLMES...
SULK!
EEH! HE'S A WONDERFUL MEDIUM, THAT DEREK. HE'S GOT THE GIFT YOU KNOW. HE ONCE GOT DANIELLA WESTBROOK'S GRANDAD ON A OUIJA BOARD.
IS THERE ANYBODY THERE? ...IS THERE AAAAAANYBODY THERE?
OOH, I WISH HE WOULD COME HERE SO AS HE COULD GET IN TOUCH WITH MY ALBERT.
HE WAS A LOVELY MAN, YOUR GRANDAD. HE NEVER CAME BACK FROM THE WAR, YOU KNOW... SNIFF!... I'D GIVE ANYTHING TO SPEAK TO HIM FROM THE OTHER SIDE... ANYTHING...
... ANYTHING UP TO £200 IN FACT.
PING!
SHORTLY...
I'M NOT SURE ABOUT THIS, JOHNNY. IF I FIND OUT YOU'RE JUST TRYING TO FLEECE YOUR GRANNY OUT OF £200 TO BUY A CHOPPER, I'LL GIVE YOU A PROPER SLIPPERING.
NO, DAD, REALLY. I HAVE THE GIFT...
GYPSY ROSE FARTPANTS 7TH FLATULIST OF A 7TH FLATULIST DEPARTED SOULS CONTACTED FROM THE OTHER SIDE £200
... NOW SILENCE EVERYBODY.
IS THERE ANYBODY THERE? ... IS THERE AAAAAANYBODY THERE?
I'M GETTING THE LETTER... G. DOES THAT MEAN ANYTHING TO ANYBODY?
GRANDAD! IT'S YOUR GRANDAD ALBERT! EEH, IT'S UNCANNY.
IF IT'S YOU, GRANDAD ALBERT, GIVE ME A SIGN. PLAY A FANFARE ON THE CELESTIAL TRUMPET.
PA-PAA PA-PAA PA-PAA PA-PAA PA-PAA PA-PAA PA-PAA PA-PAA.....
PEARL & DEAN THEME
WAFT!
...PAOW!
SNIFF!
ALBERT! IT'S YOU...
SNIFF! SNIFF! WHAT'S THAT SMELL? ...IT'S HORRIBLE...
IT'S GRANDAD'S SPIRIT. DO YOU RECOGNISE THE SMELL, GRANNY?
SNIFF!
YES. IT'S YOUR GRANDAD, ALRIGHT. HE USED TO WORK AS A LIFEGUARD AT THE MUNICIPLE SEWERAGE WORKS BEFORE THE WAR...
...HE USE TO COME HOME MINGING SOME DAYS.
ASK HIM HOW HE IS, JOHNNY. ASK HIM HOW THINGS ARE ON THE CELESTIAL PLANE.
HE SAYS HE'S VERY WELL, GRANNY. BUT THERE'S ONE THING THAT IS MAKING HIS SPIRIT RESTLESS.
SNIFF!
WHAT, JOHNNY? WHAT IS IT?
HE'S WORRIED THAT YOU WON'T PAY SOME MONEY YOU OWE TO SOMEONE BEFORE THE BIKE SHOP SHUTS...
WHO!? WHO!?!
...I'M GETTING THE LETTER... J...
JEAN!
NO...NO.
JANICE!
NO, NOT JANICE, NO.
JIM! MY COUSIN JIM!
NO. IT'S GETTING A BIT CLEARER...
...I'M GETTING SOME MORE LETTERS...
...J...O...H...N...N...Y...F...A... R...T...P...A...N...T... AND S...
DOES THAT MEAN ANYTHING TO YOU?
GOODNESS. IT'S YOU, JOHNNY!
HERE, JOHNNY. LET ME GIVE YOU THE MONEY.
YES, GIVE IT ME QUICKLY. THE VEILS ARE DRAWING CLOSED.
WELL, JOHNNY. I MUST ADMIT TO BEING SCEPTICAL AT FIRST, BUT THERE IS NO RATIONAL EXPLANATION FOR WHAT I HAVE JUST WITNESSED.
KNOCK! KNOCK! KNOCK!
I'LL GET IT.
GRANDAD SAYS THAT TWENTY POUND NOTES WILL BE FINE, GRANNY.
EEEEH! ALBERT!
12
WE ALL THOUGHT YOU WERE DEAD.
NO, LOVE. I WENT AWOL IN PARIS ON VE DAY. I'VE BEEN SHACKED UP WITH A PROSSIE FROM THE MOULIN ROUGE FOR 62 YEARS...
... BUT SHE'S HAD A STROKE SO I'VE COME BACK...
OH, ALBERT!
WHERE'S ME TEA?
WELL, YOUNG MAN!?!
COMMUNICATING WITH DEPARTED SPIRITS ON THE OTHER SIDE OF THE ETHEREAL VEIL INDEED!
SHORTLY...
YOU'RE NOT A MEDIUM, JOHNNY, BUT MY SLIPPERS ARE CERTAINLY EXTRA LARGE.
WHACK! WHACK! WHACK! WHACK! WHACK!
YOWL!
READER'S VOICE.
STOP THAT! THAT'S CHILD ABUSE. I'M REPORTING YOU TO CARTOON SOCIAL SERVICES.

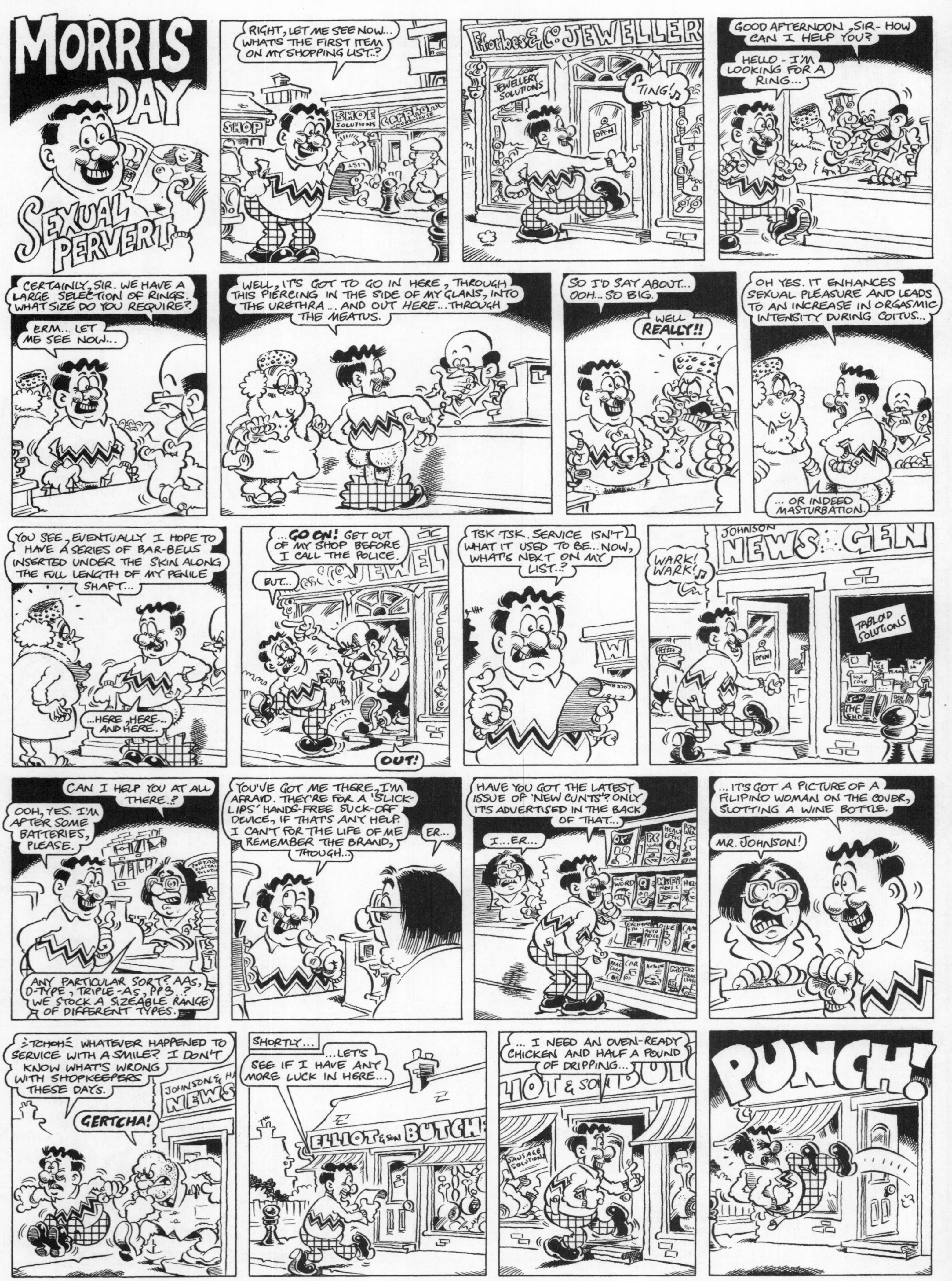
MORRIS DAY
SEXUAL PERVERT
RIGHT, LET ME SEE NOW... WHAT'S THE FIRST ITEM ON MY SHOPPING LIST..?
SHOP
SHOE SOLUTIONS
Ffordes & Co JEWELLER
JEWELLERY SOLUTIONS
OPEN
TING!
GOOD AFTERNOON, SIR- HOW CAN I HELP YOU?
HELLO - I'M LOOKING FOR A RING...
CERTAINLY, SIR. WE HAVE A LARGE SELECTION OF RINGS. WHAT SIZE DO YOU REQUIRE?
ERM... LET ME SEE NOW...
WELL, IT'S GOT TO GO IN HERE, THROUGH THIS PIERCING IN THE SIDE OF MY GLANS, INTO THE URETHRA... AND OUT HERE... THROUGH THE MEATUS.
SO I'D SAY ABOUT... OOH... SO BIG.
WELL REALLY!!
OH YES. IT ENHANCES SEXUAL PLEASURE AND LEADS TO AN INCREASE IN ORGASMIC INTENSITY DURING COITUS...
... OR INDEED MASTURBATION.
YOU SEE, EVENTUALLY I HOPE TO HAVE A SERIES OF BAR-BELLS INSERTED UNDER THE SKIN ALONG THE FULL LENGTH OF MY PENILE SHAFT...
...HERE, HERE... AND HERE..
...GO ON! GET OUT OF MY SHOP BEFORE I CALL THE POLICE.
BUT...
OUT!
TSK TSK. SERVICE ISN'T WHAT IT USED TO BE... NOW, WHAT'S NEXT ON MY LIST..?
JOHNSON NEWS GEN
WARK! WARK!
TABLOID SOLUTIONS
OPEN
CAN I HELP YOU AT ALL THERE..?
OOH, YES. I'M AFTER SOME BATTERIES, PLEASE.
ANY PARTICULAR SORT? AAs, D-TYPE, TRIPLE-As, PP3..? WE STOCK A SIZEABLE RANGE OF DIFFERENT TYPES.
YOU'VE GOT ME THERE, I'M AFRAID. THEY'RE FOR A 'SLICK-LIPS' HANDS-FREE SUCK-OFF DEVICE, IF THAT'S ANY HELP. I CAN'T FOR THE LIFE OF ME REMEMBER THE BRAND, THOUGH...
ER...
HAVE YOU GOT THE LATEST ISSUE OF 'NEW CUNTS'? ONLY ITS ADVERTISED IN THE BACK OF THAT...
I... ER...
... IT'S GOT A PICTURE OF A FILIPINO WOMAN ON THE COVER, SLOTTING A WINE BOTTLE.
MR. JOHNSON!
TCHOH! WHATEVER HAPPENED TO SERVICE WITH A SMILE? I DON'T KNOW WHAT'S WRONG WITH SHOPKEEPERS THESE DAYS.
GERTCHA!
JOHNSON & ... NEWS
SHORTLY...
...LET'S SEE IF I HAVE ANY MORE LUCK IN HERE...
ELLIOT & SON BUTCH
... I NEED AN OVEN-READY CHICKEN AND HALF A POUND OF DRIPPING...
SAUSAGE SOLUTIONS
PUNCH!

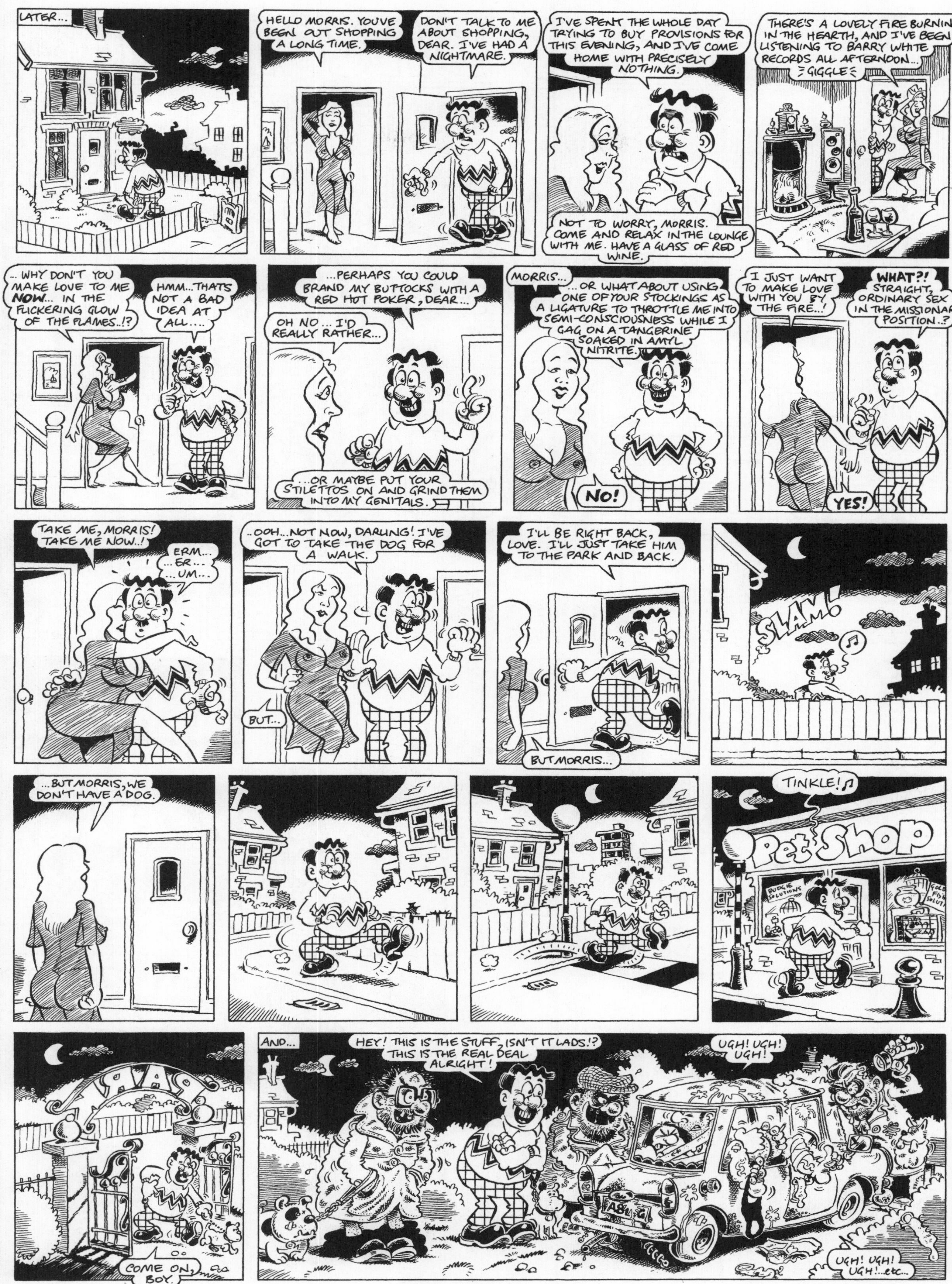
LATER...
HELLO MORRIS. YOU'VE BEEN OUT SHOPPING A LONG TIME.
DON'T TALK TO ME ABOUT SHOPPING, DEAR. I'VE HAD A NIGHTMARE.
I'VE SPENT THE WHOLE DAY TRYING TO BUY PROVISIONS FOR THIS EVENING, AND I'VE COME HOME WITH PRECISELY NOTHING.
NOT TO WORRY, MORRIS. COME AND RELAX IN THE LOUNGE WITH ME. HAVE A GLASS OF RED WINE.
THERE'S A LOVELY FIRE BURNING IN THE HEARTH, AND I'VE BEEN LISTENING TO BARRY WHITE RECORDS ALL AFTERNOON...
GIGGLE
...WHY DON'T YOU MAKE LOVE TO ME NOW... IN THE FLICKERING GLOW OF THE FLAMES..!?
HMM...THATS NOT A BAD IDEA AT ALL....
...PERHAPS YOU COULD BRAND MY BUTTOCKS WITH A RED HOT POKER, DEAR...
OH NO ... I'D REALLY RATHER...
...OR MAYBE PUT YOUR STILETTOS ON AND GRIND THEM INTO MY GENITALS.
MORRIS...
...OR WHAT ABOUT USING ONE OF YOUR STOCKINGS AS A LIGATURE TO THROTTLE ME INTO SEMI-CONSCIOUSNESS WHILE I GAG ON A TANGERINE SOAKED IN AMYL NITRITE.
NO!
I JUST WANT TO MAKE LOVE WITH YOU BY THE FIRE...!
WHAT?! STRAIGHT, ORDINARY SEX IN THE MISSIONARY POSITION..?
YES!
TAKE ME, MORRIS! TAKE ME NOW..!
ERM... ER... ...UM...
..OOH...NOT NOW, DARLING! I'VE GOT TO TAKE THE DOG FOR A WALK.
BUT...
I'LL BE RIGHT BACK, LOVE. I'LL JUST TAKE HIM TO THE PARK AND BACK.
BUT MORRIS...
SLAM!
...BUT MORRIS, WE DON'T HAVE A DOG.
TINKLE!
Pet Shop
COME ON, BOY.
AND...
HEY! THIS IS THE STUFF, ISN'T IT LADS!? THIS IS THE REAL DEAL ALRIGHT!
UGH! UGH! UGH!
UGH! UGH! UGH!...etc...

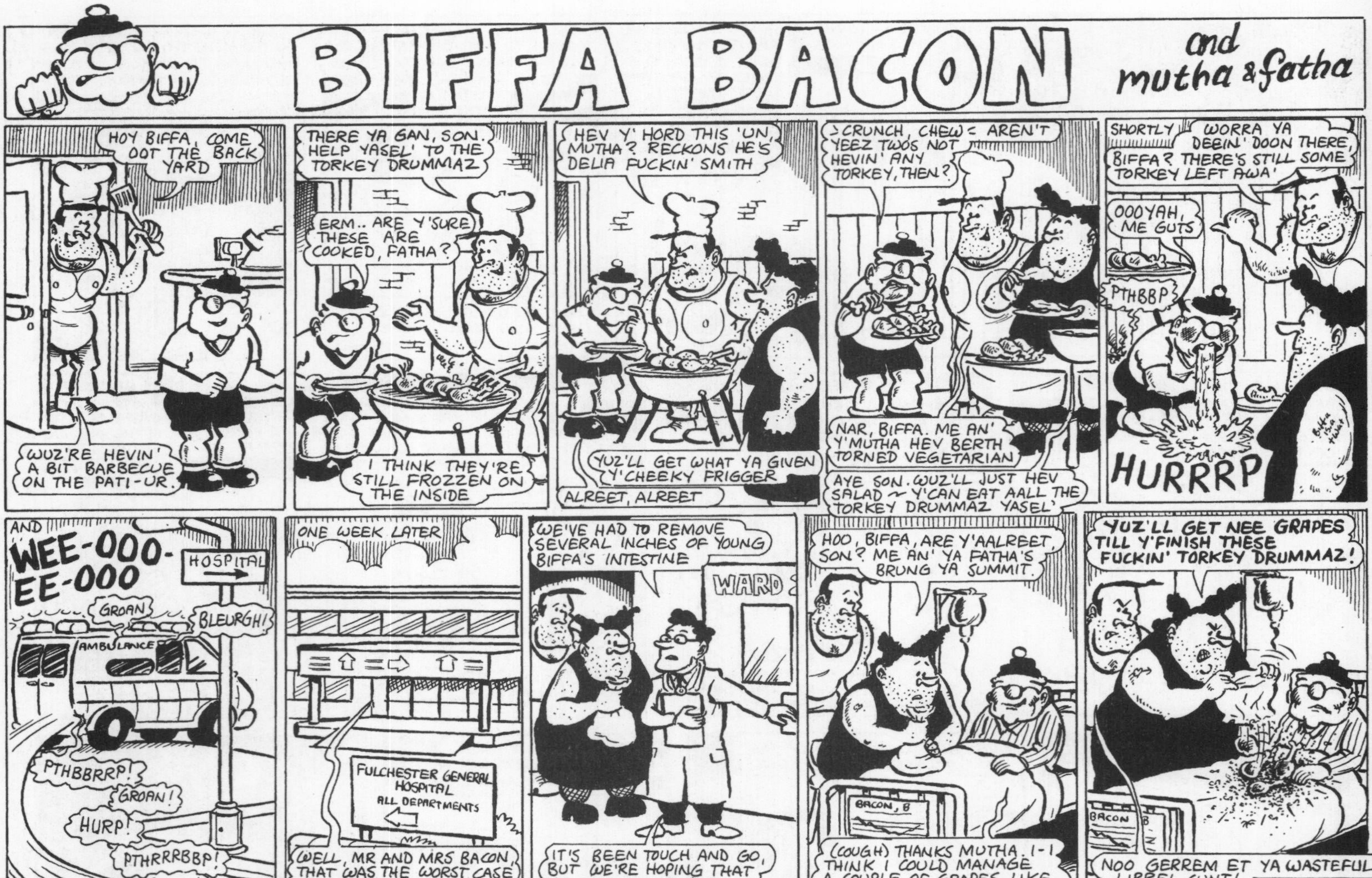
BIFFA BACON
and mutha & fatha
HOY BIFFA, COME OOT THE BACK YARD
WUZ'RE HEVIN' A BIT BARBECUE ON THE PATI-UR.
THERE YA GAN, SON. HELP YASEL' TO THE TORKEY DRUMMAZ
ERM.. ARE Y'SURE THESE ARE COOKED, FATHA?
I THINK THEY'RE STILL FROZEN ON THE INSIDE
HEV Y' HORD THIS 'UN, MUTHA? RECKONS HE'S DELIA FUCKIN' SMITH
YUZ'LL GET WHAT YA GIVEN Y'CHEEKY FRIGGER
ALREET, ALREET
≥CRUNCH, CHEW≤ AREN'T YEEZ TWO'S NOT HEVIN' ANY TORKEY, THEN?
NAR, BIFFA. ME AN' Y'MUTHA HEV BERTH TORNED VEGETARIAN
AYE SON. WUZ'LL JUST HEV SALAD ~ Y'CAN EAT AALL THE TORKEY DRUMMAZ YASEL'
SHORTLY
WORRA YA DEBIN' DOON THERE, BIFFA? THERE'S STILL SOME TORKEY LEFT AWA'
OOOYAH, ME GUTS
PTHBBP
HURRRP
AND
WEE-OOO-EE-OOO
HOSPITAL
GROAN
BLEURGH!
AMBULANCE
PTHBBRRP!
GROAN!
HURP!
PTHRRRBBP!
GROAN!
ONE WEEK LATER
FULCHESTER GENERAL HOSPITAL
ALL DEPARTMENTS
WELL, MR AND MRS BACON, THAT WAS THE WORST CASE OF FOOD POISONING I'VE EVER SEEN
WE'VE HAD TO REMOVE SEVERAL INCHES OF YOUNG BIFFA'S INTESTINE
WARD
IT'S BEEN TOUCH AND GO, BUT WE'RE HOPING THAT HE WILL MAKE A FULL RECOVERY IN TIME
HOO, BIFFA, ARE Y'AALREET, SON? ME AN' YA FATHA'S BRUNG YA SUMMIT.
BACON, B
(COUGH) THANKS MUTHA. I-I THINK I COULD MANAGE A COUPLE OF GRAPES, LIKE.
YUZ'LL GET NEE GRAPES TILL Y'FINISH THESE FUCKIN' TORKEY DRUMMAZ!
BACON, B
NOO GERREM ET YA WASTEFUL LIRREL CUNT!

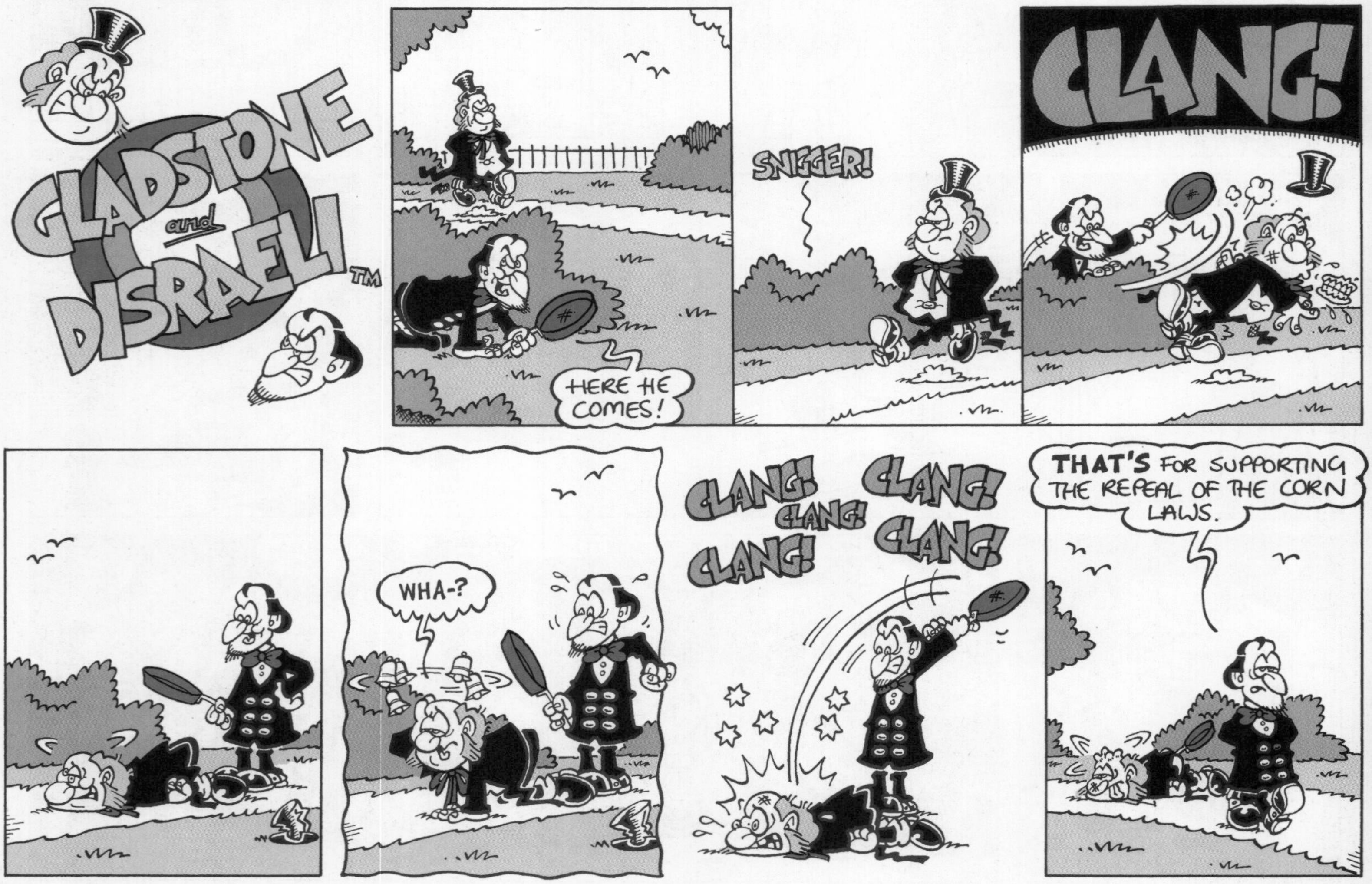
GLADSTONE and DISRAELI TM
HERE HE COMES!
SNIGGER!
CLANG!
WHA-?
CLANG! CLANG! CLANG! CLANG! CLANG!
THAT'S FOR SUPPORTING THE REPEAL OF THE CORN LAWS.

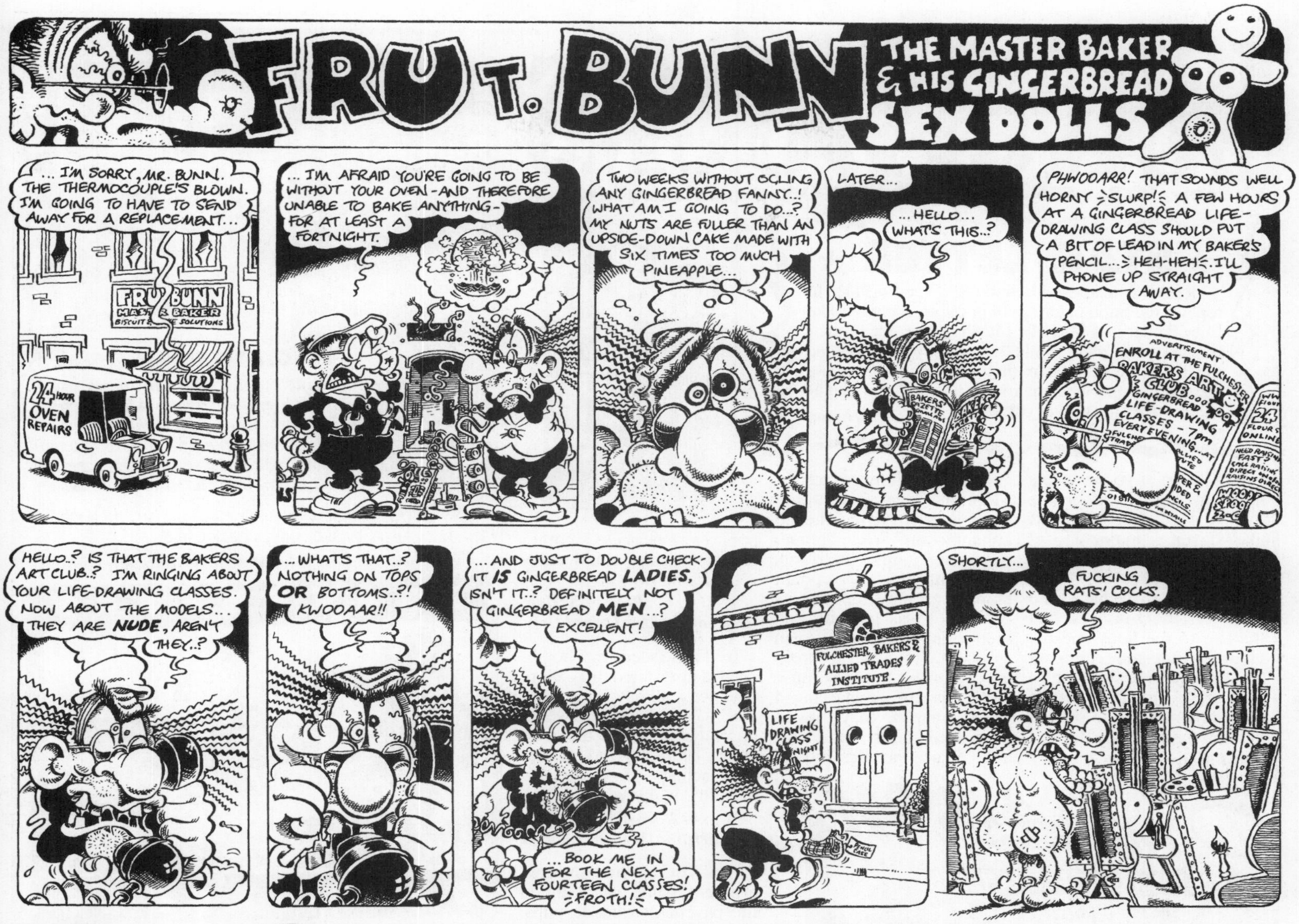
FRU T. BUNN
THE MASTER BAKER & HIS GINGERBREAD SEX DOLLS
... I'M SORRY, MR. BUNN. THE THERMOCOUPLE'S BLOWN. I'M GOING TO HAVE TO SEND AWAY FOR A REPLACEMENT...
24 HOUR OVEN REPAIRS
... I'M AFRAID YOU'RE GOING TO BE WITHOUT YOUR OVEN - AND THEREFORE UNABLE TO BAKE ANYTHING - FOR AT LEAST A FORTNIGHT.
TWO WEEKS WITHOUT OGLING ANY GINGERBREAD FANNY..! WHAT AM I GOING TO DO..? MY NUTS ARE FULLER THAN AN UPSIDE-DOWN CAKE MADE WITH SIX TIMES TOO MUCH PINEAPPLE...
LATER...
... HELLO... WHAT'S THIS..?
PHWOOARR! THAT SOUNDS WELL HORNY ≥SLURP!≤ A FEW HOURS AT A GINGERBREAD LIFE-DRAWING CLASS SHOULD PUT A BIT OF LEAD IN MY BAKER'S PENCIL... ≥HEH-HEH≤ I'LL PHONE UP STRAIGHT AWAY.
ADVERTISEMENT
ENROLL AT THE FULCHESTER BAKERS ART CLUB
GINGERBREAD LIFE-DRAWING CLASSES - 7pm EVERY EVENING
HELLO..? IS THAT THE BAKERS ART CLUB..? I'M RINGING ABOUT YOUR LIFE-DRAWING CLASSES. NOW ABOUT THE MODELS... THEY ARE NUDE, AREN'T THEY..?
... WHAT'S THAT..? NOTHING ON TOPS OR BOTTOMS..?! KWOOAAR!!
... AND JUST TO DOUBLE CHECK - IT IS GINGERBREAD LADIES, ISN'T IT..? DEFINITELY NOT GINGERBREAD MEN...? EXCELLENT!
... BOOK ME IN FOR THE NEXT FOURTEEN CLASSES! ≥FROTH!≤
FULCHESTER BAKERS & ALLIED TRADES INSTITUTE
LIFE DRAWING CLASS TONIGHT
SHORTLY...
FUCKING RATS' COCKS.

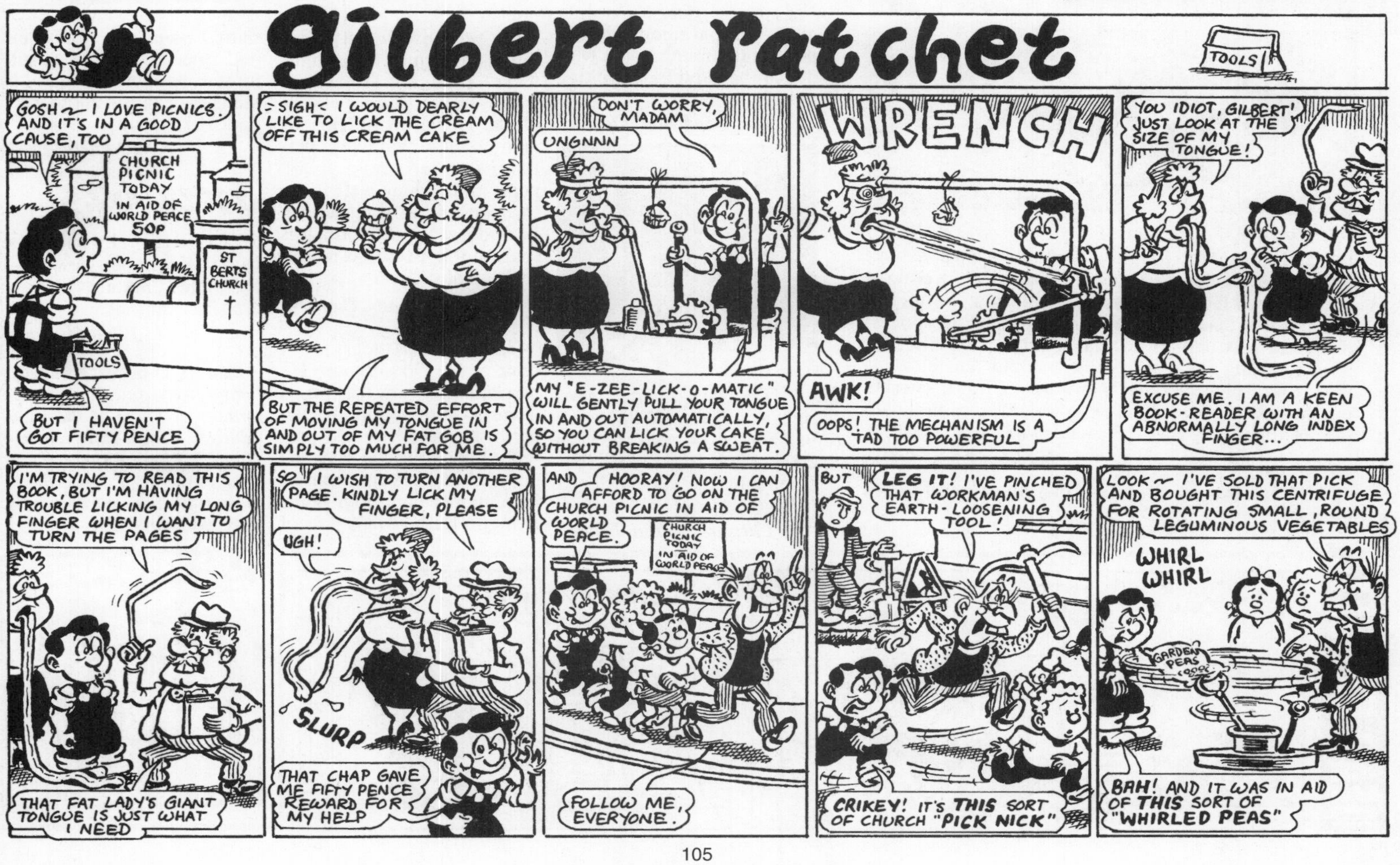
gilbert ratchet
TOOLS
GOSH ~ I LOVE PICNICS. AND IT'S IN A GOOD CAUSE, TOO
CHURCH PICNIC TODAY IN AID OF WORLD PEACE 50P
ST BERTS CHURCH
TOOLS
BUT I HAVEN'T GOT FIFTY PENCE
≥SIGH≤ I WOULD DEARLY LIKE TO LICK THE CREAM OFF THIS CREAM CAKE
BUT THE REPEATED EFFORT OF MOVING MY TONGUE IN AND OUT OF MY FAT GOB IS SIMPLY TOO MUCH FOR ME.
DON'T WORRY, MADAM
UNGNNN
MY "E-ZEE-LICK-O-MATIC" WILL GENTLY PULL YOUR TONGUE IN AND OUT AUTOMATICALLY, SO YOU CAN LICK YOUR CAKE WITHOUT BREAKING A SWEAT.
WRENCH
AWK!
OOPS! THE MECHANISM IS A TAD TOO POWERFUL
YOU IDIOT, GILBERT! JUST LOOK AT THE SIZE OF MY TONGUE!
EXCUSE ME. I AM A KEEN BOOK-READER WITH AN ABNORMALLY LONG INDEX FINGER...
I'M TRYING TO READ THIS BOOK, BUT I'M HAVING TROUBLE LICKING MY LONG FINGER WHEN I WANT TO TURN THE PAGES
THAT FAT LADY'S GIANT TONGUE IS JUST WHAT I NEED
SO I WISH TO TURN ANOTHER PAGE. KINDLY LICK MY FINGER, PLEASE
UGH!
SLURP
THAT CHAP GAVE ME FIFTY PENCE REWARD FOR MY HELP
AND HOORAY! NOW I CAN AFFORD TO GO ON THE CHURCH PICNIC IN AID OF WORLD PEACE.
CHURCH PICNIC TODAY IN AID OF WORLD PEACE
FOLLOW ME, EVERYONE.
BUT LEG IT! I'VE PINCHED THAT WORKMAN'S EARTH-LOOSENING TOOL!
CRIKEY! IT'S THIS SORT OF CHURCH "PICK NICK"
LOOK ~ I'VE SOLD THAT PICK AND BOUGHT THIS CENTRIFUGE FOR ROTATING SMALL, ROUND LEGUMINOUS VEGETABLES
WHIRL WHIRL
GARDEN PEAS
BAH! AND IT WAS IN AID OF THIS SORT OF "WHIRLED PEAS"

Letterbocks

Viz Comic, PO Box 656, North Shields NE30 4XX. e-mail: letters@viz.co.uk

★ STAR LETTER ★

• I READ with interest that the RAF have decided to replace the nude paintings of popular tit models like Lucy Pinder and Michelle Marsh on the side of their bombers with plain silhouettes for fear of offending the thousands of Muslims they are currently bombing the shit out of. I wholeheartedly applaud this display of sensitivity to another culture.

Peter Roeth, Email

1789 - 1989
POSTE VATICANE 1350

IVORY-BILLED WOODPECKER
CONSERVATION STAMP

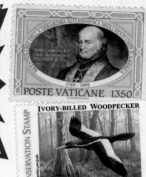

• DO ANY of your readers have any suggestions on the sort of food that elephants like? I run a major zoo in London, and we are having terrible trouble getting our elephants to eat. We have tried them on the sausages that we give to the lions and the Haribos that the chimpanzees have, but they just turn their noses up. It is getting quite urgent as three or four of them have already died.

Dr R Moreton, Regent's Park

• WITH reference to Dr Moreton's letter *(above)*, has the zoo tried giving the elephants soup? While I am no expert on animal nutrition, I could imagine an elephant blowing on the soup with its trunk if it was too hot, and then using the same organ as a straw to suck the broth up out of the bowl. Because elephants are vegetarians, I would imagine that tomato soup would be the most suitable choice, as the bits of potato and peas etc. in other vegetable soups could easily get stuck halfway up.

Prof. W Keelan, Dept. of Zoology, Oxford Univ.

• IF THE failed 21/7 bombers had just waited three more days, we'd all be calling them the 24/7 bombers. This would imply that they blow things up all day every day and, despite their actual lack of success, make them at least sound like they were good at bombing.

Christina Martin, London

• IT'S ABOUT time the government banned smoking on the pavement outside pubs. I'm sick of going for a walk along the pavement outside pubs and coming home with my clothes and hair stinking of stale smoke.

Mrs Goodchild, Finchley

Don't Ask Me

I'VE BEEN DEAD FOR 14 YEARS with Dr Magnus Pyke

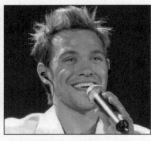

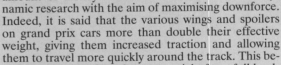

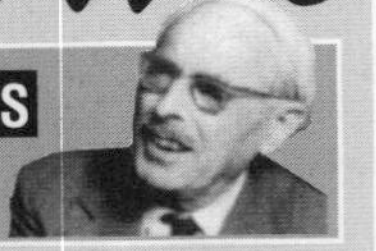

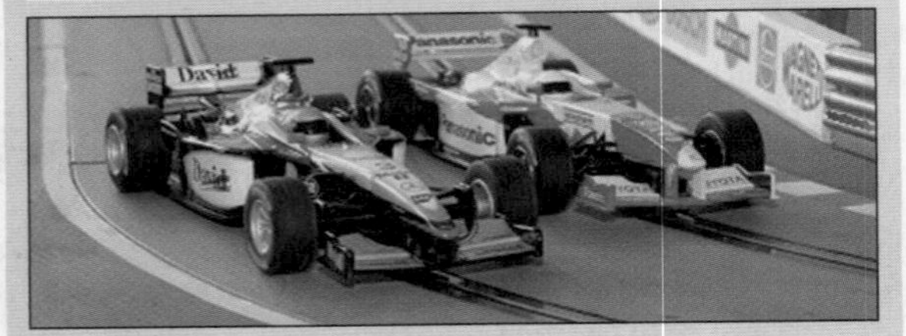

Dear Dr Pyke,

IN THE world of Formula 1 motor-racing, a huge amount of money and effort is invested in aerodynamic research with the aim of maximising downforce. Indeed, it is said that the various wings and spoilers on grand prix cars more than double their effective weight, giving them increased traction and allowing them to travel more quickly around the track. This being the case, why does the extra weight from full loads of fuel apparently slow the cars down?

D Fletcher, Godalming

***Don't ask me, Mr Fletcher. I've been dead for 14 years.**

• "I THINK I'd better leave right now," sang Will Young in 2003. As we near the year 2008, I have to say it's becoming harder and harder to believe him.

Christina Martin, London

PICTURE Requests

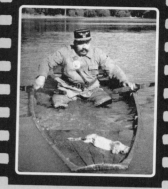

• IT WOULD make my wife's day if you could print a picture of a man in a French army uniform, in a sinking rowing boat containing a dead cat.

George, e-mail

**** Is there a very specific picture you want us to print? Perhaps you'd like to see a photo of a man riding a motorcycle with a sidecar in the shape of a giant shoe with a dog in it. Or maybe you've got a penchant for a snap of a man testing a load of vacuum cleaners by sticking his cock into them? Write in and let us know at the usual address.***

• HOW ABOUT a printing a snap of a man testing a load of vacuum cleaners by sticking his cock into them?

Mrs Marjorie Gilhooley, Cheshire

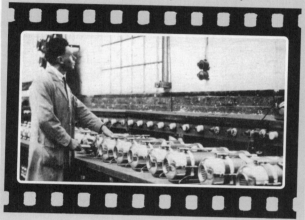

• I FOR one have never suffered any injury to my buttocks requiring treatment with criss-crossed elastoplasts. However, judging by many of the characters featured in your comic, it appears that I may well be in the minority in this respect. I wonder if any other readers share my impeccable record for gluteal safety?

Scotty, Cumbria

• MY VICAR tells me I must praise God because He presented us with the gift of a rainbow after flooding the earth. However, when I presented my girlfriend with the gift of a box of chocolates after flooding her bathroom whilst trying to flush away a pair of shitted pants, she threw me out. Once again, it's one rule for the omnipotent Creator of the Universe, and another for poor Joe Public.

PJ Public, Leeds

Jazz 625

• I CURRENTLY subscribe to NINE pay-per-view meat channels. Can any of your readers beat that?

J Fudgie, e-mail

**** Can YOU better J Fudgie's bongo telly tally? Write in and let us know at the usual address, if you have enough strength. Don't forget to mark your envelope 'I subscribe to more than nine pornographic television channels.'***

DEAD BASSET

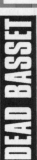

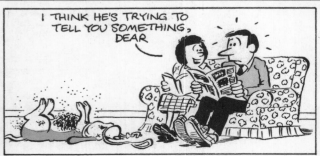

I THINK HE'S TRYING TO TELL YOU SOMETHING, DEAR
Works every time!

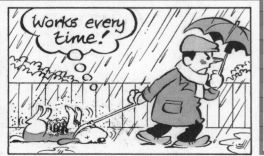

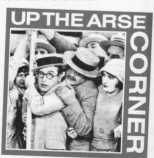

UP THE ARSE CORNER

Thou Shalt Not Grill

• WHERE in the Bible does it say that it's alright for Christians to eat sausages? In Leviticus chapter 11, God states quite clearly that nobody's allowed to eat pigs, but I can't find the bit where that ban was lifted for the C of E.

Rev. Gordon Hobbs, Ulverston

• THE PEOPLE who complained when the Crown Prosecution Service announced their decision not to bring any charges in the Cash-for-Honours case have got it wrong. The CPS only instigates criminal charges and court proceedings when it is absolutely certain that it is in possession of strong, incontrovertible evidence that points to the guilt of the offender. If the evidence is weak, inconclusive or non-existent, then the only course of action open is to throw out the case.

Barry George, Prison

• BOOKSHOPS accept money as well, so what is the point of book tokens?

Dave Thomson, e-mail

Cygnet-ure Dish

• WITH REFERENCE to Rev. Hobbs's letter *(this page)*, Leviticus chapter 11, verse 18 specifically forbids us from eating swans. Yet there's the Queen eating swans left, right and centre. If it's okay for her Majesty, as head of the Church of England, to break one of the Lord's injunctions, then what's to stop the rest of us going round murdering, stealing, coveting our neighbour's oxen and spilling our seed upon the stony ground?

F Sunderland, Sunderland

MUNICIPAL GREYHOUND TRACK
TURNSTILE
I TELL YOU, THIS COUNTRY'S GOING TO THE DOGS.

CELEBRITY SWEARS

No. 306 Osama Bin Laden

TIT ENDS.

Next Week: Bob Carolgees

TOP TIPS

KIDS. Threading a piece of string through a ping pong ball and painting it brown is ideal for a fun game of conkers that conforms with the 1974 Health & Safety Act, section 52, paragraph c.

Grant B Warner, New Malden

GOLDEN BALLS contestants. Eat greasy sausages before taking part in the programme. Then use your oily fingers to mark the 'Killer' balls with a cross so they are easy to spot when you're trying to 'Bin' them in the final round.

S Hawking, Cambridge

PARENTS. Half a cocktail stick with a blob of nail varnish on the end makes an ideal "safety match" that your children can play with without the risk of setting fire to anything.

Spud, Luton

FINAL round contestants on Jasper Carrott's Golden Balls quiz. Whether or not you come away with any money is entirely down to whether your opponent chooses to 'Split' or 'Steal', so you yourself may as well 'Steal'. That way, you double the amount, if any, that you win.

S Hawking, Cambridge

TOP TIPS

MINNIE the SPHINX
YOU HAVEN'T SEEN MY BEST GOLF CLUBS, HAVE YOU?
I CAN'T FIND THEM ANYWHERE
YEE-OW!
SMASH
GRR! NO NEED TO ASK WHO'S TAKEN MY GOLF CLUBS – THAT PESKY DAUGHTER OF OURS...
MINNIE! YOU'RE IN FOR A PROPER WHACKING!
TAKE THAT! AND THAT! AND THAT!
WHACK WHACK WHACK

Do Not Adjust Your Sets!

BY THE END of this year, men up and down the country could be BANNED from adjusting their privates in public places.

EXCLUSIVE!

Hard on the heels of new laws on hunting and smoking, the Home Office is keen to bring in a ban on nipping and rolling in pubs, restaurants, the street and the workplace. If the new bill is passed, the age-old practice of sorting out the boys in public could lead to an unlimited fine or six months imprisonment.

Home Office Minister Patricia Hewitt told the Commons that the bill was being introduced to make Britain a more decent place in time for the 2012 Olympics. "Like spitting, winding the clock is anti-social behaviour. In five years' time, the eyes of the world are going to be upon us, and we want to be seen as a modern, go-ahead society, not one that is full of men with their hands in their pockets tuning the banjo."

EROSION

But the proposed new law has not been greeted with enthusiasm from all sections of society. Shami Chakrabarti, head of Happy Shopper Amnesty International group Liberty fumed: "This is yet another example of this authoritarian government's erosion of our individual freedom. It should be every man's right to rearrange the fruitbowl whenever and wherever he pleases."

To become law, the bill would first have to go through the House of Lords, where stiff opposition is expected from traditional peers on both sides of the political divide.

Lord Turncoat-Amery, chairman of the All-Party Pocket Billiards Committee said: "A gentleman has to be allowed to stir the stew. I do it and my father did it before me, it is part of the British way of life going all the way back to the Domesday Book. I think I speak for the vast majority of British men when I say that this government will not stop me popping the mouse back in the house when I need to."

BILLY BOTTOM and his zany TOILET PRANKS
BLOODY NORA! I'VE 'AD NOWT BUT EGG PAELLA, YOUNGERS SCOTCH AN' BATTERED SQUID RINGS FOR A FORTNIGHT...
MY POOR FUCKIN' GUTS
SqueezyJet
I 'OPE Y'VE GOT A GOOD BOG BRUSH ON BOARD, LOVE. I'VE GOT A TON OF EXCESS BAGGAGE IN ME HOLD
DUTY FREE FAGS
OH, SIR! EXCUSE ME! SIR! YOU CAN'T USE THE TOILET YET, I'M AFRAID
YOU'LL HAVE TO WAIT UNTIL THE PLANE IS IN FLIGHT
EH?
BUT I'VE BEEN BAKIN ONE FOR THE LAST TWO WEEK, LOVE. I CAN'T USE THEM FOREIGN CHODDIES, ME.
I'M SORRY, SIR. I'M SURE IT WON'T BE LONG, NOW
OKAY. I'LL TRY AN' PINCH IT BACK
IT'S NOT GOIN TO BE EASY, MIND. IT'S BEEN OUT FOR A LOOK AROUND
SHORTLY...
THIS IS YOUR CAPTAIN SPEAKING. WELCOME ABOARD THIS SQUEAZYJET FLIGHT TO TEESSIDE AIRPORT...
SqueezyJet
...WE SHALL SHORTLY BE EXTINGUISHING THE SEAT BELT LIGHT, AT WHICH POINT, YOU MAY ALL GET UP AND USE THE BOG.
PING!
SECONDS OUT, ROUND ONE. 'SCUSE ME, LOVE. THAT SHITTER'S GOT MY NAME ON IT
DRINKS? PERFUME? CIGARETTES? SQUEAZYJET TEDDY BEAR?
SOD IT!
AYE, COULD I JUST SQUEEZE PAST, LOVE? I'M TOUCHIN' CLOTH 'ERE
I'M SORRY, SIR. YOU'LL HAVE TO WAIT 'TILL I REACH THE OTHER END
I ♡ SPAIN
SHORTLY...
THERE YOU GO, SIR... A STALE CHEESE SANDWICH AND A CAN OF COKE... THAT'S TWO HUNDRED AND FIFTY POUNDS, PLEASE.
ESPANIA
40 MINS LATER...
THERE YOU GO, SIR
HNNG!
EEH! ABOUT BLOODY TIME AN' ALL
OOH, NECTAR... 5, 4, 3, 2, 1... THUNDERBIRDS ARE G...
WOMEN TITS ARE GREAT
KNOCK!!! KNOCK!!
WHAT THE BLOODY HELL...?
SUN SPORT
WOMEN GOLFERS TITS GET...
WOT IS IT, LOVE? I'M TRYIN' TO 'AVE A SHITE IN 'ERE
I'M SORRY, BUT YOU'LL HAVE TO COME OUT
2 FIRST CLASS PASSENGERS NEED THE TOILET, AND I'M AFRAID THEY HAVE PRIORITY
BLOODY 'ELL! MAKE IT QUICK, WILL YOU? I'VE GOT THE MONKEY'S TOE. ... AN' IT'S A BLOODY BIG MONKEY
I'LL BE QUICK AS I CAN, PAL. ME AN' THE MISSUS ARE JUST GOING TO HAVE A MILE-HIGH TANTRIC KNEE TREMBLER
STING (BELIEVE IT OR NOT)
BAH!
SHOULDN'T BE MORE THAN TWO OR THREE HOURS.
2 HOURS LATER...
UGH!..UGH!..UGH!.. UGH!..UGH!..
POP!
AAH! THERE! ALL DONE
NOT BEFORE BLOODY TIME
BLOODY POP STARS
ZIP!
TUG!
BUT...
BOLLOCKS! I'VE BEEN HOLDIN' IT BACK THAT LONG, IT'S GOT WEDGED IN SIDEWAYS. I CAN'T BLOODY SHIFT IT.
I'LL SPARK UP A ROTHY, SEE IF I CAN GET THE BALL ROLLIN'
PUFF! PUFF! PUFF! PUFF! YES! PUFF!.. COUGH!.. PUFF! YES!..
YES...YES, HERE WE GO. EYES DOWN FOR A FULL HOUSE

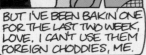

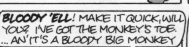

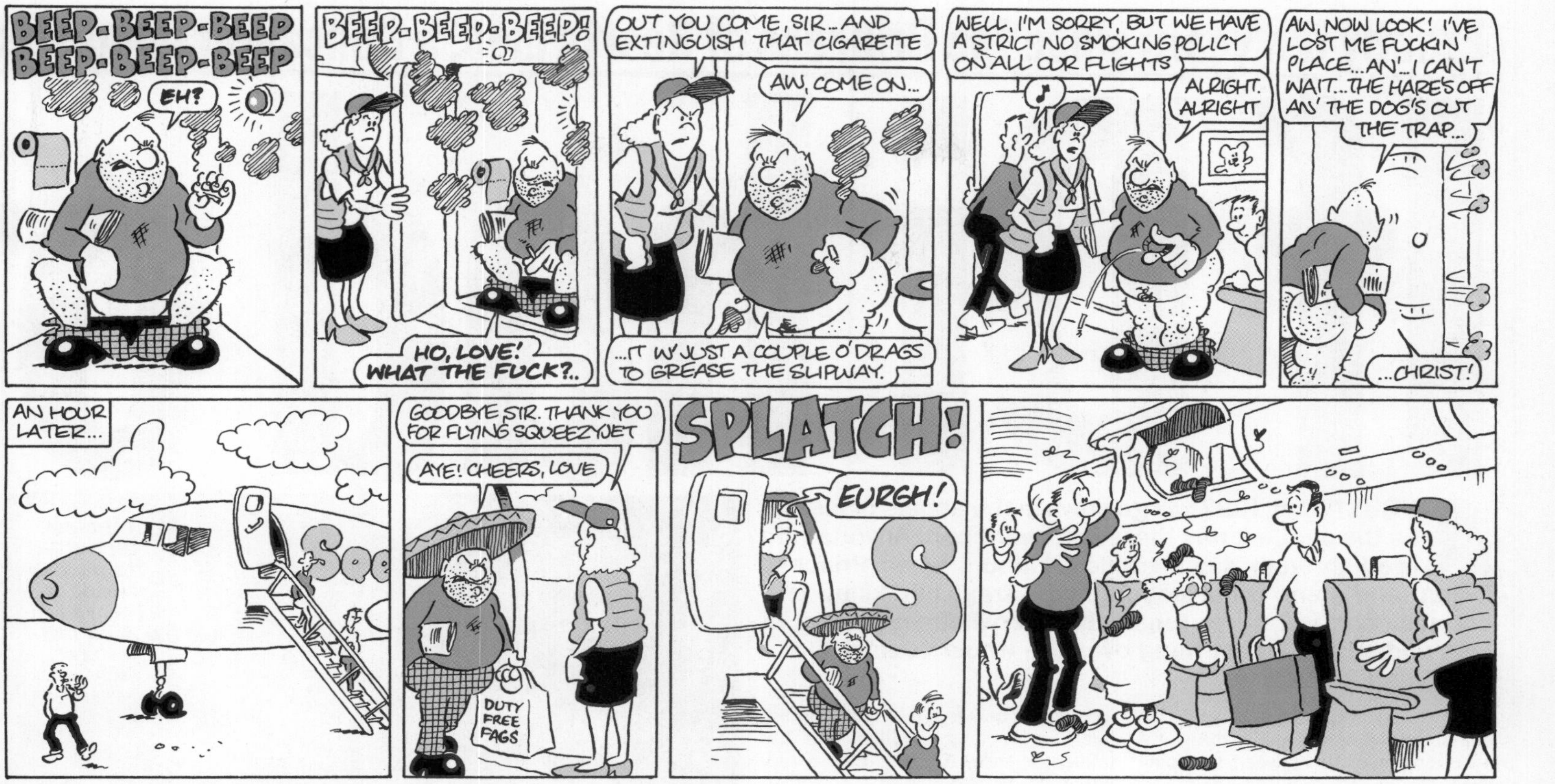
BEEP-BEEP-BEEP
BEEP-BEEP-BEEP
EH?
BEEP-BEEP-BEEP!
HO, LOVE! WHAT THE FUCK?..
OUT YOU COME, SIR... AND EXTINGUISH THAT CIGARETTE
AW, COME ON...
...IT W' JUST A COUPLE O' DRAGS TO GREASE THE SLIPWAY.
WELL, I'M SORRY, BUT WE HAVE A STRICT NO SMOKING POLICY ON ALL OUR FLIGHTS
ALRIGHT. ALRIGHT
AW, NOW LOOK! I'VE LOST ME FUCKIN' PLACE... AN'.. I CAN'T WAIT... THE HARE'S OFF AN' THE DOG'S OUT THE TRAP...
...CHRIST!
AN HOUR LATER...
GOODBYE SIR. THANK YOU FOR FLYING SQUEEZYJET
AYE! CHEERS, LOVE
DUTY FREE FAGS
SPLATCH!
EURGH!

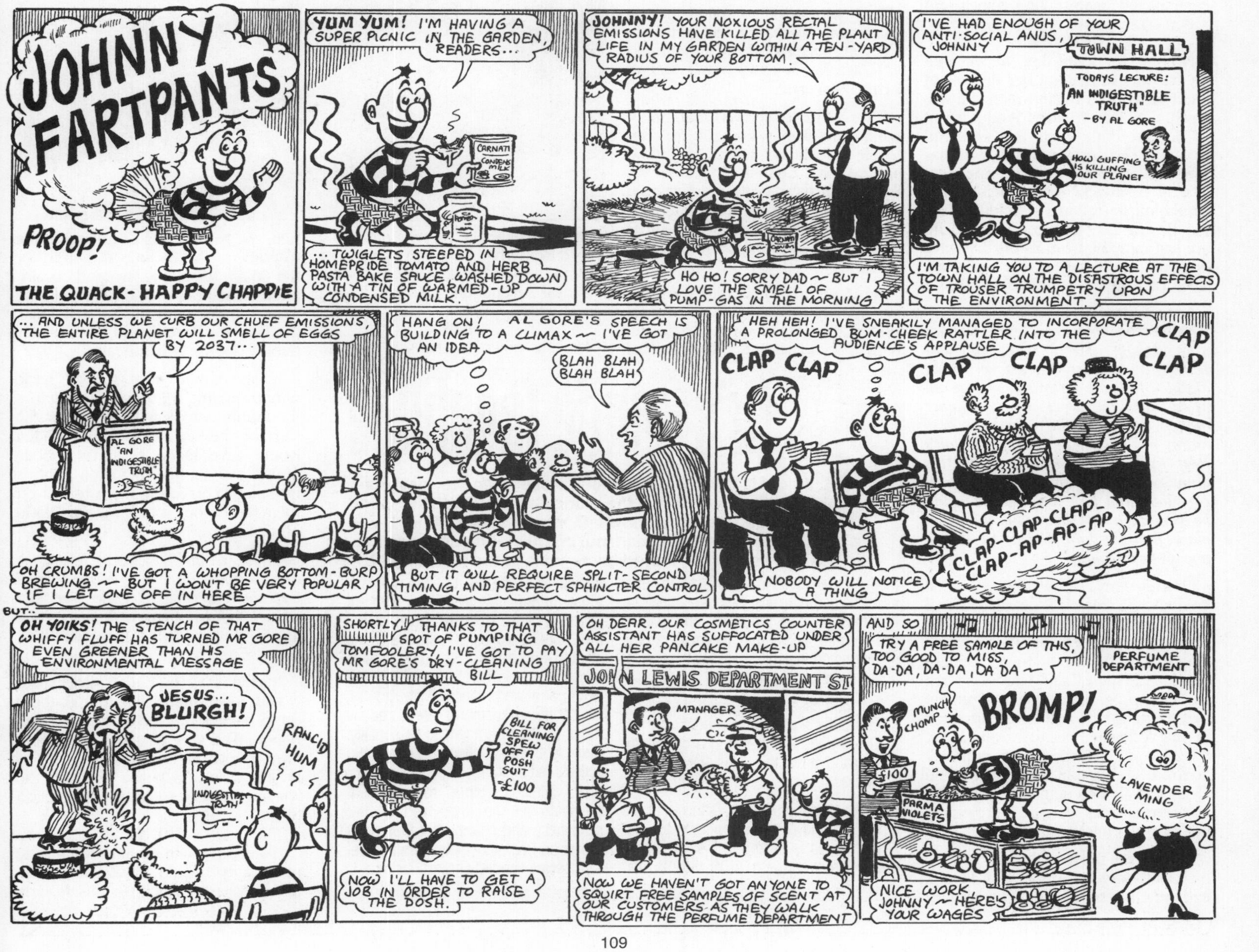
JOHNNY FARTPANTS
PROOP!
THE QUACK-HAPPY CHAPPIE
YUM YUM! I'M HAVING A SUPER PICNIC IN THE GARDEN, READERS...
...TWIGLETS STEEPED IN HOMEPRIDE TOMATO AND HERB PASTA BAKE SAUCE, WASHED DOWN WITH A TIN OF WARMED-UP CONDENSED MILK.
JOHNNY! YOUR NOXIOUS RECTAL EMISSIONS HAVE KILLED ALL THE PLANT LIFE IN MY GARDEN WITHIN A TEN-YARD RADIUS OF YOUR BOTTOM.
HO HO! SORRY DAD ~ BUT I LOVE THE SMELL OF PUMP-GAS IN THE MORNING
I'VE HAD ENOUGH OF YOUR ANTI-SOCIAL ANUS, JOHNNY
TOWN HALL
TODAYS LECTURE: "AN INDIGESTIBLE TRUTH" - BY AL GORE
HOW GUFFING IS KILLING OUR PLANET
I'M TAKING YOU TO A LECTURE AT THE TOWN HALL ON THE DISASTROUS EFFECTS OF TROUSER TRUMPETRY UPON THE ENVIRONMENT.
...AND UNLESS WE CURB OUR CHUFF EMISSIONS, THE ENTIRE PLANET WILL SMELL OF EGGS BY 2037...
AL GORE "AN INDIGESTIBLE TRUTH"
OH CRUMBS! I'VE GOT A WHOPPING BOTTOM-BURP BREWING ~ BUT I WON'T BE VERY POPULAR IF I LET ONE OFF IN HERE
HANG ON! AL GORE'S SPEECH IS BUILDING TO A CLIMAX ~ I'VE GOT AN IDEA
BLAH BLAH BLAH BLAH
BUT IT WILL REQUIRE SPLIT-SECOND TIMING, AND PERFECT SPHINCTER CONTROL
HEH HEH! I'VE SNEAKILY MANAGED TO INCORPORATE A PROLONGED BUM-CHEEK RATTLER INTO THE AUDIENCE'S APPLAUSE
CLAP CLAP CLAP CLAP CLAP CLAP
CLAP-CLAP-CLAP-CLAP-AP-AP-AP
NOBODY WILL NOTICE A THING
BUT..
OH YOIKS! THE STENCH OF THAT WHIFFY FLUFF HAS TURNED MR GORE EVEN GREENER THAN HIS ENVIRONMENTAL MESSAGE
JESUS... BLURGH!
RANCID HUM
SHORTLY!
THANKS TO THAT SPOT OF PUMPING TOMFOOLERY, I'VE GOT TO PAY MR GORE'S DRY-CLEANING BILL
BILL FOR CLEANING SPEW OFF A POSH SUIT =£100
NOW I'LL HAVE TO GET A JOB IN ORDER TO RAISE THE DOSH.
OH DEAR. OUR COSMETICS COUNTER ASSISTANT HAS SUFFOCATED UNDER ALL HER PANCAKE MAKE-UP
JOHN LEWIS DEPARTMENT ST
MANAGER
NOW WE HAVEN'T GOT ANYONE TO SQUIRT FREE SAMPLES OF SCENT AT OUR CUSTOMERS AS THEY WALK THROUGH THE PERFUME DEPARTMENT
AND SO
TRY A FREE SAMPLE OF THIS, TOO GOOD TO MISS, DA-DA, DA-DA, DA DA ~
PERFUME DEPARTMENT
MUNCH CHOMP
BROMP!
LAVENDER MING
PARMA VIOLETS
£100
NICE WORK, JOHNNY ~ HERE'S YOUR WAGES

Exactly ten years since the Princess of Hearts died, a Doncaster upholster

If Di had o

AUGUST 31st 1997 will go down in the annals of history as the saddest day there has ever been. Anyone who lived through those tragic 24 hours when Princess Diana (and some other people) were tragically killed in a car accident, will never forget the overwhelming sense of loss and sadness that hung over the whole country like a huge, dark cloud.

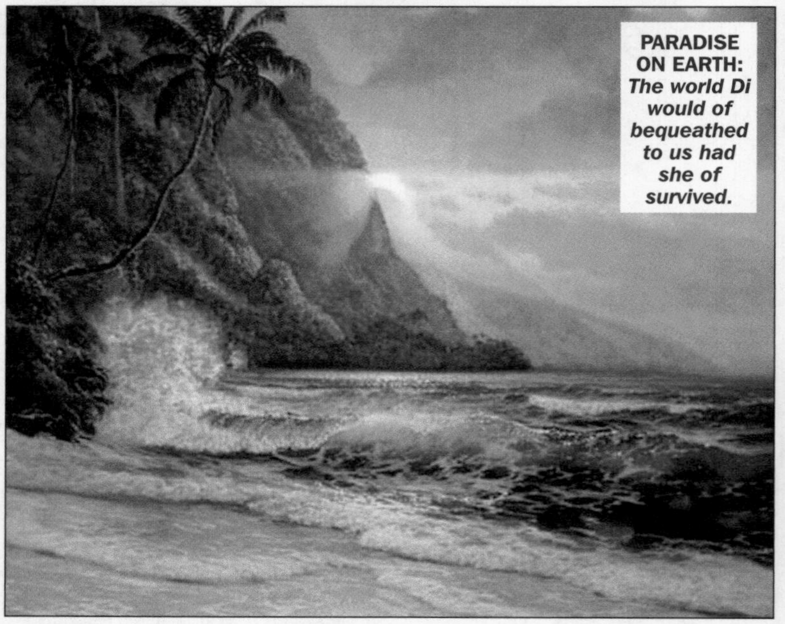

PARADISE ON EARTH: *The world Di would of bequeathed to us had she of survived.*

Before her death, Diana was famed for her tireless efforts to make the world a better place. In between shopping trips, affairs and exotic holidays, she campaigned against land mines and raised awareness of AIDS.

DREAMS

No one can doubt that she was well on the way to making her dreams of a better world a reality when she was so cruelly taken from us. And it is just as certain that, since that dreadful day in 1997, the state of the world has worsened at an ever-increasing rate. The 9/11 attacks on America, the escalating unrest in the middle east, the Boxing Day tsunami and bird flu are just some of the disasters that have befallen the planet in the ten years since Lady Diana's untimely death.

But could the Princess of Hearts really have prevented these and more tragedies from taking place? One amateur Doncaster scientist believes so. Using a state-of-the-art program, 54-year-old Mike Darbo has developed a computer model that accurately predicts how history would have differed if England's Rose had not perished in that Paris tunnel. And the unemployed upholsterer concludes that, had she lived, we would be living on a very different and happier planet from the doom-laden, war-ridden one we know today.

"Using my Commodore C64 computer, I created a detailed virtual reality model of the whole world, setting the parameters as they were on August 31st, before the tragic accident that killed Diana," said Darbo. "Then I ran the program, asking it to predict everything that would have happened in the following decade. Amazingly, the 2007 model turned out to be 100% accurate - disasters like the second Gulf war, SARS and the Cash for Honours scandal were all there on my dot-matrix printout," he added.

"Then I ran the model again, but this time as though the Princess of Hearts had lived. I factored in data for Diana's loveliness, her fairytale good looks, her heart-melting qualities and her influential style. And this time a very different picture emerged."

The program's most dramatic conclusion was that, if the Princess of Wales had not died in 1997, the infamous 9/11 Twin Towers attack would not have occurred 4 years later.

"The computer showed that, thanks to her extraordinary empathy for other people's feelings, Diana would of guessed what Osama Bin Laden was planning in the months leading up to 9/11. She would have decided to avert the forthcoming terrorist outrage by meeting face-to-face with the Al Qaida boss."

"So as not to overawe him, she would have met him in a place that he felt comfortable. The computer predicted that she would have attended a football match at Highbury, slipping out of the Royal Box at half-time and making her way to the North Bank where Osama - a loyal Arsenal fan - never missed a home match."

BOB

"Sitting down in the seat next to him, she would have encouraged him to pour out his feelings of hatred for the West. Listening sympathetically, nodding and occasionally even placing a reassuring hand on his evil knee, the People's Rose would have quickly melted Osama's black heart."

"Diana would have slipped back, unnoticed, into the Royal Box. Before the Gunners took to the field for the start of the second half, Bin Laden would have made a tearful mobile phone call to his Al Qaida cohorts in America, ordering them to call off their murderous attack on the World Trade Centre."

Thanks to the Princess of Roses, the worst terrorist atrocity in history would have been averted. But the computer predicted that Diana's influence on Middle Eastern politics would not have ended there.

"Listening to Bin Laden's grievances would have made her think about the problems that beset that troubled region. The very next day she would have jetted off to Israel in order to broker a lasting peace between the warring factions along the Gaza Strip."

NURSE

"Someone with Diana's magnetic personality would have had little difficulty in persuading the leaders

Di's Gentle Touchline

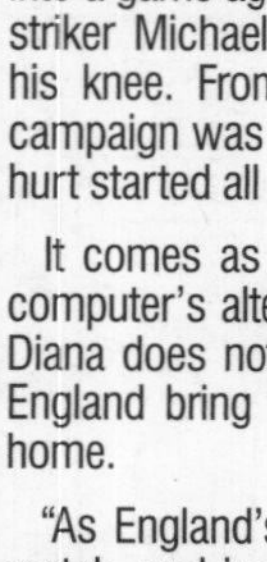

IN 2006, England came closer than they have ever come to lifting the World Cup. Under the inspired leadership of Sven Goran Eriksson and David Beckham, the team put in a blistering performance, scoring an incredible 6 goals in the tournament.

But tragedy was to strike just 2 minutes into a game against Sweden when star striker Michael Owen fell and twisted his knee. From that moment on the campaign was over and thirty years of hurt started all over again.

It comes as no surprise that in the computer's alternative model in which Diana does not perish in a car crash, England bring the Jules Verne trophy home.

"As England's Rose, Diana is at the match, and is the first person to spot that Owen is in trouble," says Darbo. "As her work with AIDS victims and people with one leg shows, she has a natural empathy with those who are suffering. And as Owen goes down, the Princess of Hearts rushes onto the pitch to comfort him. Sitting by his side and holding his hand, she chats with him in a relaxed manner. Miraculously, his shattered ligaments are cured by the power of her magnetic personality. Owen is able to continue the game and score a hat trick.

"In addition, other members of the team are so impressed by her gentleness and charm, that they don't stamp on Carvalho's knackers and get themselves sent off against Portugal."

...lly answers the question - what would the world be like...

LIVED?

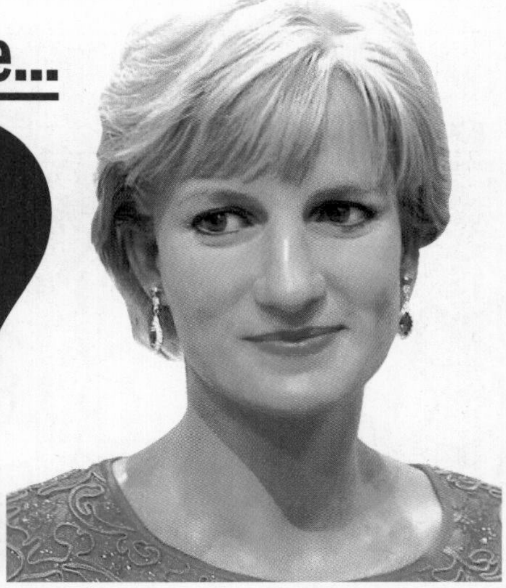

of Palestine and Israel to attend hastily-arranged summit talks in her hotel suite. Benjamin Netanyahoo and Yasser Arafat would have both jumped at the chance of meeting an international style icon whose radiant face had graced the covers of countless magazines."

"Once she had got the two bickering sides into the same room, she would have looked at them both from under her fringe. Blushing slightly, she would have explained - with a shy giggle that sounded like a cascade of silvery bells - that she didn't understand why everyone just couldn't be friends. She would then have encouraged Arafat and Netanyahoo to make up their differences and hug each other, thereby forging a permanent peace settlement between these two former enemies."

"Then she would have popped off for a private shopping trip in Tel Aviv and Jerusalem."

CABBIE

But the effects of Diana's survival would not just have been felt on a world stage. According to the computer, she would also have been a powerful force for good much closer to home.

Since her death, ASBO culture has become an increasing problem in this country's inner-city areas. Drugs, knives and hoodies have become a way of life for the disaffected youths who roam the lawless streets of our Diana-less land. But if the Rose of Hearts had survived, Britain's young people would have been following a very different path.

"The results showed that Diana would have embarked on a grueling tour of every estate in the country, meeting young people and chatting to them about their hopes, aspirations and dreams. Having herself been brought up on a Northamptonshire estate - Althorp, and having left school with just one CSE, she would have empathised with the problems faced by the younger generation. Chatting to them easily about their favourite pop stars, such as Snoopy Dog, Flavour Flav and Notorious BFG, she would quickly have won their confidence. The Princess would have inspired them to all turn their lives around, disbanding their gangs, kicking their drugs habits and respecting authority."

Di's Supersonic Lifesaver

ON 25TH July 2000, nearly 3 years after Diana's death, an Air France Concorde taking off from Charles de Gaulle Airport crashed with the loss of 113 lives. An investigation concluded that a piece of debris had been thrown up from the runway, piercing the fuel tanks of the supersonic airliner.

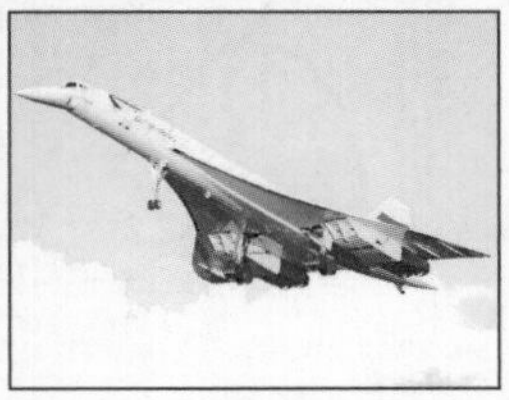

But in Mike Darbo's alternative computer model, the crash never takes place and all those lives are saved.

"In the computer's alternative version of that day, Diana is at Charles de Gaulle Airport for the opening of a hospital for orphans. The fatal piece of debris on the tarmac is too small to be spotted by any normal person. But the Princess of Hearts, with her enormous doe eyes, spots it easily. She rushes up to the air traffic control tower, pausing only to shake hands and exchange delightful pleasantries with everyone she meets. Once there, she asks for the microphone. Although against Civil Aviation Authority regulations, she is so charming that the controller hands it over immediately. In perfect French, she tells Captain, whose heart she has stolen, to abort the take off which he does with only seconds to spare."

CROW

"According to the computer model, the year after her nationwide tour there would only have been one arrest of a juvenile offender in Britain. And that would have been a seven-year-old boy in Carlton near Nottingham who had scrumped an apple from his neighbour, Mr Ridley's garden."

Once she had abolished crime in this country, Diana would have turned her attention to the other side of the Atlantic, says Darbo. His computer model proves that if she had lived, Diana would next have tackled the thorny issue of gun control in America. Once they fell under the spell of her fairy-tale charm, which would have quickly overcome any counter-arguments, the National Rifle Association would have immediately disbanded, and the US murder rate would have fallen to zero.

Noel Edmonds is a Twat

WHEN Lady Di was taken from us, our dreams of a better world went with her. In the ensuing ten years since her death we have witnessed unprecedented levels of terrorism, war and environmental catastrophe. Worse than that, the last decade has also seen the return of Noel Edmonds to our TV screens five fucking days a week.

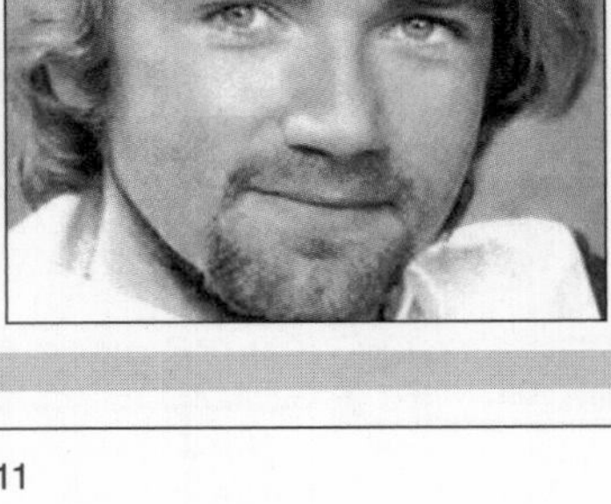

"In the program, the People's Princess of Hearts visits Edmonds at his Crinkley Bottom mansion and pleads with him not to resurrect his television career. Like all men, he instantly falls under the spell of her baby blue eyes and promises to concentrate instead on his helicopter charter business. In this alternate virtual reality world, *Deal or No Deal* is presented by Steve Penk and only runs for three weeks."

The People's Princess's fabled beauty would have continued to make world leaders go weak at the knees. Like smitten schoolboys, the World Bank and the IMF would have been putty in her hands. At her bidding, they would have re-distributed their wealth to the developing nations, spelling an end to global poverty and hunger.

COCKTAIL

As if that were not enough, England's Rose would have been unable to rest until every nuclear device on the planet had been dismantled. She would then have used her feminine powers of persuasion to make sure that the salvaged parts were used to build an automatic early-warning system for tsunamis around the Pacific Rim. She would also have called on her celebrity pals, such as Elton John, Duran Duran and Nik Kershaw, to stage a concert in Wembley Stadium, campaigning for renewable energy sources. This would have solved at a stroke the problem of global warming, rising sea levels, greenhouse gas and the ozone layer.

But perhaps the most important thing Lady Di would have done had she lived, would have been to prevent her own tragic death. Darbo's model shows that, if Diana had not perished on the night of her fatal crash, she would have managed to seize control of the speeding Mercedes from drugged driver Henri Paul, steering it skilfully to safety and shaking off the assassin's Fiat Uno which was trying to force it off the road.

"By preventing her own death, Diana would have not only saved her own life but also sixty million broken hearts," Mr Darbo added.

NEXT WEEK: Darbo runs his Program again and reveals what the world would have been like if Elvis had lived. He tells us: "If the King had managed to push that turd out on that fateful night in 1977, the Berlin Wall would still be standing and Tracey Barlow would not have been found guilty of Charlie Stubbs's murder."

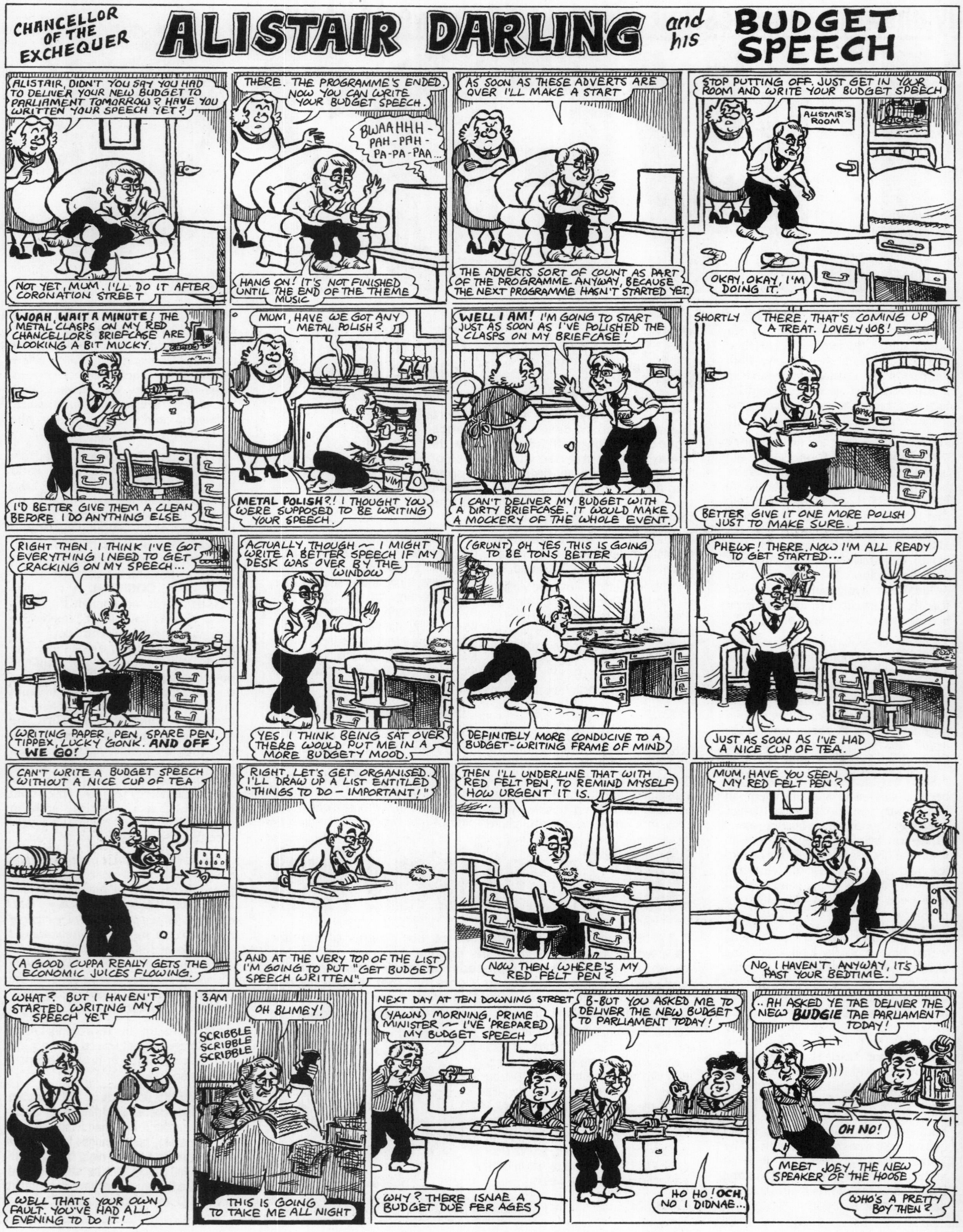
CHANCELLOR OF THE EXCHEQUER ALISTAIR DARLING and his BUDGET SPEECH
ALISTAIR, DIDN'T YOU SAY YOU HAD TO DELIVER YOUR NEW BUDGET TO PARLIAMENT TOMORROW? HAVE YOU WRITTEN YOUR SPEECH YET?
NOT YET, MUM. I'LL DO IT AFTER CORONATION STREET
THERE. THE PROGRAMME'S ENDED. NOW YOU CAN WRITE YOUR BUDGET SPEECH.
BWAAHHH-PAH-PAH-PA-PA-PAA...
HANG ON! IT'S NOT FINISHED UNTIL THE END OF THE THEME MUSIC
AS SOON AS THESE ADVERTS ARE OVER I'LL MAKE A START
THE ADVERTS SORT OF COUNT AS PART OF THE PROGRAMME ANYWAY, BECAUSE THE NEXT PROGRAMME HASN'T STARTED YET.
STOP PUTTING OFF. JUST GET IN YOUR ROOM AND WRITE YOUR BUDGET SPEECH
ALISTAIR'S ROOM
OKAY, OKAY, I'M DOING IT.
WOAH, WAIT A MINUTE! THE METAL CLASPS ON MY RED CHANCELLOR'S BRIEFCASE ARE LOOKING A BIT MUCKY.
I'D BETTER GIVE THEM A CLEAN BEFORE I DO ANYTHING ELSE
MUM, HAVE WE GOT ANY METAL POLISH?
METAL POLISH?! I THOUGHT YOU WERE SUPPOSED TO BE WRITING YOUR SPEECH.
WELL I AM! I'M GOING TO START JUST AS SOON AS I'VE POLISHED THE CLASPS ON MY BRIEFCASE!
I CAN'T DELIVER MY BUDGET WITH A DIRTY BRIEFCASE. IT WOULD MAKE A MOCKERY OF THE WHOLE EVENT.
SHORTLY
THERE, THAT'S COMING UP A TREAT. LOVELY JOB!
BETTER GIVE IT ONE MORE POLISH JUST TO MAKE SURE.
RIGHT THEN. I THINK I'VE GOT EVERYTHING I NEED TO GET CRACKING ON MY SPEECH...
WRITING PAPER, PEN, SPARE PEN, TIPPEX, LUCKY GONK. AND OFF WE GO!
ACTUALLY, THOUGH ~ I MIGHT WRITE A BETTER SPEECH IF MY DESK WAS OVER BY THE WINDOW
YES, I THINK BEING SAT OVER THERE WOULD PUT ME IN A MORE BUDGETY MOOD.
(GRUNT) OH YES, THIS IS GOING TO BE TONS BETTER
DEFINITELY MORE CONDUCIVE TO A BUDGET-WRITING FRAME OF MIND
PHEW! THERE. NOW I'M ALL READY TO GET STARTED...
JUST AS SOON AS I'VE HAD A NICE CUP OF TEA.
CAN'T WRITE A BUDGET SPEECH WITHOUT A NICE CUP OF TEA
A GOOD CUPPA REALLY GETS THE ECONOMIC JUICES FLOWING.
RIGHT, LET'S GET ORGANISED. I'LL DRAW UP A LIST ENTITLED "THINGS TO DO - IMPORTANT!"
AND AT THE VERY TOP OF THE LIST I'M GOING TO PUT "GET BUDGET SPEECH WRITTEN".
THEN I'LL UNDERLINE THAT WITH RED FELT PEN, TO REMIND MYSELF HOW URGENT IT IS.
NOW THEN, WHERE'S MY RED FELT PEN?
MUM, HAVE YOU SEEN MY RED FELT PEN?
NO, I HAVEN'T. ANYWAY, IT'S PAST YOUR BEDTIME.
WHAT? BUT I HAVEN'T STARTED WRITING MY SPEECH YET
WELL THAT'S YOUR OWN FAULT. YOU'VE HAD ALL EVENING TO DO IT!
3AM
OH BLIMEY!
SCRIBBLE SCRIBBLE SCRIBBLE
THIS IS GOING TO TAKE ME ALL NIGHT
NEXT DAY AT TEN DOWNING STREET
(YAWN) MORNING, PRIME MINISTER ~ I'VE PREPARED MY BUDGET SPEECH
WHY? THERE ISNAE A BUDGET DUE FER AGES
B-BUT YOU ASKED ME TO DELIVER THE NEW BUDGET TO PARLIAMENT TODAY!
HO HO! OCH, NO I DIDNAE...
..AH ASKED YE TAE DELIVER THE NEW BUDGIE TAE PARLIAMENT TODAY!
OH NO!
MEET JOEY, THE NEW SPEAKER OF THE HOOSE
WHO'S A PRETTY BOY THEN?

Have Your Say...

...the Bishop of Carlisle & the summer floods

THE RECENT FLOODS in the middle of June caught the whole nation by surprise, and the inhabitants of Sheffield and Hull were left counting the cost. Scientists were quick to claim that it was another effect of climate change associated with global warming. But thinking 'outside the box', *Graham Dow*, the *Bishop of Carlisle* suggested that the deluge was God's retribution for society's general degeneration, citing in particular the recent pro-gay laws that undermine marriage. *Has the Bishop got a point?* Could the unprecedented summer weather be a warning from the Almighty to change our attitudes towards homosexuality? Or is the big stupid twat talking out of his fucking arse? We went on the street to find out what YOU think?

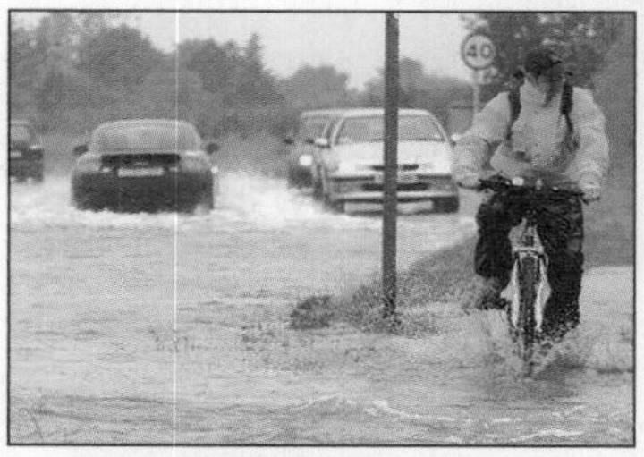

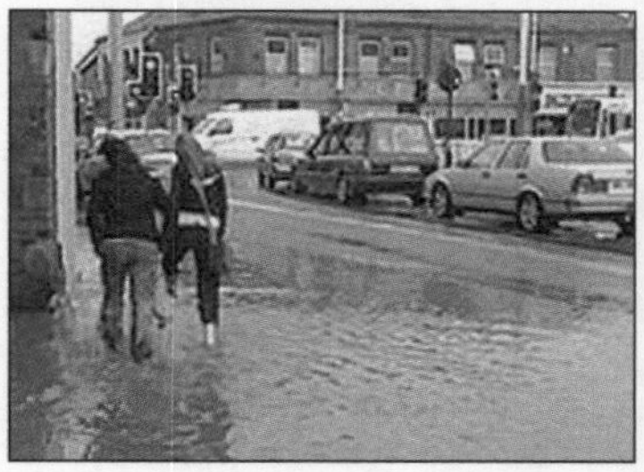

...WHAT utter nonsense Bishop Dow is talking. Does he imagine for one minute that a loving God would punish the whole of society with a flood simply because he didn't like the way some of them behaved? I don't know what books he's been reading, but it's certainly not the Bible.

Noah Johnstone, Luton

...I AM not a religious man, in fact I have been an atheist all of my adult life. But flooding in the summer just doesn't happen. I can think of no reason for the flooding of Sheffield other than divine retribution for the evils of man.

C. Hitchens, Washington

...IF THIS was a judgement on our acceptance of homosexuality, why did God choose to flood Sheffield and Hull? Why didn't we see scenes of waters cascading down the streets of Brighton, Britain's gay capital, or Elton John dragging ruined furniture onto his lawn?

Gritley Mews, Nottingham

...I'M afraid Mr Mews *(above)* has little faith in our Lord's grace. God knows that Brighton is a popular holiday resort for families. In creating the flood there, He would be spoiling the holidays for proper heterosexual couples and their children. By choosing to flood somewhere else, He has shown not only his contempt for homosexualists, but also his love of the happiness of little children.

Hillary Curtains, Corby

...MR MEWS *(letter above the one above this one)* should not be questioning God's reason for flooding Sheffield instead of elsewhere. God is omnipotent and omnipresent and can cause the greatest and smallest of things to be. If the floods occurred in Sheffield, then that is where He wanted them to occur. Perhaps the deluge was not connected with homosexuality, but was God's anger at Sheffield United for appealing to the FA to have West Ham docked points over the Carlos Tevez affair.

Rev. Arthur Plywood, Glossop

...ONCE again we hear the most ill informed words coming from the mouth of the clergy *(above letter)*. West Ham were warned by the FA not to play Tevez, yet they went ahead and played him and clawed their way out of the relegation zone. It was a clear breach of FA rules. Had the floodwaters raged down the streets of West Ham, I could believe that it was God having his say about the affair. But as they didn't, these floods have nothing to do with football. I can only think that the inhabitants of Sheffield have angered the Almighty in some other way.

Lionel Tiger, Boston

...THE FLOODS may well be God's wrath over our acceptance of homosexuality, but I've just finished watching an 18R DVD about four cheerleaders who spend the weekend alone in a log cabin in the woods. Now if a few old biddies in Sheffield get their carpets ruined so as I can watch stuff like that, quite frankly, it's a price I'm prepared to pay.

Frank Prepuce, London

...I AM a Christian, and the day before the floods, I caught my 14-year-old son abusing himself in the basest of ways in his bedroom. I hit the roof and told him that God would have his revenge. My blood ran cold when I saw the news the following day. The floods in Sheffield were God's retribution for my son's defilement of his body. And I told him so!

Edna Mental, Rhyll

...IF THE Bishop of Carlisle is right, that the floods were caused by homosexuality, the next time there is a drought perhaps we should all start bumming each other. That way we might escape another hosepipe ban.

Renton Treetops, Leigh

MONARCH CHAT

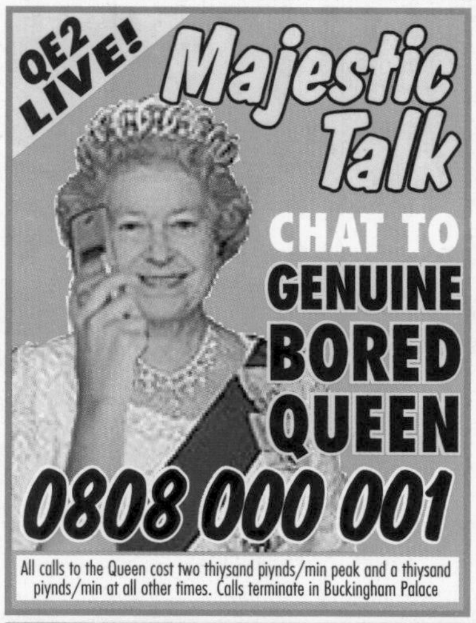

QE2 LIVE!
Majestic Talk
CHAT TO GENUINE BORED QUEEN
0808 000 001
All calls to the Queen cost two thiysand piynds/min peak and a thiysand piynds/min at all other times. Calls terminate in Buckingham Palace

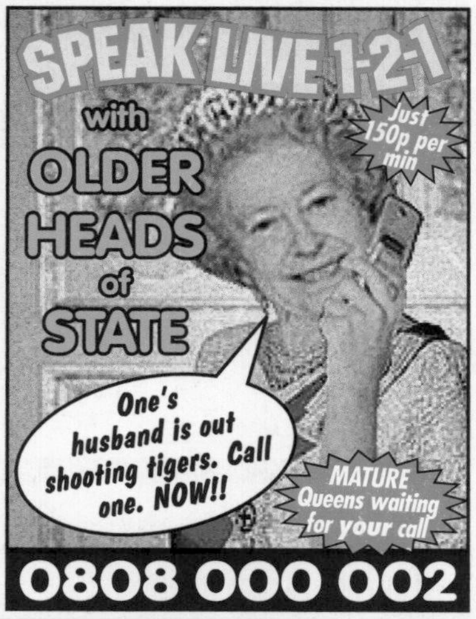

SPEAK LIVE 1-2-1
with OLDER HEADS of STATE
Just 150p per min
One's husband is out shooting tigers. Call one. NOW!!
MATURE Queens waiting for your call
0808 000 002

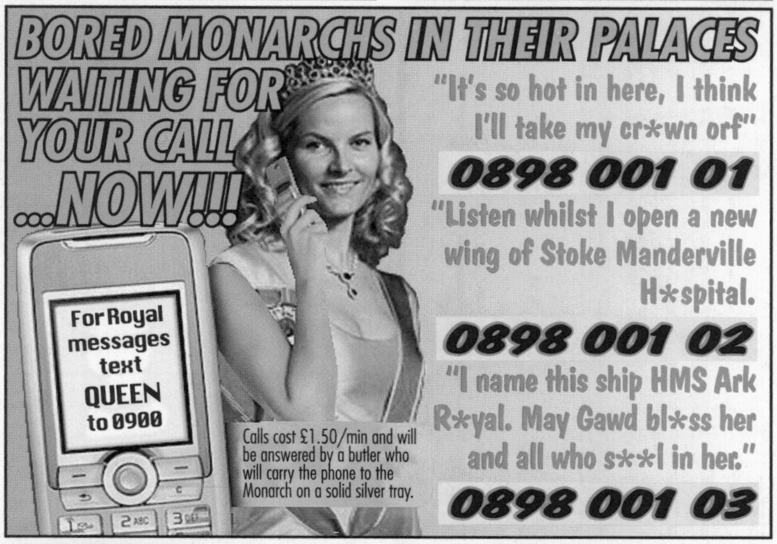

BORED MONARCHS IN THEIR PALACES WAITING FOR YOUR CALL ...NOW!!!
"It's so hot in here, I think I'll take my cr*wn orf"
0898 001 01
"Listen whilst I open a new wing of Stoke Manderville H*spital.
0898 001 02
"I name this ship HMS Ark R*yal. May Gawd bl*ss her and all who s**l in her."
0898 001 03
For Royal messages text QUEEN to 0900
Calls cost £1.50/min and will be answered by a butler who will carry the phone to the Monarch on a solid silver tray.

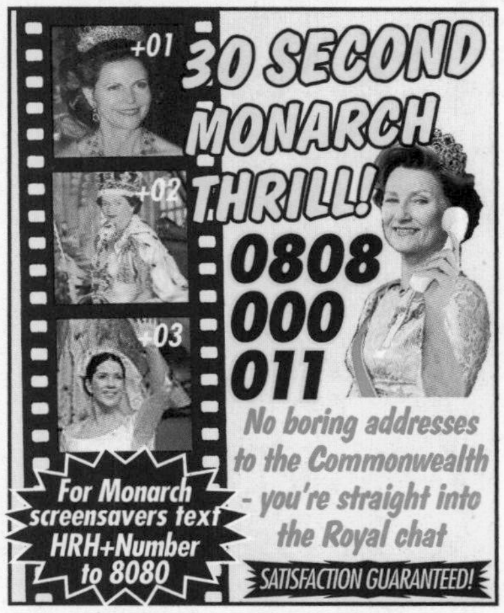

+01
+02
+03
30 SECOND MONARCH THRILL!
0808 000 011
No boring addresses to the Commonwealth - you're straight into the Royal chat
For Monarch screensavers text HRH+Number to 8080
SATISFACTION GUARANTEED!

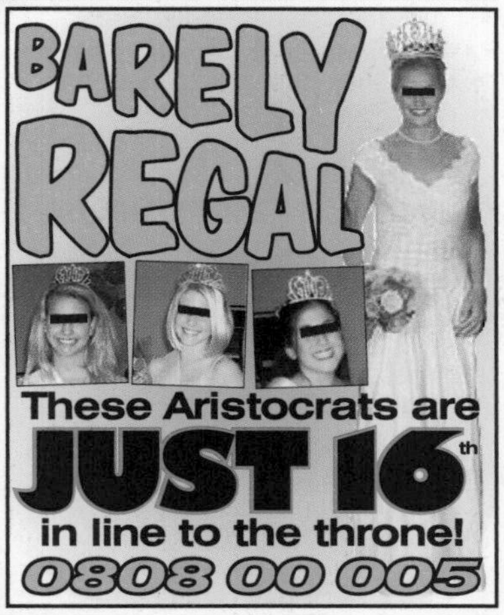

BARELY REGAL
These Aristocrats are JUST 16th in line to the throne!
0808 00 005

SMOKING BAN EVASION

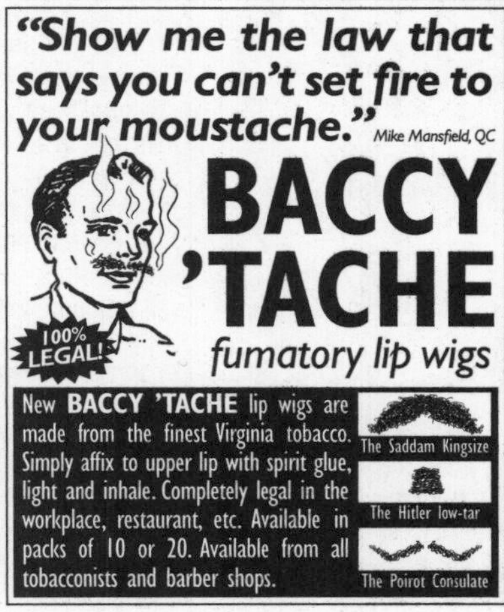

"Show me the law that says you can't set fire to your moustache." Mike Mansfield, QC
BACCY 'TACHE
fumatory lip wigs
100% LEGAL!
New BACCY 'TACHE lip wigs are made from the finest Virginia tobacco. Simply affix to upper lip with spirit glue, light and inhale. Completely legal in the workplace, restaurant, etc. Available in packs of 10 or 20. Available from all tobacconists and barber shops.
The Saddam Kingsize
The Hitler low-tar
The Poirot Consulate

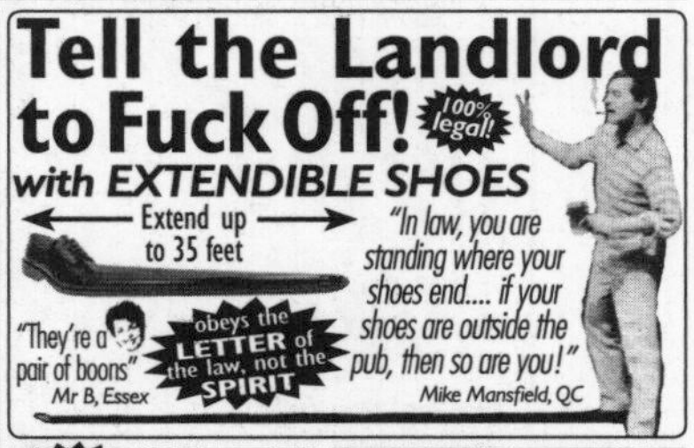

Tell the Landlord to Fuck Off!
100% legal!
with EXTENDIBLE SHOES
Extend up to 35 feet
"In law, you are standing where your shoes end.... if your shoes are outside the pub, then so are you!" Mike Mansfield, QC
"They're a pair of boons" Mr B, Essex
obeys the LETTER of the law, not the SPIRIT

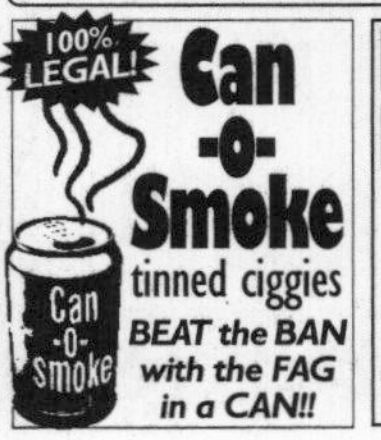

100% LEGAL!
Can -o- Smoke
tinned ciggies
BEAT the BAN with the FAG in a CAN!!

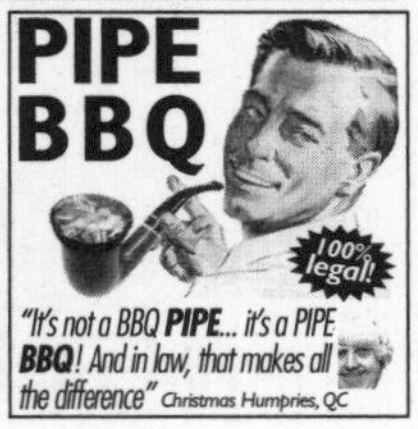

PIPE BBQ
100% legal!
"It's not a BBQ PIPE... it's a PIPE BBQ! And in law, that makes all the difference" Christmas Humpries, QC

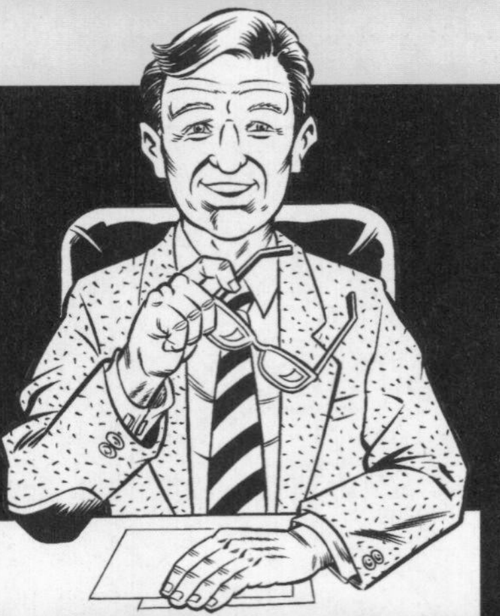

The Viz Careers Office

THIS WEEK

So you want to be A BUILDER?

MOST BOYS DREAM of being builders when they grow up, and it's a great career for any lad who is good with his hands. It's a job for life too, because new houses will always need to be built and old houses will always need to be repaired. But what exactly do they do all day? Let's look at the fascinating working life of the modern builder.

▼**A BUILDER'S** day starts very early in the morning. He goes in his van to pick up his labourers - two heavily-tattooed thugs with convictions for burglary and common assault.

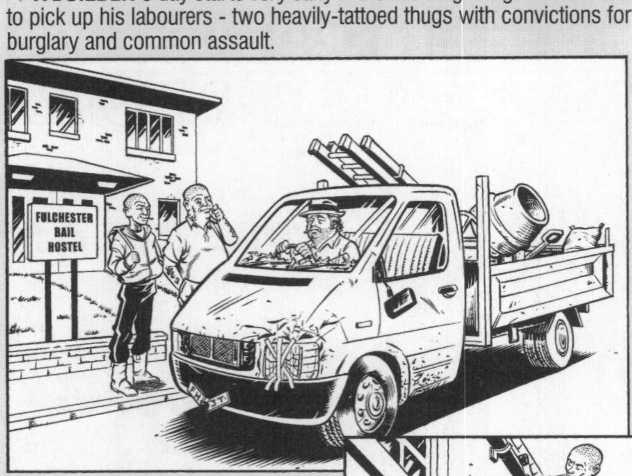
FULCHESTER
BAIL
HOSTEL

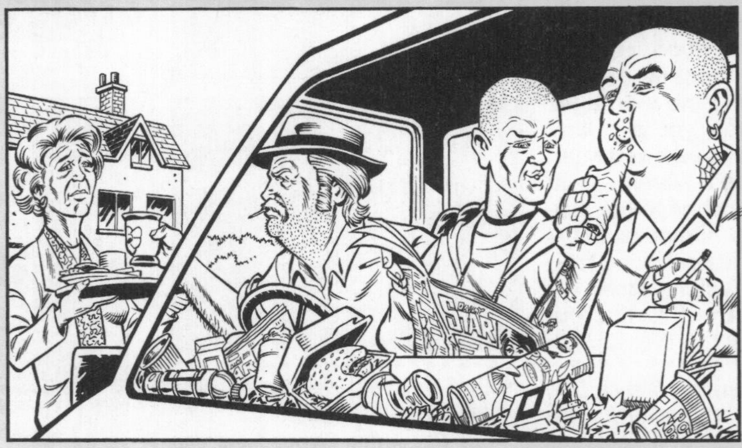

◄**IT'S OFF** to Acacia Avenue for the first job of the day - repointing Mrs Thompson's garage. Once there, they sit in the cab eating sausage rolls, reading the paper and listening to Radio One for three quarters of an hour. There's just time for a quick cup of tea with six sugars before they drop a bag of cement on the path and drive away, not to return until the following June.

►**IT'S** mid-morning and the builder is pricing up another job, this time to repair some guttering. He gives two quotes - a high one that goes through the books and a much more reasonable one for cash. While the builder surveys the job, his labourers take the opportunity to check the house for window locks and burglar alarms.

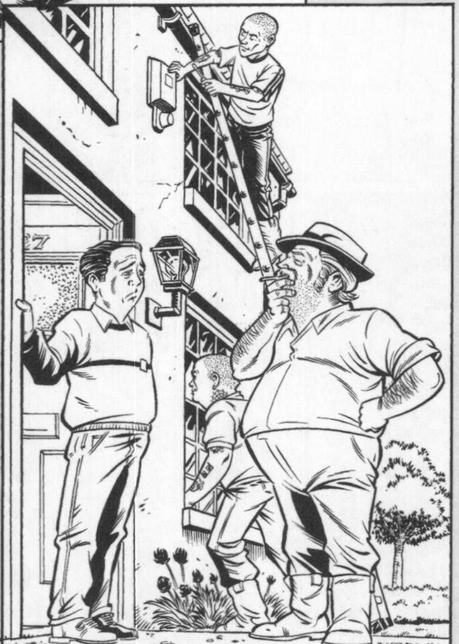

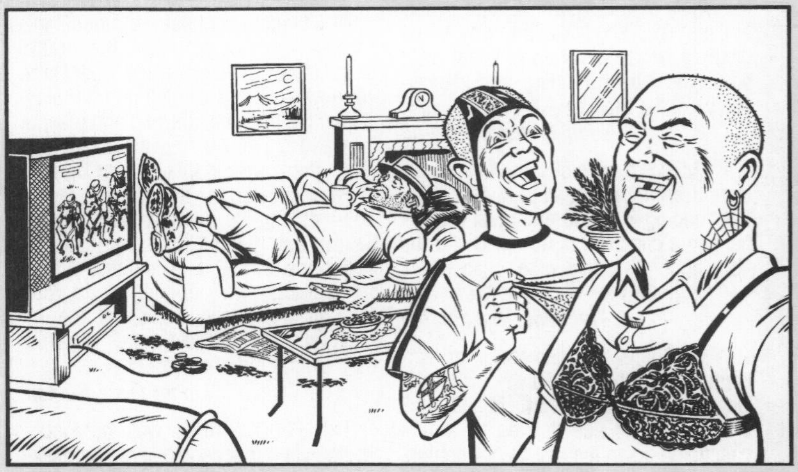

▼**FOR MANY** self-employed tradesmen, cash-flow can often be a problem, and our builder is no exception. Next, he visits a customer to chase up an unpaid £5000 bill for a loft conversion. When the householder complains that he has been waiting eighteen months and the building work hasn't started yet, the builder tells him that if he wants to cancel the job and get a cowboy in to do it, that's up to him, but he will forfeit the £25,000 he has already paid.

▲**AN HOUR** later, and it's time to get down to some hard graft at last - a spot of plastering. The owner is away, and she has left a key so that they can let themselves in. While the builder helps himself to a cup of tea and a few premium-rate phonecalls, his colleagues indulge in a little good-natured horseplay, rifling through the householder's underwear drawer.

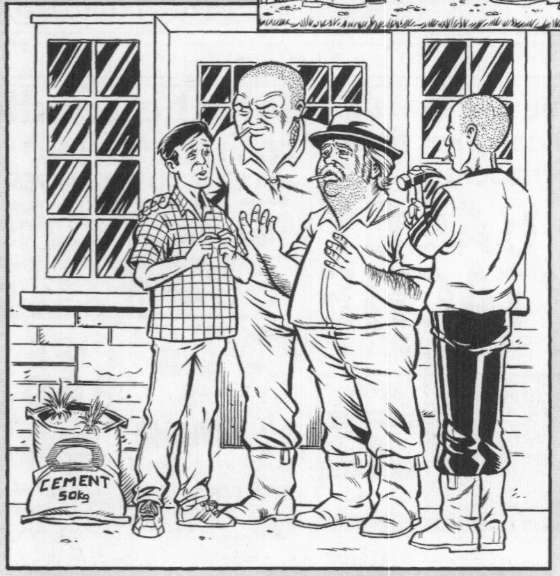
CEMENT
50kg

►**IT IS** lunchtime, but work never stops for a busy builder. An angry client calls to remonstrate with him for failing to keep an appointment. The builder tells him that he is very sorry, but his mother has been diagnosed with cancer and he is at that moment giving her a lift to hospital for her chemotherapy treatment. The shocked client apologises and tells the builder to come round only when he feels ready.

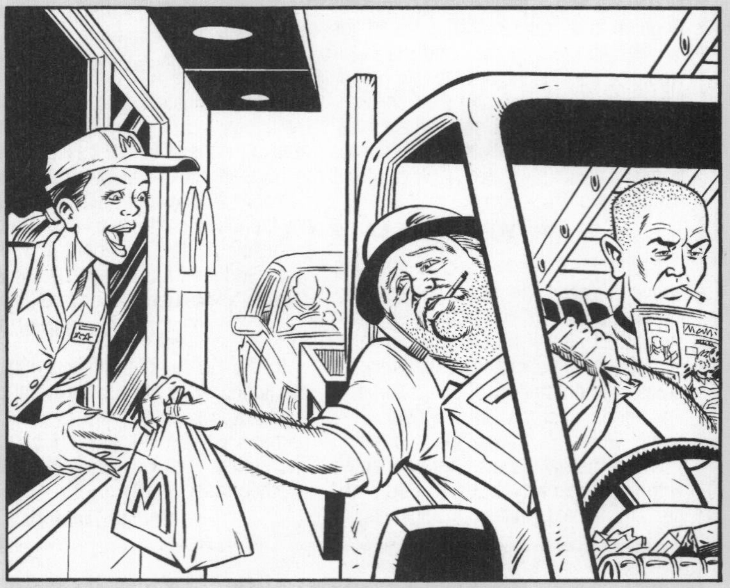

▼**IT'S** Thursday, so after lunch, the builder gives his labourers a lift to the local DSS office where they join the queue and sign on. After that, it's straight back to work.

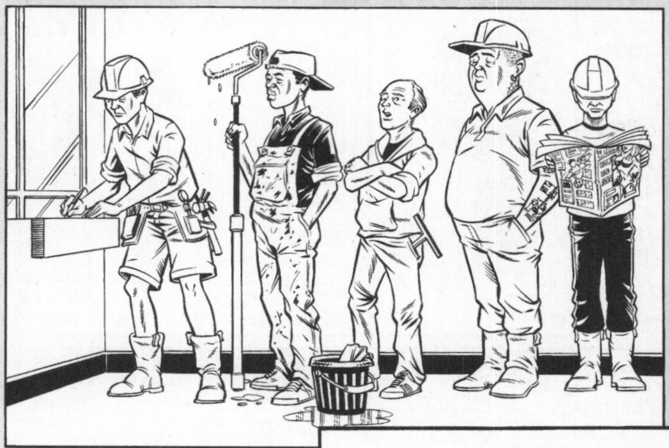

◄**OUR** builder prides himself on the quality of his work and he offers a 25-year guarantee. Here, a previous customer has made a complaint about her front door, which she claims the builder has put in upside down and back to front. However, a quick inspection reveals the cause of the problem to be roots from a tree next door growing under the house's foundations and causing the door to turn upside down and back to front.

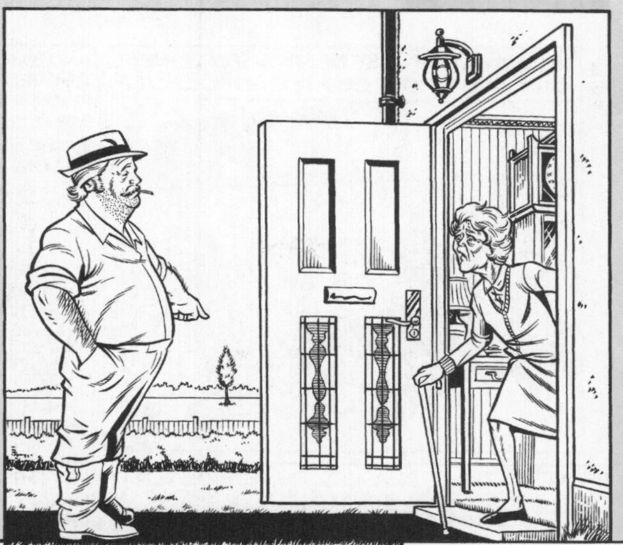

►**HIS NEXT** call-out sees our builder dealing with a problem which is quite common in older houses - rising damp. The wet summer has raised the water table, and the resulting moisture has caused the plaster to weaken and fall off the wall. Before any repair is effected, a damp-proofing course must be installed in the brickwork to ensure that there is no recurrence of the problem. Once again, the householders are out at work and have entrusted the builder with a key.

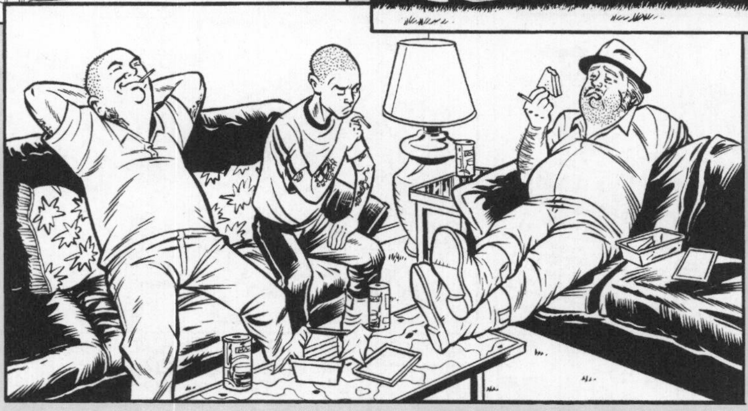

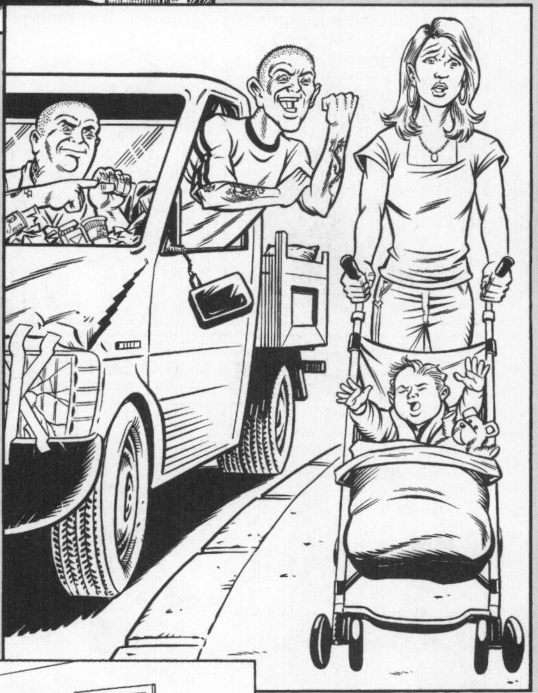

◄**LATER ON,** our builders find themselves high up on a roof of a Victorian terrace house where the wind has dislodged some tiles. Genuine Welsh slates are becoming hard to find these days, and prices have risen accordingly. So, in order to maximise profits and make the job easier and quicker, a few slates are prised off the roof of the house next door. This also has the added advantage that the builder can later go round to the neighbour's house and offer to repair their roof, where he has spotted a few missing slates.

►**ON THE** way to their next job, the builders spot an attractive woman. British builders have always had an eye for the ladies, and it is refreshing that this quaint and harmless tradition continues, even in these politically correct times. They slow down, and cheekily call out a few good-natured compliments to her.

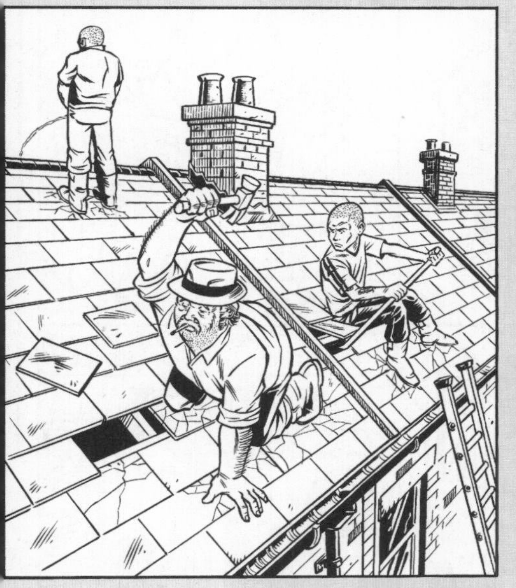

◄**HALF-WAY** through the afternoon, and the builders are laying a screed on the conservatory floor of a famous TV magician. Whilst they are waiting for the levelling compound to set, they keep themselves busy looking for pornographic polaroid photographs or home movie footage of the magician's wonderful assistant which they can sell to the News of the World.

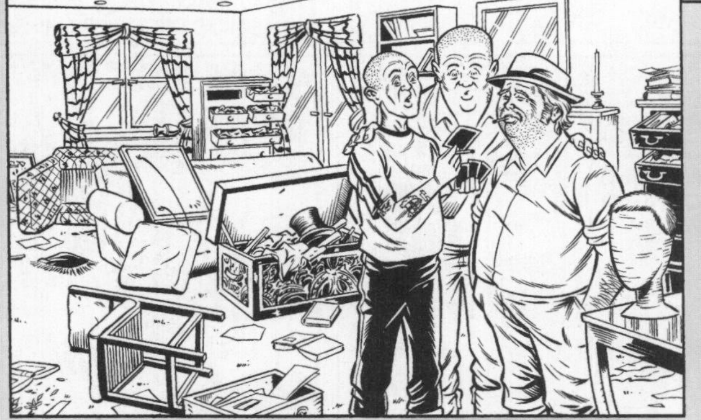

►**CONSTRUCTION** work invariably creates a lot of rubble and debris, but a good builder always cleans up after himself. Asbestos is very expensive to dispose of properly as it is subject to strict guidelines, so it has to be carefully hidden in the bottom of a skip. Loose aggregate, sand and unused cement, on the other hand, can be safely swept into the drains or flushed down the toilet.

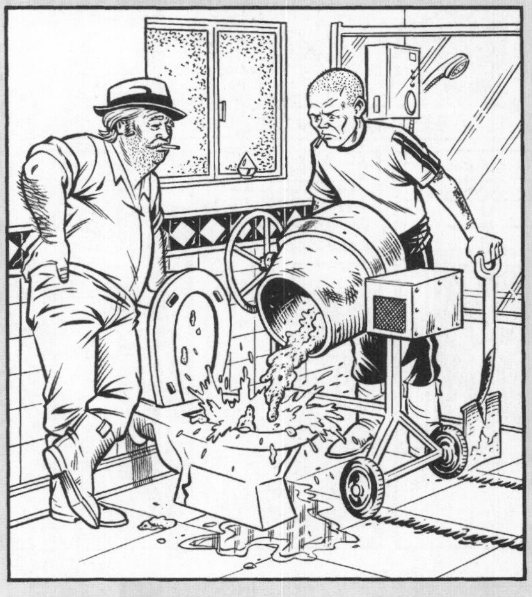

►**A BUILDER'S** work is never done, especially if you've paid him up front. Here, the builders leave a half-finished kitchen extension open to the elements in order to go and finish another kitchen extension which they left open to the elements six months previously, whose owner has taken out a private prosecution. And so another day at the sharp end of the construction industry work is done; eight new jobs started and none finished, five thousand pounds in cash, a dozen bras and several pornographic photographs of a household name in his back pocket.

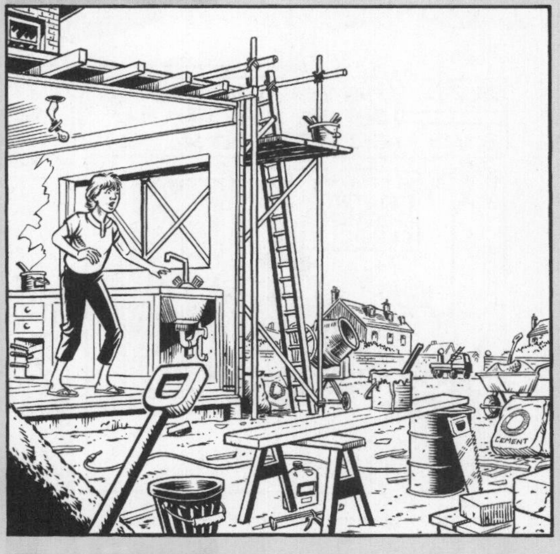

NEXT WEEK **- So you want to be a peepshow wank-booth jizzmopper?**

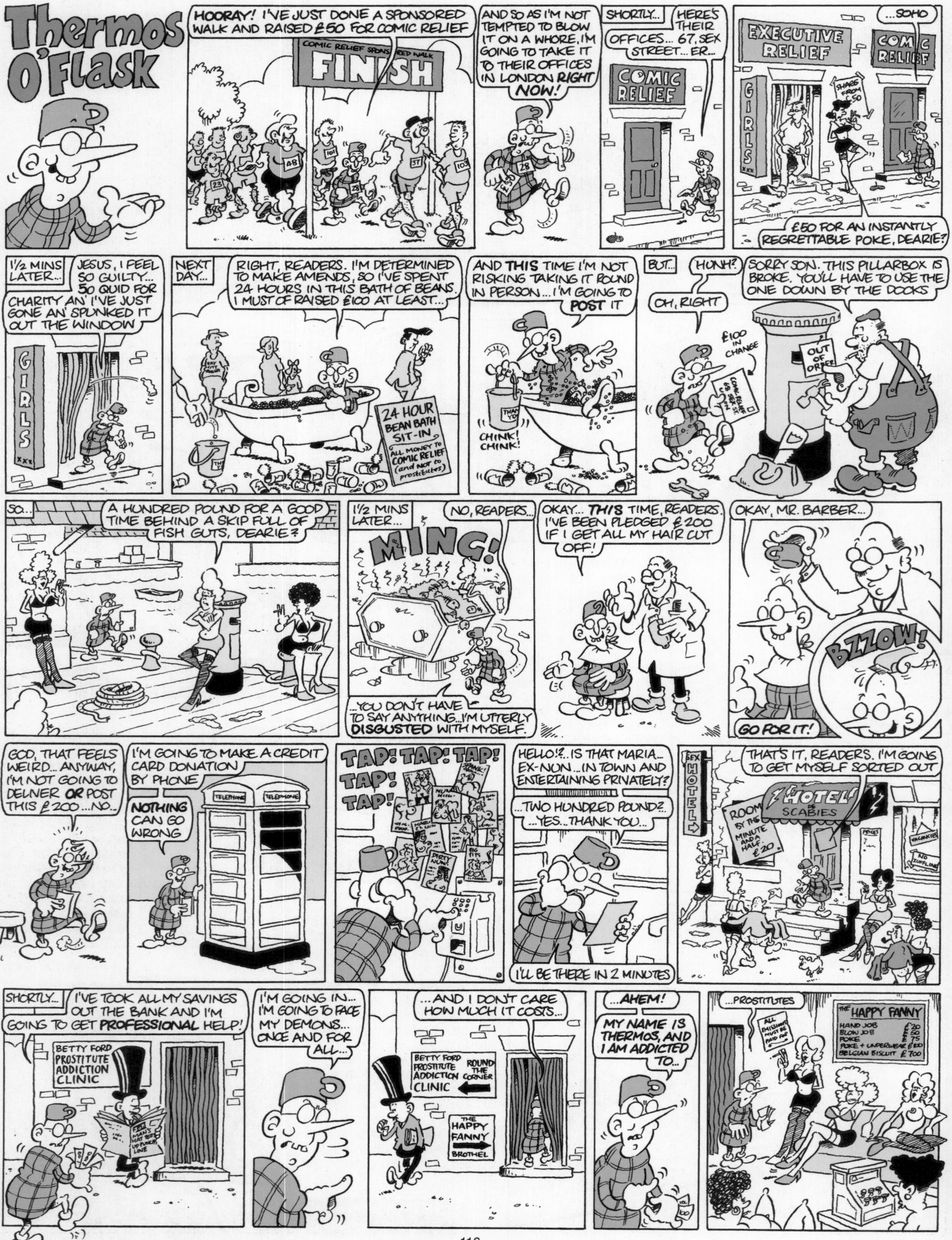
Thermos O'Flask
HOORAY! I'VE JUST DONE A SPONSORED WALK AND RAISED £50 FOR COMIC RELIEF
COMIC RELIEF SPONSORED WALK
FINISH
AND SO AS I'M NOT TEMPTED TO BLOW IT ON A WHORE, I'M GOING TO TAKE IT TO THEIR OFFICES IN LONDON RIGHT NOW!
SHORTLY...
HERE'S THEIR OFFICES... 67, SEX STREET... ER...
COMIC RELIEF
...SOHO
EXECUTIVE RELIEF
COMIC RELIEF
GIRLS
SHAGS FROM £50
£50 FOR AN INSTANTLY REGRETTABLE POKE, DEARIE?
1½ MINS LATER...
JESUS, I FEEL SO GUILTY... 50 QUID FOR CHARITY AN' I'VE JUST GONE AN' SPUNKED IT OUT THE WINDOW
GIRLS
NEXT DAY...
RIGHT, READERS. I'M DETERMINED TO MAKE AMENDS, SO I'VE SPENT 24 HOURS IN THIS BATH OF BEANS. I MUST OF RAISED £100 AT LEAST...
24 HOUR BEAN BATH SIT-IN
ALL MONEY TO COMIC RELIEF (and not to prostitutes)
AND THIS TIME I'M NOT RISKING TAKING IT ROUND IN PERSON... I'M GOING TO POST IT
CHINK! CHINK!
BUT...
HONH?
OH, RIGHT
SORRY SON. THIS PILLARBOX IS BROKE. YOU'LL HAVE TO USE THE ONE DOWN BY THE DOCKS
£100 IN CHANGE
OUT OF ORDER
SO...
A HUNDRED POUND FOR A GOOD TIME BEHIND A SKIP FULL OF FISH GUTS, DEARIE?
1½ MINS LATER...
NO, READERS...
MING!
...YOU DON'T HAVE TO SAY ANYTHING... I'M UTTERLY DISGUSTED WITH MYSELF.
OKAY... THIS TIME, READERS. I'VE BEEN PLEDGED £200 IF I GET ALL MY HAIR CUT OFF!
OKAY, MR. BARBER...
BZZOW!
GO FOR IT!
GOD, THAT FEELS WEIRD... ANYWAY, I'M NOT GOING TO DELIVER OR POST THIS £200... NO...
I'M GOING TO MAKE A CREDIT CARD DONATION BY PHONE
NOTHING CAN GO WRONG
TELEPHONE
TELEPHONE
TAP! TAP! TAP! TAP! TAP!
DIRTY NUN!
HELLO!?... IS THAT MARIA... EX-NUN... IN TOWN AND ENTERTAINING PRIVATELY?
...TWO HUNDRED POUNDS? ...YES... THANK YOU...
I'LL BE THERE IN 2 MINUTES
SEX HOTEL
THAT'S IT, READERS. I'M GOING TO GET MYSELF SORTED OUT
HOTEL DE SCABIES
ROOM BY THE MINUTE AND A HALF £20.
SHORTLY...
I'VE TOOK ALL MY SAVINGS OUT THE BANK AND I'M GOING TO GET PROFESSIONAL HELP!
BETTY FORD PROSTITUTE ADDICTION CLINIC
I'M GOING IN... I'M GOING TO FACE MY DEMONS... ONCE AND FOR ALL...
...AND I DON'T CARE HOW MUCH IT COSTS...
BETTY FORD PROSTITUTE ADDICTION CLINIC
ROUND THE CORNER
THE HAPPY FANNY BROTHEL
...AHEM!
MY NAME IS THERMOS, AND I AM ADDICTED TO...
...PROSTITUTES
THE HAPPY FANNY
HAND JOB £20
BLOW JOB 50
POKE 75
POKE + UNDERWEAR £100
BELGIAN BISCUIT £700

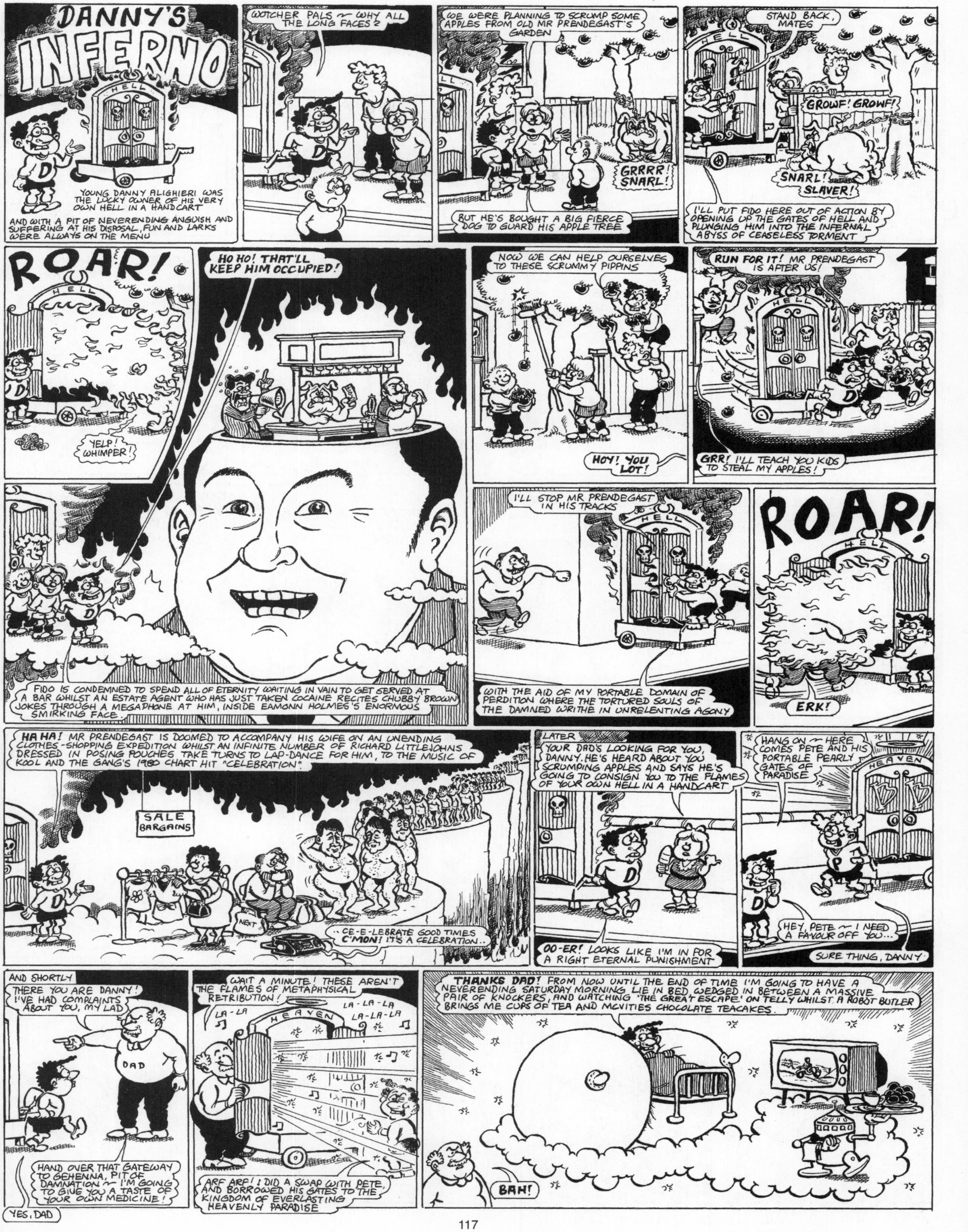
DANNY'S INFERNO
HELL
YOUNG DANNY ALIGHIERI WAS THE LUCKY OWNER OF HIS VERY OWN HELL IN A HANDCART
AND WITH A PIT OF NEVERENDING ANGUISH AND SUFFERING AT HIS DISPOSAL, FUN AND LARKS WERE ALWAYS ON THE MENU
WOTCHER PALS ~ WHY ALL THE LONG FACES?
WE WERE PLANNING TO SCRUMP SOME APPLES FROM OLD MR PRENDEGAST'S GARDEN
GRRRR! SNARL!
BUT HE'S BOUGHT A BIG FIERCE DOG TO GUARD HIS APPLE TREE
STAND BACK, MATES
GROWF! GROWF!
SNARL! SLAVER!
I'LL PUT FIDO HERE OUT OF ACTION BY OPENING UP THE GATES OF HELL AND PLUNGING HIM INTO THE INFERNAL ABYSS OF CEASELESS TORMENT
ROAR!
YELP! WHIMPER!
HO HO! THAT'LL KEEP HIM OCCUPIED!
FIDO IS CONDEMNED TO SPEND ALL OF ETERNITY WAITING IN VAIN TO GET SERVED AT A BAR WHILST AN ESTATE AGENT WHO HAS JUST TAKEN COCAINE RECITES CHUBBY BROWN JOKES THROUGH A MEGAPHONE AT HIM, INSIDE EAMONN HOLMES'S ENORMOUS SMIRKING FACE.
NOW WE CAN HELP OURSELVES TO THESE SCRUMMY PIPPINS
HOY! YOU LOT!
RUN FOR IT! MR PRENDEGAST IS AFTER US!
GRR! I'LL TEACH YOU KIDS TO STEAL MY APPLES!
I'LL STOP MR PRENDEGAST IN HIS TRACKS
WITH THE AID OF MY PORTABLE DOMAIN OF PERDITION WHERE THE TORTURED SOULS OF THE DAMNED WRITHE IN UNRELENTING AGONY
ROAR!
ERK!
HA HA! MR PRENDEGAST IS DOOMED TO ACCOMPANY HIS WIFE ON AN UNENDING CLOTHES-SHOPPING EXPEDITION WHILST AN INFINITE NUMBER OF RICHARD LITTLEJOHNS DRESSED IN POSING POUCHES TAKE TURNS TO LAP-DANCE FOR HIM, TO THE MUSIC OF KOOL AND THE GANG'S 1980 CHART HIT "CELEBRATION"
SALE BARGAINS
NEXT
...CE-E-LEBRATE GOOD TIMES C'MON! IT'S A CELEBRATION...
LATER
YOUR DAD'S LOOKING FOR YOU, DANNY. HE'S HEARD ABOUT YOU SCRUMPING APPLES AND SAYS HE'S GOING TO CONSIGN YOU TO THE FLAMES OF YOUR OWN HELL IN A HANDCART
OO-ER! LOOKS LIKE I'M IN FOR A RIGHT ETERNAL PUNISHMENT
HANG ON ~ HERE COMES PETE AND HIS PORTABLE PEARLY GATES OF PARADISE
HEAVEN
HEY, PETE ~ I NEED A FAVOUR OFF YOU...
SURE THING, DANNY
AND SHORTLY
THERE YOU ARE DANNY! I'VE HAD COMPLAINTS ABOUT YOU, MY LAD
DAD
HAND OVER THAT GATEWAY TO GEHENNA, PIT OF DAMNATION ~ I'M GOING TO GIVE YOU A TASTE OF YOUR OWN MEDICINE!
YES, DAD
WAIT A MINUTE! THESE AREN'T THE FLAMES OF METAPHYSICAL RETRIBUTION!
LA-LA
LA-LA-LA LA-LA-LA
HEAVEN
ARF ARF! I DID A SWAP WITH PETE, AND BORROWED HIS GATES TO THE KINGDOM OF EVERLASTING HEAVENLY PARADISE
THANKS DAD! FROM NOW UNTIL THE END OF TIME I'M GOING TO HAVE A NEVERENDING SATURDAY MORNING LIE IN BED, WEDGED IN BETWEEN A MASSIVE PAIR OF KNOCKERS, AND WATCHING 'THE GREAT ESCAPE' ON TELLY WHILST A ROBOT BUTLER BRINGS ME CUPS OF TEA AND MCVITIES CHOCOLATE TEACAKES.
BAH!

FRY 'T' BUNN THE MASTER BAKER AND HIS GINGERBREAD SEX DOLLS

SOON BE HOME NOW, CHELSEA LOVE. DADDY'S GOING TO BE SO PLEASED TO SEE YOU AGAIN.

DADDY! DADDY!

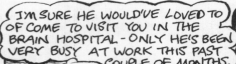

I'M SURE HE WOULD'VE LOVED TO OF COME TO VISIT YOU IN THE BRAIN HOSPITAL - ONLY HE'S BEEN VERY BUSY AT WORK THIS PAST COUPLE OF MONTHS.

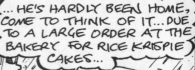

...HE'S HARDLY BEEN HOME, COME TO THINK OF IT...DUE TO A LARGE ORDER AT THE BAKERY FOR RICE KRISPIE CAKES...

PHUTT K-P-PWUFF. POP.... COUGH!

OH NO! THE ENGINE'S STOPPED..!

I'LL HAVE TO PULL OVER.

DON'T WORRY - I'LL PHONE DADDY AND GET HIM TO COME AND RESCUE US IN HIS VAN...

HELLO? FRUBERT!? OH, THANK GOD I CAUGHT YOU...I'VE GOT CHELSEA IN THE CAR AND WE'VE BROKEN DOWN ON THE BARNTON BYPASS...

WHAT'S THAT, FRUBERT..?

CHELSEA... C-H-E-L-... OUR DAUGHTER, YOU REMEMBER...?

...YES...THAT'S HER. THE ONE WITH THE LAZY EYE AND THE BUILT-UP SHOE...

OH YES. SHE'S STILL ALIVE, FRU...

...ANYWAY, LOVE, WE'RE STUCK IN A LAYBY. CAN YOU COME AND FETCH US..?

...OH, I SEE... NO...NO, I DON'T WANT THE BUSINESS TO GO BUST... IT'S JUST THAT IT'S GETTING DARK AND...

...OH, HE'S HUNG UP.

DADDY'S JUST IN THE MIDDLE OF DELIVERING A CREAM HORN AT THE MOMENT, BUT I'M SURE HE'LL BE COMING VERY SOON...

...UH!UH!...UH!UH! ...UH!UH!UH!... UH-UH-UH-UH... ...UUUUUGH!

MY MISSUS THINKS I'M AT WORK. SHE'D MURDER ME IF SHE KNEW I'D GOT YOU SET UP IN THIS LITTLE GINGERBREAD LOVENEST ON THE OTHER SIDE OF TOWN..!

...AND THAT I WAS COMING OVER HERE EVERY DAY TO BANG YOU UP YOUR DOUGHNUT...

...OVER AND OVER AGAIN...WHENEVER I WANT...

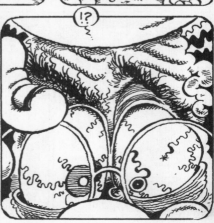

!?

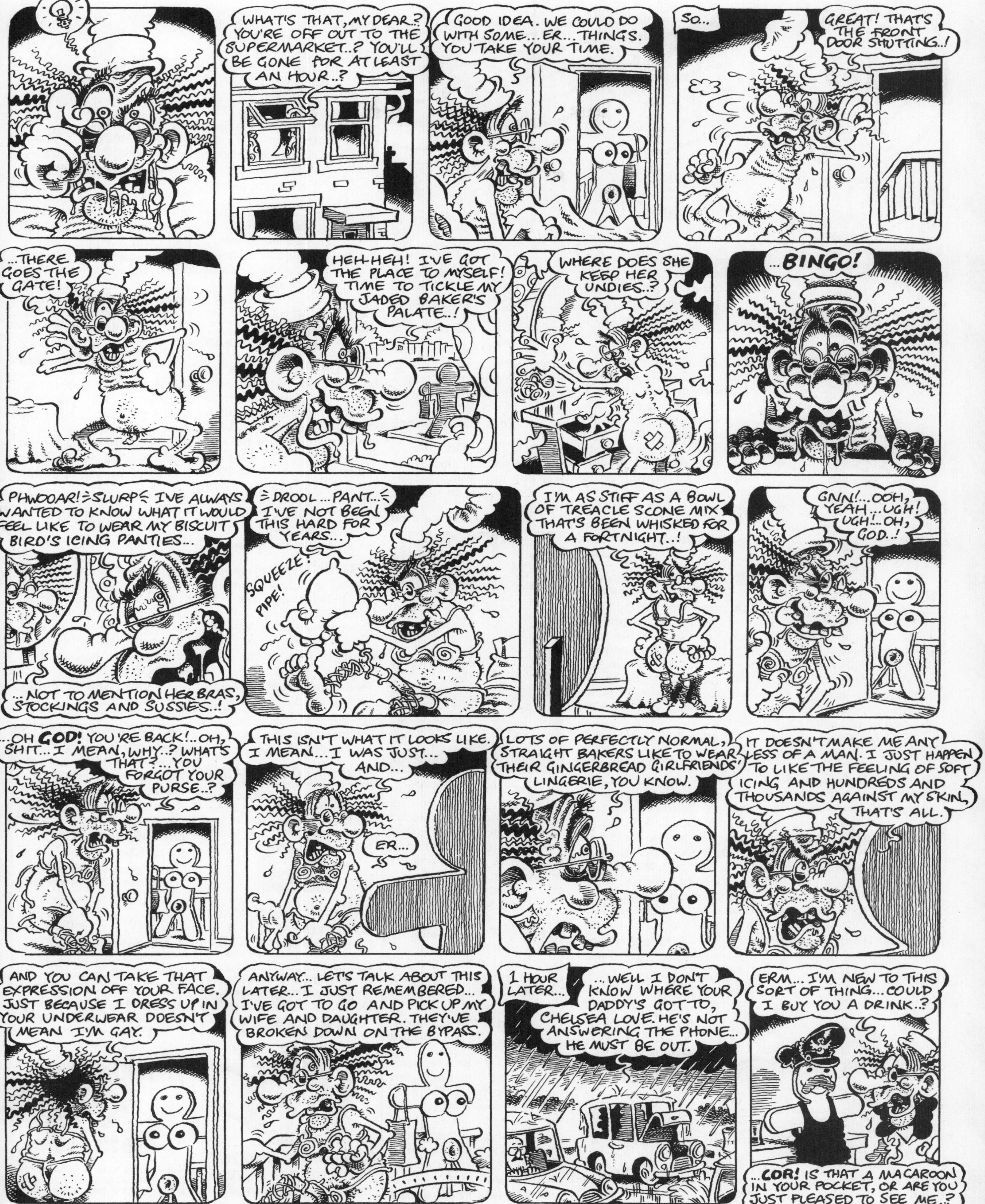
WHAT'S THAT, MY DEAR? YOU'RE OFF OUT TO THE SUPERMARKET..? YOU'LL BE GONE FOR AT LEAST AN HOUR..?
GOOD IDEA. WE COULD DO WITH SOME... ER... THINGS. YOU TAKE YOUR TIME.
SO...
GREAT! THAT'S THE FRONT DOOR SHUTTING..!
...THERE GOES THE GATE!
HEH-HEH! I'VE GOT THE PLACE TO MYSELF! TIME TO TICKLE MY JADED BAKER'S PALATE..!
WHERE DOES SHE KEEP HER UNDIES..?
...BINGO!
PHWOAR! ≥SLURP≤ I'VE ALWAYS WANTED TO KNOW WHAT IT WOULD FEEL LIKE TO WEAR MY BISCUIT BIRD'S ICING PANTIES...
...NOT TO MENTION HER BRAS, STOCKINGS AND SUSSIES..!
≥DROOL...PANT...≤ I'VE NOT BEEN THIS HARD FOR YEARS...
SQUEEZE! PIPE!
I'M AS STIFF AS A BOWL OF TREACLE SCONE MIX THAT'S BEEN WHISKED FOR A FORTNIGHT..!
GNN!...OOH, YEAH...UGH! UGH!...OH, GOD..!
...OH GOD! YOU'RE BACK!...OH, SHIT... I MEAN, WHY..? WHAT'S THAT?...YOU FORGOT YOUR PURSE..?
THIS ISN'T WHAT IT LOOKS LIKE. I MEAN... I WAS JUST... AND...
ER...
LOTS OF PERFECTLY NORMAL, STRAIGHT BAKERS LIKE TO WEAR THEIR GINGERBREAD GIRLFRIENDS' LINGERIE, YOU KNOW.
IT DOESN'T MAKE ME ANY LESS OF A MAN. I JUST HAPPEN TO LIKE THE FEELING OF SOFT ICING AND HUNDREDS AND THOUSANDS AGAINST MY SKIN, THAT'S ALL.
AND YOU CAN TAKE THAT EXPRESSION OFF YOUR FACE. JUST BECAUSE I DRESS UP IN YOUR UNDERWEAR DOESN'T MEAN I'M GAY.
ANYWAY... LET'S TALK ABOUT THIS LATER... I JUST REMEMBERED... I'VE GOT TO GO AND PICK UP MY WIFE AND DAUGHTER. THEY'VE BROKEN DOWN ON THE BYPASS.
1 HOUR LATER...
...WELL I DON'T KNOW WHERE YOUR DADDY'S GOT TO, CHELSEA LOVE. HE'S NOT ANSWERING THE PHONE... HE MUST BE OUT.
ERM... I'M NEW TO THIS SORT OF THING... COULD I BUY YOU A DRINK..?
...COR! IS THAT A MACAROON IN YOUR POCKET, OR ARE YOU JUST PLEASED TO SEE ME..?

LETTER BOCKS 169

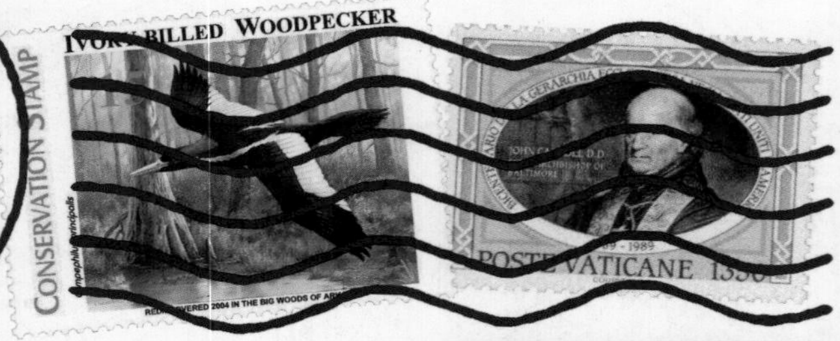

IVORY-BILLED WOODPECKER
CONSERVATION STAMP
POSTE VATICANE

Star Letter

★ I FORGOT to buy a lottery ticket last Saturday, and watched with horror as the six numbers I always choose came up. Imagine my relief when I remembered that I was JK Rowling and have money coming out of my arse. How I chuckled at my stupidity as I tossed another 3-inch thick wad of £50 notes on the fire.

JK Rowling, Edinburgh

Letterbocks Viz Comic PO Box 656, North Shields, NE30 4XX letters@viz.co.uk

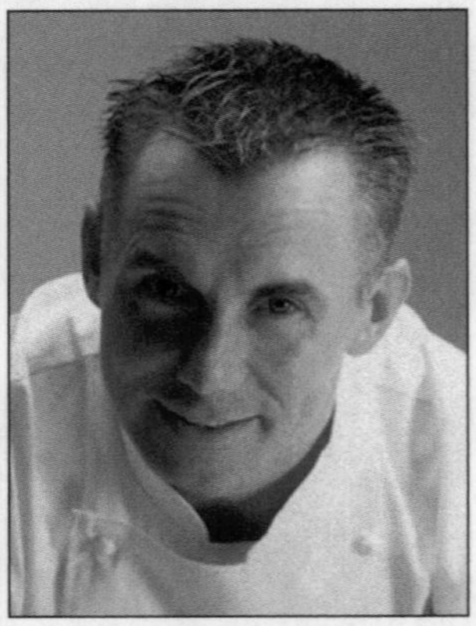

■ "THERE'S nothing better than a bit of Scotch egg," said TV chef Gary Rhodes on a recent episode of *UK Food Heroes*. Well I only hope that when he and his wife, Jennie, are making love, she remembers that her hubby doesn't consider the act as pleasurable as a bit of Scotch egg.

Frank Peterborough, London

■ I CAN'T help thinking that if baggage handlers at Glasgow Airport spent less time punching burning terrorists and more time putting suitcases onto the fucking carousel, I might not have waited an hour and a half for my bag after I got got off the plane from Toronto last week.

Chuck Jism, Newcastle

■ I READ that the same earthquake that destroyed a church in Peru killing 27 of the congregation also knocked down the wall of a prison allowing 600 convicts to escape. Now I understand that God works in mysterious ways, His wonders to perform, but I can't help thinking He was taking the piss a bit with that one.

Hazlenut Monkbottle Newcastle

■ TO THE bloke who keeps letting his dog shit on the grass opposite my house and then absent-mindedly forgetting to pick the turds up. Don't panic, I know you live at number 28, and I'll pop them through the letterbox for you. Probably late at night. And possibly on fire.

Mike Hancorn, e-mail

■ AN ELDERLY aunty of mine phoned me recently to say she would like to introduce me to her new 'gentleman friend'. Imagine my surprise when he turned out to be none other than Dr Josef Mengele, the infamous Auschwitz Dr Death. Well, I had to be civil to him for her sake, but I couldn't say I was pleased about it.

P Kaleidoscope, e-mail

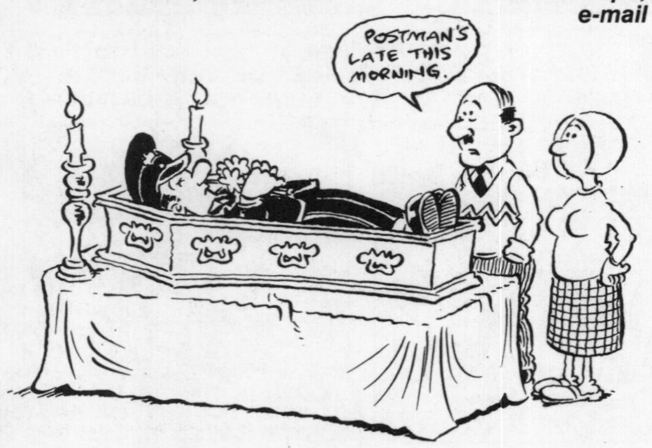

POSTMAN'S LATE THIS MORNING.

■ I'M GLAD food manufacturers include 'serving suggestions' on their labelling. I would never have thought of putting beans on toast.

Otto Pfister, e-mail

■ DOCTOR Doolittle, if you are reading this, could you pop round and tell my neighbour's dog to shut the fuck up?

Jeff Lewin, e-mail

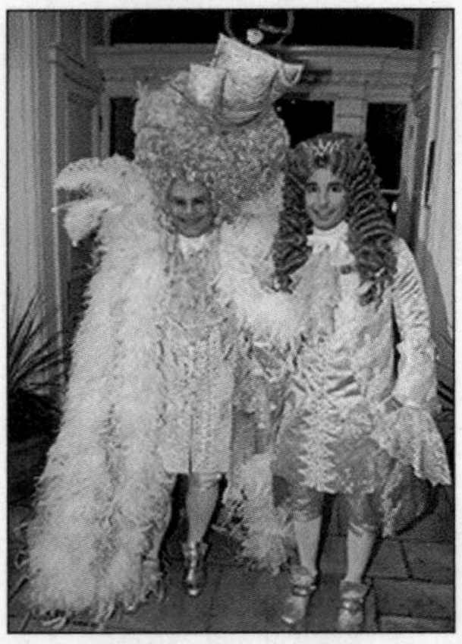

■ How selfish of Sir Elton John to go around wearing that enormous pompadour wig. Does he not realise that anyone seated behind him in the cinema, or at a concert or funeral would have a severly obstructed view?

Julie Speedie, e-mail

■ I DON'T know. Shouting "Let's all have a sing-song" at strangers in the pub really doesn't get the same reaction nowadays as it did in the 1930s.

Martin Christienson, e-mail

■ TODAY I saw a tattooed young chap in a newsagent buying a copy of *The Sun*, *Nuts* and *Zoo*. How refreshing to see the youth of today keen on getting a well-rounded view of the world from such a diverse range of publications.

David Hershman, e-mail

■ A CIRCUS came to our town last week and immediately the animal rights brigade were there in protest because it had performing lions that get plenty of exercise walking round the ring, and get fed three times a day. The same circus also had a midget that they shot out of a cannon, but I didn't see anybody protesting about that.

B Davro, e-mail

■ WHY DON'T farmers keep whales instead of cows? There's much more meat on them, and as mammals, presumably more milk. And with all the recent flooding in Gloucester there's plenty of fields for them to swim in.

Alan Heath, e-mail

■ I AM in the process of buying a car and have narrowed my choice down to two. But I don't know whether to buy the one that floats away on balloons or the one that's made of cake. I think I prefer the one made of cake, but I'd like the security of knowing that the ad had won an award before making such a big commitment.

Brian Fester, e-mail

■ FORGET 'The purple headed mountain' in *All Things Bright and Beautiful (Letterbocks p.92)*. What about verse five of *Now the Day is Over?* 'Guard the sailors tossing, on the deep blue sea.'

Rev Clair Wilson, London

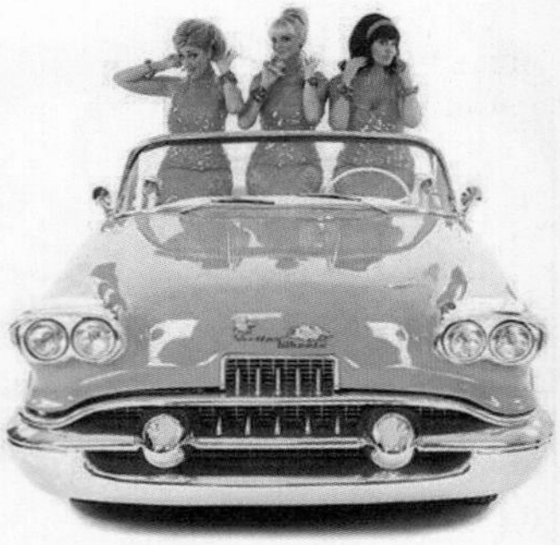

■ 'WOMEN make the safest drivers' claim those pseudo-Australian council birds in the Sheila's Wheels advert. Well having witnessed them drive backwards with their arms in the air looking the wrong way before allowing a stuffed kangaroo to take the wheel, I would beg to differ.

PO Healey, HMS Vanguard

■ I WAS never in Vietnam, so when I see helicopter blades spinning it takes me back to the time I was in a hot steamy house with a slowly rotating ceiling fan.

Paul Brelsford, e-mail

■ "YOU'LL never make anything of yourself if you persist with those idle sketches instead of knuckling down to some work," my old schoolmaster once said as I doodled in the back of my exercise book. I wish I could say that I had the last laugh, but he was right. I am terminally unemployed and sleep on a third hand mattress in a one-room bedsit.

David Shales, e-mail

OLD LADY FINANCIAL INVESTMENT

Don't trust Building Societies with *YOUR* money?

Who can blame you?

With banks going pop right, left and centre and armed robbery on the increase, it makes sense to keep YOUR money where it's safe.

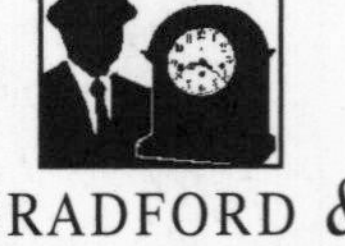

BRADFORD & BEHIND THE CLOCK

Keeping Your Money Behind a Clock on the Mantlepiece since 1878

Nationwide biscuit tin

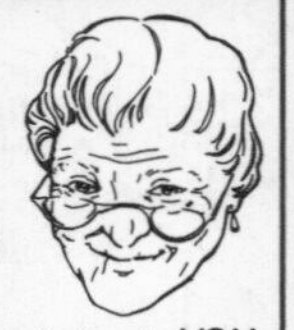

With our new *Variable Tin Account*, you can invest anything from £1 to £1m

Choose the container that suits YOU:

Investment	Account Tin
up to £1000	Shortbread
£1000~£10,000	Jacob's Biscuits for Cheese
£10,000~£50,000	Peak Frean Macaroons
over £50,000	Fox's Teatime Assortment

Old ladies - put YOUR nest-egg into NORTHERN TEAPOT

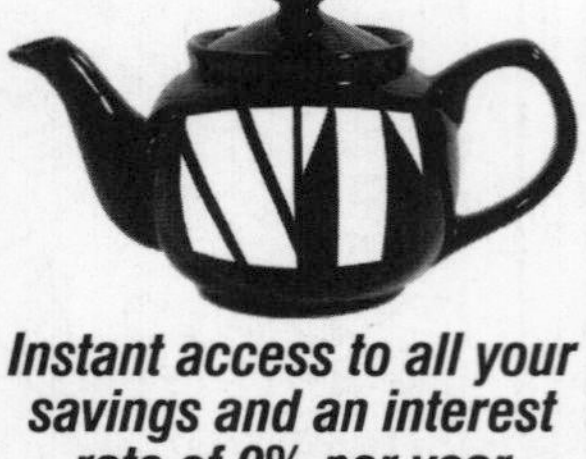

Instant access to all your savings and an interest rate of 0% per year

Are you over 90 and looking for a secure place to keep YOUR money?... Speak to

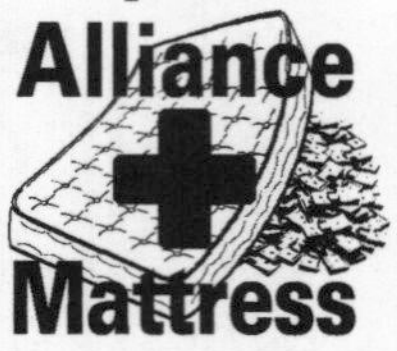

Alliance
Mattress

Your investment may be at risk from a fourteen-year-old ASBO ratboy asking for a drink of water or posing as a gas man.

I HAVE to say that until recently I was all in favour of inheritance tax. However, a few weeks ago, my elderly parents' home was valued at well above the inheritance tax threshold and I am now dead aginst it. Isn't it funny how your views change as you get older?

Chris Manning, e-mail

I RECENTLY read about a study which concluded that the longer you have to travel in an ambulance, the more likely you are to die on route to hospital. I was wondering if anyone could give me the details of who funded the research, as I am on the dole and could do with some easy money.

Nathanial, e-mail

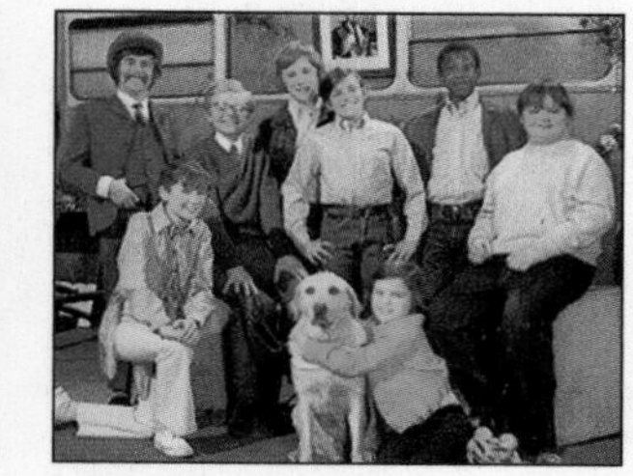

"SEE you next week..." sang the *Double Deckers* at the end of episode 17 of the popular children's TV show, aired on 30th April 1971. Thirty-six years later we are still waiting. First the *Blue Peter* debacle, now this. Are there no lengths to which the BBC will not go to mislead its younger viewers?

Albert Picture, Aberdeen

DURING a recent house hunt, it occurred to me that 'semi-detached' is a very generous term. 'Completely attached to the side of another house' is a much more accurate, although admittedly, less snappy term.

Martin Christines, e-mail

WHY doesn't President Bush pull all US troops out of Iraq and send Sylvester Stallone in with a big jagged knife?

Alan Heath
Da Nang public lavatory

IF ANY of your readers live in London, could they ask Dave out of Chas 'n' Dave to give me my banjo back?

Jack, e-mail

TOP TIPS

RADIO 5's Victoria Derbyshire. Instead of cutting racist callers off half way through their diatribe, simply don't bate them to call your phone-in show in the first place by asking loaded questions like "What would YOU do about the immigrants?"

J Thorn, Hexham

NON SMOKERS. Convince everyone that you are a sixty a day man by smearing the fingers of your right hand with iodine.

S MacRat, e-mail

DOG owners. Next time your mutt bites the postman's arse, make sure you say "well, he's never done that before."

Stu Perry the Postie, Isle of Man

US TROOPS. Catch members of the Taliban by setting large moustraps in the Tora Bora hills and baiting them with a little girl learning to read.

T Wentworth, Rhyll

FELLAS. Avoid having to do a single day's work in your life by simply wooing and marrying a queen.

P Mountbatten, London

HOUSEWIVES. Feel like a Hollywood celebrity by fitting red carpets in every room in your house. A trip to the toilet will feel like attending a film premiere.

T Jenkins, Grange Hill

MAKE people believe you are magic by vigourously shaking a bottle of talcum powder when you exit a room, thus giving the impression of you disappearing in a cloud of smoke.

Chris Lou, Martinsville

AMERICANS. Win the hearts and minds of foreign peoples by acting like every idiosyncracy of their culture is hilarious, like it's a show put on for your benefit.

Ngitibulu Ng, e-mail

DAVINA McCall. Disguise your lack of TV presenting ability by gurning excessively at any nearby camera. Nobody will notice a thing.

Podge, e-mail

CONTACT lens wearers. Keep your eyes snug and warm this winter by adding a few drops of chilli sauce to your cleaning solution.

Garry Kidwell, Stoke

B&Q. Why not replace the ten permanently unmanned checkouts in your stores with more sales shelving, giving your customers a wider range of products they can queue up for half an hour to pay for.

J Talia, North wales

SPOONERISE Rolf Harris's name. Hey Presto! You're saying it in a dog's voice.

Mr C, e-mail

TRAMPS. Avoid being constantly moved on by sleeping outside department stores and telling the police you are simply queuing early for the sales.

J King, Prison

FEEL a bit like God for the day by making some little people out of plasticine, and then judging them harshly.

Hector Plywood, Devizes

ORDINARY people. Make yourselves feel more important by carrying a bugle everywhere you go and sounding it before you enter.

L Luton, Wolverhampton

BRAZILIANS. Set your watches two hours fast. That way you might arrive wherever you are going on time for once.

C Penge, e-mail

ABSENT minded people. Don't waste money on post-it notes. Simply find an elephant that lives locally and tell them whatever it is you need remembering.

E Mail, Christinamartin

BUSINESSMEN. Fill those awkward silences in the lift by telling people made-up stories about your adventures as a sailor.

C Martin, e-mail

DRIVERS. Save money by putting much larger wheels on the back of your car. That way you will always be going downhill, thereby saving on fuel.

Daren Percy, Leigh

CLIMATE change activists. Feel less guilty about travelling by plane by breathing more shallowly whilst on holiday.

The Beed, Dudley

WHY is it that anti-pirating adverts are always on the legal DVDs? It's preaching to the converted. Surely it would be more sensible to put them on the pirate copies, instead of forcing us mugs who buy the licenced ones to sit through them.

Tugger, e-mail

IT'S ALL very well these Christians saying "Get thee behind me, Satan." If it were me, I'd want the mischievous little scamp in front of me where I could keep an eye on him.

Peter Wilson, Warwickshire

THE recent brush fires in Greece were terrible, and the loss of life tragic. But I had to laugh when I saw some Greek monks whose monastery was threatened start trying to quell the flames by waving pictures of Jesus at them. Hilarious.

T Arnold, London

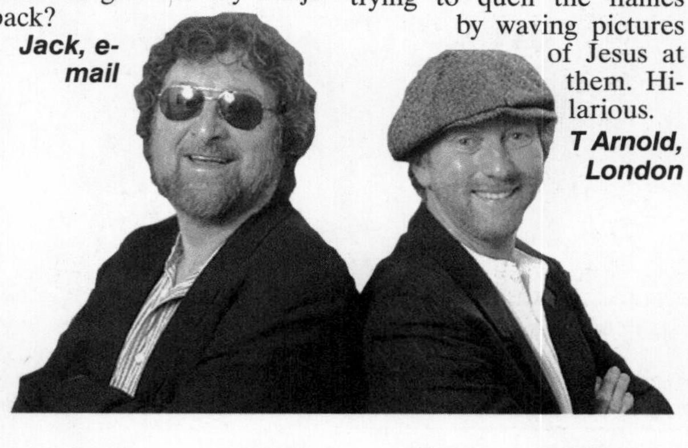

Harris for a Day

Ever wondered what it would be like to be a Harris for a day? We asked celebrities which famous Harris they would be and what they would do if they could be a Harris for a day.

Brad Pitt, *Hollywood actor*

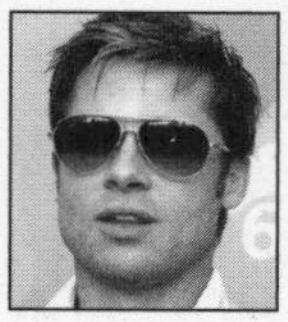

"I'd be **KEITH HARRIS**, the ventriloquist with Orville the Duck and that monkey he did with the same voice. When I was little, I always wanted to be a ventriloquist, but I could never do the b's or the m's. So if I was Keith Harris for the day, I'd go through his telephone book, get Ray Allan out of Ray Allan and Lord Charles's number, ring him up and ask him how to do it."

Tony Blair, *Former Prime Minister*

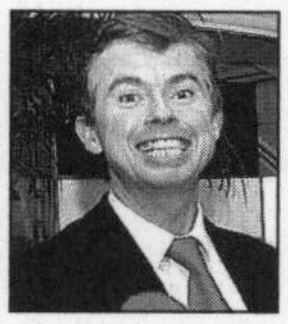

"I would be People's Artist **ROLF HARRIS**. As special envoy to the Middle east, I have to attend lots of dull meetings about relationships between Arabs and Jews. If I could stand up in the middle of one of these meetings and do a large abstract painting of some Aborigines by a watering hole, or some kangaroos and a wombat, then they might put aside their differences for a while and become united in the love of art."

Buster Bloodvessel, *Bad Manners frontman*

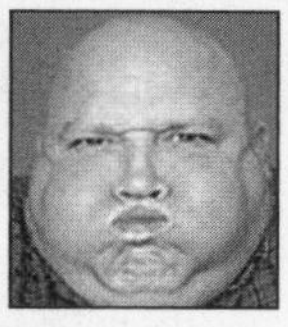

"I'd be **ANITA HARRIS**. I always thought she was really sexy, especially in *Carry On Nurse*, but you never got to see her with her kit off. So if I was her for the day, I run home and strip off in front of the mirror to see what she looked like in the rik. I might even have a crafty little feel of her knockers, too."

Oliver James, *TV Psychiatrist*

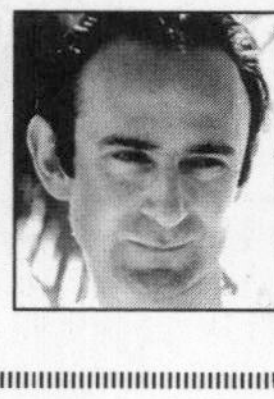

"I'd like to be psychologist **JUDITH RICH HARRIS**. In her 1988 book *The Nurture Assumption*, she challenges the commonly held belief that the personality of the adult is determined chiefly by the way they were raised by their parents. This controversial viewpoint of hers has always fascinated me. I would like to spend a day as her so I could reach into her psyche to see if any event or events in her own childhood had formulated or influenced this belief. Then I'd strip off in front of a mirror to see what her tits looked like.

BLACK BAG • THE FAITHFUL • BORDER BINLINER

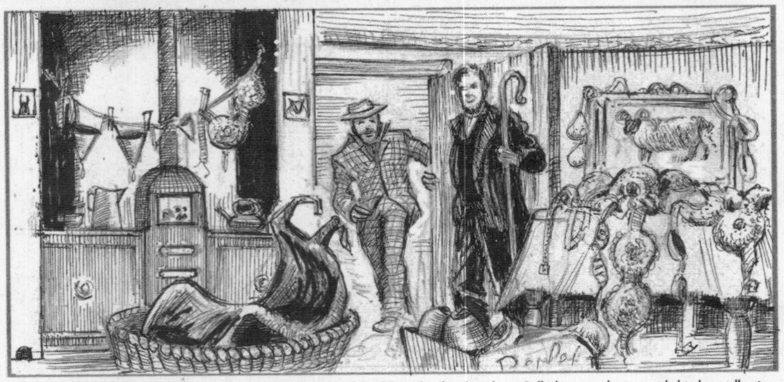

AFTER a busy day tending his sheep on the moors around Peebles, shepherd Andrew Selkirk was relaxing with his bra collection when a stranger knocked at the door of his remote croft. "I wonder can you help me?" he said. "I'm the manager of popstars Brotherhood of Man. We were on our way to a gig in Auchtermuchty when we ran out of petrol." Always willing to help a stranger for a few bawbees, Selkirk picked up his crook and shouted for his faithful border binliner, Black Bag. "Come on, laddie," he cried. "Yon sassenach needs oor help."

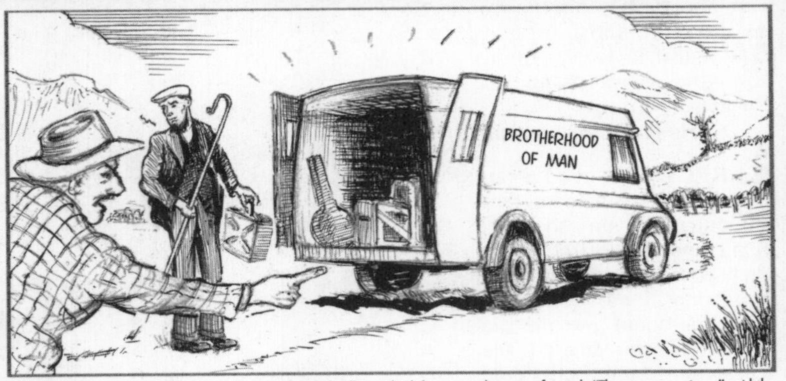
BROTHERHOOD OF MAN

AS DUSK began to fall, Selkirk, Bag and the stranger finally reached the van with a can of petrol. "There ye go, mister," said the kindly shepherd. "If ye gie me a hundred poonds for yon gallon, me an' Baggie will be on oor way." But the stranger was looking at his van with an expression of horror on his face. "My Brotherhood of Man!" he cried. "They've got out!" And it was true. The back door of the van was wide open, and there was no sign of the 1976 Eurovision wining fourpiece! "We hae tae find 'em afore the mists come doon," said Selkirk gravely.

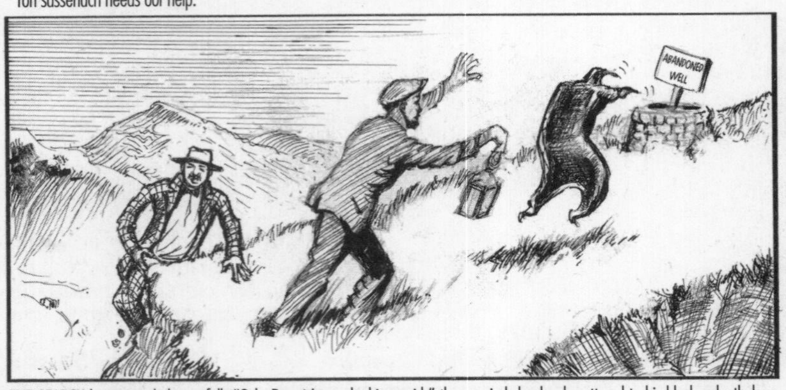
ABANDONED WELL

THE SEARCH began as darkness fell. "Och, Bag, it's nae looking guid," the worried shepherd muttered to his black polyethylene companion. "The moors at nicht are nae place for a wee pop band. And if we dinnae find 'em alive afore dawn, we willnae get oor hundred poondies." But suddenly, Black Bag flew off as fast as the highland breeze could carry him. His attention had been caught by a noise coming from an old abandoned well. "Whit is it, boy?" said Selkirk. "Is somebody doon yon well?"

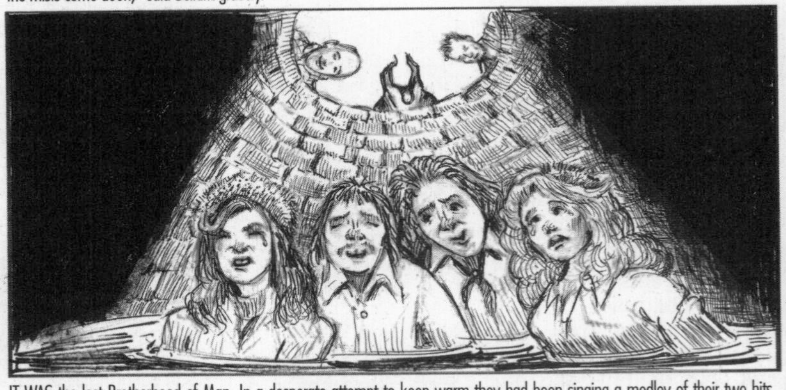

IT WAS the lost Brotherhood of Man. In a desperate attempt to keep warm they had been singing a medley of their two hits. Thanks to his keen sense of hearing, the clever binliner had heard the Wakefield-based combo from the bottom of the shaft. "It's them," cried their manager. "Thank goodness they are alive." But the shepherd scratched his chin. "Och! Dinnae get yer hopes up two' high, mister," he said. "Yon well must be fafty footies deep. I dinnae hae a rope lang enough tae lift yon popsters oot!"

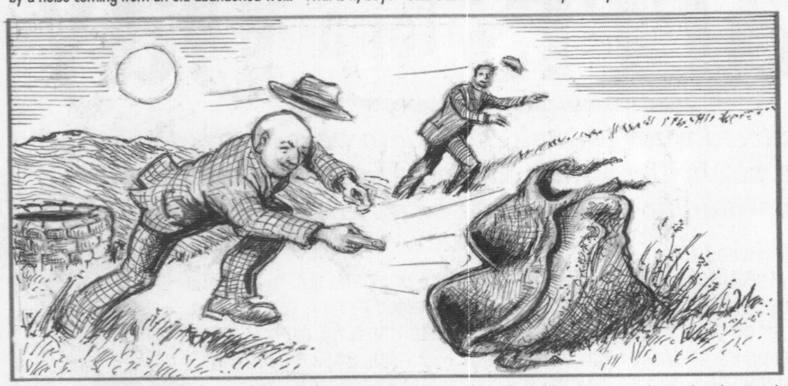

BUT Black Bag had an idea. A sudden gust twisted the quick thinking refuse sack and pinned him against a rock. "Look at that," said The Brotherhood of Man's manager. "Your binbag looks just like a woman's bra." Selkirk turned to look. "Och, aye! So he does. I hae a notion he's tryin' tae tell me something," said the shepherd. "Wait a minute, that's it! Ma bras! he want's me tae make a muckle lang rope oot o' ma collection o' brassieres." And with that, the crofter raced off across the fells towards his cottage.

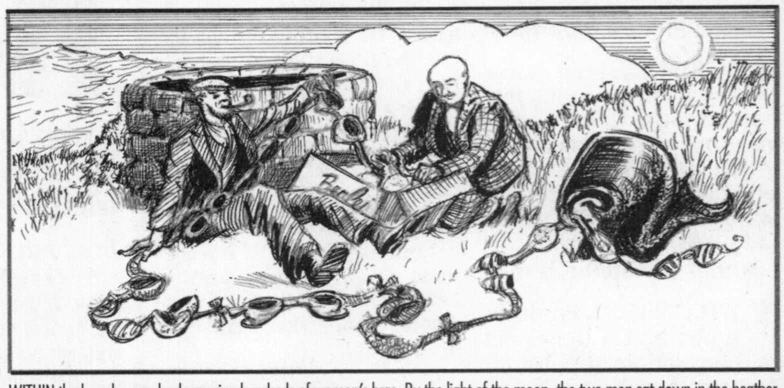

WITHIN the hour he was back carrying hundreds of women's bras. By the light of the moon, the two men sat down in the heather and set to work tying them together. "One thing is puzzling me, Mr Selkirk," said the manager. "What does a shepherd like yourself collect ladies' bras for?" Selkirk smiled to himself and puffed on his pipe. "Ach! It gets affy lonely aboot these parts, laddie, and a man has tae hae somethin' tae dae wae his handies," he chuckled. In next to no time, the long bra rope was finished.

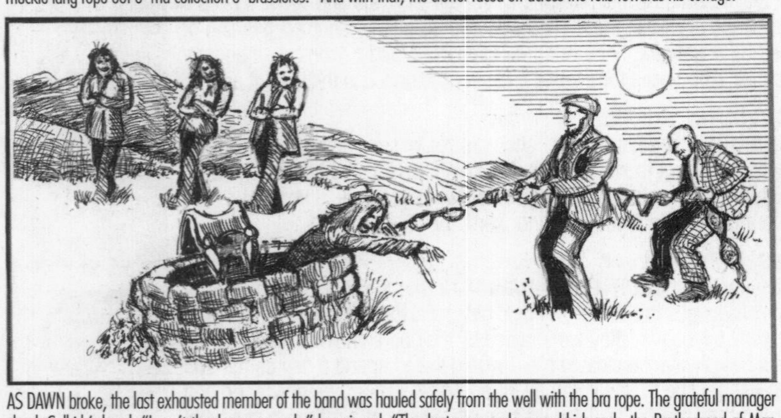

AS DAWN broke, the last exhausted member of the band was hauled safely from the well with the bra rope. The grateful manager shook Selkirk's hand. "I can't thank you enough," he grinned. "Thanks to you and your rubbish sack, the Brotherhood of Man won't miss their gig at the Peebles Agricultural Show." The shepherd's eyes lit up. "The Peebles Agricultural Show!?" he said. "Why, me and Black Bag are goin' there oor'sels. I dinnae suppose we could cadge a wee liftee in yer van, could we, the noo?"

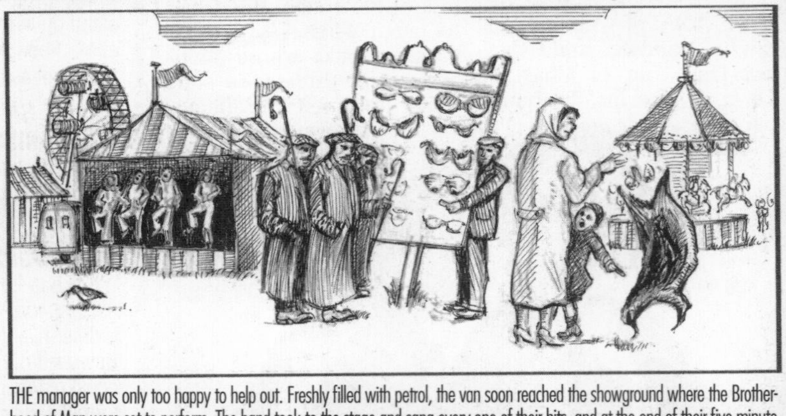

THE manager was only too happy to help out. Freshly filled with petrol, the van soon reached the showground where the Brotherhood of Man were set to perform. The band took to the stage and sang every one of their hits, and at the end of their five minute set, everyone agreed that it was one of the best Agricultural Shows the people of Peebles had seen for a good couple of years. Especially Black Bag, who was treated to a constant stream of half eaten burgers and hot dog sausages from generous passers by!

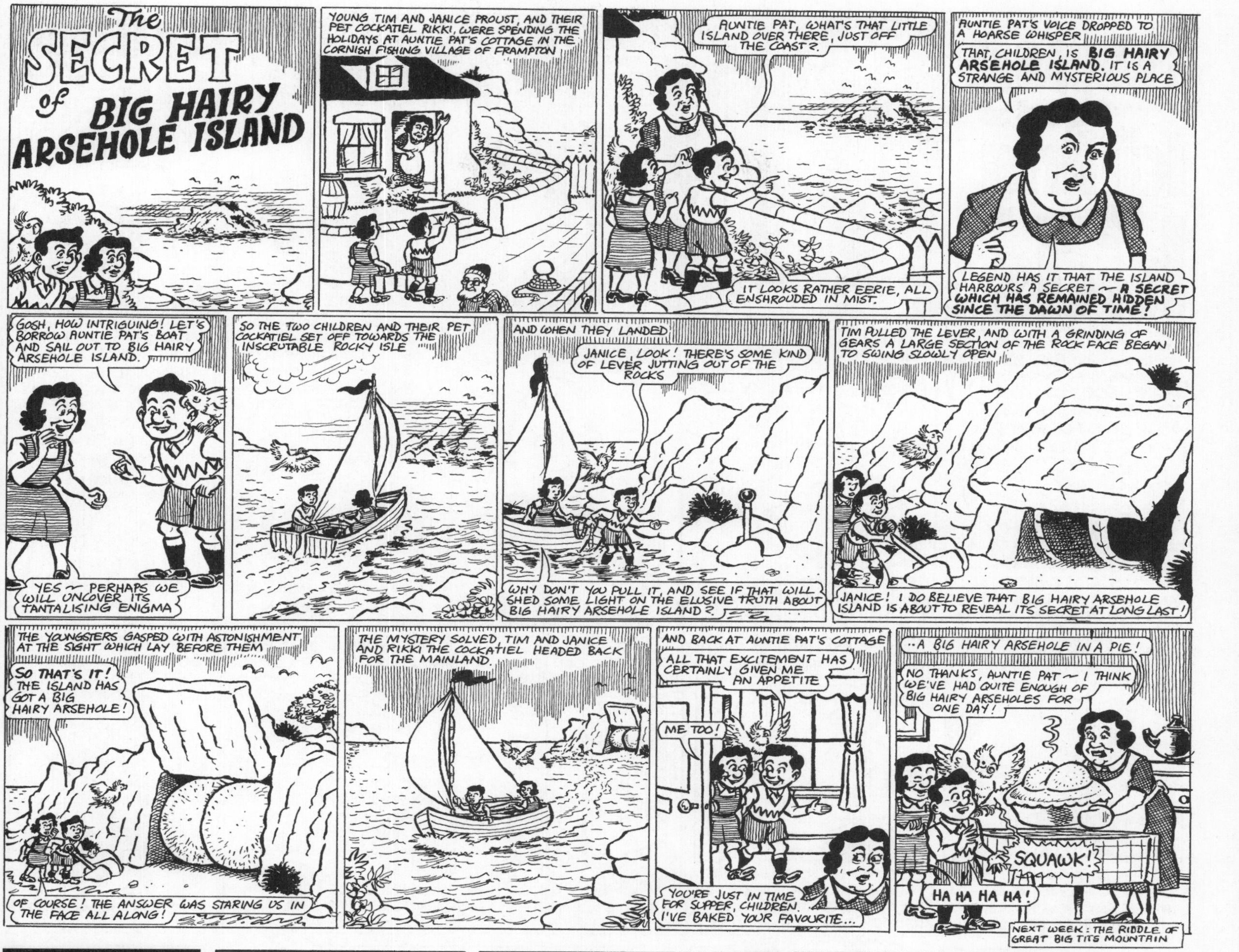
The SECRET of BIG HAIRY ARSEHOLE ISLAND
YOUNG TIM AND JANICE PROUST, AND THEIR PET COCKATIEL RIKKI, WERE SPENDING THE HOLIDAYS AT AUNTIE PAT'S COTTAGE IN THE CORNISH FISHING VILLAGE OF FRAMPTON
AUNTIE PAT, WHAT'S THAT LITTLE ISLAND OVER THERE, JUST OFF THE COAST?
IT LOOKS RATHER EERIE, ALL ENSHROUDED IN MIST.
AUNTIE PAT'S VOICE DROPPED TO A HOARSE WHISPER
THAT, CHILDREN, IS BIG HAIRY ARSEHOLE ISLAND. IT IS A STRANGE AND MYSTERIOUS PLACE
LEGEND HAS IT THAT THE ISLAND HARBOURS A SECRET ~ A SECRET WHICH HAS REMAINED HIDDEN SINCE THE DAWN OF TIME!
GOSH, HOW INTRIGUING! LET'S BORROW AUNTIE PAT'S BOAT AND SAIL OUT TO BIG HAIRY ARSEHOLE ISLAND.
YES ~ PERHAPS WE WILL UNCOVER ITS TANTALISING ENIGMA
SO THE TWO CHILDREN AND THEIR PET COCKATIEL SET OFF TOWARDS THE INSCRUTABLE ROCKY ISLE
AND WHEN THEY LANDED
JANICE, LOOK! THERE'S SOME KIND OF LEVER JUTTING OUT OF THE ROCKS
WHY DON'T YOU PULL IT, AND SEE IF THAT WILL SHED SOME LIGHT ON THE ELUSIVE TRUTH ABOUT BIG HAIRY ARSEHOLE ISLAND?
TIM PULLED THE LEVER, AND WITH A GRINDING OF GEARS A LARGE SECTION OF THE ROCK FACE BEGAN TO SWING SLOWLY OPEN
JANICE! I DO BELIEVE THAT BIG HAIRY ARSEHOLE ISLAND IS ABOUT TO REVEAL ITS SECRET AT LONG LAST!
THE YOUNGSTERS GASPED WITH ASTONISHMENT AT THE SIGHT WHICH LAY BEFORE THEM
SO THAT'S IT! THE ISLAND HAS GOT A BIG HAIRY ARSEHOLE!
OF COURSE! THE ANSWER WAS STARING US IN THE FACE ALL ALONG!
THE MYSTERY SOLVED, TIM AND JANICE AND RIKKI THE COCKATIEL HEADED BACK FOR THE MAINLAND.
AND BACK AT AUNTIE PAT'S COTTAGE
ALL THAT EXCITEMENT HAS CERTAINLY GIVEN ME AN APPETITE
ME TOO!
YOU'RE JUST IN TIME FOR SUPPER, CHILDREN. I'VE BAKED YOUR FAVOURITE...
..A BIG HAIRY ARSEHOLE IN A PIE!
NO THANKS, AUNTIE PAT ~ I THINK WE'VE HAD QUITE ENOUGH OF BIG HAIRY ARSEHOLES FOR ONE DAY!
SQUAWK!
HA HA HA HA!
NEXT WEEK: THE RIDDLE OF GREAT BIG TITS MOUNTAIN

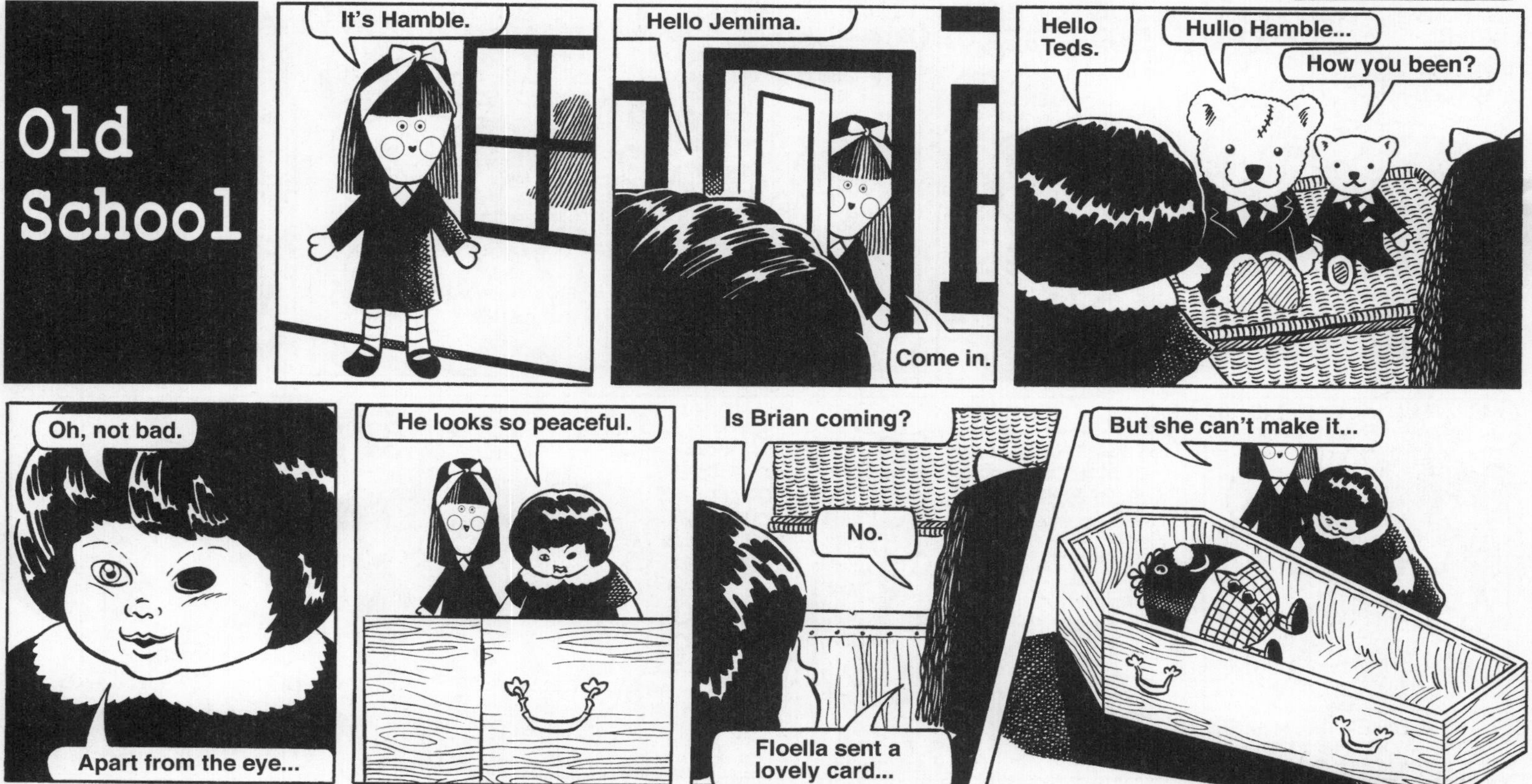
Old School
It's Hamble.
Hello Jemima.
Come in.
Hello Teds.
Hullo Hamble...
How you been?
Oh, not bad.
Apart from the eye...
He looks so peaceful.
Is Brian coming?
No.
Floella sent a lovely card...
But she can't make it...

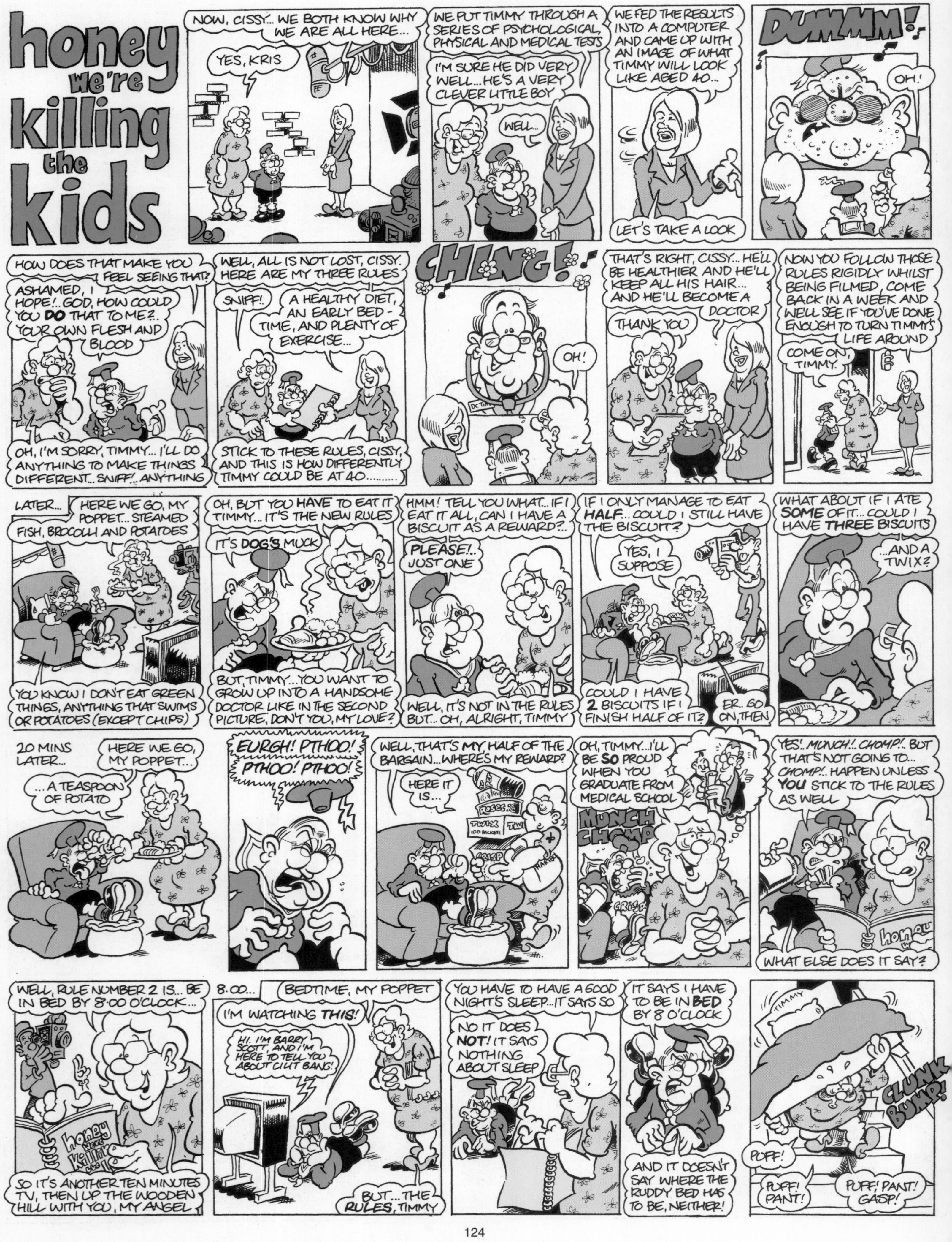
honey we're killing the kids
NOW, CISSY... WE BOTH KNOW WHY WE ARE ALL HERE...
YES, KRIS
WE PUT TIMMY THROUGH A SERIES OF PSYCHOLOGICAL, PHYSICAL AND MEDICAL TESTS
I'M SURE HE DID VERY WELL... HE'S A VERY CLEVER LITTLE BOY
WELL...
WE FED THE RESULTS INTO A COMPUTER AND CAME UP WITH AN IMAGE OF WHAT TIMMY WILL LOOK LIKE AGED 40...
LET'S TAKE A LOOK
DUMMM!
OH!
HOW DOES THAT MAKE YOU FEEL SEEING THAT?
ASHAMED, I HOPE!.. GOD, HOW COULD YOU DO THAT TO ME?.. YOUR OWN FLESH AND BLOOD
OH, I'M SORRY, TIMMY... I'LL DO ANYTHING TO MAKE THINGS DIFFERENT... SNIFF!.. ANYTHING
WELL, ALL IS NOT LOST, CISSY. HERE ARE MY THREE RULES
SNIFF!
A HEALTHY DIET, AN EARLY BED-TIME, AND PLENTY OF EXERCISE...
STICK TO THESE RULES, CISSY, AND THIS IS HOW DIFFERENTLY TIMMY COULD BE AT 40..........
CHING!
OH!
THAT'S RIGHT, CISSY... HE'LL BE HEALTHIER AND HE'LL KEEP ALL HIS HAIR... AND HE'LL BECOME A DOCTOR
THANK YOU
NOW YOU FOLLOW THOSE RULES RIGIDLY WHILST BEING FILMED, COME BACK IN A WEEK AND WE'LL SEE IF YOU'VE DONE ENOUGH TO TURN TIMMY'S LIFE AROUND
COME ON, TIMMY.
LATER...
HERE WE GO, MY POPPET... STEAMED FISH, BROCOLLI AND POTATOES
YOU KNOW I DON'T EAT GREEN THINGS, ANYTHING THAT SWIMS OR POTATOES (EXCEPT CHIPS)
OH, BUT YOU HAVE TO EAT IT TIMMY... IT'S THE NEW RULES
IT'S DOG'S MUCK
BUT, TIMMY... YOU WANT TO GROW UP INTO A HANDSOME DOCTOR LIKE IN THE SECOND PICTURE, DON'T YOU, MY LOVE?
HMM! TELL YOU WHAT... IF I EAT IT ALL, CAN I HAVE A BISCUIT AS A REWARD?...
PLEASE!.. JUST ONE
WELL, IT'S NOT IN THE RULES BUT... OH, ALRIGHT, TIMMY
IF I ONLY MANAGE TO EAT HALF... COULD I STILL HAVE THE BISCUIT?
YES, I SUPPOSE
COULD I HAVE 2 BISCUITS IF I FINISH HALF OF IT?
ER.. GO ON, THEN
WHAT ABOUT IF I ATE SOME OF IT... COULD I HAVE THREE BISCUITS
...AND A TWIX?
20 MINS LATER...
HERE WE GO, MY POPPET...
...A TEASPOON OF POTATO
EURGH! PTHOO! PTHOO! PTHOO!
WELL, THAT'S MY HALF OF THE BARGAIN... WHERE'S MY REWARD?
HERE IT IS...
ROSES
TWIX
CRISP
OH, TIMMY... I'LL BE SO PROUD WHEN YOU GRADUATE FROM MEDICAL SCHOOL
MUNCH CHOMP
YES!.. MUNCH!.. CHOMP!.. BUT THAT'S NOT GOING TO... CHOMP!.. HAPPEN UNLESS YOU STICK TO THE RULES AS WELL
WHAT ELSE DOES IT SAY?
WELL, RULE NUMBER 2 IS... BE IN BED BY 8:00 O'CLOCK...
SO IT'S ANOTHER TEN MINUTES TV, THEN UP THE WOODEN HILL WITH YOU, MY ANGEL
8.00...
BEDTIME, MY POPPET
I'M WATCHING THIS!
HI. I'M BARRY SCOTT, AND I'M HERE TO TELL YOU ABOUT CILIT BANG!
BUT... THE RULES, TIMMY
YOU HAVE TO HAVE A GOOD NIGHT'S SLEEP... IT SAYS SO
NO IT DOES NOT! IT SAYS NOTHING ABOUT SLEEP
IT SAYS I HAVE TO BE IN BED BY 8 O'CLOCK
AND IT DOESN'T SAY WHERE THE RUDDY BED HAS TO BE, NEITHER!
TIMMY
CLUNK BUMP!
POFF!
POFF! PANT!
POFF! PANT! GASP!

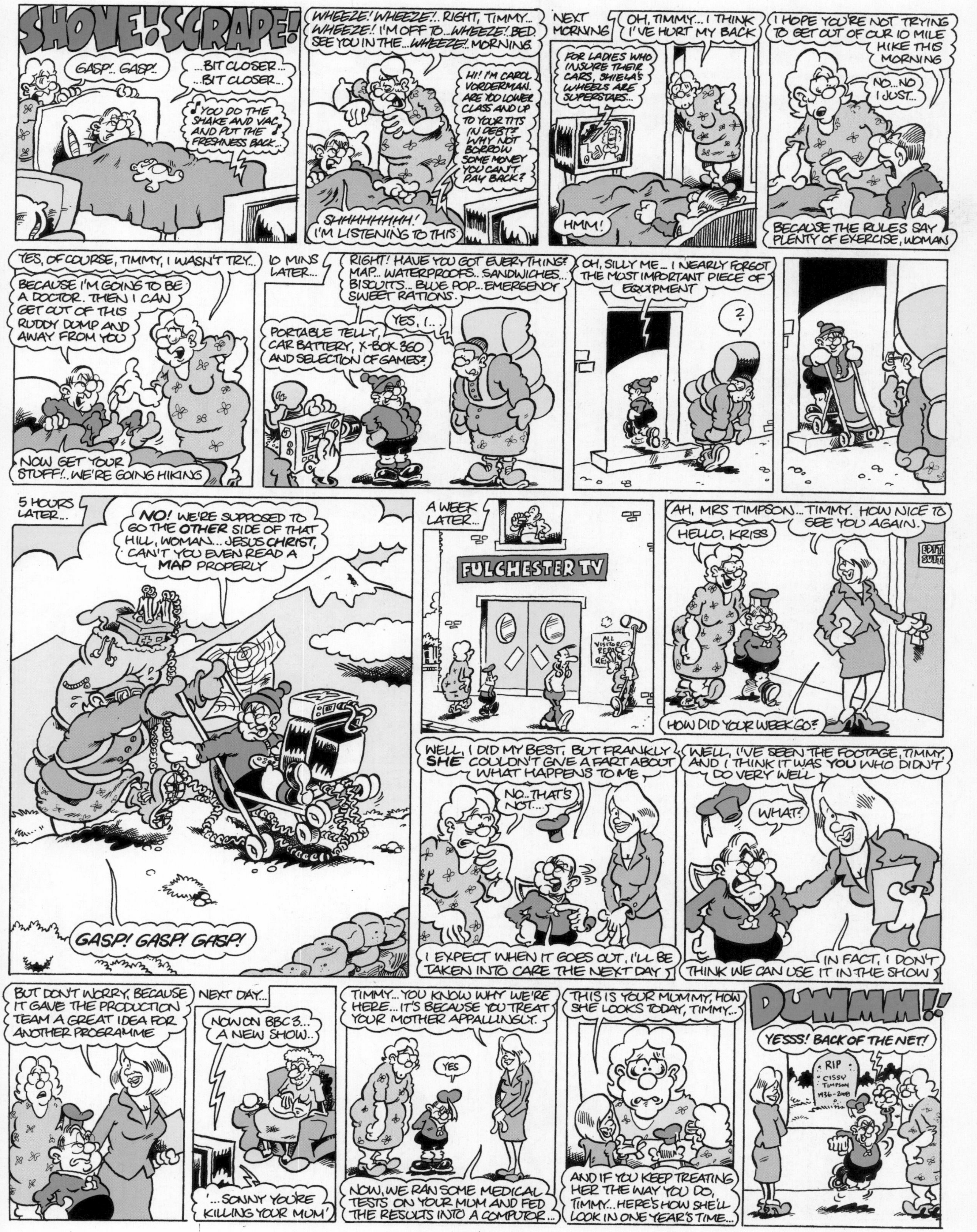
SHOVE! SCRAPE!
GASP!.. GASP!
...BIT CLOSER... ...BIT CLOSER...
YOU DO THE SHAKE AND VAC AND PUT THE FRESHNESS BACK...
WHEEZE! WHEEZE!.. RIGHT, TIMMY... WHEEZE! I'M OFF TO... WHEEZE! BED. SEE YOU IN THE... WHEEZE!.. MORNING.
HI! I'M CAROL VORDERMAN. ARE YOU LOWER CLASS AND UP TO YOUR TITS IN DEBT? WHY NOT BORROW SOME MONEY YOU CAN'T PAY BACK?
SHHHHHHHH! I'M LISTENING TO THIS
NEXT MORNING
OH, TIMMY... I THINK I'VE HURT MY BACK
FOR LADIES WHO INSURE THEIR CARS, SHIELA'S WHEELS ARE SUPERSTARS...
HMM!
I HOPE YOU'RE NOT TRYING TO GET OUT OF OUR 10 MILE HIKE THIS MORNING
NO... NO I JUST...
BECAUSE THE RULES SAY PLENTY OF EXERCISE, WOMAN
YES, OF COURSE, TIMMY, I WASN'T TRY...
BECAUSE I'M GOING TO BE A DOCTOR. THEN I CAN GET OUT OF THIS RUDDY DUMP AND AWAY FROM YOU
NOW GET YOUR STUFF!.. WE'RE GOING HIKING
10 MINS LATER...
RIGHT! HAVE YOU GOT EVERYTHING? MAP... WATERPROOFS... SANDWICHES... BISCUITS... BLUE POP... EMERGENCY SWEET RATIONS.
YES, I...
PORTABLE TELLY, CAR BATTERY, X-BOX 360 AND SELECTION OF GAMES?
OH, SILLY ME... I NEARLY FORGOT THE MOST IMPORTANT PIECE OF EQUIPMENT
?
5 HOURS LATER...
NO! WE'RE SUPPOSED TO GO THE OTHER SIDE OF THAT HILL, WOMAN... JESUS CHRIST, CAN'T YOU EVEN READ A MAP PROPERLY
GASP! GASP! GASP!
A WEEK LATER...
FULCHESTER TV
AH, MRS TIMPSON... TIMMY. HOW NICE TO SEE YOU AGAIN.
HELLO, KRISS
HOW DID YOUR WEEK GO?
WELL, I DID MY BEST, BUT FRANKLY SHE COULDN'T GIVE A FART ABOUT WHAT HAPPENS TO ME
NO.. THAT'S NOT...
I EXPECT WHEN IT GOES OUT, I'LL BE TAKEN INTO CARE THE NEXT DAY
WELL, I'VE SEEN THE FOOTAGE, TIMMY, AND I THINK IT WAS YOU WHO DIDN'T DO VERY WELL
WHAT?
IN FACT, I DON'T THINK WE CAN USE IT IN THE SHOW
BUT DON'T WORRY, BECAUSE IT GAVE THE PRODUCTION TEAM A GREAT IDEA FOR ANOTHER PROGRAMME
NEXT DAY...
NOW ON BBC 3... A NEW SHOW...
'...SONNY YOU'RE KILLING YOUR MUM'
TIMMY... YOU KNOW WHY WE'RE HERE... IT'S BECAUSE YOU TREAT YOUR MOTHER APPALLINGLY.
YES
NOW, WE RAN SOME MEDICAL TESTS ON YOUR MUM AND FED THE RESULTS INTO A COMPUTOR...
THIS IS YOUR MUMMY, HOW SHE LOOKS TODAY, TIMMY...
AND IF YOU KEEP TREATING HER THE WAY YOU DO, TIMMY... HERE'S HOW SHE'LL LOOK IN ONE YEAR'S TIME...
DUMMM!!
YESSS! BACK OF THE NET!
RIP CISSY TIMPSON 1936-2008

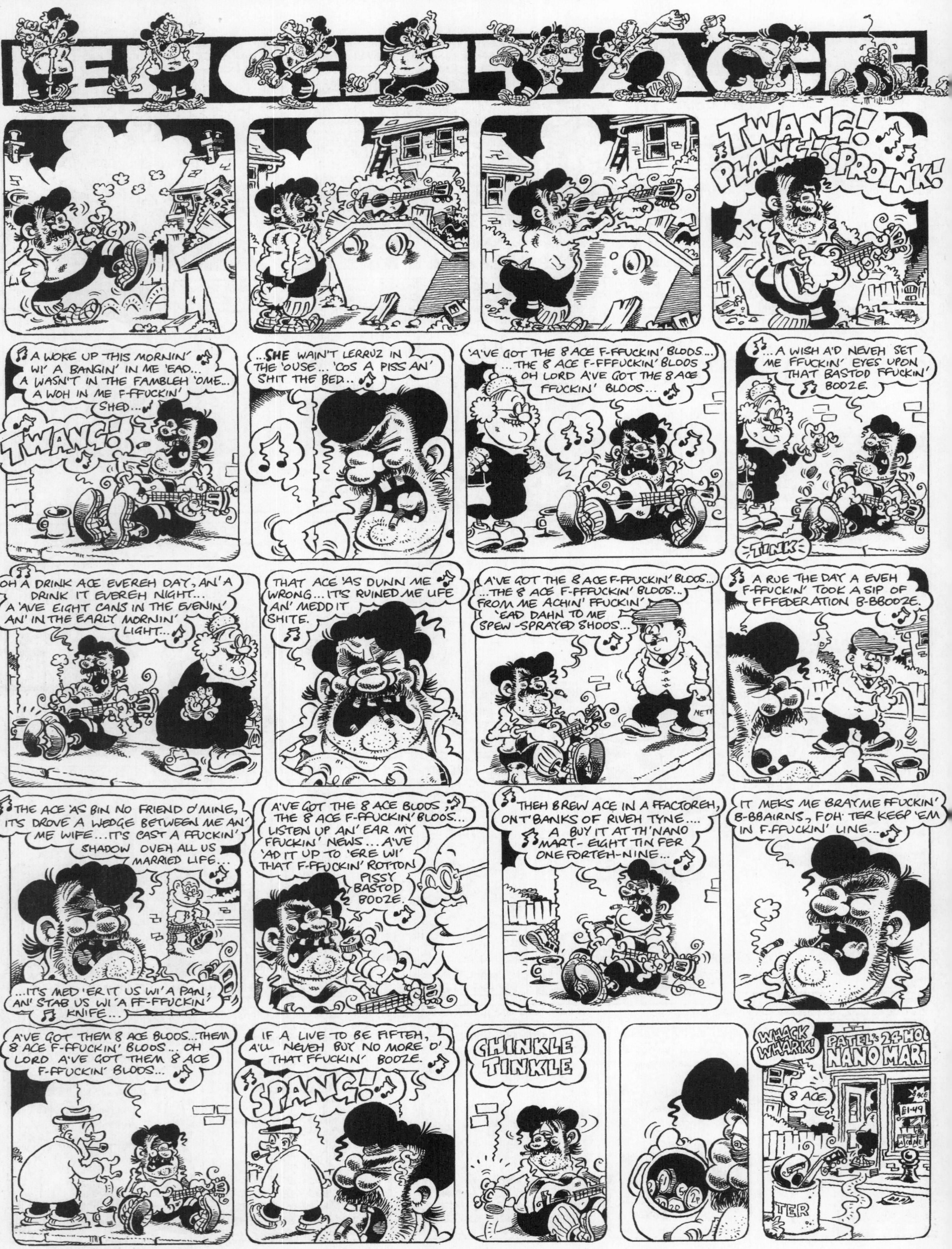

TWANG! PLANG! SPROINK!
A WOKE UP THIS MORNIN' WI' A BANGIN' IN ME 'EAD... A WASN'T IN THE FAMBLEH 'OME... A WOH IN ME F-FFUCKIN' SHED...
TWANG!
...SHE WAIN'T LERRUZ IN THE 'OUSE... 'COS A PISS AN' SHIT THE BED...
'A'VE GOT THE 8 ACE F-FFUCKIN' BLOOS... ...THE 8 ACE F-FFFUCKIN' BLOOS OH LORD A'VE GOT THE 8 ACE FFUCKIN' BLOOS...
...A WISH A'D NEVEH SET ME FFUCKIN' EYES UPON THAT BASTOD FFUCKIN' BOOZE.
TINK
OH A DRINK ACE EVEREH DAY, AN' A DRINK IT EVEREH NIGHT... A 'AVE EIGHT CANS IN THE EVENIN' AN' IN THE EARLY MORNIN' LIGHT...
THAT ACE 'AS DUNN ME WRONG... IT'S RUINED ME LIFE AN' MEDD IT SHITE.
A'VE GOT THE 8 ACE F-FFUCKIN' BLOOS... ...THE 8 ACE F-FFUCKIN' BLOOS... FROM ME ACHIN' FFUCKIN' 'EAD DAHN TO ME SPEW-SPRAYED SHOOS...
A RUE THE DAY A EVEH F-FFUCKIN' TOOK A SIP OF FFFEDERATION B-BBOOZE.
THE ACE 'AS BIN NO FRIEND O'MINE, IT'S DROVE A WEDGE BETWEEN ME AN' ME WIFE... IT'S CAST A FFUCKIN' SHADOW OVEH ALL US MARRIED LIFE...
...IT'S MED 'ER IT US WI' A PAN, AN' STAB US WI' A FF-FFUCKIN' KNIFE...
A'VE GOT THE 8 ACE BLOOS, THE 8 ACE F-FFUCKIN' BLOOS... LISTEN UP AN' 'EAR MY FFUCKIN' NEWS... A'VE 'AD IT UP TO 'ERE WI' THAT F-FFUCKIN' ROTTON PISSY BASTOD BOOZE.
THEH BREW ACE IN A FFACTOREH, ON T'BANKS OF RIVEH TYNE.... A BUY IT AT TH' NANO MART- EIGHT TIN FER ONE FORTEH-NINE...
IT MEKS ME BRAY ME FFUCKIN' B-BBAIRNS, FOH TER KEEP 'EM IN F-FFUCKIN' LINE...
A'VE GOT THEM 8 ACE BLOOS... THEM 8 ACE F-FFUCKIN' BLOOS... OH LORD A'VE GOT THEM 8 ACE F-FFUCKIN' BLOOS...
IF A LIVE TO BE FIFTEH, A'LL NEVEH BUY NO MORE 'O' THAT FFUCKIN' BOOZE.
SPANG!
CHINKLE TINKLE
WHACK WHARK!
PATEL'S 24 HOU
NANO MART
8 ACE.
£1.49
TER

Henry Kissinger's
SLIPPER TIME

Britain's Third Liveliest Letters Page about Slippers

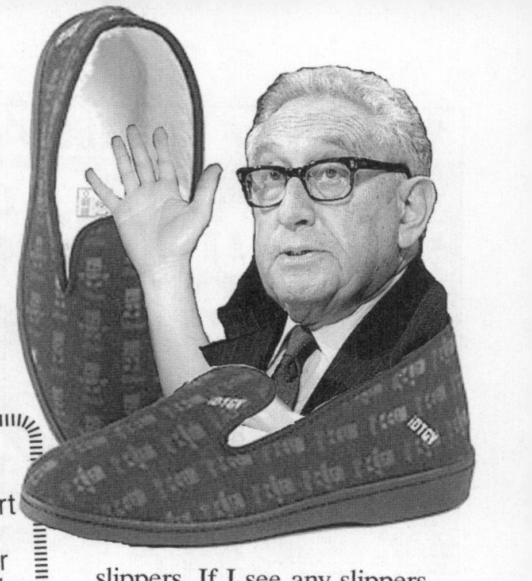

"Hi! Henry Kissinger here. Now when I'm not travelling the world trying to sort out people's problems, I like nothing more than to sit at home wearing my slippers. And so do you, if my postbag is anything to go by. So if you have any amusing stories about this most comfy of footwear, why not 'slippers' a line."

★★★★★★★★★★★★★★★★★★★★★★★★★

● **THE OTHER** day I overslept and I had to rush to get to work. When I got there, I realised I had dashed out of the house wearing my slippers! I was so embarrassed. Then I remembered that I work as a professional slipper model in a catalogue studio, and so none of my colleagues noticed.

Boyd Coddington
Corby

● **PEOPLE** say that they like nothing better than to put on their slippers of an evening and relax. That's all very well for some, but I live in Thailand, and have to check my slippers for scorpions before I put them on. Hardly a relaxing experience, I can tell you.

Ying Tong Song
Bangkok

SLIPPER FACT

If all the slippers given as Christmas presents in the UK each year were combined, they would make a piece of brown and beige checky cloth big enough to cover an area of rain forest as big as Belgium... *the size of Wales!*

SLIPPER FACT

Slippers were named after their inventor, Ernest Wellesley, Earl of Slipper and the brother of Arthur Wellesley, the 1st Duke of Wellington. Unlike his brother, Ernest never took part in any battles, preferring instead to sit at home and watch TV. But he found sitting in the house in leather shoes rather uncomfortable, and one day he asked his butler to tear off the stiff leather sole and replace it with a piece of rubber cut from one of his brother's boots. Thus, the slipper was born.

● **I ONCE** found a scorpion in my slippers. However, I wasn't surprised, as I am the tour manager of *the Scorpions*, and their lead singer Michael Schenker is always borrowing them to relax in after gigs.

Hans Schittlegruber, Berlin

● **I WROTE** in my will that I wanted to be buried in my favourite slippers so that I would be comfy in the afterlife. Image how annoyed I was when I died and got to heaven, to find that my wife had handed the undertaker my second-best slippers by mistake. I am now faced with the prospect of spending the whole of eternity in a pair of slippers I didn't want. If my widow Mabel is reading this, it is the brown ones that I wanted, and could you bring them with you when you die?

The late Hector Pilbeam
Doncaster

● **IN THE HIT TV** show The A-Team, my character BA Baracas was well known for his fear of flying. But in real life, I actually have a phobia of slippers. If I see any slippers, or even a picture of them, I break out into a cold sweat and soil my underpants. As as result, when relaxing at home I have to wear a pair of *Totes Toasties*, those thick socks with moulded grips on the sole.

Mr T, Hollywood

● **I LOVE** slippers. I've got forty pairs at least. In fact I love them so much that my wife once joked that I should change my name to Arthur Slippers. How we laughed when I reminded her that I didn't need to, as that was my name already.

Arthur Slippers, Croydon

Henry's HUNT *the* SLIPPER

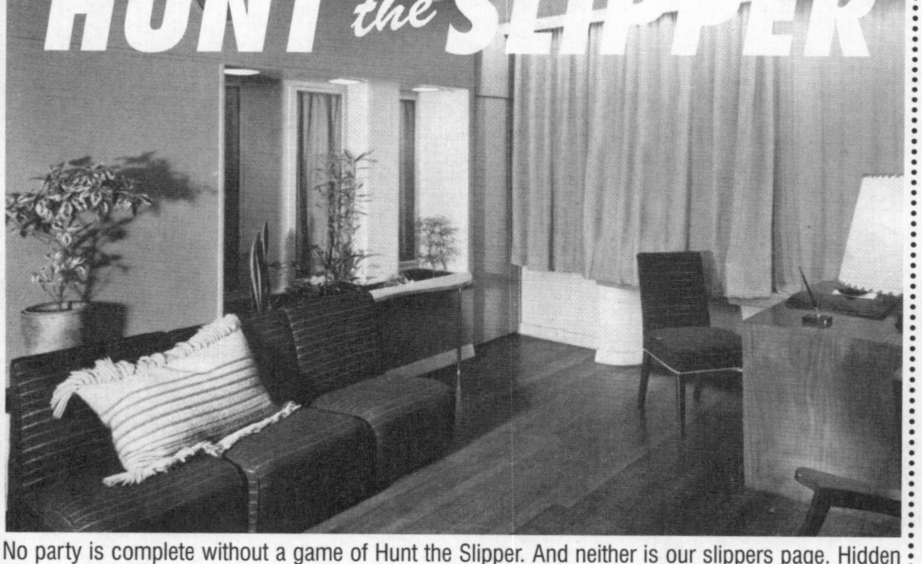

No party is complete without a game of Hunt the Slipper. And neither is our slippers page. Hidden somewhere in this front room is a slipper. All **YOU** have to do is find it. Simply write to us and tell us where you think the slipper is and we'll write back to you and tell you how hot or cold you are. Write in with another guess and we'll inform you by return of post if you are getting warmer or colder. The winner is the first person to correctly identify the hiding place of the slipper.

Last week's winner: Mr Albert Chalfont from Carlisle, who found the slipper behind the left hand cushion on the settee. A lovely pair of slippers are on their way to you, Mr Chalfont.

I think the slipper is under/behind/in/on top of (delete as appropriate) the...........................
Name...Address...
...Post Code.................................

For Official use only. You are: ☐ freezing ☐ cold ☐ cool ☐ warm ☐ hot ☐ boiling

Mark Commode's Movie *per* Slip-Ups

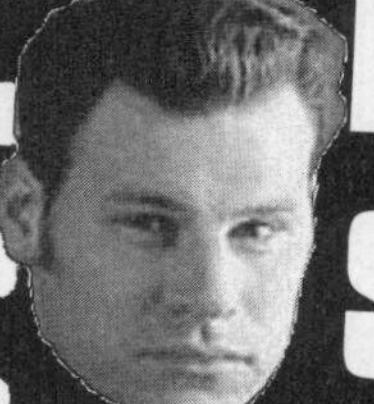

*In **1,000,000 BC**, Raquel Welch is attacked by a 500-foot long Brontosaurus. As she runs into a cave to escape, she is clearly seen wearing sabre-toothed tiger skin slippers. Strange, because slippers weren't invented until 1732, some 1,001,732 years after the film was set!*

***Citizen Kane** is hailed as the best film ever made, but even the great Orson Welles wasn't immune from slipper-ups. In the final scene where he is lying on his deathbed, the underneath of his character John Foster Kane's slippers are visible and the size, 10, can clearly be read. In real life, however, the actor Wells took a 9 1/2!*

*In the Original 1935 **King Kong**, two minutes of expensive stop frame animation had been filmed before technicians noticed that the model gorilla was wearing slippers. Too expensive to re-shoot, the footage was used. Eagle-eyed watchers will notice that when the ape begins to climb the Empire State Building he is wearing slippers, but when he gets to the top, they are gone.*

*In **Back To The Future III**, Marty McFly is seen wearing a pair of 1940s slippers. However, the film was set in 1955, 15 years after the slippers were manufactured and 30 years before the film was made. This means that in the film, the slippers were actually ten years older than actor Michael J. Fox, who at 35, was playing a character 10 years younger that the slippers he was wearing!*

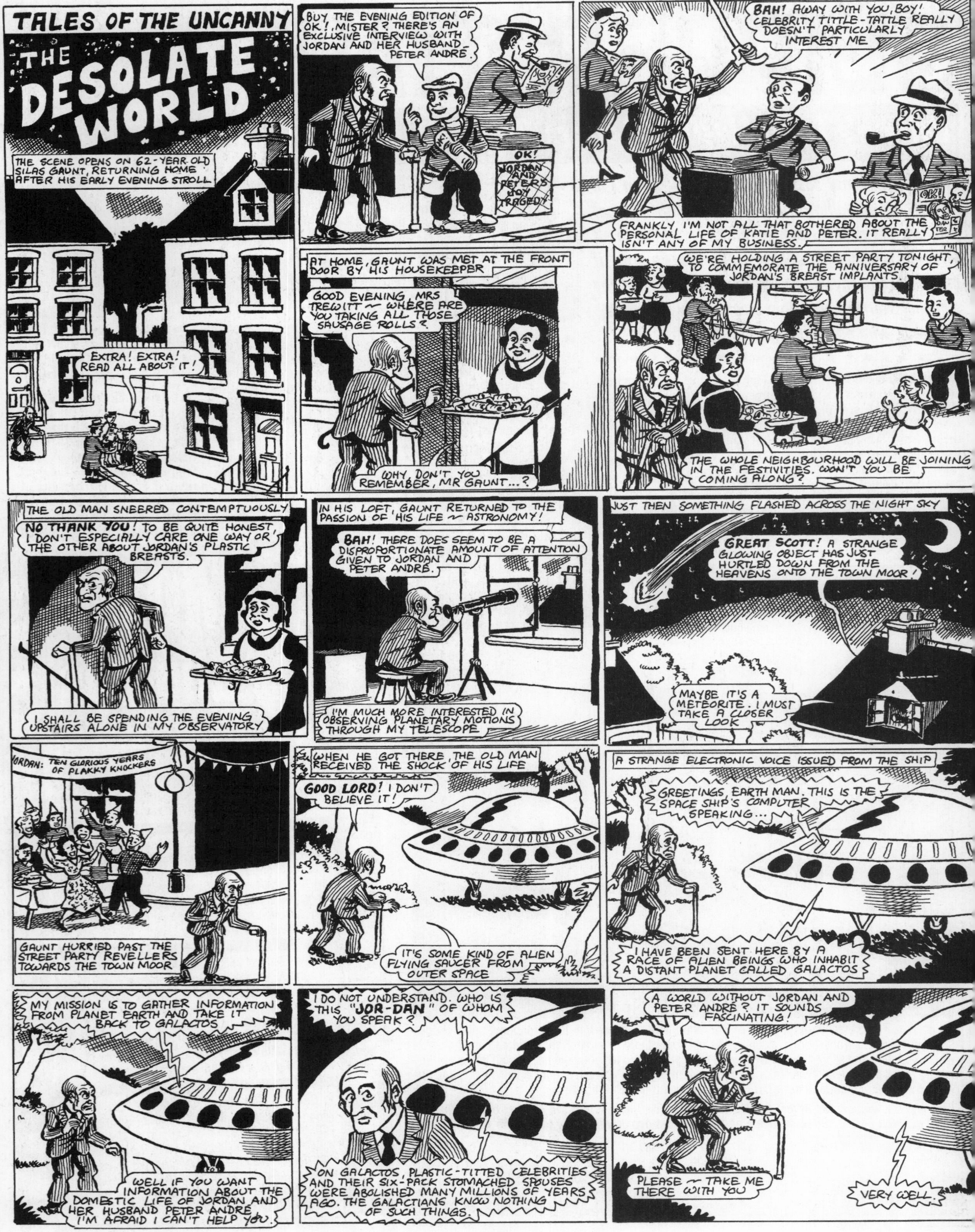
TALES OF THE UNCANNY
THE DESOLATE WORLD
THE SCENE OPENS ON 62-YEAR OLD SILAS GAUNT, RETURNING HOME AFTER HIS EARLY EVENING STROLL
EXTRA! EXTRA! READ ALL ABOUT IT!
BUY THE EVENING EDITION OF OK!, MISTER? THERE'S AN EXCLUSIVE INTERVIEW WITH JORDAN AND HER HUSBAND_ PETER ANDRÉ.
OK! JORDAN AND PETER'S JOY TRAGEDY
BAH! AWAY WITH YOU, BOY! CELEBRITY TITTLE-TATTLE REALLY DOESN'T PARTICULARLY INTEREST ME
FRANKLY, I'M NOT ALL THAT BOTHERED ABOUT THE PERSONAL LIFE OF KATIE AND PETER. IT REALLY ISN'T ANY OF MY BUSINESS.
AT HOME, GAUNT WAS MET AT THE FRONT DOOR BY HIS HOUSEKEEPER
GOOD EVENING, MRS TREWITT ~ WHERE ARE YOU TAKING ALL THOSE SAUSAGE ROLLS?
WHY, DON'T YOU REMEMBER, MR GAUNT...?
WE'RE HOLDING A STREET PARTY TONIGHT, TO COMMEMORATE THE ANNIVERSARY OF JORDAN'S BREAST IMPLANTS.
THE WHOLE NEIGHBOURHOOD WILL BE JOINING IN THE FESTIVITIES. WON'T YOU BE COMING ALONG?
THE OLD MAN SNEERED CONTEMPTUOUSLY
NO THANK YOU! TO BE QUITE HONEST, I DON'T ESPECIALLY CARE ONE WAY OR THE OTHER ABOUT JORDAN'S PLASTIC BREASTS.
I SHALL BE SPENDING THE EVENING UPSTAIRS ALONE IN MY OBSERVATORY
IN HIS LOFT, GAUNT RETURNED TO THE PASSION OF HIS LIFE ~ ASTRONOMY!
BAH! THERE DOES SEEM TO BE A DISPROPORTIONATE AMOUNT OF ATTENTION GIVEN TO JORDAN AND PETER ANDRÉ.
I'M MUCH MORE INTERESTED IN OBSERVING PLANETARY MOTIONS THROUGH MY TELESCOPE
JUST THEN SOMETHING FLASHED ACROSS THE NIGHT SKY
GREAT SCOTT! A STRANGE GLOWING OBJECT HAS JUST HURTLED DOWN FROM THE HEAVENS ONTO THE TOWN MOOR!
MAYBE IT'S A METEORITE. I MUST TAKE A CLOSER LOOK
JORDAN: TEN GLORIOUS YEARS OF PLAKKY KNOCKERS
GAUNT HURRIED PAST THE STREET PARTY REVELLERS TOWARDS THE TOWN MOOR
WHEN HE GOT THERE, THE OLD MAN RECEIVED THE SHOCK OF HIS LIFE
GOOD LORD! I DON'T BELIEVE IT!
IT'S SOME KIND OF ALIEN FLYING SAUCER FROM OUTER SPACE
A STRANGE ELECTRONIC VOICE ISSUED FROM THE SHIP
GREETINGS, EARTH MAN. THIS IS THE SPACE SHIP'S COMPUTER SPEAKING...
I HAVE BEEN SENT HERE BY A RACE OF ALIEN BEINGS WHO INHABIT A DISTANT PLANET CALLED GALACTOS
MY MISSION IS TO GATHER INFORMATION FROM PLANET EARTH AND TAKE IT BACK TO GALACTOS
WELL IF YOU WANT INFORMATION ABOUT THE DOMESTIC LIFE OF JORDAN AND HER HUSBAND PETER ANDRÉ I'M AFRAID I CAN'T HELP YOU.
I DO NOT UNDERSTAND. WHO IS THIS "JOR-DAN" OF WHOM YOU SPEAK?
ON GALACTOS, PLASTIC-TITTED CELEBRITIES AND THEIR SIX-PACK STOMACHED SPOUSES WERE ABOLISHED MANY MILLIONS OF YEARS AGO. THE GALACTIANS KNOW NOTHING OF SUCH THINGS.
A WORLD WITHOUT JORDAN AND PETER ANDRÉ? IT SOUNDS FASCINATING!
PLEASE ~ TAKE ME THERE WITH YOU
VERY WELL.

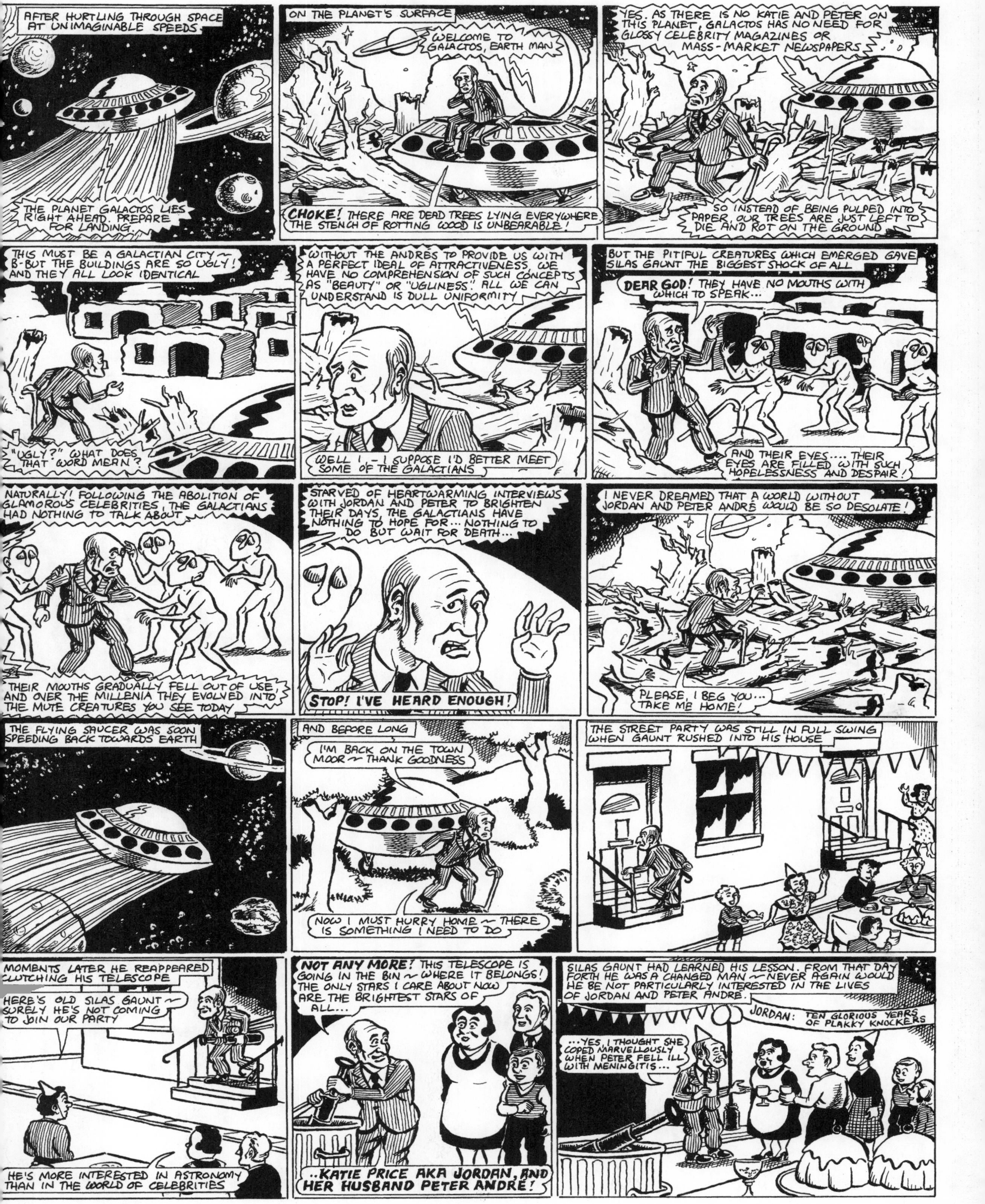
AFTER HURTLING THROUGH SPACE AT UNIMAGINABLE SPEEDS
THE PLANET GALACTOS LIES RIGHT AHEAD. PREPARE FOR LANDING.
ON THE PLANET'S SURFACE
WELCOME TO GALACTOS, EARTH MAN
CHOKE! THERE ARE DEAD TREES LYING EVERYWHERE. THE STENCH OF ROTTING WOOD IS UNBEARABLE!
YES. AS THERE IS NO KATIE AND PETER ON THIS PLANET, GALACTOS HAS NO NEED FOR GLOSSY CELEBRITY MAGAZINES OR MASS-MARKET NEWSPAPERS
SO INSTEAD OF BEING PULPED INTO PAPER, OUR TREES ARE JUST LEFT TO DIE AND ROT ON THE GROUND
THIS MUST BE A GALACTIAN CITY ~ B-BUT THE BUILDINGS ARE SO UGLY! AND THEY ALL LOOK IDENTICAL
"UGLY?" WHAT DOES THAT WORD MEAN?
WITHOUT THE ANDRÉS TO PROVIDE US WITH A PERFECT IDEAL OF ATTRACTIVENESS, WE HAVE NO COMPREHENSION OF SUCH CONCEPTS AS "BEAUTY" OR "UGLINESS". ALL WE CAN UNDERSTAND IS DULL UNIFORMITY
WELL I - I SUPPOSE I'D BETTER MEET SOME OF THE GALACTIANS
BUT THE PITIFUL CREATURES WHICH EMERGED GAVE SILAS GAUNT THE BIGGEST SHOCK OF ALL
DEAR GOD! THEY HAVE NO MOUTHS WITH WHICH TO SPEAK...
AND THEIR EYES.... THEIR EYES ARE FILLED WITH SUCH HOPELESSNESS AND DESPAIR!
NATURALLY! FOLLOWING THE ABOLITION OF GLAMOROUS CELEBRITIES, THE GALACTIANS HAD NOTHING TO TALK ABOUT
THEIR MOUTHS GRADUALLY FELL OUT OF USE, AND OVER THE MILLENIA THEY EVOLVED INTO THE MUTE CREATURES YOU SEE TODAY
STARVED OF HEARTWARMING INTERVIEWS WITH JORDAN AND PETER TO BRIGHTEN THEIR DAYS, THE GALACTIANS HAVE NOTHING TO HOPE FOR... NOTHING TO DO BUT WAIT FOR DEATH...
STOP! I'VE HEARD ENOUGH!
I NEVER DREAMED THAT A WORLD WITHOUT JORDAN AND PETER ANDRÉ WOULD BE SO DESOLATE!
PLEASE, I BEG YOU... TAKE ME HOME!
THE FLYING SAUCER WAS SOON SPEEDING BACK TOWARDS EARTH
AND BEFORE LONG
I'M BACK ON THE TOWN MOOR ~ THANK GOODNESS
NOW I MUST HURRY HOME ~ THERE IS SOMETHING I NEED TO DO
THE STREET PARTY WAS STILL IN FULL SWING WHEN GAUNT RUSHED INTO HIS HOUSE
MOMENTS LATER HE REAPPEARED CLUTCHING HIS TELESCOPE
HERE'S OLD SILAS GAUNT ~ SURELY HE'S NOT COMING TO JOIN OUR PARTY
HE'S MORE INTERESTED IN ASTRONOMY THAN IN THE WORLD OF CELEBRITIES
NOT ANY MORE! THIS TELESCOPE IS GOING IN THE BIN ~ WHERE IT BELONGS! THE ONLY STARS I CARE ABOUT NOW ARE THE BRIGHTEST STARS OF ALL...
..KATIE PRICE AKA JORDAN, AND HER HUSBAND PETER ANDRÉ!
SILAS GAUNT HAD LEARNED HIS LESSON. FROM THAT DAY FORTH HE WAS A CHANGED MAN ~ NEVER AGAIN WOULD HE BE NOT PARTICULARLY INTERESTED IN THE LIVES OF JORDAN AND PETER ANDRE.
JORDAN: TEN GLORIOUS YEARS OF PLAKKY KNOCKERS
...YES, I THOUGHT SHE COPED MARVELLOUSLY WHEN PETER FELL ILL WITH MENINGITIS...

"Stop Stuffing Cushi
Jumper or You'll be De

A WHITLEY BAY MAN has been warned that he risks a premature death if he fails to curb his habit of pushing cushions up his jumper.

Doc's Dire Warning to 35 Cushion Barry

Barry Hewitt, 29, spends every day with a staggering 35 cushions under his clothing and as a result is no longer able to live a normal life. Now he has decided to take drastic action and undergo a controversial procedure which will see the bottom of his jumper sewn to the top of his trousers. "Once it's done, there'll be no going back," he told us. "I won't be able to fit any more big cushions into my jumper, just small ones down the neck hole and up the cuffs. But I know I've made the right decision, because I can't go on living like this."

After leaving school, Hewitt worked as a self-employed plumber, but recently had to give up his job because of his cushions. "I found I was having difficulty getting into tight spaces, such as under sinks and baths," said Barry. "It was all because of the cushions stuffed into my clothes. Eventually I had to admit defeat and packed it in." Since becoming unemployed, Hewitt lives on £80 a week benefits and rarely leaves the house. "I spend my days sitting on the sofa with all cushions up my jersey watching television," he told us.

Barry's GP, Dr Kendo Nagasaki says that his patient runs many risks because of the amount of cushions he has up his jumper. "Compared to a person with no cushions up their jumper, Barry is far more likely to overheat on hot days," he told us. "Many old-fashioned cushions also fail to meet modern standards of fire-retardancy," he continued. "A carelessly-discarded cigarette end could easily send the cushions in Barry's jumper up like a rocket."

"Also, if he was at a steam rally and some of the cushions stuck up through the V-neck, they could impair his vision and he might walk out in front of a traction engine," he added. "If that happens to Barry in the next twelve months, I have no doubt he will be dead within a year."

Barry's cushion problems were evident early on in his life. "I always had a couple of cushions up my front, even when I was little," he told us. "By the time I was twenty, I was up to eighteen cushions - fourteen up my jumper and another four down the front of my trousers. But I really started to pile the cushions on when I got married eight years ago." Barry didn't realise how serious his problem had become until he saw some holiday snaps of himself. "They were pictures of me on the beach," he told us. "I couldn't believe how many cushions I had stuck up there. I looked like the Michelin Man."

Shocked Barry started a strict regime of not putting as many cushions up his jumper each day. "It was hard at first, but I stuck with it and after six months I had got myself down to twelve cushions," he said. "I felt and looked better than I had for years. Everyone said how much less ridiculous I appeared without so many cushions stuffed into my clothing."

But Barry's new, reduced-cushion lifestyle was not to last. On a Moroccan holiday with friends, he found it difficult to resist the soft furnishings that were on offer in his hotel. "The place was full of cushions and pillows," he told us. "I was like a kid in a sweet shop. I just started sticking as many of them up my jumper as I could, and before I knew it I was back up to thirty-five cushions."

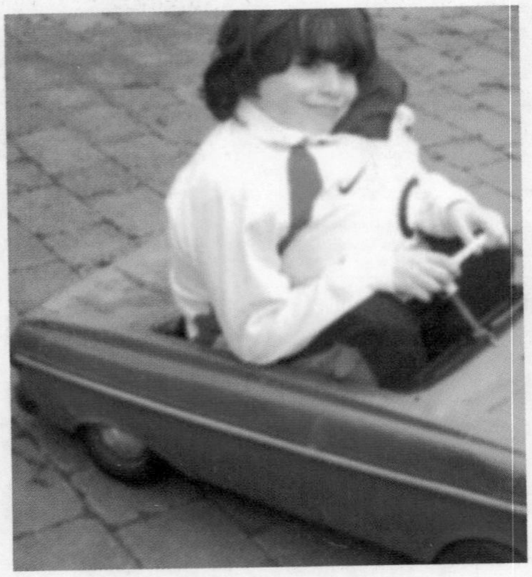

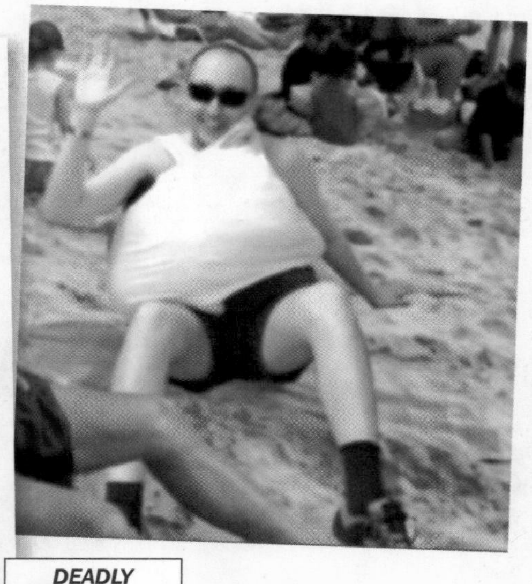

DEADLY LEGACY: Early cushions *(left)* led to beach horror snaps *(right)*.

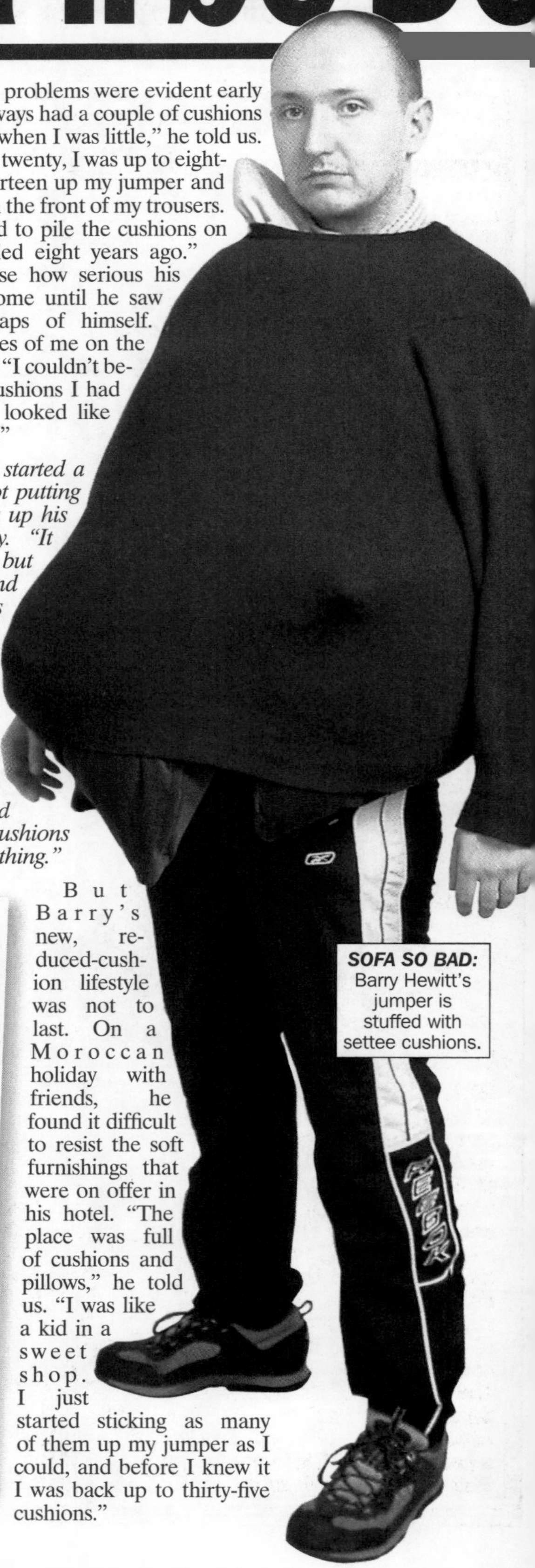

SOFA SO BAD: Barry Hewitt's jumper is stuffed with settee cushions.

s up Your

d in a Year”

Oompah Oompah, Stick It Up Your Jumper

HERE'S WHAT BARRY GETS THROUGH IN A TYPICAL DAY...

07.30	**THREE large cushions up his jumper and TWO cushions down his trousers**
09.00	TWO scatter cushions pushed down his V-neck and TWO more small cushions tucked behind the large cushions up his jumper.
10.30	**THREE more cushions**
12.00	FIVE large cushions, followed by TWO medium-sized cushions
14.30	**FOUR really big cushions**
16.00	TWO scatter cushions, a medium-sized cushion and another cushion
18.00	**THREE small cushions and ONE big cushion**
20.30	TWO quite large cushions off a sofa
23.00	**ONE big cushion and a small cushion**

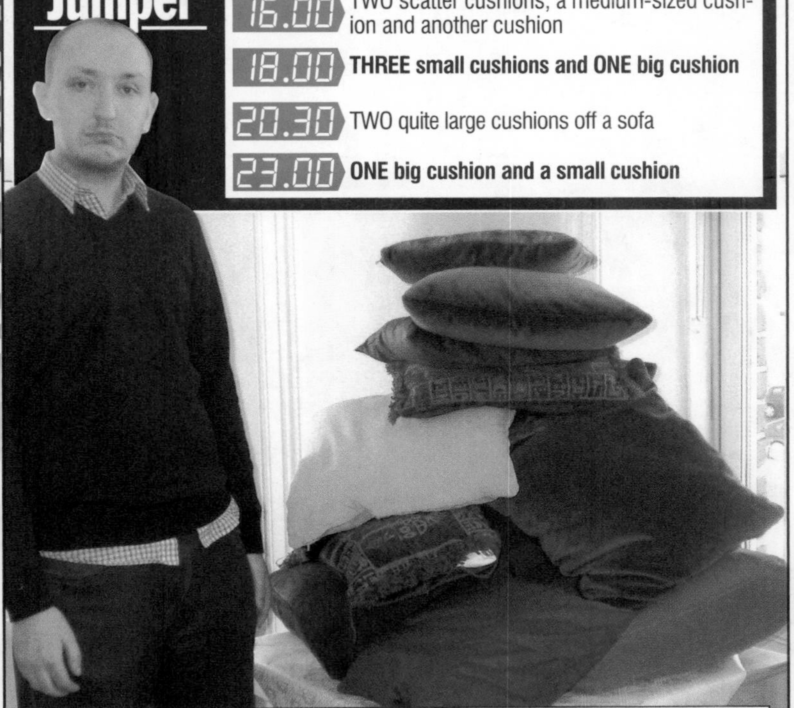

THE PROCEDURE to sew up Barry's jumper and trouser waistband will take place next Thursday at Mendys Clothing Alteration shop. Using a darning needle and a reel of cotton, a seamstress will first hem the lower ribs of the ganzy, before making a series of stitches linking the bottom of the jumper to the waistband of Barry's trousers. The whole process should take approximately 20 minutes, and will result in a garment that it is impossible to stick cushions up.

HOW IT WILL BE DONE

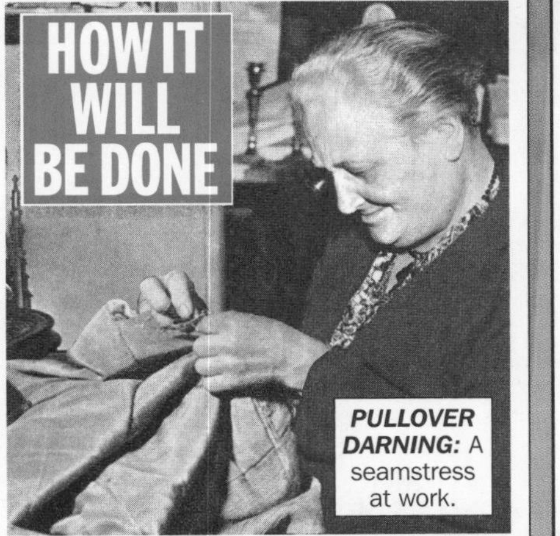

PULLOVER DARNING: A seamstress at work.

WHY PEOPLE PUSH CUSHIONS UP THEIR JUMPERS

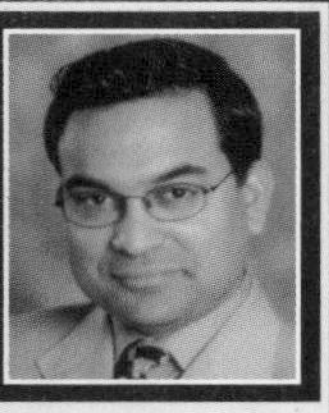

THE REASONS why a grown man would choose to stick large numbers of cushions up their jumper are still not fully understood, writes tuppenny ha'penny psychologist **DR RAJ PERSAUD**. *Most children play with cushions, sometimes pushing them up their jumpers, although few carry this particular behaviour on into adult life. The reasons why an adult male should indulge in this sort of activity past childhood are still shrouded in mystery. Whilst it is not uncommon to see infants pushing cushions up their jumpers, an explanation for why this sort of practice should carry on beyond adolescence is yet to be fully established. Examples of children pushing cushions up their jumpers are well documented, although this type of phenomenon is much less prevalent in the mature population. Where it is, the reasons for it being so remain an enigma. It is, of course, not unheard of for children to push cushions up their jumpers. It is a normal part of development, and typically ceases after puberty. Where it continues into adulthood, there is clearly a rational explanation, although what this explanation may be is not evident at present. What is evident is that young people, particularly toddlers and children, will often be seen pushing cushions up their jumpers. However, this same behaviour is much less common amongst grown-ups. At present, we are at a loss to explain why this should be, although it is clear that whilst children often experiment with pushing cushions up their jumpers, this cushion-play is rarely exhibited by them once they have passed into adulthood. The reasons why it does in some cases, though not in the majority, are yet to be fully comprehended. It is significant to note that whilst human beings between the ages of two and ten regularly display what we scientists call "cushion-stuffing behaviour," equally significant is the fact that the incidence of this behaviour rapidly declines after the upper limit of those two ages is attained, and rarely continues once the subject reaches full adult maturity. Bizarrely, in a few cases, this "cushion-stuffing behaviour" is indeed maintained by a small number of members of the adult populace, although the reasons why this situation should be the case are not in any sense clear at the present time.*

Dr Raj Persaud's book *'The Truth About Why Grown Men Push Cushions Up Their Jumpers'* (Boxtree, £16.99) **is available now from all good bookshops.**

WHY DOCTORS WRITE EXPLANITORY ARTICLES IN THE PRESS

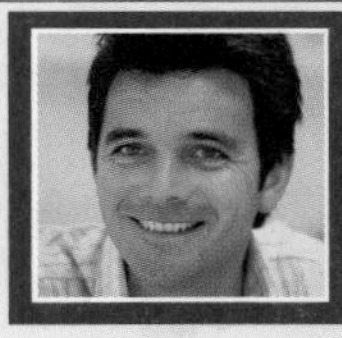

DURING the early part of their careers, many doctors experiment with attempting to write 1000 words about something they don't fully understand in a newspaper or magazine, writes **DR MARK PORTER**. *It is a perfectly natural part of their career development. However most doctors don't carry this sort of activity on into later life, effectively turning filling spaces on feature pages with inconsequential flannel and spouting shit on Richard and Judy into their main body of work. The reasons why some doctors do choose to do this are difficult to pin down with any certainty.*

Dr Mark Porter's book *'Why Doctors Write'* (Boxtree, £16.99) **is available now from all good bookshops.**

WHY I CAN'T GET A FUCKING APPOINTMENT WITH MY GP, DR. MARK PORTER

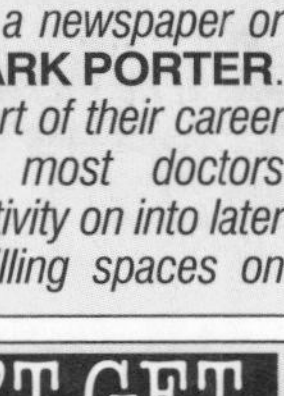

WHEN your GP is Dr Mark Porter it can be quite difficult to get an appointment to see him about your bad back, writes bus driver **LEN SHACKLETON**. *The reasons for this are quite clear. It is because he spends most of the week lolling around on TV studio sofas, waffling about anything from Britney Spears's hair to S-Club Jo's post-Big Brother depression.*

Len Shackleton's book *'The Truth About Getting an Appointment with GP Dr Mark Porter'* (Boxtree, £16.99) **is available now from all good bookshops.**

WHY THE NUMBER SIX BUS NEVER TURNS UP IN THE MORNING

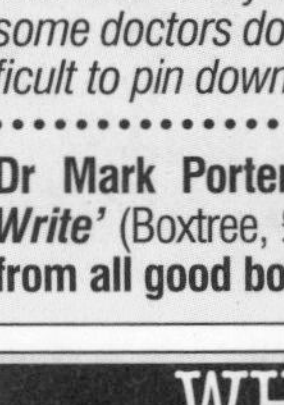

I'M TIRED of the Number 6 bus never turning up in the morning, writes pensioner **MRS EDNA CRETIS**. *And it's all because the regular driver has got a bad back that he can't get treated properly. And as often as not, he's in Waterstone's signing his new book. As a result I have to carry my shopping home.*

Mrs Edna Cretis's book *'The Dildo Decades - My Red Hot Lesbo Life with Princess Margaret'* (Boxtree, £16.99) **is available now from all good bookshops.**

MAJOR MISUNDERSTANDING

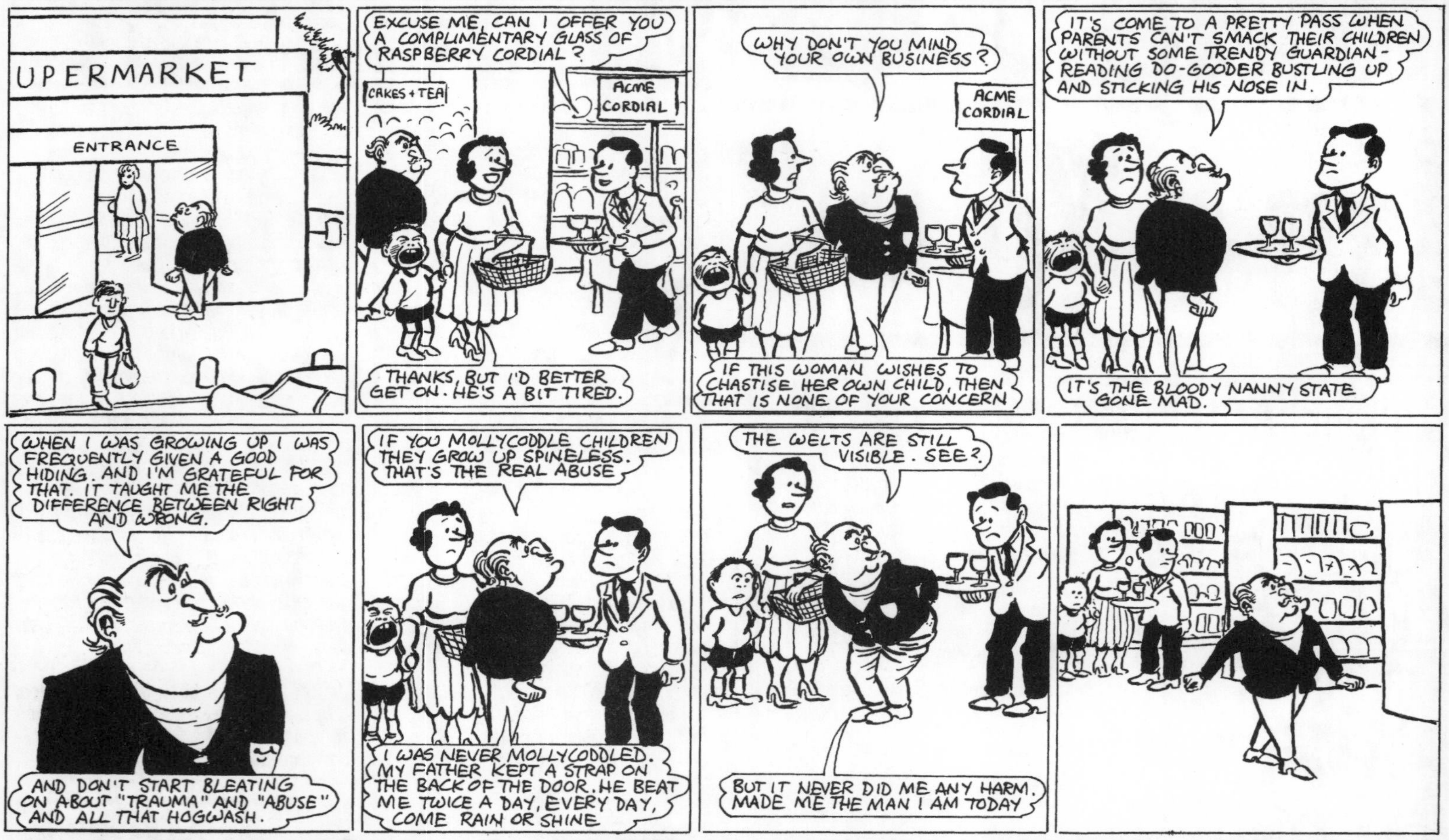
UPERMARKET
ENTRANCE
EXCUSE ME, CAN I OFFER YOU A COMPLIMENTARY GLASS OF RASPBERRY CORDIAL?
CAKES + TEA
ACME CORDIAL
THANKS, BUT I'D BETTER GET ON. HE'S A BIT TIRED.
WHY DON'T YOU MIND YOUR OWN BUSINESS?
ACME CORDIAL
IF THIS WOMAN WISHES TO CHASTISE HER OWN CHILD, THEN THAT IS NONE OF YOUR CONCERN
IT'S COME TO A PRETTY PASS WHEN PARENTS CAN'T SMACK THEIR CHILDREN WITHOUT SOME TRENDY GUARDIAN-READING DO-GOODER BUSTLING UP AND STICKING HIS NOSE IN.
IT'S THE BLOODY NANNY STATE GONE MAD.
WHEN I WAS GROWING UP I WAS FREQUENTLY GIVEN A GOOD HIDING. AND I'M GRATEFUL FOR THAT. IT TAUGHT ME THE DIFFERENCE BETWEEN RIGHT AND WRONG.
AND DON'T START BLEATING ON ABOUT "TRAUMA" AND "ABUSE" AND ALL THAT HOGWASH.
IF YOU MOLLYCODDLE CHILDREN THEY GROW UP SPINELESS. THAT'S THE REAL ABUSE
I WAS NEVER MOLLYCODDLED. MY FATHER KEPT A STRAP ON THE BACK OF THE DOOR. HE BEAT ME TWICE A DAY, EVERY DAY, COME RAIN OR SHINE
THE WELTS ARE STILL VISIBLE. SEE?
BUT IT NEVER DID ME ANY HARM. MADE ME THE MAN I AM TODAY

STARS SAVE PLANET

AT THE RECENT global series of Live Earth Concerts, the stars of pop raised awareness of the risks facing the planet as a result of climate change. Thanks to the example set by the performers, it is estimated that everyone in the world immediately changed their attitude to the earth's resources, thus pulling the planet back from the brink of Armageddon. But what do the stars do privately to combat global warming? We went backstage at Live Earth and asked them how they, personally, made a difference.

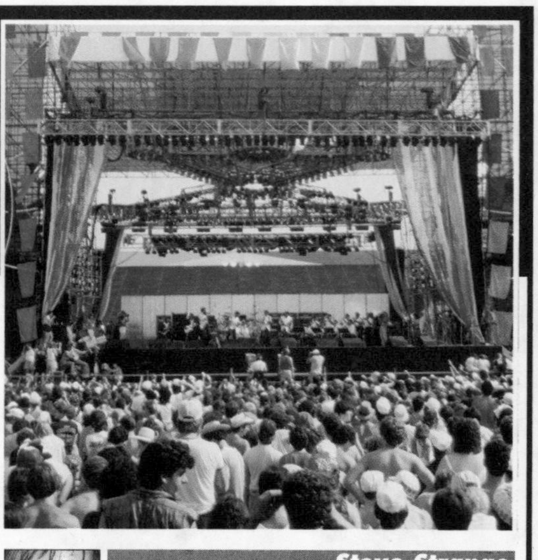

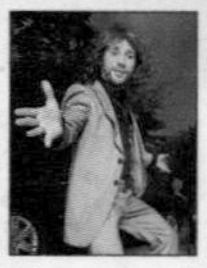

Jay Kay

...I'm very concerned about the way that mankind is using up the earth's resources. So when my new Bugatti Veyron was delivered to my estate in Tuscany, the first thing I did was drive to my local Civic Amenity Site in Buckinghamshire where I recycled the protective plastic off the leather seat upholstery.

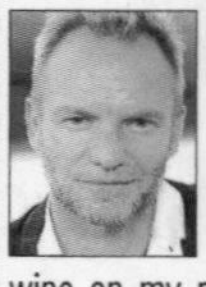

Sting

...I have tried to do my bit for the earth by turning the heating off to my servants' dormitories. I also feed them using sustainably grown food, such as potato peelings and the clippings from my croquet lawn. I also drink English wine on my private jet, because the cost to the earth of transporting champagne to my private airfield in Hampshire would be too great.

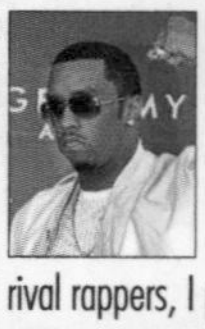

Puff Daddy

...Once fired, regular bullets made of heavy metals, such as lead, cadmium and tungsten stay around poisoning the ecosphere for decades. These toxins eventually find their way into every level of the food chain. These days when I shoot rival rappers, I pop only biodegradable caps in their ass.

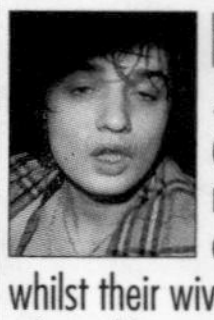

Pete Doherty

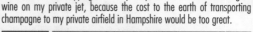

...I always try to buy ethically grown crack. I'd like to find a source of crack where the farmer gets a decent cut of money. Most times they work for a pittance, and if they complain to their drugs overlords, they are forced to watch whilst their wives have their throats cut with a machete. Also, I intend to take public transport to all my court appearances next year. That should save about 250 tons in carbon footprints.

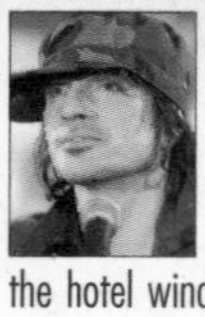

Tommy Lee

...We all have to do our bit for the environment. Me and my fellow Motley Crue band members have made a pledge that when we are on tour, we're not going to leave our TVs on 'standby' when we throw them out of the hotel window, and we are only going to drive hybrid cars into the swimming pool.

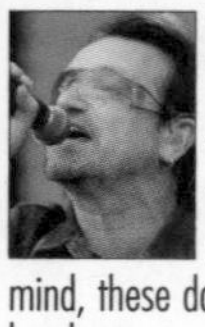

Bono

...I cringe with embarrassment when I think back to the time I chartered a Jumbo Jet to fly my hat halfway around the world. The carbon footprint of moving a hat in a 600 seat airliner doesn't bear thinking about. With this in mind, these days I usually charter a smaller Airbus 330 to transport my headwear.

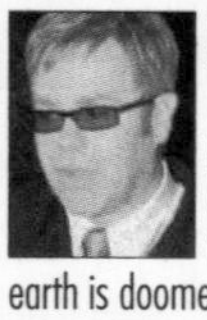

Elton John

...I have 10 pianos in each room of my 47 houses - a grand total of 23500 pianos. That's a lot of ivory on the keyboards, so I insist that it comes only from sustainably farmed elephants....We all have to do our part or else the earth is doomed.

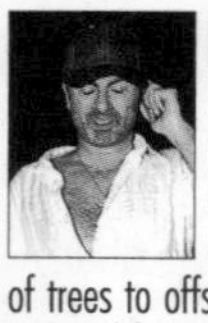

George Michael

...I am constantly being found, monged out on prescription drugs, slumped over the wheel of my car with the engine running. I realise that this is bad for the environment. So each time I do it from now on, I am going to plant an acre of trees to offset the emissions from the gridlock of traffic stuck behind me, and from the police car that drives me back to the cells.

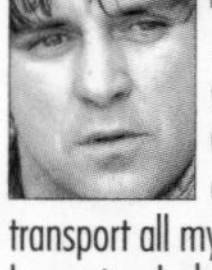

Steve Strange

...Living outdoors as I do, I am only too aware of the effects of climate change. That's why I am prepared to do my bit in order to live a green lifestyle. I never travel anywhere in a vehicle that burns fossil fuels. Instead, I transport all my belongings in recycled pram which I found in a ditch near Lampeter. I also keep my bundle in biodegradable carrier bags, which I also use to line my shoes.

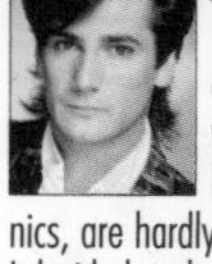

Tony Hadley

...As the lead singer of Spandau Ballet, I've spent most of my career playing to thousands of fans in huge concert venues. The logistics of such tours, with pantechnicons loaded with lighting rigs, bass stacks and stage pyrotechnics, are hardly what you would call green. So for the sake of the earth, I decided to downsize my operations. These days I'm playing much more environmentally friendly venues such as weddings, silver anniversaries and children's parties. And instead of arriving at the gig with the band in a stretched limo, I just turn up on the bus with my backing tape.

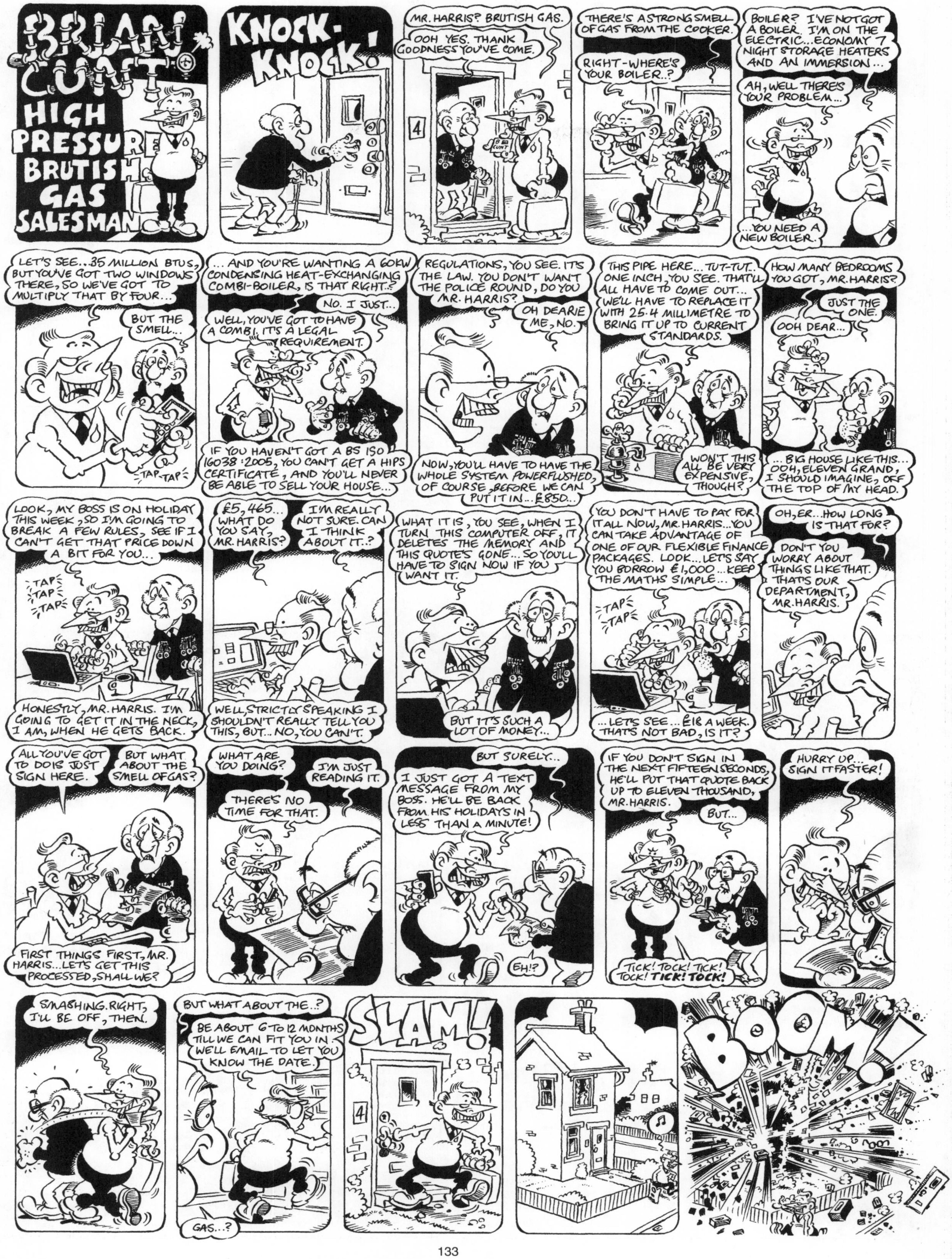
BRIAN CUNT
HIGH PRESSURE BRUTISH GAS SALESMAN
KNOCK-KNOCK!
MR. HARRIS? BRUTISH GAS.
OOH YES. THANK GOODNESS YOU'VE COME.
THERE'S A STRONG SMELL OF GAS FROM THE COOKER.
RIGHT - WHERE'S YOUR BOILER..?
BOILER? I'VE NOT GOT A BOILER. I'M ON THE ELECTRIC... ECONOMY 7 NIGHT STORAGE HEATERS AND AN IMMERSION...
AH, WELL THERE'S YOUR PROBLEM...
...YOU NEED A NEW BOILER.
LET'S SEE... 35 MILLION BTUS, BUT YOU'VE GOT TWO WINDOWS THERE, SO WE'VE GOT TO MULTIPLY THAT BY FOUR...
BUT THE SMELL...
TAP-TAP
... AND YOU'RE WANTING A 60KW CONDENSING HEAT-EXCHANGING COMBI-BOILER, IS THAT RIGHT..?
NO. I JUST...
WELL, YOU'VE GOT TO HAVE A COMBI. IT'S A LEGAL REQUIREMENT.
IF YOU HAVEN'T GOT A BS ISO 16038:2005, YOU CAN'T GET A HIPS CERTIFICATE, AND YOU'LL NEVER BE ABLE TO SELL YOUR HOUSE...
REGULATIONS, YOU SEE. IT'S THE LAW. YOU DON'T WANT THE POLICE ROUND, DO YOU MR. HARRIS?
OH DEARIE ME, NO.
NOW, YOU'LL HAVE TO HAVE THE WHOLE SYSTEM POWERFLUSHED, OF COURSE, BEFORE WE CAN PUT IT IN... £850...
THIS PIPE HERE... TUT-TUT.. ONE INCH, YOU SEE. THAT'LL ALL HAVE TO COME OUT... WE'LL HAVE TO REPLACE IT WITH 25.4 MILLIMETRE TO BRING IT UP TO CURRENT STANDARDS.
WON'T THIS ALL BE VERY EXPENSIVE, THOUGH?
HOW MANY BEDROOMS YOU GOT, MR. HARRIS?
JUST THE ONE.
OOH DEAR...
... BIG HOUSE LIKE THIS... OOH, ELEVEN GRAND, I SHOULD IMAGINE, OFF THE TOP OF MY HEAD.
LOOK, MY BOSS IS ON HOLIDAY THIS WEEK, SO I'M GOING TO BREAK A FEW RULES, SEE IF I CAN'T GET THAT PRICE DOWN A BIT FOR YOU...
TAP TAP TAP
HONESTLY, MR. HARRIS. I'M GOING TO GET IT IN THE NECK, I AM, WHEN HE GETS BACK.
£5,465... WHAT DO YOU SAY, MR. HARRIS?
I'M REALLY NOT SURE. CAN I THINK ABOUT IT..?
WELL, STRICTLY SPEAKING I SHOULDN'T REALLY TELL YOU THIS, BUT... NO, YOU CAN'T.
WHAT IT IS, YOU SEE, WHEN I TURN THIS COMPUTER OFF, IT DELETES THE MEMORY AND THIS QUOTE'S GONE... SO YOU'LL HAVE TO SIGN NOW IF YOU WANT IT.
BUT IT'S SUCH A LOT OF MONEY...
YOU DON'T HAVE TO PAY FOR IT ALL NOW, MR. HARRIS... YOU CAN TAKE ADVANTAGE OF ONE OF OUR FLEXIBLE FINANCE PACKAGES. LOOK... LET'S SAY YOU BORROW £1,000... KEEP THE MATHS SIMPLE...
TAP TAP
... LET'S SEE... £18 A WEEK. THAT'S NOT BAD, IS IT?
OH, ER... HOW LONG IS THAT FOR?
DON'T YOU WORRY ABOUT THINGS LIKE THAT. THAT'S OUR DEPARTMENT, MR. HARRIS.
ALL YOU'VE GOT TO DO IS JUST SIGN HERE.
BUT WHAT ABOUT THE SMELL OF GAS?
FIRST THINGS FIRST, MR. HARRIS... LET'S GET THIS PROCESSED, SHALL WE?
WHAT ARE YOU DOING?
I'M JUST READING IT.
THERE'S NO TIME FOR THAT.
BUT SURELY...
I JUST GOT A TEXT MESSAGE FROM MY BOSS. HE'LL BE BACK FROM HIS HOLIDAYS IN LESS THAN A MINUTE!
EH!?
IF YOU DON'T SIGN IN THE NEXT FIFTEEN SECONDS, HE'LL PUT THAT QUOTE BACK UP TO ELEVEN THOUSAND, MR. HARRIS.
BUT...
TICK! TOCK! TICK! TOCK! TICK! TOCK!
HURRY UP... SIGN IT FASTER!
SMASHING. RIGHT, I'LL BE OFF, THEN.
BUT WHAT ABOUT THE..?
BE ABOUT 6 TO 12 MONTHS TILL WE CAN FIT YOU IN. WE'LL EMAIL TO LET YOU KNOW THE DATE.
GAS...?
SLAM!
BOOM!

LETTERBOCKS

Viz Comic, PO Box 656
North Shields, NE30 4XX
e-mail: letters@viz.co.uk

STAR LETTER

According to the BBC website, 'cocaine users are getting younger'. I have always avoided illegal narcotics but now I've found out that they actually reverse the ageing process I'm going to give them a bash.

Simon Halliday, e-mail

Further to Frank Peterborough's letter *(Letterbocks p.120)* about Gary Rhodes saying 'there's nothing better than a bit of Scotch egg.' I've just heard TV Chef James Martin say that 'there's nothing worse than soft croutons.' So presumably Mr Martin doesn't consider the Holocaust as tragic an event as getting soft croutons in his soup.

Frank Plywood, e-mail

We can all thank our lucky stars that the shoe bomber Richard Reid wasn't around in the 70s. Can you imagine how many sticks of dynamite he could have sealed in a pair of Gary Glitter style platform shoes? It doesn't bear thinking about. By the way, this is the third letter I have sent you today and I'm all out of puff, so please print one of them.

Mark Richards, e-mail

A big thank you to the lady in the little black dress and strappy high heel shoes sitting on the top step at Lingfield races showing her not unattractive muff to passers by. This somewhat offset the £7.50 charged for a pint of Magners by the robbing bastards running the bars.

Uncle Road Rage, Maidstone

JOHN CARROLL D.D.
1789 - 1989
POSTE VATICANE 1350

IVORY-BILLED WOODPECKER
CONSERVATION STAMP

If the government are really committed to reducing greenhouse gasses, why don't they pass a law saying all cars must be three wheelers? If the engine drives the wheels, then surely a three wheel car will use 25% less petrol than a normal one.

T Thorn, e-mail

If J K Rowling ever wants to do another Harry Potter book, then can I suggest a storyline where he gets bummed off some tramps. An interesting twist to the story could be that they were magic tramps or something.

Jim Bowden, e-mail

Scientists really get my goat. They have had decades to come-up with a few simple discoveries like artificial gravity, time travel and hovercars. However, since the invention of CDs in the 1980s the only other major innovations have been the blue LED and thinner tellys. Hardly earth-shattering. I think we should give them till next Easter to come up with something on the list and then start turfing them out of their labs. We could let the vicars have a go and see if their creationist mumbo-jumbo can do any better.

Mark Glover, Coventry

I've just decided not to vote in Radio 2's 'Ultimate Icon' poll. Nelson Mandela and David Cassidy are both on the shortlist and I personally can't fit a cigarette paper between them when it comes to admiration for what they have achieved.

Duffers, e-mail

I wonder how they train hens to lay those 'Taste the Difference eggs' you can buy in Sainsburys. And I wonder what on earth they do to the ones who lay the economy ones?

Ada Stupid, London

Me, I like to call a spade a spade. I'm not particularly outspoken, I just think it's confusing to use any other term for it.

Hector Martingale, e-mail

While re-reading issue 135, I noticed that Nude Motorcycle Girl was riding barefoot. This is very uncomfortable as the gear lever is operated by the left foot, and in Australia, at least, illegal. Enclosed footwear must be worn. I suggest that Nude Motorcycle Girl invest in some suitable boots, perhaps calf-length soft leather with laces like the ones Jayde used to wear at SinSations adult entertainment in Mitchell.

NUDE
Motorcycle Girl

Dave, Canberra

TOP TIPS

PROSTITUTES. Helping a client to undress can be sexy, but dressing him afterwards takes him back to childhood when his mother helped him get ready for school.

Tom Brown, e-mail

EBAY sellers. Ensure that everybody looks at your item by writing "L@@K" in the title.

Andy, e-mail

THEATRE NURSES. If the surgeon you work with is called Simon, brighten up mundane procedures by refusing to pass any equipment to him until he uses the prefix "Simon Says". Remember even when he shouts "Give me the ligature, this child is DYING?!" he's probably just trying to get you out.

Ben Margerison, e-mail

DOG OWNERS. Never lose your TV remote control again. Simply sellotape it to the back of your dog, and hey presto! Whistle, and the device is at your beck and call! This can also apply to hot drinks, after intense training.

Theodore Tramp, e-mail

SKATEBOARDERS. Next time you come to a set of steps with a handrail in the middle, pick up your skateboard in one hand, grasp the handrail with the other and carefully walk down the steps. This way it won't be quite as painful on your bollocks.

Steve, e-mail

SHOPPERS. Confuse staff at Argos by stealing all the biros and replacing them with IKEA pencils.

R. Trotter, Peckham

DEVOUT Catholics. If the Lord has not yet made Himself visible, perhaps you are looking in the wrong place. Try paying more attention to the flaking paint on your walls, the rust on your frying pan or the mouldy stains on your carpet as these are the sort of places where He usually turns up.

Jon Sangham, West Ho

RECREATE the danger of a parachute jump in safety by visiting Google Earth and clicking the scroll bar until you reach the ground. Add realism to the exercise by putting a fan on blowing full in your face.

Christian Frank, Billingham

MONKS. Conduct a life of celibacy and emotional solitude without joining a monastery by simply living with my wife. It's more comfortable and you'll be able to watch TV and use the internet.

Not-So-Private Ryan, e-mail

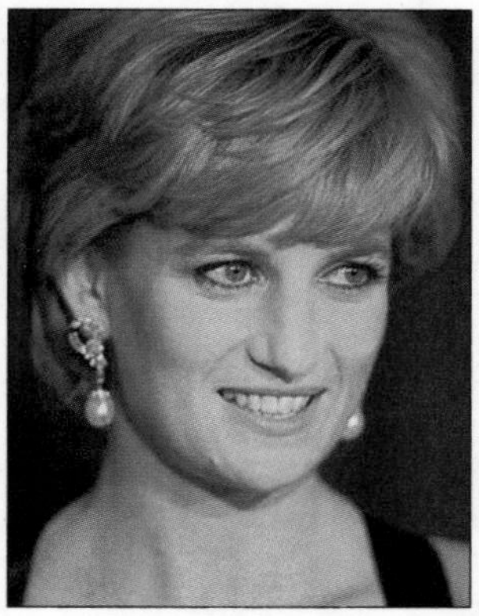

■ I was very upset whilst watching the Princess Diana memorial service last month, as I wasn't aware that she'd died. As the most famous woman in the world, you'd think the media would have made more about her death, to be honest.

Nick Pettigrew, e-mail

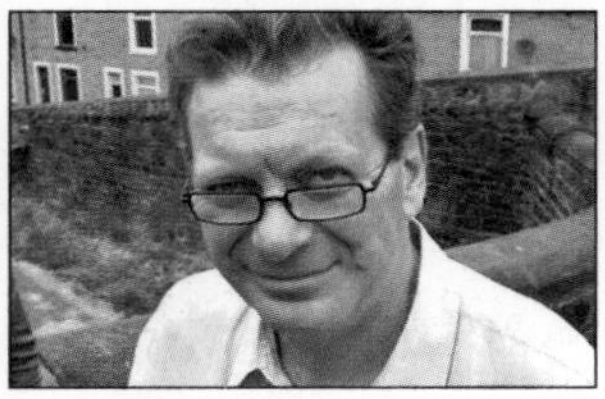

■ How nice of the authorities in Manchester to posthumously make Tony Wilson a Freeman of the city. It must be a great comfort for his widow to know that Tony's ghost can drive sheep and cattle over bridges and carry an unsheathed sword in public.

H. Cruikshanks, Manchester

■ Hats off to the Happy Mondays for rallying round to raise money for Factory Records boss Tony Wilson's life-saving cancer treatment, and shame on the authorities for refusing to put their hand in their pocket. Tony must have known who his true friends were. Having said that, if I ever find myself relying on Shaun Ryder and Bez to rustle up some sponds to keep me alive, I'll get straight off down to the coffin shop.

Spartacus Barracus, Hull

■ How about a picture of Elvis bumming a Basset Hound?

Eli Rolly, Tunbridge

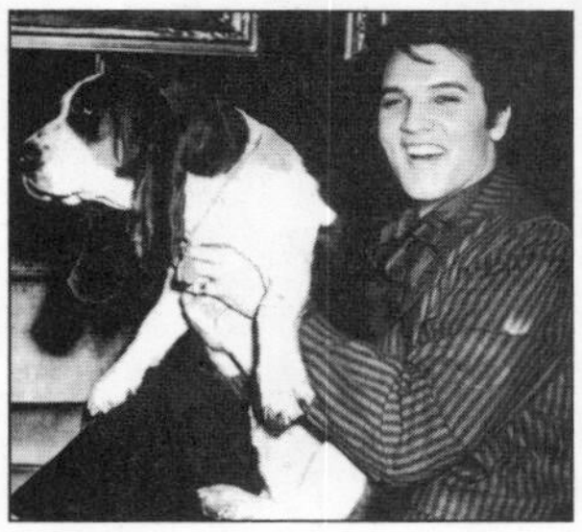

** No problem, Eli.*

■ I saw Marcel Marceau on the telly once pretending to be stuck in a box. It was brilliant. I wonder if has anybody checked in his coffin to see if he's not still pretending? I mean, a pro like him isn't going to pipe up and shout "Get me out of this box," is he?

Gerard Taylor, e-mail

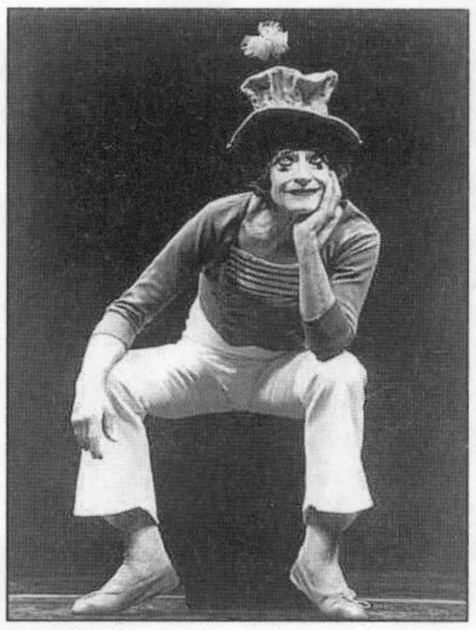

■ Although I'm sure the death of Marcel Marceau will have been upsetting for his family and friends, to be perfectly honest me and my friends couldn't care less.

Edna Margerine
Royal National Institute for the Blind

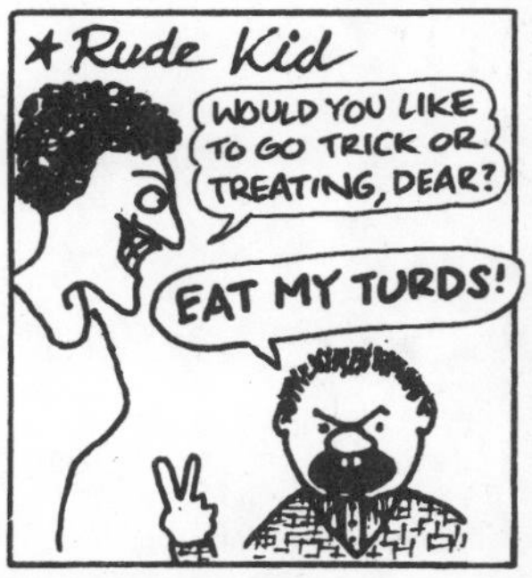

★Rude Kid
WOULD YOU LIKE TO GO TRICK OR TREATING, DEAR?
EAT MY TURDS!

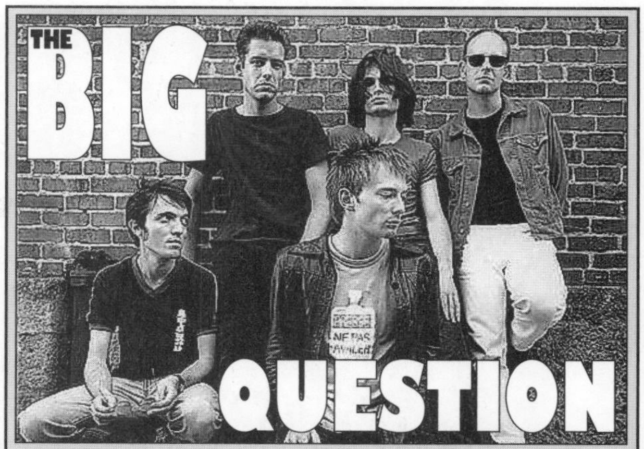

THE BIG
QUESTION

RADIOHEAD have revolutionised the music industry by making their new album *In Rainbows* available to download for whatever price fans choose to pay for it. With half of the purchasers chosing to pay nothing, and the other half paying an average of £4.20, is this a publicity stunt that has backfired on the band? Or by cutting the record companies and retail chains out of the equation, are Radiohead pointing the way to the future? We asked the wives of some notorious serial killers how much THEY would pay...

Sonia Sutcliffe ~ *wife of Yorkshire Ripper,* ***Peter.***

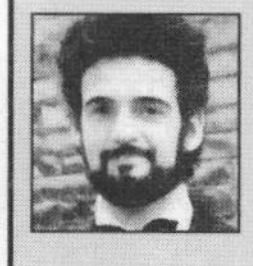

"There's been a lot said about how you can pay nothing for the album, but you have to remember that there is a mandatory 45p handling fee, so it's not really free at all. I'm not a great Radiohead fan anyway, so I probably wouldn't buy it at any price."

Primrose Shipman ~ *wife of Cheshire Death Doc,* ***Harold.***

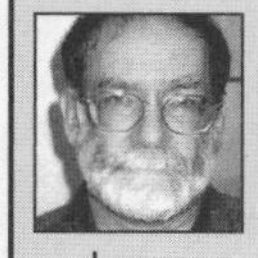

"I loved *Hail to the Thief*, but despite the hype, I was not fussed on the supposedly seminal *OK Computer*. From what I've heard of *In Rainbows*, it doesn't sound like Thom and the boys are exactly pushing back the sonic boundaries. I'll probably download it and pay no more than a pound."

Rose West ~ *wife of House of Horrors handyman* ***Fred.***

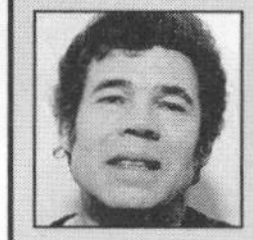

"I'm a great fan of Radiohead. I've got all their records going back to *Pablo Honey*, and for me the band just keep getting better. Unfortunately, as I'm serving a life sentence for murder, I haven't got access to the internet. So I'll have to ask a friend on the outside to download it, rip it to CD, and smuggle it into prison in a cake."

Iris Dahmer ~ *wife of gay Milwaukee Cannibal,* ***Jeffrey.***

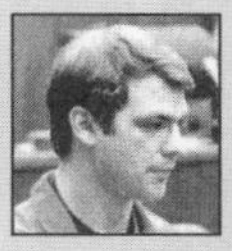

"I'm a huge music fan, but I don't like Radiohead at all, so I can't see me paying anything for *In Rainbows*. In fact, I only like Chas and Dave. Actually, only one song by them, *Rabbit*. And I only like the chorus of that. I play it all day at full volume, just the bit where the rockney twosome say 'rabbit' over and over again in turn. My husband used to say it drove him bonkers."

Ethel Christie ~ *wife of Rillington Place Ghoul,* ***John.***

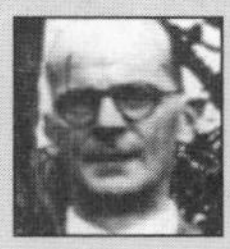

"I think it was a very brave decision of Radiohead's to let their fans decide the cost of *In Rainbows*. I would happily support their stance and pay £16 to download the album. The bread-heads and fat-cats at the record companies have it had it their own way for too long and it is time that somebody stuck it to the man. Sadly, though, back in December 1952 I became my husband's third victim, and being dead, I am unable to do my bit."

TIME TRAVEL NEWS

1 Ermine Street, between Segedunum and Vindolanda. A chariot has been in collision with a tumbril cart in ***206AD***. The Praetorian Guard say that legions are backed up for up to 6 miles in both directions, and diversions have been set up through Corstopitum.

2 Transport Sector Z. Travellers in the year ***2525*** are advised to avoid Junction Alpha 38 on the X62 Hoverway near Hull, where an anti-grav lorry has jack-knifed, spilling its load of dilithium crystals across all one hundred lanes.

3 Passengers travelling between Doncaster and Durham in ***1722*** can expect delays of up to an hour, as stagecoaches are being held up just outside York by a dandy highwayman on a glossy black steed.

4 Heathrow Intergalactic Teleport Station is experiencing severe delays of up to a microsecond on all beamings to Mars in the year ***5000***. This is as a result of increased gamma radiation in the Van Allen Belt.

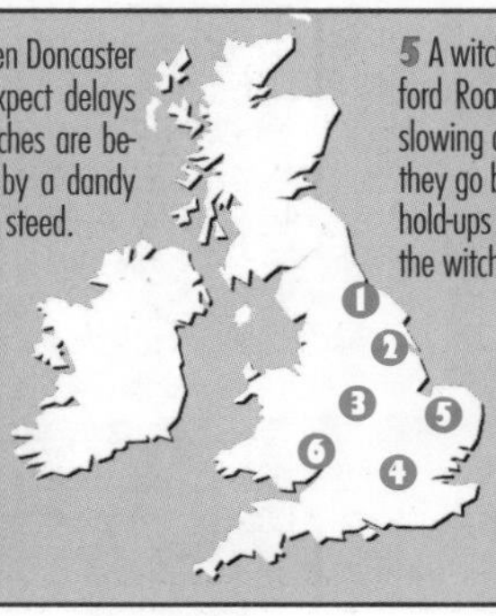

5 A witch-burning alongside the main Norwich to Sleaford Road is causing tailbacks, as rubberneckers are slowing down their haywagons to get a better look as they go by. Transport authorities in ***1567*** say that the hold-ups should ease within the next three hours when the witch's body has been purified by the flames.

6 ***20,000 BC.*** Widespread snow and ice up to half a mile thick is causing disruption to transport links throughout the country. Drivers of wooden log cars with stone wheels are advised not to venture out unless their journey is absolutely necessary.

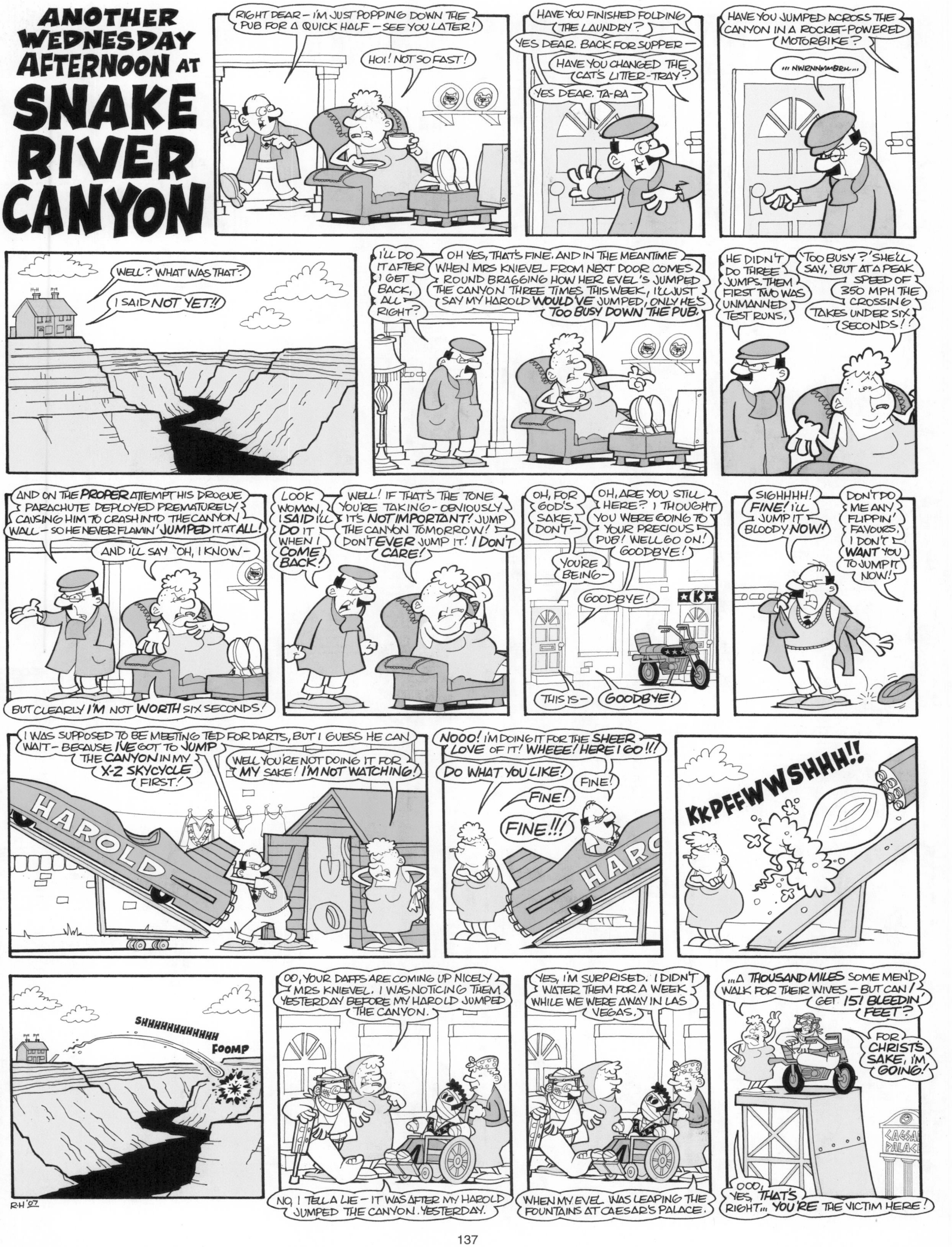
ANOTHER WEDNESDAY AFTERNOON AT SNAKE RIVER CANYON
RIGHT DEAR – I'M JUST POPPING DOWN THE PUB FOR A QUICK HALF – SEE YOU LATER!
HOI! NOT SO FAST!
HAVE YOU FINISHED FOLDING THE LAUNDRY?
YES DEAR. BACK FOR SUPPER –
HAVE YOU CHANGED THE CAT'S LITTER-TRAY?
YES DEAR. TA-RA –
HAVE YOU JUMPED ACROSS THE CANYON IN A ROCKET-POWERED MOTORBIKE?
... NWRNNMMBRH...
WELL? WHAT WAS THAT?
I SAID NOT YET!!
I'LL DO IT AFTER I GET BACK, ALL RIGHT?
OH YES, THAT'S FINE. AND IN THE MEANTIME WHEN MRS KNIEVEL FROM NEXT DOOR COMES ROUND BRAGGING HOW HER EVEL'S JUMPED THE CANYON THREE TIMES THIS WEEK, I'LL JUST SAY MY HAROLD WOULD'VE JUMPED, ONLY HE'S TOO BUSY DOWN THE PUB.
HE DIDN'T DO THREE JUMPS. THEM FIRST TWO WAS UNMANNED TEST RUNS.
'TOO BUSY?' SHE'LL SAY, 'BUT AT A PEAK SPEED OF 350 MPH THE CROSSING TAKES UNDER SIX SECONDS!'
AND ON THE PROPER ATTEMPT HIS DROGUE PARACHUTE DEPLOYED PREMATURELY CAUSING HIM TO CRASH INTO THE CANYON WALL – SO HE NEVER FLAMIN' JUMPED IT AT ALL!
AND I'LL SAY 'OH, I KNOW –
BUT CLEARLY I'M NOT WORTH SIX SECONDS!
LOOK WOMAN, I SAID I'LL DO IT WHEN I COME BACK!
WELL! IF THAT'S THE TONE YOU'RE TAKING – OBVIOUSLY IT'S NOT IMPORTANT! JUMP THE CANYON TOMORROW! DON'T EVER JUMP IT! I DON'T CARE!
OH, FOR GOD'S SAKE, DON'T –
OH, ARE YOU STILL HERE? I THOUGHT YOU WERE GOING TO YOUR PRECIOUS PUB! WELL GO ON! GOODBYE!
YOU'RE BEING –
GOODBYE!
THIS IS –
GOODBYE!
SIGHHHH! FINE! I'LL JUMP IT BLOODY NOW!
DON'T DO ME ANY FLIPPIN' FAVOURS. I DON'T WANT YOU TO JUMP IT NOW!
I WAS SUPPOSED TO BE MEETING TED FOR DARTS, BUT I GUESS HE CAN WAIT – BECAUSE I'VE GOT TO JUMP THE CANYON IN MY X-2 SKYCYCLE FIRST!
WELL YOU'RE NOT DOING IT FOR MY SAKE! I'M NOT WATCHING!
HAROLD
NOOO! I'M DOING IT FOR THE SHEER LOVE OF IT! WHEEE! HERE I GO!!!
DO WHAT YOU LIKE!
FINE!
FINE!
FINE!!!
HARO
KKPFFWWSHHH!!
SHHHHHHHHHHHH
FOOMP
OO, YOUR DAFFS ARE COMING UP NICELY MRS KNIEVEL. I WAS NOTICING THEM YESTERDAY BEFORE MY HAROLD JUMPED THE CANYON.
NO, I TELL A LIE – IT WAS AFTER MY HAROLD JUMPED THE CANYON. YESTERDAY.
YES, I'M SURPRISED. I DIDN'T WATER THEM FOR A WEEK WHILE WE WERE AWAY IN LAS VEGAS.
WHEN MY EVEL WAS LEAPING THE FOUNTAINS AT CAESAR'S PALACE.
...A THOUSAND MILES SOME MEN'D WALK FOR THEIR WIVES – BUT CAN I GET 15! BLEEDIN' FEET?
FOR CHRIST'S SAKE, I'M GOING!
OOO, YES, THAT'S RIGHT... YOU'RE THE VICTIM HERE!
R.H. '07

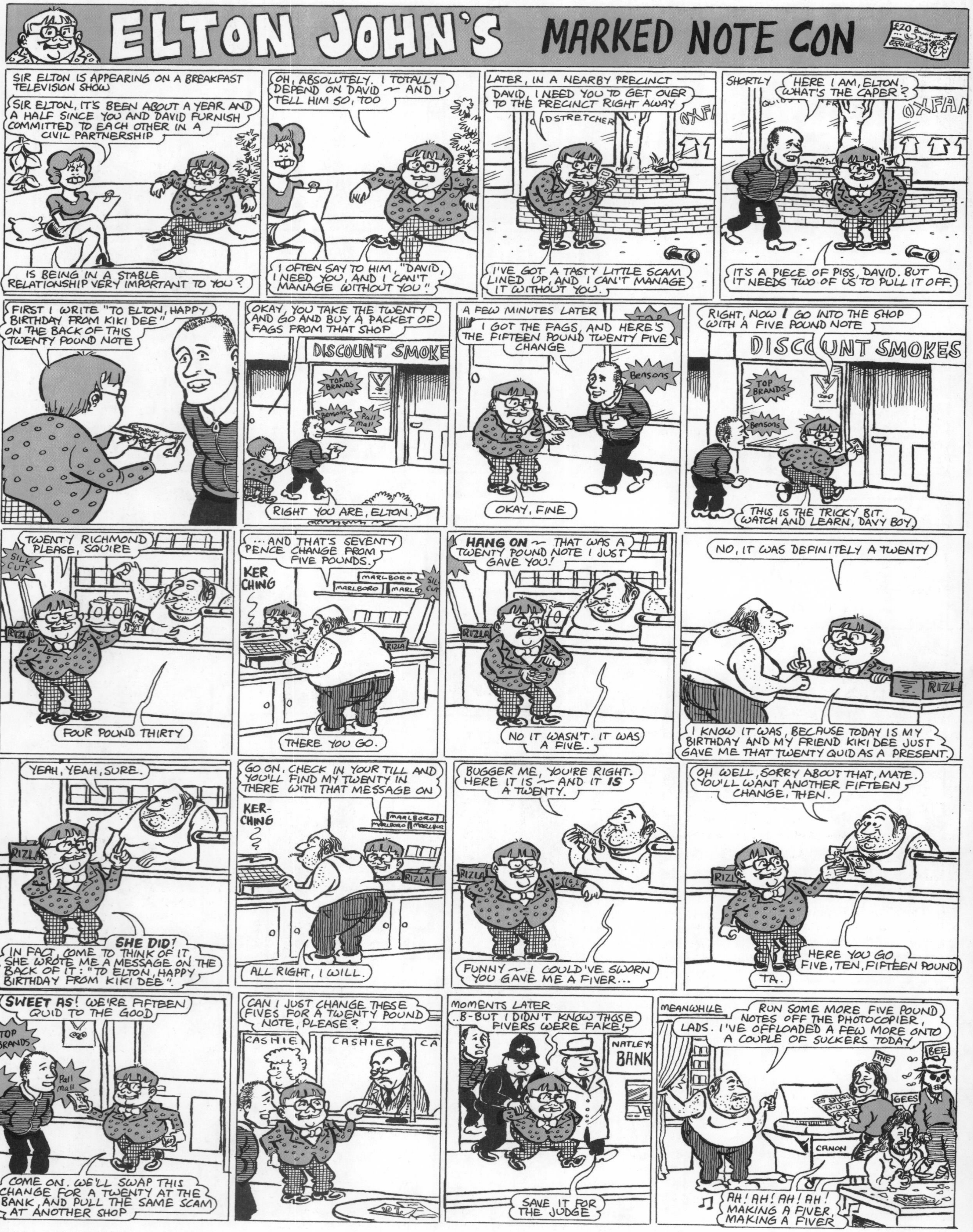

ELTON JOHN'S MARKED NOTE CON
SIR ELTON IS APPEARING ON A BREAKFAST TELEVISION SHOW
SIR ELTON, IT'S BEEN ABOUT A YEAR AND A HALF SINCE YOU AND DAVID FURNISH COMMITTED TO EACH OTHER IN A CIVIL PARTNERSHIP
IS BEING IN A STABLE RELATIONSHIP VERY IMPORTANT TO YOU?
OH, ABSOLUTELY. I TOTALLY DEPEND ON DAVID ~ AND I TELL HIM SO, TOO
I OFTEN SAY TO HIM, "DAVID, I NEED YOU, AND I CAN'T MANAGE WITHOUT YOU"
LATER, IN A NEARBY PRECINCT
DAVID, I NEED YOU TO GET OVER TO THE PRECINCT RIGHT AWAY
I'VE GOT A TASTY LITTLE SCAM LINED UP, AND I CAN'T MANAGE IT WITHOUT YOU.
SHORTLY
HERE I AM, ELTON. WHAT'S THE CAPER?
OXFAM
IT'S A PIECE OF PISS, DAVID. BUT IT NEEDS TWO OF US TO PULL IT OFF.
FIRST I WRITE "TO ELTON, HAPPY BIRTHDAY FROM KIKI DEE" ON THE BACK OF THIS TWENTY POUND NOTE
OKAY, YOU TAKE THE TWENTY AND GO AND BUY A PACKET OF FAGS FROM THAT SHOP
DISCOUNT SMOKE
TOP BRANDS
Bensons
Pall mall
RIGHT YOU ARE, ELTON.
A FEW MINUTES LATER
I GOT THE FAGS, AND HERE'S THE FIFTEEN POUND TWENTY FIVE CHANGE
Bensons
OKAY, FINE
RIGHT, NOW I GO INTO THE SHOP WITH A FIVE POUND NOTE
DISCOUNT SMOKES
TOP BRANDS
Bensons
THIS IS THE TRICKY BIT. WATCH AND LEARN, DAVY BOY.
TWENTY RICHMOND PLEASE, SQUIRE
SILK CUT
RIZLA
FOUR POUND THIRTY
...AND THAT'S SEVENTY PENCE CHANGE FROM FIVE POUNDS.
KER CHING
MARLBORO
RIZLA
THERE YOU GO.
HANG ON ~ THAT WAS A TWENTY POUND NOTE I JUST GAVE YOU!
RIZLA
NO IT WASN'T. IT WAS A FIVE.
NO, IT WAS DEFINITELY A TWENTY
RIZLA
I KNOW IT WAS, BECAUSE TODAY IS MY BIRTHDAY AND MY FRIEND KIKI DEE JUST GAVE ME THAT TWENTY QUID AS A PRESENT.
YEAH, YEAH, SURE.
RIZLA
SHE DID! IN FACT, COME TO THINK OF IT, SHE WROTE ME A MESSAGE ON THE BACK OF IT: "TO ELTON, HAPPY BIRTHDAY FROM KIKI DEE".
GO ON, CHECK IN YOUR TILL AND YOU'LL FIND MY TWENTY IN THERE WITH THAT MESSAGE ON
KER-CHING
MARLBORO
RIZLA
ALL RIGHT, I WILL.
BUGGER ME, YOU'RE RIGHT. HERE IT IS ~ AND IT IS A TWENTY.
RIZLA
FUNNY ~ I COULD'VE SWORN YOU GAVE ME A FIVER...
OH WELL, SORRY ABOUT THAT, MATE. YOU'LL WANT ANOTHER FIFTEEN CHANGE, THEN.
RIZLA
TA.
HERE YOU GO. FIVE, TEN, FIFTEEN POUND
SWEET AS! WE'RE FIFTEEN QUID TO THE GOOD
TOP BRANDS
Pall mall
COME ON. WE'LL SWAP THIS CHANGE FOR A TWENTY AT THE BANK, AND PULL THE SAME SCAM AT ANOTHER SHOP
CAN I JUST CHANGE THESE FIVES FOR A TWENTY POUND NOTE, PLEASE?
CASHIER
MOMENTS LATER
..B-BUT I DIDN'T KNOW THOSE FIVERS WERE FAKE!
NATLEYS BANK
SAVE IT FOR THE JUDGE
MEANWHILE
RUN SOME MORE FIVE POUND NOTES OFF THE PHOTOCOPIER, LADS. I'VE OFFLOADED A FEW MORE ONTO A COUPLE OF SUCKERS TODAY
THE
BEE
GEES
CANON
AH! AH! AH! AH! MAKING A FIVER, MAKING A FIVER

FANDABI-CLOTHESY

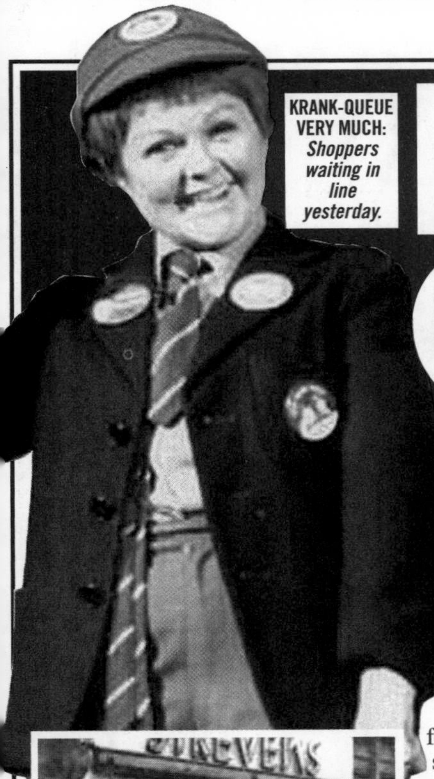

KRANK-QUEUE VERY MUCH: *Shoppers waiting in line yesterday.*

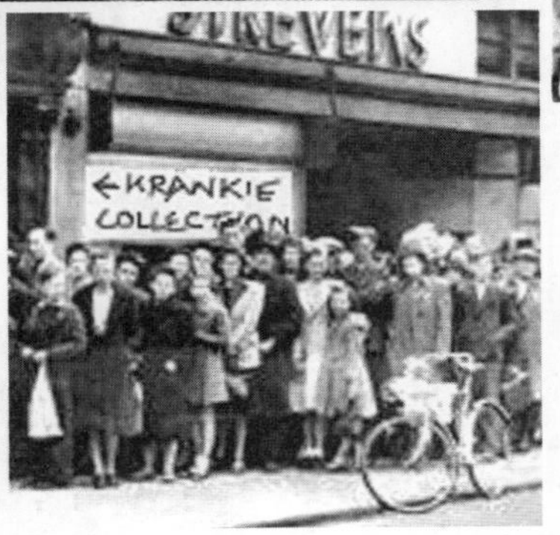

KRANKIE COLLECTION

HIGH STREET fashion chain Miss Selfridge are reporting record first week sales after becoming the latest store to launch a celebrity-endorsed clothing range. Customers queued round the block at the chain's flagship London branch eager to be first to sample the new Jeanette Krankie collection which went on sale on Monday morning.

To loud cheers and screams of excitement, Mrs Krankie appeared in the window of the Oxford Street shop for a few minutes and did a 'fandabidozi' thumbs up for photographers. The aged variety star has reportedly been paid £20 million billion for her work on the designs.

At 9.00am there was a mad scramble as shoppers fought over the exclusive new range. V-neck pullovers, baggy grey shorts and anachronistic school caps were snapped up by young women, eager to look like the iconic veteran schoolboy impersonator.

"Jeanette always looks fantastic with one sock up and one sock down and her satchel slung over her shoulder," said excited legal secretary Shaznay Freud, who had queued for eight hours to buy a tatty blazer and a pair of scuffed Clark's Commandos. Her friend, Chardonnay Jung agreed. "She's a role model to all young girls and it's great that we have finally got the chance to buy into the Jeanette Krankie look," she told Radio 4's *Today* programme.

Demand for the clothes was so heavy that Miss Selfridge bosses decided to limit purchases of the clothes to one pair of shorts and a scruffy shirt per customer, and one accessory of a tie, satchel or catapult.

The designs are due to go on sale in their 220 UK outlets next week.

Queen's Rattle Cause of Concern

ROYAL DOCTORS were left scratching their heads last night when they were unable to locate the source of a rattle in the Queen.

By LEE SCRATCH PERRY

The Duke of Edinburgh took his wife to the swanky Paddington Royal Infirmary on Tuesday after noticing an annoying noise coming from her during the State Opening of Parliament.

SOURCE

A source close to the palace told reporters: "The queen's surgeon spent a couple of hours examining her majesty, but was unable to locate the source of the noise."

Prince Philip describes the sound as a sort of metallic buzz that starts off very quiet but gets louder whenever she changes the guard. The source said: "The Duke can't locate where the noise is coming from. It sounds like it's coming from her arse, but when he puts his ear there, it seems to be coming from somewhere else. It's driving him mad."

The Queen's surgeon, Sir Cuthbert Cream told reporters: "I'm at a bit of a loss. I stripped her right down and gave her a good clean. I even had her buttocks off and greased her hips. I took her for a walk round the ward and I couldn't hear anything. But when the Duke came to collect her, he said the rattle started up again on the way home. And now she's developed a clunk when she sits for portraits."

JEWEL

"What you've got to remember is that her Majesty is 81, and you have to expect a few unexplained noises from a monarch of that age," he added.

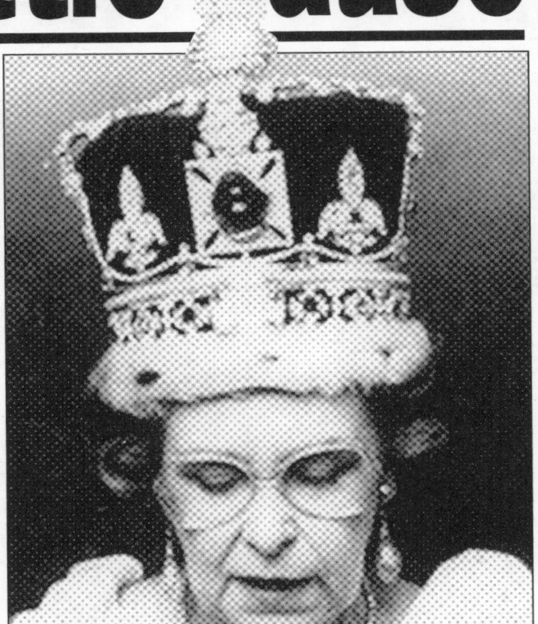

THE CRAZY WORLD OF ARTHUR BROWN

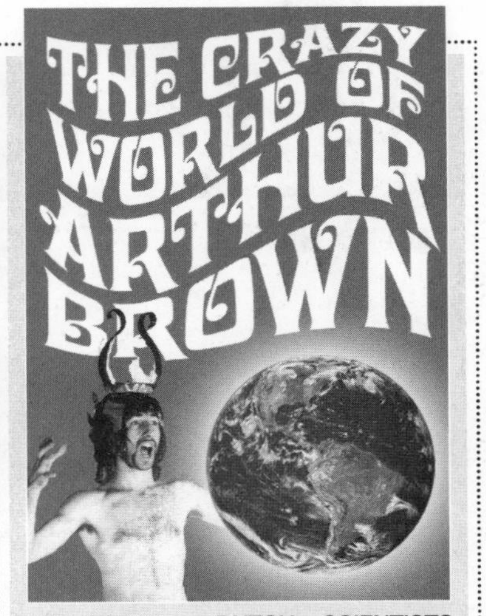

HOLLAND... DUTCH SCIENTISTS have invented a cheese that can think for itself, according to Professor Jurgen Kluivert from Amsterdam University's Department of Cheese. The cheese, a mild edam, can talk a little bit and make simple decisions. "It is not particularly intelligent, but it is definitely conscious as it begs for mercy when you grate it and screams when you put it under the grill," he told *New Scientist* magazine.

JAPAN... **A GODZILLA which rose from the sea and attacked the centre of Tokyo for several days has been killed by the Japanese army. The 200-foot high lizard appeared in the harbour after an earthquake woke it from its underwater lair where it had been hibernating since dinosaur times. Thousands of people ran screaming as the monster bit buildings and snapped busses in two before it was finally shot. "It was like something out of a Godzilla film," said passer by Takahaki Yakomoto.**

ENGLAND... SURREY HOUSEWIFE Margaret Pettigrew got the shock of her life when the answered the phone last week and found herself talking to her grandfather... who has been dead for thirty years! Mrs Pettigrew told her local paper: "He made the call in 1958, but it somehow got lost in the system, and he eventually got connected last night." British Telecom apologised for the delay, blaming a technical error at the exchange.

URUGUAY... **A DOG from Castleford has become the first animal to win a place at Oxford University. Sultan, a 5-year-old alsatian beat hundreds of other applicants to enter Magdelen College to study applied mathematics and statistics. Sultan's owner, scrap dealer Frank Pound said: "I don't know where he gets it from. The other dog we've got guarding the yard is from the same litter and he only managed a 'D' at GCSE."**

AMERICA... A KING KONG which escaped its captors and terrorised New York for several hours last week has been shot by the US Air Force. The 200-foot high gorilla had been brought back from a remote island where it was worshiped as a god by the natives. Thousands of people ran screaming as the monster clambered up the Empire State Building clutching a woman it had fallen in love with, before it was finally shot. "It was like something out of a King Kong film," said passer by Hairam Oysterburger.

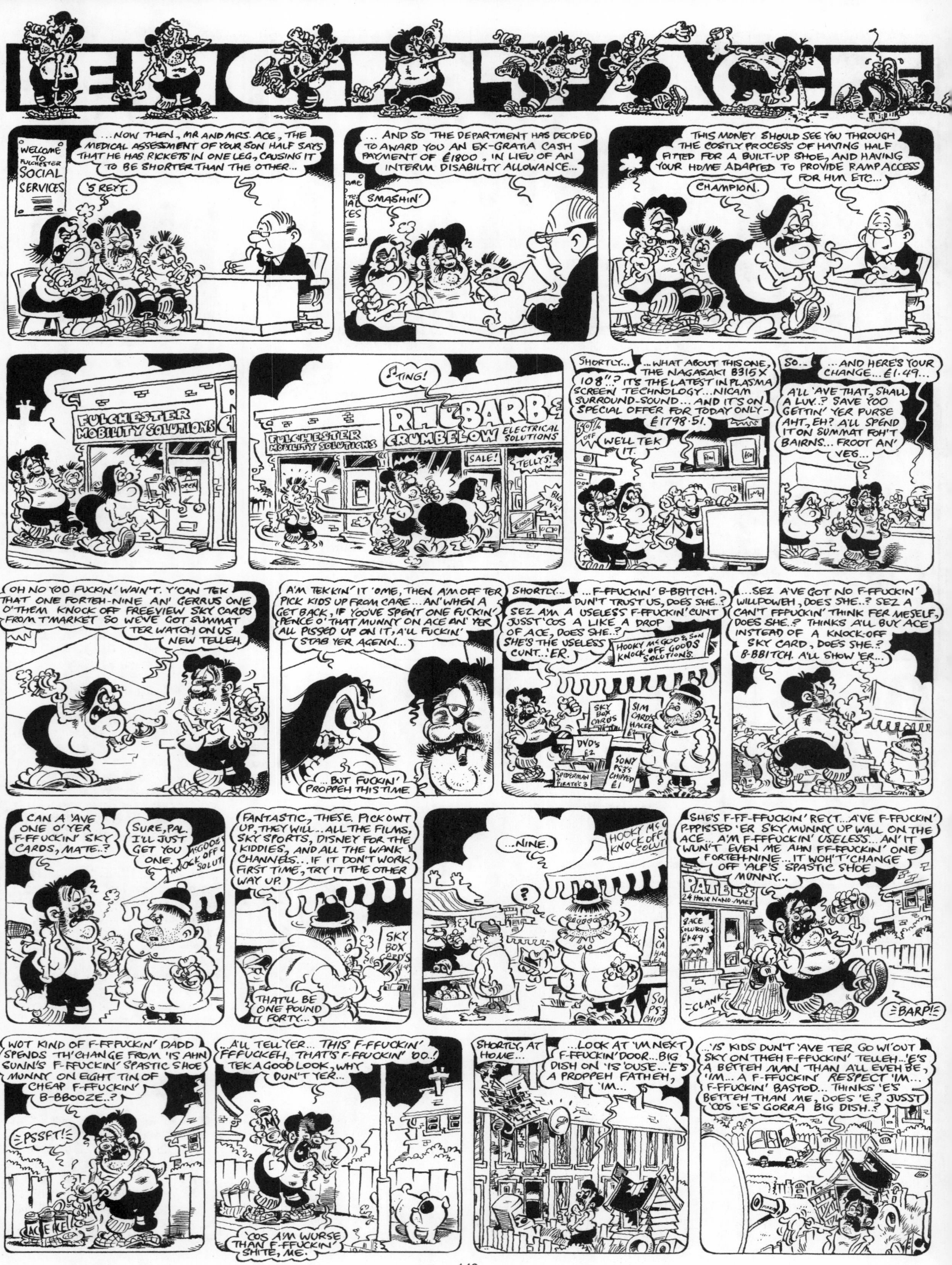
EIGHT ACE
WELCOME TO FULCHESTER SOCIAL SERVICES
...NOW THEN, MR AND MRS. ACE, THE MEDICAL ASSESSMENT OF YOUR SON HALF SAYS THAT HE HAS RICKETS IN ONE LEG, CAUSING IT TO BE SHORTER THAN THE OTHER...
'S REYT.
...AND SO THE DEPARTMENT HAS DECIDED TO AWARD YOU AN EX-GRATIA CASH PAYMENT OF £1800, IN LIEU OF AN INTERIM DISABILITY ALLOWANCE...
SMASHIN'
THIS MONEY SHOULD SEE YOU THROUGH THE COSTLY PROCESS OF HAVING HALF FITTED FOR A BUILT-UP SHOE, AND HAVING YOUR HOME ADAPTED TO PROVIDE RAMP ACCESS FOR HIM ETC...
CHAMPION.
FULCHESTER MOBILITY SOLUTIONS
TING!
RHUBARB & CRUMBELOW ELECTRICAL SOLUTIONS
SALE!
TELLYS!
BIG TVS!
SHORTLY...
...WHAT ABOUT THIS ONE, THE NAGASAKI B315X 108"? IT'S THE LATEST IN PLASMA SCREEN TECHNOLOGY...NICAM SURROUND-SOUND...AND IT'S ON SPECIAL OFFER FOR TODAY ONLY - £1798.51.
50% OFF
WE'LL TEK IT.
SO...
...AND HERE'S YOUR CHANGE...£1.49...
A'LL 'AVE THAT, SHALL A LUV..? SAVE YOO GETTIN' YER PURSE AHT, EH? A'LL SPEND IT ON SUMMAT FOH'T BAIRNS... FROOT AN' VEG...
OH NO YOO FUCKIN' WAIN'T. Y'CAN TEK THAT ONE FORTEH-NINE AN' GERRUS ONE O'THEM KNOCK OFF FREEVIEW SKY CARDS FROM T'MARKET SO WE'VE GOT SUMMAT TER WATCH ON US NEW TELLEH.
A'M TEKKIN' IT 'OME, THEN A'M OFF TER PICK KIDS UP FROM CARE... AN' WHEN A GET BACK, IF YOO'VE SPENT ONE FUCKIN' PENCE O' THAT MUNNY ON ACE AN' YER ALL PISSED UP ON IT, A'LL FUCKIN' STAB YER AGENN...
...BUT FUCKIN' PROPPEH THIS TIME.
SHORTLY...
...F-FFUCKIN' B-BBITCH. DUN'T TRUST US, DOES SHE..? SEZ A'M A USELESS F-FFUCKIN' CUNT JUSST 'COS A LIKE A DROP OF ACE, DOES SHE..? SHE'S THE USELESS CUNT...'ER.
HOOKY McGOO & SON KNOCK OFF GOODS SOLUTIONS
SKY BOX CARDS
SIM CARDS HACKED
DVD'S £2
SONY PS3'S CHIPPED £1
SPIDERMAN PIRATE'S 3
...SEZ A'VE GOT NO F-FFUCKIN' WILLPOWEH, DOES SHE..? SEZ A CAN'T FFFUCKIN' THINK FER MESELF, DOES SHE..? THINKS A'LL BUY ACE INSTEAD OF A KNOCK-OFF SKY CARD, DOES SHE..? B-BBITCH. A'LL SHOW 'ER...
CAN A 'AVE ONE O' YER F-FFUCKIN' SKY CARDS, MATE..?
SURE, PAL. I'LL JUST GET YOU ONE.
FANTASTIC, THESE. PICK OWT UP, THEY WILL...ALL THE FILMS, SKY SPORTS, DISNEY FOR THE KIDDIES, AND ALL THE WANK CHANNELS... IF IT DON'T WORK FIRST TIME, TRY IT THE OTHER WAY UP.
SKY BOX CARD'S
THAT'LL BE ONE POUND FORTY...
...NINE.
?
SHE'S F-FF-FFUCKIN' REYT... A'VE F-FFUCKIN' P-PPISSED 'ER SKY MUNNY UP WALL ON THE ACE... A'M F-FFFUCKIN' USELESS... AN' IT WUN'T EVEN ME AHN FF-FFUCKIN' ONE FORTEH-NINE... IT WOH'T CHANGE OFF 'ALF'S SPASTIC SHOE MUNNY...
PATEL'S 24 HOUR NANO-MART
8 ACE SOLUTIONS £1.49
CLANK
BARP!
WOT KIND OF F-FFUCKIN' DADD SPENDS TH'CHANGE FROM 'IS AHN SUNN'S F-FFUCKIN' SPASTIC SHOE MUNNY ON EIGHT TIN OF CHEAP F-FFUCKIN' B-BBOOZE..?
PSSFT!
...A'LL TELL YER... THIS F-FFUCKIN' FFFUCKEH, THAT'S F-FFUCKIN' OO... TEK A GOOD LOOK, WHY DUN'T YER...
'COS A'M WURSE THAN F-FFUCKIN' SHITE, ME.
SHORTLY, AT HOME...
...LOOK AT 'IM NEXT F-FFUCKIN' DOOR... BIG DISH ON 'IS 'OUSE... 'E'S A PROPPEH FATHEH, 'IM...
...'IS KIDS DUN'T 'AVE TER GO WI'OUT SKY ON THEH F-FFUCKIN' TELLEH...'E'S A BETTEH MAN THAN A'LL EVEH BE, 'IM... A F-FFUCKIN' RESPECT 'IM... F-FFUCKIN' BASTOD... THINKS 'E'S BETTEH THAN ME, DOES 'E..? JUSST 'COS 'E'S GORRA BIG DISH..?

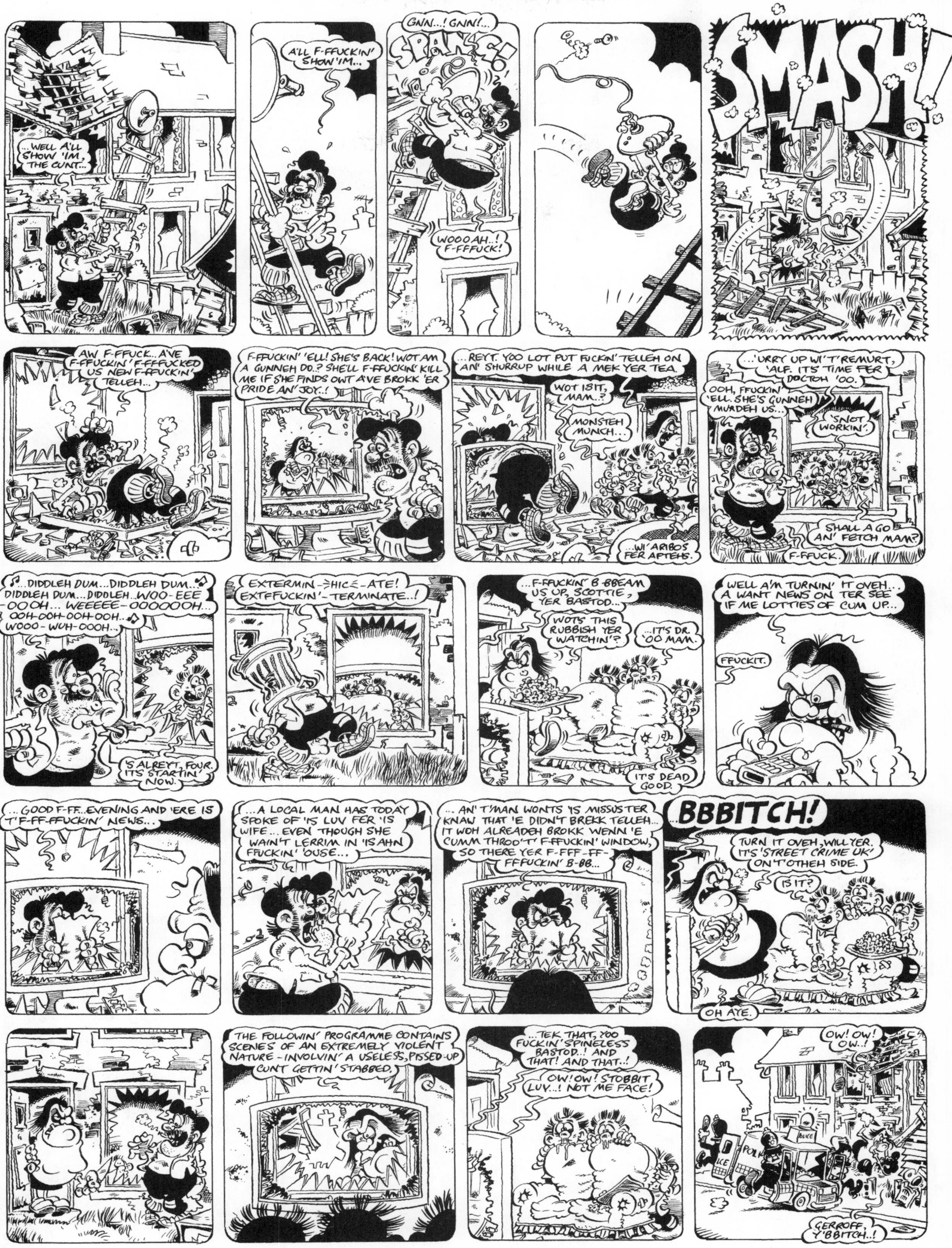

...WELL A'LL SHOW 'IM, THE CUNT...
A'LL F-FFUCKIN' SHOW 'IM...
GNN...! GNN!...
SPANG!
WOOOAH..! F-FFFUCK!
SMASH!
AW F-FFUCK... A'VE F-FFUCKIN' F-FFFUCKED US NEW F-FFUCKIN' TELLEH...
F-FFUCKIN' 'ELL! SHE'S BACK! WOT AM A GUNNEH DO..? SHE'LL F-FFUCKIN' KILL ME IF SHE FINDS OWT A'VE BROKK 'ER PRIDE AN' JOY..!
...REYT. YOO LOT PUT FUCKIN' TELLEH ON AN' SHURRUP WHILE A MEK YER TEA.
WOT IS IT, MAM..?
MONSTEH MUNCH...
...WI' ARIBOS FER APTEHS.
...'URRY UP WI' T' REMURT, 'ALF. IT'S TIME FER DOCTOH 'OO.
OOH, FFUCKIN' 'ELL. SHE'S GUNNEH MURDEH US...
'SNOT WORKIN'.
SHALL A GO AN' FETCH MAM?
F-FFUCK.
...DIDDLEH DUM...DIDDLEH DUM... DIDDLEH DUM...DIDDLEH...WOO-EEE -OOOH... WEEEEE-OOOOOOH... OOH-OOH-OOH-OOH... WOOO-WUH-OOOH...
'S ALREYT, FOUR. ITS STARTIN' NOW.
EXTERMIN-HIC-ATE! EXTFFUCKIN'-TERMINATE...!
...F-FFUCKIN' B-BBEAM US UP, SCOTTIE, YER BASTOD...
WOT'S THIS RUBBISH YER WATCHIN'?
...IT'S DR. 'OO MAM.
IT'S DEAD GOOD.
WELL A'M TURNIN' IT OVEH... A WANT NEWS ON TER SEE IF ME LOTTIES OF CUM UP...
FFUCKIT.
...GOOD F-FF...EVENING AND 'ERE IS T' F-FF-FFUCKIN' NEWS...
...A LOCAL MAN HAS TODAY SPOKE OF 'IS LUV FER 'IS WIFE... EVEN THOUGH SHE WAIN'T LERRIM IN 'IS AHN FFUCKIN' 'OUSE...
...AN' T'MAN WONTS 'IS MISSUS TER KNAW THAT 'E DIDN'T BREKK TELLEH... IT WOH ALREADEH BROKK WENN 'E CUMM THROO 'T' F-FFUCKIN' WINDOW, SO THERE YER F-FFF-FF-FFFUCKIN' B-BB...
BBBITCH!
TURN IT OVEH, WILL YER. IT'S 'STREET CRIME UK' ON T' OTHEH SIDE.
IS IT?
OH AYE.
THE FOLLOWIN' PROGRAMME CONTAINS SCENES OF AN EXTREMELY VIOLENT NATURE - INVOLVIN' A USELESS, PISSED-UP CUNT GETTIN' STABBED.
...TEK THAT, YOO FUCKIN' SPINELESS BASTOD..! AND THAT! AND THAT..!
OW! OW! STOBBIT LUV...! NOT ME FACE!
OW! OW! OW..!
GERROFF, Y' BBITCH..!

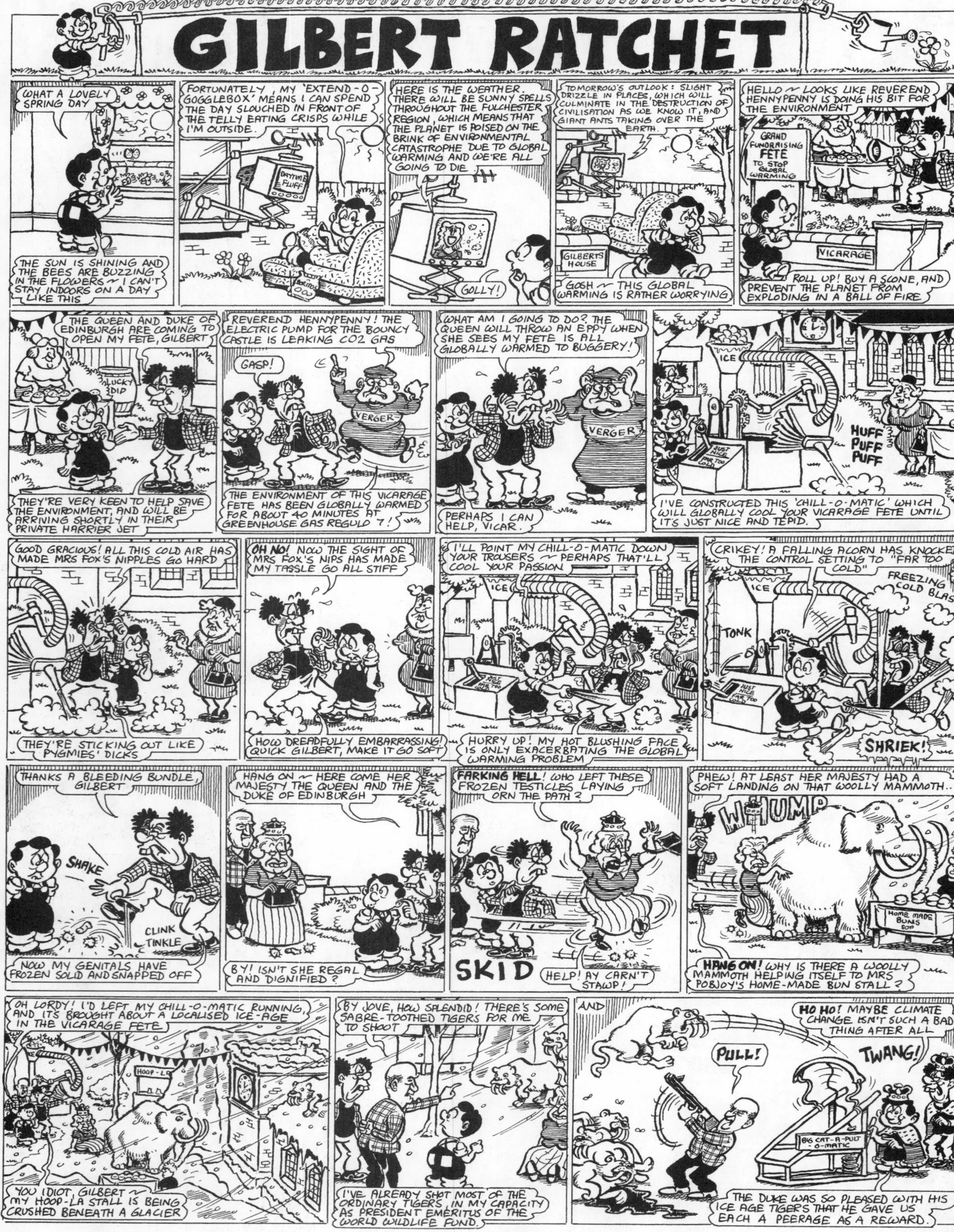
GILBERT RATCHET
WHAT A LOVELY SPRING DAY
THE SUN IS SHINING AND THE BEES ARE BUZZING IN THE FLOWERS ~ I CAN'T STAY INDOORS ON A DAY LIKE THIS
FORTUNATELY, MY 'EXTEND-O-GOGGLEBOX' MEANS I CAN SPEND THE DAY SLOUCHED IN FRONT OF THE TELLY EATING CRISPS WHILE I'M OUTSIDE.
DAYTIME FLUFF
HERE IS THE WEATHER. THERE WILL BE SUNNY SPELLS THROUGHOUT THE FULCHESTER REGION, WHICH MEANS THAT THE PLANET IS POISED ON THE BRINK OF ENVIRONMENTAL CATASTROPHE DUE TO GLOBAL WARMING AND WE'RE ALL GOING TO DIE
GOLLY!
TOMORROW'S OUTLOOK: SLIGHT DRIZZLE IN PLACES, WHICH WILL CULMINATE IN THE DESTRUCTION OF CIVILISATION AS WE KNOW IT, AND GIANT ANTS TAKING OVER THE EARTH.
GILBERTS HOUSE
GOSH ~ THIS GLOBAL WARMING IS RATHER WORRYING
HELLO ~ LOOKS LIKE REVEREND HENNYPENNY IS DOING HIS BIT FOR THE ENVIRONMENT
GRAND FUNDRAISING FETE TO STOP GLOBAL WARMING
VICARAGE
ROLL UP! BUY A SCONE, AND PREVENT THE PLANET FROM EXPLODING IN A BALL OF FIRE
THE QUEEN AND DUKE OF EDINBURGH ARE COMING TO OPEN MY FETE, GILBERT
LUCKY DIP
THEY'RE VERY KEEN TO HELP SAVE THE ENVIRONMENT, AND WILL BE ARRIVING SHORTLY IN THEIR PRIVATE HARRIER JET
REVEREND HENNYPENNY! THE ELECTRIC PUMP FOR THE BOUNCY CASTLE IS LEAKING CO2 GAS
GASP!
VERGER
THE ENVIRONMENT OF THIS VICARAGE FETE HAS BEEN GLOBALLY WARMED FOR ABOUT 40 MINUTES AT GREENHOUSE GAS REGULO 7!
WHAT AM I GOING TO DO? THE QUEEN WILL THROW AN EPPY WHEN SHE SEES MY FETE IS ALL GLOBALLY WARMED TO BUGGERY!
VERGER
PERHAPS I CAN HELP, VICAR.
ICE
HUFF PUFF PUFF
I'VE CONSTRUCTED THIS 'CHILL-O-MATIC' WHICH WILL GLOBALLY COOL YOUR VICARAGE FETE UNTIL IT'S JUST NICE AND TEPID.
GOOD GRACIOUS! ALL THIS COLD AIR HAS MADE MRS FOX'S NIPPLES GO HARD
THEY'RE STICKING OUT LIKE PYGMIES' DICKS
OH NO! NOW THE SIGHT OF MRS FOX'S NIPS HAS MADE MY TASSLE GO ALL STIFF
HOW DREADFULLY EMBARRASSING! QUICK GILBERT, MAKE IT GO SOFT
I'LL POINT MY CHILL-O-MATIC DOWN YOUR TROUSERS ~ PERHAPS THAT'LL COOL YOUR PASSION
ICE
HURRY UP! MY HOT BLUSHING FACE IS ONLY EXACERBATING THE GLOBAL WARMING PROBLEM
CRIKEY! A FALLING ACORN HAS KNOCKED THE CONTROL SETTING TO "FAR TOO COLD"
ICE
FREEZING COLD BLAST
TONK
SHRIEK!
THANKS A BLEEDING BUNDLE, GILBERT
SHAKE
CLINK TINKLE
NOW MY GENITALS HAVE FROZEN SOLID AND SNAPPED OFF
HANG ON ~ HERE COME HER MAJESTY THE QUEEN AND THE DUKE OF EDINBURGH
BY! ISN'T SHE REGAL AND DIGNIFIED?
FARKING HELL! WHO LEFT THESE FROZEN TESTICLES LAYING ORN THE PATH?
SKID
HELP! AY CARN'T STAWP!
PHEW! AT LEAST HER MAJESTY HAD A SOFT LANDING ON THAT WOOLLY MAMMOTH...
WHUMP
HOME MADE BUNS
HANG ON! WHY IS THERE A WOOLLY MAMMOTH HELPING ITSELF TO MRS POBJOY'S HOME-MADE BUN STALL?
OH LORDY! I'D LEFT MY CHILL-O-MATIC RUNNING, AND IT'S BROUGHT ABOUT A LOCALISED ICE-AGE IN THE VICARAGE FETE
HOOP-LA
YOU IDIOT, GILBERT ~ MY HOOP-LA STALL IS BEING CRUSHED BENEATH A GLACIER
BY JOVE, HOW SPLENDID! THERE'S SOME SABRE-TOOTHED TIGERS FOR ME TO SHOOT
I'VE ALREADY SHOT MOST OF THE ORDINARY TIGERS, IN MY CAPACITY AS PRESIDENT EMERITUS OF THE WORLD WILDLIFE FUND.
AND
HO HO! MAYBE CLIMATE CHANGE ISN'T SUCH A BAD THING AFTER ALL
PULL!
TWANG!
BIG CAT-A-PULT-O-MATIC
THE DUKE WAS SO PLEASED WITH HIS ICE AGE TIGERS THAT HE GAVE US EACH A PEERAGE AS A REWARD.

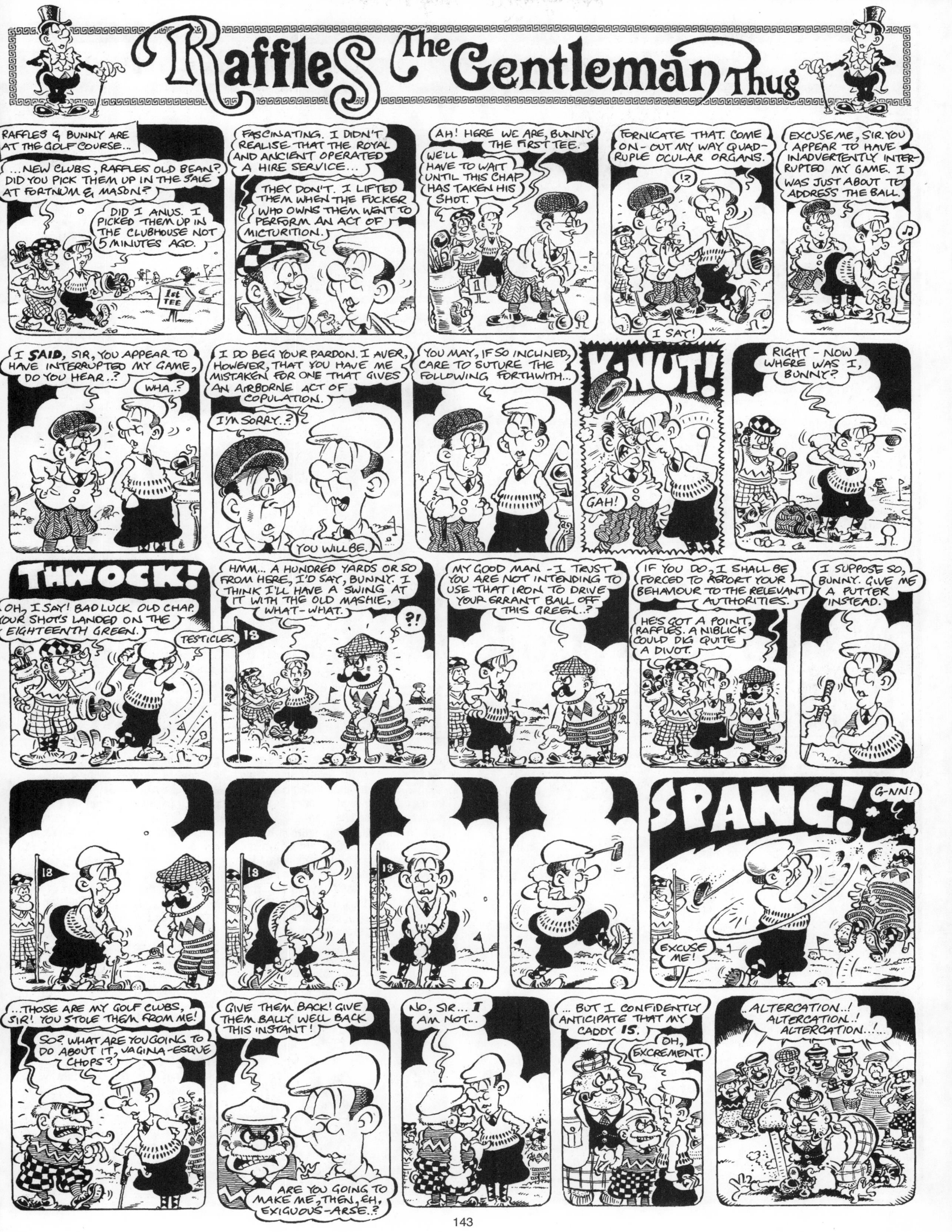
Raffles The Gentleman Thug
RAFFLES & BUNNY ARE AT THE GOLF COURSE...
...NEW CLUBS, RAFFLES OLD BEAN? DID YOU PICK THEM UP IN THE SALE AT FORTNUM & MASON?
DID I ANUS. I PICKED THEM UP IN THE CLUBHOUSE NOT 5 MINUTES AGO.
1st TEE
FASCINATING. I DIDN'T REALISE THAT THE ROYAL AND ANCIENT OPERATED A HIRE SERVICE...
THEY DON'T. I LIFTED THEM WHEN THE FUCKER WHO OWNS THEM WENT TO PERFORM AN ACT OF MICTURITION.
AH! HERE WE ARE, BUNNY. THE FIRST TEE.
WE'LL HAVE TO WAIT UNTIL THIS CHAP HAS TAKEN HIS SHOT.
FORNICATE THAT. COME ON - OUT MY WAY QUADRUPLE OCULAR ORGANS.
!?
I SAY!
EXCUSE ME, SIR. YOU APPEAR TO HAVE INADVERTENTLY INTERRUPTED MY GAME. I WAS JUST ABOUT TO ADDRESS THE BALL.
I SAID, SIR, YOU APPEAR TO HAVE INTERRUPTED MY GAME, DO YOU HEAR..?
WHA..?
I DO BEG YOUR PARDON. I AVER, HOWEVER, THAT YOU HAVE ME MISTAKEN FOR ONE THAT GIVES AN AIRBORNE ACT OF COPULATION.
I'M SORRY..?
YOU WILL BE.
YOU MAY, IF SO INCLINED, CARE TO SUTURE THE FOLLOWING FORTHWITH...
K-NUT!
GAH!
RIGHT - NOW WHERE WAS I, BUNNY?
THWOCK!
OH, I SAY! BAD LUCK OLD CHAP. YOUR SHOT'S LANDED ON THE EIGHTEENTH GREEN.
TESTICLES.
HMM... A HUNDRED YARDS OR SO FROM HERE, I'D SAY, BUNNY. I THINK I'LL HAVE A SWING AT IT WITH THE OLD MASHIE, WHAT-WHAT.
?!
MY GOOD MAN - I TRUST YOU ARE NOT INTENDING TO USE THAT IRON TO DRIVE YOUR ERRANT BALL OFF THIS GREEN..?
IF YOU DO, I SHALL BE FORCED TO REPORT YOUR BEHAVIOUR TO THE RELEVANT AUTHORITIES.
HE'S GOT A POINT, RAFFLES. A NIBLICK COULD DIG QUITE A DIVOT.
I SUPPOSE SO, BUNNY. GIVE ME A PUTTER INSTEAD.
SPANG!
G-NN!
EXCUSE ME!
...THOSE ARE MY GOLF CLUBS, SIR! YOU STOLE THEM FROM ME!
SO? WHAT ARE YOU GOING TO DO ABOUT IT, VAGINA-ESQUE CHOPS?
GIVE THEM BACK! GIVE THEM BALLY WELL BACK THIS INSTANT!
ARE YOU GOING TO MAKE ME, THEN, EH, EXIGUOUS-ARSE..?
NO, SIR... I AM NOT...
...BUT I CONFIDENTLY ANTICIPATE THAT MY CADDY IS.
OH, EXCREMENT.
...ALTERCATION..! ALTERCATION..! ALTERCATION..!...

Milton Keynes Man Spills the Beans on Ho

PEGS 'N' RUGS'

MAKING DOLLS out of clothes pegs and fashioning fireside mats from torn up rags aren't the sort of pastimes usually associated with the wild men of rock. But according to one Milton Keynes shopkeeper, these are just some of the unlikely hobbies that occupy the the men and women who front our favourite bands!

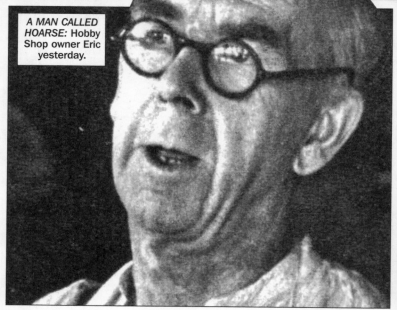

A MAN CALLED HOARSE: Hobby Shop owner Eric yesterday.

EXCLUSIVE

After 40 years running The Hobby Hoarse craft shop in Netherfield Circle shopping precinct, Eric Hoarse is shutting up shop this spring. But as he locks the door of his 100 square foot premises for the last time, it will be with a sad heart. For it will also mark the end of 4 decades serving the hobby needs of some of the greatest stars in music.

"If I told you the names of some of the people I've had through that door shopping for hobby equipment, you'd think I was making it up,"* Eric told us. *"But I'm not. Honest. And if you don't believe me, you can ask my wife."

"Only you can't at the minute, because she's staying with her sister for a few months. And anyway, she's lost her voice, so there's no point even phoning her. Anyway, I wouldn't believe anything she tells you, because she's the liar, not me," he continued.

Now, in a series of hard-hitting exposes to be serialised in Britain's third largest pastimes magazine, *The Hobbyist,* Eric has decided to lift the lid on his extraordinary career supplying hobby equipment to rock'n'roll wild men. And it's a story that will raise a few eyebrows as these exclusive extracts reveal.

Nirvana Kurt's Suicide Riddle Solved

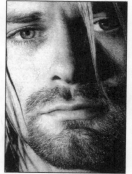

"If I've seen it once, I've seen it a thousand times. A rock star decides to take up a new hobby and comes in my shop to buy all the gear. Whether it's Robert Plant after a wine making demijohn and some corks, or Alice Cooper after some balsa wood and an X-Acto knife, it's always the same. So I didn't bat an eyelid when Kurt Cobain walked into my shop asking for some decoupage papers. I recognised him from his MTV Unplugged session, and we got chatting about decoupage.

The Nirvana vocalist told me he had decided to take up the delicate paper-cutting hobby after seeing Dawn Bibby's craft show on QVC, and he needed some supplies to make a Valentine's card for his wife Courtney Love. He chose some butterfly designs and went away. Half an hour later he was back for more of the same design.

Apparently, he had cut the butterflies out okay, but when he came to stick them down, he'd got glue all over his fingers and the shapes kept sticking to them. We had a little laugh, and I told him it was a typical beginners' mistake and not to be discouraged. But twenty minutes later, Kurt was back again with even more glue on his fingers, and his mood had darkened. I suggested he might like to try making Ms Love a card out of fuzzy felt, or perhaps dyed feathers and sequins. But Cobain was having none of it. "If I can't make this motherfuckin' card, I'm gonna shoot myself," he screamed as left my shop.

Twenty minutes later he didn't come back, so I assumed he had finally managed to stick the cut-out butterflies down. But when I turned on the radio that night, my blood ran cold. The news said that a rock star had blown his brains out in his Seattle home. I knew who it was before the newsreader even said his name.

When it comes to hobbies, you have either got it or you haven't. And I guess Kurt Cobain was simply not cut out for decoupage."

Rock 'n' Rolling Stock

"It's every schoolboy's dream to own his own model train set, complete with points, engines, carriages and scenery. So it was no surprise when headbanging AC/DC guitarist Angus Young, famous for his school uniform stage outfit, walked into my shop and told me he wanted to buy a huge Hornby 00-gauge layout. We had a chat, and I advised him that it would be best if he bought all the track and rolling stock individually so that he could get his layout exactly as he wanted it.

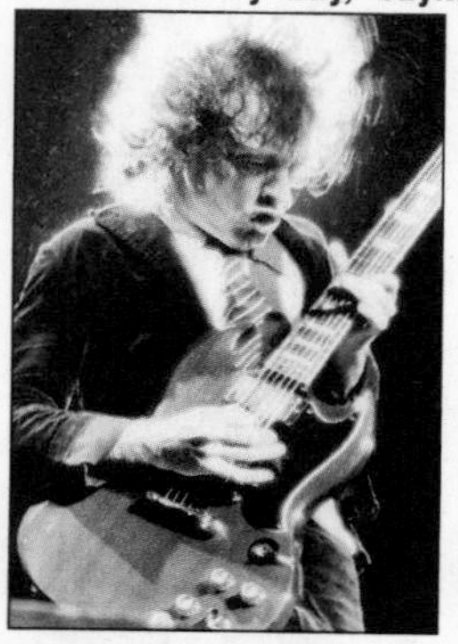

Over the next few weeks he was in and out every day, buying stations, tunnels, tiny foam rubber trees and little figures. He had just got his royalty cheque from Back in Black, and I think he must of spent all of it in my shop! Each time he came in he was more excited as he got closer to the day he was going to plug it in and try it out for the first time.

The day after the grand switch on, my shop door opened and in came AC/DC front man Bonn Scott with some bad news. Apparently Angus was in hospital with third degree flash burns to his hands after a massive explosion had ripped through his dad's loft.

Bonn told me that Angus simply didn't understand that his train set ran on 12v DC power, and in his excitement had plugged it straight into the 240v AC mains.

You would have thought that being in the group AC/DC, Young would have understood the lethal difference between direct and alternating current, and would have bought a transformer to safely operate his model railway. After all, I have them in the shop, starting at just £24.99. This was one Flick of the Switch that almost sent the schoolboy axeman on a Highway to Hell. And ironically, Flick of the Switch and Highway to Hell are the names of 2 AC/DC albums."

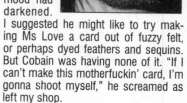

The Stars of Rock 'n' Roll Pass Their Time...

'ROCK 'N' ROLL

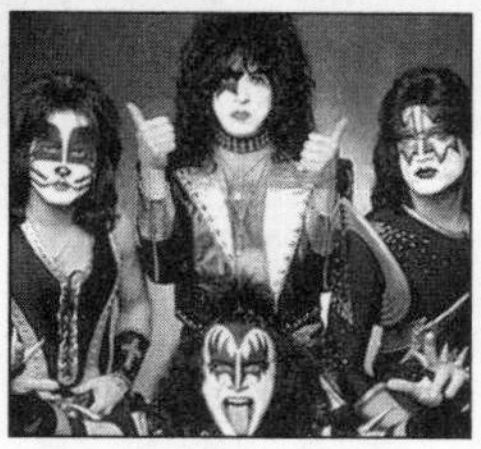

Gene's Crazy, Crazy Gonks

"I'm used to rock stars with wild, hedonistic reputations coming into my shop, so it was no surprise to me when I came out of the stockroom one day to find Gene Simmons browsing my shelves, wearing full stage makeup. The Kiss vocalist told me he was looking for a hobby to fill up his spare time in between having sex with over 4,000 women. I'd just a delivery of fun fur, Pritt-sticks and boggly plastic eyes, so I suggested he might like to try his hand at gonk-making.

It's a sad fact that nine out of ten rock stars who take up a hobby abandon it within six months, usually due to the pressures of touring, recording, and drug addiction. But Gene was different. he took to gonk-making like a duck to water. He later told me that he'd taken the first five little furry critters he'd made down to his local car boot sale and sold the lot within a couple of hours.

Since then, I don't think a week's gone by when Simmons hasn't been back to the Hobby Hoarse buying more supplies. Apparently, when his busy touring and recording schedule permits, he does three or four car boots a week, selling gonks by the dozen out of the trunk of his stretch limousine with a jacuzzi in the back.

In fact he enjoys his hobby so much that he once said to me: "Eric, if Kiss ever split up due to musical differences, or if Ace Frehley, Paul Stanley and Peter Criss all left to pursue solo careers, I wouldn't form another rock band. I'd simply make gonks for a living!""

Ted Nugent Had a Pressing Need

"Over the years, I've seen so many unusual people in my shop that nothing phazes me any more. So I didn't bat an eyelid when the door opened and in came redneck rocker Ted Nugent... riding on the back of a giant buffalo. He dismounted and shot the beast dead with a crossbow, before sheepishly wandering up to the counter.

I was surprised when he took out a wad of cash and asked to see a selection of flower presses. Pressing flowers is a popular hobby amongst old ladies and little girls, so I must confess to being a little surprised that the Motor City Madman had decided to take it up. But in this game, the customer is always right, so I showed him the presses I had in stock, which ranged from a beginner's kit at £6.99 to one capable of handling a dozen daffodils at once. Ted bought a medium-sized outfit with two-inch wing-nuts and a dozen A4 sheets of blotting paper.

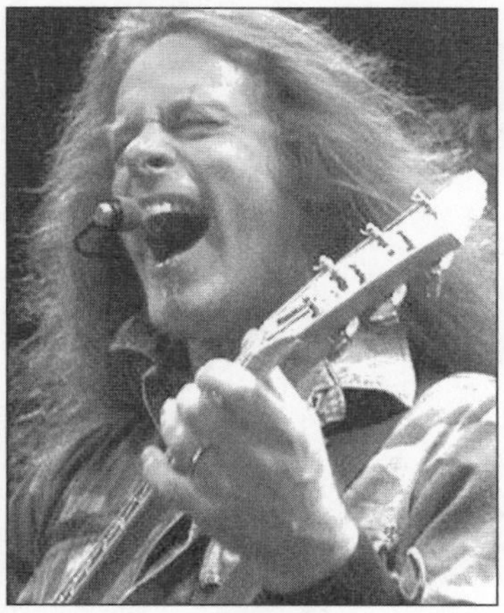

He came back the next day and bought the biggest press I had in the shop - a Rosemere 600. The Nuge has sold over 30 million albums in his career, so he didn't even flinch when I told him the price - a cool £24.99.

A couple of days later, however, I heard the familiar sound of buffalo hooves in the precinct followed by the ting of my door. It was Ted again, and he was looking for an even bigger press - fifteen feet by fifteen feet! I couldn't hold in my curiosity any longer, and I asked him what sort of flowers he was pressing to need such a big piece of equipment.

Nugent's face creased into a broad smile and he burst into laughter. As he wiped away the tears of mirth, he explained that he hadn't been pressing flowers - he'd been pressing animals! He'd already done rabbits, gophers and a small deer - but now he needed the giant press so he could handle grizzly bears, mooses and elks. Then he told me that if I ever accused him of having a "faggot" hobby like flower-pressing again, he'd drag me into the precinct and shoot me like a sick dog."

Who Moon was Wild Matchstick Man

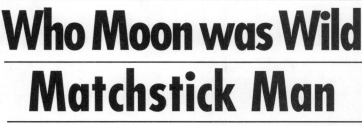

"Perhaps the man you'd least expect to see in my shop would be the Godfather of wildmen of rock, Keith Moon. But I've been in the hobby business a long time, and it was no surprise to me when the Who drummer came in wanting some advice. He'd just got back from a UK tour, and in a guest house where the band had stayed in Leeds, Moon has spotted a model Gypsy caravan made out of matchsticks. He was very impressed with it and thought he'd like to make one for himself.

Of course, I was able to supply him with the plans, glue and a craft knife which he bought on the spot. But when I suggested he buy a bag of 5000 match sticks, the late tub thumper refused. He said that he was going to ask all his rock 'n' roll friends to save the matches that they used to light their drugs with and to give them to him.

Because of the sort of circles that Moon moved in, it wasn't long before he had collected enough matches to make the caravan, and that was the last I saw of him. I assumed that he had finished the project and started on another, perhaps a galleon, or a dray horse and cart. So a few months later when Roger Daltrey came into the shop to buy some Fimo and a badge making kit, I asked him how Keith's caravan had come on. He chuckled.

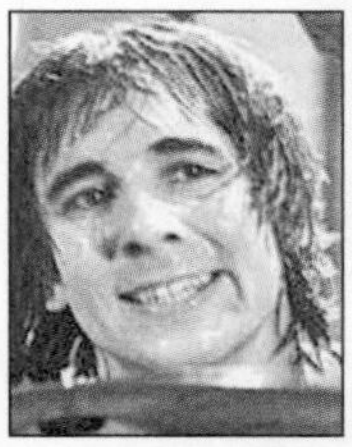

According to Daltrey, Moon had taken the matches and plans on the Who's last US tour. Instead of partying with the other band members and groupies every night, Moon had sat in his hotel room painstakingly working on his model, often till way past his bedtime. On the night of the final gig, Moon finished the caravan and joined his bandmates in the hotel bar to celebrate.

But as usual he didn't know when to stop, and in the early hours of the morning he went on a drink and drug-fuelled rampage around the hotel, setting off fire extinguishers and riding motorbikes into the lift. When he sobered up in the morning, he was gutted to discover that at the height of the previous night's madness he had pushed his beloved model off the hotel balcony and into the swimming pool twelve storeys below!"

REVEALED NEXT WEEK

ERIC REMEMBERS not being surprised the time that Starman David Bowie called in for a 5kg bag of stonecast to make a garden gnome, and remaining entirely unruffled when Motley Crue entered his shop looking for a rubber stamp of some ducklings and an ink pad.

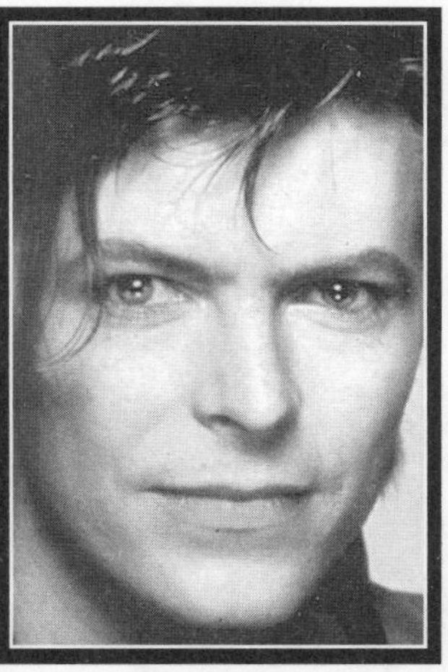

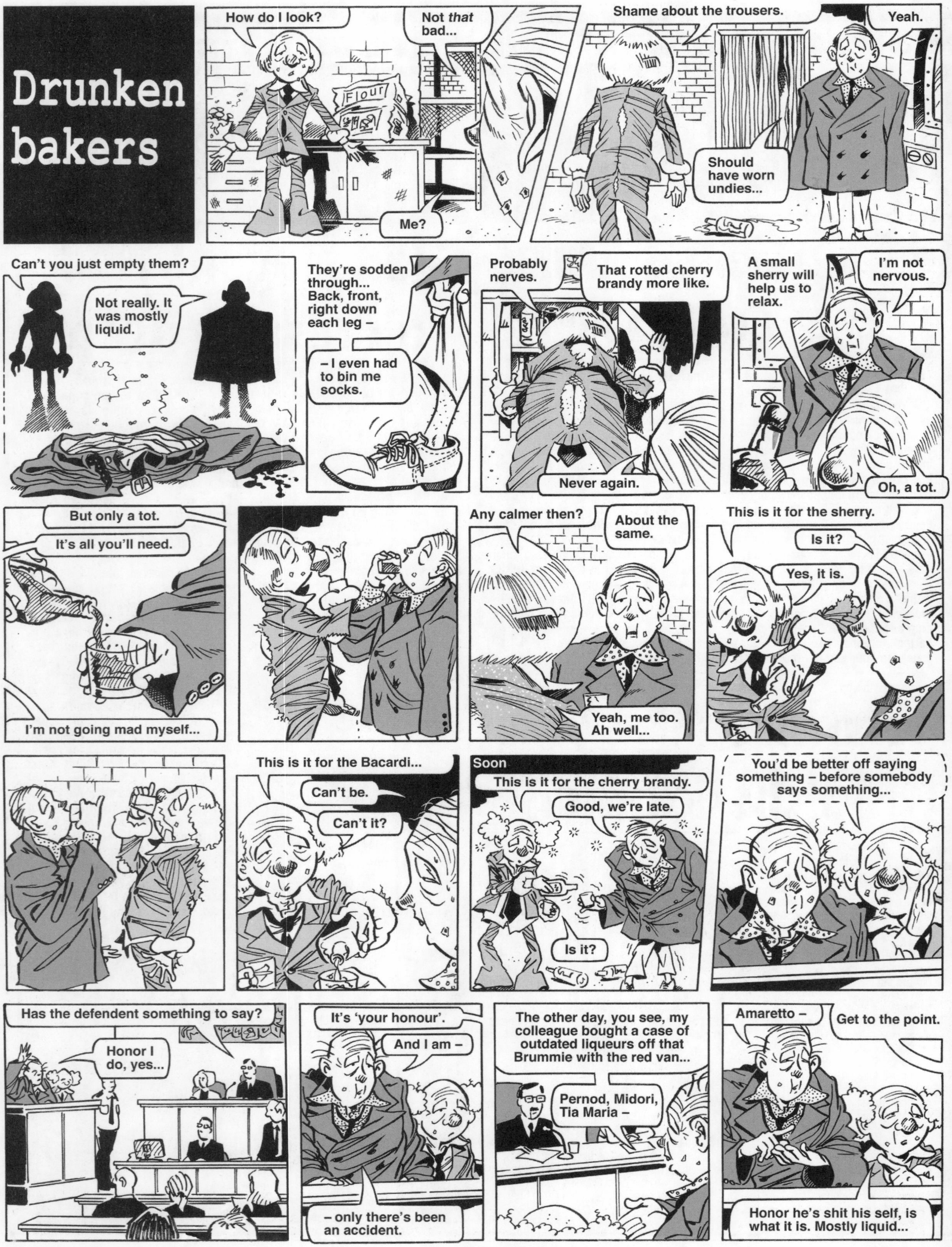
Drunken bakers
How do I look?
Not *that* bad...
Me?
Shame about the trousers.
Yeah.
Should have worn undies...
Can't you just empty them?
Not really. It was mostly liquid.
They're sodden through... Back, front, right down each leg –
– I even had to bin me socks.
Probably nerves.
That rotted cherry brandy more like.
Never again.
A small sherry will help us to relax.
I'm not nervous.
Oh, a tot.
But only a tot.
It's all you'll need.
I'm not going mad myself...
Any calmer then?
About the same.
Yeah, me too. Ah well...
This is it for the sherry.
Is it?
Yes, it is.
This is it for the Bacardi...
Can't be.
Can't it?
Soon
This is it for the cherry brandy.
Good, we're late.
Is it?
You'd be better off saying something – before somebody says something...
Has the defendent something to say?
Honor I do, yes...
It's 'your honour'.
And I am –
– only there's been an accident.
The other day, you see, my colleague bought a case of outdated liqueurs off that Brummie with the red van...
Pernod, Midori, Tia Maria –
Amaretto –
Get to the point.
Honor he's shit his self, is what it is. Mostly liquid...

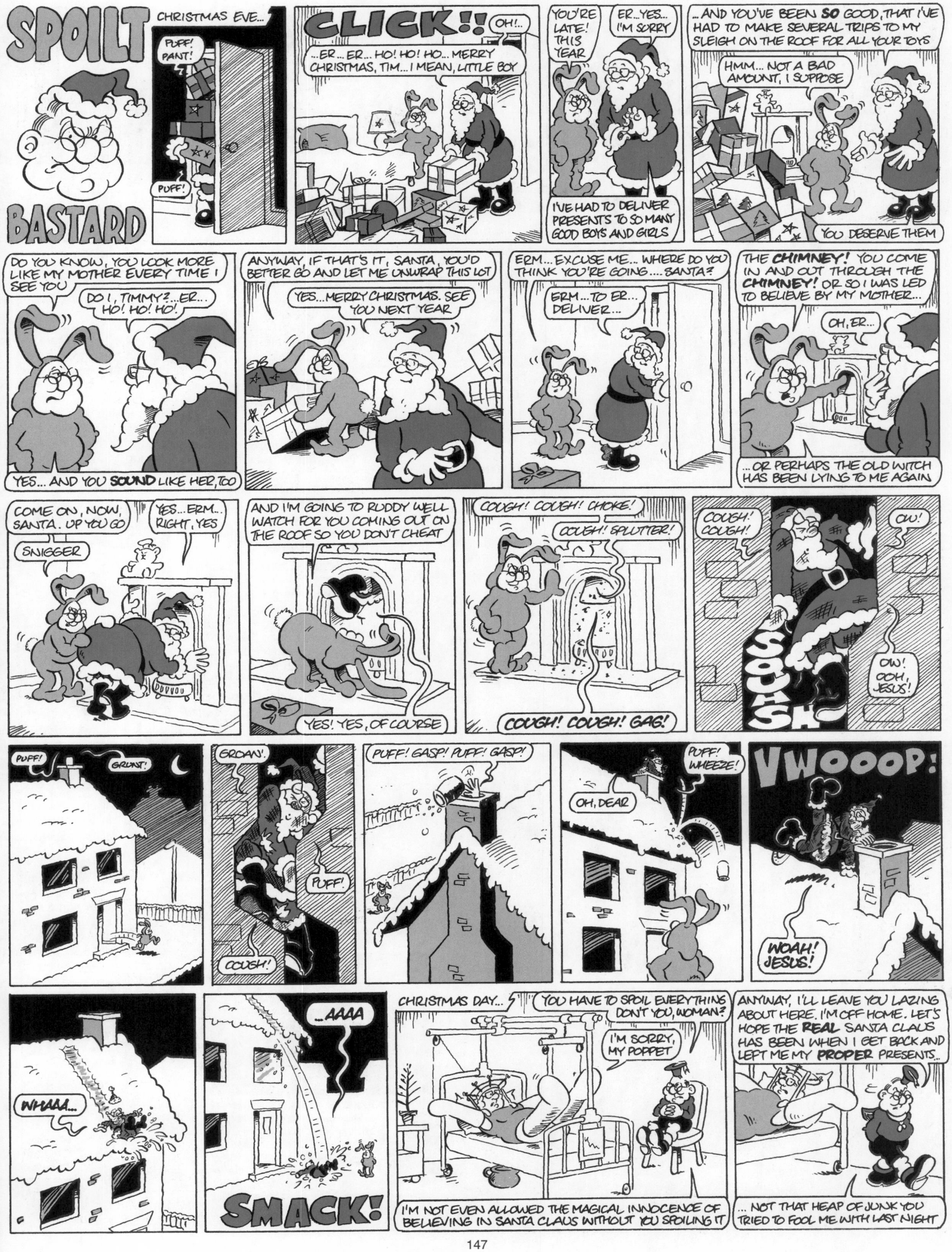
SPOILT BASTARD
CHRISTMAS EVE...
PUFF! PANT!
PUFF!
CLICK!!
OH!...
...ER...ER... HO! HO! HO... MERRY CHRISTMAS, TIM... I MEAN, LITTLE BOY
YOU'RE LATE! THIS YEAR
ER...YES... I'M SORRY
I'VE HAD TO DELIVER PRESENTS TO SO MANY GOOD BOYS AND GIRLS
...AND YOU'VE BEEN SO GOOD, THAT I'VE HAD TO MAKE SEVERAL TRIPS TO MY SLEIGH ON THE ROOF FOR ALL YOUR TOYS
HMM... NOT A BAD AMOUNT, I SUPPOSE
YOU DESERVE THEM
DO YOU KNOW, YOU LOOK MORE LIKE MY MOTHER EVERY TIME I SEE YOU
DO I, TIMMY?...ER... HO! HO! HO!
YES... AND YOU SOUND LIKE HER, TOO
ANYWAY, IF THAT'S IT, SANTA, YOU'D BETTER GO AND LET ME UNWRAP THIS LOT
YES...MERRY CHRISTMAS. SEE YOU NEXT YEAR
ERM... EXCUSE ME... WHERE DO YOU THINK YOU'RE GOING.... SANTA?
ERM... TO ER... DELIVER...
THE CHIMNEY! YOU COME IN AND OUT THROUGH THE CHIMNEY! OR SO I WAS LED TO BELIEVE BY MY MOTHER...
OH, ER...
...OR PERHAPS THE OLD WITCH HAS BEEN LYING TO ME AGAIN
COME ON, NOW, SANTA. UP YOU GO
YES...ERM... RIGHT, YES
SNIGGER
AND I'M GOING TO RUDDY WELL WATCH FOR YOU COMING OUT ON THE ROOF SO YOU DON'T CHEAT
YES! YES, OF COURSE
COUGH! COUGH! CHOKE!
COUGH! SPLUTTER!
COUGH! COUGH! GAG!
COUGH! COUGH!
OW!
SQUASH
OW! OOH, JESUS!
PUFF!
GRUNT!
GROAN!
PUFF!
COUGH!
PUFF! GASP! PUFF! GASP!
PUFF! WHEEZE!
OH, DEAR
VWOOOP!
WOAH! JESUS!
WHAAA...
...AAAA
SMACK!
CHRISTMAS DAY...
YOU HAVE TO SPOIL EVERYTHING DON'T YOU, WOMAN?
I'M SORRY, MY POPPET
I'M NOT EVEN ALLOWED THE MAGICAL INNOCENCE OF BELIEVING IN SANTA CLAUS WITHOUT YOU SPOILING IT
ANYWAY, I'LL LEAVE YOU LAZING ABOUT HERE. I'M OFF HOME. LET'S HOPE THE REAL SANTA CLAUS HAS BEEN WHEN I GET BACK AND LEFT ME MY PROPER PRESENTS...
... NOT THAT HEAP OF JUNK YOU TRIED TO FOOL ME WITH LAST NIGHT

LETTERBOCKS

Viz Comic, PO Box 656, North Shields, NE30 4XX

STAR LETTER

I was overjoyed to see David Jason on the television the other day. He is a great entertainer.

Mary Hefty, Wirral

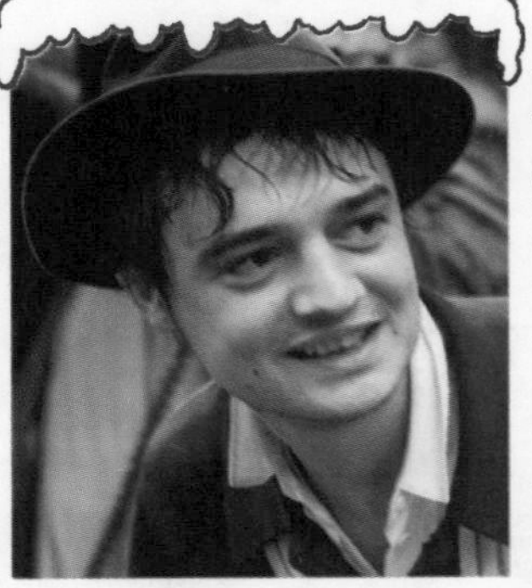

I was delighted this week when I heard the splendid news that Pete Doherty had kicked his drugs habit. Congratulations to the man. It has been a long time coming, but he has finally done it.

Edna Ballentyne, Newcastle

I don't know why Eurostar are crowing about their new train service taking just 2¼ hours to get to the French capital. Why would anyone be in a hurry to get to Paris? Quite frankly, in my opinion, the longer it takes to get there, the better. And the same goes for Brussels.

Hector Michaelmas, Diss

If the stewardess on the Jet2.Com flight 532 from Palma to Newcastle is reading this, could I please have my muffin now? I've been waiting half an hour.

S J Marston, Seat 22B

I always laugh when I see advertisements for toasters. I've had the same toaster for 38 years now and it works a treat. It was given to me on my wedding day and it still makes delicious toast. It puts these modern toasters to shame, I can tell you.

Ada Humphries, Luton

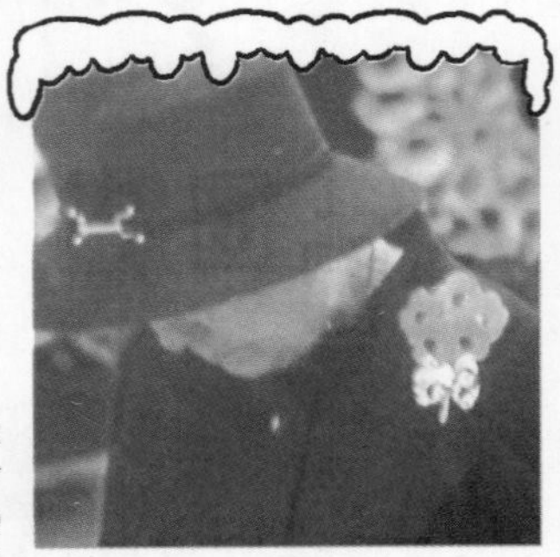

At this year's Remembrance Day parade, the Queen was wearing FIVE poppies on her lapel. This can only mean that she gave five times as much money to the poppy appeal as everyone else. Well I gave 50p for my poppy, which means she must have chucked in £2.50. What a mean gesture from the second richest woman in Britain.

H Lambert, Tring

I agree with H Lambert *(above letter)*. £2.50 is a paltry sum from the second richest woman in the country. I dare say that the richest, JK Rowling, gave more than that. I bet she gave a fiver at least.

A Duggan, Leeds

The head of MI5 says that terrorism poses a threat to every single person in the country. That doesn't worry me. I got married last week.

J Staunton, Leicester

My husband is making me something very exciting for Christmas. I don't know what is is, but he spends a lot of time in the cellar sawing things up, and then hiding things under the floorboards. I took him a cup of tea down the other day hoping to get a peek of what it is, but he held the door shut and screamed at me to leave him alone, which just piqued my curiosity all the more. It's even more exciting because he has never given me anything before in over 30 years of marriage. I can't wait for Christmas day!

Edna Potates, Croydon

Yesterday, I wrote you a letter about how pleased I was that Pete Doherty had come off drugs. Imagine my disbelief when I opened my newspaper today and read that he was back on heroin. Shame on him. I thought he had more sense.

Edna Ballentyne, Newcastle

Walking down my street today, I saw our local bishop walking in a straight line. Surely if he followed the rules of chess he should have been walking diagonally? One rule for chess players and one for the church.

I James, e-mail

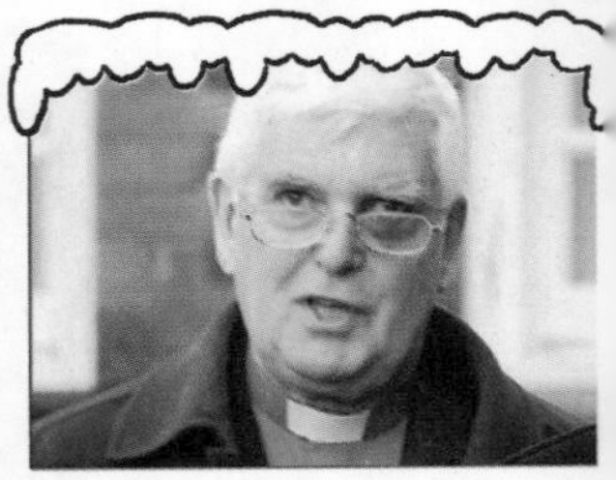

With reference to the previous letter. I live in Southwark where Tom Butler is the Bishop, and I've never seen him walking in a straight line. Especially when he's spent the afternoon at the Irish Embassy.

H Littlemore, Southwark

In reply to the letter regarding *The Double Deckers (Letterbocks, p.121)*, Doughnut was my elder brother so I ***did*** 'see him next week'. I saw him the next day, come to that. And every other day for the next 8 years that I lived with the smug, fat twat. Whoops! Sorry Doug!

JP Simmonds, Bristol

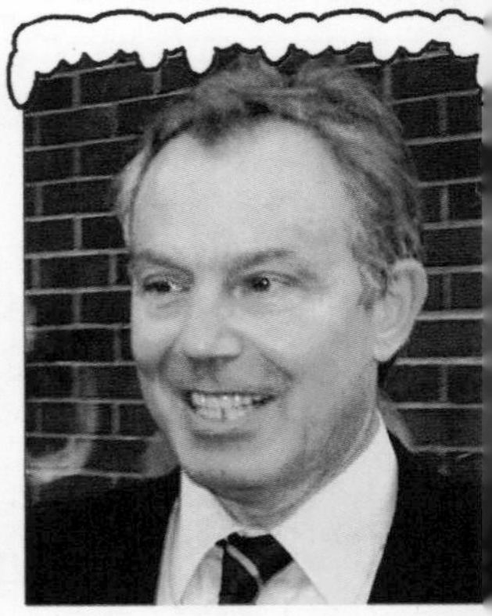

The news that Tony Blair is set to publish his memoirs for £5m fills me with disgust. What a ludcrous price for a book. I for one will be waiting until it comes out in paperback.

P Nelson, Skelmersdale

I'm livid! I read somewhere this week that the Government is going to start taxing me every time I use my feet. I for one am going to sit down for the rest of my life so they won't get their mitts on my hard earned cash!

Jim Sausage, Devizes

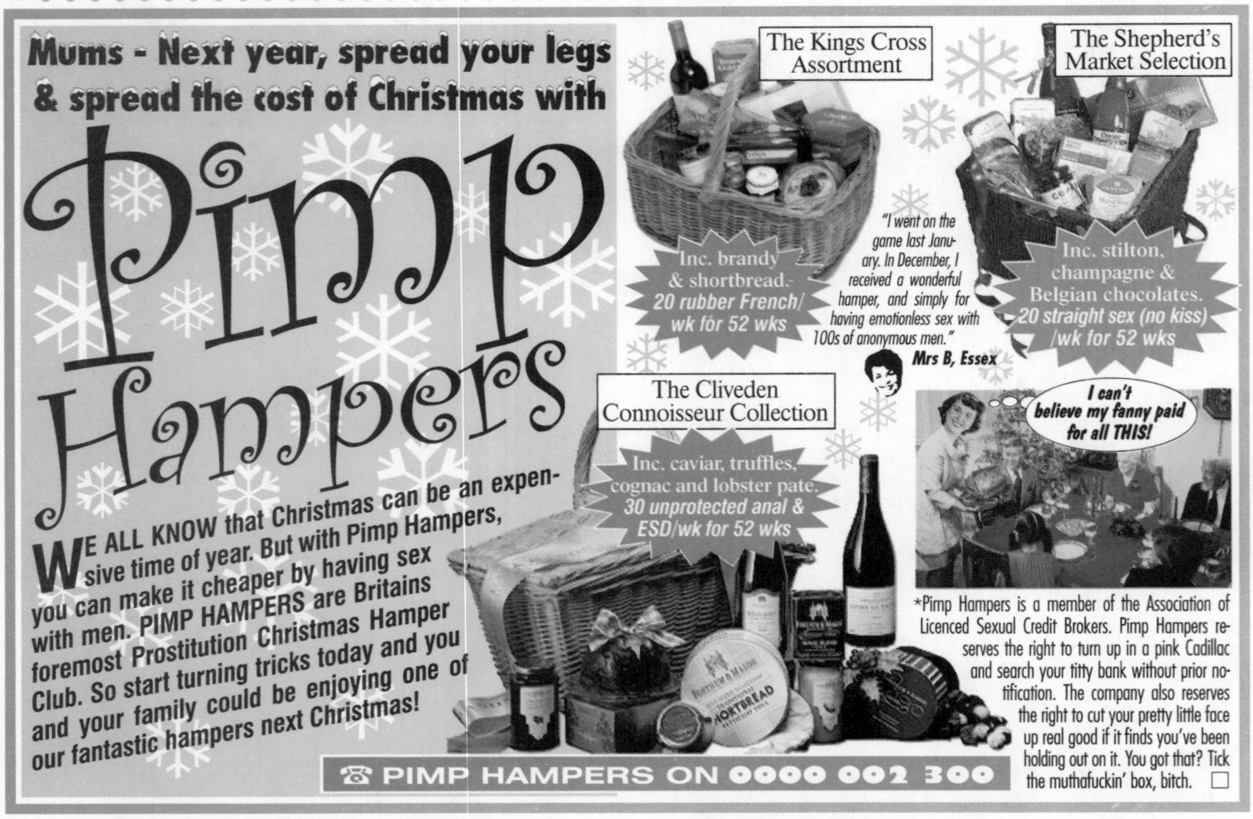

Mums - Next year, spread your legs & spread the cost of Christmas with
Pimp Hampers
The Kings Cross Assortment
Inc. brandy & shortbread. 20 rubber French/ wk for 52 wks
The Shepherd's Market Selection
Inc. stilton, champagne & Belgian chocolates. 20 straight sex (no kiss) /wk for 52 wks
"I went on the game last January. In December, I received a wonderful hamper, and simply for having emotionless sex with 100s of anonymous men."
Mrs B, Essex
The Cliveden Connoisseur Collection
Inc. caviar, truffles, cognac and lobster pate. 30 unprotected anal & ESD/wk for 52 wks
I can't believe my fanny paid for all THIS!
WE ALL KNOW that Christmas can be an expensive time of year. But with Pimp Hampers, you can make it cheaper by having sex with men. PIMP HAMPERS are Britains foremost Prostitution Christmas Hamper Club. So start turning tricks today and you and your family could be enjoying one of our fantastic hampers next Christmas!
*Pimp Hampers is a member of the Association of Licenced Sexual Credit Brokers. Pimp Hampers reserves the right to turn up in a pink Cadillac and search your titty bank without prior notification. The company also reserves the right to cut your pretty little face up real good if it finds you've been holding out on it. You got that? Tick the muthafuckin' box, bitch. ☐
☎ PIMP HAMPERS ON 0000 002 300

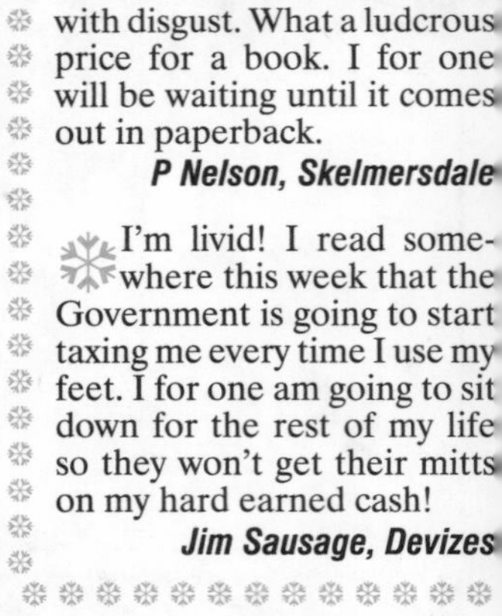

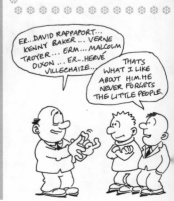

ER.. DAVID RAPPAPORT... KENNY BAKER... VERNE TROYER... ERM... MALCOLM DIXON... ER.. HERVÉ VILLECHAIZE...
THAT'S WHAT I LIKE ABOUT HIM. HE NEVER FORGETS THE LITTLE PEOPLE.

Whenever I see a very large-breasted woman, I sing the Um-Bongo song in my head. I have been doing this for about 6 months and I don't seem to able to stop.

Andrew MacBride, e-mail

I always laugh when I see people buying rolls of foil. I've had the same roll of foil for 38 years and it hasn't run out yet, not like these modern rolls which don't last five minutes.

Ada Humphries, Luton

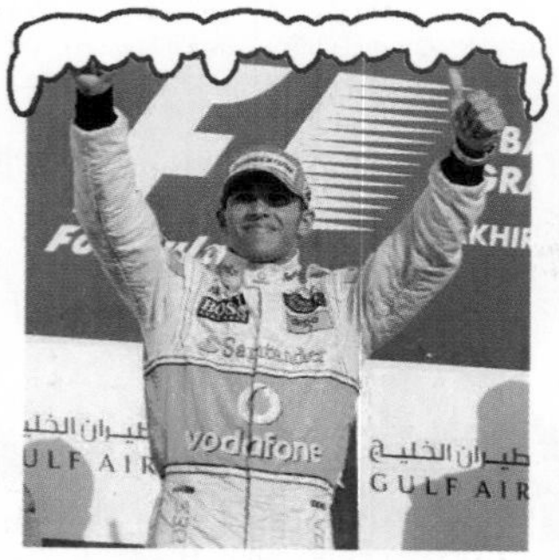

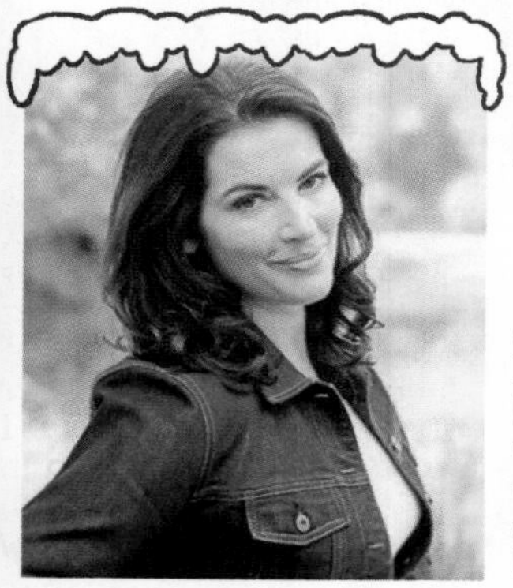

How come when Nigella licks jam off her fingers on the telly I get a raging nob-on but when my missus does it I feel slightly nauseous? Are we buying the wrong brand of jam?

Nick Pettigrew, London

Shame on Lewis Hamilton for quitting England as soon as he makes a bit of money, depriving the British coffers of his tax. You can bet your boots that when his F1 career is over, he'll be straight back to claim his dole and get on the council house list. And who will pay for it? Joe bloody Muggins, here.

JB Muggins, Here

Earlier today I wrote to you expressing my disappointment that Pete Doherty has lapsed and gone back on heroin. However, when I came back from posting the letter I put the radio on, and was delighted to hear that he had booked himself into rehab. It is splendid news that Pete has finally put his drug-riddled past behind him once and for all.

Edna Ballentyne, Newcastle

I have a tattoo of Sid the Sexist on my leg. Do I win £5? I can't send you a pic because I don't know how to work computers. I'm not Bill fuckin' Gates.

Paul Doyle, e-mail

I always laugh when I see someone buying fresh eggs. I've had the same dozen eggs in my fridge now for nearly forty years. They put these modern eggs to shame, I can tell you.

Ada Humphries, Luton

I recently nailed my knackers to the kitchen table as a sexual experiment. I won't be doing that again, let me tell you.

M Beech, London

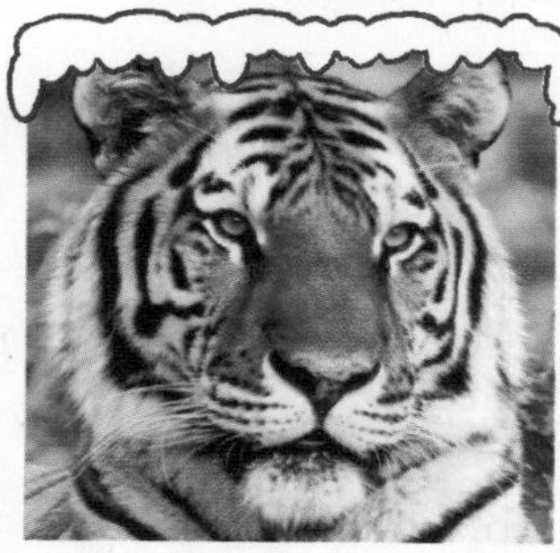

I heard that the tiger is threatened. There must be some really brave people out there. I would not dare threaten a tiger.

Alan Heath, e-mail

I was absolutely incensed when I heard off a mad bloke in a pub this week that Gordon Brown is going to be giving all the paedophiles a million pounds in cash each. Call that justice Gordon? Disgusting.

Sandra Moon-Landing
Gateshead

TOP TIPS

POSTING a letter? If you want it to arrive at its destination as soon as possible, pop a first-class stamp on it. If it's nothing urgent, pop a second-class stamp on it. Simple!

Tristram Hawks, Luton

FATTIES. Avoid your torso being surreptitiously filmed and used in a BBC news report about Britain's obesity problem by always wearing a T-shirt with 'All Newsreaders are Cunts' written on it.

J Thorn, Hexham

BIKERS! Remember to give two or three blips of your throttle, when stopping at the pub. This will remind patrons on the patio that you master a beast, likely to burst into life at any moment, of its own volition.

Chrispy, e-mail

TRICK spiders into thinking they have caught a fly by flicking cigarette ash into cobwebs.

Andy Woolfoot, Cirencester

CHINESE citizens. Improve chopstick performance by simply carving one into three points and fashioning a serrated edge on the other. Hey presto! No more chopstick based faux pas!

POB, e-mail

PUT a sawn-off piece of exhaust pipe in your mouth to fool your Dad into thinking you've swallowed his car.

Ken Leopard, e-mail

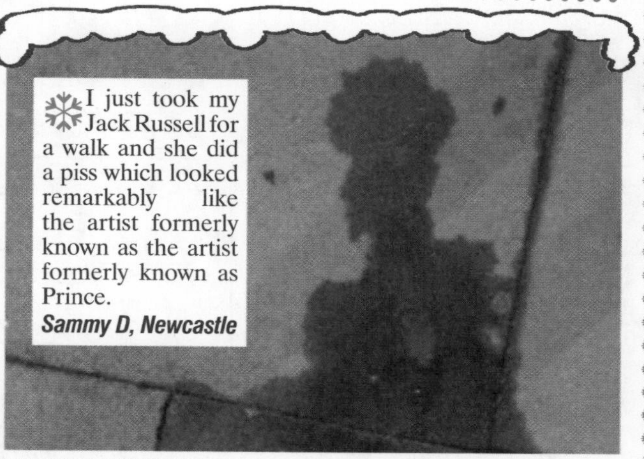

I just took my Jack Russell for a walk and she did a piss which looked remarkably like the artist formerly known as the artist formerly known as Prince.

Sammy D, Newcastle

Xmas Turkeys!

WE asked you to tell us about the most disappointing Christmas present you ever received. Here are a selection of your festive thumbs downs...

...MY aunty Joyce bought me a soap on a rope when I was 10. She's dead now, so I don't feel too bad about slagging it off.

Spud, Luton

...MY wife knitted me a jumper as a surprise. It'd taken her a year to knit, as she could only do it whilst I was out the house, and when the arthritis in her hands would allow it. It was a nice jumper I suppose, but I hadn't the heart to tell her that what I really wanted for Christmas was oral sex off a prostitute.

Hector Monkbottle, Perth

...I LIVE in a remote village in Malawi, and last Christmas a family in Surrey (whom I had never met nor heard of) bought me a goat, three chickens and half a dozen mango saplings. When I unwrapped them on Christmas morning I was so disappointed - the woman next door got an ipod shuffle and a Cyberman voice changer helmet.

Pipi Okwekwe, Malawi

...I AM a model railway enthusiast, and each Christmas my wife buys me a little something to add to my layout. Three years ago she bought me an 00-scale saddle tank locomotive in the characteristic maroon and cream livery of the post-war Great North Eastern Railway. However, my layout is a representation of a section of the GNER from the early 1930s, when the livery was a slightly darker maroon. I thought this would have been obvious to her. I spent the rest of Christmas day with my arms folded, turning my head away from her whenever she tried to ask me what was wrong.

T Potter, Morpeth

Have YOUR Say!

WITH the levels of gun crime rising on our streets, is it time to make the ownership of an illegal firearms against the law? We went onto the bullet-riddled streets to find out what YOU thought....

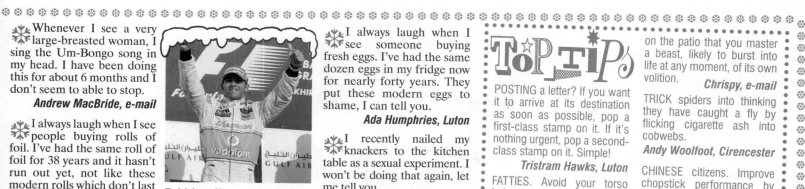

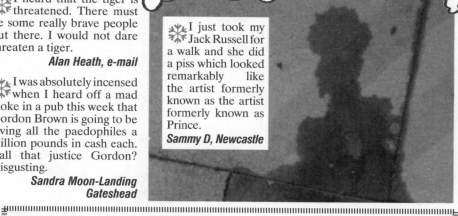

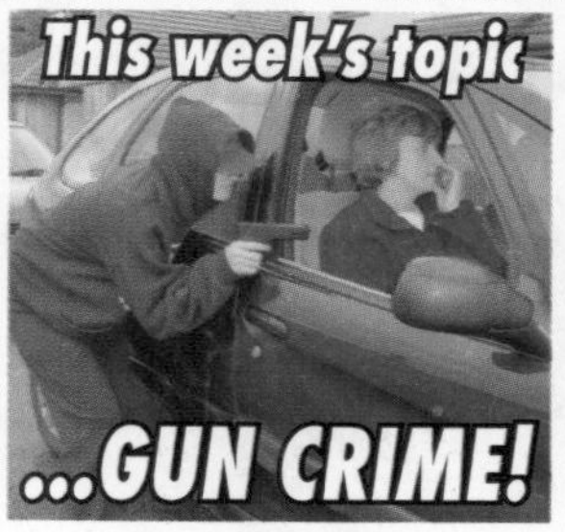
This week's topic
...GUN CRIME!

...IT IS pointless banning guns. If they were banned, robbers would simply use another sort of weapon when holding up banks and building societies, such as big daggers, candlesticks or billiard balls in a sock.

Mick Sundry, ironmonger

...IN the UK, anyone with a history of mental illness or a criminal record is not allowed to keep a gun. I would go further and say that the desire to own a gun should automatically bar a person from doing so.

Mike Whip, cheesemonger

...IF Mr Whip's suggestion *(above)* were to become law, criminals would simply pretend not to want a gun in order to get one. What's more, ordinary law-abiding people who didn't want a gun would have to pretend to want one.

Audrey Noose, fishmonger

...I AM a law abiding citizen and a member of a well-respected licensed gun club, and I can reassure the public that they are at no risk from legally-held firearms like mine. I would never hand over my weapons in the event of a ban, and if the police tried to confiscate my gun I would shoot them dead, then shoot all my family before turning the gun on myself and blowing my brains out.

Alan Fibreboard, sockmonger

...BRINGING in a ban would simply drive gun ownership underground. This would be unfair to miners, who face enough dangers as it is, what with collapsing roofs, flooding and coal gas escapes, without having to worry about getting a cap popped in their ass by a rapper.

Charlie Milk, shoemonger

...THERE is a lot of nonsense talked about the dangers of guns these days. My grandfather was shot 80 times a day from the age of sixteen and it never did him any harm. He worked as a quality control tester in a bullet-proof vest factory, and he was run over by a bus on his 90th birthday.

Lance Boil, breadmonger

...WHAT a lot of nonsense is spoken about the dangers of being run over by buses when you are 90. My grandfather was run over by 80 buses a day when he was 90 and it never did him any harm. He worked in the inspection pit of a bus garage for twenty five years after he should have retired.

T Balm, computermonger

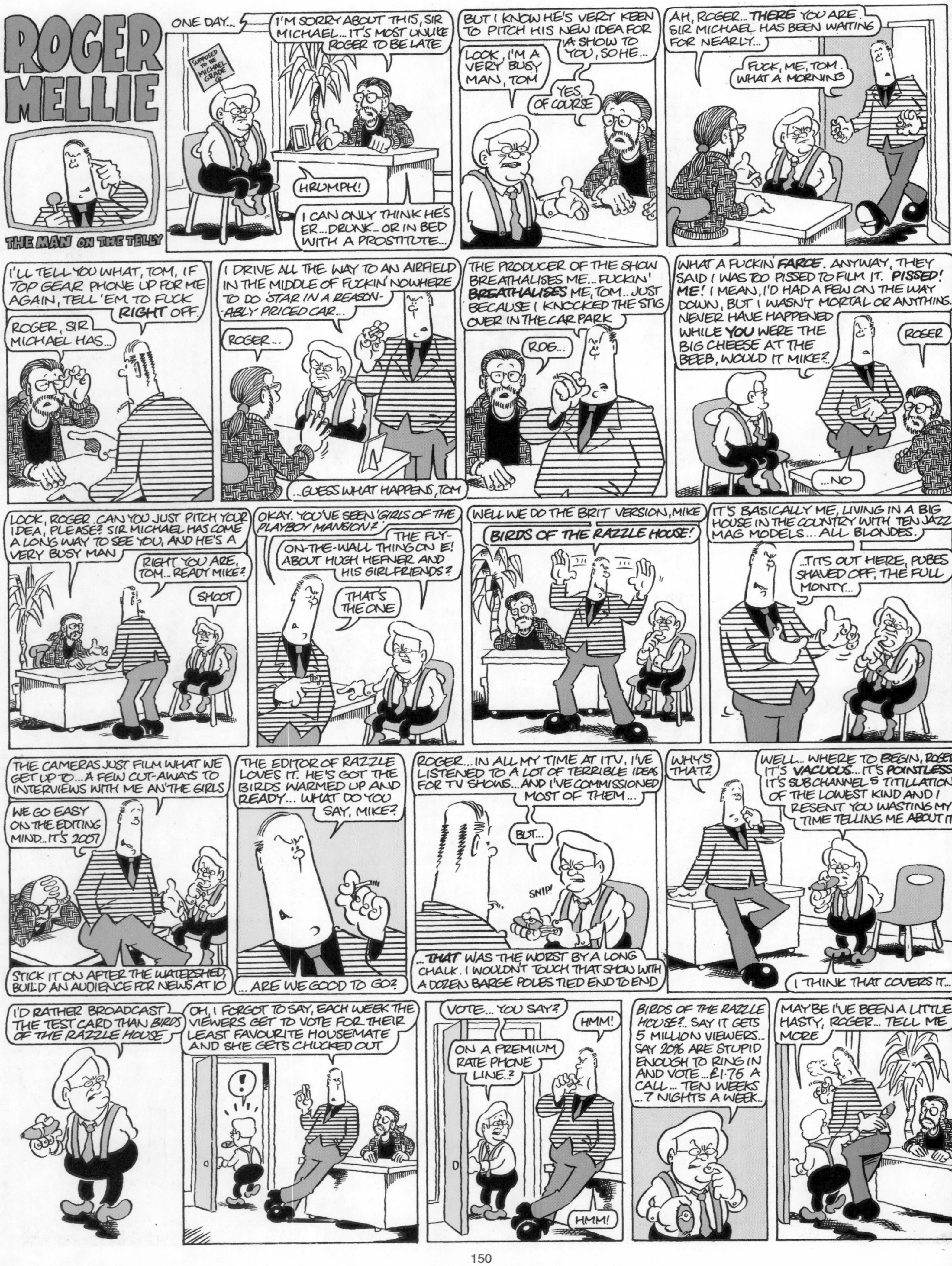
ROGER MELLIE
THE MAN ON THE TELLY
ONE DAY...
I'M SORRY ABOUT THIS, SIR MICHAEL... IT'S MOST UNLIKE ROGER TO BE LATE
SUPPOSED TO BE MICHAEL GRADE
HRUMPH!
I CAN ONLY THINK HE'S ER... DRUNK... OR IN BED WITH A PROSTITUTE...
BUT I KNOW HE'S VERY KEEN TO PITCH HIS NEW IDEA FOR A SHOW TO YOU, SO HE...
LOOK, I'M A VERY BUSY MAN, TOM
YES, OF COURSE
AH, ROGER... THERE YOU ARE. SIR MICHAEL HAS BEEN WAITING FOR NEARLY...
FUCK, ME, TOM. WHAT A MORNING
I'LL TELL YOU WHAT, TOM, IF TOP GEAR PHONE UP FOR ME AGAIN, TELL 'EM TO FUCK RIGHT OFF.
ROGER, SIR MICHAEL HAS...
I DRIVE ALL THE WAY TO AN AIRFIELD IN THE MIDDLE OF FUCKIN' NOWHERE TO DO 'STAR IN A REASON-ABLY PRICED CAR'...
ROGER...
...GUESS WHAT HAPPENS, TOM
THE PRODUCER OF THE SHOW BREATHALISES ME... FUCKIN' BREATHALISES ME, TOM... JUST BECAUSE I KNOCKED THE STIG OVER IN THE CAR PARK
ROG...
WHAT A FUCKIN' FARCE. ANYWAY, THEY SAID I WAS TOO PISSED TO FILM IT. PISSED! ME! I MEAN, I'D HAD A FEW ON THE WAY DOWN, BUT I WASN'T MORTAL OR ANYTHING.
NEVER HAVE HAPPENED WHILE YOU WERE THE BIG CHEESE AT THE BEEB, WOULD IT MIKE?
ROGER
...NO
LOOK, ROGER. CAN YOU JUST PITCH YOUR IDEA, PLEASE? SIR MICHAEL HAS COME A LONG WAY TO SEE YOU, AND HE'S A VERY BUSY MAN
RIGHT YOU ARE, TOM... READY MIKE?
SHOOT
OKAY. YOU'VE SEEN 'GIRLS OF THE PLAYBOY MANSION'?
THE FLY-ON-THE-WALL THING ON E! ABOUT HUGH HEFNER AND HIS GIRLFRIENDS?
THAT'S THE ONE
WELL WE DO THE BRIT VERSION, MIKE
BIRDS OF THE RAZZLE HOUSE!
IT'S BASICALLY ME, LIVING IN A BIG HOUSE IN THE COUNTRY WITH TEN JAZZ MAG MODELS... ALL BLONDES.
...TITS OUT HERE, PUBES SHAVED OFF, THE FULL MONTY...
THE CAMERAS JUST FILM WHAT WE GET UP TO... A FEW CUT-AWAYS TO INTERVIEWS WITH ME AN' THE GIRLS
WE GO EASY ON THE EDITING MIND... IT'S 2007
STICK IT ON AFTER THE WATERSHED, BUILD AN AUDIENCE FOR NEWS AT 10
THE EDITOR OF RAZZLE LOVES IT. HE'S GOT THE BIRDS WARMED UP AND READY... WHAT DO YOU SAY, MIKE?
...ARE WE GOOD TO GO?
ROGER... IN ALL MY TIME AT ITV, I'VE LISTENED TO A LOT OF TERRIBLE IDEAS FOR TV SHOWS... AND I'VE COMMISSIONED MOST OF THEM...
BUT...
SNIP!
...THAT WAS THE WORST BY A LONG CHALK. I WOULDN'T TOUCH THAT SHOW WITH A DOZEN BARGE POLES TIED END TO END
WHY'S THAT?
WELL... WHERE TO BEGIN, ROGER? IT'S VACUOUS... IT'S POINTLESS. IT'S SUBCHANNEL 5 TITILLATION OF THE LOWEST KIND AND I RESENT YOU WASTING MY TIME TELLING ME ABOUT IT
I THINK THAT COVERS IT...
I'D RATHER BROADCAST THE TEST CARD THAN BIRDS OF THE RAZZLE HOUSE
OH, I FORGOT TO SAY, EACH WEEK THE VIEWERS GET TO VOTE FOR THEIR LEAST FAVOURITE HOUSEMATE AND SHE GETS CHUCKED OUT
!
VOTE... YOU SAY?
HMM!
ON A PREMIUM RATE PHONE LINE?
HMM!
BIRDS OF THE RAZZLE HOUSE?.. SAY IT GETS 5 MILLION VIEWERS... SAY 20% ARE STUPID ENOUGH TO RING IN AND VOTE... £1.75 A CALL... TEN WEEKS ...7 NIGHTS A WEEK..
MAYBE I'VE BEEN A LITTLE HASTY, ROGER... TELL ME MORE

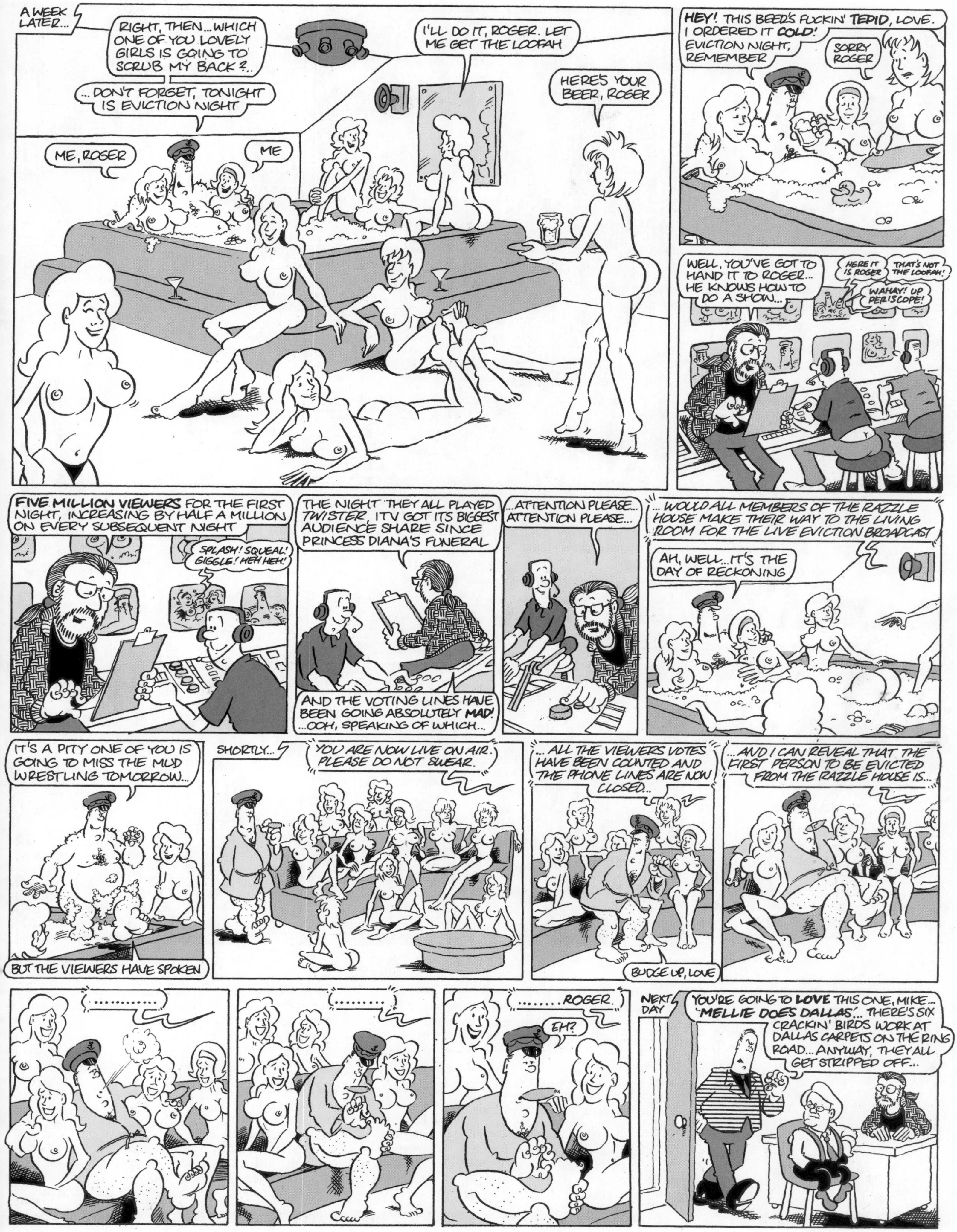
A WEEK LATER...
RIGHT, THEN... WHICH ONE OF YOU LOVELY GIRLS IS GOING TO SCRUB MY BACK?..
...DON'T FORGET, TONIGHT IS EVICTION NIGHT
I'LL DO IT, ROGER. LET ME GET THE LOOFAH
ME, ROGER
ME
HERE'S YOUR BEER, ROGER
HEY! THIS BEER'S FUCKIN' TEPID, LOVE. I ORDERED IT COLD! EVICTION NIGHT, REMEMBER
SORRY ROGER
WELL, YOU'VE GOT TO HAND IT TO ROGER... HE KNOWS HOW TO DO A SHOW...
HERE IT IS ROGER
THAT'S NOT THE LOOFAH!
WAHAY! UP PERISCOPE!
FIVE MILLION VIEWERS FOR THE FIRST NIGHT, INCREASING BY HALF A MILLION ON EVERY SUBSEQUENT NIGHT
SPLASH! SQUEAL! GIGGLE! HEH HEH!
THE NIGHT THEY ALL PLAYED TWISTER, ITV GOT ITS BIGGEST AUDIENCE SHARE SINCE PRINCESS DIANA'S FUNERAL
AND THE VOTING LINES HAVE BEEN GOING ABSOLUTELY MAD! ...OOH, SPEAKING OF WHICH...
...ATTENTION PLEASE... ATTENTION PLEASE...
...WOULD ALL MEMBERS OF THE RAZZLE HOUSE MAKE THEIR WAY TO THE LIVING ROOM FOR THE LIVE EVICTION BROADCAST
AH, WELL... IT'S THE DAY OF RECKONING
IT'S A PITY ONE OF YOU IS GOING TO MISS THE MUD WRESTLING TOMORROW...
BUT THE VIEWERS HAVE SPOKEN
SHORTLY...
YOU ARE NOW LIVE ON AIR. PLEASE DO NOT SWEAR.
...ALL THE VIEWERS VOTES HAVE BEEN COUNTED AND THE PHONE LINES ARE NOW CLOSED...
BUDGE UP, LOVE
...AND I CAN REVEAL THAT THE FIRST PERSON TO BE EVICTED FROM THE RAZZLE HOUSE IS...
....
....
........ROGER.
EH?
NEXT DAY
YOU'RE GOING TO LOVE THIS ONE, MIKE... 'MELLIE DOES DALLAS'... THERE'S SIX CRACKIN' BIRDS WORK AT DALLAS CARPETS ON THE RING ROAD... ANYWAY, THEY ALL GET STRIPPED OFF...

TODAY: Read SAS Andy's Exclusive...In his Own Words...The Story he Can NEVER Tel

CAPTIVE!

17 Year Prison Hell of SAS Torture Hero Andy

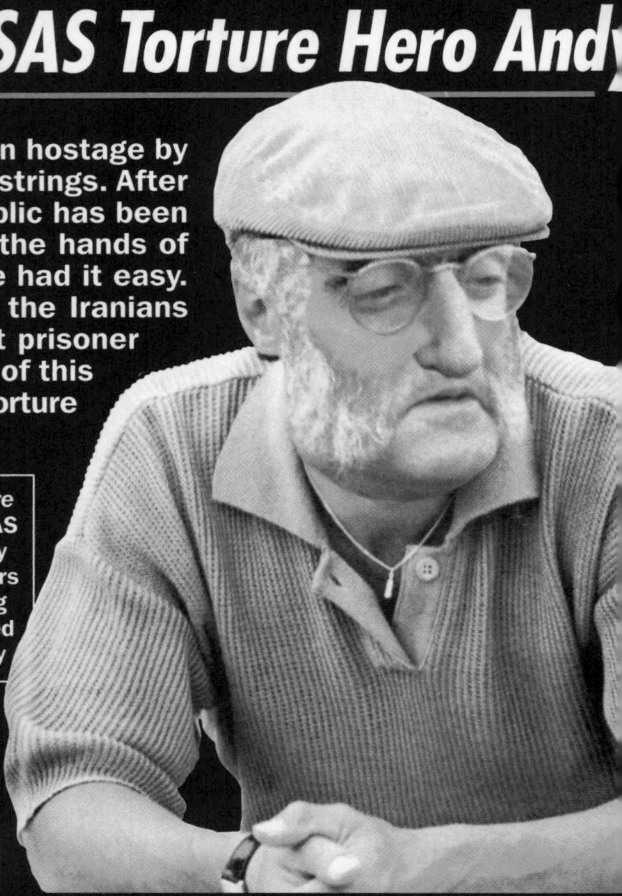

His lips are sealed: SAS hero Andy McKnackers remaining tight-lipped yesterday

THE RECENT PLIGHT of the British sailors and marines taken hostage by the vicious Iranian regime has tugged at the nation's heartstrings. After reading their six-figure stories in the gutter press, the public has been rightly outraged at the inhumane treatment they suffered at the hands of their evil captors. But one man thinks the Tehran Fifteen have had it easy. During the first Gulf War, Andy McKnackers was captured by the Iranians whilst on a routine patrol in Baghdad. Amazingly, he was kept prisoner for the next seventeen years, finally being released in January of this year. Throughout his ordeal, he was subjected to unimaginable torture and mistreatment on a daily basis, but never once cracked.

He told us: "When I turned the telly on last week and saw those sailors smiling and shaking hands with the same men who put my eyes out with red hot pokers, it made my blood boil. When I heard that they had sold their stories for hundreds of thousands of pounds, my blood boiled so much that it turned into a gas and blew out of my ears."

And he made this vow to the people of Britain. "I will never go to the papers with my story. As far as I'm concerned, what happened to me at the hands of my gaolers is a secret that will go with me to the grave. My lips are sealed, and that's an end to the matter."

Chamber of Secrets: *Andy was tortured with a dentist's chair, an Andrex puppy and a mangle.*

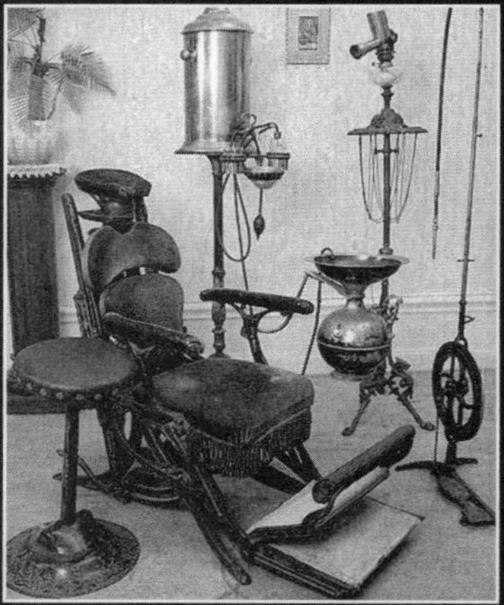

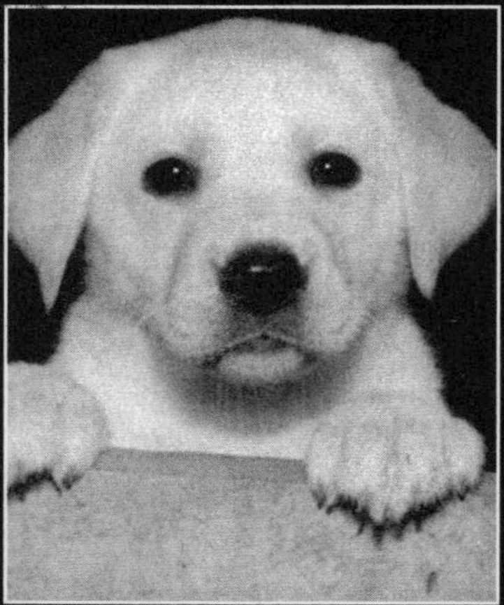

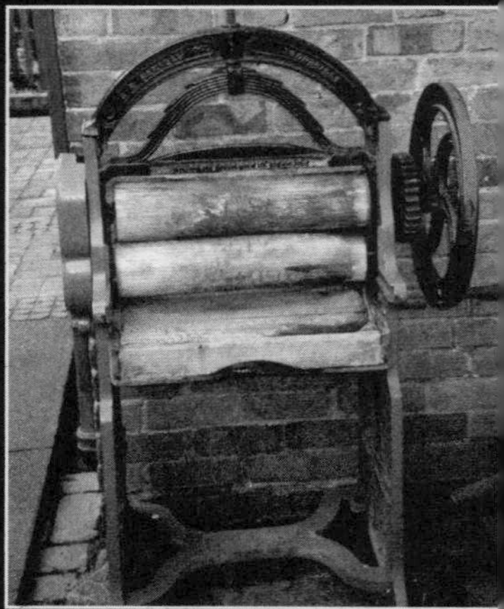

The Navy captives were pictured laughing and chatting whilst playing chess. But according to McKnackers, his treatment whilst a prisoner of the Iranians was very different.

He told us: "The first thing my captors did was throw me in a cell. Ten minutes later, an ayatollah came in and cut one of my ears off to show that he meant business."

TRAINING

"Luckily, part of my SAS training was first aid. I had a needle and thread hidden in one of my teeth, so I was able to stitch my ear back on. I'll never forget the look on the ayatollah's face the next day when he came in and found me with two ears again. He took his glasses off, rubbed them on his yashmak, then peered through them again. He couldn't believe his eyes - his expression was a picture, I can tell you!"

Over the following months, McKnackers found himself the subject of systematic torture, as the Iraqis tried to extract valuable secrets that could help the Axis of Evil in their War of Terror.

BUILT UP

"My days of captivity quickly fell into a regular routine. First thing in the morning, I would be poked with a 250,000 volt cattle prod. After breakfast, I was strapped onto the rack and stretched till lunchtime. I used to try and make my puddings last as long as possible, pretending to my captors that the jam in my roly poly or the custard on my crumble was too hot to eat, because I knew that more torture awaited me as soon as I had cleared my plate. In the afternoons it was back to the dungeon for a few hours in an iron maiden. Then, after tea, it was Chinese water torture until the blessed relief of bedtime."

This appalling treatment continued for eight years until Andy finally cracked and gave his tormentors his name. It was only after another four years of hell that he told them his rank and serial number.

"But they weren't interested in my name, rank and serial number. They wanted other information, such as secret plans and codewords, and they were prepared to go to any lengths to get it.

TAP

One day, a couple of talibans came into my cell, unlocked my shackles and lifted me down off the wall. Then they bundled me into the next room, strapped me in a dentist's chair and started drilling my teeth without an anaesthetic. They were amazed when I didn't even flinch, and took the drill out of my mouth to chec that it was working properly."

"Of course, they didn't realise that o the first day of SAS training, every re cruit has his teeth drilled. Anyone wh shows the slightest sign of discomfor clearly doesn't have what it takes t join such an elite fighting force, and i sent back to continue his career in th regular army. For all the pain I was feel ing in that dentist's chair, they might a well of been brushing my hair!"

PLUG

The first Gulf war had ended, th second had started and McKnacker was still a prisoner. After spendin more than twelve years fruitlessly torturing the SAS hardman, his captors realised that conventional means of interrogation were not getting them anywhere.

"They'd heard that Britain was a nation of animal lovers, so they brought a basket of puppies into the dungeon. They were cutest things I'd ever seen, with little waggy tails and big pleading eyes. The Iranians clearly thought that even if I wouldn't talk to save my own skin, I would tell them everything I knew to save the skin of these lovable little Andrex puppies. The head torturer started to strangle them one by one, right in front of me, whilst his accomplice asked me what I knew about Operation Desert Storm. Of course, true to form, I didn't tell them a thing."

"What they didn't realise was that on our first day of basic training in the SAS, the drill sergeant throttles a dozen week-old cocker spaniels, a basket full of kittens with bows round their necks and a fluffy yellow duckling in a beer-mug right in front of every raw recruit. Anyone who registers the slightest emotion has their career ended there and then. It's straight back to painting coal and peeling spuds for them. An Al Qaida choking Andrex puppies in front of me was like a walk in the park."

DANNY

In 2003, the world watched as victorious US troops stormed into Baghdad. Live television pictures were beamed all over the world as a giant statue of Saddam was toppled over and gleeful Iraqis queued up to hit it with their shoes. But one man who wasn't watching was Andy McKnackers who, at that very moment, was in the middle of a particularly vicious torture session in his Abu Graib dungeon.

"My captors had come up with a grisly new inquisitorial technique in order to get me to tell them the co-ordinates of a secret HQ. Even though I'd been trained to withstand incredible amounts of torture, I have to admit that my heart missed a beat when I saw what they had in store for me... a giant Victorian mangle. They fed my toes between the rollers and started winding the handle. Unless you've been fed through a mangle, you have no idea what the pain is like. It was absolute agony as my whole body was crushed to a thickness of half a millimetre. I thought my suffering was over when I came out the other side of the mangle and wafted gently down onto the floor, but nothing could of been further from the truth."

SIDNEY

"The head gaoler clapped his hands, and two Al Qaida Origami experts walked into the chamber. After thirteen years of daily torture, I thought I knew what pain was. But unless you've been folded into the shape of a bird, and then spent four days having your head

and feet pulled to make your wings flap, you simply don't know the meaning of the word. Needless to say, I remained tight-lipped about the secret HQ, and in the end my captors were forced to admit defeat. They unfolded me and stuck a bike pump up my arse, so that I popped back to my normal shape."

In 2006, even though the second Gulf war was long over, and peace had returned to the Middle East, McKnackers was still suffering daily mistreatment at the hands of his Mujahadeen tormentors.

"After sixteen years' secret incarceration, I finally decided I'd had enough. I told myself I'd have one last breakfast, then bite through the cyanide capsule I'd been hiding under my tongue since I was captured. But as I mopped up the last bits of yoke, beans and fried tomato off my plate with a slice of toast out of the rack and prepared to meet my maker, the door opened and Osama Bin Laden walked in."

ROYAL

"He explained that in 20 years as a terrorist, he had never come up against such a difficult adversary as me. In seventeen years of constant interrogation, I'd only spoken three times to tell them my name, rank and serial number. He said they'd run out of torture techniques to try on me, so they were going to set me free. Before I knew what was happening, I'd been given a suit and put on the next plane to Durham airport. I got on a bus outside the prison, and soon found myself back at the home I hadn't seen for nearly two decades."

But unlike the recent Iranian captives, McKnackers didn't go out of his way to seek publicity upon his return. Not for him the tawdry business of selling his story to the highest bidder, posing on the front of a gutter newspaper, or walking through a park talking to Trevor McDonald. And he is adamant that, having signed the Official Secrets Act when he joined the SAS, he will never speak about his experiences in the Gulf.

TYNE THEATRE AND

"Sometimes I wish I could go to the papers, if only to set the record straight. Ever since I got back from Iraq in January, there have been rumours going round the estate that I've just served seventeen years in Durham prison for burglary, assault occasioning actual bodily harm and aggravated rape. But that wasn't me. It was someone else with the same name as me, who also looks a bit like me."

"Quite a lot like me, actually. Even down to his tattoos," he added. "And I think he used to live in this house as well."

● *At his request, a percentage of the fee paid to Andy McKnackers for this interview has been donated to the Durham Prison Sex Offenders' Wing Table Tennis Club Fund, in order to buy two new bats.*

Have Your Say

I DON'T know what the 15 sailors are complaining for. They weren't treated that badly and at the end of it they were given a free suit. When I got married last year I had to buy my suit and it cost the best part of £150. Perhaps it would have been cheaper if I had joined the Navy and surrendered to the Iranians.
Frank Cob, Leeds

WHILST I abhor the actions of Iran in detaining our sailors and Royal Marines, it was nice of them to hand out souvenirs of their stay in their country when they were released. Let's hope the Americans make a similar gesture when they release the Guantanamo Bay suspects. Perhaps they could they give them an 'I heart NY' t-shirt, a wobbly Elvis and a little model of the Statue of Liberty.
Ada Brazil, Luton

I WAS disgusted that the prisoners were given party bags on being released. I was taken prisoner at the fall of Singapore in 1942 and spent four years building the Burma Railway as a prisoner of the Japanese. When I was released, I weighed three stone, and all I got was a bag with a packet of Haribos and a balloon.
Arthur Pine, Pine

I WAS fuming when I saw pictures of our detained sailors on television. There they were in clean clothes, sitting on cushions surrounded by bowls of fresh fruit. Honestly, foreign detention is more like a ruddy holiday camp these days.
Max Pea, Tring

TONY BLAIR is right when he says it was a mistake to allow the captured sailors to profit from their escapade. I suppose we'll have to wait until the PM is out of office and publishes his memoirs to find out why such a disgraceful thing was allowed to happen.
J Hazel, Redruth

ARTHUR Batchelor, the youngest captive cried himself to sleep after his evil captors called him 'Mr Bean'. Isn't it about time that calling somebody 'Mr Bean' was outlawed as a war crime under the Geneva Convention?
George Filbert, Tooting

I WAS disgusted to hear that the sailors had taken money for their stories. I took a principled stand and refused to read any of their accounts. Mind you, if Faye Turney had looked a bit more like Goldie Hawn in Private Benjamin, and gone into graphic detail about her strip search, I'd have been stood on the newsagents step waiting for them to open.
Hector Almond, Crawley

THESE service personnel wasted a golden opportunity when paraded in front of the world's TV. If I had been in their situation, I would have coughed my exact position in morse code and blinked information about how many armed people were guarding me.
Brigadier Lewis-Hewy, Hampshire

I MUST admit that when I saw those soldiers saying sorry on TV for straying into Iranian waters, I was a little suspicious. They didn't actually sound very sorry to me. One of them was actually smirking all the way through his apology. Perhaps the Ministry of Defence should teach their soldiers how to apologise convincingly by looking at their shoes.
PJ Coco, London

I WAS rather disappointed to see the service personnel apologising for straying into Iranian waters. With the whole world looking on, they should have taken the opportunity to apologise for the slave trade on behalf of everyone in Britain.
T Wall, Liverpool

HOW childish of Iran to detain our soldiers just because they wander into their territory. I suppose the Ayatollah will be bursting any footballs that are kicked over the border from Iraq next. Come on, Iran, grow up.
R Ridley, Nottingham

I LIVE next door to Mr Ridley, and he always bursts my son's footballs when he kicks them into his garden. So in my opinion, he has no right to criticise the Iranian regime.
J Drury, Nottingham

THANK goodness for the BBC News. Without them, I would be completely unaware that the mother of one of the soldiers was 'very happy' on hearing of her son's release.
R Cashew, Bristol

WORDS cannot convey my disgust at these so-called Iranians. Not only do they detain our soldiers for two weeks, but they force one of them to wear a headscarf as though she's one of them. Come on, Mr Blair, what are you waiting for? Get those B52s fuelled up.
Hector Macademia, Walls

I BELIEVE the Iranians have behaved abominably. Had they released their captives a week earlier, then Faye Turney's gripping account of her ordeal, probably to be called 'Faye - My Hell', could have been mocked up in time for the Frankfurt Book Fair. As it is, she will now have a job getting it into the bestsellers list at Christmas.
P Cann, Leeds

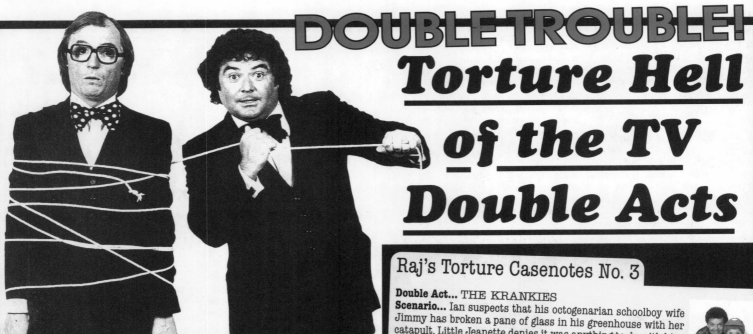

DOUBLE TROUBLE!
Torture Hell of the TV Double Acts

MEMBERS OF TV DOUBLE ACTS are usually the last people we would suspect of being torturers or their victims. But what would happen if one of them suspected that their partner was keeping secrets? How would they go about extracting that information? We asked flyweight daytime telly trick-cyclist Dr **RAJ PERSAUD** to use his unrivalled knowledge of psychology and showbiz to assess how our favourite television duos would shape up in a lighthearted series of fictitious torture chamber scenarios.

Raj's Torture Casenotes No. 1

Double Act... CANNON & BALL
Scenario... Tommy Cannon suspects that his comedy partner Bobby Ball has been repeatedly slipping petrol receipts from his wife's shopping trips into the partnership's business expense account. Ball denies the charge, so Tommy decides to torture him to find out if he is, in the words of his own famous catchphrase, "a little liar".

Raj says... *"The lads' stage act mainly consists of Ball's braces being pulled out and twanged back onto his nipples and Cannon slapping him round the face, so traditional torture techniques involving the infliction of physical pain would have little effect on the Burnley-born ex-welder. However, I imagine that there may have been a dark episode in Bobby's past, such as being molested in an aviary, which could easily have left him with a pathological fear of budgerigars. If this were indeed the case, and Cannon were to insert Ball's head through a hole in the bottom of a birdcage containing a budgie, having first tied a small bell to the end of his partner's nose, I am confident that a full confession would follow within seconds."*

Raj's Torture Casenotes No. 2

Double Act... ROBSON & JEROME
Scenario... Robson & Jerome rose to fame in Soldier Soldier and enjoyed platinum-selling pop success with a series of chart topping singles and albums. However, Robson Green has since gone on to become one of the highest-paid drama actors on British television, his ex-partner Jerome Flynn has slipped into utter obscurity. Jealous Flynn decides to torture the secret of a successful TV career out of his half-pint-sized Geordie pal.

Raj says... *"During basic training as a member of 'A' Company, 1st Battalion The King's Fusiliers in Soldier Soldier, Green will have been taught to withstand all modern forms of interrogation. However, he won't have been trained to resist medieval torture techniques, and Flynn will be able to turn this Achilles' heel to his advantage. Subjecting his friend to unimaginable torments using a variety of cruel gothic implements, such as thumbscrews, may well be enough to get him talking. But even if those don't do the trick, lifting his fingernails up with pliers and slipping quicklime underneath is guaranteed to help anyone remember their lines, even an actor as bad as Robson Green."*

Raj's Torture Casenotes No. 3

Double Act... THE KRANKIES
Scenario... Ian suspects that his octogenarian schoolboy wife Jimmy has broken a pane of glass in his greenhouse with her catapult. Little Jeanette denies it was anything to do with him, but Ian suspects she is lying through his teeth. He intends to take the cost of replacing the window out of Jimmy's pocket money, but he knows he can only do that if he gets her to confess what she has done.

Raj says... *"Unlike a real parent, Ian is unable to smack his wife's bottom in order to get her to admit breaking the window. As a professional female schoolboy, Jimmy knows all the tricks, and would certainly slip a book down the back of her shorts if she knew she was in for a proper whacking. However, she is unlikely to know a way to dodge torture techniques developed in China over 6,000 years ago. Ian could stake his wife out in the garden over a patch of bamboo plants. The pain caused by the fast-growing razor-sharp shoots digging into her skin would be a fandabidozy way to extract the truth from his mischievous wife."*

Raj's Torture Casenotes No. 4

Double Act... LITTLE & LARGE
Scenario... Roly poly funnyman Eddie Large comes back from London and tells his partner Syd Little that he has been to see Agatha Christie play The Mousetrap. Syd has heard a lot about the long-running show, and is desperate to find out whodunnit. However, at the end of each performance, the murderer swears the audience to secrecy, asking them not to reveal his or her identity. Eddie refuses to reveal this secret to Syd, who decides to torture the overweight comic until he spills the beans.

Raj says... *"Commonplace interrogation techniques, such as beating him with a rubber hose or burning the soles of his feet with a soldering iron, would simply not work on someone as large as Large. With his thick layer of subcutaneous fat to protect him, his threshold of pain will be extremely high. As a result, I believe that Supersonic Syd would cleverly opt to use Eddie's enormous weight against him by attaching him to a strappado. Hanging in excruciating agony as his shoulders are slowly wrenched out of their sockets, it is doubtful whether Large could last for more than three or four days before screaming for mercy and revealing that the detective who turns up on skis in the first scene is actually the murderer."*

Raj's Torture Casenotes No. 5

Double Act... TRINNY & SUSANNAH
Scenario... What Not to Wear fashion guru Trinny wants to fire a Trident missile straight at the heart of Beijing in order to precipitate a global thermonuclear conflict which will obliterate all human life on the planet. However, only her partner Susannah knows the 8-digit code required to initiate the doomsday launch sequence, and she's refusing to tell. Trinny decides to get the code, by whatever means it takes.

Raj says... *"I believe that this is a situation where Orwellian mental torture techniques could be Trinny's first choice. Merely by threatening to dress Susannah in a selection of last season's designer clothes and force her to attend a London Fashion Week cocktail party, I believe she could apply sufficient psychological pressure to get her TV partner to reveal the code. The thought of appearing in front of a selection of haute couture fashionistas whilst not dressed completely a la mode should be sufficient to make Susannah overcome her scruples about condemning the planet to fiery Armageddon."*

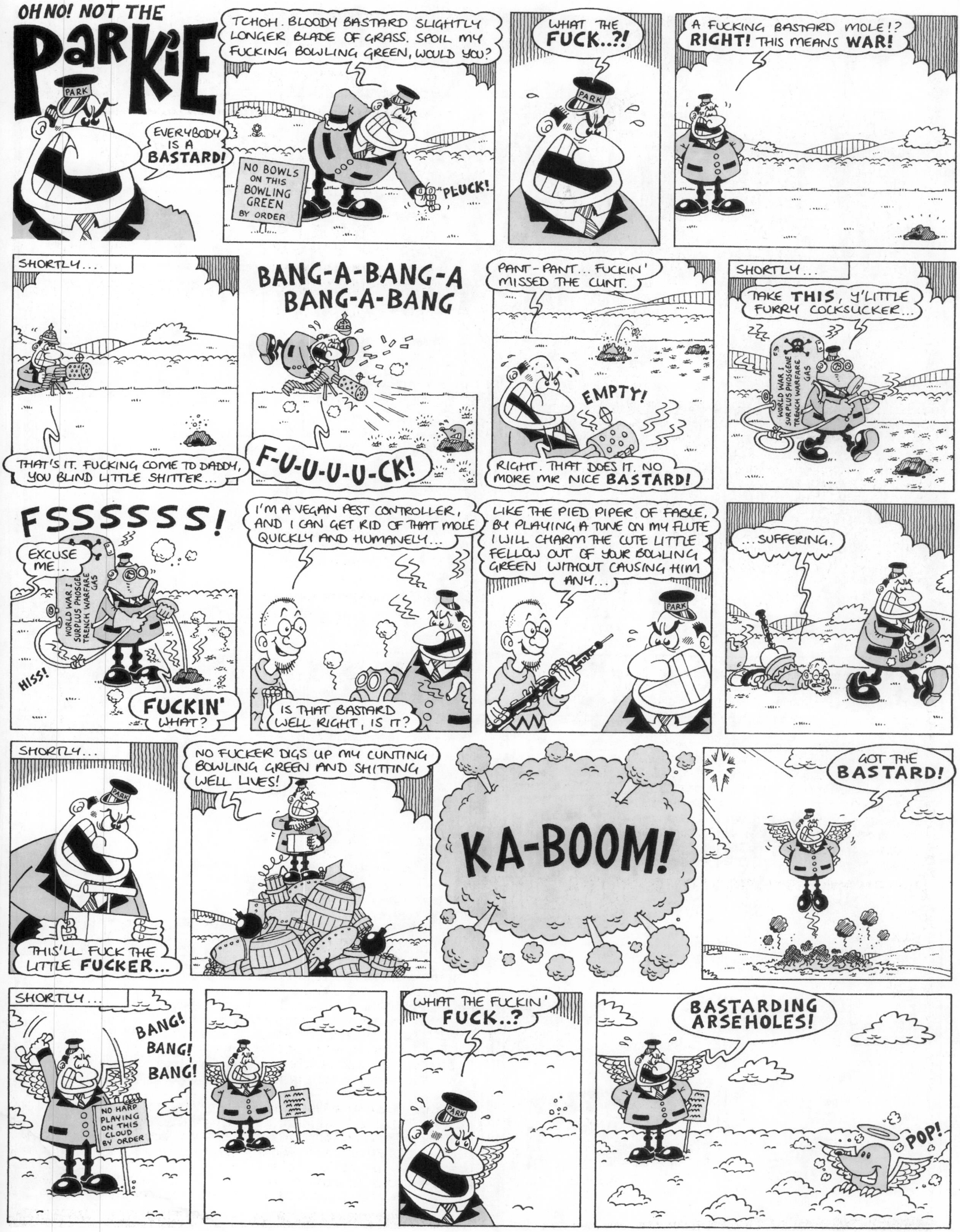
OH NO! NOT THE
PARKIE
PARK
EVERYBODY IS A BASTARD!
TCHOH. BLOODY BASTARD SLIGHTLY LONGER BLADE OF GRASS. SPOIL MY FUCKING BOWLING GREEN, WOULD YOU?
NO BOWLS ON THIS BOWLING GREEN BY ORDER
PLUCK!
WHAT THE FUCK..?!
PARK
A FUCKING BASTARD MOLE!? RIGHT! THIS MEANS WAR!
SHORTLY...
THAT'S IT. FUCKING COME TO DADDY, YOU BLIND LITTLE SHITTER...
BANG-A-BANG-A BANG-A-BANG
F-U-U-U-U-CK!
PANT-PANT... FUCKIN' MISSED THE CUNT.
EMPTY!
RIGHT. THAT DOES IT. NO MORE MR NICE BASTARD!
SHORTLY...
TAKE THIS, Y'LITTLE FURRY COCKSUCKER...
WORLD WAR I SURPLUS PHOSGENE TRENCH WARFARE GAS
FSSSSSS!
EXCUSE ME...
WORLD WAR I SURPLUS PHOSGENE TRENCH WARFARE GAS
HISS!
FUCKIN' WHAT?
I'M A VEGAN PEST CONTROLLER, AND I CAN GET RID OF THAT MOLE QUICKLY AND HUMANELY...
IS THAT BASTARD WELL RIGHT, IS IT?
LIKE THE PIED PIPER OF FABLE, BY PLAYING A TUNE ON MY FLUTE I WILL CHARM THE CUTE LITTLE FELLOW OUT OF YOUR BOWLING GREEN WITHOUT CAUSING HIM ANY...
PARK
...SUFFERING.
SHORTLY...
PARK
THIS'LL FUCK THE LITTLE FUCKER...
NO FUCKER DIGS UP MY CUNTING BOWLING GREEN AND SHITTING WELL LIVES!
KA-BOOM!
GOT THE BASTARD!
SHORTLY...
BANG! BANG! BANG!
NO HARP PLAYING ON THIS CLOUD BY ORDER
WHAT THE FUCKIN' FUCK..?
PARK
BASTARDING ARSEHOLES!
POP!

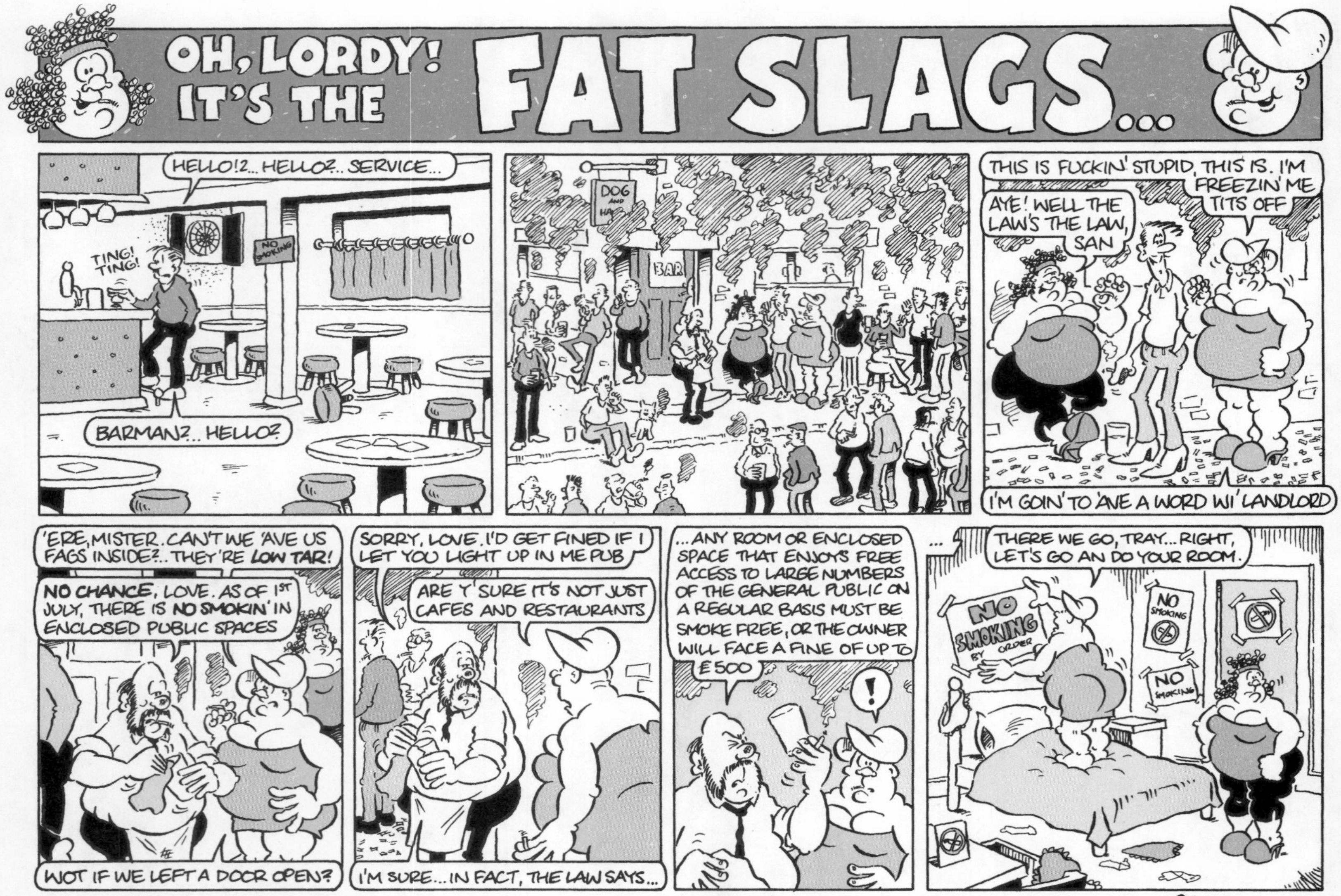
OH, LORDY! IT'S THE FAT SLAGS...
HELLO!? ... HELLO? ... SERVICE...
TING! TING!
NO SMOKING
BARMAN? ... HELLO?
DOG AND HA
BAR
THIS IS FUCKIN' STUPID, THIS IS. I'M FREEZIN' ME TITS OFF
AYE! WELL THE LAW'S THE LAW, SAN
I'M GOIN' TO 'AVE A WORD WI' LANDLORD
'ERE, MISTER. CAN'T WE 'AVE US FAGS INSIDE? .. THEY'RE LOW TAR!
NO CHANCE, LOVE. AS OF 1ST JULY, THERE IS NO SMOKIN' IN ENCLOSED PUBLIC SPACES
WOT IF WE LEFT A DOOR OPEN?
SORRY, LOVE. I'D GET FINED IF I LET YOU LIGHT UP IN ME PUB
ARE Y' SURE IT'S NOT JUST CAFES AND RESTAURANTS
I'M SURE... IN FACT, THE LAW SAYS...
...ANY ROOM OR ENCLOSED SPACE THAT ENJOYS FREE ACCESS TO LARGE NUMBERS OF THE GENERAL PUBLIC ON A REGULAR BASIS MUST BE SMOKE FREE, OR THE OWNER WILL FACE A FINE OF UP TO £500
!
...
THERE WE GO, TRAY... RIGHT, LET'S GO AN DO YOUR ROOM.
NO SMOKING BY ORDER
NO SMOKING
NO SMOKING

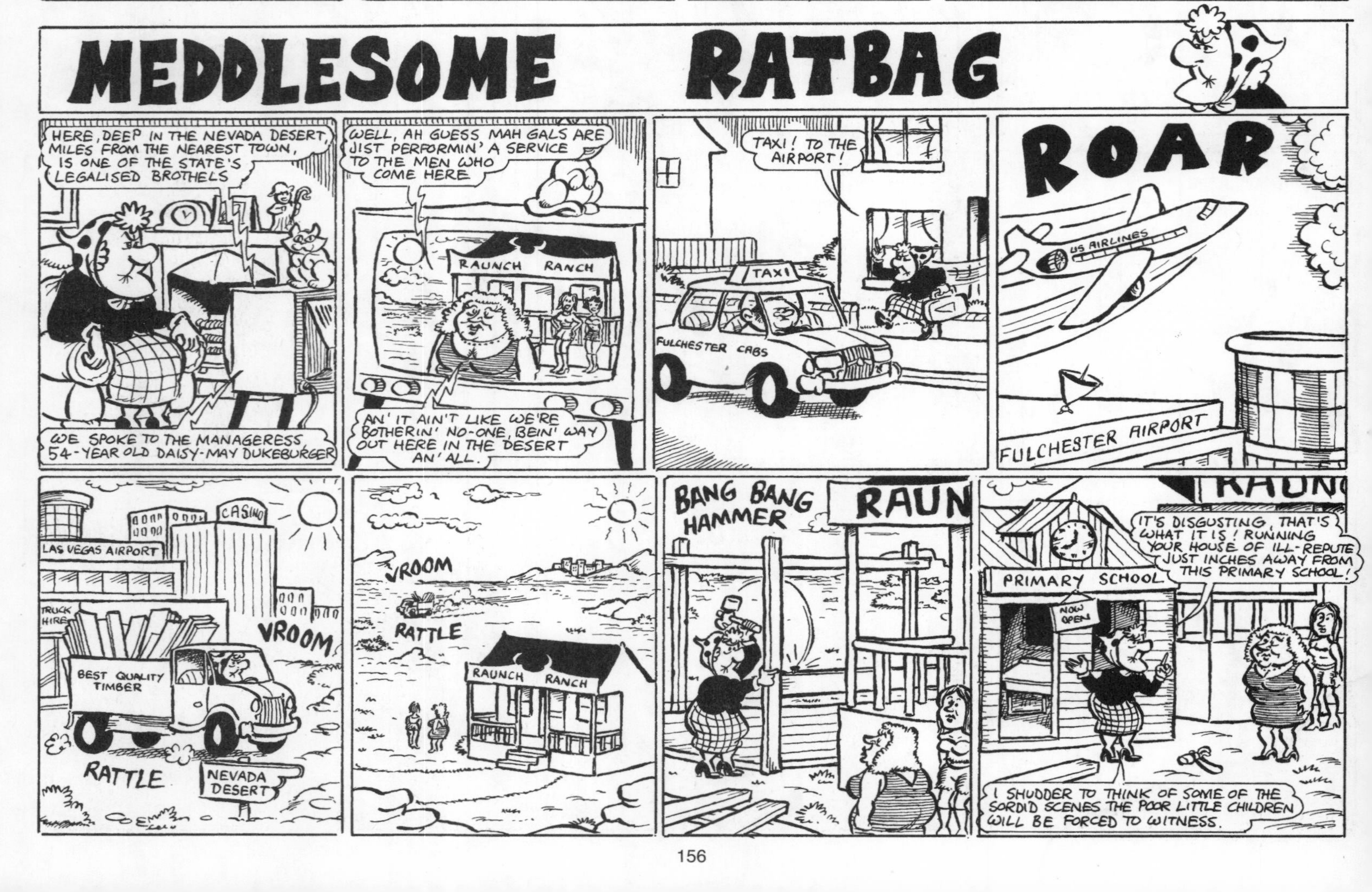
MEDDLESOME RATBAG
HERE, DEEP IN THE NEVADA DESERT, MILES FROM THE NEAREST TOWN, IS ONE OF THE STATE'S LEGALISED BROTHELS
WE SPOKE TO THE MANAGERESS 54-YEAR OLD DAISY-MAY DUKEBURGER
WELL, AH GUESS MAH GALS ARE JIST PERFORMIN' A SERVICE TO THE MEN WHO COME HERE
RAUNCH RANCH
AN' IT AIN'T LIKE WE'RE BOTHERIN' NO-ONE, BEIN' WAY OUT HERE IN THE DESERT AN' ALL.
TAXI! TO THE AIRPORT!
TAXI
FULCHESTER CABS
ROAR
US AIRLINES
FULCHESTER AIRPORT
CASINO
LAS VEGAS AIRPORT
TRUCK HIRE
BEST QUALITY TIMBER
VROOM
RATTLE
NEVADA DESERT
VROOM
RATTLE
RAUNCH RANCH
BANG BANG HAMMER
RAUN
RAUN
PRIMARY SCHOOL
NOW OPEN
IT'S DISGUSTING, THAT'S WHAT IT IS! RUNNING YOUR HOUSE OF ILL-REPUTE JUST INCHES AWAY FROM THIS PRIMARY SCHOOL!
I SHUDDER TO THINK OF SOME OF THE SORDID SCENES THE POOR LITTLE CHILDREN WILL BE FORCED TO WITNESS.

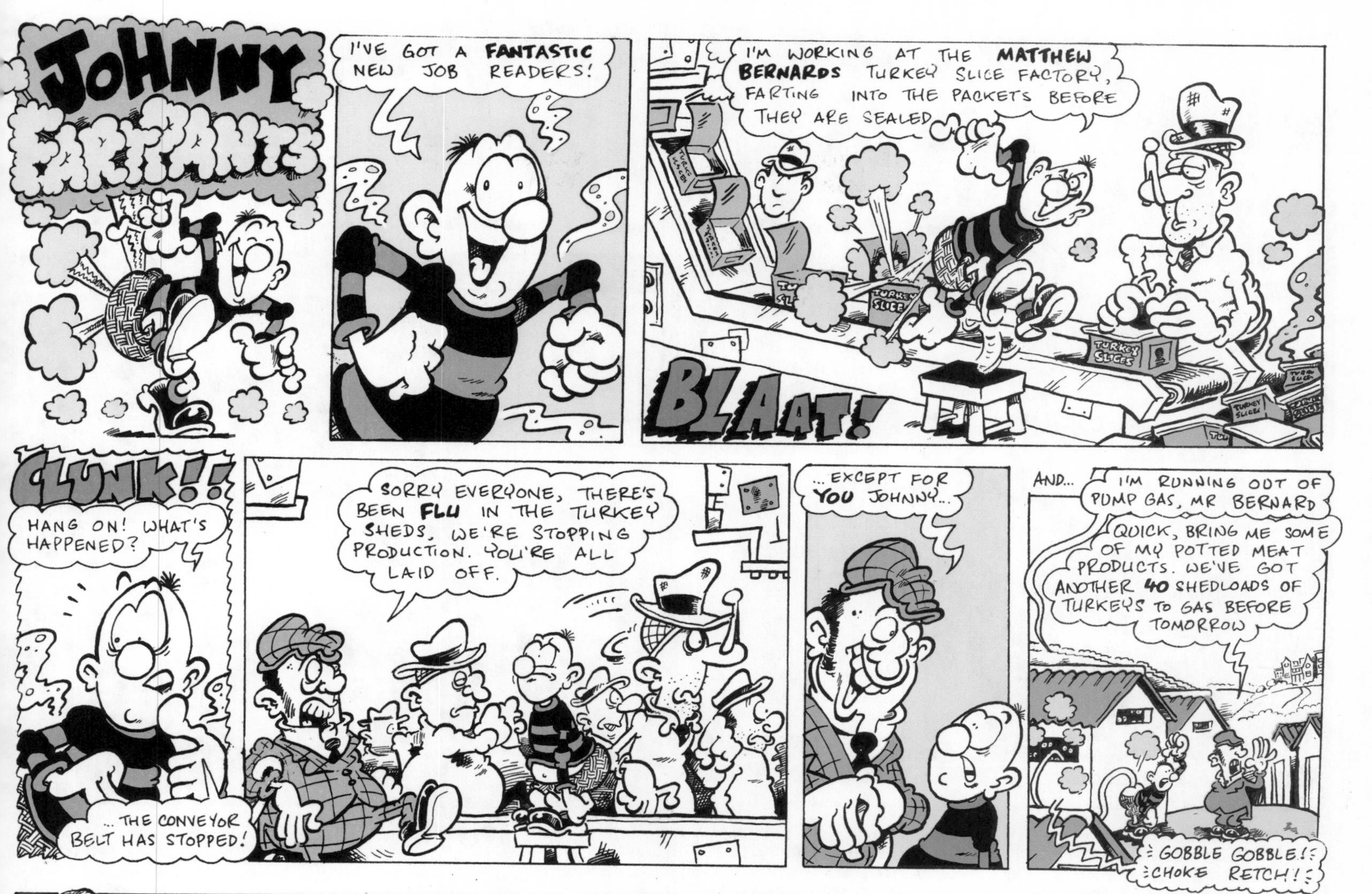
JOHNNY FARTPANTS
I'VE GOT A FANTASTIC NEW JOB READERS!
I'M WORKING AT THE MATTHEW BERNARDS TURKEY SLICE FACTORY, FARTING INTO THE PACKETS BEFORE THEY ARE SEALED
TURKEY SLICE
TURKEY SLICES
BLAAAT!
CLUNK!!
HANG ON! WHAT'S HAPPENED?
... THE CONVEYOR BELT HAS STOPPED!
SORRY EVERYONE, THERE'S BEEN FLU IN THE TURKEY SHEDS. WE'RE STOPPING PRODUCTION. YOU'RE ALL LAID OFF.
... EXCEPT FOR YOU JOHNNY...
AND...
I'M RUNNING OUT OF PUMP GAS, MR BERNARD
QUICK, BRING ME SOME OF MY POTTED MEAT PRODUCTS. WE'VE GOT ANOTHER 40 SHEDLOADS OF TURKEYS TO GAS BEFORE TOMORROW
GOBBLE GOBBLE! CHOKE RETCH!!

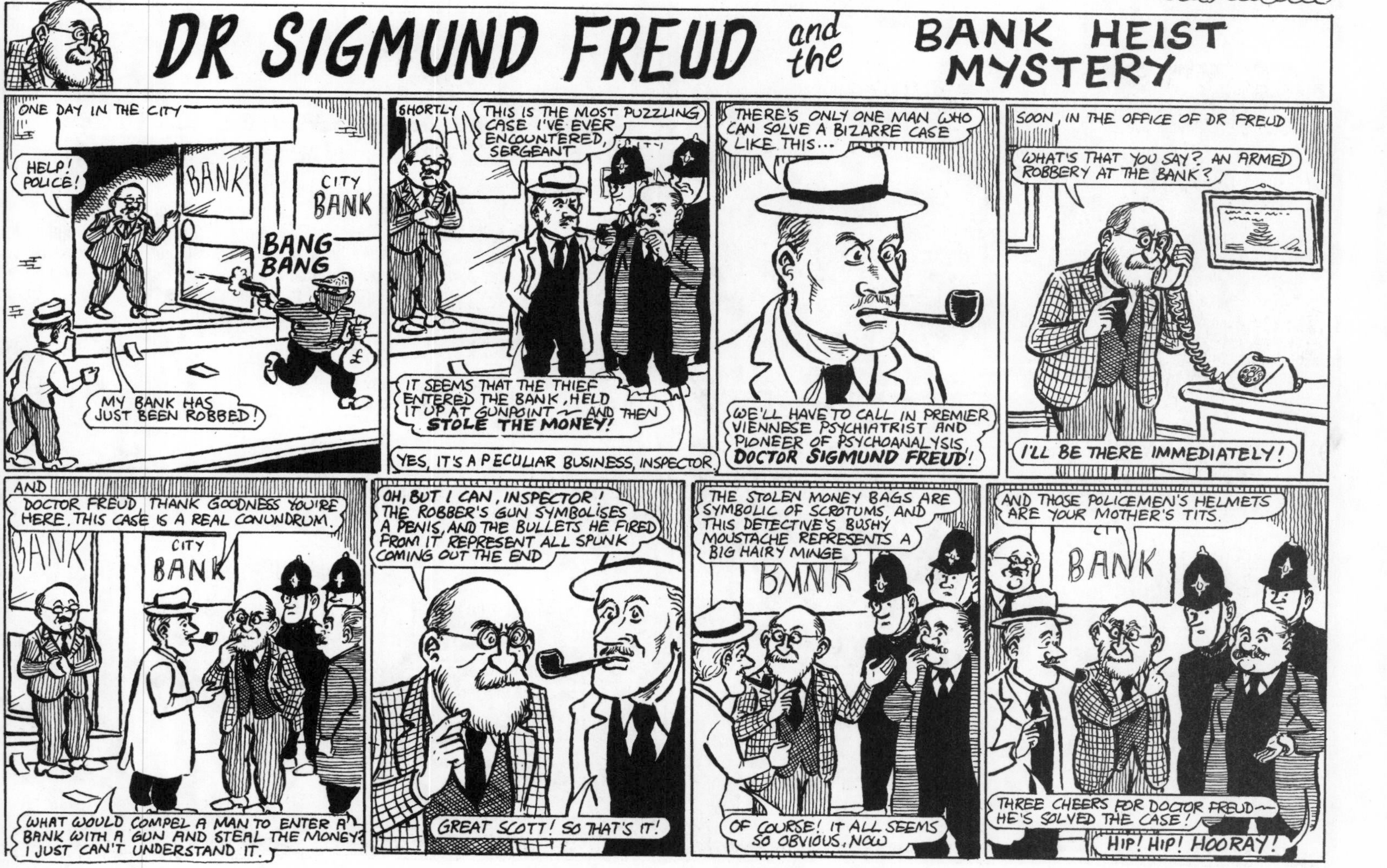
DR SIGMUND FREUD and the BANK HEIST MYSTERY
ONE DAY IN THE CITY
HELP! POLICE!
BANK
CITY BANK
BANG BANG
MY BANK HAS JUST BEEN ROBBED!
SHORTLY
THIS IS THE MOST PUZZLING CASE I'VE EVER ENCOUNTERED, SERGEANT
IT SEEMS THAT THE THIEF ENTERED THE BANK, HELD IT UP AT GUNPOINT — AND THEN STOLE THE MONEY!
YES, IT'S A PECULIAR BUSINESS, INSPECTOR
THERE'S ONLY ONE MAN WHO CAN SOLVE A BIZARRE CASE LIKE THIS...
WE'LL HAVE TO CALL IN PREMIER VIENNESE PSYCHIATRIST AND PIONEER OF PSYCHOANALYSIS, DOCTOR SIGMUND FREUD!
SOON, IN THE OFFICE OF DR FREUD
WHAT'S THAT YOU SAY? AN ARMED ROBBERY AT THE BANK?
I'LL BE THERE IMMEDIATELY!
AND
DOCTOR FREUD, THANK GOODNESS YOU'RE HERE. THIS CASE IS A REAL CONUNDRUM.
BANK
CITY BANK
WHAT WOULD COMPEL A MAN TO ENTER A BANK WITH A GUN AND STEAL THE MONEY? I JUST CAN'T UNDERSTAND IT.
OH, BUT I CAN, INSPECTOR! THE ROBBER'S GUN SYMBOLISES A PENIS, AND THE BULLETS HE FIRED FROM IT REPRESENT ALL SPUNK COMING OUT THE END
GREAT SCOTT! SO THAT'S IT!
THE STOLEN MONEY BAGS ARE SYMBOLIC OF SCROTUMS, AND THIS DETECTIVE'S BUSHY MOUSTACHE REPRESENTS A BIG HAIRY MINGE
BANK
OF COURSE! IT ALL SEEMS SO OBVIOUS, NOW
AND THOSE POLICEMEN'S HELMETS ARE YOUR MOTHER'S TITS.
BANK
THREE CHEERS FOR DOCTOR FREUD— HE'S SOLVED THE CASE!
HIP! HIP! HOORAY!

CAUGHT on CAMERA

GATSO GOTCHAS

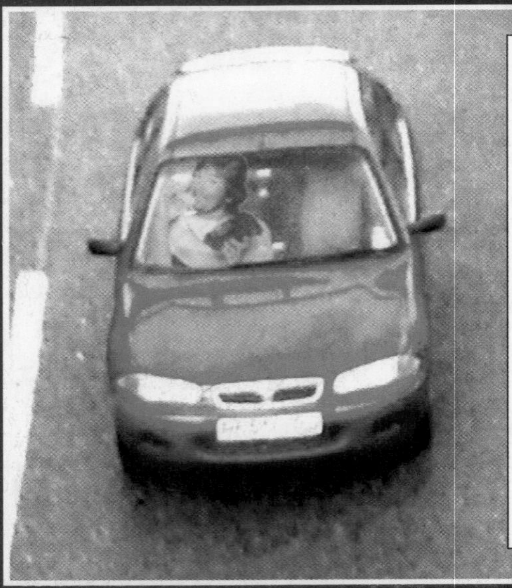

Wheel or No Wheel

TAKE a look at *Deal or No Deal* star **NOEL EDMONDS**, clocked doing 70 on the M1... steering with his knees whilst making a phone call to the banker! The tidy-bearded cuckold gets crinkly bottom marks for safe driving. If Noel hits a patch of black ice, he'll find himself facing a whirly wheel challenge that could prove every bit as fatal as the ones on his Late Late Breakfast Show!

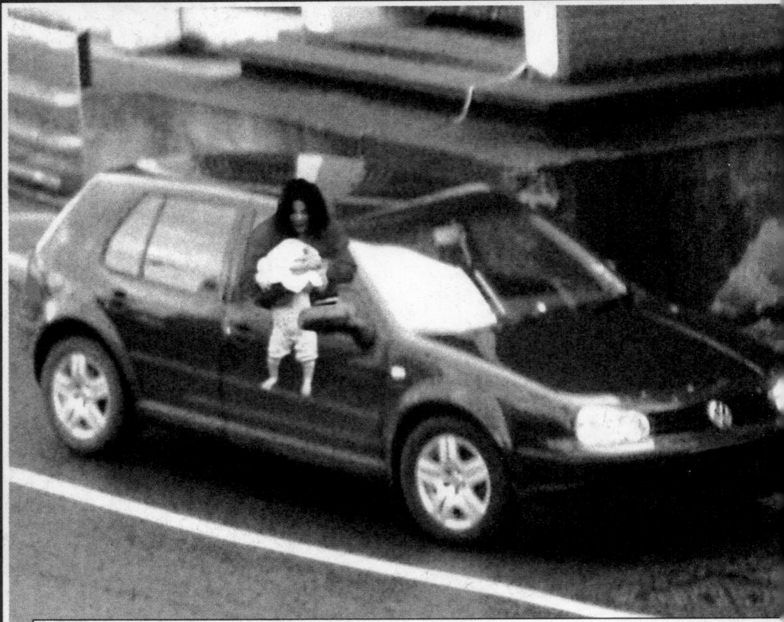

Jackson's Five Pointer

HE'S no stranger to controversy, but wacko pop legend **MICHAEL JACKSON**'s latest stunt was definitely off the wall! Cameras on the M4 caught the plastic-faced speed-ophile doing 90 in his souped-up saloon... whilst dangling baby Cushion out of the window! It may have been a thriller for Jacko, but it was certainly an example of bad driving and won him an appointment with Ludlow magistrates.

No Write of Way

FORMER London Mayoral candidate **JEFFREY ARCHER** was the author of his own misfortune when he was caught on camera hammering down the M6 whilst hammering out another utterly shit novel on his typewriter. For his misdemeanour, Cambridge magistrates fined the ex-con peer £350 - not a penny more, not a penny less.

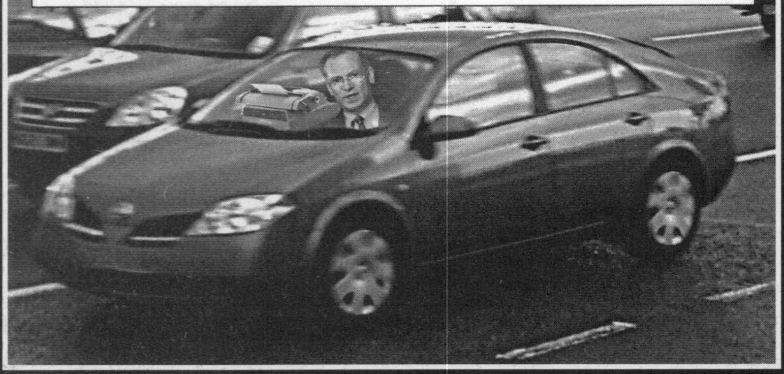

Oliver's Barmy

EATING whilst driving is bad enough, but flambeing a sirloin steak in red wine sauce whilst knocking up a blackcurrant coulis with steamed vegetables en croute whilst behind the wheel is just plain mental. But that's what Gatso cameras spotted naked chef **JAMIE OLIVER** doing on a busy bypass recently! This meal would cost you £50 in one of mockney Jamie's fancy eateries, but it cost him 3 points on his licence and a £200 fine.

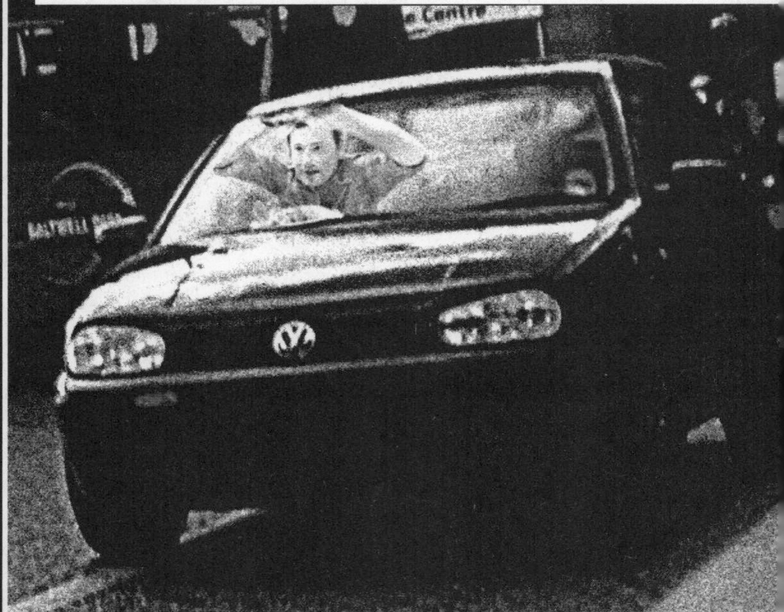

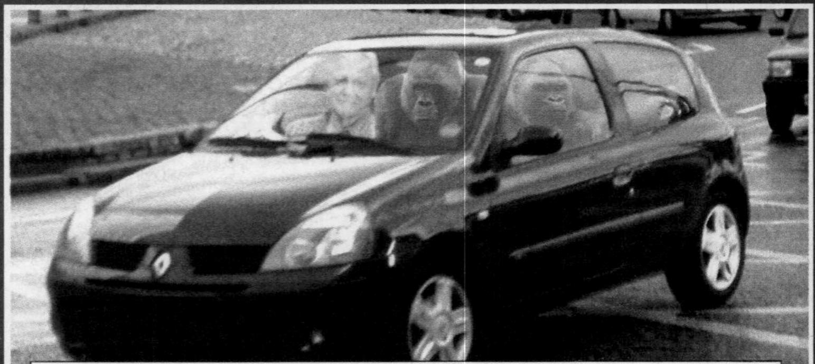

Monkey Business

POLICE went ape when they spotted *Life on Earth* host **DAVID ATTENBOROUGH** enjoying life in the fast lane... giving a lift to a 20-stone silverback gorilla! Nothing wrong with that, you might think, but get this - Sir David's monkey passenger wasn't wearing a seat belt! If he's under fourteen years old, that could mean three points on the eminent natural history presenter's licence. It's enough to send anyone bananas!